1,000 CLASSIC RECIPES

from
AROUND THE WORLD

Edited by Jo-Anne Cox
& Elizabeth Towers

p

This is a Parragon Book
This edition published in 2001

Parragon
Queen Street House
4 Queen Street
Bath BA1 1HE, UK

ISBN: 0-75253-844-6

Printed in China

Produced by Haldane Mason, London

Acknowledgements
Art Director: Ron Samuel
Publishing Director: Sydney Francis
Project Editor: Jo-Anne Cox & Elizabeth Towers
Design: dap ltd
Nutritional information: Jill Scott & Sue Baic

Material in this book has previously appeared in
*Ultimate Chinese Recipes, Ultimate Low Fat Recipes,
Ultimate Italian Recipes, Ultimate Vegetarian Recipes*

Notes
Use all metric or all imperial quantities, as the two are not interchangeable.
Cup measurements in this book are for American cups. Tablespoons are assumed to
be 15 ml. Unless otherwise stated, milk is assumed to be full fat, eggs are medium
and pepper is freshly ground black pepper.

The nutritional information provided for each recipe is per serving or per portion.
Optional ingredients, variations or serving suggestions have not been included in the
calculations. The times given for each recipe are an approximate guide only as the
preparation times may differ according to the techniques used by different people and
the cooking times may vary as a result of the type of oven used.

Contents

INTRODUCTION

This book contains 1000 classic recipes from all around the world. Each recipe contains the following information: nutritional calculations, preparation and cooking times and level of difficulty (one chef's hat means an easy recipe, rising to five chef's hats which is difficult).

Basic Recipes

The following recipes form the basis of many recipes in the book.

Cornflour (Cornstarch) Paste

Cornflour (cornstarch) paste is made by mixing 1 part cornflour (cornstarch) with about 1¹⁄₂ parts of cold water. Stir the mixture until smooth. The paste is used to thicken sauces.

Basic Pasta Dough

450 g/1 lb/4 cups durum wheat flour

4 eggs, lightly beaten

1 tbsp olive oil

salt

1 Lightly flour a work surface (counter). Sift the flour with a pinch of salt into a mound. Make a well in the centre and add the eggs and olive oil. Using a fork or your fingertips, gradually work the mixture until the ingredients are combined. Knead vigorously for 10-15 minutes

2 Set the dough aside to rest for 25 minutes, before rolling it out as thinly and evenly as possible.

Béchamel Sauce

600 m/1 pint/2½ cups

4 cloves

1 bay leaf

pinch of freshly grated nutmeg

25 g/1 oz/2 tbsp butter or margarine

25 g/1 oz/2 tbsp plain (all-purpose) flour

salt and pepper

1 Put the milk in a saucepan and add the coves, bay leaf and nutmeg. Gradually bring to the boil. Remove from the heat and leave for 15 minutes.

2 Melt the butter or margarine in another saucepan and stir in the flour to make a roux. Cook, stirring, for 1 minute. Remove the pan from the heat.

3 Strain the milk and gradually blend into the roux. Return the pan to the heat and bring to the boil, stirring, until the sauce thickens. Season with salt and pepper to taste and add any flavourings.

Basic Tomato Sauce

2 tbsp olive oil

1 small onion, chopped

1 garlic clove, chopped

400 g/14 oz can chopped tomatoes

2 tbsp chopped parsley

1 tsp dried oregano

2 bay leaves

2 tbsp tomato purée (paste)

1 tsp sugar

salt and pepper

1 Heat the oil in a pan over a medium heat and fry the onion for 2-3 minutes or until translucent. Add the garlic and fry for 1 minute. Stir in the chopped tomatoes, parsley, oregano, bay leaves, tomato purée (paste), sugar, and salt and pepper to taste.

2 Bring the sauce to the boil, then simmer, uncovered, for 15–20 minutes or until the sauce has reduced by half. Taste the sauce and adjust the seasoning if necessary. Discard the bay leaves just before serving.

Italian Red Wine Sauce

150 ml/¼ pint /⅝ cup Brown Stock (see page 8)

150 ml/¼ pint /⅔ cup Espagnole Sauce (see right)

125 ml/4 fl oz/½ cup red wine

2 tbsp red wine vinegar

4 tbsp shallots, chopped

1 bay leaf

1 thyme sprig

pepper

1 First make a demi-glace sauce. Put the Brown Stock and Espagnole Sauce in a pan and heat for 10 minutes, stirring occasionally.

2 Meanwhile, put the red wine, red wine vinegar, shallots, bay leaf and thyme in a pan, bring to the boil and reduce by three-quarters.

3 Strain the demi-glace sauce and add to the pan containing the Red Wine Sauce and leave to simmer for 20 minutes, stirring occasionally. Season with pepper to taste and strain the sauce before using.

Espagnole Sauce

2 tbsp butter

25 g/1 oz/¼ cup plain (all-purpose) flour

1 tsp tomato purée (paste)

250 ml/9 fl oz/1⅛ cups hot veal stock

1 tbsp Madeira

1½ tsp white wine vinegar

2 tbsp olive oil

25 g/1 oz bacon, diced

25 g/1 oz carrot, diced

25 g/1 oz onion, diced

15 g/½ oz celery, diced

15 g/½ oz leek, diced

15 g/½ oz fennel, diced

1 fresh thyme sprig

1 bay leaf

1 Melt the butter in a pan, add the flour and cook, stirring, until lightly coloured. Add the tomato purée (paste), then stir in the hot veal stock, Madeira and white wine vinegar and cook for 2 minutes.

2 Heat the oil in a separate pan, add the bacon, carrot, onion, celery, leek, fennel, thyme sprig and bay leaf and fry until the vegetables have softened. Remove the vegetables from the pan with a slotted spoon and drain thoroughly. Add the vegetables to the sauce and leave to simmer for 4 hours, stirring occasionally. Strain the sauce before using.

Italian Cheese Sauce

2 tbsp butter

25 g/1 oz/¼ cup plain (all-purpose) flour

300 ml/½ pint/1¼ cups hot milk

pinch of nutmeg

pinch of dried thyme

2 tbsp white wine vinegar

3 tbsp double (heavy) cream

60 g/2 oz/½ cup grated Mozzarella cheese

60 g/2 oz/½ cup Parmesan cheese

1 tsp English mustard

2 tbsp soured cream

salt and pepper

1 Melt the butter in a pan and stir in the flour. Cook, stirring, over a low heat until the roux is light in colour and crumbly in texture. Stir in the hot milk and cook, stirring, for 15 minutes until thick and smooth.

2 Add the nutmeg, thyme, white wine vinegar and season to taste. Stir in the cream and mix well.

3 Stir in the cheeses, mustard and cream and mix until the cheeses have melted and blended into the sauce.

Fresh Fish Stock

MAKES 1.75 LITRES/3 PINTS/7½ CUPS

1 head of a cod or salmon, etc, plus the
   trimmings, skin and bones or just the
   trimmings, skin and bones
1-2 onions, sliced
1 carrot, sliced
1-2 celery sticks, sliced
good squeeze of lemon juice
1 bouquet garni or 2 fresh or dried bay
   leaves

1 Wash the fish head and trimmings
   and place in a saucepan. Cover with
water and bring to the boil.

2 Remove any scum with a perforated
   spoon, then add the remaining
ingredients. Cover and simmer for about
30 minutes.

3 Strain and cool. Store in ther
   refrigerator and use within 2 days.

Brown Stock

Roast veal bones and shin of beef with
dripping (drippings) in the oven for 40
minutes. Transfer the bones to a large pan
and add sliced leeks, onion, celery and
carrots, a bouquet garni, white wine
vinegar and a thyme sprig and cover with
cold water. Simmer over a very low heat
for about 3 hours. Strain and blot the fat
from the surface with kitchen paper.

Chinese Stock

This basic stock is used in Chinese
cooking not only as the basis for soup-
making, but also whenever liquid is
required instead of plain water.

MAKES 2.5L/4½ PINTS/10 CUPS

750 g/1 lb 10 oz chicken pieces
750 g/1 lb 10 oz pork spare ribs
3.75 litres/6½ pints/15 cups cold water
3-4 pieces ginger root, crushed
3-4 spring onions (scallions), each tied into
a knot
3-4 tbsp Chinese rice wine or dry sherry

1 Trim off any excess fat from the
   chicken and spare ribs; chop them
into large pieces.

2 Place the chicken and pork in a large
   pan with the water; add the ginger
and spring onion (scallion) knots.

3 Bring to the boil, and skim off the
   scum. Reduce the heat and simmer
uncovered for at least 2-3 hours.

4 Strain the stock, discarding the
   chicken, pork, ginger and spring
onions (scallions); add the wine and return
to the boil, simmer for 2-3 minutes.

5 Refrigerate the stock when cool; it
   will keep for up to 4-5 days.
Alternatively, it can be frozen in small
containers and be defrosted as required.

Fresh Vegetable Stock

This can be kept chilled for up to three
days or frozen for up to three months.
Salt is not added when cooking the stock:
it is better to season it according to the
dish in which it its to be used.

MAKES 1.5 LITRES/2¾ PINTS/6¼ CUPS

250 g/9 oz shallots
1 large carrot, diced
1 celery stalk, chopped
½ fennel bulb
1 garlic clove
1 bay leaf
a few fresh parsley and tarragon sprigs
2 litres/ 3½ pints/8¾ cups water
pepper

1 Put all the ingredients in a large
   saucepan and bring to the boil.

2 Skim off the surface scum with a flat
   spoon and reduce to a gentle simmer.
Partially cover and cook for 45 minutes.
Leave to cool.

3 Line a sieve (strainer) with clean
   muslin (cheesecloth) and put over a
large jug or bowl. Pour the stock through
the sieve (strainer). Discard the herbs and
vegetables.

4 Cover and store in small quantities in
   the refrigerator for up to three days.

Fresh Beef Stock

MAKES: 1.75 LITRES/3 PINTS/7½ CUPS

about 1 kg/2 lb 4 oz bones from a cooked joint or raw chopped beef

2 onions, studded with 6 cloves, or sliced or chopped coarsely

2 carrots, sliced

1 leek, sliced

1–2 celery sticks, sliced

1 bouquet garni

about 2.25 litres/4 pints/2 quarts water

1 Use chopped marrow bones with a few strips of shin of beef if possible. Put in a roasting tin (pan) and cook in a preheated oven at 230°C/450°F/Gas Mark 8 for 30–50 minutes until browned.

2 Transfer to a large saucepan with the other ingredients. Bring to the boil and remove any scum from the surface with a perforated spoon.

3 Cover and simmer gently for 3–4 hours. Strain the stock and leave to cool. Remove any fat from the surface and chill. If stored for more than 24 hours the stock must be boiled every day, cooled quickly and chilled again.

4 The stock may be frozen for up to 2 months; place in a large plastic bag and seal, leaving at least 2.5 cm/1 inch of headspace to allow for expansion.

Fresh Chicken Stock

MAKES 1.75 LITRES/3 PINTS/7½ CUPS

1 kg/2 lb 4 oz chicken, skinned

2 celery sticks

1 onion

2 carrots

1 garlic clove

few sprigs of fresh parsley

2 litres/3½ pints/9 cups water

salt and pepper

1 Put all the ingredients into a large saucepan.

2 Bring to the boil. Skim away surface scum using a large flat spoon. Reduce the heat to a gentle simmer, partially cover, and cook for 2 hours. Allow to cool.

3 Line a sieve (strainer) with clean muslin (cheesecloth) and place over a large jug or bowl. Pour the stock through the sieve (strainer). The cooked chicken can be used in another recipe. Discard the other solids. Cover the stock and chill.

4 Skim away any fat that forms before using. Store in the refrigerator for 3-4 days, until required, or freeze in small batches.

Fresh Lamb Stock

MAKES 1.75 LITRES/3 PINTS/7½ CUPS

about 1 kg/2 lb 4 oz bones from a cooked joint or raw chopped lamb bones

2 onions, studded with 6 cloves, or sliced or chopped coarsely

2 carrots, sliced

1 leek, sliced

1-2 celery sticks, sliced

1 bouquet garni

about 2.25 litres/4 pints/2 quarts water

1 Chop or break up the bones and place in a large saucepan with the other ingredients.

2 Bring to the boil and remove any scum from the surface with a perforated spoon. Cover and simmer gently for 3-4 hours. Strain the stock and leave to cool.

3 Remove any fat from the surface and chill. If stored for more than 24 hours the stock must be boiled every day, cooled quickly and chilled again. The stock may be frozen for up to 2 months; place in a large plastic bag and seal, leaving at least 2.5 cm/1 inch of headspace to allow for expansion.

Soups & Starters

The traditional way to begin a meal is with a soup or starter, carefully selected to complement the following courses. In this chapter you will find a range of delicious soups from around the world to suit any occasion, for example Spicy Dal & Carrot Soup which is a variation of Indian dal, Louisiana Seafood Gumbo from New Orleans or the classic French soup, Vichysoisse. A good piece of advice, although it takes a little longer, it is always worth making your own stock to form the basis of your soups; ready-made stock cubes or granules often contain large quantities of salt and flavourings. If you prefer something other than soup there is also a range of delicious starters in this chapter, such as Spinach & Ricotta Cheese Patties or Salsa & Tortilla Chips.

Chicken & Sweetcorn Soup

A hint of chilli and sherry flavour this soup while red (bell) pepper and tomato add colour.

NUTRITIONAL INFORMATION

Calories 199   Sugars 8g
Protein ....12g   Fat 8g
Carbohydrate ...19g   Saturates 1g

5 MINS   20 MINS

SERVES 4

INGREDIENTS

1 skinless, boneless chicken breast,
 about 175 g/6 oz

2 tbsp sunflower oil

2–3 spring onions (scallions),
 thinly sliced diagonally

1 small or ½ large red
 (bell) pepper, thinly sliced

1 garlic clove, crushed

125 g/4½ oz baby sweetcorn (corn-on-the-
 cob), thinly sliced

1 litre/1¾ pints/4 cups chicken stock

200 g/7 oz can of sweetcorn
 niblets, well drained

2 tbsp sherry

2–3 tsp bottled sweet chilli sauce

2–3 tsp cornflour (cornstarch)

2 tomatoes, quartered
 and deseeded, then sliced

salt and pepper

chopped fresh coriander (cilantro)
 or parsley, to garnish

1 Cut the chicken breast into 4 strips lengthways, then cut each strip into narrow slices across the grain.

2 Heat the oil in a wok or frying pan (skillet), swirling it around until it is really hot.

3 Add the chicken and stir-fry for 3–4 minutes, moving it around the wok until it is well sealed all over and almost cooked through.

4 Add the spring onions (scallions), (bell) pepper and garlic, and stir-fry for 2–3 minutes. Add the sweetcorn and stock and bring to the boil.

5 Add the sweetcorn niblets, sherry, sweet chilli sauce and salt to taste, and simmer for 5 minutes, stirring from time to time.

6 Blend the cornflour (cornstarch) with a little cold water. Add to the soup and bring to the boil, stirring until the sauce is thickened. Add the tomato slices, season to taste and simmer for 1–2 minutes.

7 Serve the chicken and sweetcorn soup hot, sprinkled with chopped coriander (cilantro) or parsley.

Chicken Soup with Almonds

This soup can also be made using pheasant breasts. For a really gamy flavour, make game stock from the carcass and use in the soup.

NUTRITIONAL INFORMATION

Calories 219	Sugars 2g
Protein 18g	Fat 15g
Carbohydrate 2g	Saturates 2g

 10 MINS   20 MINS

SERVES 4

I N G R E D I E N T S

1 large or 2 small boneless skinned chicken breasts

1 tbsp sunflower oil

4 spring onions (scallions), thinly sliced diagonally

1 carrot, cut into julienne strips

700 ml/1¼ pints/3 cups chicken stock

finely grated rind of ½ lemon

40 g/1½ oz/⅓ cup ground almonds

1 tbsp light soy sauce

1 tbsp lemon juice

25 g/1 oz/¼ cup flaked almonds, toasted

salt and pepper

1 Cut each breast into 4 strips length-ways, then slice very thinly across the grain to give shreds of chicken.

2 Heat the oil in a wok, swirling it around until really hot.

3 Add the spring onions (scallions) and cook for 2 minutes, then add the chicken and toss it for 3-4 minutes until sealed and almost cooked through, stirring all the time. Add the carrot strips and stir.

4 Add the stock to the wok and bring to the boil. Add the lemon rind, ground almonds, soy sauce, lemon juice and plenty of seasoning. Bring back to the boil and simmer, uncovered, for 5 minutes, stirring from time to time.

5 Adjust the seasoning, add most of the toasted flaked almonds and continue to cook for a further 1-2 minutes.

6 Serve the soup very hot, in individual bowls, sprinkled with the remaining flaked almonds.

COOK'S TIP

To make game stock, break up a pheasant carcass and place in a pan with 2 litres/3½ pints/8 cups water. Bring to the boil slowly, skimming off any scum. Add 1 bouquet garni, 1 peeled onion and seasoning. Cover and simmer gently for 1½ hours. Strain, and skim any surface fat.

Lemon & Chicken Soup

This delicately flavoured summer soup is surprisingly easy to make, and tastes delicious.

NUTRITIONAL INFORMATION

Calories 506	Sugars 4g
Protein 19g	Fat 31g
Carbohydrate ...41g	Saturates 19g

  5–10 MINS 1¼ HOURS

SERVES 4

INGREDIENTS

60 g/2 oz/4 tbsp butter

8 shallots, thinly sliced

2 carrots, thinly sliced

2 celery sticks (stalks), thinly sliced

225 g/8 oz boned chicken breasts, finely chopped

3 lemons

1.2 litres/2 pints/5 cups chicken stock

225 g/8 oz dried spaghetti, broken into small pieces

150 ml/¼ pint/⅝ cup double (heavy) cream

salt and white pepper

TO GARNISH

fresh parsley sprig

3 lemon slices, halved

COOK'S TIP

You can prepare this soup up to the end of step 3 in advance, so that all you need do before serving is heat it through before adding the pasta and the finishing touches.

1 Melt the butter in a large saucepan. Add the shallots, carrots, celery and chicken and cook over a low heat, stirring occasionally, for 8 minutes.

2 Thinly pare the lemons and blanch the lemon rind in boiling water for 3 minutes. Squeeze the juice from the lemons.

3 Add the lemon rind and juice to the pan, together with the chicken stock. Bring slowly to the boil over a low heat and simmer for 40 minutes, stirring occasionally.

4 Add the spaghetti to the pan and cook for 15 minutes. Season to taste with salt and white pepper and add the cream. Heat through, but do not allow the soup to boil or it will curdle.

5 Pour the soup into a tureen or individual bowls, garnish with the parsley and half slices of lemon and serve immediately.

Chicken & Pasta Broth

This satisfying soup makes a good lunch or supper dish and you can use any vegetables you like. Children will love the tiny pasta shapes.

NUTRITIONAL INFORMATION

Calories 185	Sugars 5g
Protein 17g	Fat 5g
Carbohydrate ...20g	Saturates 1g

 5 MINS   15–20 MINS

SERVES 6

I N G R E D I E N T S

350 g/12 oz boneless chicken breasts

2 tbsp sunflower oil

1 medium onion, diced

250 g/9 oz/1 ½ cups carrots, diced

250 g/9 oz cauliflower florets

850 ml/1 ½ pints/3 ¾ cups chicken stock

2 tsp dried mixed herbs

125 g/4 ½ oz small pasta shapes

salt and pepper

Parmesan cheese (optional) and crusty
   bread, to serve

1 Using a sharp knife, finely dice the chicken, discarding any skin.

2 Heat the oil in a large saucepan and quickly sauté the chicken, onion, carrots and cauliflower until they are lightly coloured.

3 Stir in the chicken stock and dried mixed herbs and bring to the boil.

4 Add the pasta shapes to the pan and return to the boil. Cover the pan and leave the broth to simmer for 10 minutes, stirring occasionally to prevent the pasta shapes from sticking together.

5 Season the broth with salt and pepper to taste and sprinkle with Parmesan cheese, if using. Serve the broth with fresh crusty bread.

COOK'S TIP

You can use any small pasta shapes for this soup – try conchigliette or ditalini or even spaghetti broken up into small pieces. To make a fun soup for children you could add animal-shaped or alphabet pasta.

Clear Chicken & Egg Soup

This tasty chicken soup has the addition of poached eggs, making it both delicious and filling. Use fresh, home-made stock for a better flavour.

NUTRITIONAL INFORMATION

Calories 138   Sugars 1g
Protein ....16g   Fat 7g
Carbohydrate ....1g   Saturates 2g

 5 MINS   35 MINS

SERVES 4

INGREDIENTS

1 tsp salt

1 tbsp rice wine vinegar

4 eggs

850 ml/1½ pints/3¾ cups
   chicken stock

1 leek, sliced

125 g/4½ oz broccoli florets

125 g/4½ oz/1 cup shredded
   cooked chicken

2 open-cap mushrooms, sliced

1 tbsp dry sherry

dash of chilli sauce

chilli powder, to garnish

VARIATION

You could use 4 dried Chinese mushrooms, rehydrated according to the packet instructions, instead of the open-cap mushrooms, if you prefer.

1 Bring a large saucepan of water to the boil and add the salt and rice wine vinegar.

2 Reduce the heat so that it is just simmering and carefully break the eggs into the water, one at a time. Poach the eggs for 1 minute.

3 Remove the poached eggs with a slotted spoon and set aside.

4 Bring the chicken stock to the boil in a separate pan and add the leek, broccoli, chicken, mushrooms and sherry and season with chilli sauce to taste. Cook for 10–15 minutes.

5 Add the poached eggs to the soup and cook for a further 2 minutes. Carefully transfer the soup and poached eggs to 4 soup bowls. Dust with a little chilli powder and serve immediately.

Chinese Cabbage Soup

This is a piquant soup, which is slightly sweet-and-sour in flavour.
It can be served as a hearty meal or appetizer.

NUTRITIONAL INFORMATION

Calories	65	Sugars	.........7g
Protein	.........3g	Fat	..........0.5g
Carbohydrate	....11g	Saturates	.....0.1g

   5 MINS   30 MINS

SERVES 4

INGREDIENTS

450 g/1 lb pak choi

600 ml/1 pint/2½ cups vegetable
 stock

1 tbsp rice wine vinegar

1 tbsp light soy sauce

1 tbsp caster (superfine) sugar

1 tbsp dry sherry

1 fresh red chilli, thinly sliced

1 tbsp cornflour (cornstarch)

2 tbsp water

1 Wash the pak choi thoroughly under cold running water, rinse and drain. Pat dry on kitchen paper (paper towels) .

2 Trim the stems of the pak choi and shred the leaves.

3 Heat the vegetable stock in a large saucepan. Add the pak choi and cook for 10–15 minutes.

4 Mix together the rice wine vinegar, soy sauce, caster (superfine) sugar and sherry in a small bowl. Add this mixture to the stock, together with the sliced chilli.

5 Bring to the boil, lower the heat and cook for 2–3 minutes.

6 Blend the cornflour (cornstarch) with the water to form a smooth paste.

7 Gradually stir the cornflour (cornstarch) mixture into the soup. Cook, stirring constantly, until it thickens. Cook for a further 4–5 minutes.

8 Ladle the Chinese cabbage soup into individual warm serving bowls and serve immediately.

COOKS TIP

Pak choi, also known as bok choi or spoon cabbage, has long, white leaf stalks and fleshy, spoon-shaped, shiny green leaves. There are a number of varieties available, which differ mainly in size rather than flavour.

Lamb & Rice Soup

This is a very filling soup, as it contains rice and tender pieces of lamb. Serve before a light main course.

NUTRITIONAL INFORMATION

Calories	116	Sugars	0.2g
Protein	9g	Fat	4g
Carbohydrate	12g	Saturates	2g

5 MINS   35 MINS

SERVES 4

I N G R E D I E N T S

150 g/5½ oz lean lamb

50 g/1¾ oz/¼ cup rice

850 ml/1½ pints/3¾ cups
   lamb stock

1 leek, sliced

1 garlic clove, thinly sliced

2 tsp light soy sauce

1 tsp rice wine vinegar

1 medium open-cap mushroom,
   thinly sliced

salt

1 Using a sharp knife, trim any fat from the lamb and cut the meat into thin strips. Set aside until required.

2 Bring a large pan of lightly salted water to the boil and add the rice. Bring back to the boil, stir once, reduce the heat and cook for 10–15 minutes, until tender.

3 Drain the rice, rinse under cold running water, drain again and set aside until required.

4 Meanwhile, put the lamb stock in a large saucepan and bring to the boil.

5 Add the lamb strips, leek, garlic, soy sauce and rice wine vinegar to the stock in the pan. Reduce the heat, cover and leave to simmer for 10 minutes, or until the lamb is tender and cooked through.

6 Add the mushroom slices and the rice to the pan and cook for a further 2–3 minutes, or until the mushroom is completely cooked through.

7 Ladle the soup into 4 individual warmed soup bowls and serve immediately.

VARIATION

Use a few dried Chinese mushrooms, rehydrated according to the packet instructions and chopped, as an alternative to the open-cap mushroom. Add the Chinese mushrooms with the lamb in step 4.

Potato & Pesto Soup

Fresh pesto is a treat to the taste buds and very different in flavour from that available from supermarkets. Store fresh pesto in the refrigerator.

NUTRITIONAL INFORMATION

Calories 548   Sugars 0g
Protein . . . . .11g   Fat 52g
Carbohydrate . . .10g   Saturates 18g

5–10 MINS   50 MINS

SERVES 4

I N G R E D I E N T S

3 slices rindless, smoked, fatty bacon

450 g/1 lb floury potatoes

450 g/ 1 lb onions

2 tbsp olive oil

25 g/1 oz/2 tbsp butter

600 ml/1 pint/2 ½ cups chicken stock

600 ml/1 pint/2 ½ cups milk

100 g/3 ½ oz/ ¾ cup dried conchigliette

150 ml/ ¼ pint/ ⅝ cup double (heavy) cream

chopped fresh parsley

salt and pepper

freshly grated Parmesan cheese and garlic
    bread, to serve

P E S T O   S A U C E

60 g/2 oz/1 cup finely chopped fresh
    parsley

2 garlic cloves, crushed

60 g/2 oz/ ⅔ cup pine nuts (kernels),
    crushed

2 tbsp chopped fresh basil leaves

60 g/2 oz/ ⅔ cup freshly grated Parmesan
    cheese

white pepper

150 ml/ ¼ pint/ ⅝ cup olive oil

1 To make the pesto sauce, put all of the ingredients in a blender or food processor and process for 2 minutes, or blend by hand using a pestle and mortar.

2 Finely chop the bacon, potatoes and onions. Fry the bacon in a large pan over a medium heat for 4 minutes. Add the butter, potatoes and onions and cook for 12 minutes, stirring constantly.

3 Add the stock and milk to the pan, bring to the boil and simmer for 10 minutes. Add the conchigliette and simmer for a further 10-12 minutes.

4 Blend in the cream and simmer for 5 minutes. Add the parsley, salt and pepper and 2 tbsp pesto sauce. Transfer the soup to serving bowls and serve with Parmesan cheese and fresh garlic bread.

Indian Bean Soup

A thick and hearty soup, nourishing and substantial enough to serve as a main meal with wholemeal (whole wheat) bread.

NUTRITIONAL INFORMATION

Calories 237	Sugars 9g	
Protein 9g	Fat 9g	
Carbohydrate ...33g	Saturates 1g	

 20 MINS   50 MINS

SERVES 6

INGREDIENTS

4 tbsp vegetable ghee or vegetable oil

2 onions, peeled and chopped

225 g/8 oz/1½ cups potato, cut
   into chunks

225 g/8 oz/1½ cups parsnip, cut
   into chunks

225 g/8 oz/1½ cups turnip or swede
   (rutabaga), cut into chunks

2 celery sticks, sliced

2 courgettes (zucchini), sliced

1 green (bell) pepper, seeded and cut into
   1 cm/½ inch pieces

2 garlic cloves, crushed

2 tsp ground coriander

1 tbsp paprika

1 tbsp mild curry paste

1.2 litres/2 pints/5 cups vegetable stock

salt

400 g/14 oz can black-eye beans (peas),
   drained and rinsed

chopped coriander (cilantro),
   to garnish (optional)

1 Heat the ghee or oil in a saucepan, add all the prepared vegetables, except the courgettes (zucchini) and green (bell) pepper, and cook over a moderate heat, stirring frequently, for 5 minutes. Add the garlic, ground coriander, paprika and curry paste and cook, stirring constantly, for 1 minute.

2 Stir in the stock and season with salt to taste. Bring to the boil, cover and simmer over a low heat, stirring occasionally, for 25 minutes.

3 Stir in the black-eye beans (peas), sliced courgettes (zucchini) and green (bell) pepper, cover and continue cooking for a further 15 minutes, or until all the vegetables are tender.

4 Process 300 ml/½ pint/1¼ cups of the soup mixture (about 2 ladlefuls) in a food processor or blender. Return the puréed mixture to the soup in the saucepan and reheat until piping hot. Sprinkle with chopped coriander (cilantro), if using and serve hot.

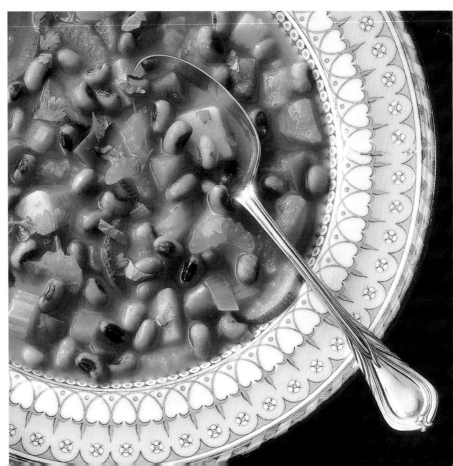

Veal & Ham Soup

Veal and ham is a classic combination, complemented here with the addition of sherry to create a richly-flavoured Italian soup.

NUTRITIONAL INFORMATION

Calories 501   Sugars 10g
Protein . . . . .38g   Fat 18g
Carbohydrate . . .28g   Saturates 10g

5 MINS   3¼ HOURS

SERVES 4

I N G R E D I E N T S

60 g/2 oz/4 tbsp butter

1 onion, diced

1 carrot, diced

1 celery stick (stalk), diced

450 g/1 lb veal, very thinly sliced

450 g/1 lb ham, thinly sliced

60 g/2 oz/ ½ cup plain (all-purpose) flour

1 litre/1 ¾ pints/4 ⅜ cups beef stock

1 bay leaf

8 black peppercorns

pinch of salt

3 tbsp redcurrant jelly

150 ml/ ¼ pint/ ⅝ cup cream sherry

100 g/3 ½ oz/ ¾ cup dried vermicelli

garlic croûtons (see Cook's Tip), to serve

1 Melt the butter in a large pan. Add the onions, carrot, celery, veal and ham and cook over a low heat for 6 minutes.

2 Sprinkle over the flour and cook, stirring constantly, for a further 2 minutes. Gradually stir in the stock, then add the bay leaf, peppercorns and salt. Bring to the boil and simmer for 1 hour.

3 Remove the pan from the heat and add the redcurrant jelly and cream sherry, stirring to combine. Set aside for about 4 hours.

4 Remove the bay leaf from the pan and discard. Reheat the soup over a very low heat until warmed through.

5 Meanwhile, cook the vermicelli in a saucepan of lightly salted boiling water for 10-12 minutes. Stir the vermicelli into the soup and transfer to soup bowls. Serve with garlic croûtons.

COOK'S TIP

To make garlic croûtons, remove the crusts from 3 slices of day-old white bread. Cut the bread into 5 mm/¼ inch cubes. Heat 3 tbsp oil over a low heat and stir-fry 1–2 chopped garlic cloves for 1–2 minutes. Remove the garlic and add the bread. Cook, stirring frequently, until golden. Remove with a slotted spoon and drain.

Chinese Potato & Pork Broth

In this recipe the pork is seasoned with traditional Chinese flavourings – soy sauce, rice wine vinegar and a dash of sesame oil.

NUTRITIONAL INFORMATION

Calories	166	Sugars	.........2g
Protein	........10g	Fat	...........5g
Carbohydrate	...26g	Saturates	.......1g

5 MINS   20 MINS

SERVES 4

INGREDIENTS

1 litre/1¾ pints/4½ cups chicken stock

2 large potatoes, diced

2 tbsp rice wine vinegar

2 tbsp cornflour (cornstarch)

4 tbsp water

125 g/4½ oz pork fillet, sliced

1 tbsp light soy sauce

1 tsp sesame oil

1 carrot, cut into very thin strips

1 tsp ginger root, chopped

3 spring onions (scallions), sliced thinly

1 red (bell) pepper, sliced

225 g/8 oz can bamboo shoots, drained

VARIATION

For extra heat, add 1 chopped red chilli or 1 tsp of chilli powder to the soup in step 5.

1 Add the chicken stock, diced potatoes and 1 tbsp of the rice wine vinegar to a saucepan and bring to the boil. Reduce the heat until the stock is just simmering.

2 Mix the cornflour (cornstarch) with the water then stir into the hot stock.

3 Bring the stock back to the boil, stirring until thickened, then reduce the heat until it is just simmering again.

4 Place the pork slices in a dish and season with the remaining rice wine vinegar, the soy sauce and sesame oil.

5 Add the pork slices, carrot strips and ginger to the stock and cook for 10 minutes. Stir in the spring onions (scallions), red (bell) pepper and bamboo shoots. Cook for a further 5 minutes. Pour the soup into warmed bowls and serve immediately.

Mussel & Potato Soup

This quick and easy soup would make a delicious summer lunch, served with fresh crusty bread.

NUTRITIONAL INFORMATION

Calories	804	Sugars	.........3g
Protein	........17g	Fat	..........68g
Carbohydrate	...32g	Saturates	......38g

 10 MINS   35 MINS

SERVES 4

INGREDIENTS

750 g/1 lb 10 oz mussels

2 tbsp olive oil

100 g/3½ oz/7 tbsp unsalted butter

2 slices rindless fatty bacon, chopped

1 onion, chopped

2 garlic cloves, crushed

60 g/2 oz/½ cup plain (all-purpose) flour

450 g/1 lb potatoes, thinly sliced

100 g/3½ oz/¾ cup dried conchigliette

300 ml/½ pint/1¼ cups double (heavy) cream

1 tbsp lemon juice

2 egg yolks

salt and pepper

TO GARNISH

2 tbsp finely chopped fresh parsley

lemon wedges

1 Debeard the mussels and scrub them under cold water for 5 minutes. Discard any mussels that do not close immediately when sharply tapped.

2 Bring a large pan of water to the boil, add the mussels, oil and a little pepper. Cook until the mussels open. (discard any mussels that remain closed.

3 Drain the mussels, reserving the cooking liquid. Remove the mussels from their shells.

4 Melt the butter in a large saucepan, add the bacon, onion and garlic and cook for 4 minutes. Carefully stir in the flour. Measure 1.2 litres/2 pints/5 cups of the reserved cooking liquid and stir it into the pan.

5 Add the potatoes to the pan and simmer for 5 minutes. Add the conchigliette and simmer for a further 10 minutes.

6 Add the cream and lemon juice, season to taste with salt and pepper, then add the mussels to the pan.

7 Blend the egg yolks with 1-2 tbsp of the remaining cooking liquid, stir into the pan and cook for 4 minutes.

8 Ladle the soup into 4 warm individual soup bowls, garnish with the chopped fresh parsley and lemon wedges and serve immediately.

Spicy Prawn (Shrimp) Soup

Lime leaves are used as a flavouring in this soup to add tartness.

NUTRITIONAL INFORMATION

Calories 217	Sugars 16g
Protein 16g	Fat 4g
Carbohydrate . . .31g	Saturates 1g

10 MINS   20 MINS

SERVES 4

INGREDIENTS

2 tbsp tamarind paste

4 red chilies, very finely chopped

2 cloves garlic, crushed

2.5 cm/1 inch piece Thai ginger, peeled and very finely chopped

4 tbsp fish sauce

2 tbsp palm sugar or caster (superfine) sugar

1.2 litres/2 pints/5 cups fish stock

8 lime leaves

100 g/3½ oz carrots, very thinly sliced

350 g/12 oz sweet potato, diced

100 g/3½ oz/1 cup baby corn cobs, halved

3 tbsp fresh coriander (cilantro), roughly chopped

100g/3½ oz cherry tomatoes, halved

225 g/8 oz fan-tail prawns (shrimp)

1 Place the tamarind paste, red chillies, garlic, ginger, fish sauce, sugar and fish stock in a preheated wok or large, heavy frying pan (skillet). Roughly tear the lime leaves and add to the wok. Bring to the boil, stirring constantly to blend the flavours.

2 Reduce the heat and add the carrot, sweet potato and baby corn cobs to the mixture in the wok.

3 Leave the soup to simmer, uncovered, for about 10 minutes, or until the vegetables are just tender.

4 Stir the coriander (cilantro), cherry tomatoes and prawns (shrimp) into the soup and heat through for 5 minutes.

5 Transfer the soup to a warm soup tureen or individual serving bowls and serve hot.

COOK'S TIP

Thai ginger or galangal is a member of the ginger family, but it is yellow in colour with pink sprouts. The flavour is aromatic and less pungent than ginger.

Shrimp Dumpling Soup

These small dumplings filled with shrimp and pork may be made slightly larger and served as dim sum on their own, if you prefer.

NUTRITIONAL INFORMATION

Calories 311	Sugars 2g
Protein 18g	Fat 8g
Carbohydrate . . .41g	Saturates 2g

🐚 🐚 🐚 🐚

🍲 20 MINS   🕐 10 MINS

SERVES 4

I N G R E D I E N T S

DUMPLINGS

150 g/5½ oz/1⅛ cups plain (all-purpose) flour

50 ml/2 fl oz/¼ cup boiling water

30 ml/1 fl oz/⅛ cup cold water

1½ tsp vegetable oil

FILLING

125 g/4½ oz minced (ground) pork

125 g/4½ oz cooked peeled shrimp, chopped

50 g/1¾ oz canned water chestnuts, drained, rinsed and chopped

1 celery stick, chopped

1 tsp cornflour (cornstarch)

1 tbsp sesame oil

1 tbsp light soy sauce

SOUP

850 ml/1½ pints/3¾ cups fish stock

50 g/1¾ oz cellophane noodles

1 tbsp dry sherry

chopped chives, to garnish

1 To make the dumplings, mix together the flour, boiling water, cold water and oil in a bowl until a pliable dough is formed.

2 Knead the dough on a lightly floured surface for 5 minutes. Cut the dough into 16 equal sized pieces.

3 Roll the dough pieces into rounds about 7.5 cm/ 3 inches in diameter.

4 Mix the filling ingredients together in a large bowl.

5 Spoon a little of the filling mixture into the centre of each round. Bring the edges of the dough together, scrunching them up to form a 'moneybag' shape. Twist the gathered edges to seal.

6 Pour the fish stock into a large saucepan and bring to the boil.

7 Add the cellophane noodles, dumplings and dry sherry to the pan and cook for 4–5 minutes, until the noodles and dumplings are tender. Garnish with chopped chives and serve immediately.

Louisiana Seafood Gumbo

Gumbo is a hearty, thick soup, almost a stew. This New Orleans classic must be served with a scoop of hot, fluffy, cooked rice.

NUTRITIONAL INFORMATION

Calories	267	Sugars 6g
Protein	........27g	Fat 8g
Carbohydrate	...24g	Saturates 1g

5 MINS   35 MINS

SERVES 4

I N G R E D I E N T S

1 tbsp plain flour

1 tsp paprika

350 g/12 oz monkfish fillets, cut into chunks

2 tbsp olive oil

1 onion, chopped

1 green (bell) pepper, cored, seeded and chopped

3 celery sticks, finely chopped

2 garlic cloves, crushed

175 g/6 oz okra, sliced

600 ml/1 pint/2½ cups vegetable stock

1 x 425 g/15 oz can chopped tomatoes

1 bouquet garni

125 g/4½ oz peeled prawns (shrimp)

juice of 1 lemon

dash of Tabasco

2 tsp Worcestershire sauce

175 g/6 oz/generous 1 cup cooked long-grain American rice

1 Mix the flour with the paprika. Add the monkfish chunks and toss to coat well.

2 Heat the olive oil in a large, heavy-based pan. Add the monkfish pieces and fry

until browned on all sides. Remove from the pan with a slotted spoon and set aside.

3 Add the onion, green (bell) pepper, celery, garlic and okra and fry gently for 5 minutes until softened.

4 Add the stock, tomatoes and bouquet garni. Bring to the boil, reduce the heat and simmer for 15 minutes.

5 Return the monkfish to the pan with the prawns (shrimp), lemon juice, Tabasco and Worcestershire sauces. Simmer for a further 5 minutes.

6 To serve, place a mound of cooked rice in each warmed, serving bowl, then ladle over the seafood gumbo.

Tuscan Veal Broth

Veal plays an important role in Italian cuisine and there are dozens of recipes for all cuts of this meat.

NUTRITIONAL INFORMATION

Calories 420   Sugars 5g
Protein . . . . .54g   Fat 7g
Carbohydrate . . .37g   Saturates 2g

2¼ HOURS   4¾ HOURS

SERVES 4

INGREDIENTS

60 g/2 oz/⅓ cup dried peas, soaked for
   2 hours and drained

900 g/2 lb boned neck of veal, diced

1.2 litres/2 pints/5 cups beef or brown
   stock (see Cook's Tip)

600 ml/1 pint/2½ cups water

60 g/2 oz/⅓ cup barley, washed

1 large carrot, diced

1 small turnip (about 175 g/6 oz), diced

1 large leek, thinly sliced

1 red onion, finely chopped

100 g/3½ oz chopped tomatoes

1 fresh basil sprig

100 g/3½ oz/¾ cup dried vermicelli

salt and white pepper

1 Put the peas, veal, stock and water into a large pan and bring to the boil over a low heat. Using a slotted spoon, skim off any scum that rises to the surface.

2 When all of the scum has been removed, add the barley and a pinch of salt to the mixture. Simmer gently over a low heat for 25 minutes.

3 Add the carrot, turnip, leek, onion, tomatoes and basil to the pan, and season with salt and pepper to taste. Leave to simmer for about 2 hours, skimming the surface from time to time to remove any scum. Remove the pan from the heat and set aside for 2 hours.

4 Set the pan over a medium heat and bring to the boil. Add the vermicelli and cook for 12 minutes. Season with salt and pepper to taste; remove and discard the basil. Ladle into soup bowls and serve immediately.

COOK'S TIP

The best brown stock is made with veal bones and shin of beef roasted with dripping (drippings) in the oven for 40 minutes. Transfer the bones to a pan and add sliced leeks, onion, celery and carrots, a bouquet garni, white wine vinegar and a thyme sprig and cover with cold water. Simmer over a very low heat for 3 hours; strain before use.

Seafood & Tofu Soup

Use prawn (shrimp), squid or scallops, or a combination of all three in this healthy soup.

NUTRITIONAL INFORMATION

Calories 97	Sugars 0g
Protein 17g	Fat 2g
Carbohydrate 3g	Saturates 0.4g

  3¹/₂ HOURS 10 MINS

SERVES 4

INGREDIENTS

250 g/9 oz seafood: peeled prawns (shrimp), squid, scallops, etc. defrosted if frozen

½ egg white, lightly beaten

1 tbsp cornflour (cornstarch) paste (see page 6)

1 cake tofu (bean curd)

700 ml/1¼ pints/3 cups Chinese Stock (see page 8)

1 tbsp light soy sauce

salt and pepper

fresh coriander (cilantro) leaves, to garnish (optional)

1 Small prawns (shrimp) can be left whole; larger ones should be cut into smaller pieces; cut the squid and scallops into small pieces.

2 If raw, mix the prawns (shrimp) and scallops with the egg white and cornflour (cornstarch) paste to prevent them from becoming tough when they are cooked. Cut the cake of tofu into about 24 small cubes.

3 Bring the stock to a rolling boil. Add the tofu and soy sauce, bring back to the boil and simmer for 1 minute.

4 Stir in the seafood, raw pieces first, pre-cooked ones last. Bring back to the boil and simmer for just 1 minute.

5 Adjust the seasoning to taste and serve, garnished with coriander, (cilantro) leaves, if liked.

COOK'S TIP

Tofu, also known as bean curd, is made from puréed yellow soya beans, which are very high in protein. Although almost tasteless, tofu absorbs the flavours of other ingredients. It is widely available in supermarkets, and Oriental and health-food stores.

Minestrone

Minestrone translates as 'big soup' in Italian. It is made all over Italy, but this version comes from Livorno, a port on the western coast.

NUTRITIONAL INFORMATION

Calories . . . . .311 Sugars 8g
Protein . . . . .12g Fat 19g
Carbohydrate . . .26g Saturates 5g

 10 MINS 30 MINS

SERVES 4

INGREDIENTS

1 tbsp olive oil

100 g/3 ½ oz pancetta ham, diced

2 medium onions, chopped

2 cloves garlic, crushed

1 potato, peeled and cut into 1 cm/
  ½ inch cubes

1 carrot, peeled and cut into chunks

1 leek, sliced into rings

¼ green cabbage, shredded

1 stick celery, chopped

450 g/1 lb can chopped tomatoes

200 g/7 oz can flageolet (small navy)
  beans, drained and rinsed

600 ml/1 pint/2 ½ cups hot ham or chicken
  stock, diluted with 600 ml/1 pint/2 ½ cups
  boiling water

bouquet garni (2 bay leaves, 2 sprigs
  rosemary and 2 sprigs thyme, tied
together)

salt and pepper

freshly grated Parmesan cheese, to serve

1 Heat the olive oil in a large saucepan. Add the diced pancetta, chopped onions and garlic and fry for about 5 minutes, stirring, or until the onions are soft and golden.

2 Add the prepared potato, carrot, leek, cabbage and celery to the saucepan. Cook for a further 2 minutes, stirring frequently, to coat all of the vegetables in the oil.

3 Add the tomatoes, flageolet (small navy) beans, hot ham or chicken stock and bouquet garni to the pan, stirring to mix. Leave the soup to simmer, covered, for 15–20 minutes or until all of the vegetables are just tender.

4 Remove the bouquet garni, season with salt and pepper to taste and serve with plenty of freshly grated Parmesan cheese.

Crab & Ginger Soup

Two classic ingredients in Chinese cooking are blended together in this recipe for a special soup.

NUTRITIONAL INFORMATION

Calories 32	Sugars 1g
Protein 6g	Fat 0.4g
Carbohydrate 1g	Saturates 0g

10 MINS   25 MINS

SERVES 4

I N G R E D I E N T S

1 carrot

1 leek

1 bay leaf

850 ml/1½ pints/3¾ cups fish stock

2 medium-sized cooked crabs

2.5-cm/1-inch piece fresh root ginger (ginger root), grated

1 tsp light soy sauce

½ tsp ground star anise

salt and pepper

1 Using a sharp knife, chop the carrot and leek into small pieces and place in a large saucepan with the bay leaf and fish stock.

2 Bring the mixture in the saucepan to the boil.

3 Reduce the heat, cover and leave to simmer for about 10 minutes, or until the vegetables are nearly tender.

4 Remove all of the meat from the cooked crabs. Break off and reserve the claws, break the joints and remove the meat, using a fork or skewer.

5 Add the crabmeat to the pan of fish stock, together with the ginger, soy sauce and star anise and bring to the boil. Leave to simmer for about 10 minutes, or until the vegetables are tender and the crab is heated through.

6 Season the soup then ladle into a warmed soup tureen or individual serving bowls and garnish with crab claws. Serve immediately.

VARIATION

If fresh crabmeat is unavailable, use drained canned crabmeat or thawed frozen crabmeat instead.

Sweetcorn & Crab Soup

Be sure to use proper creamed sweetcorn for this soup. It has a slightly mushy consistency making a deliciously thick, creamy soup.

NUTRITIONAL INFORMATION

Calories 133	Sugars 6g
Protein 10g	Fat 3g
Carbohydrate ...19g	Saturates 0.4g

 3¹/₂ HOURS   10 MINS

SERVES 4

INGREDIENTS

125 g/4½ oz crab meat (or 1 chicken breast)

¼ tsp finely chopped ginger root

2 egg whites

2 tbsp milk

1 tbsp cornflour (cornstarch) paste (see page 6)

600 ml/1 pint/2½ cups Chinese Stock (see page 8)

1 x 250 g/9 oz can American-style creamed sweetcorn

salt and pepper

finely chopped spring onions (scallions), to garnish

1 In a small bowl, flake the crab meat. Add the chopped ginger root and mix well. If using chicken breast, coarsely chop and mix with the ginger.

2 Beat the egg whites until frothy, add the milk and cornflour (cornstarch) paste and beat again until smooth.

3 Blend the crab meat or chicken into the egg-white mixture.

4 In a wok or large frying pan (skillet), bring the stock to the boil, add the sweetcorn and bring back to the boil, stirring gently.

5 Stir in the crab meat or chicken pieces and egg-white mixture.

6 Add salt and pepper to taste and stir the soup gently until the mixture is well blended.

7 Pour the soup into a warm tureen or individual serving bowls, garnish with chopped spring onions (scallions) and serve immediately.

COOK'S TIP

Always obtain the freshest possible crab, although frozen or canned will work in this recipe. The delicate, sweet flavour of crab diminishes very quickly which is why Chinese chefs tend to buy live crabs.

Tuscan Onion Soup

This soup is best made with white onions, which have a mild flavour. If you cannot get hold of them, try using large Spanish onions instead.

NUTRITIONAL INFORMATION

Calories 390   Sugars 0g
Protein . . . . .9g   Fat 33g
Carbohydrate . . .15g   Saturates 14g

 5–10 MINS   40–45 MINS

SERVES 4

INGREDIENTS

50 g/1¾ oz pancetta ham, diced

1 tbsp olive oil

4 large white onions, sliced thinly into rings

3 garlic cloves, chopped

850 ml/1½ pints/3½ cups hot chicken or
   ham stock

4 slices ciabatta or other Italian bread

50 g/1¾ oz/3 tbsp butter

75 g/2¾ oz Gruyère or Cheddar

salt and pepper

1 Dry fry the pancetta in a large saucepan for 3–4 minutes until it begins to brown. Remove the pancetta from the pan and set aside until required.

2 Add the oil to the pan and cook the onions and garlic over a high heat for 4 minutes. Reduce the heat, cover and cook for 15 minutes or until the onions are lightly caramelized.

3 Add the stock to the saucepan and bring to the boil. Reduce the heat and leave the mixture to simmer, covered, for about 10 minutes.

4 Toast the slices of ciabatta on both sides, under a preheated grill (broiler), for 2–3 minutes or until golden. Spread the ciabatta with butter and top with the Gruyère or Cheddar cheese. Cut the bread into bite-size pieces.

5 Add the reserved pancetta to the soup and season with salt and pepper to taste.

6 Pour into 4 soup bowls and top with the toasted bread.

COOK'S TIP

Pancetta is similar to bacon, but it is air- and salt-cured for about 6 months. Pancetta is available from most delicatessens and some large supermarkets. If you cannot obtain pancetta use unsmoked bacon instead.

Gazpacho

This Spanish soup is full of chopped and grated vegetables with a puréed tomato base. It requires chilling, so prepare well in advance.

NUTRITIONAL INFORMATION

Calories 140   Sugars 12g
Protein . . . . .3g   Fat 9g
Carbohydrate . . .13g   Saturates 1g

 6¹/₂ HOURS 0 MINS

SERVES 4

I N G R E D I E N T S

½ small cucumber

½ small green (bell) pepper, seeded and
    very finely chopped

500 g/1 lb 2 oz ripe tomatoes, peeled or
    400 g/14 oz can chopped tomatoes

½ onion, coarsely chopped

2–3 garlic cloves, crushed

3 tbsp olive oil

2 tbsp white wine vinegar

1–2 tbsp lemon or lime juice

2 tbsp tomato purée (paste)

450 ml/16 fl oz/scant 2 cups tomato juice

salt and pepper

TO SERVE

chopped green (bell) pepper

thinly sliced onion rings

garlic croûtons

1   Coarsely grate the cucumber into a large bowl and add the chopped green (bell) pepper.

2   Process the tomatoes, onion and garlic in a food processor or blender, then add the oil, vinegar, lemon or lime juice and tomato purée (paste) and process until smooth. Alternatively, finely chop the tomatoes and finely grate the onion, then mix both with the garlic, oil, vinegar, lemon or lime juice and tomato purée (paste).

3   Add the tomato mixture to the bowl and mix well, then add the tomato juice and mix again.

4   Season to taste, cover the bowl with clear film (plastic wrap) and chill thoroughly – for at least 6 hours and preferably longer so that the flavours have time to meld together.

5   Prepare the side dishes of green (bell) pepper, onion rings and garlic croûtons, and arrange in individual serving bowls.

6   Ladle the soup into bowls, preferably from a soup tureen set on the table with the side dishes placed around it. Hand the dishes around to allow the guests to help themselves.

Creamy Tomato Soup

This quick and easy creamy soup has a lovely fresh tomato flavour. Basil leaves complement tomatoes perfectly.

NUTRITIONAL INFORMATION

Calories 218	Sugars 10g	
Protein 3g	Fat 19g	
Carbohydrate . . .10g	Saturates 11g	

5 MINS   25–30 MINS

SERVES 4

INGREDIENTS

50 g/1 ¾ oz/3 tbsp butter

700 g/1 lb 9 oz ripe tomatoes, preferably plum, roughly chopped

850 ml/1 ½ pints/3 ¾ hot vegetable stock

50 g/1 ¾ oz/ ¼ cup ground almonds

150 ml/¼ pint/ ⅔ cup milk or single (light) cream

1 tsp sugar

2 tbsp shredded basil leaves

salt and pepper

1 Melt the butter in a large saucepan. Add the tomatoes and cook for 5 minutes until the skins start to wrinkle. Season to taste with salt and pepper.

2 Add the stock to the pan, bring to the boil, cover and simmer for 10 minutes.

3 Meanwhile, under a preheated grill (broiler), lightly toast the ground almonds until they are golden-brown. This will take only 1-2 minutes, so watch them closely.

4 Remove the soup from the heat and place in a food processor and blend the mixture to form a smooth consistency. Alternatively, mash the soup with a potato masher until smooth.

5 Pass the soup through a sieve to remove any tomato skin or pips.

6 Place the soup in the pan and return to the heat. Stir in the milk or cream, toasted ground almonds and sugar. Warm the soup through and add the shredded basil leaves just before serving.

7 Transfer the creamy tomato soup to warm soup bowls and serve hot.

COOK'S TIP

Very fine breadcrumbs can be used instead of the ground almonds, if you prefer. Toast them in the same way as the almonds and add with the milk or cream in step 6.

Pumpkin & Orange Soup

This thick, creamy soup has a wonderful, warming golden colour.
It is flavoured with orange and thyme.

NUTRITIONAL INFORMATION

Calories 111   Sugars 4g
Protein . . . . .2g   Fat 6g
Carbohydrate . . . .5g   Saturates 2g

 10 MINS   35–40 MINS

SERVES 4

INGREDIENTS

2 tbsp olive oil

2 medium onions, chopped

2 cloves garlic, chopped

900 g/2 lb pumpkin, peeled and cut into
 2.5 cm/1 inch chunks

1.5 litres /2 ¾ pints/6 ¼ cups boiling
 vegetable or chicken stock

finely grated rind and juice of 1 orange

3 tbsp fresh thyme, stalks removed

150 ml/¼ pint/⅔ cup milk

salt and pepper

crusty bread, to serve

1 Heat the olive oil in a large saucepan. Add the onions to the pan and cook for 3–4 minutes or until softened. Add the garlic and pumpkin and cook for a further 2 minutes, stirring well.

2 Add the boiling vegetable or chicken stock, orange rind and juice and 2 tablespoons of the thyme to the pan. Leave to simmer, covered, for 20 minutes or until the pumpkin is tender.

3 Place the mixture in a food processor and blend until smooth. Alternatively, mash the mixture with a potato masher until smooth. Season to taste.

4 Return the soup to the saucepan and add the milk. Reheat the soup for 3–4 minutes or until it is piping hot but not boiling.

5 Sprinkle with the remaining fresh thyme just before serving.

6 Divide the soup among 4 warm soup bowls and serve with lots of fresh crusty bread.

COOK'S TIP

Pumpkins are usually large vegetables. To make things a little easier, ask the greengrocer to cut a chunk off for you. Alternatively, make double the quantity and freeze the soup for up to 3 months.

Cream of Artichoke Soup

A creamy soup with the unique, subtle flavouring of Jerusalem artichokes and a garnish of grated carrots for extra crunch.

NUTRITIONAL INFORMATION

Calories 19	Sugars 0g
Protein 0.4g	Fat 2g
Carbohydrate . . .0.7g	Saturates 0.7g

10–15 MINS   55–60 MINS

SERVES 6

I N G R E D I E N T S

750 g/1 lb 10 oz Jerusalem artichokes

1 lemon, sliced thickly

60 g/2 oz/¼ cup butter or margarine

2 onions, chopped

1 garlic clove, crushed

1.25 litres/2¼ pints/5½ cups chicken or
   vegetable stock

2 bay leaves

¼ tsp ground mace or ground nutmeg

1 tbsp lemon juice

150 ml/¼ pint/⅔ cup single (light) cream or
   natural fromage frais

salt and pepper

TO GARNISH

coarsely grated carrot

chopped fresh parsley or coriander
   (cilantro)

1 Peel and slice the artichokes. Put into a bowl of water with the lemon slices.

2 Melt the butter or margarine in a large saucepan. Add the onions and garlic and fry gently for 3–4 minutes until soft but not coloured.

3 Drain the artichokes (discarding the lemon) and add to the pan. Mix well and cook gently for 2–3 minutes without allowing to colour.

4 Add the stock, seasoning, bay leaves, mace or nutmeg and lemon juice. Bring slowly to the boil, then cover and simmer gently for about 30 minutes until the vegetables are very tender.

5 Discard the bay leaves. Cool the soup slightly then press through a sieve (strainer) or blend in a food processor until smooth. If liked, a little of the soup may be only partially puréed and added to the rest of the puréed soup, to give extra texture.

6 Pour into a clean pan and bring to the boil. Adjust the seasoning and stir in the cream or fromage frais. Reheat gently without boiling. Garnish with grated carrot and chopped parsley or coriander (cilantro).

Indian Potato & Pea Soup

A slightly hot and spicy Indian flavour is given to this soup with the use of garam masala, chilli, cumin and coriander.

NUTRITIONAL INFORMATION

Calories 153   Sugars 6g
Protein ....6g   Fat 6g
Carbohydrate ...18g   Saturates 1g

 5 MINS   35 MINS

SERVES 4

INGREDIENTS

2 tbsp vegetable oil

225 g/8 oz floury (mealy) potatoes, diced

1 large onion, chopped

2 garlic cloves, crushed

1 tsp garam masala

1 tsp ground coriander

1 tsp ground cumin

900 ml/1½ pints/3¾ cups vegetable stock

1 red chilli, chopped

100 g/3½ oz frozen peas

4 tbsp low-fat natural yogurt

salt and pepper

chopped fresh coriander (cilantro), to garnish

1 Heat the vegetable oil in a large saucepan and add the diced potatoes, onion and garlic. Sauté gently for about 5 minutes, stirring constantly. Add the ground spices and cook for 1 minute, stirring all the time.

2 Stir in the vegetable stock and chopped red chilli and bring the mixture to the boil. Reduce the heat, cover the pan and simmer for 20 minutes.

3 Add the peas and cook for a further 5 minutes. Stir in the yogurt and season to taste.

4 Pour the soup into warmed bowls, garnish with the chopped fresh coriander (cilantro) and serve hot with warm bread.

COOK'S TIP

For slightly less heat, deseed the chilli before adding it to the soup. Always wash your hands after handling chillies as they contain volatile oils that can irritate the skin and make your eyes burn if you touch your face.

Veal & Wild Mushroom Soup

Wild mushrooms are available commercially and an increasing range of cultivated varieties is now to be found in many supermarkets.

NUTRITIONAL INFORMATION

Calories 413   Sugars 3g
Protein . . . . .28g   Fat 22g
Carbohydrate . . .28g   Saturates 12g

5 MINS   3¼ HOURS

SERVES 4

INGREDIENTS

450 g/1 lb veal, thinly sliced

450 g/1 lb veal bones

1.2 litres/2 pints/5 cups water

1 small onion

6 peppercorns

1 tsp cloves

pinch of mace

140 g/5 oz oyster and shiitake mushrooms,
    roughly chopped

150 ml/¼ pint/⅔ cup double (heavy) cream

100 g/3½ oz/¾ cup dried vermicelli

1 tbsp cornflour (cornstarch)

3 tbsp milk

salt and pepper

1 Put the veal, bones and water into a large saucepan. Bring to the boil and lower the heat. Add the onion, peppercorns, cloves and mace and simmer for about 3 hours, until the veal stock is reduced by one-third.

2 Strain the stock, skim off any fat on the surface with a slotted spoon, and pour the stock into a clean saucepan. Add the veal meat to the pan.

3 Add the mushrooms and cream, bring to the boil over a low heat and then leave to simmer for 12 minutes, stirring occasionally.

4 Meanwhile, cook the vermicelli in lightly salted boiling water for 10 minutes or until tender, but still firm to the bite. Drain and keep warm.

5 Mix the cornflour (cornstarch) and milk to form a smooth paste. Stir into the soup to thicken. Season to taste with salt and pepper and just before serving, add the vermicelli. Transfer the soup to a warm tureen and serve immediately.

COOK'S TIP

You can make this soup with the more inexpensive cuts of veal, such as breast or neck slices. These are lean and the long cooking time ensures that the meat is really tender.

Curried Parsnip Soup

Parsnips make a delicious soup as they have a slightly sweet flavour. In this recipe, spices are added to complement this sweetness.

NUTRITIONAL INFORMATION

Calories	152	Sugars	.........7g
Protein	.........3g	Fat	...........8g
Carbohydrate	...18g	Saturates	.......3g

 10 MINS 35 MINS

SERVES 4

I N G R E D I E N T S

1 tbsp vegetable oil

15 g/½ oz/1 tbsp butter

1 red onion, chopped

3 parsnips, chopped

2 garlic cloves, crushed

2 tsp garam masala

½ tsp chilli powder

1 tbsp plain (all-purpose) flour

850 ml/1½ pints/3¾ cups vegetable stock

grated rind and juice of 1 lemon

salt and pepper

lemon rind, to garnish

1 Heat the oil and butter in a large saucepan until the butter has melted. Add the onion, parsnips and garlic and sauté, stirring frequently, for about 5–7 minutes, until the vegetables have softened, but not coloured.

2 Add the garam masala and chilli powder and cook, stirring constantly, for 30 seconds. Sprinkle in the flour, mixing well and cook, stirring constantly, for a further 30 seconds.

3 Stir in the stock, lemon rind and juice and bring to the boil. Reduce the heat and simmer for 20 minutes.

4 Remove some of the vegetable pieces with a slotted spoon and reserve until required. Process the remaining soup and vegetables in a food processor or blender for about 1 minute, or until a smooth purée. Alternatively, press the vegetables through a strainer with the back of a wooden spoon.

5 Return the soup to a clean saucepan and stir in the reserved vegetables. Heat the soup through for 2 minutes until piping hot.

6 Season to taste with salt and pepper, then transfer to soup bowls, garnish with grated lemon rind and serve.

Chilli Fish Soup

Chinese mushrooms add an intense flavour to this soup which is unique.
If they are unavailable, use open-cap mushrooms, sliced.

NUTRITIONAL INFORMATION

Calories 166	Sugars 1g
Protein 23g	Fat 7g
Carbohydrate 4g	Saturates 1g

15 MINS   15 MINS

SERVES 4

INGREDIENTS

15 g/½ oz Chinese dried mushrooms

2 tbsp sunflower oil

1 onion, sliced

100 g/3½ oz/1½ cups mangetout (snow peas)

100 g/3½ oz/1½ cups bamboo shoots

3 tbsp sweet chilli sauce

1.2 litres/2 pints/5 cups fish or vegetable stock

3 tbsp light soy sauce

2 tbsp fresh coriander (cilantro), plus extra to garnish

450 g/1 lb cod fillet, skinned and cubed

COOK'S TIP

Cod is used in this recipe as it is a meaty white fish. For real luxury, use monkfish tail instead.

There are many different varieties of dried mushrooms, but shiitake are best. They are not cheap, but a small amount will go a long way.

1 Place the mushrooms in a large bowl. Pour over enough boiling water to cover and leave to stand for 5 minutes. Drain the mushrooms thoroughly in a colander. Using a sharp knife, roughly chop the mushrooms.

2 Heat the sunflower oil in a preheated wok or large frying pan (skillet). Add the sliced onion to the wok and stir-fry for 5 minutes, or until softened.

3 Add the mangetout (snow peas), bamboo shoots, chilli sauce, stock and soy sauce to the wok and bring to the boil.

4 Add the coriander (cilantro) and cod and leave to simmer for 5 minutes or until the fish is cooked through.

5 Transfer the soup to warm bowls, garnish with extra coriander (cilantro), if wished, and serve hot.

Hot & Sour Soup

This is the favourite soup in Chinese restaurants throughout the world. Strain the soaking liquid and use in other soups, sauces and casseroles.

NUTRITIONAL INFORMATION

Calories 118   Sugar 0.3g
Protein . . . . .14g   Fats 4g
Carbohydrates . . . .7g   Saturates 1g

4¼ HOURS   10 MINS

SERVES 4

I N G R E D I E N T S

4-6 dried Chinese mushrooms (Shiitake), soaked

125 g/4½ oz cooked lean pork or chicken

1 cake tofu (bean curd)

60 g/2 oz canned sliced bamboo shoots, drained

600 ml/1 pint/2½ cups Chinese Stock (see page 8) or water

1 tbsp Chinese rice wine or dry sherry

1 tbsp light soy sauce

2 tbsp rice vinegar

1 tbsp cornflour (cornstarch) paste (see page 6)

salt, to taste

½ tsp ground white pepper

2-3 spring onions (scallions), thinly sliced, to serve

1 Drain the mushrooms, squeeze dry and discard the hard stalks. Thinly slice the mushrooms. Slice the meat, tofu and bamboo shoots into narrow shreds.

2 Bring the stock or water to a rolling boil in a wok or large pan and add all the ingredients. Bring back to the boil then simmer for about 1 minute.

3 Add the wine, soy sauce and vinegar to the wok or pan.

4 Bring back to the boil once more, and add the cornflour (cornstarch) paste to thicken the soup. Gently stir the soup while it is thickening. Serve the soup hot, sprinkled with the sliced spring onions (scallions).

COOK'S TIP

There are many varieties of dried mushrooms, which add a particular flavour to Chinese cooking. Shiitake mushrooms are one of the favourite kinds. Soak in hot water for 25-30 minutes before use and cut off the hard stems.

Chick-pea & Tomato Soup

A thick vegetable soup which is a delicious meal in itself. Serve with Parmesan cheese and warm sun-dried tomato bread.

NUTRITIONAL INFORMATION

Calories 285   Sugar 11g
Protein . . . . .16g   Fats 12g
Carbohydrates . . .29g   Saturates 3g

5 MINS   15 MINS

SERVES 4

INGREDIENTS

2 tbsp olive oil

2 leeks, sliced

2 courgettes (zucchini), diced

2 garlic cloves, crushed

2 x 400 g/14 oz cans chopped
  tomatoes

1 tbsp tomato purée (paste)

1 fresh bay leaf

850 ml/1½ pints/3¾ cups chicken stock

400 g/14 oz can chick-peas (garbanzo
  beans), drained and rinsed

225 g/8 oz spinach

TO SERVE

Parmesan cheese, freshly-grated

sun-dried tomato bread

1 Heat the oil in a large saucepan, add the leeks and courgettes (zucchini) and cook briskly for 5 minutes, stirring constantly.

2 Add the garlic, tomatoes, tomato purée (paste), bay leaf, chicken stock and chick-peas (garbanzo beans).

3 Bring to the boil and simmer for 5 minutes.

4 Shred the spinach finely, add to the soup and cook for 2 minutes. Season to taste.

5 Discard the bay leaf. Serve the soup immediatly with freshly-grated Parmesan cheese and warm sun-dried tomato bread.

COOK'S TIP

Chick-peas (garbanzo beans) are used extensively in North African cuisine and are also found in Spanish, Middle Eastern and Indian cooking. They have a nutty flavour with a firm texture and are excellent canned.

Spicy Dal & Carrot Soup

This delicious, warming and nutritious soup includes a selection of spices to give it a 'kick'. It is simple to make and extremely good to eat.

NUTRITIONAL INFORMATION

Calories 173   Sugars 11g
Protein ....9g   Fat 5g
Carbohydrate ...24g   Saturates 1g

10 MINS   50 MINS

SERVES 6

INGREDIENTS

125 g/4½ oz split red lentils

1.2 litres/2 pints/5 cups vegetable stock

350 g/12 oz carrots, peeled and sliced

2 onions, peeled and chopped

1 x 250 g/9 oz can chopped tomatoes

2 garlic cloves, peeled and chopped

2 tbsp vegetable ghee or oil

1 tsp ground cumin

1 tsp ground coriander

1 fresh green chilli, seeded and chopped, or
   use 1 tsp minced chilli (from a jar)

½ tsp ground turmeric

15 ml/1 tbsp lemon juice

salt

300 ml/½ pint/1¼ cups skimmed milk

30 ml/2 tbsp chopped fresh coriander

yogurt, to serve

1 Place the lentils in a sieve and wash well under cold running water. Drain and place in a large saucepan with 850 ml/1½ pints/3½ cups of the stock, the carrots, onions, tomatoes and garlic. Bring the mixture to the boil, reduce the heat, cover and simmer for 30 minutes.

2 Meanwhile, heat the ghee or oil in a small pan, add the cumin, coriander, chilli and turmeric and fry gently for 1 minute.

3 Remove from the heat and stir in the lemon juice and salt to taste.

4 Purée the soup in batches in a blender or food processor. Return the soup to the saucepan, add the spice mixture and the remaining 300 ml/½ pint/1¼ cups stock or water and simmer for 10 minutes.

5 Add the milk to the soup, taste and adjust the seasoning according to taste.

6 Stir in the chopped coriander and reheat gently. Serve hot, with a swirl of yogurt.

Fish & Vegetable Soup

A chunky fish soup with strips of vegetables, all flavoured with ginger and lemon, makes a meal in itself.

NUTRITIONAL INFORMATION

Calories 88	Sugars 1g
Protein 12g	Fat 3g
Carbohydrate 3g	Saturates 0.5g

40 MINS   20 MINS

SERVES 4

INGREDIENTS

250 g/9 oz white fish fillets (cod, halibut, haddock, sole etc)

½ tsp ground ginger

½ tsp salt

1 small leek, trimmed

2-4 crab sticks, defrosted if frozen (optional)

1 tbsp sunflower oil

1 large carrot, cut into julienne strips

8 canned water chestnuts, thinly sliced

1.2 litres/2 pints/5 cups fish or vegetable stock

1 tbsp lemon juice

1 tbsp light soy sauce

1 large courgette (zucchini), cut into julienne strips

black pepper

1 Remove any skin from the fish and cut into cubes, about 2.5 cm/1 inch. Combine the ground ginger and salt and use to rub into the pieces of fish. Leave to marinate for at least 30 minutes.

2 Meanwhile, divide the green and white parts of the leek. Cut each part into 2.5 cm/1 inch lengths and then into julienne strips down the length of each piece, keeping the two parts separate. Slice the crab sticks into 1 cm/½ inch pieces.

3 Heat the oil in the wok, swirling it around so it is really hot. Add the white part of the leek and stir-fry for a couple of minutes, then add the carrots and water chestnuts and continue to cook for 1-2 minutes, stirring thoroughly.

4 Add the stock and bring to the boil, then add the lemon juice and soy sauce and simmer for 2 minutes.

5 Add the fish and continue to cook for about 5 minutes until the fish begins to break up a little, then add the green part of the leek and the courgettes (zucchini) and simmer for about 1 minute. Add the sliced crab sticks, if using, and season to taste with black pepper. Simmer for a further minute or so and serve piping hot.

COOK'S TIP

To skin fish, place the fillet skin-side down and insert a sharp, flexible knife at one end between the flesh and the skin. Hold the skin tightly at the end and push the knife along, keeping the blade flat against the skin.

Calabrian Mushroom Soup

The Calabrian Mountains in southern Italy provide large amounts of wild mushrooms that are rich in flavour and colour.

NUTRITIONAL INFORMATION

Calories 452	Sugars 5g	
Protein 15g	Fat 26g	
Carbohydrate ... 42g	Saturates 12g	

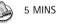

5 MINS   25–30 MINS

SERVES 4

I N G R E D I E N T S

2 tbsp olive oil

1 onion, chopped

450g/1 lb mixed mushrooms, such as ceps, oyster and button

300 ml/ ½ pint/1 ¼ cup milk

850 ml/1 ½ pints/3 ¾ cups hot vegetable stock

8 slices of rustic bread or French stick

2 garlic cloves, crushed

50 g/1 ¾ oz/3 tbsp butter, melted

75 g/2 ¾ oz Gruyère cheese, finely grated

salt and pepper

1 Heat the oil in a large frying pan (skillet) and cook the onion for 3–4 minutes or until soft and golden.

2 Wipe each mushroom with a damp cloth and cut any large mushrooms into smaller, bite-size pieces.

3 Add the mushrooms to the pan, stirring quickly to coat them in the oil.

4 Add the milk to the pan, bring to the boil, cover and leave to simmer for about 5 minutes. Gradually stir in the hot vegetable stock and season with salt and pepper to taste.

5 Under a preheated grill (broiler), toast the bread on both sides until golden.

6 Mix together the garlic and butter and spoon generously over the toast.

7 Place the toast in the bottom of a large tureen or divide it among 4 individual serving bowls and pour over the hot soup. Top with the grated Gruyère cheese and serve at once.

COOK'S TIP

Mushrooms absorb liquid, which can lessen the flavour and affect cooking properties. Therefore, carefully wipe them with a damp cloth rather than rinsing them in water.

Vichyssoise

This is a classic creamy soup made from potatoes and leeks. To achieve the delicate pale colour, be sure to use only the white parts of the leeks.

NUTRITIONAL INFORMATION

Calories 208	Sugars 5g
Protein 5g	Fat 12g
Carbohydrate . . .20g	Saturates 6g

10 MINS   40 MINS

SERVES 6

INGREDIENTS

3 large leeks

40 g/1½ oz/3 tbsp butter or margarine

1 onion, thinly sliced

500 g/1 lb 2 oz potatoes, chopped

850 ml/1½ pints/3½ cups vegetable stock

2 tsp lemon juice

pinch of ground nutmeg

¼ tsp ground coriander

1 bay leaf

1 egg yolk

150 ml/¼ pint/⅔ cup single (light) cream

salt and white pepper

TO GARNISH

freshly snipped chives

1 Trim the leeks and remove most of the green part. Slice the white part of the leeks very finely.

2 Melt the butter or margarine in a saucepan. Add the leeks and onion and fry, stirring occasionally, for about 5 minutes without browning.

3 Add the potatoes, vegetable stock, lemon juice, nutmeg, coriander and bay leaf to the pan, season to taste with salt and pepper and bring to the boil. Cover and simmer for about 30 minutes, until all the vegetables are very soft.

4 Cool the soup a little, remove and discard the bay leaf and then press through a strainer or process in a food processor or blender until smooth. Pour into a clean pan.

5 Blend the egg yolk into the cream, add a little of the soup to the mixture and then whisk it all back into the soup and reheat gently, without boiling. Adjust the seasoning to taste. Cool and then chill thoroughly in the refrigerator.

6 Serve the soup sprinkled with freshly snipped chives.

Pumpkin Soup

This is an American classic that has now become popular worldwide.
When pumpkin is out of season use butternut squash in its place.

NUTRITIONAL INFORMATION

Calories 112   Sugars 7g
Protein . . . . .4g   Fat 7g
Carbohydrate . . . .8g   Saturates 2g

 10 MINS   30 MINS

SERVES 6

INGREDIENTS

about 1 kg/2 lb 4 oz pumpkin

40 g/1½ oz/3 tbsp butter or margarine

1 onion, sliced thinly

1 garlic clove, crushed

900 ml/1½ pints/3½ cups vegetable stock

½ tsp ground ginger

1 tbsp lemon juice

3–4 thinly pared strips of orange
    rind (optional)

1–2 bay leaves or 1 bouquet garni

300 ml/½ pint/1¼ cups milk

salt and pepper

TO GARNISH

4–6 tablespoons single (light) or double
    (heavy) cream, natural yogurt
    or fromage frais

snipped chives

1 Peel the pumpkin, remove the seeds and then cut the flesh into 2.5 cm/ 1 inch cubes.

2 Melt the butter or margarine in a large, heavy-based saucepan. Add the onion and garlic and fry over a low heat until soft but not coloured.

3 Add the pumpkin and toss with the onion for 2–3 minutes.

4 Add the stock and bring to the boil over a medium heat. Season to taste with salt and pepper and add the ginger, lemon juice, strips of orange rind, if using, and bay leaves or bouquet garni. Cover and simmer over a low heat for about 20 minutes, until the pumpkin is tender.

5 Discard the orange rind, if using, and the bay leaves or bouquet garni. Cool the soup slightly, then press through a strainer or process in a food processor until smooth. Pour into a clean saucepan.

6 Add the milk and reheat gently. Adjust the seasoning. Garnish with a swirl of cream, natural yogurt or fromage frais and snipped chives, and serve.

Brown Lentil & Pasta Soup

In Italy, this soup is called *Minestrade Lentiche*. A *minestra* is a soup cooked with pasta; here, farfalline, a small bow-shaped variety, is used.

NUTRITIONAL INFORMATION

Calories 225	Sugars 1g
Protein 13g	Fat 8g
Carbohydrate ...27g	Saturates 3g

 5 MINS   25 MINS

SERVES 4

INGREDIENTS

4 rashers streaky bacon, cut into small
  squares

1 onion, chopped

2 garlic cloves, crushed

2 sticks celery, chopped

50 g/1 ¾ oz/ ¼ cup farfalline or spaghetti,
  broken into small pieces

1 x 400 g/14 oz can brown lentils, drained

1.2 litres/2 pints/5 cups hot ham or
  vegetable stock

2 tbsp chopped, fresh mint

1 Place the bacon in a large frying pan (skillet) together with the onions, garlic and celery. Dry fry for 4–5 minutes, stirring, until the onion is tender and the bacon is just beginning to brown.

2 Add the pasta to the pan (skillet) and cook, stirring, for about 1 minute to coat the pasta in the oil.

3 Add the lentils and the stock and bring to the boil. Reduce the heat and leave to simmer for 12–15 minutes or until the pasta is tender.

4 Remove the pan (skillet) from the heat and stir in the chopped fresh mint.

5 Transfer the soup to warm soup bowls and serve immeditely.

COOK'S TIP

If you prefer to use dried lentils, add the stock before the pasta and cook for 1–1¼ hours until the lentils are tender. Add the pasta and cook for a further 12–15 minutes.

Tuscan Bean Soup

A thick and creamy soup that is based on a traditional Tuscan recipe. If you use dried beans, the preparation and cooking times will be longer.

NUTRITIONAL INFORMATION

Calories . . . . . . .250 Sugars 4g
Protein . . . . .13g Fat 10g
Carbohydrate . . .29g Saturates 2g

 2 MINS   10 MINS

SERVES 4

INGREDIENTS

225 g/8 oz dried butter beans, soaked
    overnight, or 2 x 400 g/14 oz can butter
    beans

1 tbsp olive oil

2 garlic cloves, crushed

1 vegetable or chicken stock cube,
    crumbled

150 ml/¼ pint/⅔ cup milk

2 tbsp chopped fresh oregano

salt and pepper

1 If you are using dried beans that have been soaked overnight, drain them thoroughly. Bring a large pan of water to the boil, add the beans and boil for 10 minutes. Cover the pan and simmer for a further 30 minutes or until tender. Drain the beans, reserving the cooking liquid. If you are using canned beans, drain them thoroughly and reserve the liquid.

2 Heat the oil in a large frying pan (skillet) and fry the garlic for 2–3 minutes or until just beginning to brown.

3 Add the beans and 400 ml/14 fl oz/1⅔ cup of the reserved liquid to the pan (skillet), stirring. You may need to add a little water if there is insufficient liquid. Stir in the crumbled stock cube. Bring the mixture to the boil and then remove the pan from the heat.

4 Place the bean mixture in a food processor and blend to form a smooth purée. Alternatively, mash the bean mixture to a smooth consistency. Season to taste with salt and pepper and stir in the milk.

5 Pour the soup back into the pan and gently heat to just below boiling point. Stir in the chopped oregano just before serving.

Noodles in Soup

Noodles in soup are far more popular than fried noodles in China. You can use different ingredients for the dressing according to taste.

NUTRITIONAL INFORMATION

Calories 231	Sugars 1g	
Protein 18g	Fat 11g	
Carbohydrate . . .16g	Saturates 2g	

 4 HOURS   15 MINS

SERVES 4

I N G R E D I E N T S

250 g/9 oz chicken fillet, pork fillet, or any other ready-cooked meat

3-4 Chinese dried mushrooms, soaked

125 g/4½ oz canned sliced bamboo shoots, rinsed and drained

125 g/4½ oz spinach leaves, lettuce hearts, or Chinese leaves (cabbage), shredded

2 spring onions (scallions), finely shredded

250 g/9 oz egg noodles

about 600 ml/1 pint/2½ cups Chinese Stock (see page 8)

2 tbsp light soy sauce

2 tbsp vegetable oil

1 tsp salt

½ tsp sugar

2 tsp Chinese rice wine or dry sherry

a few drops sesame oil

1 tsp red chilli oil (optional)

1 Using a sharp knife or meat cleaver, cut the meat into thin shreds.

2 Squeeze dry the soaked Chinese mushrooms and discard the hard stalk.

3 Thinly shred the mushrooms, bamboo shoots, spinach leaves and spring onions (scallions).

4 Cook the noodles in boiling water according to the instructions on the packet, then drain and rinse under cold water. Place the noodles in a bowl.

5 Bring the Chinese stock to the boil, add about 1 tablespoon soy sauce and pour over the noodles. Keep warm.

6 Heat the vegetable oil in a preheated wok, add about half of the spring onions (scallions), the meat and the vegetables (mushrooms, bamboo shoots and greens). Stir-fry for about 2-3 minutes. Add all the seasonings and stir until well combined.

7 Pour the mixture in the wok over the noodles, garnish with the remaining spring onions (scallions) and serve immediately.

COOK'S TIP

Noodle soup is wonderfully satisfying and is ideal to serve on cold winter days.

Fish & Seafood Chowder

Served with warm crusty bread and a salad, this tasty soup makes a substantial lunch or supper dish.

NUTRITIONAL INFORMATION

Calories 286   Sugars 6g
Protein . . . . .30g   Fat 3g
Carbohydrate . . .31g   Saturates 1g

20 MINS   25 MINS

SERVES 4

I N G R E D I E N T S

1 kg/2 lb 4 oz mussels in their shells

1 large onion, thinly sliced

2 garlic cloves, chopped

3 bay leaves

a few stalks of parsley

a few stalks of thyme

300 ml/½ pint/1¼ cups water

225 g/8 oz smoked haddock fillets

500 g/1 lb 2 oz potatoes, peeled and diced

4 celery stalks, thickly sliced

1 x 250 g/9 oz can sweetcorn kernels, drained and rinsed

150 ml/¼ pint/⅔ cup low-fat natural yogurt

1 tsp cornflour (cornstarch)

150 ml/¼ pint/⅔ cup dry white wine, or dry cider

½ tsp cayenne pepper, or to taste

black pepper

2 tbsp chopped parsley

1 Scrub the mussels, pull off the 'beards' and rinse thoroughly. Discard any shells that remain open when tapped.

2 Put the onion, garlic, herbs, water and the mussels in a large pan. Cover and cook over high heat for 5 minutes, shaking the pan once or twice.

3 Line a colander with muslin or cheesecloth and strain the mussel liquor into a bowl. Shell the mussels. and discard the rest. Reserve the liquor.

4 Put the haddock and vegetables into a pan, add 600 ml/1 pint/2½ cups of cold water, cover and simmer for 10 minutes. Remove the fish, and skin, bone and flake it. Strain the liquor into the seafood liquor. Reserve the vegetables.

5 Return the cooking liquor to the rinsed pan, add the sweetcorn and bring to the boil. Stir together the yogurt and cornflour (cornstarch). Stir in a little of the fish liquor, then pour it into the pan. Stir the yogurt in well, then add the reserved fish and vegetables. Add the white wine, season with cayenne and black pepper and heat the soup gently, without boiling. Season and transfer to a platter, and sprinkle with the parsley.

Chicken & Coconut Soup

This fragrant soup combines citrus flavours with coconut and a hint of piquancy from chillies.

NUTRITIONAL INFORMATION

Calories 345	Sugars 2g
Protein 28g	Fat 24g
Carbohydrate 5g	Saturates 18g

  2¼ HOURS   15 MINS

SERVES 4

INGREDIENTS

350 g/12 oz/1¾ cups cooked, skinned chicken breast

125 g/4½ oz/1⅓ cups unsweetened desiccated coconut

500 ml/16 fl oz/2 cups boiling water

500 ml/18 fl oz/2 cups Fresh Chicken Stock (see page 9)

4 spring onions (scallions), white and green parts, sliced thinly

2 stalks lemon grass

1 lime

1 tsp grated ginger root

1 tbsp light soy sauce

2 tsp ground coriander

2 large fresh red chillies

1 tbsp chopped fresh coriander (cilantro)

1 tbsp cornflour (cornstarch) mixed with 2 tbsp cold water

salt and white pepper

chopped red chilli to garnish

1 Using a sharp knife, slice the chicken into thin strips.

2 Place the coconut in a heatproof bowl and pour over the boiling water. Work the coconut mixture through a sieve (strainer). Pour the coconut water into a large saucepan and add the stock.

3 Add the spring onions (scallions) to the saucepan. Slice the base of each lemon grass and discard damaged leaves. Bruise the stalks and add to the saucepan.

4 Peel the rind from the lime in large strips. Extract the juice and add to the pan with the lime strips, ginger, soy sauce and coriander. Bruise the chillies with a fork then add to the pan. Heat the pan to just below boiling point.

5 Add the chicken and fresh coriander (cilantro) to the saucepan, bring to the boil, then simmer for 10 minutes.

6 Discard the lemon grass, lime rind and red chillies. Pour the blended cornflour (cornstarch) mixture into the saucepan and stir until slightly thickened. Season with salt and white pepper to taste and serve immediatley, garnished with chopped red chilli.

Spanish Tomato Soup

This Mediterranean tomato soup is thickened with bread, as is traditional in some parts of Spain, and served with garlic bread.

NUTRITIONAL INFORMATION

Calories 297	Sugars 7g
Protein 8g	Fat 13g
Carbohydrate ...39g	Saturates 2g

 10 MINS   20 MINS

SERVES 4

INGREDIENTS

4 tbsp olive oil

1 onion, chopped

3 garlic cloves, crushed

1 green (bell) pepper, seeded and chopped

½ tsp chilli powder

500 g/1 lb 2 oz tomatoes, chopped

225 g/8 oz French or Italian bread, cubed

1 litre/1¾ pints/4 cups vegetable stock

GARLIC BREAD

4 slices ciabatta or French bread

4 tbsp olive oil

2 garlic cloves, crushed

25 g/1 oz/¼ cup grated Cheddar cheese

chilli powder, to garnish

1 Heat the olive oil in a large frying pan (skillet). Add the onion, garlic and (bell) pepper and sauté over a low heat, stirring frequently, for 2–3 minutes, or until the onion has softened.

2 Add the chilli powder and tomatoes and cook over a medium heat until the mixture has thickened.

3 Stir in the bread cubes and stock and cook for 10–15 minutes, until the soup is thick and fairly smooth.

4 Meanwhile, make the garlic bread. Toast the bread slices under a medium grill (broiler). Drizzle the oil over the top of the bread, rub with the garlic, sprinkle with the cheese and return to the grill (broiler) for 2–3 minutes, until the cheese has melted. Sprinkle with chilli powder and serve with the soup.

VARIATION

Replace the green (bell) pepper with red or orange (bell) pepper, if you prefer.

Bacon, Bean & Garlic Soup

A mouth-wateringly healthy vegetable, bean and bacon soup with a garlic flavour. Serve with granary or wholemeal (whole wheat) bread.

NUTRITIONAL INFORMATION

Calories 261	Sugars 5g
Protein 23g	Fat 8g
Carbohydrate . . .25g	Saturates 2g

 5 MINS   20 MINS

SERVES 4

INGREDIENTS

225 g/8 oz smoked back lean
  bacon slices

1 carrot, sliced thinly

1 celery stick, sliced thinly

1 onion, chopped

1 tbsp oil

3 garlic cloves, sliced

700 ml/1¼ pints/3 cups hot vegetable
  stock

200 g/7 oz can chopped tomatoes

1 tbsp chopped fresh thyme

about 400 g/14 oz can cannellini beans,
  drained

1 tbsp tomato purée (paste)

salt and pepper

grated Cheddar cheese to garnish

COOK'S TIP

For a more substantial soup add 60 g/2 oz cup small pasta shapes or short lengths of spaghetti when you add the stock and tomatoes. You will also need to add an extra 150 ml/¼ pint/⅔ cup vegetable stock.

1 Chop 2 slices of the bacon and place in a bowl. Cook on HIGH power for 3–4 minutes until the fat runs and the bacon is well cooked. Stir the bacon halfway through cooking to separate the pieces. Transfer to a plate lined with kitchen towels and leave to cool. When cool, the bacon pieces should be crisp and dry. Place the carrot, celery, onion and oil in a large bowl. Cover and cook on HIGH power for 4 minutes.

2 Chop the remaining bacon and add to the bowl with the garlic. Cover and cook on HIGH power for 2 minutes.

3 Add the stock, the contents of the can of tomatoes, the thyme, beans and tomato purée (paste). Cover and cook on HIGH power for 8 minutes, stirring halfway through. Season to taste. Ladle the soup into warmed bowls and sprinkle with the crisp bacon and grated cheese.

Mulligatawny Soup

This soup, based on Madras curry, became popular with army officers in India at the beginning of the century.

NUTRITIONAL INFORMATION

Calories ....154 Sugars 6g
Protein ....6g Fat 7g
Carbohydrate ...17g Saturates 4g

5½ HOURS   1 HOUR

SERVES 4–6

INGREDIENTS

45 g/1½ oz/3 tbsp butter or margarine

1 large onion, chopped

2 carrots, chopped

2–3 celery sticks, chopped

1 dessert apple, peeled, cored and chopped

1 tbsp plain (all-purpose) flour

1–2 tsp Madras curry powder

1–2 tsp curry paste

½ tsp ground coriander

1.25 litres/2¼ pints/5 cups Beef, Chicken or Vegetable Stock (see pages 8-9)

225 g/8 oz can chopped tomatoes

60 g/2 oz/½ cup cooked long grain rice (optional)

60–90 g/2–3 oz/⅓–½ cup cooked chicken, beef or lamb, chopped very finely

salt and pepper

poppadoms to serve (optional)

1 Melt the butter or margarine in a large saucepan and fry the onion, carrots, celery and apple, stirring occasionally, until just soft and lightly browned.

2 Stir in the flour, curry powder, curry paste and coriander and cook for a minute or so, stirring all the time.

3 Gradually add the stock and bring to the boil, stirring constantly.

4 Add the tomatoes and plenty of seasoning, cover the pan and simmer for about 45 minutes until the vegetables and apple are tender.

5 Cool the soup a little, then press through a sieve (strainer) or blend in a food processor or blender until smooth. Pour the soup into a clean pan.

6 Add the rice (if using) and the chicken or meat, adjust the seasoning and bring to the boil. Simmer gently for 5 minutes.

7 Serve the soup in warmed bowls, with poppadoms (if using).

Ravioli alla Parmigiana

This soup is traditionally served at Easter and Christmas in the province of Parma.

NUTRITIONAL INFORMATION

Calories 554   Sugars 3g
Protein ....26g   Fat 24g
Carbohydrate ...64g   Saturates 9g

4½–5 HOURS   25 MINS

SERVES 4

INGREDIENTS

285 g/10 oz Basic Pasta Dough (see page 6)

1.2 litres/2 pints/5 cups veal stock

freshly grated Parmesan cheese, to serve

FILLING

125 ml/4 fl oz/½ cup Espagnole Sauce (see page 7)

100 g/3½ oz/1 cup freshly grated Parmesan cheese

100 g/3½ oz/1⅔ cup fine white breadcrumbs

2 eggs

1 small onion, finely chopped

1 tsp freshly grated nutmeg

COOK'S TIP

It is advisable to prepare the Basic Pasta Dough (see page 6) and the Espagnole Sauce (see page 7) well in advance, or buy ready-made equivalents if you are short of time.

1 Make some pasta dough and the Espagnole Sauce (see page 7).

2 Carefully roll out 2 sheets of the pasta dough and cover with a damp tea towel (dish cloth) while you make the filling for the ravioli.

3 To make the filling, place the freshly grated Parmesan cheese, fine white breadcrumbs, eggs, Espagnole Sauce, finely chopped onion and the freshly grated nutmeg in a large mixing bowl, and mix together well.

4 Place spoonfuls of the filling at regular intervals on 1 sheet of pasta dough. Cover with the second sheet of pasta dough, then cut into squares and seal the edges.

5 Bring the veal stock to the boil in a large saucepan.

6 Add the ravioli to the pan and cook for about 15 minutes.

7 Transfer the soup and ravioli to warm serving bowls and serve, generously sprinkled with Parmesan cheese.

Consommé

A traditional clear soup made from beef bones and lean minced (ground) beef. Thin strips of vegetables provide a colourful garnish.

NUTRITIONAL INFORMATION

Calories . . . . .109 Sugars 6g
Protein . . . . . . .13g Fat 3g
Carbohydrate . . . .7g Saturates 1g

6¼ HOURS   1¼ HOURS

SERVES 4–6

I N G R E D I E N T S

1.25 litres/2¼ pints/5 cups strong Beef Stock (see page 9)

225 g/8 oz/1 cup extra lean minced (ground) beef

2 tomatoes, skinned, seeded and chopped

2 large carrots, chopped

1 large onion, chopped

2 celery sticks, chopped

1 turnip, chopped (optional)

1 bouquet garni

2–3 egg whites

shells of 2–4 eggs, crushed

1–2 tbsp sherry (optional)

salt and pepper

melba toast, to serve

TO GARNISH

julienne strips of raw carrot, turnip, celery or celeriac (celery root) or a one-egg omelette, cut into julienne strips

1 Put the stock and minced (ground) beef in a saucepan. Leave for 1 hour. Add the tomatoes, carrots, onion, celery, turnip (if using), bouquet garni, 2 of the egg whites, the crushed shells of 2 of the eggs and plenty of seasoning. Bring to almost boiling point, whisking hard all the time with a flat whisk.

2 Cover and simmer for 1 hour, taking care not to allow the layer of froth on top of the soup to break.

3 Pour the soup through a jelly bag or scalded fine cloth, keeping the froth back until the last, then pour the ingredients through the cloth again into a clean pan. The resulting liquid should be clear.

4 If the soup is not quite clear, return it to the pan with another egg white and the crushed shells of 2 more eggs. Repeat the whisking process as before and then boil for 10 minutes; strain again.

5 Add the sherry (if using) to the soup and reheat gently. Place the garnish in the warmed soup bowls and carefully pour in the soup. Serve with melba toast.

Mediterranean Fish Soup

Juicy chunks of fish and sumptuous shellfish are cooked in a flavoursome stock. Serve with toasted bread rubbed with garlic.

NUTRITIONAL INFORMATION

Calories	.316	Sugar	.4g
Protein	.53g	Fats	.7g
Carbohydrates	.5g	Saturates	.1g

1 HOUR   15 MINS

SERVES 4

INGREDIENTS

1 tbsp olive oil

1 large onion, chopped

2 garlic cloves, finely chopped

425 ml/15 fl oz/1¾ cups Fresh Fish Stock (see page 8)

150 ml/5 fl oz/⅔ cup dry white wine

1 bay leaf

1 sprig each fresh thyme, rosemary and oregano

450 g/1 lb firm white fish fillets (such as cod, monkfish or halibut), skinned and cut into 2.5 cm/1 inch cubes

450 g/1 lb fresh mussels, prepared

400 g/14 oz can chopped tomatoes

225 g/8 oz peeled prawns (shrimp), thawed if frozen

salt and pepper

sprigs of thyme, to garnish

TO SERVE

lemon wedges

4 slices toasted French bread, rubbed with cut garlic clove

1 Heat the olive oil in a large saucepan and gently fry the onion and garlic for 2–3 minutes until just softened.

2 Pour in the stock and wine and bring to the boil.

3 Tie the bay leaf and herbs together with clean string and add to the saucepan together with the fish and mussels. Stir well, cover and simmer for 5 minutes.

4 Stir in the tomatoes and prawns (shrimp) and continue to cook for a further 3–4 minutes until piping hot and the fish is cooked through.

5 Discard the herbs and any mussels that have not opened. Season to taste, then ladle into warm bowls.

6 Garnish with sprigs of fresh thyme and serve with lemon wedges and toasted bread.

Lettuce & Tofu Soup

This is a delicate, clear soup of shredded lettuce and small chunks of tofu (bean curd) with sliced carrot and spring onion (scallion).

NUTRITIONAL INFORMATION

Calories 113	Sugars 2g
Protein 5g	Fat 8g
Carbohydrate 3g	Saturates 1g

  5 MINS   15 MINS

SERVES 4

INGREDIENTS

200 g/7 oz tofu (bean curd)

2 tbsp vegetable oil

1 carrot, sliced thinly

1 cm/½ inch piece ginger root,
   cut into thin shreds

3 spring onions (scallions), sliced
   diagonally

1.2 litres/2 pints/5 cups vegetable stock

2 tbsp soy sauce

2 tbsp dry sherry

1 tsp sugar

125 g/4½ oz/1½ cups cos (romaine) lettuce,
   shredded

salt and pepper

1 Using a sharp knife, cut the tofu (bean curd) into small cubes.

2 Heat the vegetable oil in a preheated wok or large saucepan, add the tofu (bean curd) and stir-fry until browned. Remove with a perforated spoon and drain on kitchen paper (paper towels).

3 Add the carrot, ginger root and spring onions (scallions) to the wok or saucepan and stir-fry for 2 minutes.

4 Add the vegetable stock, soy sauce, sherry and sugar. Stir well to mix all the ingredients. Bring to the boil and simmer for 1 minute.

5 Add the cos (romaine) lettuce to the wok or saucepan and stir until it has just wilted.

6 Return the tofu (bean curd) to the pan to reheat. Season with salt and pepper to taste and serve the soup immediately in warmed bowls.

COOK'S TIP

For a prettier effect, score grooves along the length of the carrot with a sharp knife before slicing. This will create a flower effect as the carrot is cut into rounds. You could also try slicing the carrot on the diagonal to make longer slices.

Chicken Noodle Soup

Quick to make, this hot and spicy soup is hearty and warming. If you like your food really fiery, add a chopped dried or fresh chilli with its seeds.

NUTRITIONAL INFORMATION

Calories	196	Sugars	........4g
Protein	........16g	Fat	..........11g
Carbohydrate	....8g	Saturates	.......2g

 10 MINS 25 MINS

SERVES 4–6

I N G R E D I E N T S

1 sheet of dried egg noodles
from a 250 g/9 oz pack

1 tbsp oil

4 skinless, boneless
chicken thighs, diced

1 bunch spring onions (scallions), sliced

2 garlic cloves, chopped

2 cm/¾ inch piece fresh
ginger root, finely chopped

850 ml/1½ pints/3¾ cups chicken stock

200 ml/7 fl oz/scant 1 cup coconut milk

3 tsp red curry paste

3 tbsp peanut butter

2 tbsp light soy sauce

1 small red (bell) pepper, chopped

60 g/2 oz/½ cup frozen peas

salt and pepper

VARIATION

Green curry paste can be
used instead of red curry paste
for a less fiery flavour.

1 Put the noodles in a shallow dish and soak in boiling water as the pack directs.

2 Heat the oil in a large preheated saucepan or wok.

3 Add the diced chicken to the pan or wok and fry for 5 minutes, stirring until lightly browned.

4 Add the white part of the spring onions (scallions), the garlic and ginger and fry for 2 minutes, stirring.

5 Stir in the chicken stock, coconut milk, red curry paste, peanut butter and soy sauce.

6 Season with salt and pepper to taste. Bring to the boil, stirring, then simmer for 8 minutes, stirring occasionally.

7 Add the red (bell) pepper, peas and green spring onion tops and cook for 2 minutes.

8 Add the drained noodles and heat through. Spoon the chicken noodle soup into warmed bowls and serve with a spoon and fork.

Noodle & Mushroom Soup

This soup is very quickly and easily put together, and is cooked so that each ingredient can still be tasted in the finished dish.

NUTRITIONAL INFORMATION

Calories	74	Sugars	.........1g
Protein	........13g	Fat	..........3g
Carbohydrate	....9g	Saturates	.....0.4g

  4 HOURS   10 MINS

SERVES 4

INGREDIENTS

15 g/½ oz/¼ cup dried Chinese mushrooms
  or 125 g/4½ oz/1⅓ cups field or chestnut
  (crimini) mushrooms

1 litre/1¾ pints/4 cups hot Fresh Vegetable
  Stock (see page 8)

125 g/4½ oz thread egg noodles

2 tsp sunflower oil

3 garlic cloves, crushed

2.5 cm/1 inch piece ginger,
  shredded finely

½ tsp mushroom ketchup

1 tsp light soy sauce

125 g/4½ oz/2 cups bean sprouts

coriander (cilantro) leaves,
  to garnish

1 Soak the dried Chinese mushrooms, if using, for at least 30 minutes in 300 ml/½ pint/1¼ cups of the hot vegetable stock. Remove the stalks and discard, then slice the mushrooms. Reserve the stock.

2 Cook the noodles for 2–3 minutes in boiling water. Drain, rinse and set aside until required.

3 Heat the oil over a high heat in a wok or large, heavy frying pan (skillet). Add the garlic and ginger, stir and add the mushrooms. Stir over a high heat for 2 minutes.

4 Add the remaining vegetable stock with the reserved stock and bring to the boil. Add the mushroom ketchup and soy sauce and mix well.

5 Stir in the bean sprouts and cook until tender. Serve over the noodles, garnished with coriander (cilantro) leaves.

COOK'S TIP

Dried mushrooms are highly fragrant and add a special flavour to Chinese dishes. There are many different varieties but Shiitake are the best. Although not cheap, a small amount will go a long way and they will keep indefinitely in an airtight jar.

Vegetarian Hot & Sour Soup

This popular soup is easy to make and very filling. It can be eaten as a meal on its own or served as an appetizer before a light menu.

NUTRITIONAL INFORMATION

Calories	.61	Sugars	1g
Protein	.5g	Fat	2g
Carbohydrate	.8g	Saturates	0.2g

  30 MINS   🕐 10 MINS

SERVES 4

INGREDIENTS

4 Chinese dried mushrooms
(if unavailable, use open-cup
mushrooms)

125 g/4½ oz firm tofu (bean curd)

60 g/2 oz/1 cup canned bamboo
shoots

600 ml/1 pint/2½ cups vegetable stock
or water

60 g/2 oz/⅓ cup peas

1 tbsp dark soy sauce

2 tbsp white wine vinegar

2 tbsp cornflour (cornstarch)

salt and pepper

sesame oil to serve

1 Place the Chinese dried mushrooms in a small bowl and cover with warm water. Leave to soak for about 20–25 minutes.

2 Drain the mushrooms and squeeze out the excess water, reserving this. Remove the tough centres and cut the mushrooms into thin shreds. Shred the tofu (bean curd) and bamboo shoots.

3 Bring the stock or water to the boil in a large saucepan. Add the mushrooms, tofu (bean curd), bamboo shoots and peas. Simmer for 2 minutes.

4 Mix together the soy sauce, vinegar and cornflour (cornstarch) with 2 tablespoons of the reserved mushroom liquid.

5 Stir the soy sauce and cornflour (cornstarch) mixture into the soup with the remaining mushroom liquid. Bring to the boil and season with salt and plenty of pepper. Simmer for 2 minutes.

6 Serve in warmed bowls with a few drops of sesame oil sprinkled over the top of each.

COOK'S TIP

If you use open-cup mushrooms instead of dried mushrooms, add an extra 150 ml/ ¼ pint/⅔ cup vegetable stock or water to the soup, as these mushrooms do not need soaking.

Minted Pea & Yogurt Soup

A deliciously refreshing soup that is full of goodness. It is also extremely tasty served chilled.

NUTRITIONAL INFORMATION

Calories . . . . . . .208 Sugars 9g
Protein . . . . .10g Fat 7g
Carbohydrate . . .26g Saturates 2g

10 MINS   25 MINS

SERVES 4

INGREDIENTS

2 tbsp vegetable ghee or oil

2 onions, peeled and coarsely chopped

225 g/8 oz potato, peeled and coarsely chopped

2 garlic cloves, peeled

2.5 cm/1 inch ginger root, peeled and chopped

1 tsp ground coriander

1 tsp ground cumin

1 tbsp plain flour

850 ml/1½ pints/3½ cups vegetable stock

500 g/1 lb 2 oz frozen peas

2-3 tbsp chopped fresh mint, to taste

salt and freshly ground black pepper

150 ml/¼ pint/⅔ cup low-fat natural yogurt

½ tsp cornflour (cornstarch)

300 ml/½ pint/¼ cups skimmed milk

a little extra yogurt, for serving (optional)

mint sprigs, to garnish

1 Heat the ghee or oil in a saucepan, add the onions and potato and cook gently for 3 minutes. Stir in the garlic, ginger, coriander, cumin and flour and cook for 1 minute, stirring. Add the stock, peas and half the mint and bring to the boil, stirring. Reduce the heat, cover and simmer gently for 15 minutes.

2 Purée the soup in a blender or food processor. Return the mixture to the pan and season with salt and pepper to taste. Blend the yogurt with the cornflour (cornstarch) and stir into the soup.

3 Add the milk and bring almost to the boil, stirring all the time. Cook very gently for 2 minutes. Serve hot, sprinkled with the remaining mint and a swirl of extra yogurt, if wished.

COOK'S TIP

The yogurt is mixed with a little cornflour (cornstarch) before being added to the hot soup – this helps to stabilize the yogurt and prevents it separating when heated.

Partan Bree

This traditional Scottish soup is thickened with a purée of rice and crab meat cooked in milk. Add soured cream, if liked, at the end of cooking.

NUTRITIONAL INFORMATION

Calories	112	Sugars 5g
Protein	.........7g	Fat 2g
Carbohydrate	...18g	Saturates 0.3g

🥔 1 HOUR   🕐 35 MINS

SERVES 6

I N G R E D I E N T S

1 medium-sized boiled crab

90 g/3 oz/scant ½ cup long-grain rice

600 ml/1 pint/2½ cups skimmed milk

600 ml/1 pint/2½ cups Fish Stock
   (see page 8)

1 tbsp anchovy essence (paste)

2 tsp lime or lemon juice

1 tbsp chopped fresh parsley or 1 tsp
   chopped fresh thyme

3–4 tbsp soured cream (optional)

salt and pepper

snipped chives, to garnish

1 Remove and reserve all the brown and white meat from the crab, then crack the claws and remove and chop that meat; reserve the claw meat.

COOK'S TIP

If you are unable to buy a whole crab, use about 175 g/ 6 oz frozen crab meat and thaw thoroughly before use; or a 175 g/6 oz can of crab meat which just needs thorough draining.

2 Put the rice and milk into a saucepan and bring slowly to the boil. Cover and simmer gently for about 20 minutes.

3 Add the reserved white and brown crab meat and seasoning and simmer for a further 5 minutes.

4 Cool a little, then press through a sieve (strainer), or blend in a food processor or blender until smooth.

5 Pour the soup into a clean saucepan and add the fish stock and the reserved claw meat. Bring slowly to the boil, then add the anchovy essence (paste) and lime or lemon juice and adjust the seasoning.

6 Simmer for a further 2–3 minutes. Stir in the parsley or thyme and then swirl soured cream (if using) through each serving. Garnish with snipped chives.

Prawn (Shrimp) Gumbo

This soup is thick with onions, red (bell) peppers, rice, prawns (shrimp) and okra, which both adds flavour and acts as a thickening agent.

NUTRITIONAL INFORMATION

Calories	177	Sugar	........5g
Protein	........12g	Fats	..........8g
Carbohydrates	...15g	Saturates	......1g

 1 HOUR   45 MINS

SERVES 4–6

I N G R E D I E N T S

1 large onion, chopped finely

2 slices lean bacon, chopped finely (optional)

1–2 garlic cloves, crushed

2 tbsp olive oil

1 large or 2 small red (bell) peppers, chopped finely or minced coarsely

850 ml/1½ pints/3½ cups Fish or Vegetable Stock (see page 8)

1 fresh or dried bay leaf

1 blade mace

good pinch of ground allspice

40 g/1½ oz/3 tbsp long-grain rice

1 tbsp white wine vinegar

125–175 g/4½–6 oz okra, trimmed and sliced very thinly

90–125 g/3–4½ oz/½–⅔ cup peeled prawns (shrimp)

1 tbsp anchovy essence (paste)

2 tsp tomato purée (paste)

1–2 tbsp chopped fresh parsley

salt and pepper

TO GARNISH

whole prawns (shrimp)

sprigs of fresh parsley

1 Gently fry the onion, bacon (if using) and garlic in the oil in a large saucepan for 4–5 minutes until soft. Add the (bell) peppers to the pan and continue to fry gently for a couple of minutes.

2 Add the stock, bay leaf, mace, allspice, rice, vinegar and seasoning and bring to the boil. Cover and simmer gently for about 20 minutes, giving an occasional stir, until the rice is just tender.

3 Add the okra, prawns (shrimp), anchovy essence (paste) and tomato purée (paste), cover and simmer gently for about 15 minutes until the okra is tender and the mixture slightly thickened.

4 Discard the bay leaf and mace from the soup and adjust the seasoning. Stir in the parsley and serve each portion garnished with a whole prawn (shrimp) and parsley sprigs.

Bean Soup

Beans feature widely in Mexican cooking, and here pinto beans are used to give an interesting texture. Pinto beans require soaking overnight.

NUTRITIONAL INFORMATION

Calories 188	Sugars 9g
Protein 13g	Fat 1g
Carbohydrate ...33g	Saturates 0.3g

20 MINS   3 HOURS

SERVES 4

INGREDIENTS

175 g/6 oz pinto beans

1.25 litres/2¼ pints water

175–225 g/6–8 oz carrots, finely chopped

1 large onion, finely chopped

2–3 garlic cloves, crushed

½–1 chilli, seeded and finely chopped

1 litre /1¾ pints vegetable stock

2 tomatoes, peeled and finely chopped

2 celery sticks, very thinly sliced

salt and pepper

1 tbsp chopped coriander

(cilantro) (optional)

CROUTONS

3 slices white bread, crusts removed

oil, for deep-frying

1–2 garlic cloves, crushed

VARIATION

Pinto beans are widely available, but if you cannot find them or you wish to vary the recipe, you can use cannellini beans or black-eyed beans (peas) as an alternative.

1 Soak the beans overnight in cold water; drain and place in a pan with the water. Bring to the boil and boil vigorously for 10 minutes. Lower the heat, cover and simmer for 2 hours, or until the beans are tender.

2 Add the carrots, onion, garlic, chilli and stock and bring back to the boil. Cover and simmer for a further 30 minutes, until very tender.

3 Remove half the beans and vegetables with the cooking juices and press through a strainer or process in a food processor or blender until smooth.

4 Return the bean purée to the saucepan and add the tomatoes and celery. Simmer for 10–15 minutes, or until the celery is just tender, adding a little more stock or water if necessary.

5 Meanwhile, make the croûtons. Dice the bread. Heat the oil with the garlic in a small frying pan (skillet) and fry the croûtons until golden brown. Drain on kitchen paper (paper towels).

6 Season the soup and stir in the chopped coriander (cilantro), if using. Transfer to a warm tureen and serve immediately with the croûtons.

Jerusalem Artichoke Soup

Jerusalem artichokes are native to North America, but are also grown in Europe. They have a nutty flavour which combines well with orange.

NUTRITIONAL INFORMATION

Calories 211	Sugars 17g
Protein 7g	Fat 8g
Carbohydrate . . .29g	Saturates 4g

 10 MINS   30 MINS

SERVES 4

I N G R E D I E N T S

675 g/1½ lb Jerusalem artichokes

5 tbsp orange juice

25 g/1 oz/2 tbsp butter

1 leek, chopped

1 garlic clove, crushed

300 ml/½ pint/1¼ cups vegetable stock

150 ml/¼ pint/⅔ cup milk

2 tbsp chopped coriander (cilantro)

150 ml/¼ pint/⅔ cup natural
   (unsweetened) yogurt

grated orange rind, to garnish

1 Rinse the Jerusalem artichokes and place in a large saucepan with 2 tablespoons of the orange juice and enough water to cover. Bring to the boil, reduce the heat and cook for 20 minutes, or until the artichokes are tender.

2 Drain the artichokes, reserving 425 ml/³/₄ pint/ 2 cups of the cooking liquid. Leave the artichokes to cool, then peel and place in a large bowl. Mash the flesh with a potato masher.

3 Melt the butter in a large saucepan. Add the leek and garlic and fry over a low heat, stirring frequently, for 2–3 minutes, until the leek soft.

4 Stir in the mashed artichoke, stock, milk, remaining orange juice and reserved cooking water. Bring to the boil, then simmer for 2–3 minutes.

5 Remove a few pieces of leek with a slotted spoon and reserve. Process the remainder in a food processor for 1 minute until smooth. Alternatively, press through a strainer with the back of a spoon.

6 Return the soup to a clean saucepan and stir in the reserved leeks, coriander (cilantro) and yogurt and heat through. Transfer to individual soup bowls, garnish with orange rind and serve.

Mussels in White Wine

This soup of mussels, cooked in white wine with onions and cream, can be served as an appetizer or a main dish with plenty of crusty bread.

NUTRITIONAL INFORMATION

Calories 396   Sugars 2g
Protein ....23g   Fat 24g
Carbohydrate ....8g   Saturates 15g

5–10 MINS   25 MINS

SERVES 4

I N G R E D I E N T S

about 3 litres/5¼ pints/12 cups fresh
   mussels

60 g/2 oz/¼ cup butter

1 large onion, chopped very finely

2–3 garlic cloves, crushed

350 ml/12 fl oz/1½ cups dry white wine

150 ml/¼ pint/⅔ cup water

2 tbsp lemon juice

good pinch of finely grated lemon rind

1 bouquet garni sachet

1 tbsp plain (all-purpose) flour

4 tbsp single (light) or double (thick) cream

2–3 tbsp chopped fresh parsley

salt and pepper

warm crusty bread, to serve

1 Scrub the mussels in several changes of cold water to remove all mud, sand, barnacles, etc. Pull off all the 'beards'. All of the mussels must be tightly closed; if they don't close when given a sharp tap, they must be discarded.

2 Melt half the butter in a large saucepan. Add the onion and garlic, and fry gently until soft but not coloured.

3 Add the wine, water, lemon juice and rind, bouquet garni and plenty of seasoning. Bring to the boil then cover and simmer for 4–5 minutes.

4 Add the mussels to the pan, cover tightly and simmer for 5 minutes, shaking the pan frequently, until all the mussels have opened. Discard any mussels which have not opened. Remove the bouquet garni.

5 Remove the empty half shell from each mussel. Blend the remaining butter with the flour and whisk into the soup, a little at a time. Simmer gently for 2–3 minutes until slightly thickened.

6 Add the cream and half the parsley to the soup and reheat gently. Adjust the seasoning. Ladle the mussels and soup into warmed large soup bowls, sprinkle with the remaining parsley and serve with plenty of warm crusty bread.

Fiery Salsa

Make this Mexican-style salsa to perk up jaded palates. Its lively flavours really get the tastebuds going. Serve with hot tortilla chips.

NUTRITIONAL INFORMATION

Calories 328	Sugars 2g
Protein 4g	Fat 26g
Carbohydrate . . .21g	Saturates 5g

30 MINS 0 MINS

SERVES 4

INGREDIENTS

2 small fresh red chillies

1 tbsp lime or lemon juice

2 large ripe avocados

5 cm/2 inch piece of cucumber

2 tomatoes, peeled

1 small garlic clove, crushed

few drops of Tabasco sauce

salt and pepper

lime or lemon slices, to garnish

tortilla chips, to serve

1 Remove and discard the stem and seeds from 1 fresh red chilli. Chop the flesh very finely and place in a large mixing bowl.

2 To make a chilli 'flower' for garnish, using a small, sharp knife, slice the remaining chilli from the stem to the tip several times without removing the stem. Place in a bowl of iced water, so that the 'petals' open out.

3 Add the lime or lemon juice to the mixing bowl. Halve, stone (pit) and peel the avocados. Add the flesh to the mixing bowl and mash thoroughly with a fork. The salsa should be slightly chunky. (The lime or lemon juice prevents the avocado from turning brown.)

4 Chop the cucumber and tomatoes finely and add to the avocado mixture with the crushed garlic.

5 Stir in the Tabasco sauce and season with salt and pepper. Transfer the dip to a serving bowl. Garnish with slices of lime or lemon and the chilli flower.

6 Put the bowl on a large plate, surround with tortilla chips and serve. Do not keep this dip standing for long or it will discolour.

Figs & Parma Ham (Prosciutto)

This colourful fresh salad is delicious at any time of the year. Prosciutto di Parma is thought to be the best ham in the world.

NUTRITIONAL INFORMATION

Calories 121	Sugars 6g	
Protein 1g	Fat 11g	
Carbohydrate 6g	Saturates 2g	

 15 MINS   5 MINS

SERVES 4

INGREDIENTS

40 g/1½ oz rocket (arugula)

4 fresh figs

4 slices Parma ham (prosciutto)

4 tbsp olive oil

1 tbsp fresh orange juice

1 tbsp clear honey

1 small red chilli

1 Tear the rocket (arugula) into more manageable pieces and arrange on 4 serving plates.

2 Using a sharp knife, cut each of the figs into quarters and place them on top of the rocket (arugula) leaves.

3 Using a sharp knife, cut the Parma ham (prosciutto) into strips and scatter over the rocket (arugula) and figs.

4 Place the oil, orange juice and honey in a screw-top jar. Shake the jar until the mixture emulsifies and forms a thick dressing. Transfer to a bowl.

5 Using a sharp knife, dice the chilli, remembering not to touch your face before you have washed your hands (see Cook's Tip, below). Add the chopped chilli to the dressing and mix well.

6 Drizzle the dressing over the Parma ham (prosciutto), rocket (arugula) and figs, tossing to mix well. Serve at once.

COOK'S TIP

Chillies can burn the skin for several hours after chopping, so it is advisable to wear gloves when you are handling the very hot varieties.

Preserved Meats (Salumi)

Mix an attractive selection of these preserved meats (salumi) with olives and marinated vegetables for extra colour and variety.

NUTRITIONAL INFORMATION

Calories 227	Sugars 5g
Protein 10g	Fat 19g
Carbohydrate 5g	Saturates 1g

  10 MINS 5–10 MINS

SERVES 4

I N G R E D I E N T S

3 ripe tomatoes

3 ripe figs

1 small melon

60 g/2 oz Italian salami, sliced thinly

4 thin slices mortadella

6 slices Parma ham (prosciutto)

6 slices bresaola

4 fresh basil leaves, chopped

olive oil

90 g/3 oz/½ cup marinated olives, pitted

freshly ground black pepper, to serve

1 Slice the tomatoes thinly and cut the figs into quarters.

2 Halve the melon, scoop out the seeds, and cut the flesh into wedges.

3 Arange the meats on one half of a serving platter. Arrange the tomato slices in the centre and sprinkle with the basil leaves and oil.

4 Cover the rest of the platter with the figs and melon and scatter the olives over the meats.

5 Serve with a little extra olive oil to drizzle over the bresaola, and sprinkle with coarsely ground black pepper.

Prawn (Shrimp) Parcels

These small prawn (shrimp) bites are packed with the flavour of lime and coriander (cilantro) for a quick and tasty starter.

NUTRITIONAL INFORMATION

Calories 305	Sugars 2g	
Protein 15g	Fat 21g	
Carbohydrate . . .14g	Saturates 8g	

  15 MINS   ⏲ 20 MINS

SERVES 4

I N G R E D I E N T S

1 tbsp sunflower oil

1 red (bell) pepper, deseeded and very thinly sliced

75 g/2¾ oz/¾ cup beansprouts

finely grated zest and juice of 1 lime

1 red chili, deseeded and very finely chopped

1 cm/½ inch piece of root ginger, peeled and grated

225 g/8 oz peeled prawns (shrimp)

1 tbsp fish sauce

½ tsp arrowroot

2 tbsp chopped fresh coriander (cilantro)

8 sheets filo pastry

25 g/1 oz/2 tbsp butter

2 tsp sesame oil

oil, for frying

spring onion (scallion) tassels, to garnish

chilli sauce, to serve

COOK'S TIP

If using cooked prawns (shrimp), cook for 1 minute only otherwise the prawns (shrimp) will toughen.

1 Heat the sunflower oil in a large preheated wok. Add the red (bell) pepper and beansprouts and stir-fry for 2 minutes, or until the vegetables have softened.

2 Remove the wok from the heat and toss in the lime zest and juice, red chilli, ginger and prawns (shrimp), stirring well.

3 Mix the fish sauce with the arrowroot and stir the mixture into the wok juices. Return the wok to the heat and cook, stirring, for 2 minutes, or until the juices thicken. Toss in the coriander (cilantro) and mix well.

4 Lay the sheets of filo pastry out on a board. Melt the butter and sesame oil and brush each pastry sheet with the mixture.

5 Spoon a little of the prawn (shrimp) filling on to the top of each sheet, fold over each end, and roll up to enclose the filling.

6 Heat the oil in a large wok. Cook the parcels, in batches, for 2–3 minutes, or until crisp and golden. Garnish with spring onion (scallion) tassels and serve hot with a chilli dipping sauce.

Spicy Sweetcorn Fritters

Cornmeal can be found in most supermarkets or health food shops. Yellow in colour, it acts as a binding agent in this recipe.

NUTRITIONAL INFORMATION

Calories 213   Sugars 6g
Protein ....5g   Fat 8g
Carbohydrate ...30g   Saturates 1g

5 MINS   15 MINS

SERVES 4

INGREDIENTS

225 g/8 oz/¾ cup canned or frozen sweetcorn

2 red chillies, deseeded and very finely chopped

2 cloves garlic, crushed

10 lime leaves, very finely chopped

2 tbsp fresh coriander (cilantro), chopped

1 large egg

75 g/2¾ oz/½ cup cornmeal

100 g/3½ oz fine green beans, very finely sliced

groundnut oil, for frying

1 Place the sweetcorn, chillies, garlic, lime leaves, coriander (cilantro), egg and cornmeal in a large mixing bowl, and stir to combine.

2 Add the green beans to the ingredients in the bowl and mix well, using a wooden spoon.

3 Divide the mixture into small, evenly sized balls. Flatten the balls of mixture between the palms of your hands to form rounds.

4 Heat a little groundnut oil in a preheated wok or large frying pan (skillet) until really hot. Cook the fritters, in batches, until brown and crispy on the outside, turning occasionally.

5 Leave the fritters to drain on absorbent kitchen paper (paper towels) while frying the remaining fritters.

6 Transfer the fritters to warm serving plates and serve immediately.

COOK'S TIP

Kaffir lime leaves are dark green, glossy leaves that have a lemony-lime flavour. They can be bought from specialist Asian stores either fresh or dried. Fresh leaves impart a delicious flavour.

Crudités with Shrimp Sauce

In this recipe, fruit and vegetable crudités are served with a spicy, garlicky shrimp sauce.

NUTRITIONAL INFORMATION

Calories ....85 Sugars 11g
Protein ....7g Fat 1g
Carbohydrate ...12g Saturates 0.2g

🍲 12¹/₄ HOURS 🕐 0 MINS

SERVES 4

INGREDIENTS

about 750 g/1 lb10 oz prepared
  raw fruit and vegetables, such
  as broccoli, cauliflower, apple,
  pineapple, cucumber, celery, (bell)
  peppers and mushrooms

SAUCE

60 g/2 oz dried shrimps

1 cm/½ inch cube shrimp paste

3 garlic cloves, crushed

4 red chillies, seeded and chopped

6 stems fresh coriander (cilantro),
  coarsely chopped

juice of 2 limes

fish sauce, to taste

brown sugar, to taste

1 Soak the dried shrimps in warm water for 10 minutes.

2 To make the sauce, place the shrimp paste, drained shrimps, garlic, chillies and coriander (cilantro) in a food processor or blender and process until well chopped but not smooth.

3 Turn the sauce mixture into a bowl and add the lime juice, mixing well.

4 Add fish sauce and brown sugar to taste to the sauce. Mix well.

5 Cover the bowl tightly and chill the sauce in the refrigerator for at least 12 hours, or overnight.

6 To serve, arrange the fruit and vegetables attractively on a large serving plate. Place the prepared sauce in the centre for dipping.

COOK'S TIP

Hard-boiled quail's eggs are often added to this traditional fruit and vegetable platter and certainly would be offered on a special occasion.

Crispy Crab Wontons

These delicious wontons are a superb appetizer. Deep-fried until crisp and golden, they are delicious with a chilli dipping sauce.

NUTRITIONAL INFORMATION

Calories 266	Sugars 0.4g	
Protein 10g	Fat 17g	
Carbohydrate ...18g	Saturates 5g	

 10 MINS   15 MINS

SERVES 4

INGREDIENTS

175 g/6 oz white crabmeat, flaked

50 g/1¾ oz canned water chestnuts, drained, rinsed and chopped

1 small fresh red chilli, chopped

1 spring onion (scallion), chopped

1 tbsp cornflour (cornstarch)

1 tsp dry sherry

1 tsp light soy sauce

½ tsp lime juice

24 wonton wrappers

vegetable oil, for deep-frying

sliced lime, to garnish

1 To make the filling, mix together the crabmeat, water chestnuts, chilli, spring onion (scallion), cornflour (cornstarch), sherry, soy sauce and lime juice.

2 Spread out the wonton wrappers on a work surface (counter) and spoon one portion of the filling into the centre of each wonton wrapper.

3 Dampen the edges of the wonton wrappers with a little water and fold them in half to form triangles. Fold the two pointed ends in towards the centre, moisten with a little water to secure and then pinch together to seal.

4 Heat the oil for deep-frying in a wok or deep-fryer to 180°C–190°C/350°F–375°F, or until a cube of bread browns in 30 seconds. Fry the wontons, in batches, for 2–3 minutes, until golden brown and crisp. Remove the wontons from the oil and leave to drain on kitchen paper (paper towels).

5 Serve the wontons hot, garnished with slices of lime.

COOK'S TIP

Handle wonton wrappers carefully as they can be easily damaged. Make sure that the wontons are sealed well and secured before deep-frying to prevent the filling coming out and the wontons unwrapping.

Seven Spice Aubergines

This is a really simple dish which is perfect served with a chilli dip.

NUTRITIONAL INFORMATION

Calories 169   Sugars 2g
Protein ....2g   Fat 12g
Carbohydrate ...15g   Saturates 1g

 35 MINS   20 MINS

SERVES 4

INGREDIENTS

450 g/1 lb aubergines (eggplants),
    wiped

1 egg white

50 g/1¾ oz/3½ tbsp cornflour
    (cornstarch)

1 tsp salt

1 tbsp seven spice seasoning

oil, for deep-frying

1 Using a sharp knife, thinly slice the aubergines (eggplants). Place the aubergine (eggplant) in a colander, sprinkle with salt and leave to stand for 30 minutes. This will remove all the bitter juices.

2 Rinse the aubergine (eggplant) thoroughly and pat dry with absorbent kitchen paper (paper towels).

3 Place the egg white in a small bowl and whip until light and foamy.

4 Using a spoon, mix together the cornflour (cornstarch), salt and seven spice powder on a large plate.

5 Heat the oil for deep-frying in a large preheated wok or heavy-based frying pan (skillet).

6 Dip the aubergines (eggplants) into the egg white, and then into the cornflour (cornstarch) and seven spice mixture to coat evenly.

7 Deep-fry the coated aubergine (eggplant) slices, in batches, for 5 minutes, or until pale golden and crispy.

8 Transfer the aubergines (eggplants) to absorbent kitchen paper (paper towels) and leave to drain. Transfer the seven spice aubergines (eggplants) to serving plates and serve hot.

COOK'S TIP

The best oil to use for deep-frying is groundnut oil which has a high smoke point and mild flavour, so it will neither burn or taint the food. About 600 ml/1 pint oil is sufficient.

Bang-Bang Chicken

The cooked chicken meat is tenderized by being beaten with a rolling pin, hence the name for this very popular Szechuan dish.

NUTRITIONAL INFORMATION

Calories	82	Sugars	.........1g
Protein	........13g	Fat	..........3g
Carbohydrate	....2g	Saturates	.......1g

🍲 1¼ HOURS 🕐 40 MINS

SERVES 4

I N G R E D I E N T S

1 litre/1¾ pints/4 cups water

2 chicken quarters (breast half and leg)

1 cucumber, cut into matchstick shreds

S A U C E

2 tbsp light soy sauce

1 tsp sugar

1 tbsp finely chopped spring onions
(scallions), plus extra to garnish

1 tsp red chilli oil

¼ tsp pepper

1 tsp white sesame seeds

2 tbsp peanut butter, creamed with a little
sesame oil, plus extra to garnish

1 Bring the water to a rolling boil in a wok or a large saucepan. Add the chicken pieces, reduce the heat, cover and cook for 30-35 minutes.

2 Remove the chicken from the wok or pan and immerse in a bowl of cold water for at least 1 hour to cool it, ready for shredding.

3 Remove the chicken pieces, drain and dry on absorbent kitchen paper (paper towels). Take the meat off the bone.

4 On a flat surface, pound the chicken with a rolling pin, then tear the meat

into shreds with 2 forks. Mix the chicken with the shredded cucumber and arrange in a serving dish.

5 To serve, mix together all the sauce ingredients until thoroughly combined and pour over the chicken and cucumber in the serving dish. Sprinkle some sesame seeds and chopped spring onions (scallions) over the sauce and serve.

COOK'S TIP

Take the time to tear the chicken meat into similar-sized shreds, to make an elegant-looking dish. You can do this quite efficiently with 2 forks, although Chinese cooks would do it with their fingers.

Butterfly Prawns (Shrimp)

Use unpeeled, raw king or tiger prawns (jumbo shrimp) which are about 7-10cm (3-4 inches) long.

NUTRITIONAL INFORMATION

Calories 157   Sugars 0.3g
Protein ....8g   Fat 9g
Carbohydrate ....11g   Saturates 2g

25 MINS   10 MINS

SERVES 4

INGREDIENTS

12 raw tiger prawns (jumbo shrimp)
   in their shells

2 tbsp light soy sauce

1 tbsp Chinese rice wine or dry sherry

1 tbsp cornflour (cornstarch)

vegetable oil, for deep-frying

2 eggs, lightly beaten

8-10 tbsp breadcrumbs

salt and pepper

shredded lettuce leaves, to serve

chopped spring onions (scallions),
   either raw or soaked for about
   30 seconds in hot oil, to garnish

1 Shell and devein the prawns (shrimp) leaving the tails on. Split them in half from the underbelly about halfway along, leaving the tails still firmly attached. Mix together the salt, pepper, soy sauce, wine and cornflour (cornstarch), add the prawns (shrimp) and turn to coat. Leave to marinate for 10-15 minutes.

2 Heat the oil in a preheated wok. Pick up each prawn (shrimp) by the tail,

dip it in the beaten egg then roll it in the breadcrumbs to coat well.

3 Deep-fry the prawns (shrimp) in batches until golden brown. Remove them with a slotted spoon and drain on paper towels.

4 To serve, arrange the prawns (shrimp) neatly on a bed of lettuce leaves and garnish with spring onions (scallions).

COOK'S TIP

To devein prawns (shrimp), first remove the shell. Make a shallow cut about three-quarters of the way along the back of each prawn (shrimp), then pull out and discard the black intestinal vein.

Pork Dim Sum

These small steamed parcels are traditionally served as an appetizer and are very adaptable to your favourite fillings.

NUTRITIONAL INFORMATION

Calories 478   Sugars 3g
Protein . . . . .33g   Fat 29g
Carbohydrate . . .21g   Saturates 9g

 10 MINS   15 MINS

SERVES 4

INGREDIENTS

400 g/14 oz minced (ground) pork

2 spring onions (scallions), chopped

50 g/1¾ oz canned bamboo shoots, drained, rinsed and chopped

1 tbsp light soy sauce

1 tbsp dry sherry

2 tsp sesame oil

2 tsp caster (superfine) sugar

1 egg white, lightly beaten

4½ tsp cornflour (cornstarch)

24 wonton wrappers

1 Place the minced (ground) pork, spring onions (scallions), bamboo shoots, soy sauce, dry sherry, sesame oil, caster (superfine) sugar and beaten egg white in a large mixing bowl and mix until all the ingredients are thoroughly combined.

2 Stir in the cornflour (cornstarch), mixing until thoroughly incorporated with the other ingredients.

3 Spread out the wonton wrappers on a work surface (counter). Place a spoonful of the pork and vegetable mixture in the centre of each wonton wrapper and lightly brush the edges of the wrappers with water.

4 Bring the sides of the wrappers together in the centre of the filling, pinching firmly together.

5 Line a steamer with a clean, damp tea towel (dish cloth) and arrange the wontons inside.

6 Cover and steam for 5–7 minutes, until the dim sum are cooked through. Serve immediately.

COOK'S TIP

Bamboo steamers are designed to rest on the sloping sides of a wok above the water. They are available in a range of sizes.

Salt & Pepper Prawns

Szechuan peppercorns are very hot, adding heat and a red colour to the prawns (shrimp). They are effectively offset by the sugar in this recipe.

NUTRITIONAL INFORMATION

Calories 174   Sugars 1g
Protein ....25g   Fat 8g
Carbohydrate ....1g   Saturates 1g

5 MINS   10 MINS

SERVES 4

I N G R E D I E N T S

2 tsp salt

1 tsp black pepper

2 tsp Szechuan peppercorns

1 tsp sugar

450 g/1 lb peeled raw tiger prawns
  (jumbo shrimp)

2 tbsp groundnut oil

1 red chilli, deseeded and finely
  chopped

1 tsp freshly grated ginger

3 cloves garlic, crushed

spring onions (scallions), sliced,
  to garnish

prawn (shrimp) crackers, to serve

1 Grind the salt, black pepper and Szechuan peppercorns in a pestle and mortar.

2 Mix the salt and pepper mixture with the sugar and set aside until required.

3 Rinse the tiger prawns (jumbo shrimp) under cold running water and pat dry with absorbent kitchen paper (paper towels).

4 Heat the oil in a preheated wok or large frying pan (skillet).

5 Add the prawns (shrimp), chopped red chilli, ginger and garlic to the wok or frying pan (skillet) and stir-fry for 4–5 minutes, or until the prawns (shrimp) are cooked through.

6 Add the salt and pepper mixture to the wok and stir-fry for 1 minute, stirring constantly so it does not burn on the base of the wok.

7 Transfer the prawns (shrimp) to warm serving bowls and garnish with spring onions (scallions). Serve hot with prawn (shrimp) crackers.

COOK'S TIP

Tiger prawns (jumbo shrimp) are widely available and have a lovely meaty texture. If using cooked tiger prawns (shrimp), add them with the salt and pepper mixture in step 5 – if the cooked prawns (shrimp) are added any earlier they will toughen up and be inedible.

Deep-fried Seafood

Deep-fried seafood is popular all around the Mediterranean, where fish of all kinds is fresh and abundant.

NUTRITIONAL INFORMATION

Calories 393	Sugars 0.2g	
Protein 27g	Fat 26g	
Carbohydrate ...12g	Saturates 3g	

5 MINS   15 MINS

SERVES 4

INGREDIENTS

200 g/7 oz prepared squid

200 g/7 oz blue (raw) tiger prawns
(shrimp), peeled

150 g/5 ½ oz whitebait

oil, for deep-frying

50 g/1 ½ oz plain (all-purpose) flour

1 tsp dried basil

salt and pepper

TO SERVE

garlic mayonnaise

lemon wedges

1 Carefully rinse the squid, prawns (shrimp) and whitebait under cold running water, completely removing any dirt or grit.

2 Using a sharp knife, slice the squid into rings, leaving the tentacles whole.

3 Heat the oil in a large saucepan to 180°–190°C/350°–375°F or until a cube of bread browns in 30 seconds.

4 Place the flour in a bowl, add the basil and season with salt and pepper to taste. Mix together well.

5 Roll the squid, prawns (shrimp) and whitebait in the seasoned flour until coated all over. Carefully shake off any excess flour.

6 Cook the seafood in the heated oil, in batches, for 2–3 minutes or until crispy and golden all over. Remove all of the seafood with a perforated spoon and leave to drain thoroughly on kitchen paper.

7 Transfer the deep-fried seafood to serving plates and serve with garlic mayonnaise (see page 30) and a few lemon wedges.

Rosy Melon & Strawberries

The combination of sweet melon and strawberries macerated in rosé wine and a hint of rose water is a delightful start to a special meal.

NUTRITIONAL INFORMATION

Calories ....59 Sugars 8g
Protein ....1g Fat 0.1g
Carbohydrate ....8g Saturates 0g

2½ HOURS   0 MINS

SERVES 4

INGREDIENTS

¼ honeydew melon

½ Charentais or Cantaloupe melon

150 ml/5 fl oz/⅔ cup rosé wine

2–3 tsp rose water

175 g/6 oz small strawberries, washed and hulled

rose petals, to garnish

1 Scoop out the seeds from both melons with a spoon. Then carefully remove the skin, taking care not to remove too much flesh.

2 Cut the melon flesh into thin strips and place in a bowl. Pour over the wine and sufficient rose water to taste. Mix together gently, cover and leave to chill in the refrigerator for at least 2 hours.

3 Halve the strawberries and carefully mix into the melon.

4 Allow the melon and strawberries to stand at room temperature for about 15 minutes for the flavours to develop – if the melon is too cold, there will be little flavour.

5 Arrange on individual serving plates and serve sprinkled with a few rose petals.

COOK'S TIP

Rose water is generally available from large pharmacies and leading supermarkets as well as from more specialist food suppliers.

Crispy Wontons

Mushroom-filled crispy wontons are served on skewers with a dipping sauce flavoured with chillies.

NUTRITIONAL INFORMATION

Calories 302	Sugars 1g
Protein 3g	Fat 25
Carbohydrate ...15g	Saturates 6g

  45 MINS 20 MINS

SERVES 4

INGREDIENTS

8 wooden skewers, soaked in cold water
    for 30 minutes

1 tbsp vegetable oil

1 tbsp chopped onion

1 small garlic clove, chopped

½ tsp chopped ginger root

60 g/2 oz/½ cup flat mushrooms,
    chopped

16 wonton skins

vegetable oil, for deep-frying

salt

SAUCE

2 tbsp vegetable oil

2 spring onions (scallions),
    shredded thinly

1 red and 1 green chilli, deseeded and
    shredded thinly

3 tbsp light soy sauce

1 tbsp vinegar

1 tbsp dry sherry

pinch of sugar

1 Heat the vegetable oil in a preheated wok or frying pan (skillet).

2 Add the onion, garlic and ginger root to the wok or pan and stir-fry for 2 minutes. Stir in the mushrooms and fry for

a further 2 minutes. Season well with salt and leave to cool.

3 Place 1 teaspoon of the cooled mushroom filling in the centre of each wonton skin.

4 Bring two opposite corners of each wonton skin together to cover the mixture and pinch together to seal. Repeat with the remaining corners.

5 Thread 2 wontons on to each skewer. Heat enough oil in a large saucepan to deep-fry the wontons in batches until golden and crisp. Do not overheat the oil or the wontons will brown on the outside before they are properly cooked inside. Remove the wontons with a perforated spoon and drain on absorbent kitchen paper (paper towels).

6 To make the sauce, heat the vegetable oil in a small saucepan until quite hot or until a small cube of bread dropped in the oil browns in a few seconds. Put the spring onions (scallions) and chillies in a bowl and pour the hot oil slowly on top. Mix in the remaining ingredients.

7 Transfer the crispy wontons to a serving dish and serve with the dipping sauce.

Roasted (Bell) Peppers

These (bell) peppers can be used as an *antipasto*, as a side dish or as a relish to accompany meat and fish.

NUTRITIONAL INFORMATION

Calories . . . . . . .98 Sugars 13g
Protein . . . . .3g Fat 4g
Carbohydrate . . .15g Saturates 1g

 5 MINS   40 MINS

SERVES 4

INGREDIENTS

2 each, red, yellow and orange (bell)

  peppers

4 tomatoes, halved

1 tbsp olive oil

3 garlic cloves, chopped

1 onion, sliced in rings

2 tbsp fresh thyme

salt and pepper

1 Halve and deseed the (bell) peppers. Place them, cut-side down, on a baking tray (cookie sheet) and cook under a preheated grill (broiler) for 10 minutes.

2 Add the tomatoes to the baking tray (cookie sheet) and grill (broil) for 5 minutes, until the skins of the (bell) peppers and tomatoes are charred.

COOK'S TIP

Preserve (bell) peppers in the refrigerator by placing them in a sterilized jar and pouring olive oil over the top to seal. Or, heat 300 ml/½ pint/¼ cup white wine vinegar with a bay leaf and 4 juniper berries and bring to the boil. Pour over the (bell) peppers and set aside until cold. Pack into sterilized jars.

3 Put the (bell) peppers into a polythene bag for 10 minutes to sweat, which will make the skin easier to peel.

4 Remove the tomato skins and chop the flesh. Peel the skins from the (bell) peppers and slice the flesh into strips.

5 Heat the oil in a large frying pan (skillet) and fry the garlic and onion, stirring occasionally, for 3–4 minutes or until softened.

6 Add the (bell) peppers and tomatoes to the frying pan (skillet) and cook for 5 minutes. Stir in the fresh thyme and season to taste with salt and pepper.

7 Transfer to serving bowls and serve warm or chilled.

Vegetable Spring Rolls

There are many different versions of spring rolls throughout the Far East, a vegetable filling being the classic.

NUTRITIONAL INFORMATION

Calories 189	Sugars 4g
Protein 2g	Fat 16g
Carbohydrate 11g	Saturates 5g

10 MINS   15 MINS

SERVES 4

I N G R E D I E N T S

225 g/8 oz carrots

1 red (bell) pepper

1 tbsp sunflower oil, plus extra for frying

75 g/2¾ oz/¾ cup bean sprouts

finely grated zest and juice of 1 lime

1 red chilli, deseeded and very finely chopped

1 tbsp soy sauce

½ tsp arrowroot

2 tbsp chopped fresh coriander (cilantro)

8 sheets filo pastry

25 g/1 oz butter

2 tsp sesame oil

T O   S E R V E

chilli sauce

spring onion (scallion) tassels

1 Using a sharp knife, cut the carrots into thin sticks. Deseed the (bell) pepper and cut into thin slices.

2 Heat the sunflower oil in a large preheated wok.

3 Add the carrot, red (bell) pepper and bean sprouts and cook, stirring, for 2 minutes, or until softened. Remove the wok from the heat and toss in the lime zest and juice, and the red chilli.

4 Mix the soy sauce with the arrowroot. Stir the mixture into the wok, return to the heat and cook for 2 minutes or until the juices thicken.

5 Add the chopped fresh coriander (cilantro) to the wok and mix well.

6 Lay the sheets of filo pastry out on a board. Melt the butter and sesame oil and brush each sheet with the mixture.

7 Spoon a little of the vegetable filling at the top of each sheet, fold over each long side, and roll up.

8 Add a little oil to the wok and cook the spring rolls in batches, for 2–3 minutes, or until crisp and golden.

9 Transfer the spring rolls to a serving dish, garnish and serve hot with chilli dipping sauce.

Black Olive Pâté

This pâté is delicious served as a starter on toasted triangles of bread.
It can also be served as a cocktail snack on small rounds of fried bread.

NUTRITIONAL INFORMATION

Calories	149	Sugars	.........1g
Protein	.........2g	Fat	..........14g
Carbohydrate	....4g	Saturates	.......6g

🍞

🥟 5 MINS   🕐 5 MINS

SERVES 4

INGREDIENTS

225 g/8 oz/1½ cups pitted
   juicy black olives

1 garlic clove, crushed

finely grated rind of 1 lemon

4 tbsp lemon juice

25 g/1 oz/½ cup fresh breadcrumbs

60 g/2 oz/¼ cup full fat soft cheese

salt and pepper

lemon wedges, to garnish

TO SERVE

thick slices of bread

mixture of olive oil and butter

1 Roughly chop the olives and mix with the garlic, lemon rind and juice, breadcrumbs and soft cheese. Pound the mixture until smooth, or place in a food processor and work until fully blended. Season to taste with salt and freshly ground black pepper.

2 Store the pâté in a screw-top jar and chill for several hours before using – this allows the flavours to develop.

3 For a delicious cocktail snack, use a pastry cutter to cut out small rounds from a thickly sliced loaf.

4 Fry the bread rounds in a mixture of olive oil and butter until they are a light golden brown colour. Drain thoroughly on paper towels.

5 Top each round with a little of the pâté, garnish with lemon wedges and serve immediately. This pâté will keep chilled in an airtight jar for up to 2 weeks.

Sweet & Sour Baby Onions

This typical Sicilian dish combines honey and vinegar to give a sweet and sour flavour. Serve hot as an accompaniment or cold with cured meats.

NUTRITIONAL INFORMATION

Calories	131	Sugars	........11g
Protein	.........2g	Fat	...........6g
Carbohydrate	...19g	Saturates	.......1g

 2 MINS 🕐 15 MINS

SERVES 4

I N G R E D I E N T S

350 g/12 oz baby or pickling onions

2 tbsp olive oil

2 fresh bay leaves, torn into strips

thinly pared rind of 1 lemon

1 tbsp soft brown sugar

1 tbsp clear honey

4 tbsp red wine vinegar

1 Soak the onions in a bowl of boiling water – this will make them easier to peel. Using a sharp knife, peel and halve the onions.

2 Heat the oil in a large frying pan (skillet). Add the bay leaves and onions to the pan and cook for 5–6 minutes over a medium-high heat or until browned all over.

3 Cut the lemon rind into thin matchsticks. Add to the frying pan (skillet) with the sugar and honey. Cook for 2–3 minutes, stirring occasionally, until the onions are lightly caramelized.

4 Add the red wine vinegar to the frying pan (skillet), being careful because it will spit. Cook for about 5 minutes, stirring, or until the onions are tender and the liquid has all but disappeared.

5 Transfer the onions to a serving dish and serve at once.

COOK'S TIP

Adjust the piquancy of this dish to your liking by adding extra sugar for a sweeter, more caramelized taste or extra red wine vinegar for a sharper, tarter flavour.

Chicken or Beef Satay

In this dish, strips of chicken or beef are threaded on to skewers, grilled (broiled) and served with a spicy peanut sauce.

NUTRITIONAL INFORMATION

Calories 314	Sugars 8g
Protein 32g	Fat 16g
Carbohydrate . . .10g	Saturates 4g

  2¼ HOURS   15 MINS

SERVES 6

INGREDIENTS

4 boneless, skinned chicken breasts or
  750 g/1 lb 10 oz rump steak, trimmed

MARINADE

1 small onion, finely chopped

1 garlic clove, crushed

2.5 cm/1 inch piece ginger root, peeled
  and grated

2 tbsp dark soy sauce

2 tsp chilli powder

1 tsp ground coriander

2 tsp dark brown sugar

1 tbsp lemon or lime juice

1 tbsp vegetable oil

SAUCE

300 ml/½ pint/1¼ cups coconut milk

4 tbsp/⅓ cup crunchy peanut butter

1 tbsp fish sauce

1 tsp lemon or lime juice

salt and pepper

1 Using a sharp knife, trim any fat from the chicken or beef then cut into thin strips, about 7 cm/3 inches long.

2 To make the marinade, place all the ingredients in a shallow dish and mix well. Add the chicken or beef strips and turn in the marinade until well coated.

Cover with cling film (plastic wrap) and leave to marinate for 2 hours or stand overnight in the refrigerator.

3 Remove the meat from the marinade and thread the pieces, concertina style, on pre-soaked bamboo or thin wooden skewers.

4 Grill (broil) the chicken and beef satays for 8-10 minutes, turning and

brushing occasionally with the marinade, until cooked through.

5 Meanwhile, to make the sauce, mix the coconut milk with the peanut butter, fish sauce and lemon or lime juice in a saucepan. Bring to the boil and cook for 3 minutes. Season to taste.

6 Transfer the sauce to a serving bowl and serve with the cooked satays.

Crostini alla Fiorentina

Serve as a starter, or simply spread on small pieces of crusty fried bread (crostini) as an appetizer with drinks.

NUTRITIONAL INFORMATION

Calories 393	Sugars 2g	
Protein 17g	Fat 25g	
Carbohydrate . . .19g	Saturates 9g	

10 MINS   40-45 MINS

SERVES 4

I N G R E D I E N T S

3 tbsp olive oil

1 onion, chopped

1 celery stalk, chopped

1 carrot, chopped

1–2 garlic cloves, crushed

125 g/4½ oz chicken livers

125 g/4½ oz calf's, lamb's or pig's liver

150 ml/¼ pint/⅔ cup red wine

1 tbsp tomato purée (paste)

2 tbsp chopped fresh parsley

3–4 canned anchovy fillets, chopped finely

2 tbsp stock or water

25–40 g/1–1½ oz/2–3 tbsp butter

1 tbsp capers

salt and pepper

small pieces of fried crusty bread, to serve

chopped parsley, to garnish

1 Heat the oil in a pan, add the onion, celery, carrot and garlic, and cook gently for 4–5 minutes or until the onion is soft, but not coloured.

2 Meanwhile, rinse and dry the chicken livers. Dry the calf's or other liver, and slice into strips. Add the liver to the pan and fry gently for a few minutes until the strips are well sealed on all sides.

3 Add half of the wine and cook until it has mostly evaporated. Then add the rest of the wine, tomato purée (paste), half of the parsley, the anchovy fillets, stock or water, a little salt and plenty of black pepper.

4 Cover the pan and leave to simmer, stirring occasionally, for 15–20 minutes or until tender and most of the liquid has been absorbed.

5 Leave the mixture to cool a little, then either coarsely mince or put into a food processor and process to a chunky purée.

6 Return to the pan and add the butter, capers and remaining parsley. Heat through gently until the butter melts. Adjust the seasoning and turn out into a bowl. Serve warm or cold spread on the slices of crusty bread and sprinkled with chopped parsley.

Cauliflower Roulade

A light-as-air mixture of eggs and vegetables produces a stylish vegetarian dish that can be enjoyed hot or cold.

NUTRITIONAL INFORMATION

Calories 271	Sugars 4g
Protein 15g	Fat 20g
Carbohydrate 7g	Saturates 11g

  30 MINS 🕐 40 MINS

SERVES 6

I N G R E D I E N T S

1 small cauliflower, divided into florets

4 eggs, separated

90 g/3 oz/¾ cup grated Cheddar cheese

60 g/2 oz/¼ cup cottage cheese

pinch of grated nutmeg

½ tsp mustard powder

salt and pepper

F I L L I N G

1 bunch watercress, trimmed

60 g/2 oz/¼ cup butter

25 g/1 oz/¼ cup flour

175 ml/6 fl oz/¾ cup natural
   (unsweetened) yogurt

25 g/1 oz/¼ cup grated Cheddar cheese

60 g/2 oz/¼ cup cottage cheese

1 Line a Swiss roll tin (jelly roll pan) with baking parchment.

2 Steam the cauliflower until just tender, then drain under cold water. Process the cauliflower in a food processor or chop and press through a strainer.

3 Beat the egg yolks, then stir in the cauliflower, 60 g/2 oz/½ cup of the Cheddar and the cottage cheese. Season with nutmeg, mustard, and salt and pepper. Whisk the egg whites until stiff but not dry, then fold them in.

4 Spread the mixture evenly in the tin (pan). Bake in a preheated oven, 190°C/375°F/Gas Mark 5, for about 20-25 minutes, until risen and golden.

5 Chop the watercress, reserving a few sprigs for garnish. Melt the butter in a small pan. Cook the watercress, stirring, for 3 minutes, until wilted. Blend in the flour, then stir in the yogurt and simmer for 2 minutes. Stir in the cheeses.

6 Turn out the roulade on to a damp tea towel (dish cloth) covered with baking parchment. Peel off the paper and leave for a minute to allow the steam to escape. Roll up the roulade, including a new sheet of paper, starting from one narrow end.

7 Unroll the roulade, spread the filling to within 2.5 cm/1 inch of the edges, and roll up. Transfer to a baking tray (cookie sheet), sprinkle with the remaining Cheddar and return to the oven for 5 minutes. Serve immediately if serving hot or allow to cool completely.

Spinach & Ricotta Patties

Nudo or naked is the word used to describe this mixture, which can also be made into thin pancakes or used as a filling for tortelloni.

NUTRITIONAL INFORMATION

Calories .... .374	Sugars 4g
Protein 16g	Fat .... .31g
Carbohydrate 9g	Saturates ..... .19g

🥔 5 MINS   🕐 30 MINS

SERVES 4

I N G R E D I E N T S

450 g/1 lb fresh spinach

250 g/9 oz ricotta cheese

1 egg, beaten

2 tsp fennel seeds, lightly crushed

50 g/1¾ oz pecorino or Parmesan cheese, finely grated, plus extra to garnish

25 g/1 oz plain (all-purpose) flour, mixed with 1 tsp dried thyme

75 g/2 ¾ oz/5 tbsp butter

2 garlic cloves, crushed

salt and pepper

tomato wedges, to serve

1 Wash the spinach and trim off any long stalks. Place in a pan, cover and cook for 4–5 minutes until wilted. This will probably have to be done in batches as the volume of spinach is quite large. Place in a colander and leave to drain and cool.

2 Mash the ricotta and beat in the egg and the fennel seeds. Season with plenty of salt and pepper, then stir in the pecorino or Parmesan cheese.

3 Squeeze as much excess water as possible from the spinach and finely chop the leaves. Stir the spinach into the cheese mixture.

4 Taking about 1 tablespoon of the spinach and cheese mixture, shape it into a ball and flatten it slightly to form a patty. Gently roll in the seasoned flour. Continue this process until all of the mixture has been used up.

5 Half-fill a large frying pan (skillet) with water and bring to the boil.

Carefully add the patties and cook for 3–4 minutes or until they rise to the surface. Remove with a perforated spoon.

6 Melt the butter in a pan. Add the garlic and cook for 2–3 minutes. Pour the garlic butter over the patties, season with freshly ground black pepper and serve at once.

Little Golden Parcels

These little parcels will draw admiring gasps from your guests, but they are fairly simple to prepare.

NUTRITIONAL INFORMATION

Calories 320   Sugars 1g
Protein . . . . .6g   Fat 21g
Carbohydrate . . .28g   Saturates 5g

35 MINS   35 MINS

SERVES 4

I N G R E D I E N T S

1 garlic clove, crushed

1 tsp chopped coriander (cilantro) root

1 tsp pepper

250 g/9 oz/1 cup boiled mashed potato

175 g/6 oz/1 cup water chestnuts, chopped finely

1 tsp grated ginger root

2 tbsp ground roasted peanuts

2 tsp light soy sauce

½ tsp salt

½ tsp sugar

30 wonton sheets, defrosted

1 tsp cornflour (cornstarch), made into a paste with a little water

vegetable oil for deep-frying

fresh chives to garnish

sweet chilli sauce, to serve

1 Mix together all the ingredients except the wonton sheets, cornflour (cornstarch) and oil.

2 Keeping the remainder of the wonton sheets covered with a damp cloth, lay 4 sheets out on a work surface (counter). Put a teaspoonful of the mixture on each. Make a line of the cornflour (cornstarch) paste around each sheet, about 1 cm/ ½ inch from the edge.

3 Bring all four corners to the centre and press together to form little bags. Repeat with all the wonton sheets.

4 Heat 5 cm/2 inches of the oil in a pan until a light haze appears on top and fry the parcels, in batches of 3, until golden brown. Remove and drain on paper towels. Tie a chive around the neck of each bag to garnish, and serve with a sweet chilli sauce for dipping.

VARIATION

If wonton sheets are not available, use spring roll sheets or filo pastry, and cut the large squares down to about 10 cm/ 4 inches square.

Stewed Artichokes

This is a traditional Roman dish. The artichokes are stewed in olive oil with fresh herbs.

NUTRITIONAL INFORMATION

Calories 129	Sugars 0g
Protein 4g	Fat 8g
Carbohydrate ...10g	Saturates 1g

 5 MINS   50 MINS

SERVES 4

INGREDIENTS

4 small globe artichokes

olive oil

4 garlic cloves, peeled

2 bay leaves

finely grated rind and juice of 1 lemon

2 tbsp fresh marjoram

lemon wedges, to serve

1 Using a sharp knife, carefully peel away the tough outer leaves surrounding the artichokes. Trim the stems to about 2.5 cm/1 inch.

2 Using a knife, cut each artichoke in half and scoop out the choke (heart).

3 Place the artichokes in a large heavy-based pan. Pour over enough olive oil to half cover the artichokes in the pan.

4 Add the garlic cloves, bay leaves and half of the grated lemon rind.

5 Start to heat the artichokes gently, cover the pan and continue to cook over a low heat for about 40 minutes. It is important that the artichokes should be stewed in the oil, not fried.

6 Once the artichokes are tender, remove them with a perforated spoon and drain thoroughly. Remove the bay leaves and discard.

7 Transfer the artichokes to warm serving plates. Garnish the artichokes with the remaining grated lemon rind, fresh marjoram and a little lemon juice. Serve with lemon wedges.

COOK'S TIP

To prevent the artichokes from oxidizing and turning brown before cooking, brush them with a little lemon juice. In addition, use the oil used for cooking the artichokes for salad dressings – it will impart a lovely lemon and herb flavour.

Buttered Nut & Lentil Dip

This tasty dip is very easy to make. It is perfect to have at barbecues, as it gives your guests something to nibble while they are waiting.

NUTRITIONAL INFORMATION

Calories 395   Sugars 4g
Protein . . . . .12g   Fat 31g
Carbohydrate . . .18g   Saturates 10g

  5–10 MINS   40 MINS

SERVES 4

INGREDIENTS

60 g/2 oz/¼ cup butter

1 small onion, chopped

90 g/3 oz/⅓ cup red lentils

300 ml/½ pint/1¼ cups vegetable stock

60 g/2 oz/½ cup blanched almonds

60 g/2 oz/½ cup pine nuts

½ tsp ground coriander

½ tsp ground cumin

½ tsp grated root ginger

1 tsp chopped fresh coriander (cilantro)

salt and pepper

sprigs of fresh coriander
    (cilantro) to garnish

TO SERVE

fresh vegetable crudités

bread sticks

VARIATION

Green or brown lentils can
be used, but they will take
longer to cook than red lentils.
If you wish, substitute peanuts for
the almonds. Ground ginger can be
used instead of fresh – substitute
½ teaspoon and add it with the
other spices.

1 Melt half the butter in a saucepan
and fry the onion over a medium heat,
stirring frequently, until golden brown.

2 Add the lentils and vegetable stock.
Bring to the boil, then reduce the heat
and simmer gently, uncovered, for about
25–30 minutes, until the lentils are tender.
Drain well.

3 Melt the remaining butter in a small
frying pan (skillet). Add the almonds
and pine nuts and fry them over a low
heat, stirring frequently, until golden
brown. Remove from the heat.

4 Put the lentils, almonds and pine nuts,
with any remaining butter, into a food
processor blender. Add the ground
coriander, cumin, ginger and fresh
coriander (cilantro). Process for about
15–20 seconds, until the mixture is
smooth. Alternatively, press the lentils
through a strainer to purée them and then
mix with the finely chopped nuts, spices
and herbs.

5 Season the dip with salt and pepper
and garnish with sprigs of fresh
coriander (cilantro). Serve with fresh
vegetable crudités and bread sticks.

Filled Cucumber Cups

These attractive little cups would make an impressive appetizer at a dinner party.

NUTRITIONAL INFORMATION

Calories ....256 Sugars 7g
Protein ....10g Fat 21g
Carbohydrate ....8g Saturates 4g

10 MINS   0 MINS

SERVES 4

INGREDIENTS

1 cucumber

4 spring onions (scallions), chopped finely

4 tbsp lime juice

2 small red chillies, deseeded and chopped finely

3 tsp sugar

150 g/5½ oz/1¼ cups ground roasted peanuts

¼ tsp salt

3 shallots, sliced finely and deep-fried, to garnish

1 Wash the cucumber thoroughly and pat dry with absorbent kitchen paper (paper towels).

2 To make the cucumber cups, cut the ends off the cucumber, and divide it into 3 equal lengths. Mark a line around the centre of each one as a guide.

3 Make a zigzag cut all the way around the centre of each section, always pointing the knife towards the centre of the cucumber.

4 Pull apart the two halves. Scoop out the centre of each cup with a melon baller or teaspoon, leaving a base on the bottom of each cup.

5 Put the spring onions (scallions), lime juice, red chillies, sugar, ground roasted peanuts and salt in a bowl and mix well to combine.

6 Divide the filling evenly between the 6 cucumber cups and arrange on a serving plate.

7 Garnish the cucumber cups with the deep-fried shallots and serve.

COOK'S TIP

Cherry tomatoes can also be hollowed out very simply with a melon baller and filled with this mixture. The two look very pretty arranged together on a serving dish.

Steamed Cabbage Rolls

These small cabbage parcels are quick and easy to prepare and cook. They are ideal for a speedy starter.

NUTRITIONAL INFORMATION

Calories	162	Sugars	.......0.3g
Protein	........24g	Fat	...........7g
Carbohydrates	....2g	Saturates	.......1g

 5 MINS   20 MINS

SERVES 4

I N G R E D I E N T S

8 cabbage leaves, trimmed

225 g/8 oz skinless, boneless chicken

175 g/6 oz peeled raw or cooked prawns (shrimp)

1 tsp cornflour (cornstarch)

½ tsp chilli powder

1 egg, lightly beaten

1 tbsp vegetable oil

1 leek, sliced

1 garlic clove, thinly sliced

sliced fresh red chilli, to garnish

1 Blanch the cabbage for 2 minutes. Drain and pat dry with absorbent kitchen paper (paper towels).

2 Mince (grind) the chicken and prawns (shrimp) in a food processor. Place in a bowl with the cornflour (cornstarch), chilli powder and egg. Mix well to combine all the ingredients.

3 Place 2 tablespoons of the chicken and prawn (shrimp) mixture towards one end of each cabbage leaf. Fold the sides of the cabbage leaf around the filling and roll up.

4 Arrange the parcels, seam-side down, in a single layer on a heatproof plate and cook in a steamer for 10 minutes.

5 Meanwhile, sauté the leek and garlic in the oil for 1–2 minutes.

6 Transfer the cabbage parcels to warmed individual serving plates and garnish with red chilli slices. Serve with the leek and garlic sauté.

COOK'S TIP

Use Chinese leaves (cabbage) or Savoy cabbage for this recipe, choosing leaves of a similar size for the parcels.

Deep-fried Risotto Balls

The Italian name for this dish translates as 'telephone wires' which refers to the strings of melted Mozzarella cheese contained within the risotto balls.

NUTRITIONAL INFORMATION

Calories 280	Sugars 2g	
Protein 5g	Fat 13g	
Carbohydrate . . .35g	Saturates 3g	

 5 MINS   35-40 MINS

SERVES 4

I N G R E D I E N T S

2 tbsp olive oil

1 medium onion, finely chopped

1 garlic clove, chopped

½ red (bell) pepper, diced

150 g/5½ oz/¾ cup arborio (risotto) rice, washed

1 tsp dried oregano

400 ml/14 fl oz/1 ⅔ cup hot vegetable or chicken stock

100 ml/3 ½ fl oz/ ½ scant cup dry white wine

75 g/2 ¾ oz Mozzarella cheese

oil, for deep-frying

fresh basil sprig, to garnish

1 Heat the oil in a frying pan (skillet) and cook the onion and garlic for 3–4 minutes or until just softened.

2 Add the (bell) pepper, arborio (risotto) rice and oregano to the pan. Cook for 2–3 minutes, stirring to coat the rice in the oil.

3 Mix the stock together with the wine and add to the pan a ladleful at a time, waiting for the liquid to be absorbed by the rice before you add the next ladleful of liquid.

4 Once all of the liquid has been absorbed and the rice is tender (it should take about 15 minutes in total), remove the pan from the heat and leave until the mixture is cool enough to handle.

5 Cut the cheese into 12 pieces. Taking about 1 tablespoon of risotto, shape the mixture around the cheese pieces to make 12 balls.

6 Heat the oil until a cube of bread browns in 30 seconds. Cook the risotto balls, in batches of 4, for 2 minutes or until golden.

7 Remove the risotto balls with a perforated spoon and drain thoroughly on absorbent kitchen paper. Garnish with a sprig of basil and serve the risotto balls hot.

Onion & Mozzarella Tarts

These individual tarts are delicious hot or cold and are great for lunchboxes or picnics.

NUTRITIONAL INFORMATION

Calories . . . . . . .327 Sugars 3g
Protein . . . . .5g Fat 23g
Carbohydrate . . .25g Saturates 9g

 45 MINS   45 MINS

SERVES 4

I N G R E D I E N T S

250g/9 oz packet puff pastry, defrosted
   if frozen

2 medium red onions

1 red (bell) pepper

8 cherry tomatoes, halved

100g/3½ oz Mozzarella cheese,
   cut into chunks

8 sprigs thyme

1 Roll out the pastry to make 4 x 7.5 cm/ 3 inch squares. Using a sharp knife, trim the edges of the pastry, reserving the trimmings. Leave the pastry to chill in the refrigerator for 30 minutes.

2 Place the pastry squares on a baking tray (cookie sheet). Brush a little water along each edge of the pastry squares and use the reserved pastry trimmings to make a rim around each tart.

3 Cut the red onions into thin wedges and halve and deseed the (bell) peppers.

4 Place the onions and (bell) pepper in a roasting tin (pan). Cook under a preheated grill (broiler) for 15 minutes or until charred.

5 Place the roasted (bell) pepper halves in a polythene bag and leave to sweat for 10 minutes. Peel off the skin from the (bell) peppers and cut the flesh into strips.

6 Line the pastry squares with squares of foil. Bake in a preheated oven at 200°C/400°F/Gas Mark 6 for 10 minutes. Remove the foil squares and bake for a further 5 minutes.

7 Place the onions, (bell) pepper strips, tomatoes and cheese in each tart and sprinkle with the fresh thyme.

8 Return to the oven for 15 minutes or until the pastry is golden. Serve hot.

Onions à la Grecque

This is a well-known method of cooking vegetables
and is perfect with shallots or onions, served with a crisp salad.

NUTRITIONAL INFORMATION

Calories	200	Sugars	........26g
Protein	.........2g	Fat	...........9g
Carbohydrate	...28g	Saturates	.......1g

🕙 10 MINS   🕐 15 MINS

SERVES 4

INGREDIENTS

450 g/1 lb shallots

3 tbsp olive oil

3 tbsp clear honey

2 tbsp garlic wine vinegar

3 tbsp dry white wine

1 tbsp tomato purée (paste)

2 celery stalks, sliced

2 tomatoes, seeded and chopped

salt and pepper

chopped celery leaves, to garnish

1 Peel the shallots. Heat the oil in a large saucepan, add the shallots and cook, stirring, for 3–5 minutes, or until they begin to brown.

2 Add the honey and cook over a high heat for a further 30 seconds, then add the garlic wine vinegar and dry white wine, stirring well.

3 Stir in the tomato purée (paste), celery and tomatoes and bring the mixture to the boil. Cook over a high heat for 5–6 minutes. Season to taste and leave to cool slightly.

4 Garnish with chopped celery leaves and serve warm. Alternatively chill in the refrigerator before serving.

Courgette (Zucchini) Fritters

These tasty little fritters are great with Roasted (Bell) Peppers
(see page 84) as a relish for a drinks party.

NUTRITIONAL INFORMATION

Calories 162	Sugars 2g	
Protein 7g	Fat 6g	
Carbohydrate ...20g	Saturates 2g	

5-10 MINS   20 MINS

MAKES 16-30

INGREDIENTS

100 g/3 ½ oz self–raising flour

2 eggs, beaten

50 ml/2 fl oz milk

300 g/10 ½ oz courgettes (zucchini)

2 tbsp fresh thyme

1 tbsp oil

salt and pepper

1 Sift the self-raising flour into a large bowl and make a well in the centre. Add the eggs to the well, and using a wooden spoon, gradually draw in the flour.

2 Slowly add the milk to the mixture, stirring constantly to form a thick batter.

3 Meanwhile, wash the courgettes (zucchini). Grate the courgettes (zucchini) over a sheet of kitchen paper placed in a bowl to absorb some of the juices.

4 Add the courgettes (zucchini), thyme and salt and pepper to taste to the batter and mix thoroughly.

5 Heat the oil in a large, heavy-based frying pan (skillet). Taking a tablespoon of the batter for a medium-sized fritter or half a tablespoon of batter for a smaller-sized fritter, spoon the mixture into the hot oil and cook, in batches, for 3–4 minutes on each side.

6 Remove the fritters with a perforated spoon and drain thoroughly on absorbent kitchen paper. Keep each batch of fritters warm in the oven while making the rest. Transfer to serving plates and serve hot.

VARIATION

Try adding ½ teaspoon of dried, crushed chillies to the batter in step 4 for spicier tasting fritters.

Lentil Pâté

Red lentils are used in this spicy recipe for speed as they do not require pre-soaking. You can substitute other types of lentils, if preferred.

NUTRITIONAL INFORMATION

Calories	267	Sugars	........12g
Protein	........14g	Fat	..........8g
Carbohydrate	...37g	Saturates	.......1g

  30 MINS   1¼ HOURS

SERVES 4

I N G R E D I E N T S

1 tbsp vegetable oil, plus extra for greasing

1 onion, chopped

2 garlic cloves, crushed

1 tsp garam masala

½ tsp ground coriander

850 ml/1½ pints/3¾ cups vegetable stock

175 g/6 oz/¾ cup red lentils

1 small egg

2 tbsp milk

2 tbsp mango chutney

2 tbsp chopped parsley

chopped parsley, to garnish

salad leaves (greens) and toast, to serve

1 Heat the oil in a large saucepan and sauté the onion and garlic, stirring constantly, for 2–3 minutes. Add the spices and cook for a further 30 seconds.

2 Stir in the stock and lentils and bring the mixture to the boil. Reduce the heat and simmer for 20 minutes, until the lentils are cooked and softened. Remove the pan from the heat and drain off any excess moisture.

3 Put the mixture in a food processor and add the egg, milk, mango chutney and parsley. Process until smooth.

4 Grease and line the base of a 450 g/ 1 lb loaf tin (pan) and spoon in the mixture, levelling the surface. Cover and cook in a preheated oven, 200°C/400°F/ Gas Mark 6, for 40–45 minutes, or until firm to the touch.

5 Cool in the tin (pan) for 20 minutes, then transfer to the refrigerator.

6 Turn out the pâté on to a serving plate, slice and garnish with chopped parsley. Serve with salad leaves (greens) and toast.

VARIATION

Use other spices, such as chilli powder or Chinese five-spice powder, to flavour the pâté and add tomato relish or chilli relish instead of the mango chutney, if you prefer.

Red Curry Fishcakes

You can use almost any kind of fish fillets or seafood for these delicious fishcakes which can be eaten as an appetizer or a light meal.

NUTRITIONAL INFORMATION

Calories 203   Sugars 1g
Protein . . . . .32g   Fat 8g
Carbohydrate . . . .1g   Saturates 1g

    15 MINS   15 MINS

SERVES 6

INGREDIENTS

1 kg/2 lb 4 oz fish fillets or prepared
    seafood, such as cod, haddock, prawns
    (shrimp), crab meat or lobster

1 egg, beaten

2 tbsp chopped fresh coriander (cilantro)

Red Curry Paste (see page 218)

1 bunch spring onions (scallions), finely
    chopped

vegetable oil, for deep-frying

chilli flowers, to garnish

CUCUMBER SALAD

1 large cucumber, peeled and grated

2 shallots, peeled and grated

2 red chillies, seeded and very finely
    chopped

2 tbsp fish sauce

2 tbsp dried powdered shrimps

1½-2 tbsp lime juice

COOK'S TIP

When handling chillies be
very careful not to touch your
face or eyes: chilli juice is a
powerful irritant, and can be very
painful on the skin. Always wash
your hands after preparing chillies.

1 Place the fish in a blender or food processor with the
egg, coriander (cilantro) and curry paste and purée
until smooth and well blended.

2 Turn the mixture into a bowl, add the spring onions
(scallions) and mix well to combine.

3 Taking 2 tablespoons of the fish mixture at a time,
shape into balls, then flatten them slightly with your
fingers to make fishcakes.

4 Heat the vegetable oil in a preheated wok or frying pan
(skillet) until hot.

5 Add a few of the fishcakes to the wok or pan and
deep-fry for a few minutes until brown and cooked
through. Remove with a slotted spoon and drain on
absorbent kitchen paper (paper towels). Keep warm while
cooking the remaining fishcakes.

6 Meanwhile, to make the cucumber salad, mix the
cucumber with the shallots, chillies, fish sauce, dried
shrimps and lime juice.

7 Serve the cucumber salad immediately, with the warm
fishcakes.

Aspagarus Parcels

These small parcels are ideal as part of a main meal and irresistible as a quick snack with extra plum sauce for dipping.

NUTRITIONAL INFORMATION

Calories 194	Sugars 2g
Protein 3g	Fat 16g
Carbohydrate 11g	Saturates 4g

 5 MINS   25 MINS

SERVES 4

I N G R E D I E N T S

100 g/3½ oz fine tip asparagus

1 red (bell) pepper, deseeded and thinly sliced

50 g/1¾ oz/½ cup bean sprouts

2 tbsp plum sauce

1 egg yolk

8 sheets filo pastry

oil, for deep-frying

1 Place the asparagus, (bell) pepper and beansprouts in a large mixing bowl.

2 Add the plum sauce to the vegetables and mix until well-combined.

3 Beat the egg yolk and set aside until required.

4 Lay the sheets of filo pastry out on to a clean work surface (counter).

5 Place a little of the asparagus and red (bell) pepper filling at the top end of each filo pastry sheet. Brush the edges of the filo pastry with a little of the beaten egg yolk.

6 Roll up the filo pastry, tucking in the ends and enclosing the filling like a spring roll. Repeat with the remaining filo sheets.

7 Heat the oil for deep-frying in a large preheated wok. Carefully cook the parcels, 2 at a time, in the hot oil for 4–5 minutes or until crispy.

8 Remove the parcels with a slotted spoon and leave to drain on absorbent kitchen paper (paper towels).

9 Transfer the parcels to warm serving plates and serve immediately.

COOK'S TIP

Be sure to use fine-tipped asparagus as it is more tender than the larger stems.

Mushroom & Garlic Soufflés

These individual soufflés are very impressive starters, but must be cooked just before serving to prevent them from sinking.

NUTRITIONAL INFORMATION

Calories	179	Sugars	.........3g
Protein	.........6g	Fat	..........14g
Carbohydrate	....8g	Saturates	.......8g

10 MINS   20 MINS

SERVES 4

I N G R E D I E N T S

50 g/1¾ oz/4 tbsp butter

75 g/2¾ oz/1 cup chopped flat mushrooms,

2 tsp lime juice

2 garlic cloves, crushed

2 tbsp chopped marjoram

25 g/1 oz/¹/₄ cup plain (all-purpose) flour

225 ml/8 fl oz/1 cup milk

salt and pepper

2 eggs, separated

1 Lightly grease the inside of four 150 ml/¼ pint/²/₃ cup individual soufflé dishes with a little butter.

2 Melt 25 g/1 oz/2 tbsp of the butter in a frying pan (skillet). Add the mushrooms, lime juice and garlic and sauté for 2–3 minutes. Remove the mushroom mixture from the frying pan

COOK'S TIP

Insert a skewer into the centre of the soufflés to test if they are cooked through – it should come out clean. If not, cook for a few minutes longer, but do not overcook otherwise they will become rubbery.

 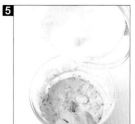

(skillet) with a slotted spoon and transfer to a mixing bowl. Stir in the marjoram.

3 Melt the remaining butter in a pan. Add the flour and cook for 1 minute, then remove from the heat. Stir in the milk and return to the heat. Bring to the boil, stirring until thickened.

4 Mix the sauce into the mushroom mixture and beat in the egg yolks.

5 Whisk the egg whites until they form peaks and fold into the mushroom mixture until fully incorporated.

6 Divide the mixture between the soufflé dishes. Place the dishes on a baking tray (cookie sheet) and cook in a preheated oven, 200°C/400°F/Gas Mark 6, for about 8–10 minutes, or until the soufflés have risen and are cooked through. Serve immediately.

Toasted Nibbles

These tiny cheese balls are rolled in fresh herbs, toasted nuts or paprika to make tasty nibbles for parties, buffets, or pre-dinner drinks.

NUTRITIONAL INFORMATION

Calories 310	Sugars 1g
Protein 15g	Fat 27g
Carbohydrate 1g	Saturates 12g

  40 MINS   5 MINS

SERVES 4

I N G R E D I E N T S

125 g/4½ oz/½ cup ricotta cheese

125 g/4½ oz/1 cup finely grated Double
   Gloucester (brick) cheese

2 tsp chopped parsley

60 g/2 oz/½ cup chopped mixed nuts

3 tbsp chopped herbs, such as parsley,
   chives, marjoram, lovage and chervil

2 tbsp mild paprika

pepper

herb sprigs, to garnish

1 Mix together the ricotta and Double Gloucester (brick) cheeses. Add the parsley and pepper and work together until thoroughly combined.

2 Form the mixture into small balls and place on a plate. Cover and chill in the refrigerator for about 20 minutes, until they are firm.

3 Scatter the chopped nuts on to a baking tray (cookie sheet) and place them under a preheated grill (broiler) until lightly browned. Take care as they can easily burn. Leave them to cool.

4 Sprinkle the nuts, herbs and paprika into 3 separate small bowls. Remove the cheese balls from the refrigerator and

divide into 3 equal piles. Roll 1 quantity of the cheese balls in the nuts, 1 quantity in the herbs and 1 quantity in the paprika until they are all well coated.

5 Arrange the coated cheese balls alternately on a large serving platter. Chill in the refrigerator until ready to serve and then garnish with sprigs of fresh herbs.

Mixed Bhajis

These small bhajis are often served as accompaniments to a main meal, but they are delicious as a starter with a small salad and yogurt sauce.

NUTRITIONAL INFORMATION

Calories 414	Sugars 7g	
Protein 9g	Fat 26g	
Carbohydrate . . .38g	Saturates 3g	

 25 MINS   30 MINS

SERVES 4

I N G R E D I E N T S

B H A J I S

175 g/6 oz/1¼ cups gram flour

1 tsp bicarbonate of soda (baking soda)

2 tsp ground coriander

1 tsp garam masala

1½ tsp turmeric

1½ tsp chilli powder

2 tbsp chopped coriander (cilantro)

1 small onion, halved and sliced

1 small leek, sliced

100 g/3½ oz cooked cauliflower

9-12 tbsp cold water

salt and pepper

vegetable oil, for deep-frying

S A U C E

150 ml/¼ pint/⅔ cup natural
   (unsweetened) yogurt

2 tbsp chopped mint

½ tsp turmeric

1 garlic clove, crushed

mint sprigs, to garnish

2 Divide the mixture into 3 and place in separate bowls. Stir the onion into one bowl, the leek into another and the cauliflower into the third bowl. Add 3-4 tbsp of water to each bowl and mix each to form a smooth paste.

1 Sift the flour, bicarbonate of soda (baking soda) and salt to taste into a mixing bowl and add the spices and fresh coriander (cilantro). Mix thoroughly.

3 Heat the oil for deep-frying in a deep fryer to 180°C/350°F or until a cube of bread browns in 30 seconds. Using 2 dessert spoons, form the mixture into

rounds and cook each in the oil for 3-4 minutes, until browned. Remove with a slotted spoon and drain well on absorbent kitchen paper (paper towels). Keep the bhajis warm in the oven while cooking the remainder.

4 Mix all of the sauce ingredients together and pour into a small serving bowl. Garnish with mint sprigs and serve with the warm bhajis.

Minted Onion Bhajis

Gram flour (also known as besan flour) is a fine yellow flour made from chick peas and is available from supermarkets and Asian food shops.

NUTRITIONAL INFORMATION

Calories . . . . .251 Sugars 7g
Protein . . . . .7g Fat 8g
Carbohydrate . . .39g Saturates 1g

5 MINS   15 MINS

MAKES 12

I N G R E D I E N T S

125 g/4½ oz/1 cup gram flour

¼ tsp cayenne pepper

¼–½ tsp ground coriander

¼–½ tsp ground cumin

1 tbsp chopped fresh mint

4 tbsp strained thick low-fat yogurt

65 ml/2½ fl oz/¼ cup cold water

1 large onion, quartered and thinly sliced

vegetable oil, for frying

salt and pepper

sprigs of mint, to garnish

1 Put the gram flour into a bowl, add the cayenne pepper, coriander, cumin and mint and season with salt and pepper to taste. Stir in the yogurt, water and sliced onion and mix well together.

2 One-third fill a large, deep frying pan with oil and heat until very hot. Drop heaped spoonfuls of the mixture, a few at a time, into the hot oil and use two forks to neaten the mixture into rough ball-shapes.

3 Fry the bhajis until golden brown and cooked through, turning frequently.

4 Drain the bhajis on absorbent kitchen paper (paper towels) and keep warm while cooking the remainder in the same way.

5 Arrange the bhajis on a platter and garnish with sprigs of fresh mint. Serve hot or warm.

COOK'S TIP

Gram flour is excellent for making batter and is used in India in place of flour. It can be made from ground split peas as well as chick-peas (garbanzo beans).

Rice Cubes with Sauce

Plain rice cubes are a good foil to any piquant dipping sauce, and they are often served with satay, to complement the dipping sauce.

NUTRITIONAL INFORMATION

Calories 317	Sugars 3g
Protein 10g	Fat 10g
Carbohydrate . . .49g	Saturates 2g

  8¼ HOURS 25 MINS

SERVES 4

INGREDIENTS

300 g/10½ oz/1½ cups jasmine rice

1.3 litres/2¼ pints/5 cups water

CORIANDER (CILANTRO) DIPPING SAUCE

1 garlic clove

2 tsp salt

1 tbsp black peppercorns

60 g/2 oz/1 cup washed coriander (cilantro), including roots and stem

3 tbsp lemon juice

175 ml/6 fl oz/¾ cup coconut milk

2 tbsp peanut butter

2 spring onions (scallions), chopped roughly

1 red chilli, deseeded and sliced

1 Grease and line a 20 x 10 x 2.5 cm 8 x 4 x 1 inch tin.

2 To make the sauce, grind together the garlic, salt, peppercorns, coriander (cilantro) and lemon juice in a pestle and mortar or blender.

3 Add the coconut milk, peanut butter, spring onions (scallions) and chilli. Grind finely. Transfer to a saucepan and bring to the boil. Leave to cool.

4 To cook the rice, do not rinse. Bring the water to the boil and add the rice.

Stir and return to a medium boil. Cook, uncovered, for 14–16 minutes until very soft. Drain thoroughly.

5 Put 125 g/4½ oz/⅔ cup of the cooked rice in a blender and purée until smooth. Alternatively, grind to a paste in a pestle and mortar.

6 Stir into the remaining cooked rice and spoon into the lined tin (pan). Level

the surface and cover with cling film (plastic wrap). Compress the rice by using either a smaller-sized tin (pan) or a small piece of board, and weigh this down with cans. Chill in the refrigerator for at least 8 hours or preferably overnight.

7 Invert the tin (pan) on to a board. Cut the rice into cubes with a wet knife. Serve with the Coriander (Cilantro) Dipping Sauce.

Hot & Crispy Noodles

These crispy noodles will add a delicious crunch to your Chinese meal. They can be served as a side dish or as an appetizer for people to share.

NUTRITIONAL INFORMATION

Calories 104   Sugars 0.3g
Protein . . . . .2g   Fat 6g
Carbohydrate . . . .11g   Saturates 1g

5 MINS   15 MINS

SERVES 4

INGREDIENTS

250 g/9 oz rice noodles

oil, for deep-frying

2 garlic cloves, chopped finely

8 spring onions (scallions), trimmed and chopped finely

1 small red or green chilli, deseeded and chopped finely

2 tbsp fish sauce

2 tbsp light soy sauce

2 tbsp lime or lemon juice

2 tbsp molasses sugar

TO GARNISH

spring onions (scallions), shredded

cucumber, sliced thinly

fresh chillies

1 Break the noodles into smaller pieces with your hands. Heat the oil for deep-frying in a wok or large frying pan (skillet) and fry small batches of the noodles until pale golden brown and puffed up. Lift the noodles out with a perforated spoon and leave to drain on kitchen paper (paper towels).

2 When all the noodles are cooked, pour off the oil, leaving 3 tbsp in the wok. Add the garlic, spring onions (scallions) and chilli, and stir-fry for 2 minutes.

3 Mix together the fish sauce, soy sauce, lime or lemon juice and sugar. Add to the wok or frying pan (skillet) and cook for 2 minutes, until the sugar has dissolved. Tip all the noodles back into the wok and toss lightly to coat with the sauce mixture.

4 Serve the noodles garnished with shredded spring onions (scallions), thinly sliced cucumber and chillies.

VARIATION

Stir-fry some uncooked peeled prawns (shrimp) or chopped raw chicken with the spring onions (scallions) and garlic in step 2. Cook for an extra 3–4 minutes to make sure they are thoroughly cooked.

Chinese Vegetable Pancakes

Chinese pancakes are made with hardly any fat – they are simply flattened white flour dough.

NUTRITIONAL INFORMATION

Calories 312	Sugars 5g
Protein 13g	Fat 19g
Carbohydrate . . .25g	Saturates 7g

5 MINS   10 MINS

SERVES 4

INGREDIENTS

1 tbsp vegetable oil

1 garlic clove, crushed

2.5 cm/1 inch piece root (fresh) ginger, grated

1 bunch spring onions (scallions), trimmed and shredded lengthwise

100 g/3½ oz mangetout (snow peas), topped, tailed and shredded

225 g/8 oz tofu (bean curd), drained and cut into 1 cm/½ inch pieces

2 tbsp dark soy sauce, plus extra to serve

2 tbsp hoisin sauce, plus extra to serve

60 g/2 oz canned bamboo shoots, drained

60 g/2 oz canned water chestnuts, drained and sliced

100 g/3½ oz bean sprouts

1 small red chilli, deseeded and sliced thinly

1 small bunch fresh chives

12 soft Chinese pancakes

TO SERVE

shredded Chinese leaves (cabbage)

1 cucumber, sliced

strips of red chilli

1 Heat the oil in a non-stick wok or a large frying pan (skillet) and stir-fry the garlic and ginger for 1 minute.

2 Add the spring onions (scallions), mangetout (snow peas), tofu (bean curd), soy and hoisin sauces. Stir-fry for 2 minutes.

3 Add the bamboo shoots, water chestnuts, bean sprouts and sliced red chilli to the pan.

4 Stir-fry gently for a further 2 minutes until the vegetables are just tender.

5 Snip the chives into 2.5 cm/1 inch lengths and stir into the mixture.

6 Heat the pancakes according to the packet instructions and keep warm.

7 Divide the vegetables and tofu (bean curd) among the pancakes. Roll up and serve with the Chinese leaves (cabbage), cucumber, chilli and extra sauce for dipping.

Pork with Chilli & Garlic

Any leftovers from this dish can be used for a number of other dishes, for example Twice-cooked Pork (see page 383).

NUTRITIONAL INFORMATION

Calories 137	Sugars 0.1g
Protein 16g	Fat 8g
Carbohydrate 1g	Saturates 2g

🄖 🄖

🧊 5 HOURS   🕐 35 MINS

SERVES 4

INGREDIENTS

500 g/1 lb 2 oz leg of pork, boned but not skinned

SAUCE

1 tsp finely chopped garlic

1 tsp finely chopped spring onions (scallions)

2 tbsp light soy sauce

1 tsp red chilli oil

½ tsp sesame oil

sprig of fresh coriander (cilantro), to garnish (optional)

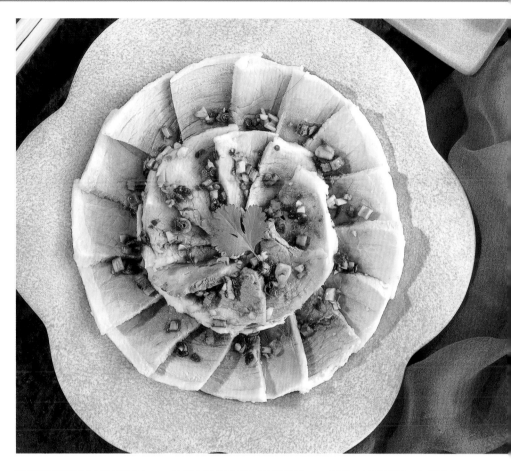

1 Place the pork, tied together in one piece, in a large saucepan, add enough cold water to cover, and bring to a rolling boil over a medium heat.

2 Using a slotted spoon, skim off the scum that rises to the surface, cover the pan with a lid and simmer gently for 25-30 minutes.

3 Leave the meat in the liquid to cool, under cover, for at least 1-2 hours.

4 Lift out the meat with 2 slotted spoons and leave to cool completely, skin-side up, for 2-3 hours.

5 To serve, cut off the skin, leaving a very thin layer of fat on top like a

ham joint. Cut the meat in small thin slices across the grain, and arrange on a plate in an overlapping pattern.

6 In a small bowl, mix together the sauce ingredients, and pour the sauce evenly over the pork.

7 Garnish the pork with a sprig of fresh coriander (cilantro), if wished, and serve at once.

COOK'S TIP

This is a very simple dish, but beautifully presented. Make sure you slice the meat as thinly and evenly as possible to make an elegantly arranged dish.

Garlic & Pine Nut Tarts

A crisp lining of bread is filled with garlic butter and pine nuts to make a delightful light meal.

NUTRITIONAL INFORMATION

Calories 435	Sugars 1g
Protein 6g	Fat 39g
Carbohydrate ...17g	Saturates 20g

20 MINS   15 MINS

SERVES 4

INGREDIENTS

4 slices wholemeal or granary bread

50 g/1¾ oz pine nuts

150 g/5½ oz/10 tbsp butter

5 garlic cloves, peeled and halved

2 tbsp fresh oregano, chopped, plus extra
  for garnish

4 black olives, halved

oregano leaves, to garnish

1 Using a rolling pin, flatten the bread slightly. Using a pastry cutter, cut out 4 circles of bread to fit your individual tart tins (pans) – they should measure about 10 cm/4 inches across. Reserve the offcuts of bread and leave them in the refrigerator for 10 minutes or until required.

VARIATION

Puff pastry can be used for the tarts. Use 200 g/7oz puff pastry to line 4 tart tins (pans). Leave the pastry to chill for 20 minutes. Line the tins (pans) with the pastry and foil and bake blind for 10 minutes. Remove the foil and bake for 3–4 minutes or until the pastry is set. Cool, then continue from step 2, adding 2 tbsp breadcrumbs to the mixture.

2 Meanwhile, place the pine nuts on a baking tray (cookie sheet). Toast the pine nuts under a preheated grill (broiler) for 2–3 minutes or until golden.

3 Put the bread offcuts, pine nuts, butter, garlic and oregano into a food processor and blend for about 20 seconds. Alternatively, pound the ingredients by hand in a mortar and pestle. The mixture should have a rough texture.

4 Spoon the pine nut butter mixture into the lined tin (pan) and top with the olives. Bake in a preheated oven at 200°C/400°F/Gas Mark 6 for 10–15 minutes or until golden.

5 Transfer the tarts to serving plates and serve warm, garnished with the fresh oregano leaves.

Mozzarella in Carriages

These deep-fried Mozzarella sandwiches are a tasty snack at any time of the day, or serve smaller triangles as an antipasto with drinks.

NUTRITIONAL INFORMATION

Calories ....379 Sugars 4g
Protein ....20g Fat 22g
Carbohydrate ...28g Saturates 5g

20 MINS · 5–10 MINS

SERVES 4

I N G R E D I E N T S

8 slices bread, preferably slightly stale,
   crusts removed

100 g/3 ½ oz Mozzarella cheese,
   sliced thickly

50 g/1 ¾ oz black olives, chopped

8 canned anchovy fillets, drained and
   chopped

16 fresh basil leaves

4 eggs, beaten

150 ml/5 floz/⅔ cup milk

oil, for deep-frying

salt and pepper

1 Cut each slice of bread into 2 triangles. Top 8 of the bread triangles with the Mozzarella slices, olives and chopped anchovies.

2 Place the basil leaves on top and season with salt and pepper to taste.

3 Lay the other 8 triangles of bread over the top and press down round the edges to seal.

4 Mix the eggs and milk and pour into an ovenproof dish. Add the sandwiches and leave to soak for about 5 minutes.

5 Heat the oil in a large saucepan to 180°–190°C/350°–375°F or until a cube of bread browns in 30 seconds.

6 Before cooking the sandwiches, squeeze the edges together again.

7 Carefully place the sandwiches in the oil and deep-fry for 2 minutes or until golden, turning once. Remove the sandwiches with a perforated spoon and drain on absorbent kitchen paper. Serve immediately while still hot.

Spanish Tortilla

This classic Spanish dish is often served as part of a tapas (appetizer) selection. A variety of cooked vegetables can be added to this recipe.

NUTRITIONAL INFORMATION

Calories 430   Sugars 6g
Protein ....16g   Fat 20g
Carbohydrate ...50g   Saturates 4g

10 MINS   35 MINS

SERVES 4

I N G R E D I E N T S

1 kg/2 lb 4 oz waxy potatoes, thinly sliced

4 tbsp vegetable oil

1 onion, sliced

2 garlic cloves, crushed

1 green (bell) pepper, seeded and diced

2 tomatoes, seeded and chopped

25 g/1 oz canned sweetcorn (corn), drained

6 large eggs, beaten

2 tbsp chopped parsley

salt and pepper

1 Parboil the potatoes in a saucepan of lightly salted boiling water for 5 minutes. Drain well.

2 Heat the oil in a large frying pan (skillet), add the potato and onions and sauté over a low heat, stirring

constantly, for 5 minutes, until the potatoes have browned.

3 Add the garlic, diced (bell) pepper, chopped tomatoes and sweetcorn (corn), mixing well.

4 Pour in the eggs and add the chopped parsley. Season well with salt and pepper. Cook for 10-12 minutes, until the underside is cooked through.

5 Remove the frying pan (skillet) from the heat and continue to cook the tortilla under a preheated medium grill (broiler) for 5-7 minutes, or until the tortilla is set and the top is golden brown.

6 Cut the tortilla into wedges or cubes, depending on your preference, and transfer to serving dishes. Serve with salad. In Spain tortillas are served hot, cold or warm.

COOK'S TIP

Ensure that the handle of your pan is heatproof before placing it under the grill (broiler) and be sure to use an oven glove when removing it as it will be very hot.

Cheese, Garlic & Herb Pâté

This wonderful soft cheese pâté is fragrant with the aroma of fresh herbs and garlic. Serve with triangles of Melba toast for a perfect starter.

NUTRITIONAL INFORMATION

Calories . . . . . . .392 Sugars 1g
Protein . . . . .17g Fat 28g
Carbohydrate . . .18g Saturates 18g

  20 MINS   10 MINS

SERVES 4

I N G R E D I E N T S

15 g/½ oz/1 tbsp butter

1 garlic clove, crushed

3 spring onions (scallions), finely chopped

125 g/4½ oz/½ cup full-fat soft cheese

2 tbsp chopped mixed herbs,
    such as parsley, chives, marjoram,
    oregano and basil

175 g/6 oz/1½ cups finely grated mature
    (sharp) Cheddar cheese

pepper

4–6 slices of white bread from a
    medium-cut sliced loaf

mixed salad leaves (greens) and cherry
tomatoes, to serve

T O   G A R N I S H

ground paprika

herb sprigs

1 Melt the butter in a small frying pan (skillet) and gently fry the garlic and spring onions (scallions) together for 3–4 minutes, until softened. Allow to cool.

2 Beat the soft cheese in a large mixing bowl until smooth, then add the garlic and spring onions (scallions). Stir in the herbs, mixing well.

3 Add the Cheddar and work the mixture together to form a stiff paste. Cover and chill until ready to serve.

4 To make the Melba toast, toast the slices of bread on both sides, and then cut off the crusts. Using a sharp bread knife, cut through the slices horizontally to make very thin slices. Cut into triangles and then lightly grill (broil) the untoasted sides until golden.

5 Arrange the mixed salad leaves (greens) on 4 serving plates with the cherry tomatoes. Pile the cheese pâté on top and sprinkle with a little paprika. Garnish with sprigs of fresh herbs and serve with the Melba toast.

Crispy Seaweed

This tasty Chinese starter is not all that it seems – the 'seaweed' is in fact pak choi which is then fried, salted and tossed with pine kernels.

NUTRITIONAL INFORMATION

Calories	214	Sugars	. . . . .14g
Protein	. . . . .6g	Fat	. . . . .15g
Carbohydrate	. . .15g	Saturates	. . . . . . .2g

10 MINS   5 MINS

SERVES 4

INGREDIENTS

1 kg/2 lb 4 oz pak choi

groundnut oil, for deep-frying (about 850 ml/1½ pints/3¾ cups)

1 tsp salt

1 tbsp caster (superfine) sugar

50 g/1¾ oz/2½ tbsp toasted pine kernels (nuts)

1 Rinse the pak choi leaves under cold running water and then pat dry thoroughly with absorbent kitchen paper (paper towels).

2 Discarding any tough outer leaves, roll each pak choi leaf up, then slice

through thinly so that the leaves are finely shredded. Alternatively, use a food processor to shred the pak choi.

3 Heat the groundnut oil in a large wok or heavy-based frying pan (skillet).

4 Carefully add the shredded pak choi leaves to the wok or frying pan (skillet) and fry for about 30 seconds or until they shrivel up and become crispy

(you will probably need to do this in several batches, depending on the size of the wok).

5 Remove the crispy seaweed from the wok with a slotted spoon and drain on absorbent kitchen paper (paper towels).

6 Transfer the crispy seaweed to a large bowl and toss with the salt, sugar and pine kernels (nuts). Serve immediately.

COOK'S TIP

The tough, outer leaves of pak choi are discarded as these will spoil the overall taste and texture of the dish.

Use savoy cabbage instead of the pak choi if it is unavailable, drying the leaves thoroughly before frying.

Dumplings in Yogurt Sauce

Adding a baghaar (seasoned oil dressing) just before serving makes this a mouth-watering accompaniment to any meal.

NUTRITIONAL INFORMATION

Calories 719   Sugars 9g
Protein . . . . .9g   Fat 60g
Carbohydrate . . .38g   Saturates 7g

🍲 35 MINS   🕐 35 MINS

SERVES 4

INGREDIENTS

DUMPLINGS

100 g/3½ oz/¾ cup gram flour

1 tsp chilli powder

½ tsp bicarbonate of soda (baking soda)

1 medium onion, finely chopped

2 green chillies

coriander (cilantro) leaves

150 ml/¼ pint/⅔ cup water

300 ml/½ pint/1¼ cups vegetable oil

salt

YOGURT SAUCE

300 ml/½ pint/1¼ cups natural
   (unsweetened) yogurt

3 tbsp gram flour

150 ml/¼ pint/⅔ cup water

1 tsp chopped root ginger

1 tsp crushed garlic

1½ tsp chilli powder

½ tsp turmeric

1 tsp ground coriander

1 tsp ground cumin

SEASONED DRESSING

150 ml/¼ pint/⅔ cup vegetable oil

1 tsp white cumin seeds

6 dried red chillies

1 To make the dumplings, sift the gram flour into a large bowl. Add the chilli powder, ½ teaspoon salt, bicarbonate of soda (baking soda), onion, green chillies and coriander (cilantro) and mix. Add the water and mix to form a thick paste. Heat the oil in a frying pan (skillet). Place teaspoonfuls of the paste in the oil and fry over a medium heat, turning once, until a crisp golden brown. Set aside.

2 To make the sauce, place the yogurt in a bowl and whisk with the gram flour and the water. Add all of the spices and 1½ teaspoons salt and mix well.

3 Press this mixture through a large strainer into a saucepan. Bring to a boil over a low heat, stirring constantly. If the yogurt sauce becomes too thick, add a little extra water.

4 Pour the sauce into a deep serving dish and arrange all the dumplings on top. Set aside and keep warm.

5 To make the dressing, heat the oil in a frying pan (skillet). Add the white cumin seeds and the dried red chillies and fry until darker in colour and giving off their aroma. Pour the dressing over the dumplings and serve hot.

Vegetable & Nut Samosas

These delicious little fried pastries are really quite simple to make. Serve them hot or cold as a starter to an Indian meal.

NUTRITIONAL INFORMATION

Calories 343   Sugars 2g
Protein ....5g   Fat 26g
Carbohydrate ...24g   Saturates 5g

🥟 30 MINS   🕐 40 MINS

MAKES 12

I N G R E D I E N T S

350 g/12 oz potatoes, diced

salt

125 g/4½ oz/1 cup frozen peas

3 tbsp vegetable oil

1 onion, chopped

2.5 cm/1 inch piece of root
    ginger, chopped

1 garlic clove, crushed

1 tsp garam masala

2 tsp mild curry paste

½ tsp cumin seeds

2 tsp lemon juice

60 g/2 oz/½ cup unsalted cashews,
    coarsely chopped

vegetable oil, for shallow frying

coriander (cilantro) sprigs, to garnish

mango chutney, to serve

PASTRY

225 g/8 oz/2 cups plain (all-
    purpose) flour

60 g/2 oz/¼ cup butter

6 tbsp warm milk

1 Cook the potatoes in a saucepan of boiling, salted water for 5 minutes. Add the peas and cook for a further 4 minutes, or until the potatoes are tender. Drain well. Heat the oil in a frying pan (skillet) and fry the onion, potato and pea mixture, ginger, garlic and spices for 2 minutes. Stir in the lemon juice and cook gently, uncovered, for 2 minutes. Remove from the heat, slightly mash the potato and peas, then add the cashews, mix well and season with salt.

2 To make the pastry, put the flour in a bowl and rub in the butter. Mix in the milk to form a dough. Knead lightly and divide into 6 portions. Form each into a ball and roll out to an 18 cm/7 inch round. Cut each one in half.

3 Divide the filling equally between the semi-circles of pastry, spreading it out to within 5 mm/¼ inch of the edges. Brush the edges of pastry all the way round with water and fold over to form triangular shapes, sealing the edges well together to enclose the filling completely.

4 Heat the vegetable oil in a frying pan (skillet) to 180°C/ 350°F or until a cube of bread browns in 30 seconds. Fry the samosas, a few at a time, turning frequently until golden brown and heated through. Drain on kitchen paper (paper towels) and keep warm while cooking the remainder. Garnish with coriander (cilantro) sprigs and serve hot.

Money Bags

These traditional steamed dumplings can be eaten on their own or dipped in a mixture of soy sauce, sherry and slivers of ginger root.

NUTRITIONAL INFORMATION

Calories 315   Sugars 3g
Protein . . . . .8g   Fat 8g
Carbohydrate . . .56g   Saturates 1g

45 MINS   20 MINS

SERVES 4

I N G R E D I E N T S

3 Chinese dried mushrooms
(if unavailable, use thinly sliced
open-cup mushrooms)

250 g/9 oz/2 cups plain (all-purpose) flour

1 egg, beaten

75 ml/3 fl oz/⅓ cup water

1 tsp baking powder

¾ tsp salt

2 tbsp vegetable oil

2 spring onions (scallions), chopped

90 g/3 oz/½ cup sweetcorn kernels

½ red chilli, deseeded and chopped

1 tbsp brown bean sauce

1 Place the dried mushrooms in a small bowl, cover with warm water and leave to soak for 20–25 minutes.

2 To make the wrappers, sift the plain (all-purpose) flour into a bowl. Add the beaten egg and mix in lightly. Stir in the water, baking powder and salt. Mix to make a soft dough.

3 Knead the dough lightly on a floured board. Cover with a damp tea towel (dish cloth) and set aside for 5–6 minutes. This allows the baking powder time to activate, so that the dumplings swell when steaming.

4 Drain the mushrooms, squeezing them dry. Remove the tough centres and chop the mushrooms.

5 Heat the vegetable oil in a wok or large frying pan (skillet) and stir-fry the mushrooms, spring onions (scallions), sweetcorn and chilli for 2 minutes.

6 Stir in the brown bean sauce and remove from the heat.

7 Roll the dough into a large sausage and cut into 24 even-sized pieces. Roll each piece out into a thin round and place a teaspoonful of the filling in the centre. Gather up the edges to a point, pinch together and twist to seal.

8 Stand the dumplings in an oiled steaming basket. Place over a saucepan of simmering water, cover and steam for 12–14 minutes before serving.

Spinach Filo Baskets

If you use frozen spinach, it only needs to be thawed and drained before being mixed with the cheeses and seasonings.

NUTRITIONAL INFORMATION

Calories ....533 Sugars 3g
Protein ....24g Fat 38g
Carbohydrate ...26g Saturates 22g

 55 MINS   30 MINS

MAKES 2

INGREDIENTS

125 g/4½ oz/3 cups fresh leaf spinach,
    washed and chopped roughly, or
    90 g/3 oz/½ cup thawed frozen spinach

2–4 spring onions (scallions), trimmed and
    chopped, or 1 tbsp finely chopped onion

1 garlic clove, crushed

2 tbsp grated Parmesan cheese

90 g/3 oz/¾ cup grated mature (sharp)
    Cheddar cheese

pinch of ground allspice

1 egg yolk

4 sheets filo pastry

25 g/1 oz/2 tbsp butter, melted

salt and pepper

2 spring onions (scallions), to garnish

1 If using fresh spinach, cook it in the minimum of boiling salted water for 3–4 minutes, until tender. Drain very thoroughly, using a potato masher to remove excess liquid, then chop and put into a bowl. If using frozen spinach, simply drain and chop.

2 Add the spring onions (scallions) or onion, garlic, cheeses, allspice, egg yolk and seasoning, and mix well.

3 Grease 2 individual Yorkshire pudding tins (muffin pans), or ovenproof dishes or tins (pans) about 12 cm/5 inches in diameter, and 4 cm/1½ inches deep. Cut the filo pastry sheets in half to make 8 pieces and brush each lightly with melted butter.

4 Place one piece of filo pastry in a tin (pan) or dish and then cover with a second piece at right angles to the first. Add two more pieces at right angles, so that all the corners are in different places. Line the other tin (pan) in the same way.

5 Spoon the spinach mixture into the 'baskets' and cook in a preheated oven, 180°C/350°F/Gas Mark 4, for about 20 minutes, or until the pastry is golden brown. Garnish with a spring onion (scallion) tassel and serve hot or cold.

6 Make spring onion (scallion) tassels about 30 minutes before required. Trim off the root end and cut to a length of 5–7 cm/2–3 inches. Make a series of cuts from the green end to within 2 cm/¾ inch of the other end. Place in a bowl of iced water to open out. Drain well before use.

Vegetable Medley

This is a colourful dish of shredded vegetables in a fresh garlic and honey dressing. It is delicious served with crusty bread.

NUTRITIONAL INFORMATION

Calories 209	Sugars 10g
Protein 2g	Fat 14g
Carbohydrate ... 20g	Saturates 2g

 15 MINS   5 MINS

SERVES 4

INGREDIENTS

2 tbsp olive oil

1 potato, cut into thin strips

1 fennel bulb, cut into thin strips

2 carrots, grated

1 red onion, cut into thin strips

chopped chives and fennel fronds,
   to garnish

DRESSING

3 tbsp olive oil

1 tbsp garlic wine vinegar

1 garlic clove, crushed

1 tsp Dijon mustard

2 tsp clear honey

salt and pepper

1 Heat the olive oil in a frying pan (skillet), add the potato and fennel slices and cook over a medium heat for about 2–3 minutes, until beginning to brown. Remove from the frying pan (skillet) with a slotted spoon and drain on kitchen paper (paper towels).

2 Arrange the carrot, red onion, potato and fennel in separate piles on a serving platter.

3 Mix the dressing ingredients together and pour over the vegetables. Toss well and sprinkle with chopped chives and fennel fronds. Serve immediately or leave in the refrigerator until required.

VARIATION

Use mixed, grilled (bell) peppers or shredded leeks in this dish for variety, or add bean sprouts and a segmented orange, if you prefer.

Fried Tofu with Peanut Sauce

This is a very sociable dish if put in the centre of the table where people can help themselves with cocktail sticks.

NUTRITIONAL INFORMATION

Calories 338   Sugars 9g
Protein . . . . .16g   Fat 22g
Carbohydrate . . .21g   Saturates 4g

5 MINS   20 MINS

SERVES 4

INGREDIENTS

500 g/1 lb 2 oz marinated or plain tofu
(bean curd)

2 tbsp rice vinegar

2 tbsp sugar

1 tsp salt

3 tbsp smooth peanut butter

½ tsp chilli flakes

3 tbsp barbecue sauce

1 litre/1¾ pints/4 cups sunflower oil

2 tbsp sesame oil

BATTER

4 tbsp plain (all-purpose) flour

2 eggs, beaten

4 tbsp milk

½ tsp baking powder

½ tsp chilli powder

COOK'S TIP

Tofu (bean curd) is made from puréed soya beans. It is white, with a soft cheese-like texture, and is sold in blocks, either fresh or vacuum-packed. Although it has a bland flavour, it blends well with other ingredients, and absorbs the flavours of spices and sauces.

1 Cut the tofu (bean curd) into 2.5 cm/1 inch triangles. Set aside until required.

2 Combine the rice vinegar, sugar and salt in a saucepan. Bring to the boil and then simmer for 2 minutes.

3 Remove the sauce from the heat and add the smooth peanut butter, chilli flakes and barbecue sauce, stirring well until thoroughly blended.

4 To make the batter, sift the plain (all-purpose) flour into a bowl, make a well in the centre and add the eggs. Draw in the flour, adding the milk slowly. Stir in the baking powder and chilli powder.

5 Heat both the sunflower oil and sesame oil in a deep-fryer or large saucepan until a light haze appears on top.

6 Dip the tofu (bean curd) triangles into the batter and deep-fry until golden brown. You may need to do this in batches. Drain on absorbent kitchen paper (paper towels).

7 Transfer the tofu (bean curd) triangles to a serving dish and serve with the peanut sauce.

Barbecue Spare Ribs

This is a simplified version of the half saddle of pork ribs seen hanging in the windows of Cantonese restaurants.

NUTRITIONAL INFORMATION

Calories 271   Sugars 4g
Protein . . . . .13g   Fat 22g
Carbohydrate . . . .5g   Saturates 8g

6½ HOURS   50 MINS

SERVES 4

I N G R E D I E N T S

500 g/1 lb 2 oz pork finger spare ribs

1 tbsp sugar

1 tbsp light soy sauce

1 tbsp dark soy sauce

3 tbsp hoi-sin sauce

1 tbsp rice wine or dry sherry

4-5 tbsp water or Chinese Stock
(see page 8)

mild chilli sauce, to dip

coriander (cilantro) leaves, to garnish

1 Using a sharp knife, trim off any excess fat from the spare ribs and cut into pieces. Place the ribs in a baking dish.

2 Mix together the sugar, light and dark soy sauce, hoi-sin sauce and wine. Pour over the ribs in the baking dish. Turn to coat the ribs thoroughly in the mixture and leave to marinate for about 2-3 hours.

3 Add the water or Chinese stock to the ribs and spread them out in the dish. Roast in a preheated hot oven for 15 minutes.

4 Turn the ribs over, lower the oven temperature and cook for 30-35 minutes longer.

5 To serve, chop each rib into 3-4 small, bite-sized pieces with a large knife or Chinese cleaver and arrange neatly on a serving dish.

6 Pour the sauce from the baking dish over the spare ribs and garnish with a few coriander (cilantro) leaves. Place some mild chilli sauce into a small dish and serve with the ribs as a dip. Serve immediately.

COOK'S TIP

Finger ribs are specially small, thin ribs. Ask your local butcher to cut some if you can't find the right size in the supermarket. Don't throw away any trimmings from the ribs – they can be used for soup or stock.

Son-in-Law Eggs

This recipe is supposedly so called because it is an easy dish for a son-in-law to cook to impress his new mother-in-law!

NUTRITIONAL INFORMATION

Calories . . . . . . .229 Sugars 8g
Protein . . . . .9g Fat 18g
Carbohydrate . . . .8g Saturates 3g

15 MINS   15 MINS

SERVES 4

I N G R E D I E N T S

6 eggs, hard-boiled (hard-cooked)
  and shelled

4 tbsp sunflower oil

1 onion, sliced thinly

2 fresh red chillies, sliced

2 tbsp sugar

1 tbsp water

2 tsp tamarind pulp

1 tbsp liquid seasoning, such
  as Maggi

rice, to serve

1 Prick the hard-boiled (hard-cooked) eggs 2 or 3 times with a cocktail stick (toothpick).

2 Heat the sunflower oil in a wok and fry the eggs until crispy and golden. Drain on absorbent kitchen paper (paper towels).

3 Halve the eggs lengthways and put on a serving dish.

4 Reserve one tablespoon of the oil, pour off the rest, then heat the tablespoonful in the wok. Cook the onion and chillies over a high heat until golden and slightly crisp. Drain on kitchen paper (paper towels).

5 Heat the sugar, water, tamarind pulp and liquid seasoning in the wok and simmer for 5 minutes until thickened.

6 Pour the sauce over the eggs and spoon over the onion and chillies. Serve immediately with rice.

COOK'S TIP

Tamarind pulp is sold in oriental stores, and is quite sour. If it is not available, use twice the amount of lemon juice in its place.

Vegetables with Tahini Dip

This tasty dip is great for livening-up simply-cooked vegetables.
You can vary the vegetables according to the season.

NUTRITIONAL INFORMATION

Calories 126	Sugars 7g	
Protein 11g	Fat 6g	
Carbohydrate 8g	Saturates 1g	

5 MINS   20 MINS

SERVES 4

I N G R E D I E N T S

225 g/8 oz small broccoli florets

225 g/8 oz small cauliflower florets

225 g/8 oz asparagus, sliced into 5 cm/
 2 inch lengths

2 small red onions, quartered

1 tbsp lime juice

2 tsp toasted sesame seeds

1 tbsp chopped fresh chives, to garnish

H O T   T A H I N I   &
G A R L I C   D I P

1 tsp sunflower oil

2 garlic cloves, crushed

½–1 tsp chilli powder

2 tsp tahini (sesame seed paste)

150 ml/¼ pint/⅔ cup low-fat natural
 fromage frais

2 tbsp chopped fresh chives

salt and pepper

1 Line the base of a steamer with baking parchment and arrange the vegetables on top.

2 Bring a wok or large saucepan of water to the boil, and place the steamer on top. Sprinkle with lime juice and steam for 10 minutes.

3 To make the hot tahini & garlic dip, heat the sunflower oil in a small non-stick saucepan, add the garlic, chilli powder and seasoning to taste and fry gently for 2–3 minutes until the garlic is softened.

4 Remove the saucepan from the heat and stir in the tahini (sesame seed paste) and fromage frais. Return to the heat and cook gently for 1–2 minutes without boiling. Stir in the chives.

5 Remove the vegetables from the steamer and place on a warmed serving platter. Sprinkle with the sesame seeds and garnish with chopped chives. Serve with the hot dip.

Avocado Margherita

The colours of the tomatoes, basil and Mozzarella cheese in this patriotic recipe represent the colours of the Italian flag.

NUTRITIONAL INFORMATION

Calories 249	Sugars 2g
Protein 4g	Fat 24g
Carbohydrate 4g	Saturates 6g

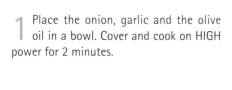 5-10 MINS   10-15 MINS

SERVES 4

I N G R E D I E N T S

1 small red onion, sliced

1 garlic clove, crushed

1 tbsp olive oil

2 small tomatoes

2 avocados, halved and pitted

4 fresh basil leaves, torn into shreds

60 g/2 oz Mozzarella cheese, sliced thinly

salt and pepper

fresh basil leaves, to garnish

mixed salad leaves, to serve

1 Place the onion, garlic and the olive oil in a bowl. Cover and cook on HIGH power for 2 minutes.

2 Meanwhile, skin the tomatoes by cutting a cross in the base of the tomatoes and placing them in a small bowl. Pour on boiling water and leave for about 45 seconds. Drain and then plunge into cold water. The skins will slide off without too much difficulty.

3 Arrange the avocado halves on a plate with the narrow ends pointed towards the centre. Spoon the onions into the hollow of each half.

4 Cut and slice the tomatoes in half. Divide the tomatoes, basil and thin slices of Mozzarella between the avocado halves. Season with salt and pepper to taste.

5 Cook on MEDIUM power for 5 minutes or until the avocados are heated through and the cheese has melted. Transfer the avocados to serving plates, garnish with basil leaves and serve with mixed salad leaves.

VARIATION

If you are using a combination microwave oven with grill (broiler) – arrange the avocados on the low rack of the grill (broiler), or on the glass turntable. Cook on combination grill (broiler) 1 and LOW power for 8 minutes until browned and bubbling.

Crispy-Fried Vegetables

A hot and sweet dipping sauce makes the perfect accompaniment to fresh vegetables coated in a light batter and deep-fried.

NUTRITIONAL INFORMATION

Calories	258	Sugars	........11g
Protein	.........6g	Fat	...........9g
Carbohydrate	...39g	Saturates	......11g

40 MINS   10 MINS

SERVES 4

I N G R E D I E N T S

vegetable oil for deep-frying

500 g/1 lb 2 oz selection of vegetables, such as cauliflower, broccoli, mushrooms, courgettes (zucchini), (bell) peppers and baby sweetcorn, cut into even-sized pieces

B A T T E R

125 g/4½ oz/1 cup plain (all-purpose) flour

½ tsp salt

1 tsp caster (superfine) sugar

1 tsp baking powder

3 tbsp vegetable oil

200 ml/7 fl oz/scant 1 cup warm water

S A U C E

6 tbsp light malt vinegar

2 tbsp fish sauce or light soy sauce

2 tbsp water

1 tbsp soft brown sugar

pinch of salt

2 garlic cloves, crushed

2 tsp grated ginger root

2 red chillies, deseeded and chopped finely

2 tbsp chopped fresh coriander (cilantro)

1 To make the batter, sift the flour, salt, sugar and baking powder into a bowl. Add the oil and most of the water. Whisk together to make a smooth batter, adding extra water to give it the consistency of single cream. Chill for 20–30 minutes.

2 Meanwhile, make the sauce. Heat the vinegar, fish sauce or soy sauce, water, sugar and salt until boiling. Remove from the heat and leave to cool.

3 Mix together the garlic, ginger, chillies and coriander (cilantro). Add the cooled vinegar mixture and stir well to combine.

4 Heat the oil for deep-frying in a wok. Dip the vegetables in the batter and fry, in batches, until crisp and golden – about 2 minutes. Drain on kitchen paper (paper towels). Serve the vegetables accompanied by the dipping sauce.

Butterfly Prawns (Shrimp)

These prawns (shrimp) look stunning when presented on the skewers, and they will certainly be an impressive prelude to the main meal.

NUTRITIONAL INFORMATION

Calories 183	Sugars 0g	
Protein 28g	Fat 8g	
Carbohydrate 0g	Saturates 1g	

4½ HOURS   10 MINS

SERVES 2–4

INGREDIENTS

500 g/1 lb 2 oz or 16 raw tiger prawns (shrimp), shelled, leaving tails intact

juice of 2 limes

1 tsp cardamom seeds

2 tsp cumin seeds, ground

2 tsp coriander seeds, ground

½ tsp ground cinnamon

1 tsp ground turmeric

1 garlic clove, crushed

1 tsp cayenne pepper

2 tbsp oil

cucumber slices, to garnish

1 Soak 8 wooden skewers in water for 20 minutes. Cut the prawns (shrimp) lengthways in half down to the tai and flatten out to a symmetrical shape.

2 Thread a prawn (shrimp) on to 2 wooden skewers, with the tail between them, so that, when laid flat, the skewers hold the prawn (shrimp) in shape. Thread another 3 prawns (shrimp) on to these 2 skewers in the same way.

3 Repeat until you have 4 sets of 4 prawns (shrimp) each.

4 Lay the skewered prawns (shrimp) in a non-porous, non-metallic dish, and sprinkle over the lime juice.

5 Combine the spices and the oil, and coat the prawns (shrimp) well in the mixture. Cover the prawns (shrimp) and chill for 4 hours.

6 Cook over a hot barbecue (grill) or in a grill (broiler) pan lined with foil under a preheated grill (broiler) for 6 minutes, turning once.

7 Serve immediately, garnished with cucumber and accompanied by a sweet chutney – walnut chutney is ideal.

Tofu Sandwiches

Slices of tofu (beancurd) are sandwiched together with a cucumber and cream cheese filling and coated in batter.

NUTRITIONAL INFORMATION

Calories 398	Sugars 8g
Protein 13g	Fat 24g
Carbohydrate . . .35g	Saturates 7g

40 MINS   15 MINS

MAKES 28

I N G R E D I E N T S

4 Chinese dried mushrooms (if unavailable, use thinly sliced open-cup mushrooms)

275 g/9½ oz tofu (bean curd)

½ cucumber, grated

1 cm/½ inch piece ginger root, grated

60 g/2 oz/¼ cup cream cheese

salt and pepper

B A T T E R

125 g/4½ oz/1 cup plain (all-purpose) flour

1 egg, beaten

125 ml/4 fl oz/½ cup water

½ tsp salt

2 tbsp sesame seeds

vegetable oil for deep-frying

S A U C E

150 ml/¼ pint/⅔ cup natural (unsweetened) yogurt

2 tsp honey

2 tbsp chopped fresh mint

1 Place the dried mushrooms in a small bowl and cover with warm water. Leave to soak for 20–25 minutes.

2 Drain the mushrooms, squeezing out the excess water. Remove the tough centres and chop the mushrooms.

3 Drain the tofu (bean curd) and slice thinly. Then cut each slice to make 2.5 cm/1 inch squares.

4 Squeeze the excess liquid from the cucumber and mix the cucumber with the mushrooms, grated ginger and cream cheese. Season well with salt and pepper. Use as a filling to sandwich slices of tofu (bean curd) together to make about 28 sandwiches.

5 To make the batter, sift the flour into a bowl. Beat in the egg, water and salt to make a thick batter. Stir in the sesame seeds. Heat the oil in a wok. Coat the sandwiches in the batter and deep-fry in batches until golden. Remove and drain on kitchen paper (paper towels).

6 To make the dipping sauce, combine the yogurt, honey and mint. Serve with the tofu (bean curd) sandwiches.

Root Croustades

This colourful combination of grated root vegetables and mixed (bell) peppers would make a stunning dinner-party dish.

NUTRITIONAL INFORMATION

Calories 304	Sugars 17g	
Protein 6g	Fat 19g	
Carbohydrate ...28g	Saturates 3g	

2½ HOURS   1¼ HOURS

SERVES 4

I N G R E D I E N T S

1 orange (bell) pepper

1 red (bell) pepper

1 yellow (bell) pepper

3 tbsp olive oil

2 tbsp red wine vinegar

1 tsp French mustard

1 tsp clear honey

salt and pepper

flat leaf parsley sprigs, to garnish

green vegetables, to serve

C R O U S T A D E S

225 g/8 oz potatoes, coarsely grated

225 g/8 oz carrots, coarsely grated

350 g/12 oz celeriac (celery root),
    coarsely grated

1 garlic clove, crushed

1 tbsp lemon juice

25 g/1 oz/2 tbsp butter or
    margarine, melted

1 egg, beaten

1 tbsp vegetable oil

1 Place the (bell) peppers on a baking tray (cookie sheet) and bake in a preheated oven, 190°C/375°F/Gas Mark 5, for 35 minutes, turning after 20 minutes.

2 Cover with a tea towel (dish cloth) and leave to cool for 10 minutes.

3 Peel the skin from the cooked (bell) peppers; cut in half and discard the seeds. Thinly slice the flesh into strips and place in a shallow dish.

4 Put the oil, vinegar, mustard, honey and seasoning in a small screw-top jar and shake well to mix. Pour over the (bell) pepper strips, mix well and set aside to marinate for 2 hours.

5 To make the croustades, put the potatoes, carrots and celeriac (celery root) in a mixing bowl and toss in the garlic and lemon juice.

6 Mix in the melted butter or margarine and the egg. Season to taste with salt and pepper. Divide the mixture into 8 and pile on to 2 baking trays (cookie sheets) lined with baking parchment, forming each into a 10 cm/4 inch round. Brush with oil.

7 Bake in a preheated oven, 220°C/ 425°F/Gas Mark 7, for 30–35 minutes, until the croustades are crisp around the edges and golden. Carefully transfer to a warmed serving dish. Heat the (bell) peppers and the marinade for 2–3 minutes until warmed through. Spoon the (bell) peppers over the croustades, garnish with flat leaf parsley and serve immediately with green vegetables.

Tofu (Bean Curd) Tempura

Crispy coated vegetables and tofu (bean curd) accompanied by a sweet, spicy dip give a real taste of the Orient in this Japanese-style dish.

NUTRITIONAL INFORMATION

Calories 582	Sugars 10g	
Protein 16g	Fat 27g	
Carbohydrate . . .65g	Saturates 4g	

 15 MINS   🕑 20 MINS

SERVES 4

I N G R E D I E N T S

125 g/4½ oz baby courgettes (zucchini)

125 g/4½ oz baby carrots

125 g/4½ oz baby corn cobs

125 g/4½ oz baby leeks

2 baby aubergines (eggplants)

225 g/8 oz tofu (bean curd)

vegetable oil, for deep-frying

julienne strips of carrot, root ginger and
    baby leek to garnish

noodles, to serve

B A T T E R

2 egg yolks

300 ml/½ pint/1¼ cups water

225 g/8 oz/2 cups plain (all-purpose) flour

D I P P I N G   S A U C E

5 tbsp mirin or dry sherry

5 tbsp Japanese soy sauce

2 tsp clear honey

1 garlic clove, crushed

1 tsp grated root ginger

1 Slice the courgettes (zucchini) and carrots in half lengthways. Trim the corn. Trim the leeks at both ends. Quarter the aubergines (eggplants). Cut the tofu (bean curd) into 2.5 cm/1 inch cubes.

2 To make the batter, mix the egg yolks with the water. Sift in 175 g/6 oz/1½ cups of the flour and beat with a balloon whisk to form a thick batter. Don't worry if there are any lumps. Heat the oil for deep-frying to 180°C/350°F or until a cube of bread browns in 30 seconds.

3 Place the remaining flour on a large plate and toss the vegetables and tofu (bean curd) until lightly coated.

4 Dip the tofu (bean curd) in the batter and deep-fry for 2–3 minutes, until lightly golden. Drain on kitchen paper (paper towels) and keep warm.

5 Dip the vegetables in the batter and deep-fry, a few at a time, for 3–4 minutes, until golden. Drain and place on a warmed serving plate.

6 To make the dipping sauce, mix all the ingredients together. Serve with the vegetables and tofu (bean curd), accompanied with noodles and garnished with julienne strips of vegetables.

Spring Rolls

This classic Chinese dish is very popular in the West. Serve hot or chilled with a soy sauce or hoisin dip.

NUTRITIONAL INFORMATION

Calories 442   Sugars 4g
Protein ....23g   Fat 21g
Carbohydrate ...42g   Saturates 3g

45 MINS   45 MINS

SERVES 4

INGREDIENTS

175 g/6 oz cooked pork, chopped

75 g/2¾ oz cooked chicken, chopped

1 tsp light soy sauce

1 tsp light brown sugar

1 tsp sesame oil

1 tsp vegetable oil

225 g/8 oz bean sprouts

25 g/1 oz canned bamboo shoots,
    drained, rinsed and chopped

1 green (bell) pepper, seeded and
    chopped

2 spring onions (scallions), sliced

1 tsp cornflour (cornstarch)

2 tsp water

vegetable oil, for deep-frying

SKINS

125 g/4½ oz/1⅛ cups plain (all-purpose)
    flour

5 tbsp cornflour (cornstarch)

450 ml/16 fl oz/2 cups water

3 tbsp vegetable oil

1 Mix the pork, chicken, soy sauce, sugar and sesame oil. Cover and marinate for 30 minutes.

2 Heat the vegetable oil in a preheated wok. Add the bean sprouts, bamboo shoots, (bell) pepper and spring onions (scallions) to the wok and stir-fry for 2–3 minutes. Add the meat and the marinade to the wok and stir-fry for 2–3 minutes.

3 Blend the cornflour (cornstarch) with the water and stir the mixture into the wok. Set aside to cool completely.

4 To make the skins, mix the flour and cornflour (cornstarch) and gradually stir in the water, to make a smooth batter.

5 Heat a small, oiled frying pan (skillet). Swirl one-eighth of the batter over the base and cook for 2–3 minutes. Repeat with the remaining batter. Cover the skins with a damp tea towel (dish cloth) while frying the remaining skins.

6 Spread out the skins and spoon one-eighth of the filling along the centre of each. Brush the edges with water and fold in the sides, then roll up.

7 Heat the oil for deep-frying in a wok to 180°C/350°F. Cook the spring rolls, in batches, for 2–3 minutes, or until golden and crisp. Remove from the oil with a slotted spoon, drain and serve immediately.

Barbecue Pork (Char Siu)

Also called honey-roasted pork, these are the strips of reddish meat sometimes seen hanging in the windows of Cantonese restaurants.

NUTRITIONAL INFORMATION

Calories 250   Sugar 8g
Protein ....27g   Fat 10g
Carbohydrate ....9g   Saturates 3g

4¼ HOURS   30 MINS

SERVES 4

INGREDIENTS

500 g/1 lb 2 oz pork fillet

150 ml/¼ pint/⅔ cup boiling water

1 tbsp honey, dissolved with a little hot water

MARINADE

1 tbsp sugar

1 tbsp crushed yellow bean sauce

1 tbsp light soy sauce

1 tbsp hoisin sauce

1 tbsp oyster sauce

½ tsp chilli sauce

1 tbsp brandy or rum

1 tsp sesame oil

shredded lettuce, to serve

1 Using a sharp knife or meat cleaver, cut the pork into strips about 2.5 cm/1 inch thick and 18-20 cm/7-8 inches long and place in a large shallow dish. Mix the marinade ingredients together and pour over the pork, turning until well coated. Cover, and leave to marinate for at least 3-4 hours, turning occasionally.

2 Remove the pork strips from the dish with a slotted spoon, reserving the marinade. Arrange the pork strips on a rack over a baking tin (pan). Place the tin

(pan) in a preheated oven and pour in the boiling water. Roast the pork for about 10-15 minutes.

3 Lower the oven temperature. Baste the pork strips with the reserved marinade and turn over using metal tongs. Roast for a further 10 minutes.

4 Remove the pork from the oven, brush with the honey syrup, and

lightly brown under a medium hot grill (broiler) for about 3-4 minutes, turning once or twice.

5 To serve, allow the pork to cool slightly before cutting it. Cut across the grain into thin slices and arrange neatly on a bed of shredded lettuce. Make a sauce by boiling the marinade and the drippings in the baking tin (pan) for a few minutes, strain and pour over the pork.

Chick-peas & Parma Ham

Prosciutto is used in this recipe. It is a cured ham, which is air- and salt-dried for up to 1 year. There are many different varieties available.

NUTRITIONAL INFORMATION

Calories 180	Sugars 2g	
Protein 12g	Fat 7g	
Carbohydrate ...18g	Saturates 1g	

10 MINS   15 MINS

SERVES 4

INGREDIENTS

1 tbsp olive oil

1 medium onion, thinly sliced

1 garlic clove, chopped

1 small red (bell) pepper, deseeded and cut
    into thin strips

200 g/7 oz Parma ham (prosciutto),
    cut into cubes

400g/14 oz can chick-peas (garbanzo
    beans), drained and rinsed

1 tbsp chopped parsley, to garnish

crusty bread, to serve

COOK'S TIP

Whenever possible, use fresh herbs when cooking. They are becoming more readily available, especially since the introduction of 'growing' herbs, small pots of herbs which you can buy from the supermarket or greengrocer and grow at home. This ensures the herbs are fresh and also provides a continuous supply.

1 Heat the oil in a frying pan (skillet). Add the onion, garlic and (bell) pepper and cook for 3–4 minutes or until the vegetables have softened. Add the Parma ham (prosciutto) to the pan (skillet) and fry for 5 minutes or until the ham (prosciutto) is just beginning to brown.

2 Add the chick-peas (garbanzo beans) to the pan (skillet) and cook, stirring, for 2–3 minutes until warmed through.

3 Sprinkle with chopped parsley and transfer to warm serving plates. Serve with lots of fresh crusty bread.

Cured Meats, Olives & Tomatoes

This is a typical *antipasto* dish with the cold cured meats, stuffed olives and fresh tomatoes, basil and balsamic vinegar.

NUTRITIONAL INFORMATION

Calories	312	Sugars	.........1g
Protein	........12g	Fat	..........28g
Carbohydrate	....2g	Saturates	.......1g

 10 MINS 5 MINS

SERVES 4

I N G R E D I E N T S

4 plum tomatoes

1 tbsp balsamic vinegar

6 canned anchovy fillets, drained and rinsed

2 tbsp capers, drained and rinsed

125 g/4½ oz green olives, pitted

175 g/6 oz mixed, cured meats, sliced

8 fresh basil leaves

1 tbsp extra virgin olive oil

salt and pepper

crusty bread, to serve

1 Using a sharp knife, cut the tomatoes into evenly-sized slices. Sprinkle the tomato slices with the balsamic vinegar and a little salt and pepper to taste, and set aside.

2 Chop the anchovy fillets into pieces measuring about the same length as the olives.

3 Push a piece of anchovy and a caper into each olive.

4 Arrange the sliced meat on 4 individual serving plates together with the tomatoes, filled olives and basil leaves.

5 Lightly drizzle the olive oil over the sliced meat, tomatoes and olives.

6 Serve the cured meats, olives and tomatoes with plenty of fresh crusty bread.

COOK'S TIP

The cured meats for this recipe are up to your individual taste. They can include a selection of Parma ham (prosciutto), pancetta, bresaola (dried salt beef) and salame di Milano (pork and beef sausage).

Olive & Anchovy Pâté

The flavour of olives is accentuated by the anchovies. Serve the pâté as an appetizer on thin pieces of toast with a very dry white wine.

NUTRITIONAL INFORMATION

Calories 214	Sugars 1g	
Protein 2g	Fat 22g	
Carbohydrate 1g	Saturates 8g	

5–10 MINS ⏱ 35 MINS

SERVES 4

I N G R E D I E N T S

175 g/6 oz black olives, pitted and chopped

finely grated rind and juice of 1 lemon

50 g/1½ oz unsalted butter

4 canned anchovy fillets, drained and rinsed

2 tbsp extra virgin olive oil

15 g/½ oz ground almonds

fresh herbs, to garnish

1 If you are making the pâté by hand, chop the olives very finely and then mash them along with the lemon rind, juice and butter, using a fork or potato masher. Alternatively, place the roughly chopped olives, lemon rind, juice and butter in a food processor and blend until all of the ingredients are finely chopped.

2 Chop the drained anchovies and add them to the olive and lemon mixture. Mash the pâté by hand or blend in a food processor for 20 seconds.

3 Gradually whisk in the olive oil and stir in the ground almonds. Place the black olive pâté in a serving bowl. Leave the pâté to chill in the refrigerator for about 30 minutes. Serve the pâté accompanied by thin pieces of toast, if wished.

COOK'S TIP

This pâté will keep for up to 5 days in a serving bowl in the refrigerator if you pour a thin layer of extra-virgin olive oil over the top of the pâté to seal it. Then use the oil to brush on the toast before spreading the pâté.

Feta Cheese Tartlets

These crisp-baked bread cases, filled with sliced tomatoes, feta cheese, black olives and quail's eggs, are quick to make and taste delicious.

NUTRITIONAL INFORMATION

Calories 570   Sugars 3g
Protein . . . . .14g   Fat 42g
Carbohydrate . . .36g   Saturates 23g

30 MINS   10 MINS

SERVES 4

I N G R E D I E N T S

8 slices bread from a medium-cut large loaf

125 g/4½ oz/ ½ cup butter, melted

125 g/4½ oz feta cheese,
    cut into small cubes

4 cherry tomatoes, cut into wedges

8 pitted black or green olives, halved

8 quail's eggs, hard-boiled (hard-cooked)

2 tbsp olive oil

1 tbsp wine vinegar

1 tsp wholegrain mustard

pinch of caster (superfine) sugar

salt and pepper

parsley sprigs, to garnish

1 Remove the crusts from the bread. Trim the bread into squares and flatten each piece with a rolling pin.

2 Brush the bread with melted butter, and then arrange them in bun or muffin tins (pans). Press a piece of crumpled foil into each bread case to secure in place. Bake in a preheated oven, 190°C/375°F/Gas Mark 5, for about 10 minutes, or until crisp and browned.

3 Meanwhile, mix together the feta cheese, tomatoes and olives. Shell the eggs and quarter them. Mix together the olive oil, vinegar, mustard and sugar. Season to taste with salt and pepper.

4 Remove the bread cases from the oven and discard the foil. Leave to cool.

5 Just before serving, fill the bread cases with the cheese and tomato mixture. Arrange the eggs on top and spoon over the dressing. Garnish with parsley sprigs.

Potato Skins with Guacamole

Although avocados do contain fat, if they are used in small quantities you can still enjoy their creamy texture.

NUTRITIONAL INFORMATION

Calories 399   Sugars 4g
Protein ....10g   Fat 15g
Carbohydrate ...59g   Saturates 4g

45 MINS   1³/₄ HOURS

SERVES 4

INGREDIENTS

4 x 225g/8 oz baking potatoes

2 tsp olive oil

coarse sea salt and pepper

chopped fresh chives, to garnish

GUACAMOLE DIP

175 g/6 oz ripe avocado

1 tbsp lemon juice

2 ripe, firm tomatoes, chopped finely

1 tsp grated lemon rind

100 g/3½ oz/½ cup low-fat soft cheese
   with herbs and garlic

4 spring onions (scallions), chopped
   finely

a few drops of Tabasco sauce

salt and pepper

1 Bake the potatoes in a preheated oven at 200°C/400°F/Gas Mark 6 for 1¼ hours. Remove from the oven and allow to cool for 30 minutes. Reset the oven to 220°C/425°F/Gas Mark 7.

2 Halve the potatoes lengthwise and scoop out 2 tablespoons of the flesh. Slice in half again. Place on a baking tray (cookie) sheet and brush the flesh side lightly with oil. Sprinkle with salt and pepper. Bake for a further 25 minutes until golden and crisp.

3 To make the guacamole dip, mash the avocado with the lemon juice. Add the remaining ingredients and mix.

4 Drain the potato skins on paper towels and transfer to a warmed serving platter. Garnish with chives. Pile the avocado mixture into a serving bowl.

COOK'S TIP

Mash the leftover potato flesh with natural yogurt and seasoning, and serve as an accompaniment to meat, fish and vegetarian dishes.

Spicy Fried Tofu Triangles

Marinated tofu (bean curd) is ideal in this recipe for added flavour, although the spicy coating is very tasty with plain tofu (bean curd).

NUTRITIONAL INFORMATION

Calories . . . . . . .224 Sugars 17g
Protein . . . . .10g Fat 13g
Carbohydrate . . .18g Saturates 2g

1¼ HOURS   10 MINS

SERVES 4

INGREDIENTS

1 tbsp sea salt

4½ tsp Chinese five-spice powder

3 tbsp light brown sugar

2 garlic cloves, crushed

1 tsp grated fresh root ginger

2 x 225 g/8 oz cakes tofu (bean curd)

vegetable oil, for deep-frying

2 leeks, shredded and halved

shredded leek, to garnish

1 Mix together the salt, Chinese five-spice powder, sugar, garlic and ginger in a bowl and transfer to a plate.

2 Cut the tofu (bean curd) cakes in half diagonally to form two triangles. Cut each triangle in half and then in half again to form 16 triangles.

3 Roll the tofu (bean curd) triangles in the spice mixture, turning to coat thoroughly. Set aside for 1 hour.

4 Heat the vegetable oil for deep-frying in a wok until it is almost smoking.

5 Reduce the heat slightly, add the tofu (bean curd) triangles and fry for 5 minutes, until golden brown. Remove

the tofu (bean curd) from the wok with a slotted spoon, set aside and keep warm until required.

6 Add the leeks to the wok and stir-fry for 1 minute. Remove from the wok and drain on kitchen paper (paper towels).

7 Arrange the leeks on a warm serving plate and place the fried tofu (bean curd) on top. Garnish with the fresh shredded leek and serve immediately.

COOK'S TIP

Fry the tofu (bean curd) in batches and keep each batch warm until all of the tofu (bean curd) has been fried and is ready to serve.

Pancake Rolls

This classic *dim sum* dish is adaptable to almost any filling of your choice. Here the traditional mixture of pork and pak choi is used.

NUTRITIONAL INFORMATION

Calories	488	Sugars	........19g
Protein	........16g	Fat	..........24g
Carbohydrate	...55g	Saturates	.......4g

20 MINS   20 MINS

SERVES 4

I N G R E D I E N T S

4 tsp vegetable oil

1-2 garlic cloves, crushed

225 g/8 oz minced (ground) pork

225/8 oz pak choi, shredded

4½ tsp light soy sauce

½ tsp sesame oil

8 spring roll skins, 25 cm/10 inches square, thawed if frozen

oil, for deep-frying

C H I L L I   S A U C E

60 g/2 oz/¼ cup caster (superfine) sugar

50 ml/2 fl oz/¼ cup rice vinegar

2 tbsp water

2 red chillies, finely chopped

1 Heat the oil in a preheated wok. Add the garlic and stir-fry for 30 seconds. Add the pork and stir-fry for 2–3 minutes, until lightly coloured.

2 Add the pak choi, soy sauce and sesame oil to the wok and stir-fry for 2–3 minutes. Remove from the heat and set aside to cool.

3 Spread out the spring roll skins on a work surface (counter) and spoon 2 tablespoons of the pork mixture along one edge of each. Roll the skin over once and

fold in the sides. Roll up completely to make a sausage shape, brushing the edges with a little water to seal. Set the pancake rolls aside for 10 minutes to seal firmly.

4 To make the chilli sauce, heat the sugar, vinegar and water in a small saucepan, stirring until the sugar dissolves. Bring the mixture to the boil and boil rapidly until a light syrup forms. Remove from the heat and stir in the

chopped red chillies. Leave the sauce to cool before serving.

5 Heat the oil for deep-frying in a wok until almost smoking. Reduce the heat slightly and fry the pancake rolls, in batches if necessary, for 3–4 minutes, until golden brown. Remove from the oil with a slotted spoon and drain on absorbent kitchen paper (paper towels). Serve with the chilli sauce.

Deep-Fried Spare Ribs

The spare ribs should be chopped into small bite-sized pieces before or after cooking.

NUTRITIONAL INFORMATION

Calories 177   Sugars 0.2g
Protein ....6g   Fat 14g
Carbohydrate ....6g   Saturates 4g

 5 MINS   2¼ HOURS

SERVES 4

INGREDIENTS

8-10 finger spare ribs

1 tsp five-spice powder or 1 tbsp mild curry powder

1 tbsp rice wine or dry sherry

1 egg

2 tbsp flour

vegetable oil, for deep-frying

1 tsp finely shredded spring onions (scallions)

1 tsp finely shredded fresh green or red hot chillies, seeded

salt and pepper

Spicy Salt and Pepper (see page 80), to serve

1 Chop the ribs into 3-4 small pieces. Place the ribs in a bowl with salt, pepper, five-spice or curry powder and the wine. Turn to coat the ribs in the spices and leave to marinate for 1-2 hours.

2 Mix the egg and flour together to make a batter. Dip the ribs in the batter one by one to coat well.

3 Heat the oil in a preheated wok until smoking. Deep-fry the ribs for 4-5 minutes, then remove with chopsticks or a slotted spoon and drain on kitchen paper (paper towels).

4 Reheat the oil over a high heat and deep-fry the ribs once more for another minute. Remove and drain again on kitchen paper (paper towels).

5 Pour 1 tablespoon of the hot oil over the spring onions (scallions) and chillies and leave for 30-40 seconds. Serve the ribs with Spicy Salt and Pepper, garnished with the shredded spring onions (scallions) and chillies.

COOK'S TIP

To make finger ribs, cut the sheet of spare ribs into individual ribs down each side of the bones. These ribs are then chopped into bite-sized pieces for deep-frying.

Roasted Seafood

Vegetables become deliciously sweet and juicy when they are roasted, and they go particularly well with fish and seafood.

NUTRITIONAL INFORMATION

Calories ....280 Sugars 5g
Protein ....15g Fat 12g
Carbohydrate ...28g Saturates 2g

15 MINS   50 MINS

SERVES 4

INGREDIENTS

600 g/1 lb 5 oz new potatoes

3 red onions, cut into wedges

2 courgettes (zucchini), sliced into chunks

8 garlic cloves, peeled

2 lemons, cut into wedges

4 sprigs rosemary

4 tbsp olive oil

350 g/12 oz shell-on prawns (shrimp),
    preferably uncooked

2 small squid, chopped into rings

4 tomatoes, quartered

1 Scrub the potatoes to remove any excess dirt. Cut any large potatoes in half. Place the potatoes in a large roasting tin (pan), together with the onions, courgettes (zucchini), garlic, lemon and rosemary sprigs.

2 Pour over the oil and toss to coat all of the vegetables in the oil. Cook in a preheated oven, at 200°C/400°F/Gas Mark 6, for 40 minutes, turning occasionally, until the potatoes are tender.

3 Once the potatoes are tender, add the prawns (shrimp), squid and tomatoes, tossing to coat them in the oil, and roast for 10 minutes. All of the vegetables should be cooked through and slightly charred for full flavour.

4 Transfer the roasted seafood and vegetables to warm serving plates and serve hot.

VARIATION

Most vegetables are suitable for roasting in the oven. Try adding 450 g/1 lb pumpkin, squash or aubergine (eggplant), if you prefer.

Tuna Stuffed Tomatoes

Deliciously sweet roasted tomatoes are filled with home-made lemon mayonnaise and tuna.

NUTRITIONAL INFORMATION

Calories ....196 Sugars 2g
Protein ....9g Fat 17g
Carbohydrate ....2g Saturates 3g

5-10 MINS   25 MINS

SERVES 4

INGREDIENTS

4 plum tomatoes

2 tbsp sun-dried tomato paste

2 egg yolks

2 tsp lemon juice

finely grated rind of 1 lemon

4 tbsp olive oil

115g/4 oz can tuna, drained

2 tbsp capers, rinsed

salt and pepper

TO GARNISH

2 sun-dried tomatoes, cut into strips

fresh basil leaves

1 Halve the tomatoes and scoop out the seeds. Divide the sun-dried tomato paste among the tomato halves and spread around the inside of the skin.

2 Place on a baking tray (cookie sheet) and roast in a preheated oven at 200°C/400°F/Gas Mark 6 for 12–15 minutes. Leave to cool slightly.

3 Meanwhile, make the mayonnaise. In a food processor, blend the egg yolks and lemon juice with the lemon rind until smooth. Once mixed and with the motor still running slowly, add the olive oil. Stop the processor as soon as the mayonnaise has thickened. Alternatively, use a hand whisk, beating the mixture continuously until it thickens.

4 Add the tuna and capers to the mayonnaise and season.

5 Spoon the tuna mayonnaise mixture into the tomato shells and garnish with sun-dried tomato strips and basil leaves. Return to the oven for a few minutes or serve chilled.

COOK'S TIP

For a picnic, do not roast the tomatoes, just scoop out the seeds, drain, cut-side down on absorbent kitchen paper for 1 hour, and fill with the mayonnaise mixture. They are firmer and easier to handle this way. If you prefer, shop-bought mayonnaise may be used instead – just stir in the lemon rind.

Crab Ravioli

These small parcels are made from won ton wrappers, filled with mixed vegetables and crabmeat for a melt-in-the-mouth starter.

NUTRITIONAL INFORMATION

Calories 292   Sugars 1g
Protein ....25g   Fat 17g
Carbohydrate ....11g   Saturates 5g

     20 MINS   25 MINS

SERVES 4

INGREDIENTS

450 g/1 lb crabmeat (fresh or canned and drained)

½ red (bell) pepper, seeded and finely diced

125 g/4½ oz Chinese leaves (cabbage), shredded

25 g/1 oz bean sprouts, roughly chopped

1 tbsp light soy sauce

1 tsp lime juice

16 wonton wrappers

1 small egg, beaten

2 tbsp peanut oil

1 tsp sesame oil

salt and pepper

1 Mix together the crabmeat, (bell) pepper, Chinese leaves (cabbage), bean sprouts, soy sauce and lime juice. Season and leave to stand for 15 minutes.

2 Spread out the wonton wrappers on a work surface (counter). Spoon a little of the crabmeat mixture into the centre of each wrapper. Brush the edges with egg and fold in half, pushing out any air. Press the edges together to seal.

3 Heat the peanut oil in a preheated wok or frying pan (skillet). Fry the ravioli, in batches, for 3–4 minutes, turning, until browned. Remove with a slotted spoon and drain on kitchen paper (paper towels).

4 Heat any remaining filling in the wok or frying pan (skillet) over a gentle heat until hot. Serve the ravioli with the hot filling and sprinkled with sesame oil.

COOK'S TIP

Make sure that the edges of the ravioli are sealed well and that all of the air is pressed out to prevent them from opening during cooking.

Smoked Fish & Potato Pâté

This smoked fish pâté is given a tart fruity flavour by the gooseberries, which complement the fish perfectly.

NUTRITIONAL INFORMATION

Calories 418	Sugars 4g
Protein 18g	Fat 25g
Carbohydrate . . .32g	Saturates 6g

20 MINS   10 MINS

SERVES 4

INGREDIENTS

650 g/1 lb 7 oz floury (mealy) potatoes, diced

300 g/10½ oz smoked mackerel, skinned and flaked

75 g/2¾ oz cooked gooseberries

2 tsp lemon juice

2 tbsp low-fat crème fraîche

1 tbsp capers

1 gherkin, chopped

1 tbsp chopped dill pickle

1 tbsp chopped fresh dill

salt and pepper

lemon wedges, to garnish

toast or warm crusty bread, to serve

1 Cook the diced potatoes in a saucepan of boiling water for 10 minutes until tender, then drain well.

2 Place the cooked potatoes in a food processor or blender.

3 Add the skinned and flaked smoked mackerel and process for 30 seconds until fairly smooth. Alternatively, place the ingredients in a bowl and mash with a fork.

4 Add the cooked gooseberries, lemon juice and crème fraîche to the fish and potato mixture. Blend for a further 10 seconds or mash well.

5 Stir in the capers, chopped gherkin and dill pickle, and chopped fresh dill. Season well with salt and pepper.

6 Turn the fish pâté into a serving dish, garnish with lemon wedges and serve with slices of toast or warm crusty bread cut into chunks or slices.

COOK'S TIP

Use stewed, canned or bottled cooked gooseberries for convenience and to save time, or when fresh gooseberries are out of season.

Shrimp Rolls

This variation of a spring roll is made with shrimps, stir-fried with shallots, carrot, cucumber, bamboo shoots and rice.

NUTRITIONAL INFORMATION

Calories 388   Sugars 2g
Protein ....9g   Fat 25g
Carbohydrate ...33g   Saturates 6g

10 MINS   15 MINS

SERVES 4

I N G R E D I E N T S

2 tbsp vegetable oil

3 shallots, chopped very finely

1 carrot, cut into matchstick pieces

7 cm/3 inch piece of cucumber, cut into matchstick pieces

60 g/2 oz/½ cup bamboo shoots, shredded finely

125 g/4½ oz/½ cup peeled (small) shrimps

90 g/3 oz/½ cup cooked long-grain rice

1 tbsp fish sauce or light soy sauce

1 tsp sugar

2 tsp cornflour (cornstarch), blended in 2 tbsp cold water

8 × 25 cm/10 inch spring roll wrappers

oil for deep-frying

salt and pepper

plum sauce, to serve

T O   G A R N I S H

spring onion (scallion) brushes (see page 515)

sprigs of fresh coriander (cilantro)

1 Heat the oil in a wok and add the shallots, carrot, cucumber and bamboo shoots. Stir-fry briskly for 2–3 minutes. Add the shrimps and cooked rice, and cook for a further 2 minutes. Season.

2 Mix together the fish sauce or soy sauce, sugar and blended cornflour (cornstarch). Add to the stir-fry and cook, stirring constantly, for about 1 minute, until thickened. Leave to cool slightly.

3 Place spoonfuls of the shrimp and vegetable mixture on the spring roll wrappers. Dampen the edges and roll them up to enclose the filling completely.

4 Heat the oil for deep-frying and fry the spring rolls until crisp and golden brown. Drain on paper towels. Serve the rolls garnished with spring onion (scallion) brushes and fresh coriander (cilantro) and accompanied by the plum sauce.

Vegetable Fritters

These mixed vegetable fritters are coated in a light batter and deep-fried until golden. They are ideal with the sweet and sour dipping sauce.

NUTRITIONAL INFORMATION

Calories	479	Sugars	........18g
Protein	.........8g	Fat	..........32g
Carbohydrate	...42g	Saturates	.......5g

20 MINS   20 MINS

SERVES 4

I N G R E D I E N T S

100 g/3½ oz/¾ cup wholemeal (whole
    wheat) flour

pinch of cayenne pepper

4 tsp olive oil

12 tbsp cold water

100 g/3½ oz broccoli florets

100 g/3½ oz cauliflower florets

50 g/1¾ oz mangetout (snow peas)

1 large carrot, cut into batons

1 red (bell) pepper, seeded and sliced

2 egg whites, beaten

oil, for deep-frying

salt

S A U C E

150 ml/¼ pint/⅔ cup pineapple juice

150 ml/¼ pint/⅔ cup vegetable stock

2 tbsp white wine vinegar

2 tbsp light brown sugar

2 tsp cornflour (cornstarch)

2 spring onions (scallions), chopped

1 Sift the flour and a pinch of salt into a mixing bowl and add the cayenne pepper. Make a well in the centre and gradually beat in the oil and cold water to make a smooth batter.

2 Cook the vegetables in boiling water for 5 minutes and drain well.

3 Whisk the egg whites until they form peaks and gently fold them into the flour batter.

4 Dip the vegetables into the batter, turning to coat well. Drain off any excess batter. Heat the oil for deep-frying in a deep-fryer to 180°C/350°F or until a cube of bread browns in 30 seconds. Fry the coated vegetables, in batches, for 1–2 minutes, until golden. Remove from the oil with a slotted spoon and drain on kitchen paper (paper towels).

5 Place all of the sauce ingredients in a pan and bring to the boil, stirring, until thickened and clear. Serve with the fritters.

Tzatziki & Black Olive Dip

Tzatziki is a Greek dish, made with yogurt, mint and cucumber.
It tastes superb with warm pitta (pocket) bread.

NUTRITIONAL INFORMATION

Calories 381   Sugars 8g
Protein . . . . .11g   Fat 15g
Carbohydrate . . .52g   Saturates 2g

  1 HOUR   3 MINS

SERVES 4

I N G R E D I E N T S

½ cucumber

225 g/8 oz/1 cup thick natural
   (unsweetened) yogurt

1 tbsp chopped mint

salt and pepper

4 pitta (pocket) breads

D I P

2 garlic cloves, crushed

125 g/4½ oz/1 cup pitted black olives

4 tbsp olive oil

2 tbsp lemon juice

1 tbsp chopped parsley

TO GARNISH

mint sprigs

parsley sprigs

COOK'S TIP

Sprinkling the cucumber
with salt draws out some of its
moisture, making it crisper. If
you are in a hurry, you can omit
this procedure. Use green olives
instead of black ones if you prefer.

1 To make the tzatziki, peel the cucumber and chop roughly. Sprinkle it with salt and leave to stand for 15–20 minutes. Rinse with cold water and drain well.

2 Mix the cucumber, yogurt and mint together. Season to taste with salt and pepper and transfer to a serving bowl. Cover and chill for 20–30 minutes.

3 To make the black olive dip, put the crushed garlic and olives into a blender or food processor and process for 15–20 seconds. Alternatively, chop them very finely.

4 Add the olive oil, lemon juice and parsley to the blender or food processor and process for a few more seconds. Alternatively, mix with the chopped garlic and olives and mash together. Season with salt and pepper.

5 Wrap the pitta (pocket) breads in foil and place over a barbecue for 2–3 minutes, turning once to warm through. Alternatively, heat in the oven or under the grill (broiler). Cut into pieces and serve with the tzatziki and black olive dip, garnished with sprigs of fresh mint and parsley.

Spinach Roulade

A delicious savoury roll, stuffed with mozzarella and broccoli. Serve as a main course or as an appetizer, in which case it would easily serve six.

NUTRITIONAL INFORMATION

Calories . . . . . . .287 Sugars 8g
Protein . . . . .23g Fat 12g
Carbohydrate . . . .8g Saturates 6g

15 MINS   25 MINS

SERVES 4

I N G R E D I E N T S

500 g/1 lb 2 oz small spinach leaves

2 tbsp water

4 eggs, separated

½ tsp ground nutmeg

salt and pepper

300 ml/½ pint/1¼ cups sugocasa,
   to serve

F I L L I N G

175 g/6 oz small broccoli florets

25 g/1 oz/¼ cup freshly grated
   Parmesan cheese

175 g/6 oz/1½ cups grated
   mozzarella cheese

1 Wash the spinach and pack, still wet, into a large saucepan. Add the water. Cover with a tight-fitting lid and cook over a high heat for 4–5 minutes, until reduced and soft. Drain thoroughly, squeezing out excess water. Chop finely and pat dry.

2 Mix the spinach with the egg yolks, seasoning and nutmeg. Whisk the egg whites until very frothy but not too stiff, and fold into the spinach mixture.

3 Grease and line a 32 x 23 cm/ 13 x 9 inch Swiss roll tin (jelly roll pan). Spread the mixture in the tin (pan) and smooth the surface. Bake in a preheated oven, 220°C/425°F/Gas Mark 7, for about 12–15 minutes, until firm to the touch and golden.

4 Meanwhile, cook the broccoli florets in lightly salted boiling water for 4–5 minutes, until just tender. Drain and keep warm.

5 Sprinkle Parmesan on a sheet of baking parchment. Turn the base on to it and peel away the lining paper. Sprinkle with mozzarella and top with broccoli.

6 Hold one end of the paper and roll up the spinach base like a Swiss (jelly) roll. Heat the sugocasa and spoon on to warmed serving plates. Slice the roulade and place on top of the sugocasa.

Poultry, Meat & Game

This chapter features exciting ways of cooking poultry, meat and game to offer a variety of satisfying meals. Dishes range from easy, economical mid-week suppers to sophisticated and elegant meals for special occasions. There are also tempting recipes to liven up a summer barbecue. The dishes bring together a wide range of flavours and ingredients from around the world, from classics such as Spaghetti Bolognese to less well-known but equally delicious dishes such as Kung Po Chicken with Cashews and Lamb Do Pyaza. There are also variations on old favourites, for example Pheasant Lasagne or Mediterranean-style Sunday Roast. Experiment with the ever increasing range of ingredients that are now available from a supermarket near you!

Jerk Chicken

This is perhaps one of the best known Caribbean dishes. The 'jerk' in the name refers to the hot spicy coating.

NUTRITIONAL INFORMATION

Calories . . . . . . .158 Sugars 0.4g
Protein . . . . .29g Fat 4g
Carbohydrate . . . .2g Saturates 1g

24 HOURS   30 MINS

SERVES 4

INGREDIENTS

4 lean chicken portions

1 bunch spring onions (scallions), trimmed

1–2 Scotch Bonnet chillies, deseeded

1 garlic clove

5 cm/2 inch piece root (fresh) ginger, peeled and roughly chopped

½ tsp dried thyme

½ tsp paprika

¼ tsp ground allspice

pinch ground cinnamon

pinch ground cloves

4 tbsp white wine vinegar

3 tbsp light soy sauce

pepper

1 Rinse the chicken portions and pat them dry on absorbent kitchen paper. Place them in a shallow dish.

2 Place the spring onions (scallions), chillies, garlic, ginger, thyme, paprika, allspice, cinnamon, cloves, wine vinegar, soy sauce and pepper to taste in a food processor and process until smooth.

3 Pour the spicy mixture over the chicken. Turn the chicken portions over so that they are well coated in the marinade.

4 Transfer the chicken portions to the refrigerator and leave to marinate for up to 24 hours.

5 Remove the chicken from the marinade and barbecue (grill) over medium hot coals for about 30 minutes, turning the chicken over and basting occasionally with any remaining marinade, until the chicken is browned and cooked through.

6 Transfer the chicken portions to individual serving plates and serve at once.

Chicken Marengo

Napoleon's chef was ordered to cook a sumptuous meal on the eve of the battle of Marengo – this feast of flavours was the result.

NUTRITIONAL INFORMATION

Calories 521	Sugars 6g
Protein 47g	Fat 19g
Carbohydrate . . .34g	Saturates 8g

🄖 🄖 🄖

🥘 20 MINS   🕐 50 MINS

SERVES 4

INGREDIENTS

1 tbsp olive oil

8 chicken pieces

300 g/10½ oz passata (tomato paste)

200 ml/7 fl oz/¾ cup white wine

2 tsp dried mixed herbs

8 slices white bread

40 g/1½ oz butter, melted

2 garlic cloves, crushed

100 g/3½ oz mixed mushrooms
   (such as button, oyster and ceps)

40 g/1½ oz black olives, chopped

1 tsp sugar

fresh basil, to garnish

1 Using a sharp knife, remove the bone from each of the chicken pieces.

2 Heat the oil in a large frying pan (skillet). Add the chicken pieces and cook for 4–5 minutes, turning occasionally, or until browned all over.

3 Add the passata (tomato paste), wine and mixed herbs to the frying pan (skillet). Bring to the boil and then leave to simmer for 30 minutes or until the chicken is tender and the juices run clear when a skewer is inserted into the thickest part of the meat.

4 Mix the melted butter and crushed garlic together. Lightly toast the slices of bread and brush with the garlic butter.

5 Add the remaining oil to a separate frying pan (skillet) and cook the mushrooms for 2–3 minutes or until just browned.

6 Add the olives and sugar to the chicken mixture and warm through.

7 Transfer the chicken and sauce to serving plates. Serve with the bruschetta (fried bread) and fried mushrooms.

Chicken Lasagne

This variation of the traditional beef dish has layers of pasta and chicken or turkey baked in red wine, tomatoes and a delicious cheese sauce.

NUTRITIONAL INFORMATION

Calories	550	Sugars	........11g
Protein	........35g	Fat	.........29g
Carbohydrate	...34g	Saturates	......12g

20 MINS   1¼ HOURS

SERVES 4

INGREDIENTS

350 g/12 oz fresh lasagne (about 9 sheets)

   or 150 g/5½ oz dried lasagne

   (about 9 sheets)

1 tbsp olive oil

1 red onion, finely chopped

1 garlic clove, crushed

100 g/3½ oz mushrooms, wiped and sliced

350 g/12 oz chicken or turkey breast, cut

   into chunks

150 ml/¼ pint/⅔ cup red wine, diluted with

   100 ml/3½ fl oz/scant ⅓ cup water

250 g/9 oz passata (sieved tomatoes)

1 tsp sugar

BECHAMEL SAUCE

75 g/2¾ oz/5 tbsp butter

50 g/1¾ oz plain (all-purpose) flour

600 ml/1 pint/2½ cups milk

1 egg, beaten

75 g/2¾ oz Parmesan cheese, grated

salt and pepper

1 Cook the lasagne in a pan of boiling water according to the instructions on the packet. Lightly grease a deep ovenproof dish.

2 Heat the oil in a pan. Add the onion and garlic and cook for 3–4 minutes. Add the mushrooms and chicken and stir-fry for 4 minutes or until the meat browns.

3 Add the wine, bring to the boil, then simmer for 5 minutes. Stir in the passata (sieved tomatoes) and sugar and cook for 3–5 minutes until the meat is tender and cooked through. The sauce should have thickened, but still be quite runny.

4 To make the Béchamel Sauce, melt the butter in a pan, stir in the flour and cook for 2 minutes. Remove the pan from the heat and gradually add the milk, mixing to form a smooth sauce. Return the pan to the heat and bring to the boil, stirring until thickened. Leave to cool slightly, then beat in the egg and half of the cheese. Season to taste.

5 Place 3 sheets of lasagne in the base of the dish and spread with half of the chicken mixture. Repeat the layers. Top with the last 3 sheets of lasagne, pour over the Béchamel Sauce and sprinkle with the Parmesan. Bake in a preheated oven, at 190°C/375°F/Gas Mark 5, for 30 minutes until golden and the pasta is cooked.

Jamaican Hot Pot

A tasty way to make chicken joints go a long way, this hearty casserole is spiced with the warm, subtle flavour of ginger.

NUTRITIONAL INFORMATION

Calories	277	Sugars	.........6g
Protein	........33g	Fat	...........7g
Carbohydrate	...22g	Saturates	......1g

🥔 5 MINS   🕐 1¼ HOURS

SERVES 4

I N G R E D I E N T S

2 tsp sunflower oil

4 chicken drumsticks

4 chicken thighs

1 medium onion

750 g/1 lb 10 oz piece squash or pumpkin, peeled

1 green (bell) pepper

2.5 cm/1 inch fresh ginger root, chopped finely

425 g/15 oz can chopped tomatoes

300ml/½ pint/1¼ cups chicken stock

60 g/2 oz/¼ cup split lentils

garlic salt and cayenne pepper

350 g/12 oz can sweetcorn (corn-on-the-cob)

1 Heat the oil in a large flameproof casserole and fry the chicken joints, turning frequently, until they are golden all over.

2 Peel and slice the onion.

3 Using a sharp knife, cut the squash or pumpkin into dice.

4 Deseed and slice the green (bell) pepper.

5 Drain any excess fat from the pan and add the onion, pumpkin and pepper. Gently fry for a few minutes. Add the ginger, tomatoes, stock and lentils. Season with garlic salt and cayenne.

6 Cover and place in a preheated oven, 190°C/375°F/Gas Mark 5, for about 1 hour, until the vegetables are tender and the juices from the chicken run clear.

7 Add the drained corn and cook for a further 5 minutes. Season to taste and serve with crusty bread.

Italian Chicken Spirals

These little foil parcels retain all the natural juices of the chicken while cooking conveniently over the pasta while it boils.

NUTRITIONAL INFORMATION

Calories 367	Sugars 1g
Protein 33g	Fat 12g
Carbohydrate ...35g	Saturates 2g

20 MINS   20 MINS

SERVES 4

INGREDIENTS

4 skinless, boneless chicken breasts

25 g/1 oz/1 cup fresh basil leaves

15 g/½ oz/2 tbsp hazelnuts

1 garlic clove, crushed

250 g/9 oz/2 cups wholemeal (whole wheat) pasta spirals

2 sun-dried tomatoes or fresh tomatoes

1 tbsp lemon juice

1 tbsp olive oil

1 tbsp capers

60 g/2 oz/½ cup black olives

1 Beat the chicken breasts with a rolling pin to flatten evenly.

2 Place the basil and hazelnuts in a food processor and process until finely chopped. Mix with the garlic and salt and pepper to taste.

3 Spread the basil mixture over the chicken breasts and roll up from one short end to enclose the filling. Wrap the chicken roll tightly in foil so that they hold their shape, then seal the ends well.

4 Bring a pan of lightly salted water to the boil and cook the pasta for 8–10 minutes or until tender, but still firm to the bite. Meanwhile, place the chicken parcels in a steamer or colander set over the pan, cover tightly, and steam for 10 minutes.

5 Using a sharp knife, dice the tomatoes.

6 Drain the pasta and return to the pan with the lemon juice, olive oil, tomatoes, capers and olives. Heat through.

7 Pierce the chicken with a skewer to make sure that the juices run clear and not pink (this shows that the chicken is cooked through). Slice the chicken, arrange over the pasta and serve.

COOK'S TIP

Sun-dried tomatoes have a wonderful, rich flavour but if they're unavailable, use fresh tomatoes instead.

Thai Red Chicken

This is a really colourful dish, the red of the tomatoes perfectly complementing the orange of the sweet potato.

NUTRITIONAL INFORMATION

Calories 249	Sugars 14g	
Protein 26g	Fat 7g	
Carbohydrate ...22g	Saturates 2g	

10 MINS   35 MINS

SERVES 4

INGREDIENTS

1 tbsp sunflower oil

450 g/1 lb lean boneless, skinless chicken

2 cloves garlic, crushed

2 tbsp Thai red curry paste

2 tbsp fresh grated galangal or root ginger

1 tbsp tamarind paste

4 lime leaves

225 g/8 oz sweet potato

600 ml/1 pint/2½ cups coconut milk

225 g/8 oz cherry tomatoes, halved

3 tbsp chopped fresh coriander (cilantro)

cooked jasmine or Thai fragrant rice, to serve

1 Heat the sunflower oil in a large preheated wok.

2 Thinly slice the chicken. Add the chicken to the wok and stir-fry for 5 minutes.

3 Add the garlic, curry paste, galangal or root ginger, tamarind and lime leaves to the wok and stir-fry for about 1 minute.

4 Using a sharp knife, peel and dice the sweet potato. Add the coconut milk and sweet potato to the mixture in the wok and bring to the boil. Allow to bubble over a medium heat for 20 minutes, or until the juices start to thicken and reduce.

5 Add the cherry tomatoes and coriander (cilantro) to the curry and cook for a further 5 minutes, stirring occasionally. Transfer to serving plates and serve hot with cooked jasmine or Thai fragrant rice.

COOK'S TIP

Galangal is a spice very similar to ginger and is used to replace the latter in Thai cuisine. It can be bought fresh from Oriental food stores but is also available dried and as a powder. The fresh root, which is not as pungent as ginger, needs to be peeled before slicing to use.

Lemon Chicken

This is on everyone's list of favourite Chinese dishes, and it is so simple to make. Serve with stir-fried vegetables for a truly delicious meal.

NUTRITIONAL INFORMATION

Calories	272	Sugars 1g
Protein	. . . . .36g	Fat 11g
Carbohydrate	. . . .5g	Saturates 2g

5 MINS   15 MINS

SERVES 4

INGREDIENTS

vegetable oil, for deep-frying

650 g/1 lb 7 oz skinless, boneless
 chicken, cut into strips

lemon slices and shredded spring onion
 (scallion), to garnish

SAUCE

1 tbsp cornflour (cornstarch)

6 tbsp cold water

3 tbsp fresh lemon juice

2 tbsp sweet sherry

½ tsp caster (superfine) sugar

1 Heat the oil for deep-frying in a preheated wok or frying pan (skillet) to 180°C/350°F or until a cube of bread browns in 30 seconds.

2 Reduce the heat and stir-fry the chicken strips for 3–4 minutes, until cooked through.

3 Remove the chicken with a slotted spoon, set aside and keep warm. Drain the oil from the wok.

4 To make the sauce, mix the cornflour (cornstarch) with 2 tablespoons of the water to form a paste.

5 Pour the lemon juice and remaining water into the mixture in the wok.

6 Add the sweet sherry and caster (superfine) sugar and bring to the boil, stirring until the sugar has completely dissolved.

7 Stir in the cornflour mixture and return to the boil. Reduce the heat and simmer, stirring constantly, for 2-3 minutes, until the sauce is thickened and clear.

8 Transfer the chicken to a warm serving plate and pour the sauce over the top.

9 Garnish the chicken with the lemon slices and shredded spring onion (scallion) and serve immediately.

COOK'S TIP

If you would prefer to use chicken portions rather than strips, cook them in the oil, covered, over a low heat for about 30 minutes, or until cooked through.

Chicken Cacciatora

This is a popular Italian classic in which browned chicken quarters are cooked in a tomato and (bell) pepper sauce.

NUTRITIONAL INFORMATION

Calories	397	Sugars	........4g
Protein	........37g	Fat	..........17g
Carbohydrate	...22g	Saturates	.......4g

 20 MINS   1 HOUR

SERVES 4

INGREDIENTS

1 roasting chicken, about 1.5 kg/ 3 lb 5 oz,
   cut into 6 or 8 serving pieces

125 g/4½ oz/1 cup plain (all-purpose) flour

3 tbsp olive oil

150 ml/¼ pint/⅔ cup dry white wine

1 green (bell) pepper, deseeded and sliced

1 red (bell) pepper, deseeded and sliced

1 carrot, chopped finely

1 celery stalk, chopped finely

1 garlic clove, crushed

200 g/7 oz can of chopped tomatoes

salt and pepper

1 Rinse and pat dry the chicken pieces with paper towels. Lightly dust them with seasoned flour.

2 Heat the oil in a large frying pan (skillet). Add the chicken and fry over a medium heat until browned all over. Remove from the pan and set aside.

3 Drain off all but 2 tablespoons of the fat in the pan. Add the wine and stir for a few minutes. Then add the (bell) peppers, carrots, celery and garlic, season with salt and pepper to taste and simmer together for about 15 minutes.

4 Add the chopped tomatoes to the pan. Cover and simmer for 30 minutes, stirring often, until the chicken is completely cooked through.

5 Check the seasoning before serving piping hot.

Chicken with a Yogurt Crust

A spicy, Indian-style coating is baked around lean chicken to give a full flavour. Serve with a tomato, cucumber and coriander (cilantro) relish.

NUTRITIONAL INFORMATION

Calories . . . . . . .176 Sugars 5g
Protein . . . . .30g Fat 4g
Carbohydrate . . . .5g Saturates 1g

 10 MINS   35 MINS

SERVES 4

I N G R E D I E N T S

1 garlic clove, crushed

2.5 cm/1 inch piece root (fresh) ginger, finely chopped

1 fresh green chilli, deseeded and finely chopped

6 tbsp low-fat natural (unsweetened) yogurt

1 tbsp tomato purée (paste)

1 tsp ground turmeric

1 tsp garam masala

1 tbsp lime juice

4 boneless, skinless chicken breasts, each 125 g/4½ oz

salt and pepper

wedges of lime or lemon, to serve

R E L I S H

4 medium tomatoes

¼ cucumber

1 small red onion

2 tbsp fresh coriander (cilantro), chopped

1 Preheat the oven to 190°C/375°F/Gas Mark 5.

2 Place the garlic, ginger, chilli, yogurt, tomato purée (paste), spices, lime juice and seasoning in a bowl and mix to combine all the ingredients.

3 Wash and pat dry the chicken breasts with absorbent kitchen paper (paper towels) and place them on a baking sheet.

4 Brush or spread the spicy yogurt mix over the chicken and bake in the oven for 30–35 minutes until the meat is tender and cooked through.

5 Meanwhile, make the relish. Finely chop the tomatoes, cucumber and onion and mix together with the coriander (cilantro). Season with salt and pepper to taste, cover and chill in the refrigerator until required.

6 Drain the cooked chicken on absorbent kitchen paper (paper towels) and serve hot with the relish and lemon or lime wedges. Alternatively, allow to cool, chill for at least 1 hour and serve sliced as part of a salad.

Chicken in Spicy Yogurt

Make sure the barbecue (grill) is really hot before you start cooking. The coals should be white and glow red when fanned.

NUTRITIONAL INFORMATION

Calories 74	Sugars 2g	
Protein 9g	Fat 4g	
Carbohydrate 2g	Saturates 1g	

4³/₄ HOURS   25 MINS

SERVES 6

INGREDIENTS

3 dried red chillies

2 tbsp coriander seeds

2 tsp turmeric

2 tsp garam masala

4 garlic cloves, crushed

½ onion, chopped

2.5cm/1 inch piece fresh ginger root, grated

2 tbsp lime juice

1 tsp salt

125 ml/4 fl oz/½ cup low-fat natural (unsweetened) yogurt

1 tbsp oil

2 kg/4 lb 8 oz lean chicken, cut into 6 pieces, or 6 chicken portions

TO SERVE

chopped tomatoes

diced cucumber

sliced red onion

cucumber and yogurt

1 Grind together the chillies, coriander seed, turmeric, garam masala, garlic, onion, ginger, lime juice and salt with a pestle and mortar or grinder.

2 Gently heat a frying pan (skillet) and add the spice mixture. Stir until

fragrant, about 2 minutes, and turn into a shallow non-porous dish.

3 Add the natural (unsweetened) yogurt and the oil to the spice paste and mix well to combine.

4 Remove the skin from the chicken portions and make three slashes in the flesh of each piece. Add the chicken to the dish containing the yogurt and spice mixture and coat the pieces completely in the marinade. Cover with cling film (plastic wrap) and chill for at least 4 hours. Remove the dish from the refrigerator and leave covered at room temperature for 30 minutes before cooking.

5 Wrap the chicken pieces in foil, sealing well so the juices cannot escape.

6 Cook the chicken pieces over a very hot barbecue (grill) for about 15 minutes, turning once.

7 Remove the foil, with tongs, and brown the chicken on the barbecue (grill) for 5 minutes.

8 Serve the chicken with the chopped tomatoes, diced cucumber, sliced red onion and the yogurt and cucumber mixture.

Spanish Chicken Casserole

Tomatoes, olives, peppers and potatoes, with a splash of Spanish red wine, make this a marvellous peasant-style dish.

NUTRITIONAL INFORMATION

Calories 293   Sugar 6g
Protein . . . . .15g   Fats 12g
Carbohydrates . . .26g   Saturates 2g

 10 MINS   1¼ HOURS

SERVES 4

INGREDIENTS

25 g/1 oz/¼ cup plain (all-purpose) flour

1 tsp salt

pepper

1 tbsp paprika

4 chicken portions

3 tbsp olive oil

1 large onion, chopped

2 garlic cloves, crushed

6 tomatoes, chopped, or 425 g/15 oz can chopped tomatoes

1 green (bell) pepper, cored, deseeded and chopped

150 ml/¼ pint/⅔ cup Spanish red wine

300 ml/½ pint/1¼ cups chicken stock

3 medium potatoes, peeled and quartered

12 pitted black olives

1 bay leaf

crusty bread, to serve

1 Put the plain (all-purpose) flour, salt, pepper and paprika into a large polythene bag.

2 Rinse the chicken portions and pat dry with kitchen paper (paper towels). Put them into the bag and shake to coat in the seasoned flour.

3 Heat the oil in a large flameproof casserole dish. Add the chicken portions and cook over a medium–high heat for 5–8 minutes until well-browned on each side. Lift out of the casserole with a perforated spoon and set aside.

4 Add the onion and garlic to the casserole and cook for a few minutes until browned. Add the tomatoes and (bell) pepper and cook for 2–3 minutes.

5 Return the chicken to the casserole. Add the wine, stock and potatoes, and then the olives and bay leaf. Cover and bake in a preheated oven at 190°C/375°F/ Gas Mark 5 for 1 hour until the chicken is tender.

6 Check the seasoning, adding more salt and pepper if necessary. Serve the chicken casserole hot with chunks of crusty bread.

Stir-Fried Ginger Chicken

The oranges add colour and piquancy to this refreshing dish, which complements the chicken well.

NUTRITIONAL INFORMATION

Calories	289	Sugars	........15g
Protein	........20g	Fat	...........9g
Carbohydrate	...17g	Saturates	.......2g

 5 MINS   20 MINS

SERVES 4

INGREDIENTS

2 tbsp sunflower oil

1 onion, sliced

175 g/6 oz carrots, cut into thin sticks

1 clove garlic, crushed

350 g/12 oz boneless skinless chicken breasts

2 tbsp fresh ginger, peeled and grated

1 tsp ground ginger

4 tbsp sweet sherry

1 tbsp tomato purée (tomato paste)

1 tbsp demerara sugar

100 ml/3½ fl oz/⅓ cup orange juice

1 tsp cornflour (cornstarch)

1 orange, peeled and segmented

fresh snipped chives, to garnish

1 Heat the oil in a large preheated wok. Add the onion, carrots and garlic and stir-fry over a high heat for 3 minutes or until the vegetables begin to soften.

2 Slice the chicken into thin strips. Add to the wok with the fresh and ground ginger. Stir-fry for a further 10 minutes, or until the chicken is well cooked through and golden in colour.

3 Mix together the sherry, tomato purée (tomato paste), sugar, orange juice and cornflour (cornstarch) in a bowl. Stir the mixture into the wok and heat through until the mixture bubbles and the juices start to thicken.

4 Add the orange segments and carefully toss to mix.

5 Transfer the stir-fried chicken to warm serving bowls and garnish with freshly snipped chives. Serve immediately.

COOK'S TIP

Make sure that you do not continue cooking the dish once the orange segments have been added in step 4, otherwise they will break up.

Chicken Chop Suey

Chop suey is a well known and popular dish based on bean sprouts and soy sauce with a meat or vegetable flavouring.

NUTRITIONAL INFORMATION

Calories 337   Sugars 7g
Protein . . . . .32g   Fat 18g
Carbohydrate . . .14g   Saturates 3g

 25 MINS   15 MINS

SERVES 4

I N G R E D I E N T S

4 tbsp light soy sauce

2 tsp light brown sugar

500 g/1 lb 2 oz skinless, boneless chicken
    breasts

3 tbsp vegetable oil

2 onions, quartered

2 garlic cloves, crushed

350 g/12 oz bean sprouts

3 tsp sesame oil

1 tbsp cornflour (cornstarch)

3 tbsp water

425 ml/¾ pint/2 cups chicken stock

shredded leek, to garnish

VARIATION

This recipe may be made with strips of lean steak, pork or with mixed vegetables. Change the type of stock accordingly.

1 Mix the soy sauce and sugar together, stirring until the sugar has dissolved.

2 Trim any fat from the chicken and cut into thin strips. Place the meat in a shallow dish and spoon the soy mixture over them, turning to coat. Marinate in the refrigerator for 20 minutes.

3 Heat the oil in a wok and stir-fry the chicken for 2–3 minutes, until golden brown. Add the onions and garlic and cook for a further 2 minutes. Add the bean sprouts, cook for 4–5 minutes, then add the sesame oil.

4 Mix the cornflour (cornstarch) and water to form a smooth paste. Pour the stock into the wok, add the cornflour (cornstarch) paste and bring to the boil, stirring until the sauce is thickened and clear. Serve, garnished with shredded leek.

Chicken with Rice & Peas

The secret of this dish is that it must be brown in colour, which is achieved by caramelizing the chicken first.

NUTRITIONAL INFORMATION

Calories . . . . Sugars . . . .
Protein . . . . Fat . . . .
Carbohydrate . . . . . . Saturates . . . .

10 MINS   1 HOUR

SERVES 6

I N G R E D I E N T S

1 onion, chopped

2 garlic cloves

1 tbsp chopped fresh chives

1 tbsp chopped fresh thyme

2 celery stalks with leaves, chopped

350 ml/12 fl oz/1½ cups water

½ fresh coconut, chopped

liquid from 1 fresh coconut

500 g/1 lb 2 oz can pigeon peas or kidney beans, drained

1 red chilli, deseeded and sliced thinly

2 tbsp groundnut oil

2 tbsp caster (superfine) sugar

1.5 kg/3 lb 5 oz chicken pieces

250 g/9 oz/1¼ cups white long-grain rice, rinsed and drained

salt and pepper

celery leaves, to garnish

1 Put the onion, garlic, chives, thyme, celery and 4 tablespoons of the water into a food processor. Blend until smooth.

2 Alternatively, chop the onion and celery very finely, then grind with the garlic and herbs in a pestle and mortar, gradually mixing in the water. Pour into a saucepan and set aside.

3 Put the chopped coconut and liquid into the food processor and mix to a thick milk, adding water if necessary. Alternatively, finely grate the coconut and mix with the liquid. Add to the onion and celery mixture. Stir in the drained pigeon peas or kidney beans and chilli. Cook over a low heat for 15 minutes, then season.

4 Put the oil and sugar in a heavy-based casserole and cook over a moderate heat until the sugar begins to caramelize. Add the chicken and cook for 15–20 minutes, turning frequently, until browned all over.

5 Stir in the coconut mixture, the rice and remaining water. Bring to the boil, then reduce the heat, cover and simmer for 20 minutes until the chicken and rice are tender and the liquid has been absorbed. Garnish with celery leaves.

Yellow Bean Chicken

Ready-made yellow bean sauce is available from large supermarkets and Chinese food stores.It is made from yellow soya beans and is quite salty.

NUTRITIONAL INFORMATION

Calories . . . . . . .234 Sugars 1g
Protein . . . . .26g Fat 12g
Carbohydrate . . . .6g Saturates 2g

 25 MINS   10 MINS

SERVES 4

I N G R E D I E N T S

450 g/1 lb skinless, boneless chicken breasts

1 egg white, beaten

1 tbsp cornflour (cornstarch)

1 tbsp rice wine vinegar

1 tbsp light soy sauce

1 tsp caster (superfine) sugar

3 tbsp vegetable oil

1 garlic clove, crushed

1-cm/½-inch piece fresh root ginger, grated

1 green (bell) pepper, seeded and diced

2 large mushrooms, sliced

3 tbsp yellow bean sauce

yellow or green (bell) pepper strips, to garnish

1 Trim any fat from the chicken and cut the meat into 2.5-cm/1-inch cubes.

2 Mix the egg white and cornflour (cornstarch) in a shallow bowl. Add the chicken and turn in the mixture to coat. Set aside for 20 minutes.

3 Mix the rice wine vinegar, soy sauce and caster (superfine) sugar in a bowl.

4 Remove the chicken from the egg white mixture.

5 Heat the oil in a preheated wok, add the chicken and stir-fry for 3–4 minutes, until golden brown. Remove the chicken from the wok with a slotted spoon, set aside and keep warm.

6 Add the garlic, ginger, (bell) pepper and mushrooms to the wok and stir-fry for 1–2 minutes.

7 Add the yellow bean sauce and cook for 1 minute. Stir in the vinegar mixture and return the chicken to the wok. Cook for 1–2 minutes and serve hot, garnished with (bell) pepper strips.

VARIATION

Black bean sauce would work equally well with this recipe. Although this would affect the appearance of the dish, as it is much darker in colour, the flavours would be compatible.

Pan-Cooked Chicken

Artichokes are a familiar ingredient in Italian cookery. In this dish, they are used to delicately flavour chicken.

NUTRITIONAL INFORMATION

Calories . . . . . . .296 Sugars 2g
Protein . . . . .27g Fat 15g
Carbohydrate . . . .7g Saturates 6g

15 MINS   55 MINS

SERVES 4

I N G R E D I E N T S

4 chicken breasts, part boned

25 g/1 oz/2 tbsp butter

2 tbsp olive oil

2 red onions, cut into wedges

2 tbsp lemon juice

150 ml/¼ pt/⅔ cup dry white wine

150 ml/¼ pt/⅔ cup chicken stock

2 tsp plain (all-purpose) flour

400 g/14 oz can artichoke halves,
    drained and halved

salt and pepper

chopped fresh parsley, to garnish

1 Season the chicken with salt and pepper to taste. Heat the oil and 15 g/½ oz/1 tablespoon of the butter in a large frying pan (skillet). Add the chicken and fry for 4–5 minutes on each side until lightly golden. Remove from the pan using a slotted spoon.

2 Toss the onion in the lemon juice, and add to the frying pan (skillet). Gently fry, stirring, for 3–4 minutes until just beginning to soften.

3 Return the chicken to the pan. Pour in the wine and stock, bring to the boil, cover and simmer gently for 30 minutes.

4 Remove the chicken from the pan, reserving the cooking juices, and keep warm. Bring the juices to the boil, and boil rapidly for 5 minutes.

5 Blend the remaining butter with the flour to form a paste. Reduce the juices to a simmer and spoon the paste into the frying pan (skillet), stirring until thickened.

6 Adjust the seasoning according to taste, stir in the artichoke hearts and cook for a further 2 minutes. Pour the mixture over the chicken and garnish with chopped parsley.

Baked Chicken & Chips

Traditionally, this dish is deep-fried, but the low-fat version is just as mouthwatering. Serve with chunky potato wedge chips.

NUTRITIONAL INFORMATION

Calories 361	Sugars 2g	
Protein 24g	Fat 8g	
Carbohydrate . . .51g	Saturates 2g	

10 MINS   35 MINS

SERVES 4

I N G R E D I E N T S

4 baking potatoes, each 225 g/8 oz

1 tbsp sunflower oil

2 tsp coarse sea salt

2 tbsp plain (all-purpose) flour

pinch of cayenne pepper

½ tsp paprika pepper

½ tsp dried thyme

8 chicken drumsticks, skin removed

1 medium egg, beaten

2 tbsp cold water

6 tbsp dry white breadcrumbs

salt and pepper

T O   S E R V E

low-fat coleslaw salad

sweetcorn relish

1 Preheat the oven to 200°C/400°F/Gas Mark 6. Wash and scrub the potatoes and cut each into 8 equal portions. Place in a clean plastic bag and add the oil. Seal and shake well to coat.

2 Arrange the potato wedges, skin side down, on a non-stick baking tray (cookie sheet), sprinkle over the sea salt and bake in the oven for 30–35 minutes until they are tender and golden.

3 Meanwhile, mix the flour, spices, thyme and seasoning together on a plate. Press the chicken drumsticks into the seasoned flour to lightly coat.

4 On one plate mix together the egg and water. On another plate sprinkle the breadcrumbs. Dip the chicken drumsticks first in the egg and then in the breadcrumbs. Place on a non-stick baking tray (cookie sheet).

5 Bake the chicken drumsticks alongside the potato wedges for 30 minutes, turning after 15 minutes, until both potatoes and chicken are tender and cooked through.

6 Drain the potato wedges thoroughly on absorbent kitchen paper (paper towels) to remove any excess fat and serve with the chicken, accompanied with low-fat coleslaw and sweetcorn relish.

Kung Po Chicken

In this recipe, cashew nuts are used but peanuts, walnuts or almonds can be substituted, if preferred.

NUTRITIONAL INFORMATION

Calories 294   Sugars 3g
Protein ....21g   Fat 18g
Carbohydrate ...10g   Saturates 4g

10 MINS   5 MINS

SERVES 4

INGREDIENTS

250–300 g/9–10½ oz chicken meat, boned and skinned

¼ tsp salt

⅓ egg white

1 tsp cornflour (cornstarch) paste (see page 6)

1 medium green (bell) pepper, cored and seeded

4 tbsp vegetable oil

1 spring onion (scallion), cut into short sections

a few small slices of ginger root

4–5 small dried red chillies, soaked, seeded and shredded

2 tbsp crushed yellow bean sauce

1 tsp rice wine or dry sherry

125 g/4½ oz roasted cashew nuts

a few drops of sesame oil

boiled rice, to serve

1 Cut the chicken into small cubes about the size of sugar lumps. Place the chicken in a small bowl and mix with a pinch of salt, the egg white and the cornflour (cornstarch) paste, in that order.

2 Cut the green (bell) pepper into cubes or triangles about the same size as the chicken pieces.

3 Heat the oil in a wok, add the chicken and stir-fry for 1 minute. Remove with a slotted spoon and keep warm.

4 Add the spring onion (scallion), ginger, chillies and green (bell) pepper. Stir-fry for 1 minute, then add the chicken with the yellow bean sauce and wine. Blend well and stir-fry for another minute. Finally stir in the cashew nuts and sesame oil. Serve hot with boiled rice.

VARIATION

Any nuts can be used in place of the cashew nuts, if preferred. The important point is the crunchy texture, which is very much a feature of Szechuan cooking.

Wild Mushroom Lasagne

You can use your favourite mushrooms, such as chanterelles or oyster mushrooms, for this delicately flavoured dish.

NUTRITIONAL INFORMATION

Calories 708   Sugars 17g

Protein . . . . .35g   Fat 35g

Carbohydrate . . .57g   Saturates 14g

40 MINS   1³/₄ HOURS

SERVES 4

I N G R E D I E N T S

butter, for greasing

14 sheets pre-cooked lasagne

850 ml/1½ pints/3¾ cups Béchamel Sauce (see page 6)

75 g/3 oz/1 cup grated Parmesan cheese

WILD MUSHROOM SAUCE

2 tbsp olive oil

2 garlic cloves, crushed

1 large onion, finely chopped

225 g/8 oz wild mushrooms, sliced

300 g/10½ oz/2½ cups minced (ground) chicken

80 g/3 oz chicken livers, finely chopped

115 g/4 oz Parma ham (prosciutto), diced

150 ml/¼ pint/⅔ cup Marsala

285g/10 oz can chopped tomatoes

1 tbsp chopped fresh basil leaves

2 tbsp tomato purée (paste)

salt and pepper

1 To make the chicken and wild mushroom sauce, heat the olive oil in a large saucepan. Add the garlic, onion and mushrooms and cook, stirring frequently, for 6 minutes.

2 Add the minced (ground) chicken, chicken livers and Parma ham (prosciutto) and cook over a low heat for 12 minutes, or until the meat has browned.

3 Stir the Marsala, tomatoes, basil and tomato purée (paste) into the mixture in the pan and cook for 4 minutes. Season with salt and pepper to taste, cover and leave to simmer for 30 minutes. Uncover the pan, stir and leave to simmer for a further 15 minutes.

4 Lightly grease an ovenproof dish with butter. Arrange sheets of lasagne over the base of the dish, spoon over a layer of wild mushroom sauce, then spoon over a layer of Béchamel Sauce. Place another layer of lasagne on top and repeat the process twice, finishing with a layer of Béchamel Sauce. Sprinkle over the grated cheese and bake in a preheated oven at 190°C/375°F/Gas Mark 5 for 35 minutes until golden brown and bubbling. Serve immediately.

Chicken & Noodle One-Pot

Flavoursome chicken and vegetables cooked with Chinese egg noodles in a coconut sauce. Serve in deep soup bowls.

NUTRITIONAL INFORMATION

Calories 256	Sugars 7g	
Protein 30g	Fat 8g	
Carbohydrate ...18g	Saturates 2g	

5 MINS   20 MINS

SERVES 4

INGREDIENTS

1 tbsp sunflower oil

1 onion, sliced

1 garlic clove, crushed

2.5 cm/1 inch root ginger, peeled and grated

1 bunch spring onions (scallions), sliced diagonally

500 g/1 lb 2 oz chicken breast fillet, skinned and cut into bite-sized pieces

2 tbsp mild curry paste

450 ml/16 fl oz/2 cups coconut milk

300 ml/½ pint/1¼ cups chicken stock

250 g/9 oz Chinese egg noodles

2 tsp lime juice

salt and pepper

basil sprigs, to garnish

1 Heat the sunflower oil in a wok or large, heavy-based frying pan (skillet).

2 Add the onion, garlic, ginger and spring onions (scallions) to the wok and stir-fry for 2 minutes until softened.

3 Add the chicken and curry paste and stir-fry for 4 minutes, or until the vegetables and chicken are golden brown. Stir in the coconut milk, stock and salt and pepper to taste, and mix well.

4 Bring to the boil, break the noodles into large pieces, if necessary, add to the pan, cover and simmer for about 6-8 minutes until the noodles are just tender, stirring occasionally.

5 Add the lime juice and adjust the seasoning, if necessary.

6 Serve the chicken and noodle one-pot at once in deep soup bowls, garnished with basil sprigs.

COOK'S TIP

If you enjoy hot flavours, substitute the mild curry paste in the above recipe with hot curry paste (found in most supermarkets) but reduce the quantity to1 tablespoon.

Mustard Baked Chicken

Chicken pieces are cooked in a succulent, mild mustard sauce, then coated in poppy seeds and served on a bed of fresh pasta shells.

NUTRITIONAL INFORMATION

Calories	652	Sugars	.........5g
Protein	........51g	Fat	..........31g
Carbohydrate	...46g	Saturates	......12g

10 MINS   35 MINS

SERVES 4

I N G R E D I E N T S

8 chicken pieces (about 115 g/4 oz each)

60g/2 oz/4 tbsp butter, melted

4 tbsp mild mustard (see Cook's Tip)

2 tbsp lemon juice

1 tbsp brown sugar

1 tsp paprika

3 tbsp poppy seeds

400 g/14 oz fresh pasta shells

1 tbsp olive oil

salt and pepper

1 Arrange the chicken pieces in a single layer in a large ovenproof dish.

2 Mix together the butter, mustard, lemon juice, sugar and paprika in a bowl and season with salt and pepper to taste. Brush the mixture over the upper

surfaces of the chicken pieces and bake in a preheated oven at 200°C/400°F/Gas Mark 6 for 15 minutes.

3 Remove the dish from the oven and carefully turn over the chicken pieces. Coat the upper surfaces of the chicken with the remaining mustard mixture, sprinkle the chicken pieces with poppy seeds and return to the oven for a further 15 minutes.

4 Meanwhile, bring a large saucepan of lightly salted water to the boil. Add the pasta shells and olive oil and cook for 8–10 minutes or until tender, but still firm to the bite.

5 Drain the pasta thoroughly and arrange on a warmed serving dish. Top the pasta with the chicken, pour over the sauce and serve immediately.

COOK'S TIP

Dijon is the type of mustard most often used in cooking, as it has a clean and only mildly spicy flavour. German mustard has a sweet-sour taste, with Bavarian mustard being slightly sweeter. American mustard is mild and sweet.

Coconut Chicken Curry

Okra or ladies fingers are slightly bitter in flavour. The pineapple and coconut in this recipe offsets them in both colour and flavour.

NUTRITIONAL INFORMATION

Calories 456   Sugars 21g
Protein . . . . .29g   Fat 29g
Carbohydrate . . .22g   Saturates 17g

 5 MINS   45 MINS

SERVES 4

I N G R E D I E N T S

2 tbsp sunflower oil or 25 g

450 g/1 lb boneless, skinless chicken
    thighs or breasts

150 g/5½ oz/1 cup okra

1 large onion, sliced

2 cloves garlic, crushed

3 tbsp mild curry paste

300 ml/½ pint/2¼ cups chicken stock

1 tbsp fresh lemon juice

100 g/3½ oz/½ cup creamed coconut,
    coarsely grated

175 g/6 oz/1¼ cups fresh or canned
    pineapple, cubed

150 ml/¼ pint/⅔ cup thick, natural
    (unsweetened) yogurt

2 tbsp chopped fresh coriander (cilantro)

freshly boiled rice, to serve

TO GARNISH

lemon wedges

fresh coriander (cilantro) sprigs

1 Heat the oil in a wok. Cut the chicken
into bite-sized pieces, add to the wok
and stir-fry until evenly browned.

2 Using a sharp knife, trim the okra.
Add the onion, garlic and okra to the
wok and cook for a further 2–3 minutes,
stirring constantly.

3 Mix the curry paste with the chicken
stock and lemon juice and pour into
the wok. Bring to the boil, cover and leave
to simmer for 30 minutes.

4 Stir the grated coconut into the curry
and cook for about 5 minutes.

5 Add the pineapple, yogurt and
coriander (cilantro) and cook for
2 minutes, stirring. Garnish and serve.

COOK'S TIP

Score around the top of
the okra with a knife before
cooking to release the sticky
glue-like substance which
is bitter in taste.

Grilled (Broiled) Chicken

This Italian-style dish is richly flavoured with pesto, which is a mixture of basil, olive oil, pine nuts and Parmesan cheese.

NUTRITIONAL INFORMATION

Calories 787   Sugars 6g
Protein . . . . .45g   Fat 38g
Carbohydrate . . .70g   Saturates 9g

 10 MINS   25 MINS

SERVES 4

I N G R E D I E N T S

8 part-boned chicken thighs

olive oil, for brushing

400 ml/14 fl oz/1⅓ cups passata
   (sieved tomatoes)

125 ml/4 fl oz/½ cup green or
   red pesto sauce

12 slices French bread

90 g/3 oz/1 cup freshly grated
   Parmesan cheese

60 g/2 oz/½ cup pine nuts or flaked
   (slivered) almonds

salad leaves, to serve

1 Arrange the chicken in a single layer in a wide flameproof dish and brush lightly with oil. Place under a preheated grill (broiler) for about 15 minutes, turning occasionally, until golden brown.

COOK'S TIP

Although leaving the skin on the chicken means that it will have a higher fat content, many people like the rich taste and crispy skin especially when it is blackened by the barbecue (grill). The skin also keeps in the cooking juices.

2 Pierce the chicken with a skewer to test if it is cooked through – the juices will run clear, not pink, when it is ready.

3 Pour off any excess fat. Warm the passata (sieved tomatoes) and half the pesto sauce in a small pan and pour over the chicken. Grill (broil) for a few more minutes, turning until coated.

4 Meanwhile, spread the remaining pesto on to the slices of bread. Arrange the bread over the chicken and sprinkle with the Parmesan cheese. Scatter the pine nuts over the cheese. Grill (broil) for 2–3 minutes, or until browned and bubbling. Serve with salad leaves.

Chilli Coconut Chicken

This tasty dish combines the flavours of lime, peanut, coconut and chilli. You'll find coconut cream in most supermarkets or delicatessens.

NUTRITIONAL INFORMATION

Calories ....348 Sugars 2g
Protein ....36g Fat 21g
Carbohydrate ....3g Saturates 8g

 5 MINS   15 MINS

SERVES 4

I N G R E D I E N T S

150 ml/¼ pint/⅔ cup hot chicken stock

25 g/1 oz/⅓ cup coconut cream

1 tbsp sunflower oil

8 skinless, boneless chicken thighs,
    cut into long, thin strips

1 small red chilli, sliced thinly

4 spring onions (scallions),
    sliced thinly

4 tbsp smooth or crunchy peanut butter

finely grated rind and juice of 1 lime

1 fresh red chilli and spring onion (scallion)
    tassel, to garnish

boiled rice, to serve

1 Pour the chicken stock into a measuring jug or small bowl. Crumble the coconut cream into the chicken stock and stir the mixture until the coconut cream dissolves.

2 Heat the oil in a preheated wok or large heavy pan.

3 Add the chicken strips and cook, stirring, until the chicken turns a golden colour.

4 Stir in the chopped red chilli and spring onions (scallions) and cook gently for a few minutes.

5 Add the peanut butter, coconut cream and chicken stock mixture, lime rind, lime juice and simmer, uncovered, for about 5 minutes, stirring frequently to prevent the mixture sticking to the base of the wok or pan.

6 Transfer the chilli coconut chicken to a warm serving dish, garnish with the red chilli and spring onion (scallion) tassel and serve with boiled rice.

COOK'S TIP

Serve jasmine rice with this spicy dish. It has a fragrant aroma that is well-suited to the flavours in this dish.

Chicken with Black Bean Sauce

This tasty chicken stir-fry is quick and easy to make and is full of fresh flavours and crunchy vegetables.

NUTRITIONAL INFORMATION

Calories 205   Sugars 4g
Protein ....25g   Fat 9g
Carbohydrate ....6g   Saturates 2g

40 MINS   10 MINS

SERVES 4

INGREDIENTS

425 g/15 oz chicken breasts,
  sliced thinly

pinch of salt

pinch of cornflour

2 tbsp oil

1 garlic clove, crushed

1 tbsp black bean sauce

1 each small red and green (bell) pepper,
  cut into strips

1 red chilli, chopped finely

75 g/2¾ oz/1 cup mushrooms, sliced

1 onion, chopped

6 spring onions (scallions), chopped

salt and pepper

SEASONING

½ tsp salt

½ tsp sugar

3 tbsp chicken stock

1 tbsp dark soy sauce

2 tbsp beef stock

2 tbsp rice wine

1 tsp cornflour (cornstarch), blended
  with a little rice wine

1 Put the chicken strips in a bowl. Add a pinch of salt and a pinch of cornflour and cover with water. Leave to stand for 30 minutes.

2 Heat 1 tablespoon of the oil in a wok or deep-sided frying pan (skillet) and stir-fry the chicken for 4 minutes.

3 Remove the chicken to a warm serving dish and clean the wok.

4 Add the remaining oil to the wok and add the garlic, black bean sauce, green and red (bell) peppers, chilli, mushrooms, onion and spring onions (scallions). Stir-fry for 2 minutes then return the chicken to the wok.

5 Add the seasoning ingredients, fry for 3 minutes and thicken with a little of the cornflour (cornstarch) blend. Serve with fresh noodles.

Chilli Chicken Meatballs

These tender chicken and sweetcorn nuggets are served with a sweet and sour sauce.

NUTRITIONAL INFORMATION

Calories 196   Sugars 12g
Protein ....26g   Fat 4g
Carbohydrate ...15g   Saturates 1g

 2½ HOURS   25 MINS

SERVES 4

INGREDIENTS

450 g/1 lb lean chicken, minced (ground)

4 spring onions (scallions), trimmed and finely chopped, plus extra to garnish

1 small red chilli, deseeded and finely chopped

2.5 cm/1 inch piece root (fresh) ginger, finely chopped

100 g/3½ oz can sweetcorn (no added sugar or salt), drained

salt and white pepper

boiled jasmine rice, to serve

SAUCE

150 ml/5 fl oz/⅔ cup Fresh Chicken Stock (see page 9)

100 g/3½ oz cubed pineapple in natural juice, drained, with 4 tbsp reserved juice

1 medium carrot, cut into thin strips

1 small red (bell) pepper, deseeded and diced, plus extra to garnish

1 small green (bell) pepper, deseeded and diced

1 tbsp light soy sauce

2 tbsp rice vinegar

1 tbsp caster (superfine) sugar

1 tbsp tomato purée (paste)

2 tsp cornflour (cornstarch) mixed to a paste with 4 tsp cold water

1 To make the meatballs, place the chicken in a bowl and mix with the spring onions (scallions), chilli, ginger, seasoning and sweetcorn.

2 Divide into 16 portions and form each into a ball. Bring a saucepan of water to the boil. Arrange the meatballs on baking parchment in a steamer or large sieve (strainer), place over the water, cover and steam for 10–12 minutes.

3 To make the sauce, pour the stock and pineapple juice into a pan and bring to the boil. Add the carrot and (bell) peppers, cover and simmer for 5 minutes. Add the remaining ingredients stirring until thickened. Season and set aside.

4 Drain the meatballs and transfer to a serving plate. Garnish with snipped chives and serve with boiled rice and the sauce (re-heated if necessary).

Barbecued Chicken Legs

Just the thing to put on the barbecue – chicken legs, coated with a spicy, curry-like butter, then grilled until crispy and golden.

NUTRITIONAL INFORMATION

Calories ....660 Sugars 4g
Protein ....34g Fat 57g
Carbohydrate ....4g Saturates 30g

5 MINS   20 MINS

SERVES 4

I N G R E D I E N T S

12 chicken drumsticks

S P I C E D   B U T T E R

175 g/6 oz/¾ cup butter

2 garlic cloves, crushed

1 tsp grated ginger root

2 tsp ground turmeric

4 tsp cayenne pepper

2 tbsp lime juice

3 tbsp mango chutney

T O   S E R V E

crisp green seasonal salad

boiled rice

VARIATION

This spicy butter mixture would be equally effective on grilled chicken or turkey breast fillets. Skin before coating with the mixture.

1 To make the Spiced Butter mixture, beat the butter with the garlic, ginger, turmeric, cayenne pepper, lime juice and chutney until well blended.

2 Using a sharp knife, slash each chicken leg to the bone 3-4 times.

3 Cook the drumsticks over a moderate barbecue (grill) for about 12-15 minutes or until almost cooked.

Alternatively, grill (broil) the chicken for about 10-12 minutes until almost cooked, turning halfway through.

4 Spread the chicken legs liberally with the butter mixture and continue to cook for a further 5-6 minutes, turning and basting frequently with the butter until golden and crisp. Serve the chicken legs hot or cold with a crisp green salad and rice.

Chicken with Green Olives

Olives are a popular flavouring for poultry and game in the Apulia region of Italy, where this recipe originates.

NUTRITIONAL INFORMATION

Calories 614	Sugars 6g	
Protein 34g	Fat 30g	
Carbohydrate . . .49g	Saturates 11g	

 15 MINS   🕐 1½ HOURS

SERVES 4

I N G R E D I E N T S

3 tbsp olive oil

25 g/1 oz/2 tbsp butter

4 chicken breasts, part boned

1 large onion, finely chopped

2 garlic cloves, crushed

2 red, yellow or green (bell) peppers, cored,
  seeded and cut into large pieces

250 g/9 oz button mushrooms, sliced
  or quartered

175 g/6 oz tomatoes, skinned and halved

150 ml/¼ pint/⅔ cup dry white wine

175 g/6 oz/1½ cups stoned (pitted)
  green olives

4–6 tbsp double (heavy) cream

400 g/14 oz dried pasta

salt and pepper

chopped flat leaf parsley, to garnish

1 Heat 2 tbsp of the oil and the butter in a frying pan (skillet). Add the chicken breasts and fry until golden brown all over. Remove the chicken from the pan.

2 Add the onion and garlic to the pan and fry over a medium heat until beginning to soften. Add the (bell) peppers and mushrooms and cook for 2–3 minutes.

3 Add the tomatoes and season to taste with salt and pepper. Transfer the vegetables to a casserole and arrange the chicken on top.

4 Add the wine to the pan and bring to the boil. Pour the wine over the chicken. Cover and cook in a preheated oven at 180°C/350°F/Gas Mark 4 for 50 minutes.

5 Add the olives to the casserole and mix in. Pour in the cream, cover and return to the oven for 10–20 minutes.

6 Meanwhile, bring a large pan of lightly salted water to the boil. Add the pasta and the remaining oil and cook for 8–10 minutes or until tender, but still firm to the bite. Drain the pasta well and transfer to a serving dish.

7 Arrange the chicken on top of the pasta, spoon over the sauce, garnish with the parsley and serve immediately. Alternatively, place the pasta in a large serving bowl and serve separately.

Chicken with Peanut Sauce

A tangy stir-fry with a strong peanut flavour. Serve with freshly boiled rice or noodles.

NUTRITIONAL INFORMATION

Calories 538   Sugars 5g
Protein . . . . .45g   Fat 36g
Carbohydrate . . .10g   Saturates 16g

10 MINS   10 MINS

SERVES 4

I N G R E D I E N T S

4 boneless, skinned chicken breasts, about 625 g/1 lb 6 oz

4 tbsp soy sauce

4 tbsp sherry

3 tbsp crunchy peanut butter

350 g/12 oz courgettes (zucchini), trimmed

2 tbsp sunflower oil

4-6 spring onions (scallions), thinly sliced diagonally

1 x 250 g/9 oz can bamboo shoots, well drained and sliced

salt and pepper

4 tbsp desiccated (shredded) coconut, toasted

1 Cut the chicken into thin strips across the grain and season lightly with salt and pepper.

2 Stir the soy sauce in a bowl with the sherry and peanut butter until smooth and well blended.

3 Cut the courgettes (zucchini) into 5 cm/2 inch lengths and then cut into sticks about 5mm/¼ inch thick.

4 Heat the oil in a preheated wok, swirling it around until it is really hot.

5 Add the spring onions (scallions) and stir-fry for a minute or so then add the chicken strips and stir-fry for 3-4 minutes until well sealed and almost cooked.

6 Add the courgettes (zucchini) and bamboo shoots and continue to stir-fry for 1-2 minutes.

7 Add the peanut butter mixture and heat thoroughly, stirring all the time so everything is coated in the sauce as it thickens.

8 Adjust the seasoning to taste and serve the chicken very hot, sprinkled with toasted coconut.

VARIATION

This dish can also be made with turkey fillet or pork fillet. For coconut lovers dissolve 25 g/1 oz creamed coconut in 2-3 tablespoons boiling water and add to the soy sauce mixture before adding to the wok

Spicy Peanut Chicken

This quick dish has many variations, but this version includes the classic combination of peanuts, chicken and chillies.

NUTRITIONAL INFORMATION

Calories 342	Sugars 3g	
Protein 25g	Fat 24g	
Carbohydrate 6g	Saturates 5g	

5 MINS   10 MINS

SERVES 4

I N G R E D I E N T S

300 g/10½ oz skinless, boneless chicken breast

2 tbsp peanut oil

125 g/4½ oz/1 cup shelled peanuts

1 fresh red chilli, sliced

1 green (bell) pepper, seeded and cut into strips

fried rice, to serve

S A U C E

150 ml/¼ pint/⅔ cup chicken stock

1 tbsp Chinese rice wine or dry sherry

1 tbsp light soy sauce

1½ tsp light brown sugar

2 garlic cloves, crushed

1 tsp grated fresh root ginger

1 tsp rice wine vinegar

1 tsp sesame oil

1 Trim any fat from the chicken and cut the meat into 2.5-cm/1-inch cubes. Set aside until required.

2 Heat the peanut oil in a preheated wok or frying pan (skillet).

3 Add the peanuts to the wok and stir-fry for 1 minute. Remove the peanuts with a slotted spoon and set aside.

4 Add the chicken to the wok and cook for 1–2 minutes.

5 Stir in the chilli and green (bell) pepper and cook for 1 minute. Remove from the wok with a slotted spoon and set aside.

6 Put half of the peanuts in a food processor and process until almost smooth. If necessary, add a little stock to form a softer paste. Alternatively, place them in a plastic bag and crush them with a rolling pin.

7 To make the sauce, add the chicken stock, Chinese rice wine or dry sherry, light soy sauce, slight brown sugar, crushed garlic cloves, grated fresh root ginger and rice wine vinegar to the wok.

8 Heat the sauce without boiling and stir in the peanut purée, remaining peanuts, chicken, sliced red chilli and green (bell) pepper strips. Mix well until all the ingredients are thoroughly combined.

9 Sprinkle the sesame oil into the wok, stir and cook for 1 minute. Transfer the spicy peanut chicken to a warm serving dish and serve hot with fried rice.

Garlic & Lime Chicken

Garlic and coriander (cilantro) flavour the chicken breasts which are served with a caramelised sauce, sharpened with lime juice.

NUTRITIONAL INFORMATION

Calories 280	Sugars 7g	
Protein 26g	Fat 17g	
Carbohydrate 7g	Saturates 8g	

 10 MINS   25 MINS

SERVES 4

INGREDIENTS

4 large skinless, boneless
  chicken breasts

50 g/1¾ oz/3 tbsp garlic butter,
  softened

3 tbsp chopped fresh coriander
  (cilantro)

1 tbsp sunflower oil

finely grated zest and juice of 2 limes,
  plus extra zest, to garnish

25 g/1 oz/4 tbsp palm sugar or
  demerara (brown crystal) sugar

TO SERVE

boiled rice

lemon wedges

1 Place each chicken breast between 2 sheets of cling film (plastic wrap) and pound with a rolling pin until flattened to about 1 cm/½ inch thick.

2 Mix together the garlic butter and coriander (cilantro) and spread over each flattened chicken breast. Roll up like a Swiss roll and secure with a cocktail stick (toothpick).

3 Heat the sunflower oil in a preheated wok or heavy-based frying pan (skillet).

4 Add the chicken rolls to the wok or pan and cook, turning, for 15–20 minutes or until cooked through.

5 Remove the chicken from the wok and transfer to a board. Cut each chicken roll into slices.

6 Add the lime zest, juice and sugar to the wok and heat gently, stirring, until the sugar has dissolved. Raise the heat and allow to bubble for 2 minutes.

7 Arrange the chicken on warmed serving plates and spoon the pan juices over to serve.

8 Garnish the garlic and lime chicken with extra lime zest, if desired

COOK'S TIP

Be sure to check that the chicken is cooked through before slicing and serving. Cook over a gentle heat so as not to overcook the outside, while the inside remains raw.

Chicken Scallops

Served in scallop shells, this makes a stylish presentation for a starter or a light lunch.

NUTRITIONAL INFORMATION

Calories . . . . . . .532 Sugars 3g
Protein . . . . .25g Fat 34g
Carbohydrate . . .33g Saturates 14g

20 MINS   25 MINS

SERVES 4

INGREDIENTS

175 g/6 oz short-cut macaroni, or other short pasta shapes

3 tbsp vegetable oil, plus extra for brushing

1 onion, chopped finely

3 rashers unsmoked collar or back bacon, rind removed, chopped

125 g/4½ oz button mushrooms, sliced thinly or chopped

175 g/6 oz/¾ cup cooked chicken, diced

175 ml/6 fl oz/¾ cup crème fraîche

4 tbsp dry breadcrumbs

60 g/2 oz/½ cup mature (sharp) Cheddar, grated

salt and pepper

flat-leaf parsley sprigs, to garnish

1 Cook the pasta in a large pan of boiling salted water, to which you have added 1 tablespoon of the oil, for 8–10 minutes or until tender. Drain the pasta, return to the pan and cover.

2 Heat the grill (broiler) to medium. Heat the remaining oil in a pan over medium heat and fry the onion until it is translucent. Add the chopped bacon and mushrooms and cook for 3–4 minutes, stirring once or twice.

3 Stir in the pasta, chicken and crème fraîche and season to taste with salt and pepper.

4 Brush four large scallop shells with oil. Spoon in the chicken mixture and smooth to make neat mounds.

5 Mix together the breadcrumbs and cheese, and sprinkle over the top of the shells. Press the topping lightly into the chicken mixture, and grill (broil) for 4–5 minutes, until golden brown and bubbling. Garnish with sprigs of flat-leaf parsley, and serve hot.

Sweet Mango Chicken

The sweet, scented flavour of mango gives this dish its characteristic sweetness.

NUTRITIONAL INFORMATION

Calories 244	Sugars 18g
Protein 27g	Fat 7g
Carbohydrate ...2.1g	Saturates 2g

 10 MINS   15 MINS

SERVES 4

I N G R E D I E N T S

1 tbsp sunflower oil

6 skinless, boneless chicken thighs

1 ripe mango

2 cloves garlic, crushed

225 g/8 oz leeks, shredded

100 g/3½ oz/1 cup bean sprouts

150 ml/¼ pint/⅔ cup mango juice

1 tbsp white wine vinegar

2 tbsp clear honey

2 tbsp tomato ketchup

1 tsp cornflour (cornstarch)

1 Heat the sunflower oil in a large preheated wok.

2 Cut the chicken into bite-sized cubes, add to the wok and stir-fry over a high heat for 10 minutes, tossing frequently until the chicken is cooked through and golden in colour.

3 Peel and slice the mango and add to the wok with the garlic, leeks and bean sprouts. Stir-fry for a further 2–3 minutes, or until softened.

4 Mix together the mango juice, white wine vinegar, honey, tomato ketchup and cornflour (cornstarch). Pour into the wok and stir-fry for a further 2 minutes, or until the juices start to thicken.

5 Transfer to a warmed serving dish and serve immediately.

COOK'S TIP

Mango juice is available in jars from most supermarkets and is quite thick and sweet. If it is unavailable, purée and sieve a ripe mango and add a little water to make up the required quantity.

Ginger Chicken & Corn

Chicken wings and corn in a sticky ginger marinade are designed to be eaten with the fingers – there's no other way!

NUTRITIONAL INFORMATION

Calories 123   Sugars 3g
Protein ....14g   Fat 6g
Carbohydrate ....3g   Saturates 1g

 10 MINS   20 MINS

SERVES 6

I N G R E D I E N T S

3 cobs fresh sweetcorn (corn-on-the-cob)

12 chicken wings

2.5cm/1 inch piece fresh ginger root

6 tbsp lemon juice

4 tsp sunflower oil

1 tbsp golden caster (superfine) sugar

jacket potatoes or salad, to serve

1 Remove the husks and silks from the corn. Using a sharp knife, cut each cob into 6 slices.

2 Place the corn in a large bowl with the chicken wings.

3 Peel and grate the ginger root or chop finely. Place in a bowl and add the lemon juice, sunflower oil and golden caster (superfine) sugar. Mix together until well combined.

4 Toss the corn and chicken in the ginger mixture to coat evely.

5 Thread the corn and chicken wings alternately on to metal or pre-soaked wooden skewers, to make turning easier.

6 Cook under a preheated moderately hot grill (broiler) or barbecue (grill) for 15–20 minutes, basting with the gingery glaze and turning frequently until the corn is golden brown and tender and the chicken is cooked. Serve with jacket potatoes or salad.

COOK'S TIP

Cut off the wing tips before grilling (broiling) as they burn very easily. Or you can cover them with small pieces of foil.

Chicken with Bean Sprouts

This is the basic Chicken Chop Suey to be found in almost every Chinese restaurant and takeaway all over the world.

NUTRITIONAL INFORMATION

Calories	153	Sugars	.........4g
Protein	.........9g	Fat	..........10g
Carbohydrate	....8g	Saturates	.......1g

  3¹/₂ HOURS 🕐 10 MINS

SERVES 4

INGREDIENTS

125 g/4½ oz chicken breast fillet, skinned

1 tsp salt

¼ egg white, lightly beaten

2 tsp cornflour (cornstarch) paste
   (see page 6)

about 300 ml/½ pint/1¼ cups vegetable oil

1 small onion, thinly shredded

1 small green (bell) pepper, cored, seeded
   and thinly shredded

1 small carrot, thinly shredded

125 g/4½ oz fresh beansprouts

½ tsp sugar

1 tbsp light soy sauce

1 tsp rice wine or dry sherry

2-3 tbsp Chinese Stock (see page 8)

a few drops of sesame oil

chilli sauce, to serve

COOK'S TIP

Chop Suey actually originated in San Francisco at the turn of the century when Chinese immigrants were first settling there, and was first devised as a handy dish for using up leftovers.

1 Using a sharp knife or meat cleaver, cut the chicken into thin shreds and place in a bowl.

2 Add a pinch of the salt, the egg white and cornflour (cornstarch) paste to the chicken and mix well.

3 Heat the vegetable oil in a preheated wok or large frying pan (skillet).

4 Add the chicken and stir-fry for about 1 minute, stirring to separate the shreds. Remove with a slotted spoon and drain on kitchen paper (paper towels).

5 Pour off the oil, leaving about 2 tablespoons in the wok. Add the onion, green (bell) pepper and carrot and stir-fry for about 2 minutes.

6 Add the bean sprouts and stir-fry for a few seconds.

7 Add the chicken with the remaining salt, sugar, soy sauce and rice wine or dry sherry, blend well and add the Chinese stock or water.

8 Sprinkle the stir-fry with the sesame oil and serve with the chilli sauce.

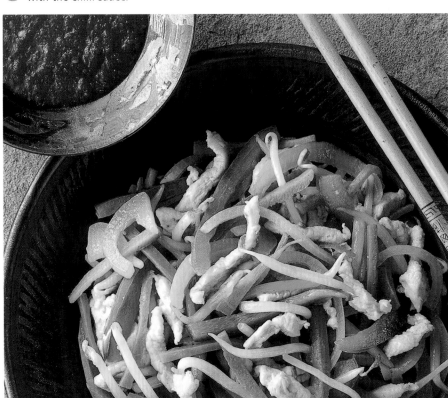

Orange Chicken Stir-Fry

Chicken thighs are inexpensive, meaty portions which are readily available. Although not as tender as breast, it is perfect for stir-frying.

NUTRITIONAL INFORMATION

Calories 267   Sugars 11g
Protein ....23g   Fat 11g
Carbohydrate ...15g   Saturates 2g

10 MINS   15 MINS

SERVES 4

INGREDIENTS

3 tbsp sunflower oil

350 g/12 oz boneless chicken thighs, skinned and cut into thin strips

1 onion, sliced

1 clove garlic, crushed

1 red (bell) pepper, deseeded and sliced

75 g/2¾ oz/1¼ cups mangetout (snow peas)

4 tbsp light soy sauce

4 tbsp sherry

1 tbsp tomato purée (tomato paste)

finely grated rind and juice of 1 orange

1 tsp cornflour (cornstarch)

2 oranges

100 g/3½ oz/1 cup bean sprouts

cooked rice or noodles, to serve

1 Heat the oil in a large preheated wok. Add the chicken and stir-fry for 2–3 minutes or until sealed on all sides.

2 Add the onion, garlic, (bell) pepper and mangetout (snow peas) to the wok. Stir-fry for a further 5 minutes, or until the vegetables are just tender and the chicken is completely cooked through.

3 Mix together the soy sauce, sherry, tomato purée (tomato paste), orange rind and juice and the cornflour (cornstarch). Add to the wok and cook, stirring, until the juices start to thicken.

4 Using a sharp knife, peel and segment the oranges. Add the segments to the mixture in the wok with the bean sprouts and heat through for a further 2 minutes.

5 Transfer the stir-fry to serving plates and serve at once with cooked rice or noodles.

COOK'S TIP

Bean sprouts are sprouting mung beans and are a regular ingredient in Chinese cooking. They require very little cooking and may even be eaten raw, if wished.

Poussin with Dried Fruits

Baby chickens are ideal for a one or two portion meal, and cook very easily and quickly for a special dinner – either in the oven or microwave.

NUTRITIONAL INFORMATION

Calories	316	Sugars	23g
Protein	23g	Fat	15g
Carbohydrate	23g	Saturates	2g

🍲 35 MINS   🕐 30 MINS

SERVES 2

INGREDIENTS

125 g/4½ oz/¾ cup dried apples, peaches and prunes

125 ml/4 floz/½ cup boiling water

2 baby chickens

25 g/1 oz/⅓ cup walnut halves

1 tbsp honey

1 tsp ground allspice

1 tbsp walnut oil

salt and pepper

vegetables and new potatoes, to serve

1 Place the fruits in a bowl, cover with the water and leave to stand for about 30 minutes.

2 Cut the chickens in half down the breastbone using a sharp knife, or leave whole.

3 Mix the fruit and any juices with the walnuts, honey and allspice and divide between two small roasting bags or squares of foil.

4 Brush the chickens with walnut oil and sprinkle with salt and pepper then place on top of the fruits.

5 Close the roasting bags or fold the foil over to enclose the chickens and bake on a baking sheet in a preheated oven, 190°C/375°F/Gas Mark 5, for 25–30 minutes or until the juices run clear. To cook in a microwave, use microwave roasting bags and cook on high/100% power for 6–7 minutes each, depending on size.

6 Transfer the poussin to a warm plate and serve hot with fresh vegetables and new potatoes.

VARIATION

Alternative dried fruits that can be used in this recipe are cherries, mangoes or paw-paws (papayas).

Chicken & Potato Bake

Make this when new potatoes are in season. A medium onion or a few shallots can be substituted for the spring onions (scallions).

NUTRITIONAL INFORMATION

Calories 323   Sugars 9g
Protein . . . . .30g   Fat 10g
Carbohydrate . . .29g   Saturates 2g

🍲 10 MINS   🕙 1¼ HOURS

SERVES 4

I N G R E D I E N T S

2 tbsp olive oil

4 lean chicken breasts

1 bunch spring onions (scallions), trimmed
and chopped

350 g/12 oz young spring carrots, scrubbed
and sliced

125 g/4½ oz dwarf green beans, trimmed
and sliced

600 ml/1 pint/2½ cups chicken stock

350 g/12 oz small new potatoes, scrubbed

1 small bunch mixed fresh herbs, such as
thyme, rosemary, bay and parsley

salt and pepper

2 tbsp cornflour (cornstarch)

2–3 tbsp cold water

sprigs of fresh mixed herbs, to garnish

1 Heat the oil in a large flameproof casserole and add the chicken breasts. Gently fry for 5–8 minutes until browned on both sides. Lift from the casserole with a perforated spoon and set aside.

2 Add the spring onions (scallions), carrots and green beans and gently fry for 3–4 minutes.

3 Return the chicken to the casserole and pour in the stock. Add the potatoes and herbs. Season, bring to the boil, then cover the casserole and transfer to the oven. Bake in a preheated oven at 190°C/375°F/Gas Mark 5 for 40–50 minutes until the potatoes are tender.

4 Blend the cornflour (cornstarch) with the cold water. Add to the casserole, stirring until blended and thickened. Cover and cook for a further 5 minutes. Garnish with fresh herbs and serve.

COOK'S TIP

Use your favourite combination of herbs for this dish. If fresh herbs are unavailable, use half the quantity of dried mixed herbs. Alternatively, use a bouquet garni sachet which is usually a combination of bay, thyme and parsley.

Szechuan Chilli Chicken

In China, the chicken pieces are chopped through the bone for this dish, but if you do not possess a cleaver, use filleted chicken meat.

NUTRITIONAL INFORMATION

Calories	218	Sugars	. . . . .4g
Protein	. . . . .23g	Fat	. . . . .9g
Carbohydrate	. . . .8g	Saturates	. . . . . . .2g

4 HOURS   15 MINS

SERVES 4

INGREDIENTS

500 g/1 lb 2 oz chicken thighs

¼ tsp pepper

1 tbsp sugar

2 tsp light soy sauce

1 tsp dark soy sauce

1 tbsp rice wine or dry sherry

2 tsp cornflour (cornstarch)

2-3 tbsp vegetable oil

1-2 garlic cloves, crushed

2 spring onions (scallions), cut into
    short sections, with the green
    and white parts separated

4-6 small dried red chillies, soaked and
    seeded

2 tbsp crushed yellow bean sauce

about 150 ml/¼ pint/⅔ cup Chinese Stock
    (see page 8) or water

1 Cut or chop the chicken thighs into bite-sized pieces and marinate with the pepper, sugar, soy sauce, wine and cornflour (cornstarch) for 25-30 minutes.

2 Heat the oil in a pre-heated wok and stir-fry the chicken for about 1–2 minutes until lightly brown. Remove with a slotted spoon, transfer to a warm dish and reserve. Add the garlic, the white parts of the spring onions (scallions), the chillies and yellow bean sauce to the wok and stir-fry for about 30 seconds.

3 Return the chicken to the wok, stirring constantly for about 1-2 minutes, then add the stock or water, bring to the boil and cover. Braise over a medium heat for 5-6 minutes, stirring once or twice. Garnish with the green parts of the spring onions (scallions) and serve immediately.

COOK'S TIP

One of the striking features of Szechuan cooking is the quantity of chillies used. Food generally in this region is much hotter than elsewhere in China – people tend to keep a string of dry chillies hanging from the eaves of their houses.

Chicken & Ginger Stir-fry

The pomegranate seeds add a sharp Chinese flavour to this Indian stir-fry. Serve in the summer with a spicy rice salad or a mixed green salad.

NUTRITIONAL INFORMATION

Calories	291	Sugars	.........0g
Protein	........41g	Fat	..........14g
Carbohydrate	....0g	Saturates	......3g

🕙 10 MINS   ⏱ 25 MINS

SERVES 4

I N G R E D I E N T S

3 tbsp oil

700 g/1 lb 9 oz lean skinless, boneless chicken breasts, cut into 5 cm/2 inch strips

3 garlic cloves, crushed

3.5 cm/1½ inch piece fresh ginger root, cut into strips

1 tsp pomegranate seeds, crushed

½ tsp ground turmeric

1 tsp garam masala

2 fresh green chillies, sliced

½ tsp salt

4 tbsp lemon juice

grated rind of 1 lemon

6 tbsp chopped fresh coriander (cilantro)

125 ml/4 fl oz/½ cup chicken stock

naan bread, to serve

1 Heat the oil in a wok or large frying pan (skillet) and stir-fry the chicken until golden brown all over. Remove from the pan and set aside.

2 Add the garlic, ginger and pomegranate seeds to the pan and fry in the oil for 1 minute taking care not to let the garlic burn.

3 Stir in the turmeric, garam masala and chillies, and fry for 30 seconds.

4 Return the chicken to the pan and add the salt, lemon juice, lemon rind, coriander (cilantro) and stock. Stir the chicken well to make sure it is coated in the sauce.

5 Bring the mixture to the boil, then lower the heat and simmer for 10–15 minutes until the chicken is thoroughly cooked. Serve with warm naan bread.

COOK'S TIP

Stir-frying is perfect for low-fat diets as only a little oil is needed. Cooking the food over a high temperature ensures that food is sealed and cooked quickly to hold in the flavour.

Chicken with Orange Sauce

The refreshing combination of chicken and orange sauce makes this a perfect dish for a warm summer evening.

NUTRITIONAL INFORMATION

Calories 797   Sugars 28g
Protein ....59g   Fat 25g
Carbohydrate ...77g   Saturates 6g

15 MINS   25 MINS

SERVES 4

INGREDIENTS

30 ml/1 fl oz/⅛ cup rapeseed oil

3 tbsp olive oil

4 x 225 g/8 oz chicken suprêmes

150 ml/¼ pint/⅔ cup orange brandy

15 g/½ oz/2 tbsp plain (all-purpose) flour

150 ml/¼ pint/⅔ cup freshly squeezed
   orange juice

25 g/1 oz courgette (zucchini), cut into
   matchstick strips

25 g/1 oz red (bell) pepper, cut into
   matchstick strips

25 g/1 oz leek, finely shredded

400 g/14 oz dried wholemeal
   (whole-wheat) spaghetti

3 large oranges, peeled and cut into
   segments

rind of 1 orange, cut into very fine strips

2 tbsp chopped fresh tarragon

150 ml/¼ pint/⅔ cup fromage frais or
   ricotta cheese

salt and pepper

fresh tarragon leaves, to garnish

1 Heat the rapeseed oil and 1 tablespoon of the olive oil in a frying pan (skillet). Add the chicken and cook quickly until golden brown. Add the orange brandy and cook for 3 minutes. Sprinkle over the flour and cook for 2 minutes.

2 Lower the heat and add the orange juice, courgette (zucchini), (bell) pepper and leek and season. Simmer for 5 minutes until the sauce has thickened.

3 Meanwhile, bring a pan of salted water to the boil. Add the spaghetti and 1 tablespoon of the olive oil and cook for 10 minutes. Drain the spaghetti, transfer to a serving dish and drizzle over the remaining oil.

4 Add half of the orange segments, half of the orange rind, the tarragon and fromage frais or ricotta cheese to the sauce in the pan and cook for 3 minutes.

5 Place the chicken on top of the pasta, pour over a little sauce, garnish with orange segments, rind and tarragon. Serve immediately.

Green Chicken Stir-Fry

Tender chicken is mixed with a selection of spring greens and flavoured with yellow bean sauce in this crunchy stir-fry.

NUTRITIONAL INFORMATION

Calories	297	Sugars	.........5g
Protein	........30g	Fat	..........16g
Carbohydrate	....8g	Saturates	.......3g

 5 MINS   15 MINS

SERVES 4

I N G R E D I E N T S

2 tbsp sunflower oil

450 g/1 lb skinless, boneless chicken breasts

2 cloves garlic, crushed

1 green (bell) pepper

100 g/3½ oz/1½ cups mangetout (snow peas)

6 spring onions (scallions), sliced, plus extra to garnish

225 g/8 oz spring greens or cabbage, shredded

160 g/5¾ oz jar yellow bean sauce

50 g/1¾ oz/3 tbsp roasted cashew nuts

1 Heat the sunflower oil in a large preheated wok.

2 Slice the chicken into thin strips and add to the wok together with the garlic. Stir-fry for about 5 minutes or until the chicken is sealed on all sides and beginning to turn golden.

3 Using a sharp knife, deseed the green (bell) pepper and cut into thin strips.

4 Add the mangetout (snow peas), spring onions (scallions), green (bell) pepper strips and spring greens or cabbage to the wok. Stir-fry for a further 5 minutes or until the vegetables are just tender.

5 Stir in the yellow bean sauce and heat through for about 2 minutes or until the mixture starts to bubble.

6 Scatter the roasted cashew nuts into the wok.

7 Transfer the stir-fry to warm serving plates and garnish with extra spring onions (scallions), if desired. Serve the stir-fry immediately.

COOK'S TIP

Do not add salted cashew nuts to this dish otherwise the dish will be too salty.

Lemon & Sesame Chicken

Sesame seeds have a strong flavour which adds nuttiness to recipes. They are perfect for coating these thin chicken strips.

NUTRITIONAL INFORMATION

Calories	273	Sugars	.........5g
Protein	........29g	Fat	..........13g
Carbohydrate	....11g	Saturates	.......3g

10 MINS   10 MINS

SERVES 4

INGREDIENTS

4 boneless, skinless chicken breasts

1 egg white

25 g/1 oz/2 tbsp sesame seeds

2 tbsp vegetable oil

1 onion, sliced

1 tbsp demerara (brown crystal) sugar

finely grated zest and juice of 1 lemon

3 tbsp lemon curd

200 g/7 oz can water chestnuts, drained

lemon zest, to garnish

COOK'S TIP

Water chestnuts are commonly added to Chinese recipes for their crunchy texture as they do not have a great deal of flavour.

1 Place the chicken breasts between 2 sheets of cling film (plastic wrap) and pound with a rolling pin to flatten. Slice the chicken into thin strips.

2 Whisk the egg white until light and foamy. Dip the chicken strips into the egg white, then coat in the sesame seeds.

3 Heat the oil in a wok and stir-fry the onion for 2 minutes until softened.

4 Add the chicken to the wok and stir-fry for 5 minutes, or until the chicken turns golden.

5 Mix the sugar, lemon zest, lemon juice and lemon curd and add to the wok. Allow it to bubble slightly.

6 Slice the water chestnuts thinly, add to the wok and cook for 2 minutes. Garnish with lemon zest and serve hot.

Chicken with Lime Stuffing

A cheesy stuffing is tucked under the breast skin of the chicken to give added flavour and moistness to the meat.

NUTRITIONAL INFORMATION

Calories	236	Sugars	.........1g
Protein	........28g	Fat	..........12g
Carbohydrate	....3g	Saturates	......7g

10 MINS   2 HOURS

SERVES 4

INGREDIENTS

1 chicken, weighing 2.25 kg/5 lb

oil for brushing

225 g/8 oz/1⅓ cups courgette (zucchini)

25 g/1 oz/2 tbsp butter

juice of 1 lime

lime slices and shreds of lime rind,
to garnish

STUFFING

90 g/3 oz/½ cup courgette (zucchini)

90 g/3 oz/¾ cup low-fat soft cheese

finely grated rind of 1 lime

2 tbsp fresh breadcrumbs

salt and pepper

1 To make the stuffing, trim and coarsely grate the courgette (zucchini) and mix with the cheese, lime rind, breadcrumbs, salt and pepper.

2 Carefully ease the skin away from the breast of the chicken with the fingertips, taking care not to split it.

3 Push the stuffing under the skin, to cover the breast evenly.

4 Place in a baking tin (pan), brush with oil and roast in a preheated oven, 190°C/375°F/Gas Mark 5, for 20 minutes

per 500 g/1 lb 2 oz plus 20 minutes, or until the chicken juices run clear when pierced with a skewer.

5 Meanwhile, trim the remaining courgettes (zucchini) and cut into long, thin strips with a potato peeler or sharp knife. Sauté in the butter and lime juice until just tender, then serve with the chicken. Garnish the chicken with lime slices and shreds of lime rind and serve immediately.

COOK'S TIP

For quicker cooking, finely grate the courgettes (zucchini) rather than cutting them into strips.

Chicken Wontons

These deliciously crispy nibbles make an ideal introduction to a Chinese meal. Here they are filled with a chicken and mushroom mixture.

NUTRITIONAL INFORMATION

Calories 285	Sugars 1g
Protein 16g	Fat 19g
Carbohydrate ...14g	Saturates 5g

 20 MINS   35 MINS

SERVES 4

INGREDIENTS

250 g/9 oz boneless chicken breast, skinned

60 g/2 oz/⅔ cup mushrooms

1 garlic clove

2 shallots

1 tbsp fish sauce or mushroom ketchup

1 tbsp chopped fresh coriander (cilantro)

2 tbsp vegetable oil

about 50 wonton wrappers

oil, for deep-frying

salt and pepper

sliced spring onion (scallion), to garnish

sweet chilli sauce, to serve

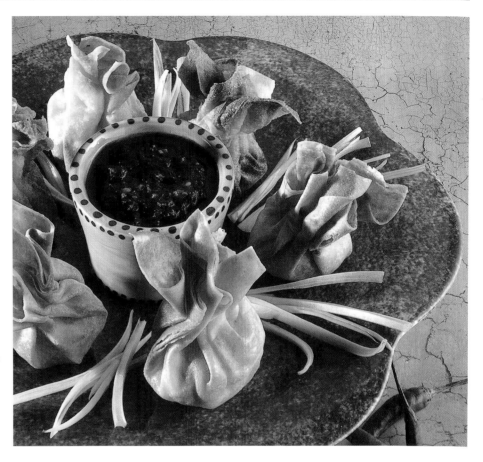

1 Put the chicken, mushrooms, garlic, shallots, fish sauce or mushroom ketchup and coriander (cilantro) into a blender or food processor. Blend for 10–15 seconds. Alternatively, chop all the ingredients finely and mix together well.

2 Heat the vegetable oil in a wok or frying pan (skillet) and add the chicken mixture. Stir-fry for about 8 minutes, breaking up the mixture as it cooks, until it browns. Transfer to a bowl and leave to cool for 10–15 minutes.

3 Place the wonton wrappers on a clean, damp tea towel (dish cloth).

Layering 2 wrappers together at a time, place teaspoonfuls of the chicken mixture into the middle. Dampen the edges with water, then make small pouches, pressing the edges together to seal. Repeat with the remaining wrappers until all the mixture is used.

4 Heat the oil for deep-frying in a wok or deep fat fryer. Fry the wontons, a few at a time, for about 2–3 minutes until

golden brown. Remove the won tons from the oil with a perforated spoon and drain on kitchen paper (paper towels). Keep warm while frying the remaining wontons.

5 Transfer the wontons to a warmed serving platter and garnish with the sliced spring onion (scallion). Serve at once, accompanied by some sweet chilli sauce.

Filipino Chicken

Tomato ketchup is a very popular ingredient in Asian dishes, as it imparts a zingy sweet-sour flavour.

NUTRITIONAL INFORMATION

Calories 197   Sugars 7g
Protein ....28g   Fat 4g
Carbohydrate ....8g   Saturates 1g

2³/₄ HOURS   20 MINS

SERVES 4

INGREDIENTS

1 can lemonade or lime-and-lemonade

2 tbsp gin

4 tbsp tomato ketchup

2 tsp garlic salt

2 tsp Worcestershire sauce

4 lean chicken suprêmes or breast fillets

salt and pepper

TO SERVE

thread egg noodles

1 green chilli, chopped finely

2 spring onions (scallions), sliced

1 Combine the lemonade or lime-and-lemonade, gin, tomato ketchup, garlic salt, Worcestershire sauce and seasoning in a large non-porous dish.

2 Put the chicken supremes into the dish and make sure that the marinade covers them completely.

3 Leave to marinate in the refrigerator for 2 hours. Remove and leave covered at room temperature for 30 minutes.

4 Place the chicken over a medium barbecue (grill) and cook for 20 minutes.

5 Turn the chicken once, halfway through the cooking time.

6 Remove from the barbecue (grill) and leave to rest for 3–4 minutes before serving.

7 Serve with egg noodles, tossed with a little green chilli and spring onions (scallions).

COOK'S TIP

Cooking the meat on the bone after it has reached room temperature means that it cooks in a shorter time, which ensures that the meat remains moist right through to the bone.

Italian-style Sunday Roast

A mixture of cheese, rosemary and sun-dried tomatoes is stuffed under the chicken skin, then roasted with garlic, potatoes and vegetables.

NUTRITIONAL INFORMATION

Calories 488   Sugars 6g
Protein . . . . .37g   Fat 23g
Carbohydrate . . .34g   Saturates 11g

  35 MINS   1¹/₂ HOURS

SERVES 6

I N G R E D I E N T S

2.5 kg/5 lb 8 oz chicken

sprigs of fresh rosemary

175 g/6 oz/¾ cup feta cheese,
    coarsely grated

2 tbsp sun-dried tomato paste

60 g/2 oz/4 tbsp butter, softened

1 bulb garlic

1 kg/2 lb 4 oz new potatoes, halved if large

1 each red, green and yellow (bell) pepper,
    cut into chunks

3 courgettes (zucchini), sliced thinly

2 tbsp olive oil

2 tbsp plain (all-purpose) flour

600 ml/1 pint/2½ cups chicken stock

salt and pepper

1 Rinse the chicken inside and out with cold water and drain well. Carefully cut between the skin and the top of the breast meat using a small pointed knife. Slide a finger into the slit and carefully enlarge it to form a pocket. Continue until the skin is completely lifted away from both breasts and the top of the legs.

2 Chop the leaves from 3 rosemary stems. Mix with the feta cheese, sun-dried tomato paste, butter and pepper to taste, then spoon under the skin. Put the chicken in a large roasting tin (pan), cover with foil and cook in a preheated oven, 190°C/375°F/Gas Mark 5, for 20 minutes per 500 g/1 lb 2 oz, plus 20 minutes.

3 Break the garlic bulb into cloves but do not peel. Add the vegetables to the chicken after 40 minutes.

4 Drizzle with oil, tuck in a few stems of rosemary and season with salt and pepper. Cook for the remaining calculated time, removing the foil for the last 40 minutes to brown the chicken.

5 Transfer the chicken to a serving platter. Place some of the vegetables around the chicken and transfer the remainder to a warmed serving dish. Pour the fat out of the roasting tin (pan) and stir the flour into the remaining pan juices. Cook for 2 minutes then gradually stir in the stock. Bring to the boil, stirring until thickened. Strain into a sauce boat and serve with the chicken.

Parma-wrapped Chicken

There is a delicious surprise of creamy herb and garlic soft cheese hidden inside these chicken parcels!

NUTRITIONAL INFORMATION

Calories	272	Sugars	.........4g
Protein	........29g	Fat	..........13g
Carbohydrate	....4g	Saturates	.......6g

20 MINS 25 MINS

SERVES 4

I N G R E D I E N T S

4 chicken breasts, skin removed

100 g/3½ oz full fat soft cheese, flavoured with herbs and garlic

8 slices Parma ham (prosciutto)

150 ml/¼ pint/⅔ cup red wine

150 ml/¼ pint/⅔ cup chicken stock

1 tbsp brown sugar

1 Using a sharp knife, make a horizontal slit along the length of each chicken breast to form a pocket.

2 Beat the cheese with a wooden spoon to soften it. Spoon the cheese into the pocket of the chicken breasts.

3 Wrap 2 slices of Parma ham (prosciutto) around each chicken breast and secure firmly in place with a length of string.

4 Pour the wine and chicken stock into a large frying pan (skillet) and bring to the boil. When the mixture is just starting to boil, add the sugar and stir well to dissolve.

5 Add the chicken breasts to the mixture in the frying pan (skillet). Leave to simmer for 12–15 minutes or until the chicken is tender and the juices run clear when a skewer is inserted into the thickest part of the meat.

6 Remove the chicken from the pan, set aside and keep warm.

7 Reheat the sauce and boil until reduced and thickened. Remove the string from the chicken and cut into slices. Pour the sauce over the chicken to serve.

VARIATION

Try adding 2 finely chopped sun-dried tomatoes to the soft cheese in step 2, if you prefer.

Red Chicken Curry

The chicken is cooked with a curry paste using red chillies. It is a fiery hot sauce – for a milder version, reduce the number of chillies used.

NUTRITIONAL INFORMATION

Calories 331   Sugars 5g
Protein . . . . .36g   Fat 17g
Carbohydrate . . . .7g   Saturates 3g

10 MINS   10 MINS

SERVES 4

INGREDIENTS

4 tbsp vegetable oil

2 garlic cloves, crushed

400 ml/14 fl oz/1¾ cups coconut milk

6 chicken breast fillets, skinned and
   cut into bite-sized pieces

125 ml/4 fl oz/½ cup chicken stock

2 tbsp fish sauce

sliced red and green chillies,
   to garnish

boiled rice, to serve

RED CURRY PASTE

8 dried red chillies, seeded
   and chopped

2.5 cm/1 inch galangal or ginger root,
   peeled and sliced

3 stalks lemon grass, chopped

1 garlic clove, peeled

2 tsp shrimp paste

1 kaffir lime leaf, chopped

1 tsp ground coriander

¾ tsp ground cumin

1 tbsp chopped fresh coriander
   (cilantro)

1 tsp salt and black pepper

1 To make the red curry paste, place all the ingredients in a food processor or blender and process until smooth.

2 Heat the vegetable oil in a large, heavy-based pan or wok. Add the garlic and cook for 1 minute or until it turns golden.

3 Stir in the red curry paste and cook for 10-15 seconds.

4 Gradually add the coconut milk, stirring constantly (don't worry if the mixture starts to look curdled at this stage).

5 Add the chicken pieces and turn in the sauce mixture to coat. Cook gently for about 3-5 minutes or until almost tender.

6 Stir in the chicken stock and fish sauce, mixing well, then cook for a further 2 minutes.

7 Transfer the chicken curry to a warmed serving dish and garnish with sliced red and green chillies. Serve with rice.

Peanut Sesame Chicken

Sesame and peanuts give extra crunch and flavour to this stir-fry and the fruit juice glaze gives a lovely shiny coating to the sauce.

NUTRITIONAL INFORMATION

Calories 435	Sugars 10g	
Protein 38g	Fat 26g	
Carbohydrate ...14g	Saturates 4g	

10 MINS   15 MINS

SERVES 4

I N G R E D I E N T S

2 tbsp vegetable oil

2 tbsp sesame oil

500g/1 lb 2 oz boneless, skinned chicken breasts, sliced into strips

250 g/9 oz broccoli, divided into small florets

250 g/9 oz baby or dwarf corn, halved if large

1 small red (bell) pepper, cored, seeded and sliced

2 tbsp soy sauce

250 ml/9 fl oz/1 cup orange juice

2 tsp cornflour (cornstarch)

2 tbsp toasted sesame seeds

60 g/2 oz/⅓ cup roasted, shelled, unsalted peanuts

rice or noodles, to serve

1 Heat the vegetable oil and sesame oil in a large, heavy-based frying pan (skillet) or wok until smoking. Add the chicken strips and stir-fry until browned, about 4-5 minutes.

2 Add the broccoli, corn and red (bell) pepper and stir-fry for a further 1-2 minutes.

3 Meanwhile, mix the soy sauce with the orange juice and cornflour (cornstarch). Stir into the chicken and vegetable mixture, stirring constantly until the sauce has slightly thickened and a glaze develops.

4 Stir in the sesame seeds and peanuts, mixing well. Heat the stir-fry for a further 3-4 minutes.

5 Transfer the stir-fry to a warm serving dish and serve with rice or noodles.

COOK'S TIP

Make sure you use the unsalted variety of peanuts or the dish will be too salty, as the soy sauce adds saltiness.

Cheesy Baked Chicken

Cheese and mustard, and a simple, crispy coating, make a delicious combination for this healthy dish.

NUTRITIONAL INFORMATION

Calories 225	Sugars 1g
Protein 32g	Fat 7g
Carbohydrate 9g	Saturates 3g

 5 MINS   35 MINS

SERVES 4

I N G R E D I E N T S

1 tbsp skimmed milk

2 tbsp prepared English mustard

60 g/2oz/1 cup grated low-fat mature (sharp) Cheddar cheese

3 tbsp plain (all-purpose) flour

2 tbsp chopped fresh chives

4 skinless, boneless chicken breasts

T O   S E R V E

jacket potatoes and fresh vegetables

crisp salad

1 Mix together the milk and mustard in a bowl. Mix the cheese with the flour and chives on a plate.

2 Dip the chicken into the milk and mustard mixture, brushing with a pastry brush to coat evenly.

3 Dip the chicken breasts into the cheese mixture, pressing to coat them evenly all over.

4 Place on a baking tray (cookie sheet) and spoon any spare cheese coating on top.

5 Bake the chicken in a preheated oven, 200°C/400°F/Gas Mark 6, for 30–35 minutes, or until golden brown and the juices run clear, not pink, when pierced with a skewer.

6 Serve the chicken hot, with jacket potatoes and fresh vegetables, or serve cold, with a crisp salad.

COOK'S TIP

Part-boned chicken breasts are very suitable for pan-cooking and casseroling, as they stay moist and tender. Try using chicken quarters if part-boned breasts are unavailable.

Karahi Chicken

A karahi is an extremely versatile two-handled metal pan, similar to a wok. Food is always cooked over a high heat in a karahi.

NUTRITIONAL INFORMATION

Calories 270	Sugars 1g	
Protein 41g	Fat 11g	
Carbohydrate 1g	Saturates 2g	

5 MINS   20 MINS

SERVES 4

I N G R E D I E N T S

2 tbsp ghee

3 garlic cloves, crushed

1 onion, chopped finely

2 tbsp garam masala

1 tsp coriander seeds, ground

½ tsp dried mint

1 bay leaf

750 g/1 lb 10 oz lean boneless chicken
    meat, diced

200 ml/7 fl oz/scant 1 cup chicken stock

1 tbsp fresh coriander (cilantro), chopped

salt

warm naan bread or chapatis, to serve

1 Heat the ghee in a karahi, wok or a large, heavy frying pan (skillet). Add the garlic and onion. Stir-fry for about 4 minutes until the onion is golden.

2 Stir in the garam masala, ground coriander, mint and bay leaf.

3 Add the chicken and cook over a high heat, stirring occasionally, for about 5 minutes. Add the stock and simmer for 10 minutes, until the sauce has thickened and the chicken juices run clear when the meat is tested with a sharp knife.

4 Stir in the fresh coriander (cilantro) and mix well, salt to taste and serve immediately with warm naan bread or chapatis.

COOK'S TIP

Always heat a kahari or wok before you add the oil to help maintain the high temperature.

Crispy Stuffed Chicken

An attractive main course of chicken breasts filled with mixed (bell) peppers and set on a sea of red (bell) peppers and tomato sauce.

NUTRITIONAL INFORMATION

Calories 196	Sugars 4g	
Protein 29g	Fat 6g	
Carbohydrate 6g	Saturates 2g	

20 MINS   50 MINS

SERVES 4

INGREDIENTS

4 boneless chicken breasts, about 150 g/
5½ oz each, skinned

4 sprigs fresh tarragon

½ small orange (bell) pepper, deseeded and
sliced

½ small green (bell) pepper, deseeded and
sliced

15 g/½ oz wholemeal breadcrumbs

1 tbsp sesame seeds

4 tbsp lemon juice

1 small red (bell) pepper, halved and
deseeded

200 g/7 oz can chopped tomatoes

1 small red chilli, deseeded and chopped

¼ tsp celery salt

salt and pepper

fresh tarragon, to garnish

1 Preheat the oven to 200°C/400°F/Gas Mark 6. Slit the chicken breasts with a small, sharp knife to create a pocket in each. Season inside each pocket.

2 Place a sprig of tarragon and a few slices of orange and green (bell) peppers in each pocket. Place the chicken breasts on a non-stick baking tray (cookie sheet) and sprinkle over the breadcrumbs and sesame seeds.

3 Spoon 1 tablespoon lemon juice over each chicken breast and bake in the oven for 35–40 minutes until the chicken is tender and cooked through.

4 Meanwhile, preheat the grill (broiler) to hot. Arrange the red (bell) pepper halves, skin side up, on the rack and cook for 5–6 minutes until the skin blisters. Leave to cool for 10 minutes, then peel off the skins.

5 Put the red (bell) pepper in a blender, add the tomatoes, chilli and celery salt and process for a few seconds. Season to taste. Alternatively, finely chop the red (bell) pepper and press through a sieve with the tomatoes and chilli.

6 When the chicken is cooked, heat the sauce, spoon a little on to a warm plate and arrange a chicken breast in the centre. Garnish with tarragon and serve.

Chicken with Whisky Sauce

After cooking with stock and vegetables, chicken breasts are served with a velvety sauce made from whisky and low-fat crème fraîche.

NUTRITIONAL INFORMATION

Calories ....337 Sugars 6g
Protein ....37g Fat 15g
Carbohydrate ....6g Saturates 8g

5 MINS   30 MINS

SERVES 4

I N G R E D I E N T S

25 g/1 oz/2 tbsp butter

60 g/2 oz/½ cup shredded leeks

60 g/2 oz/⅓ cup diced carrot

60 g/2 oz/¼ cup diced celery

4 shallots, sliced

600 ml/1 pint/2½ cups chicken stock

6 chicken breasts

50 ml/2 fl oz/¼ cup whisky

200 ml/7 fl oz/1 cup low-fat crème fraîche

2 tbsp freshly grated horseradish

1 tsp honey, warmed

1 tsp chopped fresh parsley

salt and pepper

parsley, to garnish

TO SERVE

vegetable patty

mashed potato

fresh vegetables

1 Melt the butter in a large saucepan and add the leeks, carrot, celery and shallots. Cook for 3 minutes, add half the chicken stock and cook for about 8 minutes.

2 Add the remaining chicken stock, and bring to the boil. Add the chicken breasts and cook for 10 minutes.

3 Remove the chicken and thinly slice. Place on a large, hot serving dish and keep warm.

4 In another saucepan, heat the whisky until reduced by half. Strain the chicken stock through a fine sieve, add to the pan and reduce the liquid by half.

5 Add the crème fraîche, the horseradish and the honey. Heat gently and add the chopped fresh parsley and salt and pepper to taste.

6 Pour a little of the whisky sauce around the chicken and pour the remaining sauce into a sauceboat to serve.

7 Serve with a vegetable patty made from the leftover vegetables, mashed potato and fresh vegetables. Garnish with parsley.

Chicken Tikka Masala

Try serving the chicken with mango chutney, lime pickle and cucumber raita. Add poppadoms and rice to make a delicious meal.

NUTRITIONAL INFORMATION

Calories 353   Sugars 8g
Protein ....44g   Fat 16g
Carbohydrate ....8g   Saturates 2g

2¼ HOURS   50 MINS

SERVES 4

INGREDIENTS

½ onion, chopped coarsely

60 g/2 oz/3 tbsp tomato purée (paste)

1 tsp cumin seeds

2.5 cm/1 inch piece ginger root, chopped

3 tbsp lemon juice

2 garlic cloves, crushed

2 tsp chilli powder

750 g/1 lb 10 oz boneless chicken

salt and pepper

fresh mint sprigs, to garnish

MASALA SAUCE

2 tbsp ghee

1 onion, sliced

1 tbsp black onion seeds

3 garlic cloves, crushed

2 fresh green chillies, chopped

200 g/7 oz can tomatoes

125 ml/4 fl oz/½ cup low-fat natural yogurt

125 ml/4 fl oz/½ cup coconut milk

1 tbsp chopped fresh coriander (cilantro)

1 tbsp chopped fresh mint

2 tbsp lemon or lime juice

½ tsp garam masala

sprigs of fresh mint, to garnish

1 Combine the first seven ingredients and seasoning in a food processor or blender and then transfer to a bowl. Cut chicken into 4 cm/1½ inch cubes. Stir into the bowl and leave for 2 hours.

2 Make the masala sauce. Heat the ghee in a saucepan, add the onion and stir over a medium heat for 5 minutes. Add the spices and garlic. Add the tomatoes, yogurt and coconut milk, bring to the boil, then simmer for 20 minutes.

3 Divide the chicken evenly between 8 oiled skewers and cook under a preheated very hot grill (broiler) for 15 minutes, turning frequently. Remove chicken and add to the sauce. Stir in the herbs, lemon or lime juice, and garam masala. Serve garnished with mint sprigs.

Chicken with Chilli & Basil

Chicken drumsticks are cooked in a delicious sauce and served with deep-fried basil for colour and flavour.

NUTRITIONAL INFORMATION

Calories 196	Sugars 2g
Protein 23g	Fat 10g
Carbohydrate 3g	Saturates 2g

 5 MINS   🕐 30 MINS

SERVES 4

I N G R E D I E N T S

8 chicken drumsticks

2 tbsp soy sauce

1 tbsp sunflower oil

1 red chilli

100 g/3½ oz carrots, cut into thin sticks

6 celery stalks, cut into sticks

3 tbsp sweet chilli sauce

oil, for frying

about 50 fresh basil leaves

1 Remove the skin from the chicken drumsticks if desired. Make 3 slashes in each drumstick. Brush the drumsticks with the soy sauce.

2 Heat the sunflower oil in a preheated wok and fry the drumsticks for 20 minutes, turning frequently, until they are cooked through.

3 Deseed and finely chop the chilli. Add the chilli, carrots and celery to the wok and cook for a further 5 minutes. Stir in the chilli sauce, cover and allow to bubble gently whilst preparing the basil leaves.

4 Heat a little oil in a heavy based pan. Carefully add the basil leaves – stand well away from the pan and protect

your hand with a tea towel (dish cloth) as they may spit a little. Cook the basil leaves for about 30 seconds or until they begin to curl up but not brown. Leave the leaves to drain on absorbent kitchen paper (paper towels).

5 Arrange the cooked chicken, vegetables and pan juices on to a warm serving plate, garnish with the deep-fried crispy basil leaves and serve immediately.

COOK'S TIP

Basil has a very strong flavour which is perfect with chicken and Chinese flavourings. You could use baby spinach instead of the basil, if you prefer.

Chinese Chicken Rice

This is a really colourful main meal or side dish which tastes just as good as it looks.

NUTRITIONAL INFORMATION

Calories	324	Sugars	.........4g
Protein	........24g	Fat	..........10g
Carbohydrate	...37g	Saturates	.......2g

5 MINS   25 MINS

SERVES 4

INGREDIENTS

350 g/12 oz/1¾ cups long-grain white rice

1 tsp turmeric

2 tbsp sunflower oil

350 g/12 oz skinless, boneless chicken breasts or thighs, sliced

1 red (bell) pepper, deseeded and sliced

1 green (bell) pepper, deseeded and sliced

1 green chilli, deseeded and finely chopped

1 medium carrot, coarsely grated

150 g/5½ oz/1½ cups bean sprouts

6 spring onions (scallions), sliced, plus extra to garnish

2 tbsp soy sauce

salt

1 Place the rice and turmeric in a large saucepan of lightly salted water and cook until the grains of rice are just tender, about 10 minutes. Drain the rice thoroughly and press out any excess water with kitchen paper (paper towels)

2 Heat the sunflower oil in a large preheated wok or frying pan (skillet).

3 Add the strips of chicken to the wok or frying pan (skillet) and stir-fry over a high heat until the chicken is just beginning to turn a golden colour.

4 Add the sliced (bell) peppers and green chilli to the wok and stir-fry for 2–3 minutes.

5 Add the cooked rice to the wok, a little at a time, tossing well after each addition until well combined and the grains of rice are separated.

6 Add the carrot, bean sprouts and spring onions (scallions) to the wok and stir-fry for a further 2 minutes.

7 Drizzle with the soy sauce and toss to combine.

8 Transfer the Chinese chicken rice to a warm serving dish, garnish with extra spring onions (scallions), if wished and serve at once.

Sage Chicken & Rice

Cooking in a single pot means that all of the flavours are retained. This is a substantial meal that needs only a salad and some crusty bread.

NUTRITIONAL INFORMATION

Calories	247	Sugars	.........5g
Protein	........26g	Fat	...........5g
Carbohydrate	...25g	Saturates	......2g

 10 MINS   ⏱ 50 MINS

SERVES 4

I N G R E D I E N T S

1 large onion, chopped

1 garlic clove, crushed

2 sticks celery, sliced

2 carrots, diced

2 sprigs fresh sage

300 ml/½ pint/1¼ cups chicken stock

350 g/12 oz boneless, skinless chicken breasts

225 g/8 oz/1⅓ cups mixed brown and wild rice

400 g/14 oz can chopped tomatoes

dash of Tabasco sauce

2 medium courgettes (zucchini), trimmed and thinly sliced

100 g/3½ oz lean ham, diced

salt and pepper

fresh sage, to garnish

TO SERVE

salad leaves

crusty bread

1 Place the pieces of onion, garlic, celery, carrots and sprigs of fresh sage in a large saucepan and pour in the chicken stock.

2 Bring to the boil, cover the pan and simmer for 5 minutes.

3 Cut the chicken into 2.5 cm/1 inch cubes and stir into the pan with the vegetables. Cover the pan and continue to cook for a further 5 minutes.

4 Stir in the mixed brown and wild rice and chopped tomatoes.

5 Add a dash of Tabasco sauce to taste and season well. Bring to the boil, cover and simmer for 25 minutes.

6 Stir in the sliced courgettes (zucchini) and diced ham and continue to cook, uncovered, for a further 10 minutes, stirring occasionally, until the rice is just tender.

7 Remove and discard the sprigs of sage.

8 Garnish with sage leaves and serve with a salad and fresh crusty bread.

Oyster Sauce Noodles

Chicken and noodles are cooked and then tossed in an oyster sauce and egg mixture in this delicious recipe.

NUTRITIONAL INFORMATION

Calories 278   Sugars 2g
Protein ....30g   Fat 12g
Carbohydrate ...13g   Saturates 3g

5 MINS   25 MINS

SERVES 4

INGREDIENTS

250 g/9 oz egg noodles

450 g/1 lb chicken thighs

2 tbsp groundnut oil

100 g/3½ oz carrots, sliced

3 tbsp oyster sauce

2 eggs

3 tbsp cold water

1 Place the egg noodles in a large bowl or dish. Pour enough boiling water over the noodles to cover and leave to stand for 10 minutes.

2 Meanwhile, remove the skin from the chicken thighs. Cut the chicken flesh into small pieces, using a sharp knife.

VARIATION

Flavour the eggs with soy sauce or hoisin sauce as an alternative to the oyster sauce, if you prefer.

3 Heat the groundnut oil in a large preheated wok or frying pan (skillet), swirling the oil around the base of the wok until it is really hot.

4 Add the pieces of chicken and the carrot slices to the wok and stir-fry for about 5 minutes.

5 Drain the noodles thoroughly. Add the noodles to the wok and stir-fry for a further 2–3 minutes or until the noodles are heated through.

6 Beat together the oyster sauce, eggs and 3 tablespoons of cold water. Drizzle the mixture over the noodles and stir-fry for a further 2–3 minutes or until the eggs set.

7 Transfer the mixture in the wok to warm serving bowls and serve hot.

Risotto à la Milanese

This famous dish is known throughout the world, and it is perhaps the best known of all Italian risottos, although there are many variations.

NUTRITIONAL INFORMATION

Calories 857	Sugars 1g	
Protein 57g	Fat 38g	
Carbohydrate ...72g	Saturates 21g	

 5 MINS   55 MINS

SERVES 4

I N G R E D I E N T S

125 g/4½ oz/½ cup butter

900 g/2 lb chicken meat, sliced thinly

1 large onion, chopped

500 g/1 lb 2 oz/2½ cups risotto rice

600 ml/1 pint/2½ cups chicken stock

150 ml/¼ pint/⅔ cup white wine

1 tsp crumbled saffron

salt and pepper

60 g/2 oz/½ cup grated Parmesan cheese,
    to serve

1 Heat 60 g/2 oz/4 tbsp of butter in a deep frying pan (skillet), and fry the chicken and onion until golden brown.

2 Add the rice, stir well, and cook for 15 minutes.

3 Heat the stock until boiling and gradually add to the rice. Add the white wine, saffron, salt and pepper to taste and mix well. Simmer gently for 20 minutes, stirring occasionally, and adding more stock if the risotto becomes too dry.

4 Leave to stand for 2–3 minutes and just before serving, add a little more stock and simmer for 10 minutes. Serve the risotto, sprinkled with the grated Parmesan cheese and the remaining butter.

Sweet-Sour Chicken

This sweet-citrusy chicken is delicious hot or cold. Sesame-flavoured noodles are the ideal accompaniment for the hot version.

NUTRITIONAL INFORMATION

Calories 248   Sugars 8g
Protein . . . . .30g   Fat 8g
Carbohydrate . . .16g   Saturates 2g

 5 MINS   25 MINS

SERVES 4

I N G R E D I E N T S

4 boneless chicken breasts, about 125 g/
  4½ oz each

2 tbsp clear honey

1 tbsp dark soy sauce

1 tsp lemon rind, finely grated

1 tbsp lemon juice

salt and pepper

TO GARNISH

1 tbsp fresh chives, chopped

lemon rind, grated

NOODLES

225 g/8 oz rice noodles

2 tsp sesame oil

1 tbsp sesame seeds

1 tsp lemon rind, finely grated

1 Preheat the grill (broiler) to medium. Skin and trim the chicken breasts to remove any excess fat, then wash and pat them dry with absorbent kitchen paper. Using a sharp knife, score the chicken breasts with a criss-cross pattern on both sides (making sure that you do not cut all the way through the meat).

2 Mix together the honey, soy sauce, lemon rind and juice in a small bowl, and then season well with black pepper.

3 Arrange the chicken breasts on the grill (broiler) rack and brush with half the honey mixture. Cook for 10 minutes, turn over and brush with the remaining mixture. Cook for a further 8–10 minutes or until cooked through.

4 Meanwhile, prepare the noodles according to the instructions on the packet. Drain well and transfer to a warm serving bowl. Mix the noodles with the sesame oil, sesame seeds and the lemon rind. Season and keep warm.

5 Drain the chicken and serve with a small mound of noodles, garnished with chopped chives and grated lemon rind.

VARIATION

For a different flavour, replace the lemon with orange or lime. If you prefer, serve the chicken with boiled rice or pasta, which you can flavour with sesame seeds and citrus rind in the same way.

Braised Chicken

This is a delicious way to cook a whole chicken. It has a wonderful glaze, which is served as a sauce.

NUTRITIONAL INFORMATION

Calories 294   Sugars 9g
Protein ....31g   Fat 15g
Carbohydrate ...10g   Saturates 3g

5 MINS   1¼ HOURS

SERVES 4

INGREDIENTS

1.5 kg/3 lb 5 oz chicken

3 tbsp vegetable oil

1 tbsp peanut oil

2 tbsp dark brown sugar

5 tbsp dark soy sauce

150 ml/¼ pint/⅔ cup water

2 garlic cloves, crushed

1 small onion, chopped

1 fresh red chilli, chopped

celery leaves and chives,
    to garnish

1   Preheat a large wok or large frying pan (skillet).

2   Clean the chicken inside and out with damp kitchen paper (paper towels).

3   Put the vegetable oil and peanut oil in the wok, add the dark brown sugar and heat gently until the sugar caramelizes.

4   Stir the soy sauce into the wok. Add the chicken and turn it in the mixture to coat thoroughly on all sides.

5   Add the water, garlic, onion and chilli. Cover and simmer, turning the chicken occasionally, for about 1 hour, or until cooked through. Test by piercing a thigh with the point of a knife or a skewer – the juices will run clear when the chicken is cooked.

6   Remove the chicken from the wok and set aside. Increase the heat and reduce the sauce in the wok until thickened. Transfer the chicken to a serving plate, garnish with celery leaves and chives and serve with the sauce.

COOK'S TIP

For a spicier sauce, add 1 tbsp finely chopped fresh root ginger and 1 tbsp ground Szechuan peppercorns with the chilli in step 5.

Cumin-spiced Chicken

Cumin seeds are more frequently associated with Indian cooking, but they are used in this Chinese recipe for their earthy flavour.

NUTRITIONAL INFORMATION

Calories 245	Sugars 9g	
Protein 28g	Fat 10g	
Carbohydrate 11g	Saturates 2g	

 5 MINS   15 MINS

SERVES 4

I N G R E D I E N T S

450 g/1 lb boneless, skinless chicken
  breasts

2 tbsp sunflower oil

1 clove garlic, crushed

1 tbsp cumin seeds

1 tbsp grated fresh ginger root

1 red chilli, deseeded and sliced

1 red (bell) pepper, deseeded and sliced

1 green (bell) pepper, deseeded and sliced

1 yellow (bell) pepper, deseeded and sliced

100 g/3½ oz/1 cup bean sprouts

350 g/12 oz pak choi or other green leaves

2 tbsp sweet chilli sauce

3 tbsp light soy sauce

deep-fried crispy ginger, to garnish (see
  Cook's Tip)

COOK'S TIP

To make the deep-fried ginger garnish, peel and thinly slice a large piece of root ginger. Carefully lower the slices of ginger into a wok or small pan of hot oil and cook for about 30 seconds. Transfer to kitchen paper and leave to drain thoroughly.

1 Using a sharp knife, slice the chicken breasts into thin strips.

2 Heat the oil in a large preheated wok.

3 Add the chicken to the wok and stir-fry for 5 minutes.

4 Add the garlic, cumin seeds, ginger and chilli to the wok, stirring to mix.

5 Add all the (bell) peppers to the wok and stir-fry for a further 5 minutes.

6 Toss in the bean sprouts and pak choi together with the sweet chilli sauce and soy sauce and continue to cook until the pak choi leaves start to wilt.

7 Transfer to warm serving bowls and garnish with deep-fried ginger (see Cook's Tip).

Fragrant Spiced Chicken

The combination of chicken and chick-peas (garbanzo beans) is particlarly good. Use the canned variety for a quick meal.

NUTRITIONAL INFORMATION

Calories 343   Sugars 5g
Protein . . . . .28g   Fat 16g
Carbohydrate . . .24g   Saturates 3g

5 MINS   30 MINS

SERVES 4

I N G R E D I E N T S

3 tbsp ghee or vegetable oil

8 small chicken portions, such as thighs or drumsticks

1 large onion, peeled and chopped

2 garlic cloves, peeled and crushed

1-2 fresh green chillies, seeded and chopped, or use 1-2 tsp minced chilli (from a jar)

2 tsp ground cumin

2 tsp ground coriander

1 tsp garam masala

1 tsp ground turmeric

1 x 400 g/14 oz can chopped tomatoes

150 ml/¼ pint/⅔ cup water

1 tbsp chopped fresh mint

1 x 400 g/14 oz can chick-peas (garbanzo beans), drained

salt

1 tbsp chopped fresh coriander (cilantro)

low-fat natural yogurt, to serve (optional)

1 Heat the ghee or oil in a large saucepan and fry the chicken.

2 Fry the pieces all over until sealed and lightly golden. Remove from the pan. Add the onion, garlic, chilli and spices and cook very gently for 2 minutes, stirring frequently.

3 Stir in the tomatoes, water, mint and chick-peas (garbanzo beans). Mix well, return the chicken portions to the pan, season with salt, then cover and simmer gently for about 20 minutes or until the chicken is tender.

4 Taste and adjust the seasoning if necessary, then sprinkle with the chopped coriander (cilantro) and serve hot, drizzled with yogurt (if using).

VARIATION

Canned black-eyed beans and red kidney beans also make delicious additions to this spicy chicken dish. Be sure to drain and rinse canned beans before adding to the pan.

Chicken & Balsamic Vinegar

A rich caramelized sauce, flavoured with balsamic vinegar and wine, adds a piquant flavour. The chicken needs to be marinated overnight.

NUTRITIONAL INFORMATION

Calories	148	Sugars	.......0.2g
Protein	........11g	Fat	...........8g
Carbohydrate	...0.2g	Saturates	.......3g

 10 MINS   35 MINS

SERVES 4

INGREDIENTS

4 chicken thighs, boned

2 garlic cloves, crushed

200 ml/7 fl oz/¾ cup red wine

3 tbsp white wine vinegar

1 tbsp oil

15 g/½ oz/1 tbsp butter

6 shallots

3 tbsp balsamic vinegar

2 tbsp fresh thyme

salt and pepper

cooked polenta or rice, to serve

1 Using a sharp knife, make a few slashes in the skin of the chicken. Brush the chicken with the crushed garlic and place in a non-metallic dish.

2 Pour the wine and white wine vinegar over the chicken and season with salt and pepper to taste. Cover and leave to marinate in the refrigerator overnight.

3 Remove the chicken pieces with a perforated spoon, draining well, and reserve the marinade.

4 Heat the oil and butter in a frying pan (skillet). Add the shallots and cook for 2–3 minutes or until they begin to soften.

5 Add the chicken pieces to the pan and cook for 3-4 minutes, turning, until browned all over. Reduce the heat and add half of the reserved marinade. Cover and cook for 15–20 minutes, adding more marinade when necessary.

6 Once the chicken is tender, add the balsamic vinegar and thyme and cook for a further 4 minutes.

7 Transfer the chicken and marinade to serving plates and serve with polenta or rice.

COOK'S TIP

To make the chicken pieces look a little neater, use wooden skewers to hold them together or secure them with a length of string.

Speedy Peanut Pan-fry

Thread egg noodles are the ideal accompaniment to this quick dish because they can be cooked quickly and easily while the stir-fry sizzles.

NUTRITIONAL INFORMATION

Calories 563	Sugars 7g
Protein 45g	Fat 33g
Carbohydrate ...22g	Saturates 7g

  5 MINS   15 MINS

SERVES 4

INGREDIENTS

300 g/10½ oz/2 cups courgettes (zucchini)

250 g/9 oz/1⅓ cups baby corn (corn-on-the-cob)

250 g/9 oz thread egg noodles

2 tbsp corn oil

1 tbsp sesame oil

8 boneless chicken thighs or 4 breasts, sliced thinly

300 g/10½ oz/3¾ cups button mushrooms

350 g/12 oz/1½ cups bean sprouts

4 tbsp smooth peanut butter

2 tbsp soy sauce

2 tbsp lime or lemon juice

60 g/2 oz/½ cup roasted peanuts

salt and pepper

coriander (cilantro), to garnish

1 Using a sharp knife, trim and thinly slice the courgettes (zucchini) and baby corn (corn-on-the-cob). Set the vegetables aside until required.

2 Cook the noodles in lightly salted boiling water for 3–4 minutes.

3 Meanwhile, heat the corn oil and sesame oil in a large wok or frying pan (skillet) and fry the chicken over a fairly high heat for 1 minute.

4 Add the courgettes (zucchini), corn and mushrooms and stir-fry for 5 minutes.

5 Add the bean sprouts, peanut butter, soy sauce, lime or lemon juice and pepper, then cook for a further 2 minutes.

6 Drain the noodles thoroughly. Scatter with the roasted peanuts and serve with the noodles. Garnish with fresh coriander (cilantro).

COOK'S TIP

Try serving this stir-fry with rice sticks. These are broad, pale, translucent ribbon noodles made from ground rice.

Chicken on Crispy Noodles

Blanched noodles are fried in the wok until crisp and brown, and then topped with a shredded chicken sauce for a delightfully tasty dish.

NUTRITIONAL INFORMATION

Calories . . . . . . .376 Sugars 2g
Protein . . . . .15g Fat 27g
Carbohydrate . . .17g Saturates 4g

 35 MINS 25 MINS

SERVES 4

INGREDIENTS

225 g/8 oz skinless, boneless chicken breasts, shredded

1 egg white

5 tsp cornflour (cornstarch)

225 g/8 oz thin egg noodles

300 ml/½ pint/1⅓ cups vegetable oil

600 ml/1 pint/2½ cups chicken stock

2 tbsp dry sherry

2 tbsp oyster sauce

1 tbsp light soy sauce

1 tbsp hoisin sauce

1 red (bell) pepper, seeded and very thinly sliced

2 tbsp water

3 spring onions (scallions), chopped

1 Mix together the chicken, egg white and 2 teaspoons of the cornflour (cornstarch) in a bowl. Leave to stand for at least 30 minutes.

2 Blanch the noodles in boiling water for 2 minutes, then drain thoroughly.

3 Heat the vegetable oil in a preheated wok. Add the noodles, spreading them to cover the base of the wok. Cook over a low heat for about 5 minutes, until the noodles are browned on the underside.

Flip the noodles over and brown on the other side. Remove from the wok when crisp and browned, place on a serving plate and keep warm. Drain the oil from the wok.

4 Add 300 ml/½ pint/1¼ cups of the chicken stock to the wok. Remove from the heat and add the chicken, stirring well so that it does not stick. Return to the heat and cook for 2 minutes. Drain, discarding the stock.

5 Wipe the wok with kitchen paper (paper towels) and return to the heat. Add the sherry, sauces, (bell) pepper and the remaining stock and bring to the boil. Blend the remaining cornflour (cornstarch) with the water and stir it into the mixture.

6 Return the chicken to the wok and cook over a low heat for 2 minutes. Place the chicken on top of the noodles and sprinkle with spring onions (scallions).

Chinese Risotto

Risotto is a creamy Italian dish made with arborio or risotto rice. This Chinese version is simply delicious!

NUTRITIONAL INFORMATION

Calories 436	Sugars 7g
Protein 13g	Fat 14g
Carbohydrate ...70g	Saturates 4g

 5 MINS   25 MINS

SERVES 4

INGREDIENTS

2 tbsp groundnut oil

1 onion, sliced

2 cloves garlic, crushed

1 tsp Chinese five-spice powder

225 g/8 oz Chinese sausage, sliced

225 g/8 oz carrots, diced

1 green (bell) pepper, deseeded and diced

275 g/9½oz/1⅓ cups risotto rice

850 ml/1½ pints/1¾ cups vegetable or chicken stock

1 tbsp fresh chives

1 Heat the groundnut oil in a large preheated wok or heavy-based frying pan (skillet).

2 Add the onion slices, crushed garlic and Chinese five-spice powder to the wok or frying pan (skillet) and stir-fry for 1 minute.

3 Add the Chinese sausage, carrots and green (bell) pepper to the wok and stir to combine.

4 Stir in the risotto rice and cook for 1 minute.

5 Gradually add the vegetable or chicken stock, a little at a time, stirring constantly until the liquid has been completely absorbed and the rice grains are tender.

6 Snip the chives with a pair of clean kitchen scissors and stir into the wok with the last of the stock.

7 Transfer the Chinese risotto to warm serving bowls and serve immediately.

COOK'S TIP

Chinese sausage is highly flavoured and is made from chopped pork fat, pork meat and spices. Use a spicy Portuguese sausage if Chinese sausage is unavailable.

Chicken Chow Mein

This classic dish requires no introduction as it is already a favourite amongst most Chinese food-eaters.

NUTRITIONAL INFORMATION

Calories ....230 Sugars 2g
Protein ....19g Fat 11g
Carbohydrate ...14g Saturates 2g

 5 MINS   20 MINS

SERVES 4

I N G R E D I E N T S

250 g/9 oz packet medium egg
  noodles

2 tbsp sunflower oil

275 g/9½ oz cooked chicken breasts,
  shredded

1 clove garlic, finely chopped

1 red (bell) pepper, deseeded and thinly
  sliced

100 g/3½ oz shiitake mushrooms,
  sliced

6 spring onions (scallions), sliced

100 g/3½ oz/1 cup bean sprouts

3 tbsp soy sauce

1 tbsp sesame oil

1 Place the egg noodles in a large bowl or dish and break them up slightly. Pour over enough boiling water to cover the noodles and leave to stand.

2 Heat the sunflower oil in a large preheated wok. Add the shredded chicken, finely chopped garlic, (bell) pepper slices, mushrooms, spring onions (scallions) and bean sprouts to the wok and stir-fry for about 5 minutes.

3 Drain the noodles thoroughly. Add the noodles to the wok, toss well and stir-fry for a further 5 minutes.

4 Drizzle the soy sauce and sesame oil over the chow mein and toss until well combined.

5 Transfer the chicken chow mein to warm serving bowls and serve immediately.

VARIATION

You can make the chow mein with a selection of vegetables for a vegetarian dish, if you prefer.

Quick Chicken Noodles

Chicken and fresh vegetables are flavoured with ginger and Chinese five-spice powder in this speedy stir-fry.

NUTRITIONAL INFORMATION

Calories 266   Sugars 4g
Protein ....25g   Fat 13g
Carbohydrate ...12g   Saturates 2g

10 MINS   15 MINS

SERVES 4

INGREDIENTS

175 g/6 oz Chinese thread egg noodles

2 tbsp sesame or vegetable oil

25 g/1 oz/¼ cup peanuts

1 bunch spring onions (scallions), sliced

1 green (bell) pepper, deseeded and cut into
thin strips

1 large carrot, cut into matchsticks

125 g/4½ oz cauliflower, broken into small
florets

350 g/12 oz skinless, boneless chicken, cut
into strips

250 g/9 oz mushrooms, sliced

1 tsp finely grated ginger root

1 tsp Chinese five-spice powder

1 tbsp chopped fresh coriander (cilantro)

1 tbsp light soy sauce

salt and pepper

fresh chives, to garnish

chicken to the pan. Stir-fry over a high heat for 4–5 minutes.

1 Put the noodles in a large bowl and cover with boiling water. Leave to soak for 6 minutes.

2 Heat the oil in a wok and stir-fry the peanuts for 1 minute until browned. Remove from the wok and leave to drain.

3 Add the spring onions (scallions), (bell) pepper, carrot, cauliflower and

4 Drain the noodles thoroughly and add to the wok. Add the mushrooms and stir-fry for 2 minutes. Add the ginger, five-spice and coriander (cilantro); stir-fry for 1 minute.

5 Season with soy sauce and salt and pepper. Sprinkle with the peanuts, garnish and serve.

VARIATION

Instead of ginger root, ½ teaspoon ground ginger can be used. Vary the vegetables according to what is in season. Make the most of bargains bought from your greengrocer or market.

Chicken & Lobster on Penne

While this is certainly a treat to get the taste buds tingling,
it is not as extravagant as it sounds.

NUTRITIONAL INFORMATION

Calories 696	Sugars 4g
Protein 59g	Fat 32g
Carbohydrate ...45g	Saturates 9g

🍲 20 MINS   🕐 30 MINS

SERVES 6

INGREDIENTS

butter, for greasing

6 chicken breasts

450 g/1 lb dried penne rigate

6 tbsp extra virgin olive oil

90 g/3 oz/1 cup freshly grated
   Parmesan cheese

salt

FILLING

115 g/4 oz lobster meat, chopped

2 shallots, very finely chopped

2 figs, chopped

1 tbsp Marsala

2 tbsp breadcrumbs

1 large egg, beaten

salt and pepper

1 Grease 6 pieces of foil large enough to enclose each chicken breast and lightly grease a baking tray (cookie sheet).

2 Place all of the filling ingredients into a mixing bowl and blend together thoroughly with a spoon.

3 Cut a pocket in each chicken breast with a sharp knife and fill with the lobster mixture. Wrap each chicken breast in foil, place the parcels on the greased baking tray (cookie sheet) and bake in a preheated oven at 200°C/400°F/Gas Mark 6 for 30 minutes.

4 Meanwhile, bring a large pan of lightly salted water to the boil. Add the pasta and 1 tablespoon of the olive oil and cook for about 10 minutes, or until tender but still firm to the bite. Drain the pasta thoroughly and transfer to a large serving plate. Sprinkle over the remaining olive oil and the grated Parmesan cheese, set aside and keep warm.

5 Carefully remove the foil from around the chicken breasts. Slice the breasts very thinly, arrange over the pasta and serve immediately.

COOK'S TIP

The cut of chicken known as
suprême consists of the breast
and wing. It is always skinned.

Mediterranean Chicken

This recipe uses ingredients found in the Languedoc area of France, where cooking over hot embers is a way of life.

NUTRITIONAL INFORMATION

Calories ....143 Sugars 4g
Protein ....13g Fat 8g
Carbohydrate ....4g Saturates 2g

2³/₄ HOURS   40 MINS

SERVES 4

INGREDIENTS

4 tbsp low-fat natural yogurt

3 tbsp sun-dried tomato paste

1 tbsp olive oil

15 g/½ oz/¼ cup fresh basil leaves, lightly crushed

2 garlic cloves, chopped roughly

4 chicken quarters

green salad, to serve

1 Combine the yogurt, tomato paste, olive oil, basil leaves and garlic in a small bowl and stir well to mix.

2 Put the marinade into a bowl large enough to hold the chicken quarters in a single layer. Add the chicken quarters. Make sure that the chicken pieces are thoroughly coated in the marinade.

3 Leave to marinate in the refrigerator for 2 hours. Remove and leave covered at room temperature for 30 minutes.

4 Place the chicken over a medium barbecue and cook for 30–40 minutes, turning frequently. Test for readiness by piercing the flesh at the thickest part – usually at the top of the drumstick. If the juices that run out are clear, it is cooked through.

5 Serve hot with a green salad. It is also delicious eaten cold.

VARIATION

For a marinade with an extra zingy flavour combine 2 garlic cloves, coarsely chopped, the juice of 2 lemons and 3 tbsp olive oil, and cook in the same way.

Chicken & Seafood Parcels

These mouth-watering mini-parcels of chicken and prawns (shrimp) on a bed of pasta will delight your guests.

NUTRITIONAL INFORMATION

Calories 799   Sugars 5g
Protein . . . . .50g   Fat 45g
Carbohydrate . . .51g   Saturates 13g

45 MINS   25 MINS

SERVES 4

I N G R E D I E N T S

60 g/2 oz/4 tbsp butter, plus extra
   for greasing

4 x 200 g/7 oz chicken suprêmes, trimmed

115 g/4 oz large spinach leaves, trimmed
   and blanched in hot salted water

4 slices of Parma ham (prosciutto)

12–16 raw tiger prawns (shrimp), shelled
   and deveined

450 g/1 lb dried tagliatelle

1 tbsp olive oil

3 leeks, shredded

1 large carrot, grated

150 ml/¼ pint/⅔ cup thick mayonnaise

2 large cooked beetroot (beet)

salt

1 Grease 4 large pieces of foil and set aside. Place each suprême between 2 pieces of baking parchment and pound with a rolling pin to flatten.

2 Divide half of the spinach between the suprêmes, add a slice of ham to each and top with more spinach. Place 3–4 prawns (shrimp) on top of the spinach. Fold the pointed end of the suprême over the prawns (shrimp), then fold over again to form a parcel. Wrap in foil, place on a baking tray (cookie sheet) and bake in a preheated oven at 200°C/400°F/Gas Mark 6 for 20 minutes.

3 Meanwhile, bring a saucepan of salted water to the boil. Add the pasta and oil and cook for 8–10 minutes or until tender. Drain and transfer to a serving dish.

4 Melt the butter in a frying pan (skillet). Fry the leeks and carrots for 3 minutes. Transfer the vegetables to the centre of the pasta.

5 Work the mayonnaise and 1 beetroot (beet) in a food processor or blender until smooth. Rub through a strainer and pour around the pasta and vegetables.

6 Cut the remaining beetroot (beet) into diamond shapes and place them neatly around the mayonnaise. Remove the foil from the chicken and, using a sharp knife, cut the suprêmes into thin slices. Arrange the chicken and prawn (shrimp) slices on top of the vegetables and pasta, and serve.

Chicken Pasta Bake

Tender lean chicken is baked with pasta in a creamy low-fat sauce which contrasts well with the fennel and the sweetness of the raisins.

NUTRITIONAL INFORMATION

Calories 380	Sugars 15g	
Protein 39g	Fat 14g	
Carbohydrate ...27g	Saturates 6g	

15 MINS   45 MINS

SERVES 4

I N G R E D I E N T S

2 bulbs fennel

2 medium red onions, finely shredded

1 tbsp lemon juice

125 g/4½ oz button mushrooms

1 tbsp olive oil

225 g/8 oz penne (quills)

60 g/2 oz/⅓ cup raisins

225 g/8 oz lean, boneless cooked chicken, skinned and shredded

375 g/13 oz low-fat soft cheese with garlic and herbs

125 g/4½ oz low-fat Mozzarella cheese, thinly sliced

2 tbsp Parmesan cheese, grated

salt and pepper

chopped fennel fronds, to garnish

1 Preheat the oven to 200°C/400°F/Gas Mark 6. Trim the fennel, reserving the green fronds, and slice the bulbs thinly.

2 Generously coat the onions in the lemon juice. Quarter the mushrooms.

3 Heat the oil in a large frying pan (skillet) and fry the fennel, onion and mushrooms for 4–5 minutes, stirring, until just softened. Season well, transfer the mixture to a large bowl and set aside.

4 Bring a pan of lightly salted water to the boil and cook the penne (quills) according to the instructions on the packet until just cooked. Drain and mix the pasta with the vegetables.

5 Stir the raisins and chicken into the pasta mixture. Soften the soft cheese by beating it, then mix into the pasta and chicken – the heat from the pasta should make the cheese melt slightly.

6 Put the mixture into an ovenproof baking dish and transfer to a baking tray (cookie sheet). Arrange slices of Mozzarella cheese over the top and sprinkle with the grated Parmesan.

7 Bake in the oven for 20–25 minutes until golden-brown.

8 Garnish with chopped fennel fronds and serve hot.

Chicken Jalfrezi

This is a quick and tasty way to use leftover roast chicken. The sauce can also be used for any cooked poultry, lamb or beef.

NUTRITIONAL INFORMATION

Calories 270
Sugars 3g
Protein 36g
Fat 11g
Carbohydrate 7g
Saturates 2g

 25 MINS   15 MINS

SERVES 4

I N G R E D I E N T S

1 tsp mustard oil

3 tbsp vegetable oil

1 large onion, chopped finely

3 garlic cloves, crushed

1 tbsp tomato purée (paste)

2 tomatoes, skinned and chopped

1 tsp ground turmeric

½ tsp cumin seeds, ground

½ tsp coriander seeds, ground

½ tsp chilli powder

½ tsp garam masala

1 tsp red wine vinegar

1 small red (bell) pepper, chopped

125 g/4½ oz/1 cup frozen broad (fava) beans

500 g/1 lb 2 oz cooked chicken, cut into bite-sized pieces

salt

sprigs of fresh coriander (cilantro), to garnish

1 Heat the mustard oil in a large, frying pan (skillet) set over a high heat for about 1 minute until it begins to smoke.

2 Add the vegetable oil, reduce the heat and then add the onion and the garlic. Fry the garlic and onion until they are golden.

3 Add the tomato purée (paste), chopped tomatoes, turmeric, ground cumin and coriander seeds, chilli powder, garam masala and wine vinegar to the frying pan (skillet). Stir the mixture until fragrant.

4 Add the red (bell) pepper and broad (fava) beans and stir for 2 minutes until the pepper is softened. Stir in the chicken, and salt to taste.

5 Simmer gently for 6–8 minutes until the chicken is heated through and the beans are tender.

6 Serve garnished with sprigs of coriander (cilantro).

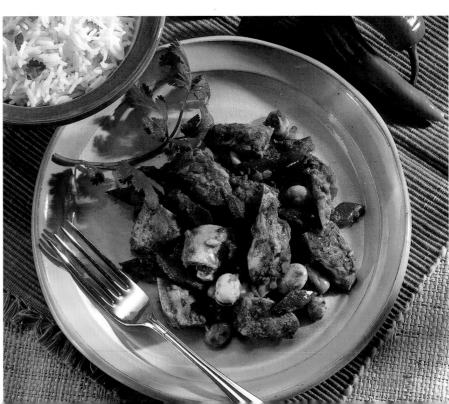

Celery & Cashew Chicken

Stir-fry yellow bean sauce gives this quick and easy Chinese dish a really authentic taste. Pecan nuts can be used in place of the cashews.

NUTRITIONAL INFORMATION

Calories 549	Sugars 24g	
Protein 41g	Fat 31g	
Carbohydrate . . .28g	Saturates 5g	

5 MINS   10 MINS

SERVES 4

I N G R E D I E N T S

3-4 boneless, skinned chicken breasts, about 625g/1 lb 6 oz

2 tbsp sunflower or vegetable oil

125 g/4½ oz/1 cup cashew nuts (unsalted)

4-6 spring onions (scallions), thinly sliced diagonally

5-6 celery sticks, thinly sliced diagonally

1 x 175 g/6 oz jar stir-fry yellow bean sauce

salt and pepper

celery leaves, to garnish (optional)

plain boiled rice, to serve

1 Using a sharp knife or metal cleaver, cut the chicken into thin slices across the grain.

2 Heat the oil in a preheated wok or large frying pan (skillet), swirling it around until it is really hot.

3 Add the cashew nuts and stir-fry until they begin to brown but do not allow them to burn.

4 Add the chicken and stir-fry until well sealed and almost cooked through.

5 Add the spring onions (scallions) and celery and continue to stir-fry for 2–3 minutes, stirring the food well around the wok.

6 Add the stir-fry yellow bean sauce to the wok or frying pan (skillet) and season lightly with salt and pepper.

7 Toss the mixture in the wok until the chicken and vegetables are thoroughly coated with the sauce and piping hot.

8 Serve at once with plain boiled rice, garnished with celery leaves, if liked.

VARIATION

This recipe can be adapted to use turkey fillets or steaks, or pork fillet or boneless steaks. Cut the turkey or pork lengthwise first, then slice thinly across the grain. Alternatively, cut into 2 cm/½ inch cubes.

Marinated Chicken Kebabs

Pieces of chicken marinated in yogurt, chutney and spices make meltingly tender kebabs, and are cooked quickly in the microwave.

NUTRITIONAL INFORMATION

Calories 180   Sugars 11g
Protein ....24g   Fat 5g
Carbohydrate ....11g   Saturates 1g

  1¼ HOURS   15 MINS

SERVES 4

INGREDIENTS

1 tbsp peach chutney

3 tbsp low-fat natural yogurt

½ tsp ground cumin

pinch of mixed (apple pie) spice

squeeze of lemon juice

3 chicken breast fillets, cut into even pieces

½ red (bell) pepper, cut into 16 even chunks

1 courgette (zucchini), cut into 16 slices

8 button mushrooms

salt and pepper

CHIVE & MINT DRESSING

150 ml/¼ pint/⅔ cup low-fat natural yogurt

2 tbsp low-fat mayonnaise

skimmed milk

1 tbsp chopped fresh chives

1 tbsp chopped fresh mint

mixed salad, to serve

TO GARNISH

sprigs of fresh mint

fresh chives

mixed salad, to serve

1 Mix the chutney, yogurt, spices and lemon juice together in a bowl. Season to taste.

2 Add the chicken to the bowl. Mix well and leave in a cool place to marinate for 1 hour.

3 Thread the red (bell) pepper, courgette (zucchini), chicken and mushrooms on to 8 long wooden skewers.

4 Arrange 4 skewers on a large plate or microwave rack. Cook on HIGH power for 6 minutes, turning over and rearranging halfway through. Repeat with the remaining 4 kebabs.

5 To make the chive and mint dressing, mix together all the ingredients and season with salt and pepper to taste. Spoon the dressing over the kebabs and garnish with mint and chives. Serve with a mixed salad.

Lime Fricassée of Chicken

The addition of lime juice and lime rind adds a delicious tangy flavour to this chicken stew.

NUTRITIONAL INFORMATION

Calories	235	Sugars	........3g
Protein	........20g	Fat	..........6g
Carbohydrate	...26g	Saturates	......1g

15 MINS   1¾ HOURS

SERVES 4

INGREDIENTS

2 tbsp oil

1 large chicken, cut into small portions

60 g/2 oz/½ cup flour, seasoned

500 g/1 lb 2 oz baby onions or shallots, sliced

1 each green and red (bell) pepper, sliced thinly

150 ml/¼ pint/⅔ cup chicken stock

juice and rind of 2 limes

2 chillies, chopped

2 tbsp oyster sauce

1 tsp Worcestershire sauce

salt and pepper

1 Heat the oil in a large frying pan (skillet). Coat the chicken pieces in the seasoned flour and cook for about 4 minutes until browned all over.

2 Transfer the chicken to a large casserole. Sprinkle with the onions.

3 Slowly fry the (bell) peppers in the juices in the frying pan.

4 Add the chicken stock, lime juice and rind and cook for a further 5 minutes.

5 Add the chillies, oyster sauce and Worcestershire sauce, mixing well.

6 Season to taste with salt and pepper, then pour the (bell) peppers and juices over the chicken and onions.

7 Cover the casserole with a lid or cooking foil.

8 Cook in the centre of a preheated oven, 190°C/375°F/Gas Mark 5, for 1½ hours until the chicken is very tender, then serve.

COOK'S TIP

Try this casserole with a cheese scone (biscuit) topping. About 30 minutes before the end of cooking time, simply top with rounds cut from cheese scone (biscuit) pastry.

Yellow Bean Noodles

Cellophane or thread noodles are excellent re-heated, unlike other noodles which must be served as soon as they are ready.

NUTRITIONAL INFORMATION

Calories 212   Sugars 0.5g
Protein . . . . .28g   Fat 7g
Carbohydrate . . .10g   Saturates 2g

5 MINS   30 MINS

SERVES 4

I N G R E D I E N T S

175 g/6 oz cellophane noodles

1 tbsp peanut oil

1 leek, sliced

2 garlic cloves, crushed

450 g/1 lb minced (ground) chicken

425 ml/¾ pint/1 cup chicken stock

1 tsp chilli sauce

2 tbsp yellow bean sauce

4 tbsp light soy sauce

1 tsp sesame oil

chopped chives, to garnish

1 Place the cellophane noodles in a bowl, pour over boiling water and soak for 15 minutes.

2 Drain the noodles thoroughly and cut into short lengths with a pair of kitchen scissors.

3 Heat the oil in a wok or frying pan (skillet) and stir-fry the leek and garlic for 30 seconds.

4 Add the chicken to the wok and stir-fry for 4–5 minutes, until the chicken is completely cooked through.

5 Add the chicken stock, chilli sauce, yellow bean sauce and soy sauce to the wok and cook for 3–4 minutes.

6 Add the drained noodles and sesame oil to the wok and cook, tossing to mix well, for 4–5 minutes.

7 Spoon the mixture into warm serving bowls, sprinkle with chopped chives and serve immediately.

COOK'S TIP

Cellophane noodles are available from many supermarkets and all Chinese supermarkets.

Chicken with (Bell) Peppers

Red (bell) pepper or celery can also be used in recipe, the method is the same.

NUTRITIONAL INFORMATION

Calories 113	Sugars 1g	
Protein 17g	Fat 3g	
Carbohydrate 4g	Saturates 1g	

🥘 5 MINS   🕐 5 MINS

SERVES 4

I N G R E D I E N T S

300 g/10½ oz boned, skinned chicken
    breast

1 tsp salt

½ egg white

2 tsp cornflour (cornstarch) paste (see
    page 6)

1 medium green (bell) pepper, cored and
    seeded

300 ml/½ pint/1¼ cups vegetable oil

1 spring onion (scallion), finely shredded

a few strips of ginger root, thinly shredded

1-2 red chillies, seeded and thinly
    shredded

½ tsp sugar

1 tbsp rice wine or dry sherry

a few drops of sesame oil

1 Cut the chicken breast into strips. Mix
the chicken with a pinch of the salt,
the egg white and cornflour (cornstarch).

2 Cut the green (bell) pepper into thin
shreds.

3 Heat the oil in a preheated wok, and
deep-fry the chicken strips in batches
for about 1 minute, or until the chicken
changes colour. Remove the chicken strips
with a slotted spoon, pat dry on kitchen
paper (paper towels) and keep warm.

4 Pour off the excess oil from the wok,
leaving about 1 tablespoon. Add the
spring onion (scallion), ginger, chillies
and green (bell) pepper and stir-fry for
1 minute.

5 Return the chicken to the wok with
the remaining salt, the sugar and
wine or sherry. Stir-fry for another
minute, sprinkle with sesame oil and serve
immediately.

COOK'S TIP

Rice wine is used every-
where in China for both cooking and drinking. Made from
glutinous rice, it is known as
'yellow wine' because of its rich
amber colour. Sherry is the best
substitute as a cooking ingredient.

Spicy Tomato Chicken

These low-fat, spicy skewers are cooked in a matter of minutes – assemble ahead of time and store in the fridge until you need them.

NUTRITIONAL INFORMATION

Calories . . . . . . .195 Sugars 11g
Protein . . . . .28g Fat 4g
Carbohydrate . . .12g Saturates 1g

 10 MINS   10 MINS

SERVES 4

I N G R E D I E N T S

500 g/1 lb 2 oz skinless, boneless chicken
　breasts

3 tbsp tomato purée (paste)

2 tbsp clear honey

2 tbsp Worcestershire sauce

1 tbsp chopped fresh rosemary

250 g/9 oz cherry tomatoes

sprigs of rosemary, to garnish

couscous or rice, to serve

1 Cut the chicken into 2.5 cm/1 inch chunks and place in a bowl.

2 Mix together the tomato purée (paste), honey, Worcestershire sauce and rosemary. Add to the chicken, stirring to coat evenly.

3 Alternating the chicken pieces and cherry tomatoes, thread them on to eight wooden skewers.

4 Spoon over any remaining glaze. Cook under a preheated hot grill (broiler)

for 8–10 minutes, turning occasionally, until the chicken is thoroughly cooked.

5 Serve on a bed of couscous or rice and garnish with sprigs of rosemary.

COOK'S TIP

Couscous is made from semolina that has been made into separate grains. It usually just needs moistening or steaming before serving.

Pot-Roast Orange Chicken

This colourful, nutritious pot-roast could be served for a family meal or for a special dinner. Add more vegetables if you're feeding a crowd.

NUTRITIONAL INFORMATION

Calories 302   Sugar 17g

Protein . . . . .29g   Fats 11g

Carbohydrates . . .22g   Saturates 2g

 10 MINS   2 HOURS

SERVES 4

INGREDIENTS

2 tbsp sunflower oil

1 chicken, weighing about 1.5 kg/3 lb 5 oz

2 large oranges

2 small onions, quartered

500 g/1 lb 2 oz/2 cups small whole carrots or thin carrots, cut into 5 cm/ 2 inch lengths

150ml/¼ pint/⅔ cup orange juice

2 tbsp brandy

2 tbsp sesame seeds

1 tbsp cornflour (cornstarch)

salt and pepper

1 Heat the oil in a large flameproof casserole and fry the chicken, turning occasionally until evenly browned.

2 Cut one orange in half and place half inside the cavity of the chicken. Place the chicken in a large, deep casserole. Arrange the onions and carrots around the chicken. Season with salt and pepper and pour over the orange juice.

3 Cut the remaining oranges into thin wedges and tuck around the chicken, among the vegetables.

4 Cover and cook in a preheated oven, 180°C/350°F/Gas Mark 4, for about 1½ hours, or until the chicken juices run clear when pierced, and the vegetables are tender. Remove the lid and sprinkle with the brandy and sesame seeds. Return to the oven for 10 minutes.

5 To serve, lift the chicken on to a large platter and add the vegetables. Skim any excess fat from the juices. Blend the cornflour with 1 tablespoon cold water, then stir into the juices and bring to the boil, stirring all the time. Adjust to taste, then serve the sauce with the chicken.

Golden Chicken Risotto

Long-grain rice can be used instead of risotto rice, but it won't give you the traditional, creamy texture that is typical of Italian risottos.

NUTRITIONAL INFORMATION

Calories 701   Sugars 7g
Protein . . . . .35g   Fat 26g
Carbohydrate . . .88g   Saturates 8g

 10 MINS   30 MINS

SERVES 4

INGREDIENTS

2 tbsp sunflower oil

15 g/ ½ oz/1 tbsp butter or margarine

1 medium leek, thinly sliced

1 large yellow (bell) pepper, diced

3 skinless, boneless chicken breasts, diced

350 g/12 oz arborio (risotto) rice

a few strands of saffron

1.5 litres/2 ¾ pints/6 ¼ cups chicken stock

200 g/7 oz can sweetcorn
   (corn-on-the-cob)

60 g/2 oz/ ½ cup toasted unsalted peanuts

60 g/2 oz/ ½ cup grated Parmesan cheese

salt and pepper

1 Heat the sunflower oil and butter or margarine in a large saucepan. Fry the leek and (bell) pepper for 1 minute, then stir in the chicken and cook, stirring until golden brown.

2 Stir in the arborio (risotto) rice and cook for 2–3 minutes.

3 Stir in the saffron strands and salt and pepper to taste. Add the chicken stock, a little at a time, cover and cook over a low heat, stirring occasionally, for about 20 minutes, or until the rice is tender and most of the liquid has been absorbed. Do not let the risotto dry out – add more stock if necessary.

4 Stir in the sweetcorn (corn-on-the-cob), peanuts and Parmesan cheese, then season with salt and pepper to taste. Serve hot.

COOK'S TIP

Risottos can be frozen, before adding the Parmesan cheese, for up to 1 month, but remember to reheat this risotto thoroughly as it contains chicken.

Barbecued (Grilled) Chicken

You need a bit of brute force to prepare the chicken, but once marinated it's an easy and tasty candidate for the barbecue (grill).

NUTRITIONAL INFORMATION

Calories 129	Sugars 0g
Protein 22g	Fat 5g
Carbohydrate 0g	Saturates 1g

2¹/₂ HOURS   30 MINS

SERVES 4

I N G R E D I E N T S

1.5 kg/3 lb 5 oz chicken

grated rind of 1 lemon

4 tbsp lemon juice

2 sprigs rosemary

1 small red chilli, chopped finely

150 ml/¼ pint/⅔ cup olive oil

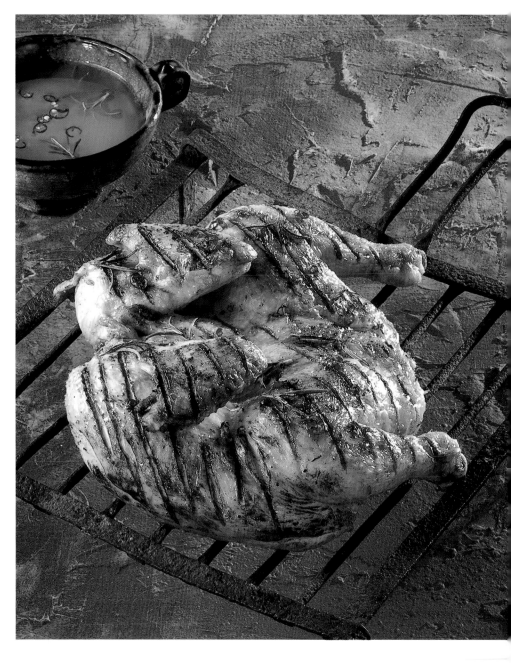

1 Split the chicken down the breast bone and open it out. Trim off excess fat, and remove the parson's nose, wing and leg tips. Break the leg and wing joints to enable you to pound it flat. This ensures that it cooks evenly. Cover the split chicken with clingfilm (plastic wrap) and pound it as flat as possible with a rolling pin.

2 Mix the lemon rind and juice, rosemary sprigs, chilli and olive oil together in a small bowl. Place the chicken in a large dish and pour over the marinade, turning the chicken to coat it evenly. Cover the dish and leave the chicken to marinate for at least 2 hours.

3 Cook the chicken over a hot barbecue (the coals should be white, and red when fanned) for about 30 minutes, turning it regularly until the skin is golden and crisp. To test if it is cooked, pierce one of the chicken thighs; the juices will run clear, not pink, when it is ready. Serve.

Boned Chicken & Parmesan

It's really very easy to bone a whole chicken, but if you prefer, you can ask your butcher to do this for you.

NUTRITIONAL INFORMATION

Calories	578	Sugars	.......0.4g
Protein	........42g	Fat	..........42g
Carbohydrate	....9g	Saturates	......15g

 35 MINS 1½ HOURS

SERVES 6

INGREDIENTS

1 chicken, weighing about 2.25 kg/5 lb

8 slices Mortadella or salami

125 g/4½ oz/2 cups fresh white or
   brown breadcrumbs

125 g/4½ oz/1 cup freshly grated
   Parmesan cheese

2 garlic cloves, crushed

6 tbsp chopped fresh basil or parsley

1 egg, beaten

pepper

fresh spring vegetables, to serve

1 Bone the chicken, keeping the skin intact. Dislocate each leg by breaking it at the thigh joint. Cut down each side of the backbone, taking care not to pierce the breast skin.

2 Pull the backbone clear of the flesh and discard. Remove the ribs, severing any attached flesh with a sharp knife.

3 Scrape the flesh from each leg and cut away the bone at the joint with a knife or shears.

4 Use the bones for stock. Lay out the boned chicken on a board, skin side down. Arrange the Mortadella slices over the chicken, overlapping slightly.

5 Put the breadcrumbs, Parmesan, garlic and basil or parsley in a bowl. Season

with pepper to taste and mix together well. Stir in the beaten egg to bind the mixture together. Spoon the mixture down the middle of the boned chicken, roll the meat around it and then tie securely with string.

6 Place in a roasting dish and brush lightly with olive oil. Roast in a preheated oven, 200°C/400°F/Gas Mark 6, for 1½ hours or until the juices run clear when pierced.

7 Serve hot or cold, in slices, with fresh spring vegetables.

VARIATION

Replace the Mortadella with rashers of streaky bacon, if preferred.

Chicken with Vermouth

The aromatic flavours of vermouth makes a good base for the sauce, and when partnered with refreshing grapes ensures a delicious meal.

NUTRITIONAL INFORMATION

Calories	.271	Sugars	.5g
Protein	.31g	Fat	.4g
Carbohydrate	...22g	Saturates	.1g

2¼ HOURS 45 MINS

SERVES 4

INGREDIENTS

4 × 175 g/6 oz 'part-boned' chicken breasts, skinned

150 ml/¼ pint/⅔ cup dry white vermouth

150 ml/¼ pint/⅔ cup Fresh Chicken Stock (see page 9)

2 shallots, sliced thinly

about 400 g/13 oz can artichoke hearts, drained and halved

125 g/4½ oz/¾ cup seedless green grapes

1 tbsp cornflour (cornstarch) mixed with tbsp cold water

salt and pepper

watercress sprigs to garnish

freshly cooked vegetables to serve

1 Cook the chicken in a heavy-based non-stick frying pan (skillet) for 2–3 minutes on each side until sealed. Drain on kitchen paper (paper towels).

2 Rinse out the pan, then add the dry vermouth and stock. Bring to the boil and add the shallots and chicken.

3 Cover and simmer for 35 minutes. Season to taste.

4 Stir in the artichokes and grapes and heat through for 2–3 minutes.

5 Stir in the cornflour (cornstarch) mixture until thickened. Garnish the chicken with watercress sprigs and serve with freshly cooked vegetables.

COOK'S TIP

Vermouth is a mixture of wines. It is fortified, and enriched with a secret blend of herbs and spices. It is available in sweet and dry forms. Dry white wine would make a suitable substitute in this recipe.

Cajun Chicken Gumbo

This complete main course is cooked in one saucepan. If you're cooking for one, halve the ingredients – the cooking time should stay the same.

NUTRITIONAL INFORMATION

Calories	425	Sugars	.........8g
Protein	........34g	Fat	..........12g
Carbohydrate	...48g	Saturates	......3g

 5 MINS　　 25 MINS

SERVES 2

INGREDIENTS

1 tbsp sunflower oil

4 chicken thighs

1 small onion, diced

2 sticks (stalks) celery, diced

1 small green (bell) pepper, diced

90 g/3 oz/½ cup long grain rice

300 ml/½ pint/1¼ cups chicken stock

1 small red chilli

225 g/8 oz okra

15 ml/1 tbsp tomato purée (paste)

salt and pepper

COOK'S TIP

The whole chilli makes the dish hot and spicy – if you prefer a milder flavour, discard the seeds of the chilli.

1 Heat the oil in a wide pan and fry the chicken until golden. Remove the chicken from the pan.

2 Stir in the onion, celery and pepper and fry for 1 minute. Pour off any excess oil.

3 Add the rice and fry, stirring for a further minute. Add the stock and heat until boiling. Thinly slice the chilli and trim the okra. Add to the pan with the tomato purée (paste). Season to taste.

4 Return the chicken to the pan and stir. Cover tightly and simmer gently for 15 minutes, or until the rice is tender, the chicken is thoroughly cooked and the liquid absorbed. Stir occasionally and if it becomes too dry, add a little extra stock.

Festive Apple Chicken

The stuffing in this recipe is cooked under the breast skin so all the flavour sealed in, and the chicken stays really moist and succulent.

NUTRITIONAL INFORMATION

Calories 219   Sugars 7g
Protein . . . . .29g   Fat 8g
Carbohydrate . . . .9g   Saturates 4g

🄖 🄖 🄖

🍲 10 MINS   🕐 2¼ HOURS

SERVES 6

I N G R E D I E N T S

1 chicken, weighing 2 kg/4½ lb

2 dessert apples

15 g/½ oz/1 tbsp butter

1 tbsp redcurrant jelly

parsley, to garnish

S T U F F I N G

15 g/½ oz/1 tbsp butter

1 small onion, chopped finely

60 g/2 oz mushrooms, chopped finely

60 g/2 oz lean smoked ham, chopped finely

25 g/1 oz/½ cup fresh breadcrumbs

1 tbsp chopped fresh parsley

1 crisp eating apple

1 tbsp lemon juice

oil, to brush

salt and pepper

1 To make the stuffing, melt the butter and fry the onion gently, stirring until softened. Stir in the mushrooms and cook over a moderate heat for 2–3 minutes. Remove from the heat and stir in the ham, breadcrumbs and the chopped parsley.

2 Core the apple, leaving the skin on, and grate coarsely. Add the stuffing mixture to the apple with the lemon juice. Season to taste.

3 Loosen the breast skin of the chicken and carefully spoon the stuffing mixture under it, smoothing evenly with your hands.

4 Place the chicken in a roasting tin (pan) and brush lightly with oil.

5 Roast the chicken in a preheated oven, 190°C/375°F/Gas Mark 5, for 25 minutes per 500 g/1 lb 2 oz plus 25 minutes, or until there is no trace of pink in the juices when the chicken is pierced through the thickest part with a skewer. If the breast starts to brown too much, cover the chicken with foil.

6 Core and slice the remaining apples and sauté in the butter until golden. Stir in the redcurrant jelly and warm through until melted. Serve the chicken garnished with the apple and parsley.

Roast Baby Chickens

Poussins are stuffed with lemon grass and lime leaves, coated with a spicy marinade, then roasted until crisp and golden.

NUTRITIONAL INFORMATION

Calories ....183 Sugars 1g
Protein ....30g Fat 7g
Carbohydrate ....1g Saturates 2g

  10 MINS 55 MINS

SERVES 4

INGREDIENTS

4 small poussins, weighing about
350-500 g/12 oz-1 lb 2 oz each

coriander (cilantro) leaves and lime
wedges, to garnish

a mixture of wild rice and Basmati rice,
to serve

MARINADE

4 garlic cloves, peeled

2 fresh coriander roots

1 tbsp light soy sauce

salt and pepper

STUFFING

4 blades lemon grass

4 kaffir lime leaves

4 slices ginger root

about 6 tbsp coconut milk, to brush

1 Wash the chickens and dry on kitchen paper (paper towels).

2 Place all the ingredients for the marinade in a small blender and purée until smooth. Alternatively, grind to a paste in a pestle and mortar. Season to taste with salt and pepper.

3 Rub this marinade mixture into the skin of the chickens, using the back of a spoon to spread it evenly over the skins.

4 Place a blade of lemon grass, a lime leaf and a piece of ginger in the cavity of each chicken.

5 Place the chickens in a roasting pan and brush lightly with the coconut milk. Roast for about 30 minutes in a preheated oven.

6 Remove from the oven, brush again with coconut milk, return to the oven

and cook for a further 15-25 minutes, until golden and cooked through, depending upon the size of the chickens. The chickens are cooked when the juices from the thigh run clear and are not tinged at all with pink.

7 Serve the baby chickens with the pan juices poured over. Garnish with coriander (cilantro) leaves and lime wedges and serve with rice.

Cashew Chicken

Yellow bean sauce is available from large supermarkets. Try to buy a chunky sauce rather than a smooth sauce for texture.

NUTRITIONAL INFORMATION

Calories	398	Sugars	........2g
Protein	........31g	Fat	..........27g
Carbohydrate	....8g	Saturates	.......4g

10 MINS   15 MINS

SERVES 4

INGREDIENTS

450 g/1 lb boneless chicken breasts

2 tbsp vegetable oil

1 red onion, sliced

175 g/6 oz/1½ cups flat mushrooms, sliced

100 g/3½ oz/⅓ cup cashew nuts

75 g/2¾ oz jar yellow bean sauce

fresh coriander (cilantro), to garnish

egg fried rice or plain boiled rice, to serve

1 Using a sharp knife, remove the excess skin from the chicken breasts, if desired. Cut the chicken into small, bite-sized chunks.

2 Heat the vegetable oil in a preheated wok or frying pan (skillet).

3 Add the chicken to the wok and stir-fry for 5 minutes.

4 Add the red onion and mushrooms to the wok and continue to stir-fry for a further 5 minutes.

5 Place the cashew nuts on a baking tray (cookie sheet) and toast under a preheated medium grill (broiler) until just browning – toasting nuts brings out their flavour.

6 Toss the toasted cashew nuts into the wok together with the yellow bean sauce and heat through.

7 Allow the sauce to bubble for 2–3 minutes.

8 Transfer the chop suey to warm serving bowls and garnish with fresh coriander (cilantro). Serve hot with egg fried rice or plain boiled rice.

VARIATION

Chicken thighs could be used instead of the chicken breasts for a more economical dish.

Garlic Chicken Cassoulet

This is a cassoulet with a twist – it is made with chicken instead of duck and lamb. If you use canned beans, the result will be just as tasty.

NUTRITIONAL INFORMATION

Calories 550	Sugars 2g
Protein 60g	Fat 19g
Carbohydrate . . .26g	Saturates 4g

🍳 5 MINS   🕐 2¼ HOURS

SERVES 4

I N G R E D I E N T S

4 tbsp sunflower oil

900 g/2 lb chicken meat, chopped

225 g/8 oz/3 cups mushrooms, sliced

16 shallots

6 garlic cloves, crushed

1 tbsp plain (all-purpose) flour

225 ml/8 fl oz/1 cup white wine

225 ml/8 fl oz/1 cup chicken stock

1 bouquet garni (1 bay leaf, sprig thyme, celery, parsley & sage tied with string)

400 g/14 oz can borlotti beans

salt and pepper

1   Heat the sunflower oil in an ovenproof casserole and fry the chicken until browned all over. Remove from the casserole with a slotted spoon.

2   Add the mushrooms, shallots and garlic to the oil in the casserole and cook for 4 minutes.

3   Return the chicken to the casserole and sprinkle with the flour then cook for a further 2 minutes.

4   Add the wine and stock, stir until boiling then add the bouquet garni. Season well with salt and pepper.

5   Stir in the borlotti beans.

6   Cover and place in the centre of a preheated oven, 150°C/300°F/Gas Mark 2, for 2 hours.

7   Remove the bouquet garni and serve piping hot.

COOK'S TIP

Add chunks of potatoes and other vegetables, such as carrots and celery, for a delicious one-pot meal.

Orange Turkey with Rice

This is a good way to use up left-over rice. Use fresh or canned sweet pink grapefruit for an interesting alternative to the orange.

NUTRITIONAL INFORMATION

Calories ....337 Sugars 12g
Protein ....32g Fat 7g
Carbohydrate ...40g Saturates 1g

30 MINS   40 MINS

SERVES 4

INGREDIENTS

1 tbsp olive oil

1 medium onion, chopped

450 g/1 lb skinless lean turkey (such as fillet), cut into thin strips

300 ml/½ pint/1¼ cups unsweetened orange juice

1 bay leaf

225 g/8 oz small broccoli florets

1 large courgette (zucchini), diced

1 large orange

350 g/12 oz/6 cups cooked brown rice

salt and pepper

tomato and onion salad, to serve

TO GARNISH

25 g/1 oz pitted black olives in brine, drained and quartered

shredded basil leaves

1 Heat the oil in a large frying pan (skillet) and fry the onion and turkey, stirring, for 4–5 minutes until lightly browned.

2 Pour in the orange juice and add the bay leaf and seasoning. Bring to the boil and simmer for 10 minutes.

3 Meanwhile, bring a large saucepan of water to the boil and cook the broccoli florets, covered, for 2 minutes. Add the diced courgette (zucchini), bring back to the boil, cover and cook for a further 3 minutes (do not overcook). Drain and set aside.

4 Using a sharp knife, peel off the skin and white pith from the orange.

5 Thinly slice down the orange to make round slices, then halve each slice.

6 Stir the broccoli, courgette (zucchini), rice and orange slices into the turkey mixture. Gently mix together and season, then heat through for a further 3–4 minutes until piping hot.

7 Transfer the turkey rice to warm serving plates and garnish with black olives and shredded basil leaves. Serve the turkey with a fresh tomato and onion salad.

Turkey with Cranberry Glaze

Traditional Christmas ingredients are given a Chinese twist in this stir-fry which containing cranberries, ginger, chestnuts and soy sauce!

NUTRITIONAL INFORMATION

Calories 167   Sugars 11g
Protein . . . . .8g   Fat 7g
Carbohydrate . . .20g   Saturates 1g

5 MINS   15 MINS

SERVES 4

INGREDIENTS

1 turkey breast

2 tbsp sunflower oil

15 g/½ oz/2 tbsp stem ginger

50 g/1¾ oz/½ cup fresh or frozen cranberries

100 g/3½ oz/¼ cup canned chestnuts

4 tbsp cranberry sauce

3 tbsp light soy sauce

salt and pepper

1 Remove any skin from the turkey breast. Using a sharp knife, thinly slice the turkey breast.

2 Heat the sunflower oil in a large preheated wok or heavy-based frying pan (skillet).

3 Add the turkey to the wok and stir-fry for 5 minutes, or until cooked through.

4 Using a sharp knife, finely chop the stem ginger.

5 Add the ginger and the cranberries to the wok or frying pan (skillet) and stir-fry for 2–3 minutes or until the cranberries have softened.

6 Add the chestnuts, cranberry sauce and soy sauce, season to taste with salt and pepper and allow to bubble for 2–3 minutes.

7 Transfer the turkey stir-fry to warm serving dishes and serve immediately.

COOK'S TIP

It is very important that the wok is very hot before you stir-fry. Test by by holding your hand flat about 7.5 cm/3 inches above the base of the interior – you should be able to feel the heat radiating from it.

Curried Turkey with Apricots

An easy-to-prepare supper dish of lean turkey in a fruit curry sauce served on a bed of spicy rice.

NUTRITIONAL INFORMATION

Calories 377   Sugars 19g
Protein ....33g   Fat 6g
Carbohydrate ...51g   Saturates 1g

2¹/₂ HOURS   30 MINS

SERVES 4

INGREDIENTS

1 tbsp vegetable oil

1 large onion, chopped

450 g/1 lb skinless turkey breast, cut into 2.5 cm/1 inch cubes

3 tbsp mild curry paste

300 ml/½ pint/1¼ cups Fresh Chicken Stock (see page 9)

175 g/6 oz frozen peas

400 g/14 oz can apricot halves in natural juice

50 g/1¾ oz/⅓ cup sultanas (golden raisins)

350 g/12 oz/6 cups Basmati rice, freshly cooked

1 tsp ground coriander

4 tbsp fresh coriander (cilantro), chopped

1 green chilli, deseeded and sliced

salt and pepper

1 Heat the oil in a large saucepan and gently fry the onion and turkey for 4–5 minutes until the onion has softened but not browned and the turkey is a light golden colour.

2 Stir in the curry paste. Pour in the stock, stirring, and bring to the boil. Cover and simmer for 15 minutes. Stir in the peas and bring back to the boil. Cover and simmer for 5 minutes.

3 Drain the apricots, reserving the juice, and cut into thick slices. Add to the curry, stirring in a little of the juice if the mixture is becoming dry. Add the sultanas and cook for 2 minutes.

4 Mix the rice with the ground and fresh coriander (cilantro), stir in the sliced green chilli and season well. Transfer the rice to warm plates and top with the curry.

VARIATION

Peaches can be used instead of the apricots if you prefer. Cook in exactly the same way.

Duck with Leek & Cabbage

Duck is a strongly-flavoured meat which benefits from the added citrus peel to counteract this rich taste.

NUTRITIONAL INFORMATION

Calories 192	Sugars 5g
Protein 26g	Fat 7g
Carbohydrate 6g	Saturates 2g

🥘 10 MINS   🕙 40 MINS

SERVES 4

I N G R E D I E N T S

4 duck breasts

350 g/12 oz green cabbage,
  thinly shredded

225 g/8 oz leeks, sliced

finely grated zest of 1 orange

6 tbsp oyster sauce

1 tsp toasted sesame seeds,
  to serve

1 Heat a large wok and dry-fry the duck breasts, with the skin on, for about 5 minutes on each side (you may need to do this in 2 batches).

2 Remove the duck breasts from the wok and transfer to a clean board.

3 Using a sharp knife, cut the duck breasts into thin slices.

4 Remove all but 1 tablespoon of the fat from the duck left in the wok; discard the rest.

5 Using a sharp knife, thinly shred the green cabbage.

6 Add the leeks, green cabbage and orange zest to the wok and stir-fry for about 5 minutes, or until the vegetables have softened.

7 Return the duck to the wok and heat through for 2–3 minutes.

8 Drizzle the oyster sauce over the mixture in the wok, toss well until all the ingredients are combined and then heat through.

9 Scatter the stir-fry with toasted sesame seeds, transfer to a warm serving dish and serve hot.

VARIATION

Use Chinese leaves (cabbage) for a lighter, sweeter flavour instead of the green cabbage, if you prefer.

Duck with Pineapple

For best results, use ready-cooked duck meat, widely available from Chinese restaurants and takeaways.

NUTRITIONAL INFORMATION

Calories 187   Sugars 7g
Protein ....10g   Fat 12g
Carbohydrate ....11g   Saturates 2g

 25 MINS   10 MINS

SERVES 4

INGREDIENTS

125-175 g/4½-6 oz cooked duck meat

3 tbsp vegetable oil

1 small onion, thinly shredded

2-3 slices ginger root, thinly shredded

1 spring onion (scallion), thinly shredded

1 small carrot, thinly shredded

125 g/4½ oz canned pineapple, cut into small slices

½ tsp salt

1 tbsp red rice vinegar

2 tbsp syrup from the pineapple

1 tbsp cornflour (cornstarch) paste (see page 6)

black bean sauce, to serve (optional)

1 Using a sharp knife or metal cleaver, cut the cooked duck meat into thin even-sized strips and set aside until required.

2 Heat the oil in a preheated wok or large heavy-based frying pan (skillet).

3 Add the shredded onion and stir-fry until the shreds are opaque.

4 Add the slices of ginger root, spring onion (scallion) shreds and carrot shreds to the wok and stir-fry for about 1 minute.

5 Add the duck shreds and pineapple to the wok together with the salt, rice vinegar and the pineapple syrup. Stir until the mixture is well blended.

6 Add the cornflour (cornstarch) paste and stir for 1-2 minutes until the sauce has thickened.

7 Transfer to a serving dish and serve with black bean sauce, if desired.

COOK'S TIP

Red rice vinegar is made from fermented rice. It has a distinctive dark colour and depth of flavour. If unavailable, use red wine vinegar, which is similar in flavour.

Duck with Broccoli & Peppers

This is a colourful dish using different coloured (bell) peppers
and broccoli to make it both tasty and appealing to the eye.

NUTRITIONAL INFORMATION

Calories 261   Sugars 3g
Protein . . . . .26g   Fat 13g
Carbohydrate . . . .11g   Saturates 2g

 35 MINS   15 MINS

SERVES 4

INGREDIENTS

1 egg white

2 tbsp cornflour (cornstarch)

450 g/1 lb skinless, boneless duck meat

vegetable oil, for deep-frying

1 red (bell) pepper, seeded and diced

1 yellow (bell) pepper, seeded and diced

125 g/4½ oz small broccoli florets

1 garlic clove, crushed

2 tbsp light soy sauce

2 tsp Chinese rice wine or dry sherry

1 tsp light brown sugar

125 ml/4 fl oz/½ cup chicken stock

2 tsp sesame seeds

1 In a mixing bowl, beat together the
egg white and cornflour (cornstarch).

2 Using a sharp knife, cut the duck into
2.5-cm/1-inch cubes and stir into the
egg white mixture. Leave to stand for
30 minutes.

3 Heat the oil for deep-frying in a
preheated wok or heavy-based frying
pan (skillet) until almost smoking.

4 Remove the duck from the egg white
mixture, add to the wok and fry in the
oil for 4–5 minutes, until crisp. Remove

the duck from the oil with a slotted spoon
and drain on kitchen paper (paper towels).

5 Add the (bell) peppers and broccoli to
the wok and fry for 2–3 minutes.
Remove with a slotted spoon and drain on
kitchen paper (paper towels).

6 Pour all but 2 tablespoons of the oil
from the wok and return to the heat.
Add the garlic and stir-fry for 30 seconds.

Stir in the soy sauce, Chinese rice wine or
sherry, sugar and chicken stock and bring
to the boil.

7 Stir in the duck and reserved
vegetables and cook for 1–2 minutes.

8 Carefully spoon the duck and
vegetables on to a warmed serving
dish and sprinkle with the sesame seeds.
Serve immediately.

Duck with Ginger & Lime

Just the thing for a lazy summer day – roasted duck sliced and served with a dressing made of ginger, lime juice, sesame oil and fish sauce.

NUTRITIONAL INFORMATION

Calories	529	Sugars	.........3g
Protein	........38g	Fat	..........41g
Carbohydrate	....3g	Saturates	.......6g

20 MINS   25 MINS

SERVES 4

INGREDIENTS

3 boneless Barbary duck breasts, about 250 g/9 oz each

salt

DRESSING

125 ml/4 fl oz/½ cup olive oil

2 tsp sesame oil

2 tbsp lime juice

grated rind and juice of 1 orange

2 tsp fish sauce

1 tbsp grated ginger root

1 garlic clove, crushed

2 tsp light soy sauce

3 spring onions (scallions), finely chopped

1 tsp sugar

about 250 g/9 oz assorted salad leaves

orange slices, to garnish (optional)

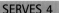

1 Wash the duck breasts, dry on kitchen paper (paper towels), then cut in half. Prick the skin all over with a fork and season well with salt. Place the duck pieces, skin-side down, on a wire rack or trivet over a roasting tin (pan).

2 Cook the duck in a preheated oven for 10 minutes, then turn over and cook for a further 12-15 minutes, or until the duck is cooked, but still pink in the centre, and the skin is crisp.

3 To make the dressing, beat the olive oil and sesame oil with the lime juice, orange rind and juice, fish sauce, grated ginger root, garlic, light soy sauce, spring onions (scallions) and sugar until well blended.

4 Remove the duck from the oven, and allow to cool. Using a sharp knife, cut the duck into thick slices.

5 Add a little of the dressing to moisten and coat the duck.

6 To serve, arrange assorted salad leaves on a serving dish. Top with the sliced duck breasts and drizzle with the remaining salad dressing.

7 Garnish with orange slices, if using, then serve at once.

Aromatic & Crispy Duck

As it is very time-consuming to make the pancakes, buy ready-made ones from Oriental stores, or use crisp lettuce leaves as the wrapper.

NUTRITIONAL INFORMATION

Calories 169	Sugars 1g
Protein 7g	Fat 11g
Carbohydrate 7g	Saturates 3g

🍲 9¼ HOURS   🕐 3¼ HOURS

SERVES 4

INGREDIENTS

2 large duckling quarters

1 tsp salt

3-4 pieces star anise

1 tsp Szechuan red peppercorns

1 tsp cloves

2 cinnamon sticks, broken into pieces

2-3 spring onions (scallions), cut into short sections

4-5 small slices ginger root

3-4 tbsp rice wine or dry sherry

vegetable oil, for deep-frying

TO SERVE

12 ready-made pancakes or 12 crisp lettuce leaves

hoisin or plum sauce

¼ cucumber, thinly shredded

3-4 spring onions (scallions), thinly shredded

1 Rub the duck with the salt and arrange the star anise, peppercorns, cloves and cinnamon on top. Sprinkle with the spring onions (scallions), ginger and wine and marinate for at least 3-4 hours.

2 Arrange the duck pieces on a plate that will fit inside a bamboo steamer. Pour some hot water into a wok, place the bamboo steamer on top, sitting on a trivet. Add the duck and cover with the bamboo lid. Steam the duck over a high heat for 2-3 hours, until tender and cooked through. Top up the hot water from time to time as required. Remove the duck and leave to cool for at least 4-5 hours so the duck becomes crispy.

3 Pour off the water and wipe the wok dry. Pour in the oil and heat until smoking. Deep-fry the duck pieces, skin-side down, for 4-5 minutes or until crisp and brown. Remove and drain.

4 To serve, scrape the meat off the bone, place about 1 teaspoon of hoisin or plum sauce on the centre of a pancake (or lettuce leaf), add a few pieces of cucumber and spring onion (scallion) with a portion of the duck meat. Wrap up to form a small parcel and eat with your fingers.

Peking Duck

No Chinese cookery book would be complete without this famous recipe in which crispy skinned duck is served with pancakes and a tangy sauce.

NUTRITIONAL INFORMATION

Calories	357	Sugars	........48g
Protein	........20g	Fat	..........10g
Carbohydrate	...49g	Saturates	.......2g

6¹/₄ HOURS   1¹/₂ HOURS

SERVES 4

I N G R E D I E N T S

1.8 kg/4 lb duck

1.75 litres/3 pints/7½ cups boiling water

4 tbsp clear honey

2 tsp dark soy sauce

2 tbsp sesame oil

125 ml/4 fl oz/½ cup hoisin sauce

125 g/4½ oz/⅔ cup caster (superfine) sugar

125 ml/4 fl oz/½ cup water

carrot strips, to garnish

Chinese pancakes, cucumber matchsticks and spring onions (scallions), to serve

1 Place the duck on a rack set over a roasting tin (pan) and pour 1.2 litres/2 pints/5 cups of the boiling water over it.

2 Remove the duck and rack and discard the water. Pat dry with absorbent kitchen paper (paper towels), replace the duck and the rack and set aside for several hours.

3 In a small bowl, mix together the clear honey, remaining boiling water and dark soy sauce, until they are thoroughly combined.

4 Brush the mixture over the skin and inside the duck. Reserve the remaining glaze. Set the duck aside for 1 hour, until the glaze has dried.

5 Coat the duck with another layer of glaze. Let dry and repeat until all of the glaze is used.

6 Heat the sesame oil in a saucepan and add the hoisin sauce, caster (superfine) sugar and water. Simmer for 2-3 minutes, until thickened. Leave to cool and then refrigerate until required.

7 Cook the duck in a preheated oven, at 190°C/375°F/Gas Mark 5, for 30 minutes. Turn the duck over and cook for 20 minutes. Turn the duck again and cook for 20-30 minutes, or until cooked through and the skin is crisp.

8 Remove the duck from the oven and set aside for 10 minutes.

9 Meanwhile, heat the pancakes in a steamer for 5-7 minutes or according to the instructions on the packet. Cut the skin and duck meat into strips, garnish with the carrot strips and serve with the pancakes, sauce, cucumber and spring onions (scallions).

Roast Duck with Apple

The richness of the duck meat contrasts well with the apricot sauce. If duckling portions are unavailable, use a whole bird cut into joints.

NUTRITIONAL INFORMATION

Calories 316   Sugars 38g
Protein . . . . .25g   Fat 6g
Carbohydrate . . .40g   Saturates 1g

10 MINS   1½ HOURS

SERVES 4

INGREDIENTS

4 duckling portions, 350 g/12 oz each

4 tbsp dark soy sauce

2 tbsp light muscovado sugar

2 red-skinned apples

2 green-skinned apples

juice of 1 lemon

2 tbsp clear honey

few bay leaves

salt and pepper

assorted fresh vegetables, to serve

SAUCE

400 g/14 oz can apricots, in natural juice

4 tbsp sweet sherry

1 Preheat the oven to 190°C/375°F/Gas Mark 5. Wash the duck and trim away any excess fat. Place on a wire rack over a roasting pan and prick all over with a fork.

2 Brush the duck with the soy sauce. Sprinkle over the sugar and season with pepper. Cook in the oven, basting occasionally, for 50–60 minutes until the meat is cooked through – the juices should run clear when a skewer is inserted into the thickest part of the meat.

3 Meanwhile, core the apples and cut each into 6 wedges. Place in a small roasting tin and mix with the lemon juice and honey. Add a few bay leaves and season. Cook alongside the duck, basting occasionally, for 20–25 minutes until tender. Discard the bay leaves.

4 To make the sauce, place the apricots in a blender or food processor together with the juice from the can and the sherry. Process for a few seconds until smooth. Alternatively, mash the apricots with a fork until smooth and mix with the juice and sherry.

5 Just before serving, heat the apricot purée (paste) in a small pan. Remove the skin from the duck and pat the flesh with kitchen paper to absorb any fat. Serve the duck with the apple wedges, apricot sauce and fresh vegetables.

VARIATION

Fruit complements duck perfectly. Use canned pineapple in natural juice for a delicious alternative.

Barbecued (Grilled) Duckling

The sweet, spicy marinade used in this recipe gives the duckling a subtle flavour of the Orient.

NUTRITIONAL INFORMATION

Calories 249   Sugars 20g
Protein ....27g   Fat 6g
Carbohydrate ...23g   Saturates 2g

 6¼ HOURS   30 MINS

SERVES 4

I N G R E D I E N T S

3 cloves garlic, crushed

150 ml/5 fl oz/⅔ cup light soy sauce

5 tbsp light muscovado sugar

2.5 cm/1 inch piece root (fresh) ginger, grated

1 tbsp chopped, fresh coriander (cilantro)

1 tsp five-spice powder

4 duckling breasts

sprig of fresh coriander (cilantro),
    to garnish (optional)

1 To make the marinade, mix together the garlic, soy sauce, sugar, grated ginger, chopped coriander (cilantro) and five-spice powder in a small bowl until well combined.

2 Place the duckling breasts in a shallow, non-metallic dish and pour over the marinade. Carefully turn over the duckling so that it is fully coated with the marinade on both sides.

3 Cover the bowl with cling film (plastic wrap) and leave to marinate for 1–6 hours, turning the duckling once or twice so that the marinade is fully absorbed.

4 Remove the duckling from the marinade, reserving the marinade for basting.

5 Barbecue (grill) the duckling breasts over hot coals for about 20–30 minutes, turning and basting frequently with the reserved marinade, using a pastry brush.

6 Cut the duckling into slices and transfer to warm serving plates. Serve the barbecued (grilled) duckling garnished with a sprig of fresh coriander (cilantro), if using.

COOK'S TIP

Duckling is quite a fatty meat so there is no need to add oil to the marinade. However, you must remember to oil the barbecue (grill) rack to prevent the duckling from sticking. Oil the barbecue (grill) rack well away from the barbecue (grill) to avoid any danger of a flare-up.

Duck with Pineapple

The pineapple and plum sauce add a sweetness and fruity flavour to this colourful recipe which blends well with the duck.

NUTRITIONAL INFORMATION

Calories	.241	Sugars	.7g
Protein	.26g	Fat	.8g
Carbohydrate	.16g	Saturates	.2g

5 MINS   25 MINS

SERVES 4

INGREDIENTS

4 duck breasts

1 tsp Chinese five-spice powder

1 tbsp cornflour (cornstarch)

1 tbsp chilli oil

225 g/8 oz baby onions, peeled

2 cloves garlic, crushed

100 g/3½ oz/1 cup baby corn cobs

175 g/6 oz/1¼ cups canned pineapple chunks

6 spring onions (scallions), sliced

100 g/3½ oz/1 cup bean sprouts

2 tbsp plum sauce

1 Remove any skin from the duck breasts. Cut the duck into thin slices.

2 Mix the five-spice powder and the cornflour (cornstarch). Toss the duck in the mixture until well coated.

3 Heat the oil in a preheated wok. Stir-fry the duck for 10 minutes, or until just begining to crispen around the edges. Remove from the wok and set aside.

4 Add the onions and garlic to the wok and stir-fry for 5 minutes, or until softened. Add the baby corn cobs and stir-fry for a further 5 minutes. Add the pineapple, spring onions (scallions) and bean sprouts and stir-fry for 3–4 minutes. Stir in the plum sauce.

5 Return the cooked duck to the wok and toss until well mixed. Transfer to warm serving dishes and serve hot.

COOK'S TIP

Buy pineapple chunks in natural juice rather than syrup for a fresher flavour. If you can only obtain pineapple in syrup, rinse it in cold water and drain thoroughly before using.

Tasmanian Duck

Some of the best cherries in the world are grown in Tasmania, hence the title for this recipe, though dried cherries from any country can be used.

NUTRITIONAL INFORMATION

Calories 259   Sugars 12g
Protein . . . . .24g   Fat 12g
Carbohydrate . . .12g   Saturates 2g

5 MINS   35 MINS

SERVES 4

I N G R E D I E N T S

4 duck breasts

60 g/2 oz/½ cup dried cherries

125 ml/4 fl oz/½ cup water

4 tbsp lemon juice

2 large leeks, quartered, or 8 baby leeks

2 tbsp olive oil

2 tbsp balsamic vinegar

2 tbsp port

2 tsp pink peppercorns

1 Using a sharp knife, make 3 slashes in the fat of the duck breasts in one direction, and 3 in the other.

2 Put the dried cherries, water and lemon juice into a small saucepan. Bring to the boil. Remove from the heat and leave to cool.

3 Turn a large foil tray upside-down, make several holes in the bottom with a skewer and put it over a hot barbecue (grill). Put the duck into the tray. Cover with foil and cook for 20 minutes.

4 Brush the leeks with olive oil and cook on the open barbecue (grill) for 5–7 minutes, turning constantly.

5 Remove the duck from the tray and cook on the open barbecue (grill) for

5 minutes, skin-side down, while you make the sauce.

6 Stir the balsamic vinegar into the cooking sauces in the tray, scraping any bits from the bottom. Add to the cherries in the saucepan. Return to the heat – either the hob (stove top) or barbecue (grill) – and stir in the port and

pink peppercorns. Bring to the boil and cook for 5 minutes, until the sauce has thickened slightly.

7 Serve the duck piping hot, pour over the cherry sauce, and accompany with the leeks.

Ginger Beef with Chilli

Serve these fruity, hot and spicy steaks with noodles. Use a non-stick ridged frying pan (skillet) to cook with a minimum of fat.

NUTRITIONAL INFORMATION

Calories 179	Sugars 8g
Protein 21g	Fat 6g
Carbohydrate 8g	Saturates 2g

🧊 40 MINS   🕐 10 MINS

SERVES 4

INGREDIENTS

4 lean beef steaks (such as rump, sirloin or fillet), 100 g/3½ oz each

2 tbsp ginger wine

2.5 cm/1 inch piece root (fresh) ginger, finely chopped

1 garlic clove, crushed

1 tsp ground chilli

1 tsp vegetable oil

salt and pepper

red chilli strips, to garnish

TO SERVE

freshly cooked noodles

2 spring onions (scallions), shredded

RELISH

225 g/8 oz fresh pineapple

1 small red (bell) pepper

1 red chilli

2 tbsp light soy sauce

1 piece stem ginger in syrup, drained and chopped

1 Trim any excess fat from the beef if necessary. Using a meat mallet or covered rolling pin, pound the steaks until 1 cm/½ inch thick. Season on both sides and place in a shallow dish.

2 Mix the ginger wine, root (fresh) ginger, garlic and chilli and pour over the meat. Cover and chill for 30 minutes.

3 Meanwhile, make the relish. Peel and finely chop the pineapple and place it in a bowl. Halve, deseed and finely chop the (bell) pepper and chilli. Stir into the pineapple together with the soy sauce and stem ginger. Cover and chill until required.

4 Brush a grill (broiler) pan with the oil and heat until very hot. Drain the beef and add to the pan, pressing down to seal. Lower the heat and cook for 5 minutes. Turn the steaks over and cook for a further 5 minutes.

5 Drain the steaks on kitchen paper and transfer to serving plates. Garnish with chilli strips, and serve with noodles, spring onions (scallions) and the relish.

Spaghetti Bolognese

The original recipe takes about 4 hours to cook and should be left over night to allow the flavours to mingle. This version is much quicker.

NUTRITIONAL INFORMATION

Calories . . . . .591 Sugars 7g
Protein . . . . .29g Fat 24g
Carbohydrate . . .64g Saturates 9g

 20 MINS   1 HR 5 MINS

SERVES 4

INGREDIENTS

1 tbsp olive oil

1 onion, finely chopped

2 garlic cloves, chopped

1 carrot, scraped and chopped

1 stick celery, chopped

50 g/1¾ oz pancetta or streaky bacon, diced

350 g/12 oz lean minced beef

400 g/14 oz can chopped tomatoes

2 tsp dried oregano

125 ml/4 fl oz/scant ½ cup red wine

2 tbsp tomato purée (paste)

salt and pepper

675 g/1½ lb fresh spaghetti or 350 g/12 oz
    dried spaghetti

1 Heat the oil in a large frying pan (skillet). Add the onions and cook for 3 minutes.

2 Add the garlic, carrot, celery and pancetta or bacon and sauté for 3–4 minutes or until just beginning to brown.

3 Add the beef and cook over a high heat for another 3 minutes or until all of the meat is brown.

4 Stir in the tomatoes, oregano and red wine and bring to the boil. Reduce the heat and leave to simmer for about 45 minutes.

5 Stir in the tomato purée (paste) and season with salt and pepper.

6 Cook the spaghetti in a pan of boiling water for 8–10 minutes until tender, but still has 'bite'. Drain thoroughly.

7 Transfer the spaghetti to a serving plate and pour over the bolognese sauce. Toss to mix well and serve hot.

VARIATION

Try adding 25 g/1 oz dried porcini, soaked for 10 minutes in 2 tablespoons of warm water, to the bolognese sauce in step 4, if you wish.

Shepherd's Pie

Minced (ground) lamb or beef cooked with onions, carrots, herbs and tomatoes and with a topping of piped creamed potatoes.

NUTRITIONAL INFORMATION

Calories 378   Sugars 8g
Protein . . . . .33g   Fat 12g
Carbohydrate . . .37g   Saturates 4g

10 MINS   1¹/₂ HOURS

SERVES 4–5

I N G R E D I E N T S

700 g/1 lb 9 oz lean minced (ground) or lamb or beef

2 onions, chopped

225 g/8 oz carrots, diced

1–2 garlic cloves, crushed

1 tbsp plain (all-purpose) flour

200 ml/7 fl oz/scant 1 cup beef stock

200 g/7 oz can chopped tomatoes

1 tsp Worcestershire sauce

1 tsp chopped fresh sage or oregano or ½ tsp dried sage or oregano

750 g–1 kg/1½–2 lb potatoes

25 g/1 oz/2 tbsp margarine

3–4 tbsp skimmed milk

125 g/4½ oz button mushrooms, sliced (optional)

salt and pepper

1 Place the meat in a heavy-based saucepan with no extra fat and cook gently, stirring frequently, until the meat begins to brown.

2 Add the onions, carrots and garlic and continue to cook gently for about 10 minutes. Stir in the flour and cook for a minute or so, then gradually stir in the stock and tomatoes and bring to the boil.

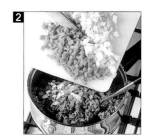

3 Add the Worcestershire sauce, seasoning and herbs, cover the pan and simmer gently for about 25 minutes, giving an occasional stir.

4 Cook the potatoes in boiling salted water until tender, then drain thoroughly and mash, beating in the margarine, seasoning and sufficient milk to give a piping consistency. Place in a piping bag fitted with a large star nozzle (tip).

5 Stir the mushrooms (if using) into the meat and adjust the seasoning. Turn into a shallow ovenproof dish.

6 Pipe the potatoes evenly over the meat. Cook in a preheated oven at 200°C/400°F/Gas Mark 6 for about 30 minutes until piping hot and the potatoes are golden brown.

VARIATION

If liked, a mixture of boiled potatoes and parsnips or swede may be used for the topping.

Oyster Sauce Beef

The vegetables used in this recipe can be varied as you wish – use your personal favourites.

NUTRITIONAL INFORMATION

Calories	462	Sugars	........2g
Protein	........16g	Fat	.........42g
Carbohydrate	....4g	Saturates	.......8g

4 HOURS   10 MINS

SERVES 4

I N G R E D I E N T S

300 g/10½ oz beef steak

1 tsp sugar

1 tbsp light soy sauce

1 tsp rice wine or dry sherry

1 tsp cornflour (cornstarch) paste
  (see page 6)

½ small carrot

60 g/2 oz mangetout (snow peas)

60 g/2 oz canned bamboo shoots

60 g/2 oz canned straw mushrooms

about 300 ml/½ pint/1¼ cups vegetable oil

1 spring onion (scallion), cut into short
  sections

2-3 small slices ginger root

½ tsp salt

2 tbsp oyster sauce

2-3 tbsp Chinese Stock (see page 8) or
  water

1 Cut the beef into small, thin slices. Place in a shallow dish with the sugar, soy sauce, wine and cornflour (cornstarch) paste and leave to marinate for 25-30 minutes.

2 Slice the carrot, mangetout (snow peas), bamboo shoots and straw mushrooms into roughly the same size pieces as each other.

3 Heat the oil in a wok and add the beef slices. Stir-fry for 1 minute, then remove and keep warm.

4 Pour off the oil, leaving about 1 tablespoon in the wok. Add the sliced vegetables with the spring onion (scallion) and ginger and stir-fry for about 2 minutes. Add the salt, beef and oyster sauce with stock or water. Blend well until heated through and serve.

VARIATION

You can use whatever vegetables are available for this dish, but it is important to get a good contrast of colour – don't use all red or all green for example.

Beef Goulash

Slow, gentle cooking is the secret to this superb goulash – it really brings out the flavour of the ingredients.

NUTRITIONAL INFORMATION

Calories	386	Sugars	........10g
Protein	........44g	Fat	..........16g
Carbohydrate	...17g	Saturates	......5g

 10 MINS   2¼ HOURS

SERVES 4

INGREDIENTS

2 tbsp vegetable oil

1 large onion, chopped

1 garlic clove, crushed

750 g/1 lb 10 oz lean stewing steak

2 tbsp paprika

425 g/15 oz can chopped tomatoes

2 tbsp tomato purée (paste)

1 large red (bell) pepper, deseeded and chopped

175 g/6 oz mushrooms, sliced

600 ml/1 pint/2½ cups beef stock

1 tbsp cornflour (cornstarch)

1 tbsp water

4 tbsp low-fat natural yogurt

salt and pepper

paprika for sprinkling

chopped fresh parsley, to garnish

long grain rice and wild rice, to serve

1 Heat the vegetable oil in a large frying pan (skillet) and cook the onion and garlic for 3–4 minutes.

2 Cut the stewing steak into chunks and cook over a high heat for 3 minutes until browned all over. Add the paprika and stir well, then add the chopped tomatoes, tomato purée (paste),

(bell) pepper and mushrooms. Cook for 2 minutes, stirring frequently.

3 Pour in the beef stock. Bring to the boil, then reduce the heat. Cover and simmer for 1½–2 hours until the meat is tender.

4 Blend the cornflour (cornstarch) with the water, then add to the saucepan, stirring until thickened and smooth. Cook

for 1 minute, then season with salt and pepper to taste.

5 Put the natural yogurt in a serving bowl and sprinkle with a little paprika.

6 Transfer the beef goulash to a warm serving dish, garnish with chopped fresh parsley and serve with rice and yogurt.

Crispy Shredded Beef

A very popular Szechuan dish served in most Chinese restaurants all over the world.

NUTRITIONAL INFORMATION

Calories 341   Sugars 17g
Protein . . . . .20g   Fat 17g
Carbohydrate . . .29g   Saturates 4g

3¹/₂ HOURS   15 MINS

SERVES 4

I N G R E D I E N T S

300-350 g/10½-12 oz beef steak (such as topside or rump)

2 eggs

¼ tsp salt

4-5 tbsp plain (all-purpose) flour

vegetable oil, for deep-frying

2 medium carrots, finely shredded

2 spring onions (scallions), thinly shredded

1 garlic clove, finely chopped

2-3 small fresh green or red chillies, seeded and thinly shredded

4 tbsp sugar

3 tbsp rice vinegar

1 tbsp light soy sauce

2-3 tbsp Chinese Stock (see page 8) or water

1 tsp cornflour (cornstarch) paste (see page 6)

1 Cut the steak across the grain into thin strips. Beat the eggs in a bowl with the salt and flour, adding a little water if necessary. Add the beef strips to the batter and mix well until coated.

2 Heat the oil in a preheated wok until smoking. Add the beef strips and deep-fry for 4-5 minutes, stirring to separate the shreds. Remove with a slotted spoon and drain on absorbent kitchen paper (paper towels).

3 Add the carrots to the wok and deep-fry for about 1-1½ minutes, then remove with a slotted spoon and drain.

4 Pour off the excess oil, leaving about 1 tablespoon in the wok. Add the spring onions (scallions), garlic, chillies and carrots and stir-fry for 1 minute.

5 Add the sugar, rice vinegar, light soy sauce and Chinese stock or water to the wok, blend well and bring to the boil.

6 Stir in the cornflour (cornstarch) paste and simmer for a few minutes to thicken the sauce.

7 Return the beef to the wok and stir until the shreds of meat are well coated with the sauce. Serve hot.

Layered Meat Loaf

The cheese-flavoured pasta layer comes as a pleasant surprise inside this lightly spiced meat loaf.

NUTRITIONAL INFORMATION

Calories	.412	Sugars	.3g
Protein	.21g	Fat	.30g
Carbohydrate	.15g	Saturates	.13g

🥘 35 MINS   🕐 1½ HOURS

SERVES 6

INGREDIENTS

25 g/1 oz/2 tbsp butter, plus extra

    for greasing

1 small onion, finely chopped

1 small red (bell) pepper, cored, seeded

    and chopped

1 garlic clove, chopped

450 g/1 lb/4 cups minced (ground) beef

25 g/1 oz/½ cup white breadcrumbs

½ tsp cayenne pepper

1 tbsp lemon juice

½ tsp grated lemon rind

2 tbsp chopped fresh parsley

90 g/3 oz/¾ cup dried short pasta,

    such as fusilli

1 tbsp olive oil

4 bay leaves

250 ml/9 fl oz/1 cup Italian Cheese Sauce

    (see page 7)

175 g/6 oz fatty bacon, rinds removed

salt and pepper

salad leaves (greens), to serve

1 Melt the butter in a pan over a medium heat and fry the onion and (bell) pepper for about 3 minutes. Stir in the garlic and cook for 1 minute.

2 Put the meat into a bowl and mash with a wooden spoon until sticky. Add the onion mixture, breadcrumbs, cayenne pepper, lemon juice, lemon rind and parsley. Season and set aside.

3 Bring a pan of salted water to the boil. Add the pasta and oil and cook for 8–10 minutes, until almost tender. Drain and stir into the Italian Cheese Sauce.

4 Grease a 1 kg/2 lb l4 oz oaf tin (pan) and arrange the bay leaves in the base. Stretch the bacon slices with the back of a knife and line the base and sides of the tin (pan) with them. Spoon in half the meat mixture and smooth the surface. Cover with the pasta mixed with Italian Cheese Sauce, then spoon in the remaining meat mixture. Level the top and cover with foil.

5 Bake the meat loaf in a preheated oven, at 180°C/350°F/Gas Mark 4, for 1 hour or until the juices run clear when a skewer is inserted into the centre and the loaf has shrunk away from the sides. Pour off any fat and turn out the loaf on to a serving dish. Serve with salad leaves (greens).

Boiled Beef & Carrots

Serve this old favourite with vegetables and herby dumplings for a substantial one-pot meal.

NUTRITIONAL INFORMATION

Calories 459	Sugars 2g
Protein 31g	Fat 22g
Carbohydrate . . .35g	Saturates 10g

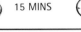

15 MINS   2³/₄ HOURS

SERVES 6

INGREDIENTS

about 1.75 kg/3½ lb joint of salted silverside or topside

2 onions, quartered, or 5–8 small onions

8–10 cloves

2 bay leaves

1 cinnamon stick

2 tbsp brown sugar

4 large carrots, sliced thickly

1 turnip, quartered

½ swede, sliced thickly

1 large leek, sliced thickly

25 g/1 oz/2 tbsp butter or margarine

25 g/1 oz/4 tbsp plain (all-purpose) flour

½ tsp dried mustard powder

salt and pepper

DUMPLINGS

225 g/8 oz/2 cups self-raising flour

½ tsp dried sage

90 g/3 oz/ ½ cup shredded vegetable suet

about 150 ml/¼ pint/⅔ cup water

1 Put the beef in a large saucepan, add the onions, cloves, bay leaves, cinnamon and sugar and sufficient water to cover the meat. Bring slowly to the boil, remove any scum from the surface, cover and simmer gently for 1 hour.

2 Add the carrots, turnip, swede and leeks, cover and simmer for a further 1¼ hours until the beef is tender.

3 Meanwhile, make the dumplings. Sift the flour into a bowl, season well and mix in the herbs and suet. Add sufficient water to mix to a softish dough.

4 Divide the dough into 8 pieces, roughly shape into balls and place on top of the beef and vegetables. Replace the lid and simmer for 15–20 minutes.

5 Place the beef, vegetables and dumplings in a serving dish. Measure 300 ml/½ pint/1¼ cups of the cooking liquid into a pan. Blend the margarine with the flour then gradually whisk into the pan. Bring to the boil and simmer until thickened. Stir in the mustard, adjust the seasoning and serve with the beef.

Peppered Beef Cashew

A simple but stunning dish of tender strips of beef mixed with crunchy cashew nuts, coated in a hot sauce. Serve with rice noodles.

NUTRITIONAL INFORMATION

Calories 403	Sugars 7g	
Protein 26g	Fat 29g	
Carbohydrate 11g	Saturates 9g	

  10 MINS 10 MINS

SERVES 4

INGREDIENTS

1 tbsp groundnut or sunflower oil

1 tbsp sesame oil

1 onion, sliced

1 garlic clove, crushed

1 tbsp grated ginger root

500 g/1 lb 2 oz fillet or rump steak, cut into thin strips

2 tsp palm sugar

2 tbsp light soy sauce

1 small yellow (bell) pepper, cored, seeded and sliced

1 red (bell) pepper, cored, seeded and sliced

4 spring onions (scallions), chopped

2 celery sticks, chopped

4 large open-cap mushrooms, sliced

4 tbsp roasted cashew nuts

3 tbsp stock or white wine

1 Heat the oils in a large, heavy-based frying pan (skillet) or wok. Add the onion, garlic and ginger and stir-fry for about 2 minutes until softened.

2 Add the steak strips and stir-fry for a further 2-3 minutes, until the meat has browned.

3 Add the sugar and soy sauce, stirring to mix well.

4 Add the (bell) peppers, spring onions (scallions), celery, mushrooms and cashews, mixing well.

5 Add the stock or white wine and stir-fry for 2-3 minutes until the beef is cooked through and the vegetables are tender-crisp.

6 Serve the stir-fry immediately with rice noodles.

COOK'S TIP

Palm sugar is a thick brown sugar with a slightly caramel taste. It is sold in cakes, or in small containers. If not available, use soft dark brown or demerara (brown crystal) sugar.

Ma-po Tofu

Ma-Po was the wife of a Szechuan chef who created this popular dish in the middle of the 19th century.

NUTRITIONAL INFORMATION

Calories	....	235
Protein	....	16g
Carbohydrate	....3g	

Sugars	....	1g
Fat	....	18g
Saturates	....	4g

3¹/₂ HOURS   15 MINS

SERVES 4

INGREDIENTS

3 cakes tofu (bean curd)

3 tbsp vegetable oil

125 g/4½ oz coarsely minced (ground) beef

½ tsp finely chopped garlic

1 leek, cut into short sections

½ tsp salt

1 tbsp black bean sauce

1 tbsp light soy sauce

1 tsp chilli bean sauce

3-4 tbsp Chinese Stock (see page 8) or water

2 tsp cornflour (cornstarch) paste (see page 6)

a few drops sesame oil

black pepper

finely chopped spring onions (scallions), to garnish

1 Cut the tofu (bean curd) into 1 cm/½ inch cubes, handling it carefully.

2 Bring some water to the boil in a small pan or a wok, add the tofu (bean curd) and blanch for 2-3 minutes to harden. Remove and drain well.

3 Heat the oil in a preheated wok. Add the minced (ground) beef and garlic and stir-fry for about 1 minute, or until the colour of the beef changes. Add the leek, salt and sauces and blend well.

4 Add the stock or water followed by the tofu (bean curd). Bring to the boil and braise gently for 2-3 minutes.

5 Add the cornflour (cornstarch) paste, and stir until the sauce has thickened. Sprinkle with sesame oil and black pepper, garnish and serve hot.

COOK'S TIP

Tofu has been an important element in Chinese cooking for more than 1000 years. It is made of yellow soya beans, which are soaked, ground and mixed with water. Tofu is highly nutritious, being rich in protein and low in fat.

Beef & Tomato Gratin

A satisfying bake of lean minced beef, courgettes (zucchini) and tomatoes cooked in a low-fat 'custard' with a cheesy crust.

 10 MINS   🕑 1¼ HOURS

SERVES 4

INGREDIENTS

350 g/12 oz lean beef, minced (ground)

1 large onion, finely chopped

1 tsp dried mixed herbs

1 tbsp plain (all-purpose) flour

300 ml/½ pint/1¼ cups beef stock

1 tbsp tomato purée (paste)

2 large tomatoes, thinly sliced

4 medium courgettes (zucchini), thinly
   sliced

2 tbsp cornflour (cornstarch)

300 ml/½ pint/1¼ cups skimmed milk

150 ml/5 fl oz/⅔ cup low-fat natural
   fromage frais (unsweetened yogurt)

1 medium egg yolk

4 tbsp Parmesan cheese, freshly grated

salt and pepper

TO SERVE

crusty bread

steamed vegetables

1 Preheat the oven to 190°C/375°F/Gas
   Mark 5. In a large frying pan (skillet),
dry-fry the beef and onion for 4–5
minutes until browned.

2 Stir in the dried mixed herbs, flour,
   beef stock and tomato purée (paste),
and season. Bring to the boil and simmer
for 30 minutes until the mixture has
thickened.

3 Transfer the beef mixture to an
   ovenproof gratin dish. Cover with a
layer of the sliced tomatoes and then add
a layer of sliced courgettes (zucchini).
Blend the cornflour (cornstarch) with a
little milk. Pour the remaining milk into a
saucepan and bring to the boil. Add the

cornflour (cornstarch) mixture and cook,
stirring, for 1–2 minutes until thickened.
Remove from the heat and beat in the
fromage frais (yogurt) and egg yolk.
Season well.

4 Spread the white sauce over the layer
   of courgettes (zucchini). Place the
dish on to a baking sheet and sprinkle
with grated Parmesan. Bake in the oven
for 25–30 minutes until golden-brown.
Serve with crusty bread and vegetables.

Beef & Orange Curry

A citrusy, spicy blend of tender chunks of tender beef with the tang of orange and the warmth of Indian spices.

NUTRITIONAL INFORMATION

Calories 345   Sugars 24g
Protein . . . . .28g   Fat 13g
Carbohydrate . . .31g   Saturates 3g

5¼ HOURS   1¼ HOURS

SERVES 4

INGREDIENTS

1 tbsp vegetable oil

225 g/8 oz shallots, halved

2 garlic cloves, crushed

450 g/1 lb lean rump or sirloin beef,
    trimmed and cut into 2 cm/¾ inch cubes

3 tbsp curry paste

450 ml/16 fl oz/2 cups Fresh Beef Stock
    (see page 9)

4 medium oranges

2 tsp cornflour (cornstarch)

salt and pepper

2 tbsp fresh coriander (cilantro), chopped,
    to garnish

basmati rice, freshly boiled, to serve

RAITA

½ cucumber, finely diced

3 tbsp chopped fresh mint

150 ml/5 fl oz/⅔ cup low-fat natural yogurt

1 Heat the oil in a large saucepan. Gently fry the shallots, garlic and the cubes of beef for 5 minutes, stirring occasionally, until the beef is evenly browned all over.

2 Blend together the curry paste and stock. Add the mixture to the beef and stir to mix thoroughly. Bring to the boil, cover and simmer for about 1 hour.

3 Grate the rind of one orange. Extract the juice from the orange and from one other. Peel the other two oranges, removing the pith. Slice between each segment and remove the flesh.

4 Blend the cornflour (cornstarch) with the orange juice. At the end of the cooking time, stir the orange rind into the beef along with the orange and cornflour (cornstarch) mixture. Bring to the boil and

simmer, stirring, for 3–4 minutes until the sauce thickens. Season to taste and stir in the orange segments.

5 To make the raita, mix the cucumber with the mint and stir in the yogurt. Season with salt and pepper to taste.

6 Serve the curry with rice and the cucumber raita, garnished with the chopped coriander (cilantro).

Beef & Black Bean Sauce

It is not necessary to use the expensive cuts of beef steak for this recipe: the meat will be tender as it is cut into small thin slices and marinated.

NUTRITIONAL INFORMATION

Calories 392   Sugars 2g
Protein ....13g   Fat 36g
Carbohydrate ....3g   Saturates 7g

3¹⁄₄ HOURS   10 MINS

SERVES 4

INGREDIENTS

250-300 g/9-10½ oz beef steak (such as rump)

1 small onion

1 small green (bell) pepper, cored and seeded

about 300 ml/½ pint/1¼ cups vegetable oil

1 spring onion (scallion), cut into short sections

a few small slices of ginger root

1-2 small green or red chillies, seeded and sliced

2 tbsp crushed black bean sauce

MARINADE

½ tsp bicarbonate of soda (baking soda) or baking powder

½ tsp sugar

1 tbsp light soy sauce

2 tsp rice wine or dry sherry

2 tsp cornflour (cornstarch) paste (see page 6)

2 tsp sesame oil

1 Using a sharp knife or meat cleaver, cut the beef into small thin strips.

2 To make the marinade, mix together all the ingredients in a shallow dish. Add the beef strips, turn to coat and leave to marinate for at least 2-3 hours.

3 Cut the onion and green (bell) pepper into small cubes.

4 Heat the vegetable oil in a pre-heated wok or large frying pan (skillet). Add the beef strips and stir-fry for about 1 minute, or until the colour changes. Remove the beef strips with a slotted spoon and drain on absorbent kitchen paper (paper towels). Keep warm and set aside until required.

5 Pour off the excess oil, leaving about 1 tablespoon in the wok. Add the spring onion (scallion), ginger, chillies, onion and green (bell) pepper and stir-fry for about 1 minute.

6 Add the black bean sauce and stir until smooth. Return the beef strips to the wok, blend well and stir-fry for another minute. Transfer the stir-fry to a warm serving dish and serve hot.

Rich Beef Stew

This slow-cooked beef stew is flavoured with oranges, red wine and porcini mushrooms.

NUTRITIONAL INFORMATION

Calories	388	Sugars	........15g
Protein	........30g	Fat	..........21g
Carbohydrate	...16g	Saturates	.......9g

45 MINS   1³/₄ HOURS

SERVES 4

I N G R E D I E N T S

1 tbsp oil

15 g/½ oz/1 tbsp butter

225 g/8 oz baby onions, peeled and halved

600 g/1 lb 5 oz stewing steak, diced into
   4 cm/1½ inch chunks

300 ml/½ pint/1¼ cup beef stock

150 ml/¼ pint/⅔ cup red wine

4 tbsp chopped oregano

1 tbsp sugar

1 orange

25 g/1 oz porcini or other dried mushrooms

225 g/8 oz fresh plum tomatoes

cooked rice or potatoes, to serve

1 Heat the oil and butter in a large frying pan (skillet). Add the onions and sauté for 5 minutes or until golden. Remove the onions with a perforated spoon, set aside and keep warm.

2 Add the beef to the pan and cook, stirring, for 5 minutes or until browned all over.

3 Return the onions to the frying pan (skillet) and add the stock, wine, oregano and sugar, stirring to mix well. Transfer the mixture to an ovenproof casserole dish.

4 Pare the rind from the orange and cut it into strips. Slice the orange flesh into rings. Add the orange rings and the rind to the casserole. Cook in a preheated oven, at 180°C/350°F/Gas Mark 4, for 1¼ hours.

5 Soak the porcini mushrooms for 30 minutes in a small bowl containing 4 tablespoons of warm water.

6 Peel and halve the tomatoes. Add the tomatoes, porcini mushrooms and their soaking liquid to the casserole. Cook for a further 20 minutes until the beef is tender and the juices thickened. Serve with cooked rice or potatoes.

Tamarind Beef Balti

Tamarind has been used in Asian cooking for centuries and gives a sour fruity flavour to the sauce.

NUTRITIONAL INFORMATION

Calories 280   Sugars 7g
Protein . . . . .35g   Fat 12g
Carbohydrate . . . .7g   Saturates 4g

 12 HOURS   35 MINS

SERVES 4

I N G R E D I E N T S

125 g/4½ oz tamarind block, broken into pieces

150 ml/¼ pint/⅔ cup water

2 tbsp tomato purée (paste)

1 tbsp granulated sugar

2.5 cm/1 inch piece ginger root, chopped

1 garlic clove, chopped

½ tsp salt

1 onion, chopped

2 tbsp oil

1 tsp cumin seeds

1 tsp coriander seeds

1 tsp brown mustard seeds

4 curry leaves

750 g/1 lb 10 oz lean braising steak, cut into 2.5 cm/1 inch cubes and par-cooked

1 red (bell) pepper, cut in half, sliced

2 fresh green chillies, deseeded and sliced

1 tsp garam masala

1 tbsp chopped fresh coriander (cilantro), to garnish

1 Soak the tamarind overnight in the water. Strain the soaked tamarind, keeping the liquid.

2 Put the tamarind, tomato purée (paste), sugar, ginger, garlic, salt and onion into a food processor or blender and mix to a smooth purée. Alternatively, mash the ingredients together in a bowl.

3 Heat the oil in a Balti pan or wok, add the cumin, coriander seeds, mustard seeds and curry leaves, and cook until the spices start popping.

4 Stir the beef into the spices and stir-fry for 2–4 minutes until the meat is browned.

5 Add the red (bell) pepper, chillies, garam masala, tamarind mixture and reserved tamarind liquid and cook for 20–25 minutes.

6 Serve the beef garnished with fresh coriander (cilantro).

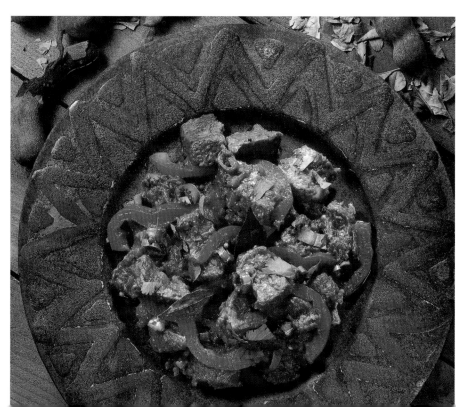

Beef Teriyaki

This Japanese-style teriyaki sauce complements barbecued (grilled) beef, but it can also be used to accompany chicken or salmon.

NUTRITIONAL INFORMATION

Calories ....184 Sugars 6g
Protein ....24g Fat 5g
Carbohydrate ....8g Saturates 2g

2¼ HOURS   15 MINS

SERVES 4

INGREDIENTS

450 g/1 lb extra thin lean beef steaks

8 spring onions (scallions), trimmed and cut into short lengths

1 yellow (bell) pepper, deseeded and cut into chunks

green salad, to serve

SAUCE

1 tsp cornflour (cornstarch)

2 tbsp dry sherry

2 tbsp white wine vinegar

3 tbsp soy sauce

1 tbsp dark muscovado sugar

1 clove garlic, crushed

½ tsp ground cinnamon

½ tsp ground ginger

1 Place the meat in a shallow, non-metallic dish.

2 To make the sauce, combine the cornflour (cornstarch) with the sherry, then stir in the remaining sauce ingredients. Pour the sauce over the meat and leave to marinate for at least 2 hours.

3 Remove the meat from the sauce. Pour the sauce into a small saucepan.

4 Cut the meat into thin strips and thread these, concertina-style, on to pre-soaked wooden skewers, alternating each strip of meat with the prepared pieces of spring onion (scallion) and (bell) pepper.

5 Gently heat the sauce until it is just simmering, stirring occasionally.

6 Barbecue (grill) the kebabs over hot coals for 5–8 minutes, turning and basting the beef and vegetables occasionally with the reserved teriyaki sauce.

7 Arrange the skewers on serving plates and pour the remaining sauce over the kebabs. Serve with a green salad.

Mexican Beef

Strips of beef cooked with (bell) peppers and onion and carrot in a tomato and chilli sauce are prepared quickly in the microwave.

NUTRITIONAL INFORMATION

Calories 513   Sugars 7g
Protein . . . . .33g   Fat 23g
Carbohydrate . . .46g   Saturates 8g

 30 MINS   35 MINS

SERVES 4

I N G R E D I E N T S

225 g/8 oz/1 generous cup brown rice

700 ml/1¼ pints/3 cups boiling water

½ tsp salt

2 tbsp oil

1 onion, sliced into rings

1 carrot, cut into thin matchsticks

½ each red, green and yellow (bell) peppers

½–1 fresh green chilli, deseeded and chopped

1 garlic clove, crushed

500 g/1 lb 2 oz rump steak, cut into strips

225 g/8 oz/scant 1 cup canned tomatoes

1 tbsp tomato purée (paste)

2 tsp cornflour (cornstarch)

sprigs of fresh coriander (cilantro), to garnish

salt and pepper

S A L S A

tomatoes, skinned and chopped

2 spring onions (scallions), chopped

1 small fresh green chilli, deseeded and chopped

2 tbsp lime juice

1 tbsp chopped fresh coriander (cilantro)

8 flour tortillas

1 Place the rice in a large bowl. Add the boiling water and salt. Cover and cook on HIGH power for 15 minutes. Leave to stand, covered, for 5 minutes before draining.

2 Place the oil, onion and carrot in a large bowl. Cover and cook on HIGH power for 2 minutes. Slice the (bell) peppers, and add with the chilli, garlic and steak to the bowl. Cover and cook on HIGH power for 4 minutes, stirring once.

3 Add the canned tomatoes, tomato purée (paste) and seasoning. Mix the cornflour (cornstarch) with a little water, then stir into the bowl. Cover and cook on MEDIUM power for 10 minutes.

4 To make the salsa, mix together the tomatoes, spring onions (scallions), chilli, lime juice and coriander (cilantro). Season and leave to stand for 10 minutes.

5 Heat the tortillas on HIGH power for 40 seconds, covered, or according to the packet instructions.

6 Garnish the beef with fresh coriander (cilantro) sprigs and serve with the tortillas, rice and salsa.

Beef & Beans

The green of the beans complements the dark colour of the beef, served in a rich sauce.

NUTRITIONAL INFORMATION

Calories	.381	Sugars	.3g
Protein	.25g	Fat	.27g
Carbohydrate	.10g	Saturates	.8g

 35 MINS   15 MINS

SERVES 4

I N G R E D I E N T S

450 g/1 lb rump or fillet steak, cut into
2.5-cm/1-inch pieces

M A R I N A D E

2 tsp cornflour (cornstarch)

2 tbsp dark soy sauce

2 tsp peanut oil

S A U C E

2 tbsp vegetable oil

3 garlic cloves, crushed

1 small onion, cut into 8

225 g/8 oz thin green beans, halved

25 g/1 oz/¼ cup unsalted cashews

25 g/1 oz canned bamboo shoots, drained
and rinsed

2 tsp dark soy sauce

2 tsp Chinese rice wine or dry sherry

125 ml/4 fl oz/½ cup beef stock

2 tsp cornflour (cornstarch)

4 tsp water

salt and pepper

1 To make the marinade, mix together the cornflour (cornstarch), soy sauce and peanut oil.

2 Place the steak in a shallow glass bowl. Pour the marinade over the steak, turn to coat thoroughly, cover and leave to marinate in the refrigerator for at least 30 minutes.

3 To make the sauce, heat the oil in a preheated wok. Add the garlic, onion, beans, cashews and bamboo shoots and stir-fry for 2–3 minutes.

4 Remove the steak from the marinade, drain, add to the wok and stir-fry for 3–4 minutes.

5 Mix the soy sauce, Chinese rice wine or sherry and beef stock together. Blend the cornflour (cornstarch) with the water and add to the soy sauce mixture, mixing to combine.

6 Stir the mixture into the wok and bring the sauce to the boil, stirring until thickened and clear. Reduce the heat and leave to simmer for 2–3 minutes. Season to taste and serve immediately.

Carrot-Topped Beef Pie

This is a variation of an old favourite, where a creamy mashed potato and carrot topping is piled thickly on to a delicious beef pie filling.

NUTRITIONAL INFORMATION

Calories 352	Sugars 6g	
Protein 28g	Fat 11g	
Carbohydrate ...38g	Saturates 6g	

10 MINS   1¼ HOURS

SERVES 4

INGREDIENTS

450 g/1 lb lean ground beef

1 onion, chopped

1 garlic clove, crushed

1 tbsp plain (all-purpose) flour

300 ml/½ pint/1¼ cups beef stock

2 tbsp tomato purée (paste)

1 celery stick, chopped

3 tbsp chopped fresh parsley

1 tbsp Worcestershire sauce

675 g/1½ lb floury (mealy) potatoes, diced

2 large carrots, diced

25 g/1 oz/2 tbsp butter

3 tbsp skimmed milk

salt and pepper

1 Dry fry the beef in a large pan set over a high heat for 3-4 minutes or until sealed. Add the onion and garlic and cook for a further 5 minutes, stirring.

2 Add the flour and cook for 1 minute. Gradually blend in the beef stock and tomato purée (paste). Stir in the celery, 1 tbsp of the parsley and the Worcestershire sauce. Season to taste.

3 Bring the mixture to the boil, then reduce the heat and simmer for 20-

25 minutes. Spoon the beef mixture into a 1.1 litre/2 pint/5 cup pie dish.

4 Meanwhile, cook the potatoes and carrots in a saucepan of boiling water for 10 minutes. Drain and mash them together.

5 Stir the butter, milk and the remaining parsley into the potato and

carrot mixture and season with salt and pepper to taste. Spoon the potato on top of the beef mixture to cover it completely; alternatively, pipe the potato with a piping (pastry) bag.

6 Cook the corrot-topped beef pie in a preheated oven, 190°C/375°F/Gas Mark 5, for 45 minutes or until cooked through. Serve piping hot.

Beef, Tomato & Olive Kebabs

These kebabs (kabobs) have a Mediterranean flavour. The sweetness of the tomatoes and the sharpness of the olives makes them rather more-ish.

NUTRITIONAL INFORMATION

Calories 166	Sugars 1g
Protein 12g	Fat 12g
Carbohydrate 1g	Saturates 3g

 45 MINS   15 MINS

SERVES 8

INGREDIENTS

450 g/1 lb rump or sirloin steak

16 cherry tomatoes

16 large green olives, pitted

focaccia bread, to serve

BASTE

4 tbsp olive oil

1 tbsp sherry vinegar

1 clove garlic, crushed

salt and pepper

FRESH TOMATO RELISH

1 tbsp olive oil

½ red onion, chopped finely

1 clove garlic, chopped

6 plum tomatoes, deseeded, skinned
  and chopped

2 pitted green olives, sliced

1 tbsp chopped, fresh parsley

1 tbsp lemon juice

1 Using a sharp knife, trim any fat from the beef and cut the meat into about 24 evenly-sized pieces.

2 Thread the pieces of beef on to 8 wooden skewers, alternating the meat with the cherry tomatoes and the green olives.

3 To make the baste, combine the oil, vinegar, garlic and salt and pepper to taste in a bowl.

4 To make the relish, heat the oil in a small pan and fry the onion and garlic for 3–4 minutes until softened. Add the tomatoes and olives and cook for 2–3 minutes until the tomatoes have softened slightly. Stir in the parsley and lemon juice and season with salt and pepper to taste. Set aside and keep warm or leave to chill.

5 Barbecue (grill) the kebabs (kabobs) on an oiled rack over hot coals for 5–10 minutes, basting and turning frequently. Serve with the tomato relish and slices of focaccia.

COOK'S TIP

The kebabs (kabobs), baste and relish can be prepared several hours in advance, avoiding the need for any last minute rush. For a simple meal, serve with crusty fresh bread and a mixed salad.

Beef & Bok Choy

In this recipe, a colourful selection of vegetables is stir-fried with tender strips of steak.

NUTRITIONAL INFORMATION

Calories 369	Sugars 9g	
Protein 29g	Fat 23g	
Carbohydrate ...12g	Saturates 8g	

15 MINS   🕐 5 MINS

SERVES 4

INGREDIENTS

1 large head of bok choy, about 250-275 g/9-9½ oz, torn into large pieces

2 tbsp vegetable oil

2 garlic cloves, crushed

500 g/1 lb 2 oz rump or fillet steak, cut into thin strips

150 g/5½ oz mangetout (snow peas), trimmed

150 g/5½ oz baby or dwarf corn

6 spring onions (scallions), chopped

2 red (bell) peppers, cored, seeded and thinly sliced

2 tbsp oyster sauce

1 tbsp fish sauce

1 tbsp sugar

rice or noodles, to serve

1 Steam the bok choy over boiling water until just tender. Keep warm.

2 Heat the oil in a large, heavy-based frying pan (skillet) or wok, add the garlic and steak strips and stir-fry until just browned, about 1-2 minutes.

3 Add the mangetout (snow peas), baby corn, spring onions (scallions), red (bell) pepper, oyster sauce, fish sauce and sugar to the pan, mixing well. Stir-fry for a further 2-3 minutes until the vegetables are just tender, but still crisp.

4 Arrange the bok choy leaves in the base of a heated serving dish and spoon the beef and vegetable mixture into the centre.

5 Serve the stir-fry immediately, with rice or noodles.

COOK'S TIP

Bok choy is one of the most important ingredients in this dish. If unavailable, use Chinese leaves (cabbage), kai choy (mustard leaves) or pak choy.

Rogan Josh

This is one of the best-known curries. Rogan Josh means 'red curry', and is so-called because of the red chillies in the recipe.

NUTRITIONAL INFORMATION

Calories 248	Sugars 2g
Protein 35g	Fat 11g
Carbohydrate 2g	Saturates 5g

 10 MINS   1³/₄ HOURS

SERVES 6

INGREDIENTS

2 tbsp ghee

1 kg/2 lb 4 oz lean braising steak, cut into 2.5 cm/1 inch cubes

1 onion, chopped finely

3 garlic cloves

2.5 cm/1 inch piece ginger root, grated

4 fresh red chillies, chopped

4 green cardamom pods

4 cloves

2 tsp coriander seeds

2 tsp cumin seeds

1 tsp paprika

1 tsp salt

1 bay leaf

125 ml/4 fl oz/¼ cup low-fat yogurt

2.5 cm/1 inch piece cinnamon stick

150 ml/¼ pint/⅔ cup hot water

¼ tsp garam masala

pepper

1 Heat the ghee in a large flameproof casserole and brown the meat in batches. Remove the meat from the casserole and set aside in a bowl.

2 Add the chopped onion to the ghee and stir over a high heat for 3–4 minutes.

3 Grind together the garlic, ginger, chillies, cardamom, cloves, coriander, cumin, paprika and salt. Add the spice paste and bay leaf to the casserole and stir until fragrant.

4 Return the meat and any juices in the bowl to the casserole and simmer for 2–3 minutes. Gradually stir the yogurt into the casserole keeping the sauce simmering.

5 Stir in the cinnamon stick and hot water, and pepper to taste.

6 Cover the casserole and cook in a preheated oven, 180°C/350°F/Gas Mark 4, for 1¼ hours until the meat is very tender and the sauce is slightly reduced. Discard the cinnamon stick and stir in the garam masala. Remove surplus oil from the surface of the casserole before serving.

Cantonese Fried Noodles

This dish is usually served as a snack or light meal. It may also be served as an accompaniment to plain meat and fish dishes.

NUTRITIONAL INFORMATION

Calories 385   Sugars 6g
Protein . . . . .38g   Fat 17g
Carbohydrate . . .21g   Saturates 4g

 5 MINS   15 MINS

SERVES 4

I N G R E D I E N T S

350 g/12 oz egg noodles

3 tbsp vegetable oil

675 g/1½ lb lean beef steak, cut into thin strips

125 g/4½ oz green cabbage, shredded

75 g/2¾ oz bamboo shoots

6 spring onions (scallions), sliced

25 g/1 oz green beans, halved

1 tbsp dark soy sauce

2 tbsp beef stock

1 tbsp dry sherry

1 tbsp light brown sugar

2 tbsp chopped parsley, to garnish

1 Cook the noodles in a saucepan of boiling water for 2-3 minutes. Drain well, rinse under cold running water and drain thoroughly again.

2 Heat 1 tablespoon of the oil in a preheated wok or frying pan (skillet), swirling it around until it is really hot

3 Add the noodles and stir-fry for 1-2 minutes. Drain the noodles and set aside until required.

4 Heat the remaining oil in the wok. Add the beef and stir-fry for 2-3 minutes. Add the cabbage, bamboo shoots, spring onions (scallions) and beans to the wok and stir-fry for 1-2 minutes.

5 Add the soy sauce, beef stock, dry sherry and light brown sugar to the wok, stirring to mix well.

6 Stir the noodles into the mixture in the wok, tossing to mix well. Transfer to serving bowls, garnish with chopped parsley and serve immediately.

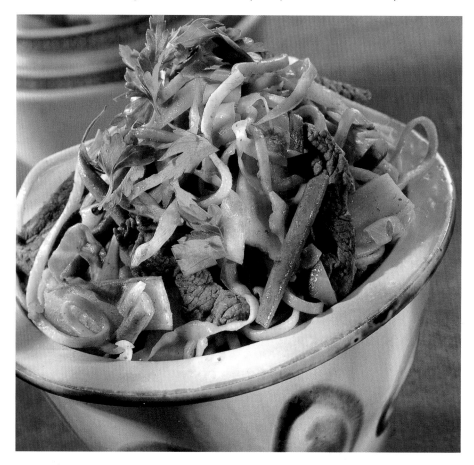

VARIATION

You can vary the vegetables in this dish depending on seasonal availability or whatever you have at hand – try broccoli, green (bell) pepper or spinach.

Beef with Crispy Noodles

Crispy noodles are terrific and may also be served on their own as a side dish, sprinkled with sugar and salt.

NUTRITIONAL INFORMATION

Calories 244	Sugars 9g
Protein 20g	Fat 10g
Carbohydrate . . .19g	Saturates 2g

 5 MINS   30 MINS

SERVES 4

I N G R E D I E N T S

225 g/8 oz medium egg noodles

350 g/12 oz beef fillet

2 tbsp sunflower oil

1 tsp ground ginger

1 clove garlic, crushed

1 red chilli, deseeded and very finely chopped

100 g/3½ oz carrots, cut into thin sticks

6 spring onions (scallions), sliced

2 tbsp lime marmalade

2 tbsp soy sauce

oil, for frying

1 Place the noodles in a large dish or bowl. Pour over enough boiling water to cover the noodles and leave to stand for about 10 minutes while you stir-fry the rest of the ingredients.

2 Using a sharp knife, thinly slice the beef fillet.

3 Heat the sunflower oil in a large preheated wok or frying pan (skillet).

4 Add the beef and ground ginger to the wok or frying pan (skillet) and stir-fry for about 5 minutes.

5 Add the crushed garlic, chopped red chilli, carrots and spring onions (scallions) to the wok and stir-fry for a further 2–3 minutes.

6 Add the lime marmalade and soy sauce to the wok and allow to bubble for 2 minutes. Remove the chilli beef and ginger mixture, set aside and keep warm until required.

7 Heat the oil for frying in the wok or frying pan (skillet).

8 Drain the noodles thoroughly and pat dry with absorbent kitchen paper (paper towels). Carefully lower the noodles into the hot oil and cook for 2–3 minutes or until crispy. Drain the noodles on absorbent kitchen paper (paper towels).

9 Divide the noodles between 4 warm serving plates and top with the chilli beef and ginger mixture. Serve immediately.

Egg Noodles with Beef

Quick and easy, this mouth-watering Chinese-style noodle dish can be cooked in minutes.

NUTRITIONAL INFORMATION

Calories	329	Sugars	........3g
Protein	........23g	Fat	..........16g
Carbohydrate	...20g	Saturates	.......4g

10 MINS   15 MINS

SERVES 4

I N G R E D I E N T S

285 g/10 oz egg noodles

3 tbsp walnut oil

2.5 cm/1 inch piece fresh root ginger,
   cut into thin strips

5 spring onions (scallions), finely
   shredded

2 garlic cloves, finely chopped

1 red (bell) pepper, cored, seeded and
   thinly sliced

100 g/3½ oz button mushrooms, thinly
   sliced

350 g/12 oz fillet steak, cut into
   thin strips

1 tbsp cornflour (cornstarch)

5 tbsp dry sherry

3 tbsp soy sauce

1 tsp soft brown sugar

225 g/8 oz/1 cup bean sprouts

1 tbsp sesame oil

salt and pepper

spring onion (scallion) strips,
   to garnish

1 Bring a large saucepan of water to the boil. Add the egg noodles and cook according to the instructions on the packet. Drain the noodles, rinse under cold running water, drain thoroughly again and set aside.

2 Heat the walnut oil in a preheated wok until it is really hot.

3 Add the grated fresh root ginger, shredded spring onions (scallions) and chopped garlic and stir-fry for 45 seconds.

4 Add the red (bell) pepper, button mushrooms and steak and stir-fry for 4 minutes. Season to taste with salt and pepper.

5 Mix together the cornflour (cornstarch), dry sherry and soy sauce in a small jug to form a paste, and pour into the wok. Sprinkle over the brown sugar and stir-fry all of the ingredients for a further 2 minutes.

6 Add the bean sprouts, drained noodles and sesame oil to the wok, stir and toss together for 1 minute.

7 Transfer the stir-fry to warm serving dishes, garnish with strips of spring onion (scallion) and serve.

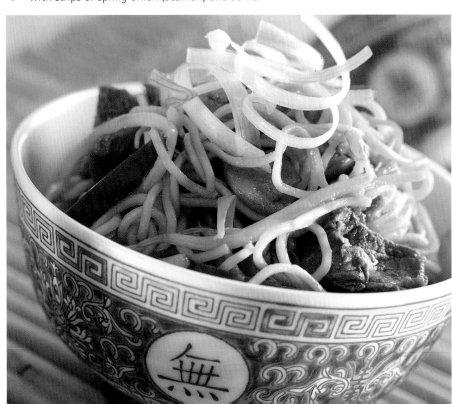

Beef in Barolo

Barolo is a famous wine from the Piedmont area of Italy. Its mellow flavour is the key to this dish, so don't stint on the quality of the wine.

NUTRITIONAL INFORMATION

Calories ....744 Sugars 1g
Protein ....66g Fat 43g
Carbohydrate ....1g Saturates 16g

15 MINS   2¼ HOURS

SERVES 4

INGREDIENTS

4 tbsp oil

1 kg/2 lb 4 oz piece boned rolled rib of
    beef, or piece of silverside (round)

2 garlic cloves, crushed

4 shallots, sliced

1 tsp chopped fresh rosemary

1 tsp chopped fresh oregano

2 celery stalks, sliced

1 large carrot, diced

2 cloves

1 bottle Barolo wine

freshly grated nutmeg

salt and pepper

cooked vegetables, such as broccoli, carrots
    and new potatoes, to serve

1 Heat the oil in a flameproof casserole and brown the meat all over. Remove the meat from the casserole.

2 Add the garlic, shallots, herbs, celery, carrot and cloves and fry for 5 minutes.

3 Replace the meat on top of the vegetables. Pour in the wine. Cover the casserole and simmer gently for about 2 hours until tender. Remove the meat from the casserole, slice and keep warm.

4 Rub the contents of the pan through a sieve (strainer) or purée in a blender, adding a little hot beef stock if necessary. Season with nutmeg, salt and pepper.

5 Serve the meat with the sauce and accompanied by cooked vegetables, such as broccoli, carrots and new potatoes, if wished.

Fresh Spaghetti & Meatballs

This well-loved Italian dish is famous across the world. Make the most of it by using high-quality steak for the meatballs.

NUTRITIONAL INFORMATION

Calories 665   Sugars 9g
Protein ....39g   Fat 24g
Carbohydrate ...77g   Saturates 8g

 45 MINS   1¼ HOURS

SERVES 4

I N G R E D I E N T S

150 g/5½ oz/2½ cups brown breadcrumbs

150 ml/¼ pint/⅔ cup milk

25 g/1 oz/2 tbsp butter

25 g/1 oz/¼ cup wholemeal
   (whole-wheat) flour

200 ml/7 fl oz/⅞ cup beef stock

400 g/14 oz can chopped tomatoes

2 tbsp tomato purée (paste)

1 tsp sugar

1 tbsp finely chopped fresh tarragon

1 large onion, chopped

450 g/1 lb/4 cups minced steak

1 tsp paprika

4 tbsp olive oil

450 g/1 lb fresh spaghetti

salt and pepper

fresh tarragon sprigs, to garnish

1 Place the breadcrumbs in a bowl, add the milk and set aside to soak for about 30 minutes.

2 Melt half of the butter in a pan. Add the flour and cook, stirring constantly, for 2 minutes. Gradually stir in the beef stock and cook, stirring constantly, for a further 5 minutes. Add the tomatoes, tomato purée (paste), sugar and tarragon. Season well and simmer for 25 minutes.

3 Mix the onion, steak and paprika into the breadcrumbs and season to taste. Shape the mixture into 14 meatballs.

4 Heat the oil and remaining butter in a frying pan (skillet) and fry the meatballs, turning, until brown all over. Place in a deep casserole, pour over the tomato sauce, cover and bake in a preheated oven, at 180°C/350°F/Gas Mark 4, for 25 minutes.

5 Bring a large saucepan of lightly salted water to the boil. Add the fresh spaghetti, bring back to the boil and cook for about 2–3 minutes or until tender, but still firm to the bite.

6 Meanwhile, remove the meatballs from the oven and allow them to cool for 3 minutes. Serve the meatballs and their sauce with the spaghetti, garnished with tarragon sprigs.

Pathan Beef Stir-Fry

Although the meat can be left in the marinade overnight, this is a quick and tasty dish to make.

NUTRITIONAL INFORMATION

Calories 325   Sugars 6g
Protein ....41g   Fat 15g
Carbohydrate ....7g   Saturates 5g

 2¼ HOURS   15 MINS

SERVES 4

INGREDIENTS

750 g/1 lb 10 oz fillet of lean beef, cut into 2.5 cm/1 inch strips

2 tbsp vegetable oil

1 onion

2.5 cm/1 inch piece ginger root, cut into strips

1 fresh red chilli, deseeded and sliced

2 carrots, cut into strips

1 green (bell) pepper, cut into strips

1 tsp garam masala

1 tbsp toasted sesame seeds

MARINADE

1 tsp dried fenugreek

1 tsp brown mustard seeds, ground

1 tsp ground cinnamon

1 tsp ground cumin

1 garlic clove, crushed

150 ml/¼ pint/⅔ cup low-fat natural yogurt

1 To make the marinade, mix the ingredients together in a bowl.

2 Mix the beef with the marinade, then cover and leave to marinate for 1–2 hours, or overnight in the refrigerator.

3 Heat the oil in a Balti pan or wok, add the onion and stir-fry until softened.

4 Stir in the ginger, chilli, carrots and green (bell) pepper and stir-fry for 1 minute.

5 Add the garam masala and beef with its marinade to the vegetables, and stir-fry for 8–10 minutes until the beef is tender; it is best if it is still pinkish inside.

6 Stir in the toasted sesame seeds and serve the stir-fry immediately.

VARIATION

Any selection of vegetables can be added to the stir-fry, which is a good way to use up any vegetables left over in the refrigerator, but add them to the beef for just long enough to heat through.

Creamed Strips of Sirloin

This quick and easy dish tastes superb and would make a delicious treat for a special occasion.

NUTRITIONAL INFORMATION

Calories 796	Sugars 2g	
Protein 29g	Fat 63g	
Carbohydrate ...26g	Saturates 39g	

15 MINS   30 MINS

SERVES 4

INGREDIENTS

75 g/3 oz/6 tbsp butter

450 g/1 lb sirloin steak, trimmed
  and cut into thin strips

175 g/6 oz button mushrooms, sliced

1 tsp mustard

pinch of freshly grated root ginger

2 tbsp dry sherry

150 ml/¼ pint/⅔ cup double (heavy) cream

salt and pepper

4 slices hot toast, cut into triangles,
  to serve

PASTA

450 g/1 lb dried rigatoni

2 tbsp olive oil

2 fresh basil sprigs

115 g/4 oz/8 tbsp butter

1 Melt the butter in a large frying pan (skillet) and gently fry the steak over a low heat, stirring frequently, for 6 minutes. Using a slotted spoon, transfer the steak to an ovenproof dish and keep warm.

2 Add the sliced mushrooms to the frying pan (skillet) and cook for 2–3 minutes in the juices remaining in the pan. Add the mustard, ginger, salt and pepper. Cook for 2 minutes, then add the sherry and cream. Cook for a further 3 minutes, then pour the cream sauce over the steak.

3 Bake the steak and cream mixture in a preheated oven, at 90°C/375°F/Gas Mark 5, for 10 minutes.

4 Meanwhile, cook the pasta. Bring a large saucepan of lightly salted water to the boil. Add the rigatoni, olive oil and 1 of the basil sprigs and boil rapidly for 10 minutes, until tender but still firm to the bite. Drain the pasta and transfer to a warm serving plate. Toss the pasta with the butter and garnish with a sprig of basil.

5 Serve the creamed steak strips with the pasta and triangles of warm toast.

COOK'S TIP

Dried pasta will keep for up to 6 months. Keep it in the packet and reseal it once you have opened it, or transfer the pasta to an airtight jar.

Beef Daube

This dish is very French but also very, very New Orleans, especially when the beef is perked up with Tabasco and Cajun spices.

NUTRITIONAL INFORMATION

Calories	.251	Sugars	.2g
Protein	.31g	Fat	.10g
Carbohydrate	.8g	Saturates	.3g

  10 MINS   3¼ HOURS

SERVES 6–8

I N G R E D I E N T S

2 tbsp olive oil

1 large onion, cut into wedges

2 celery sticks, chopped

1 green (bell) pepper, cored, seeded and chopped

1 kg/2¼ lb lean braising steak, cubed

60 g/2 oz/½ cup plain flour, seasoned with salt and pepper

600 ml/1 pint/2½ cups beef stock

2 garlic cloves, crushed

150 ml/¼ pint/⅔ cup red wine

2 tbsp red wine vinegar

2 tbsp tomato purée (paste)

½ tsp Tabasco

1 tsp chopped fresh thyme

2 bay leaves

½ tsp Cajun spice mix

French bread, to serve

1 Heat the oil in a large heavy-based, flameproof casserole. Add the onion wedges and cook until browned on all sides. Remove with a slotted spoon and set aside.

2 Add the celery and (bell) pepper to the pan and cook until softened.

Remove the vegetables with a slotted spoon and set aside.

3 Coat the meat in the seasoned flour, add to the pan and sauté until browned on all sides.

4 Add the stock, garlic, wine, vinegar, tomato purée (paste), Tabasco and thyme and heat gently.

5 Return the onions, celery and peppers to the pan. Tuck in the bay leaves and sprinkle with the Cajun seasoning.

6 Bring to the boil, transfer to the oven and cook for 2½–3 hours, or until the meat and vegetables are tender.

7 Serve the beef daube with French bread.

Sicilian Spaghetti

This delicious Sicilian dish originated as a handy way of using up leftover cooked pasta.

NUTRITIONAL INFORMATION

Calories 797   Sugars 7g
Protein ....31g   Fat 60g
Carbohydrate ...35g   Saturates 16g

30 MINS   1¹/₂ HOURS

SERVES 4

INGREDIENTS

150 ml/¼ pint/⅔ cup olive oil, plus extra
   for brushing

2 aubergines (eggplant)

350 g/12 oz/3 cups minced (ground) beef

1 onion, chopped

2 garlic cloves, crushed

2 tbsp tomato purée (paste)

400 g/14 oz can chopped tomatoes

1 tsp Worcestershire sauce

1 tsp chopped fresh marjoram or oregano
   or ½ tsp dried marjoram or oregano

60 g/2 oz/½ cup stoned (pitted) black
   olives, sliced

1 green, red or yellow (bell) pepper, cored,
   seeded and chopped

175 g/6 oz dried spaghetti

115 g/4 oz/1 cup freshly grated
   Parmesan cheese

salt and pepper

fresh oregano or parsley sprigs,
   to garnish

1 Brush a 20 cm/8 inch loose-based round cake tin (pan) with oil, line the base with baking parchment and brush with oil.

2 Slice the aubergines (eggplant). Heat a little oil in a pan and fry the aubergines (eggplant) in batches for 3–4 minutes or until browned on both sides. Add more oil, as necessary. Drain on kitchen paper (kitchen towels).

3 Put the minced (ground) beef, onion and garlic in a saucepan and cook over a medium heat, stirring occasionally, until browned. Add the tomato purée (paste), tomatoes, Worcestershire sauce, marjoram or oregano and salt and pepper to taste. Leave to simmer, stirring occasionally, for 10 minutes. Add the olives and (bell) pepper and cook for a further 10 minutes.

4 Bring a pan of salted water to the boil. Add the spaghetti and 1 tbsp oil and cook for 8–10 minutes until tender, but still firm to the bite. Drain and turn the spaghetti into a bowl. Add the meat mixture and cheese and toss with 2 forks.

5 Arrange aubergine (eggplant) slices over the base and up the sides of the tin (pan). Add the spaghetti, pressing down firmly, and then cover with the rest of the aubergine (eggplant) slices. Bake in a preheated oven at 200°C/400°F/Gas Mark 6 for 40 minutes. Leave to stand for 5 minutes, then invert on to a serving dish. Discard the baking parchment. Garnish with the fresh herbs and serve.

Pizzaiola Steak

This has a Neapolitan sauce, using the delicious red tomatoes so abundant in that area, but canned ones make an excellent alternative.

NUTRITIONAL INFORMATION

Calories 371	Sugars 7g	
Protein 43g	Fat 19g	
Carbohydrate 7g	Saturates 5g	

25 MINS   30 MINS

SERVES 4

I N G R E D I E N T S

2 x 400 g/14 oz cans peeled tomatoes or
   750 g/1 lb 10 oz fresh tomatoes

4 tbsp olive oil

2–3 garlic cloves, crushed

1 onion, chopped finely

1 tbsp tomato purée (paste)

1½ tsp chopped fresh marjoram or oregano
   or ¾ tsp dried marjoram or oregano

4 thin sirloin or rump steaks

2 tbsp chopped fresh parsley

1 tsp sugar

salt and pepper

fresh herbs, to garnish (optional)

sauté potatoes, to serve

1 If using canned tomatoes, purée them in a food processor, then sieve to remove the seeds. If using fresh tomatoes, peel, remove the seeds and chop finely.

2 Heat half of the oil in a pan and fry the garlic and onions very gently for about 5 minutes, or until softened.

3 Add the tomatoes, seasoning, tomato purée (paste) and chopped herbs to the pan. If using fresh tomatoes add 4 tablespoons water too, and then simmer

very gently for 8–10 minutes, giving an occasional stir.

4 Meanwhile, trim the steaks if necessary and season. Heat the remaining oil in a frying pan (skillet) and fry the steaks quickly on both sides to seal, then continue until cooked to your liking – 2 minutes for rare, 3–4 minutes for medium, or 5 minutes for well done. Alternatively, cook the steaks under a hot grill (broiler) after brushing lightly with oil.

5 When the sauce has thickened a little, adjust the seasoning and stir in the chopped parsley and sugar.

6 Pour off the excess fat from the pan containing the steaks and add the tomato sauce. Reheat gently and serve at once, with the sauce spooned over and around the steaks. Garnish with sprigs of fresh herbs, if liked. Sauté potatoes and a green vegetable make very good accompaniments.

Beef Chow Mein

Chow Mein must be the best-known and most popular noodle dish on any Chinese menu. You can use any meat or vegetables instead of beef.

NUTRITIONAL INFORMATION

Calories	341	Sugars	.........3g
Protein	........27g	Fat	..........17g
Carbohydrate	...20g	Saturates	.......4g

10 MINS   20 MINS

SERVES 4

INGREDIENTS

450 g/1 lb egg noodles

4 tbsp peanut oil

450 g/1 lb lean beef steak, cut into thin strips

2 garlic cloves, crushed

1 tsp grated fresh root ginger

1 green (bell) pepper, thinly sliced

1 carrot, thinly sliced

2 celery sticks, sliced

8 spring onions (scallions)

1 tsp dark brown sugar

1 tbsp dry sherry

2 tbsp dark soy sauce

few drops of chilli sauce

1 Cook the noodles in a saucepan of boiling salted water for 4-5 minutes. Drain well, rinse under cold running water and drain again thoroughly.

2 Toss the noodles in 1 tablespoon of the peanut oil.

3 Heat the remaining oil in a preheated wok. Add the beef and stir-fry for 3-4 minutes, stirring constantly.

4 Add the crushed garlic and grated fresh root ginger to the wok and stir-fry for 30 seconds.

5 Add the (bell) pepper, carrot, celery and spring onions (scallions) and stir-fry for about 2 minutes.

6 Add the dark brown sugar, dry sherry, dark soy sauce and chilli sauce to the mixture in the wok and cook, stirring, for 1 minute.

7 Stir in the noodles, mixing well, and cook until completely warmed through.

8 Transfer the noodles to warm serving bowls and serve immediately.

VARIATION

A variety of different vegetables may be used in this recipe for colour and flavour – try broccoli, red (bell) peppers, green beans or baby sweetcorn cobs.

Spicy Beef

In this recipe beef is marinated in a five-spice and chilli marinade for a spicy flavour.

NUTRITIONAL INFORMATION

Calories 246	Sugars 2g	
Protein 21g	Fat 13g	
Carbohydrate ...10g	Saturates 3g	

1¼ HOURS   10 MINS

SERVES 4

INGREDIENTS

225 g/8 oz fillet steak

2 garlic cloves, crushed

1 tsp powdered star anise

1 tbsp dark soy sauce

spring onion (scallion) tassels, to garnish

SAUCE

2 tbsp vegetable oil

1 bunch spring onions (scallions), halved
 lengthways

1 tbsp dark soy sauce

1 tbsp dry sherry

¼ tsp chilli sauce

150 ml/¼ pint/⅔ cup water

2 tsp cornflour (cornstarch)

4 tsp water

1 Cut the steak into thin strips and place in a shallow dish.

2 Mix together the garlic, star anise and dark soy sauce in a bowl.

3 Pour the sauce mixture over the steak strips, turning them to coat thoroughly. Cover and leave to marinate in the refrigerator for at least 1 hour.

4 To make the sauce, heat the oil in a preheated wok or large frying pan (skillet). Reduce the heat and stir-fry the spring onions (scallions) for 1-2 minutes.

5 Remove the spring onions (scallions) from the wok with a slotted spoon, drain on absorbent kitchen paper (paper towels) and set aside until required.

6 Add the beef to the wok, together with the marinade, and stir-fry for 3-4 minutes. Return the spring onions (scallions) to the wok and add the soy sauce, sherry, chilli sauce and two thirds of the water.

7 Blend the cornflour (cornstarch) with the remaining water and stir into the wok. Bring to the boil, stirring until the sauce thickens and clears.

8 Transfer to a warm serving dish, garnish and serve immediately.

Beef & Broccoli Stir-fry

This is a great combination of ingredients in terms of colour and flavour, and it is so simple and quick to prepare.

NUTRITIONAL INFORMATION

Calories 232   Sugars 1g
Protein . . . . .12g   Fat 19g
Carbohydrate . . . .4g   Saturates 6g

4¼ HOURS   15 MINS

SERVES 4

I N G R E D I E N T S

225 g/8 oz lean steak, trimmed

2 garlic cloves, crushed

dash of chilli oil

1-cm/½-inch piece fresh root ginger, grated

½ tsp Chinese five-spice powder

2 tbsp dark soy sauce

2 tbsp vegetable oil

150 g/5½ oz broccoli florets

1 tbsp light soy sauce

150 ml/¼ pint/⅔ cup beef stock

2 tsp cornflour (cornstarch)

4 tsp water

carrot strips, to garnish

1 Using a sharp knife, cut the steak into thin strips and place in a shallow glass dish.

2 Mix together the garlic, chilli oil, grated ginger, Chinese five-spice powder and dark soy sauce in a small bowl and pour over the beef, tossing to coat the strips evenly.

3 Cover the bowl and leave the meat to marinate in the refrigerator for several hours to allow the flavours to develop fully.

4 Heat 1 tablespoon of the vegetable oil in a preheated wok or large frying pan (skillet). Add the broccoli and stir-fry over a medium heat for 4–5 minutes. Remove from the wok with a slotted spoon and set aside until required.

5 Heat the remaining oil in the wok. Add the steak together with the marinade, and stir-fry for 2–3 minutes, until the steak is browned and sealed.

6 Return the broccoli to the wok and stir in the light soy sauce and stock.

7 Blend the cornflour (cornstarch) with the water to form a smooth paste and stir into the wok. Bring to the boil, stirring, until thickened and clear. Cook for 1 minute. Transfer the beef & broccoli stir-fry to a warm serving dish, arrange the carrot strips in a lattice on top and serve immediately.

Roman Pan-fried Lamb

Chunks of tender lamb, pan-fried with garlic and stewed in red wine are a real Roman dish.

NUTRITIONAL INFORMATION

Calories 299   Sugars 1g
Protein ....31g   Fat 16g
Carbohydrate ....1g   Saturates 7g

15 MINS   50 MINS

SERVES 4

INGREDIENTS

1 tbsp oil

15 g/½ oz/1 tbsp butter

600 g/1 lb 5 oz lamb (shoulder or leg),
    cut into 2.5 cm/1 inch chunks

4 garlic cloves, peeled

3 sprigs thyme, stalks removed

6 canned anchovy fillets

150 ml/¼ pint/⅔ cup red wine

150 ml/¼ pint/⅔ cup lamb or
    vegetable stock

1 tsp sugar

50 g/1¾ oz black olives, pitted and halved

2 tbsp chopped parsley, to garnish

mashed potato, to serve

1 Heat the oil and butter in a large frying pan (skillet). Add the lamb and cook for 4–5 minutes, stirring, until the meat is browned all over.

2 Using a pestle and mortar, grind together the garlic, thyme and anchovies to make a smooth paste.

3 Add the wine and lamb or vegetable stock to the frying pan (skillet). Stir in the garlic and anchovy paste together with the sugar.

4 Bring the mixture to the boil, reduce the heat, cover and simmer for 30–40 minutes or until the lamb is tender. For the last 10 minutes of the cooking time, remove the lid to allow the sauce to reduce slightly.

5 Stir the olives into the sauce and mix to combine.

6 Transfer the lamb and the sauce to a serving bowl and garnish. Serve with creamy mashed potatoes.

COOK'S TIP

Rome is the capital of both the region of Lazio and Italy and thus has become a focal point for specialities from all over Italy. Food from this region tends to be fairly simple and quick to prepare, all with plenty of herbs and seasonings giving really robust flavours.

Lamb with Bay & Lemon

These lamb chops quickly become more elegant when the bone is removed to make noisettes.

NUTRITIONAL INFORMATION

Calories ....268 Sugars 0.2g
Protein ....24g Fat 16g
Carbohydrate ...0.2g Saturates 7g

10 MINS   35 MINS

SERVES 4

INGREDIENTS

4 lamb chops

1 tbsp oil

15 g/½ oz/1 tbsp butter

150 ml/¼ pint/⅔ cup white wine

150 ml/¼ pint/⅔ cup lamb or
   vegetable stock

2 bay leaves

pared rind of 1 lemon

salt and pepper

1 Using a sharp knife, carefully remove the bone from each lamb chop, keeping the meat intact. Alternatively, ask the butcher to prepare the lamb noisettes for you.

2 Shape the meat into rounds and secure with a length of string.

3 In a large frying pan (skillet), heat together the oil and butter until the mixture starts to froth.

4 Add the lamb noisettes to the frying pan (skillet) and cook for 2–3 minutes on each side or until browned all over.

5 Remove the frying pan (skillet) fom the heat, drain off all of the excess fat and discard.

6 Return the frying pan (skillet) to the heat. Add the wine, stock, bay leaves and lemon rind to the frying pan (skillet) and cook for 20–25 minutes or until the lamb is tender. Season the lamb noisettes and sauce to taste with a little salt and pepper.

7 Transfer to serving plates. Remove the string from each noisette and serve with the sauce.

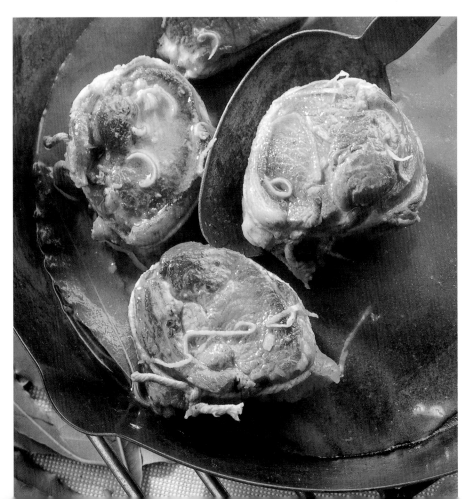

COOK'S TIP

Your local butcher will offer you good advice on how to prepare the lamb noisettes, if you are wary of preparing them yourself.

Lamb Kebabs with Herbs

Serve the kebabs sizzling hot, and the cucumber and yoghurt sauce as cool as can be – it is a delicious partnership.

NUTRITIONAL INFORMATION

Calories ....238 Sugars 7g
Protein ....21g Fat 14g
Carbohydrate ....7g Saturates 5g

2¼ HOURS   15 MINS

SERVES 4

I N G R E D I E N T S

1 kg/2 lb 4 oz lean leg of lamb, trimmed of fat

3 tbsp olive oil

1 tbsp red wine vinegar

juice of ½ lemon

3 tbsp low-fat natural yogurt

1 tbsp dried oregano

2 large garlic cloves, crushed

2 dried bay leaves, crumbled

4 fresh bay leaves

2 tbsp chopped parsley

salt and pepper

S A U C E

300 ml/½ pint/1¼ cups low-fat natural yogurt

1 garlic clove, crushed

¼ tsp salt

½ small cucumber, peeled and finely chopped

3 tbsp finely chopped mint

pinch of paprika

1 Cut the lamb into cubes about 4-5 cm/1½-2 inches square. Pat dry with kitchen paper (paper towels) to ensure that the meat stays crisp and firm on the outside when grilled (broiled).

2 Whisk together the olive oil, wine vinegar, lemon juice and yogurt. Stir in the oregano, garlic and crumbled bay leaves and season with salt and pepper. Place the meat cubes in the marinade and stir until well coated in the mixture. Cover and place in the refrigerator for at least 2 hours.

3 Meanwhile, make the sauce. Place the natural yogurt in a large bowl. Stir in the garlic, salt, cucumber and mint. Cover with cling film (plastic wrap) and set aside in the refrigerator until required.

4 Heat the grill (broiler) to high. With a slotted spoon, lift the meat from the marinade and shake off any excess liquid. Divide the meat into 4 equal portions. Thread the meat and the fresh bay leaves on to 4 skewers.

5 Grill (broil) the kebabs for about 4 minutes on each side, basting frequently with the marinade. At this stage the meat should be crisp on the outside and slightly pink on the inside. If you prefer lamb well done, cook the kebabs for a little longer.

6 Sprinkle the kebabs with parsley and serve at once. Sprinkle the paprika over the sauce and serve chilled.

Turkish Lamb Stew

A delicious blend of flavours with lamb, onions and tomatoes, complete with potatoes to make the perfect one-pot dish for two.

NUTRITIONAL INFORMATION

Calories	442	Sugars	.........5g
Protein	........41g	Fat	..........17g
Carbohydrate	...35g	Saturates	......7g

10 MINS   1¼ HOURS

SERVES 2

I N G R E D I E N T S

350 g/12 oz lean boneless lamb

1 large or 2 small onions

1 garlic clove, crushed

½ red, yellow or green (bell) pepper, diced roughly

300 ml/½ pint/1¼ cups stock

1 tbsp balsamic vinegar

2 tomatoes, peeled and chopped roughly

1½ tsp tomato purée (paste)

1 bay leaf

½ tsp dried sage

½ tsp dried dillweed

350 g/12 oz potatoes

6–8 black olives, halved and pitted

salt and pepper

1 Cut the piece of lamb into cubes of about 2 cm/³⁄₄ inch, discarding any excess fat or gristle.

2 Place in a non-stick saucepan with no extra fat and heat gently until the fat runs and the meat begins to seal.

3 Cut the onion into 8 wedges. Add to the lamb with the garlic and fry for a further 3–4 minutes.

4 Add the (bell) pepper, stock, vinegar, tomatoes, tomato purée (paste), bay leaf, sage, dillweed and seasoning. Cover and simmer gently for 30 minutes.

5 Peel the potatoes and cut into 2 cm/³⁄₄ inch cubes. Add to the stew and stir well. If necessary, add a little more boiling stock or water if it seems a little dry. Cover the pan again and simmer for a further 25–30 minutes, or until tender.

6 Add the olives and adjust the seasoning. Simmer for a further 5 minutes and serve with vegetables or a salad and crusty bread.

COOK'S TIP

A good accompaniment would be a salad made of shredded white cabbage, Little Gem lettuce, coarsely grated carrot, diced avocado or cucumber and spring onions (scallions).

Lamb with Garlic Sauce

This dish contains Szechuan pepper which is quite hot and may be replaced with black pepper, if preferred.

NUTRITIONAL INFORMATION

Calories 320   Sugars 2g
Protein . . . . .25g   Fat 21g
Carbohydrate . . . .4g   Saturates 6g

 35 MINS   10 MINS

SERVES 4

I N G R E D I E N T S

450 g/1 lb lamb fillet or loin

2 tbsp dark soy sauce

2 tsp sesame oil

2 tbsp Chinese rice wine or dry sherry

½ tsp Szechuan pepper

4 tbsp vegetable oil

4 garlic cloves, crushed

60 g/2 oz water chestnuts, quartered

1 green (bell) pepper, seeded and sliced

1 tbsp wine vinegar

1 tbsp sesame oil

rice or noodles, to serve

1 Cut the lamb into 2.5-cm/1-inch pieces and place in a shallow dish.

2 Mix together 1 tablespoon of the soy sauce, the sesame oil, Chinese rice wine or sherry and Szechuan pepper. Pour the mixture over the lamb, turning to coat, and leave to marinate for 30 minutes.

3 Heat the vegetable oil in a preheated wok. Remove the lamb from the marinade and add to the wok, together with the garlic. Stir-fry for 2–3 minutes.

4 Add the water chestnuts and (bell) pepper and stir-fry for 1 minute.

5 Add the remaining soy sauce and the wine vinegar, mixing together well.

6 Add the sesame oil and cook, stirring constantly, for 1–2 minutes, or until the lamb is cooked through.

7 Transfer the lamb and garlic sauce to a warm serving dish and serve immediately with rice or noodles.

COOK'S TIP

Chinese chives, also known as garlic chives, would make an appropriate garnish.

Sesame oil is used as a flavouring, rather than for frying, as it burns readily, hence it is added at the end of cooking.

Masala Kebabs

Indian kebab dishes are not necessarily cooked on a skewer; they can also be served in a dish and are always dry dishes with no sauce.

NUTRITIONAL INFORMATION

Calories 294	Sugars 0g
Protein 35g	Fat 17g
Carbohydrate 0g	Saturates 7g

1¼ HOURS   20 MINS

SERVES 4

I N G R E D I E N T S

1 dried bay leaf

2.5 cm/1 inch piece ginger root, chopped

2.5 cm/1 inch cinnamon stick

1 tsp coriander seeds

½ tsp salt

1 tsp fennel seeds

1 tsp chilli powder

1 tsp garam masala

1 tsp lemon juice

1 tsp ground turmeric

1 tbsp oil

750 g/1 lb 10 oz lamb neck fillet

T O   G A R N I S H

sprigs of fresh coriander (cilantro)

lemon wedges

T O   S E R V E

bread

chutney

1 Use a food processor, blender or pestle and mortar to grind together the bay leaf, ginger, cinnamon, coriander seeds, salt, fennel seeds and chilli powder.

2 Combine this spice mix with the garam masala, lemon juice, turmeric and oil in a large bowl.

3 Cut the lamb into 5 mm/¼ inch slices. Add to the spice mix and leave to marinate at room temperature for about 1 hour, or in the refrigerator for 3 hours or overnight.

4 Spread out the pieces of lamb on a baking sheet and cook in a preheated oven, 200°C/400°F/Gas Mark 6, for 20 minutes until well done. Transfer the pieces of lamb to paper towels to drain any excess fat.

5 Thread 3 or 4 pieces of meat on to each skewer and garnish with sprigs of fresh coriander (cilantro) and lemon wedges.

6 Serve the masala kebabs hot with bread and chutney.

Lamb with Olives

This is a very simple dish, and the chilli adds a bit of spiciness. It is quick to prepare and makes an ideal supper dish.

NUTRITIONAL INFORMATION

Calories	....	.577
Protein	....	62g
Carbohydrate	....	1g

Sugars	....	.1g
Fat	....	.33g
Saturates	......	10g

15 MINS   1 1/2 HOURS

SERVES 4

INGREDIENTS

1.25 kg/2 lb 12 oz boned leg of lamb

90 ml/3 fl oz/⅓ cup olive oil

2 garlic cloves, crushed

1 onion, sliced

1 small red chilli, cored, deseeded and
  chopped finely

175 ml/6 fl oz/¾ cup dry white wine

175 g/6 oz/1 cup pitted black olives

salt

chopped fresh parsley, to garnish

1 Using a sharp knife, cut the lamb into 2.5 cm/1 inch cubes.

2 Heat the oil in a frying pan (skillet) and fry the garlic, onion and chilli for 5 minutes.

3 Add the meat and wine and cook for a further 5 minutes.

4 Stir in the olives, then transfer the mixture to a casserole. Place in a preheated oven, 180°C/350°F/Gas Mark 4, and cook for 1 hour 20 minutes or until the meat is tender. Season with salt to taste, and serve garnished with chopped fresh parsley.

Moroccan Lamb Kebabs

Marinated in Moroccan spices, these barbecued (grilled) kebabs have a mild spicy flavour. Add the chilli if you like a bit of zip to your meat.

NUTRITIONAL INFORMATION

Calories 348	Sugars 2g
Protein 30g	Fat 24g
Carbohydrate 2g	Saturates 10g

  2¼ HOURS 10 MINS

SERVES 4

I N G R E D I E N T S

450 g/1 lb lean lamb

1 lemon

1 red onion

4 small courgettes (zucchini)

couscous, to serve (see Cook's Tip)

M A R I N A D E

grated rind and juice of 1 lemon

2 tbsp olive oil

1 clove garlic, crushed

1 red chilli, sliced (optional)

1 tsp ground cinnamon

1 tsp ground ginger

½ tsp ground cumin

½ tsp ground coriander

1 Cut the lamb into large, evenly-sized chunks.

2 To make the marinade, combine the lemon rind and juice, oil, garlic, chilli (if using), ground cinnamon, ginger, cumin and coriander in a large non-metallic dish.

3 Add the meat to the marinade, tossing to coat the meat completely. Cover and leave to marinate in the refrigerator for at least 2 hours or preferably overnight.

4 Cut the lemon into 8 pieces. Cut the onion into wedges, then separate each wedge into 2 pieces.

5 Using a canelle knife (or potato peeler), cut thin strips of peel from the courgettes (zucchini), then cut the courgettes (zucchini) into chunks.

6 Remove the meat from the marinade, reserving the liquid for basting. Thread the meat on to skewers alternating with the onion, lemon and courgette (zucchini).

7 Barbecue (grill) over hot coals for 8–10 minutes, turning and basting with the reserved marinade. Serve on a bed of couscous (see Cook's Tip, below).

COOK'S TIP

Serve these kebabs with couscous. Allowing 60 g/2 oz couscous per person, soak the couscous in cold water for about 20 minutes until softened. Drain and steam for 10 minutes or until piping hot.

Lamb with Satay Sauce

This recipe demonstrates the classic serving of lamb satay – lamb marinated in chilli and coconut and threaded on to wooden skewers.

NUTRITIONAL INFORMATION

Calories	.501	Sugars	.6g
Protein	.34g	Fat	.37g
Carbohydrate	.9g	Saturates	.10g

 35 MINS   25 MINS

SERVES 4

I N G R E D I E N T S

450 g/1 lb lamb loin fillet

1 tbsp mild curry paste

150 ml/5 fl oz/⅔ cup coconut milk

2 cloves garlic, crushed

½ tsp chilli powder

½ tsp cumin

S A T A Y   S A U C E

1 tbsp corn oil

1 onion, diced

6 tbsp crunchy peanut butter

1 tsp tomato purée (paste)

1 tsp fresh lime juice

100 ml/3½ fl oz/1⅓ cup cold water

1 Using a sharp knife, thinly slice the lamb and place in a large dish.

2 Mix together the curry paste, coconut milk, garlic, chilli powder and cumin in a bowl. Pour over the lamb, toss well, cover and marinate for 30 minutes.

3 To make the satay sauce. Heat the oil in a large wok and stir-fry the onion for 5 minutes, then reduce the heat and cook for 5 minutes.

4 Stir in the peanut butter, tomato purée (paste), lime juice and water.

5 Thread the lamb on to wooden skewers, reserving the marinade.

6 Grill (broil) the lamb skewers under a hot grill (broiler) for 6–8 minutes, turning once.

7 Add the reserved marinade to the wok, bring to the boil and cook for 5 minutes. Serve the lamb skewers with the satay sauce.

COOK'S TIP

Soak the wooden skewers in cold water for 30 minutes before grilling (broiling) to prevent the skewers from burning.

Lamb & Potato Masala

To create delicious Indian dishes at home – simply open a can of curry sauce, add a few interesting ingredients and you have a splendid meal.

NUTRITIONAL INFORMATION

Calories 513	Sugars 6g
Protein 40g	Fat 27g
Carbohydrate . . .30g	Saturates 8g

15 MINS   1½ HOURS

SERVES 4

INGREDIENTS

750 g/1 lb 10 oz lean lamb (from the leg)

3 tbsp ghee or vegetable oil

500 g/1 lb 2 oz potatoes, peeled and cut in large 2.5 cm/1 inch pieces

1 large onion, peeled, quartered and sliced

2 garlic cloves, peeled and crushed

175 g/6 oz mushrooms, thickly sliced

1 x 283 g/10 oz can Tikka Masala Curry Sauce

300 ml/½ pint/1¼ cups water

salt

3 tomatoes, halved and cut into thin slices

125g/4½ oz spinach, washed and stalks trimmed

sprigs of mint, to garnish

1 Cut the lamb into 2.5 cm/1 inch cubes. Heat the ghee or oil in a large pan, add the lamb and fry over moderate heat for 3 minutes or until sealed all over. Removethe lamb from the pan.

2 Add the potatoes, onion, garlic and mushrooms and fry for 3-4 minutes, stirring frequently.

3 Stir the curry sauce and water into the pan, add the lamb, mix well and season with salt to taste. Cover and cook very gently for 1 hour or until the lamb is tender and cooked through, stirring occasionally.

4 Add the sliced tomatoes and the spinach to the pan, pushing the leaves well down into the mixture, then cover and cook for a further 10 minutes until the spinach is cooked and tender.

5 Garnish with mint sprigs and serve hot.

COOK'S TIP

Spinach leaves wilt quickly during cooking, so if the leaves are young and tender add them whole to the mixture; larger leaves may be coarsely shredded, if wished, before adding to the pan.

Lamb Cutlets with Rosemary

A classic combination of flavours, this dish would make a perfect Sunday lunch. Serve with tomato and onion salad and jacket potatoes.

NUTRITIONAL INFORMATION

Calories 560   Sugars 1g
Protein . . . . .48g   Fat 40g
Carbohydrate . . . .1g   Saturates 13g

 1¼ HOURS   15 MINS

SERVES 4

I N G R E D I E N T S

8 lamb cutlets

5 tbsp olive oil

2 tbsp lemon juice

1 clove garlic, crushed

½ tsp lemon pepper

salt

8 sprigs rosemary

jacket potatoes, to serve

S A L A D

4 tomatoes, sliced

4 spring onions (scallion), sliced diagonally

D R E S S I N G

2 tbsp olive oil

1 tbsp lemon juice

1 clove garlic, chopped

¼ tsp fresh rosemary, chopped finely

1 Trim the lamb chops by cutting away the flesh with a sharp knife to expose the tips of the bones.

2 Place the oil, lemon juice, garlic, lemon pepper and salt in a shallow, non-metallic dish and whisk with a fork to combine.

3 Lay the sprigs of rosemary in the dish and place the lamb on top. Leave to marinate for at least 1 hour, turning the lamb cutlets once.

4 Remove the chops from the marinade and wrap a little kitchen foil around the bones to stop them from burning.

5 Place the rosemary sprigs on the rack and place the lamb on top. Barbecue (grill) for 10–15 minutes, turning once.

6 Meanwhile make the salad and dressing. Arrange the tomatoes on a serving dish and scatter the spring onions (scallions) on top. Place all the ingredients for the dressing in a screw-top jar, shake well and pour over the salad. Serve with the lamb cutlets and jacket potatoes.

COOK'S TIP

Choose medium to small baking potatoes if you want to cook jacket potatoes on the barbecue (grill). Scrub them well, prick with a fork and wrap in buttered kitchen foil. Bury them in the hot coals and barbecue (grill) for 50–60 minutes.

Hot Lamb

This is quite a spicy dish, using 2 chillies in the sauce. Halve the number of chillies to reduce the heat or seed the chillies before using if desired.

NUTRITIONAL INFORMATION

Calories 323   Sugars 4g
Protein ....26g   Fat 22g
Carbohydrate ....5g   Saturates 7g

25 MINS   15 MINS

SERVES 4

INGREDIENTS

450 g/1 lb lean, boneless lamb

2 tbsp hoisin sauce

1 tbsp dark soy sauce

1 garlic clove, crushed

2 tsp grated fresh root ginger

2 tbsp vegetable oil

2 onions, sliced

1 fennel bulb, sliced

4 tbsp water

SAUCE

1 large fresh red chilli, cut into thin strips

1 fresh green chilli, cut into thin strips

2 tbsp rice wine vinegar

2 tsp light brown sugar

2 tbsp peanut oil

1 tsp sesame oil

VARIATION

Use beef, pork or duck instead of the lamb and vary the vegetables, using leeks or celery instead of the onion and fennel.

1 Cut the lamb into 2.5-cm/1-inch cubes and place in a glass dish.

2 Mix together the hoisin sauce, soy sauce, garlic and ginger and pour over the lamb, turning to coat well. Leave to marinate for 20 minutes.

3 Heat the oil in a preheated wok and stir-fry the lamb for 1–2 minutes. Add the onions and fennel and cook for a further 2 minutes, or until they are just beginning to brown. Stir in the water, cover and cook for 2–3 minutes.

4 To make the sauce, place all the ingredients in a pan and cook over a low heat for 3-4 minutes, stirring.

5 Transfer the lamb and onions to a serving dish, toss lightly in the sauce and serve immediately.

Irish Stew with Dumplings

This traditional recipe makes a hearty stew with fluffy parsley dumplings. Cubes of lean lamb shoulder could be used in place of the cutlets.

NUTRITIONAL INFORMATION

Calories 576	Sugars 4g	
Protein 27g	Fat 28g	
Carbohydrate ...55g	Saturates 12g	

10 MINS   1¹⁄₄ HOURS

SERVES 4

INGREDIENTS

2 tbsp vegetable oil

2 large onions, sliced

1 leek, sliced

1 large carrot, sliced

2 celery sticks, sliced

850 ml/1½ pints/3¾ cups lamb stock

750 g/1 lb 10 oz lean lamb cutlets, trimmed

60 g/2 oz/⅓ cup pearl barley

2 large potatoes, peeled and cut into large chunks

salt and pepper

chopped fresh parsley, to garnish

DUMPLINGS

90 g/3 oz self-raising flour

25 g/1 oz/¼ cup porridge oats

2 tbsp chopped fresh parsley

pinch of salt

60 g/2 oz vegetable suet

chilled water, to mix

1 First make the dumplings. Put the flour, oats, parsley and salt into a large mixing bowl. Stir in the suet. Add sufficient chilled water to make a soft, but not sticky, dough. Shape into 8 dumplings, cover with a tea towel and set aside.

2 Heat the vegetable oil in a large saucepan and gently fry the onions, leek, carrot and celery for 5 minutes, without browning.

3 Add the stock, lamb and pearl barley to the saucepan. Bring to the boil and then reduce the heat. Cover and simmer for 20 minutes.

4 Add the potatoes and cook for a further 20 minutes. Add the dumplings to the saucepan. Cover and simmer for 15–20 minutes until the dumplings are light and fluffy.

5 Season the stew with salt and pepper, garnish with parsley and serve immediately while still hot.

Lamb with Mushroom Sauce

Use a lean cut of lamb, such as fillet, for this recipe for both flavour and tenderness.

NUTRITIONAL INFORMATION

Calories 219   Sugars 1g
Protein . . . . .21g   Fat 14g
Carbohydrate . . . .4g   Saturates 4g

5 MINS   10 MINS

SERVES 4

I N G R E D I E N T S

350 g/12 oz lean boneless lamb, such as
  fillet or loin

2 tbsp vegetable oil

3 garlic cloves, crushed

1 leek, sliced

175 g/6 oz large mushrooms, sliced

½ tsp sesame oil

fresh red chillies, to garnish

S A U C E

1 tsp cornflour (cornstarch)

4 tbsp light soy sauce

3 tbsp Chinese rice wine or dry sherry

3 tbsp water

½ tsp chilli sauce

1 Using a sharp knife or meat cleaver, cut the lamb into thin strips.

2 Heat the vegetable oil in a preheated wok or large frying pan (skillet).

3 Add the lamb strips, garlic and leek and stir-fry for about 2-3 minutes.

4 To make the sauce, mix together the cornflour (cornstarch), soy sauce, Chinese rice wine or dry sherry, water and chilli sauce and set aside.

5 Add the sliced mushrooms to the wok and stir-fry for 1 minute.

6 Stir in the prepared sauce and cook for 2–3 minutes, or until the lamb is cooked through and tender.

7 Sprinkle the sesame oil over the top and transfer the lamb and mushrooms to a warm serving dish. Garnish with red chillies and serve immediately.

VARIATION

The lamb can be replaced with lean steak or pork fillet (tenderloin) in this classic recipe from Beijing. You could also use 2-3 spring onions (scallions), 1 shallot or 1 small onion instead of the leek, if you prefer.

Barbecued Butterfly Lamb

The appearance of the lamb as it is opened out to cook on the barbecue gives this dish its name. Marinate the lamb in advance if possible.

NUTRITIONAL INFORMATION

Calories 733	Sugars 6g
Protein 69g	Fat 48g
Carbohydrate 6g	Saturates 13g

 6¼ HOURS   🕐 1 HOUR

SERVES 4

INGREDIENTS

boned leg of lamb, about 1.8 kg/4 lb

8 tbsp balsamic vinegar

grated rind and juice of 1 lemon

150 ml/¼ pint/⅔ cup sunflower oil

4 tbsp chopped, fresh mint

2 cloves garlic, crushed

2 tbsp light muscovado sugar

salt and pepper

TO SERVE

grilled (broiled) vegetables

green salad leaves

1 Open out the boned leg of lamb so that its shape resembles a butterfly. Thread 2–3 skewers through the meat in order to make it easier to turn on the barbecue (grill).

2 Combine the balsamic vinegar, lemon rind and juice, oil, mint, garlic, sugar and salt and pepper to taste in a non-metallic dish that is large enough to hold the lamb.

3 Place the lamb in the dish and turn it over a few times so that the meat is coated on both sides with the marinade. Leave to marinate for at least 6 hours or preferably overnight, turning occasionally.

4 Remove the lamb from the marinade and reserve the liquid for basting.

5 Place the rack about 15 cm/6 inches above the coals and barbecue (grill) the lamb for about 30 minutes on each side, turning once and basting frequently with the marinade.

6 Transfer the lamb to a chopping board and remove the skewers. Cut the lamb into slices across the grain and serve.

COOK'S TIP

If you prefer, cook the lamb for half the cooking time in a preheated oven at 180°C/350°F/ Gas Mark 4, then finish off on the barbecue (grill).

Persian Lamb

Chargrilling and lamb seem to be made for each other, and all over the Middle East both lamb and mutton are enjoyed in this way.

NUTRITIONAL INFORMATION

Calories	235	Sugars	........4g
Protein	........15g	Fat	..........9g
Carbohydrate	...25g	Saturates	......3g

🧊 3¹/₄ HOURS   🕐 25 MINS

SERVES 4–6

I N G R E D I E N T S

2 tbsp chopped fresh mint

225 ml/8 fl oz/1 cup low-fat natural yogurt

4 garlic cloves, crushed

¼ tsp pepper

6 lean lamb chops

2 tbsp lemon juice

T A B B O U L E H

250 g/9 oz/2 cups couscous

500 ml/18 fl oz/2 cups boiling water

2 tbsp olive oil

2 tbsp lemon juice

½ onion, chopped finely

4 tomatoes, chopped

25 g/1 oz/½ cup fresh coriander (cilantro), chopped

2 tbsp chopped fresh mint

salt and pepper

1 For the marinade, combine the mint, yogurt, garlic and pepper.

2 Put the chops into a non-porous dish and rub all over with the lemon juice. Pour the marinade over the chops. Cover and marinate for 2–3 hours.

3 To make the tabbouleh. Put the couscous into a heatproof bowl and pour over the boiling water. Leave for 5 minutes. Drain and put into a sieve (strainer). Steam over a pan of barely simmering water for 8 minutes. Toss in the oil and lemon juice. Add the onion, tomato and herbs. Season and set aside.

4 Cook the lamb over a medium barbecue (grill) for 15 minutes, turning once. Serve with the tabbouleh.

COOK'S TIP

Yogurt is a useful ingredient as a base for a marinade. The bland taste is a good medium for many flavours such as herbs, citrus fruit, spices and oils.

Lamb with Lime Leaves

Groundnut oil is used here for flavour – it is a common oil used for stir-frying.

NUTRITIONAL INFORMATION

Calories	302	Sugars	........15g
Protein	........24g	Fat	..........16g
Carbohydrate	...17g	Saturates	.......6g

5 MINS   35 MINS

SERVES 4

I N G R E D I E N T S

2 red chillies

2 tbsp groundnut oil

2 cloves garlic, crushed

4 shallots, chopped

2 stalks lemon grass, sliced

6 lime leaves

1 tbsp tamarind paste

25 g/1 oz/2 tbsp palm sugar

450 g/1 lb lean lamb (leg or loin fillet)

600 ml/1 pint/2½ cups coconut milk

175 g/6 oz cherry tomatoes, halved

1 tbsp chopped fresh coriander (cilantro)

fragrant rice, to serve

1 Using a sharp knife, deseed and very finely chop the red chillies.

2 Heat the oil in a large preheated wok or frying pan (skillet).

3 Add the garlic, shallots, lemon grass, lime leaves, tamarind paste, palm sugar and chillies to the wok and stir-fry for about 2 minutes.

4 Using a sharp knife, cut the lamb into thin strips or cubes. Add the lamb to the wok or frying pan (skillet) and stir-fry for about 5 minutes, tossing well so that the lamb is evenly coated in the spice mixture.

5 Pour the coconut milk into the wok and bring to the boil. Reduce the heat and leave to simmer for 20 minutes.

6 Add the tomatoes and coriander (cilantro) to the wok and leave to simmer for 5 minutes. Transfer to serving plates and serve hot with fragrant rice.

COOK'S TIP

When buying fresh coriander (cilantro), look for bright green, unwilted leaves. To store it, wash and dry the leaves, leaving them on the stem. Wrap the leaves in damp kitchen paper (paper towels) and keep them in a plastic bag in the refrigerator.

Five-spice Lamb

Chinese five-spice powder is a blend of cinnamon, fennel, star anise, ginger and cloves, all finely ground together.

NUTRITIONAL INFORMATION

Calories 361	Sugars 3g	
Protein 35g	Fat 22g	
Carbohydrate 5g	Saturates 8g	

  1¼ HOURS ⏱ 10 MINS

SERVES 4

I N G R E D I E N T S

625 g/1 lb 6 oz lean boneless lamb (leg or fillet)

2 tsp Chinese five-spice powder

3 tbsp sunflower oil

1 red (bell) pepper, cored, seeded and thinly sliced

1 green (bell) pepper, cored, seeded and thinly sliced

1 yellow or orange (bell) pepper, cored, seeded and thinly sliced

4-6 spring onions (scallions), thinly sliced diagonally

175 g/6 oz French (green) or fine beans, cut into 4 cm/1½ inch lengths

2 tbsp soy sauce

4 tbsp sherry

salt and pepper

Chinese noodles, to serve

TO GARNISH

strips of red and yellow (bell) pepper

fresh coriander (cilantro) leaves

1 Cut the lamb into narrow strips, about 4 cm/1½ inches long, across the grain. Place in a bowl, add the five-spice powder and ¼ teaspoon salt, mix well and leave to marinate, covered, in a cool place for at least an hour and up to 24 hours.

2 Heat half the oil in the wok, swirling it around until really hot. Add the lamb and stir-fry briskly for 3-4 minutes until almost cooked through. Remove from the pan and set aside.

3 Add the remaining oil to the wok and when hot add the (bell) peppers and spring onions (scallions). Stir-fry for 2-3 minutes, then add the beans and stir for a minute or so.

4 Add the soy sauce and sherry to the wok and when hot return the lamb and any juices to the wok. Stir-fry for 1-2 minutes until the lamb is really hot again and thoroughly coated in the sauce. Season to taste.

5 Serve the Five-spice Lamb with Chinese noodles, garnished with strips of red and green (bell) pepper and fresh coriander (cilantro).

Sesame Lamb Stir-Fry

This is a very simple, but delicious dish, in which lean pieces of lamb are cooked in sugar and soy sauce and then sprinkled with sesame seeds.

NUTRITIONAL INFORMATION

Calories ....276 Sugars 4g
Protein ....25g Fat 18g
Carbohydrate ....5g Saturates 6g

   5 MINS   10 MINS

SERVES 4

INGREDIENTS

450 g/1 lb boneless lean lamb

2 tbsp peanut oil

2 leeks, sliced

1 carrot, cut into matchsticks

2 garlic cloves, crushed

85 ml/3 fl oz/⅓ cup lamb or vegetable stock

2 tsp light brown sugar

1 tbsp dark soy sauce

4½ tsp sesame seeds

1 Using a sharp knife, cut the lamb into thin strips.

2 Heat the peanut oil in a preheated wok or large frying pan (skillet) until it is really hot.

3 Add the lamb and stir-fry for 2–3 minutes. Remove the lamb from the wok with a slotted spoon and set aside until required.

4 Add the leeks, carrot and garlic to the wok or frying pan (skillet) and stir-fry in the remaining oil for 1–2 minutes.

5 Remove the vegetables from the wok with a slotted spoon and set aside.

6 Drain any remaining oil from the wok. Place the lamb or vegetable stock,

light brown sugar and dark soy sauce in the wok and add the lamb. Cook, stirring constantly to coat the lamb, for 2–3 minutes.

7 Sprinkle the sesame seeds over the top, turning the lamb to coat.

8 Spoon the leek, carrot and garlic mixture on to a warm serving dish and top with the lamb. Serve immediately.

COOK'S TIP

Be careful not to burn the sugar in the wok when heating and coating the meat, otherwise the flavour of the dish will be spoiled.

Lamb Hotpot

This classic recipe using lamb cutlets layered between sliced potatoes, kidneys, onions and herbs makes a perfect meal on a cold winter's day.

NUTRITIONAL INFORMATION

Calories	420	Sugars	........2g
Protein	........41g	Fat	..........15g
Carbohydrate	...31g	Saturates	......8g

 15 MINS   2 HOURS

SERVES 4

INGREDIENTS

675 g/1½ lb lean lamb neck cutlets

2 lamb's kidneys

675 g/1½ lb waxy potatoes, scrubbed and sliced thinly

1 large onion, sliced thinly

2 tbsp chopped fresh thyme

150 ml/¼ pint/⅔ cup lamb stock

25 g/1 oz/2 tbsp butter, melted

salt and pepper

fresh thyme sprigs, to garnish

1 Remove any excess fat from the lamb. Skin and core the kidneys and cut them into slices.

2 Arrange a layer of potatoes in the base of a 1.8 litre/3 pint/3½ cup ovenproof dish.

3 Arrange the lamb neck cutlets on top of the potatoes and cover with the sliced kidneys, onion and chopped thyme.

4 Pour the lamb stock over the meat and season to taste with salt and pepper.

5 Layer the remaining potato slices on top, overlapping to completely cover the meat and sliced onion.

6 Brush the potato slices with the butter, cover the dish and cook in a preheated oven, 180°C/350°F/Gas Mark 4, for 1½ hours.

7 Remove the lid and cook for a further 30 minutes until golden brown on top.

8 Garnish with fresh thyme sprigs and serve hot.

VARIATION

Traditionally, oysters are also included in this tasty hotpot. Add them to the layers along with the kidneys, if wished.

Lamb Do Pyaza

Do Pyaza usually indicates a dish of meat cooked with plenty of onions, and in this recipe the onions are cooked in two different ways.

NUTRITIONAL INFORMATION

Calories 433	Sugars 6g
Protein 42g	Fat 27g
Carbohydrate 7g	Saturates 8g

 10 MINS   1³/₄ HOURS

SERVES 4

INGREDIENTS

2 tbsp ghee or vegetable oil

2 large onions, sliced finely

4 garlic cloves, 2 of them crushed

750 g/1 lb 10 oz lean boneless lamb, cut into 2.5 cm/1 inch cubes

1 tsp chilli powder

2.5 cm/1 inch piece ginger root, grated

2 fresh green chillies, chopped

½ tsp ground turmeric

175 ml/6 fl oz/½ cup low-fat natural yogurt

2 cloves

2.5 cm/1 inch piece cinnamon stick

300 ml/½ pint/1¼ cups water

2 tbsp chopped fresh coriander (cilantro)

3 tbsp lemon juice

salt and pepper

naan bread, to serve

1 Heat the ghee or oil in a large saucepan and add 1 of the onions and all the garlic. Cook for 2–3 minutes, stirring constantly.

2 Add the lamb and brown all over. Remove and set aside. Add the chilli powder, ginger, chillies and turmeric and stir for a further 30 seconds.

3 Add plenty of salt and pepper, the yogurt, cloves, cinnamon and water.

4 Return the lamb to the pan. Bring to the boil then simmer for 10 minutes.

5 Transfer the mixture to an ovenproof dish and cook uncovered in a preheated oven, 180°C/350°F/Gas Mark 4, for 40 minutes.

6 Adjust the seasoning, if necessary, stir in the remaining onion and cook uncovered for a further 40 minutes.

7 Add the fresh coriander (cilantro) and lemon juice.

8 Transfer the lamb do pyaza to a warm serving dish and serve with naan bread.

Hot Pot Chops

A Hot Pot is a lamb casserole, made with carrots and onions and with a potato topping. The chops used here are an interesting alternative.

NUTRITIONAL INFORMATION

Calories 250	Sugars 2g
Protein 27g	Fat 12g
Carbohydrate 8g	Saturates 5g

10 MINS   30 MINS

SERVES 4

INGREDIENTS

4 lean, boneless lamb leg steaks, about 125 g/4½ oz each

1 small onion, thinly sliced

1 medium carrot, thinly sliced

1 medium potato, thinly sliced

1 tsp olive oil

1 tsp dried rosemary

salt and pepper

fresh rosemary, to garnish

freshly steamed green vegetables, to serve

1 Preheat the oven to 180°C/350°F/Gas Mark 4. Using a sharp knife, trim any excess fat from the lamb steaks.

2 Season both sides of the steaks with salt and pepper and arrange them on a baking tray.

3 Alternate layers of sliced onion, carrot and potato on top of each lamb steak.

4 Brush the tops of the potato lightly with oil, season well with salt and pepper to taste and then sprinkle with a little dried rosemary.

5 Bake the hot pot chops in the oven for 25–30 minutes until the lamb is tender and cooked through.

6 Drain the lamb on absorbent kitchen paper (paper towels) and transfer to a warmed serving plate.

7 Garnish with fresh rosemary and serve accompanied with a selection of green vegetables.

VARIATION

This recipe would work equally well with boneless chicken breasts. Pound the chicken slightly with a meat mallet or covered rolling pin so that the pieces are the same thickness throughout.

Lamb & Tomato Koftas

These little meatballs, served with a minty yogurt dressing, can be prepared well in advance, ready to cook when required.

NUTRITIONAL INFORMATION

Calories 183	Sugars 5g
Protein 15g	Fat 11g
Carbohydrate 5g	Saturates 4g

15 MINS   10 MINS

SERVES 4

INGREDIENTS

225 g/8 oz finely minced lean lamb

1½ onions, peeled

1-2 garlic cloves, peeled and crushed

1 dried red chilli, finely chopped (optional)

2-3 tsp garam masala

2 tbsp chopped fresh mint

2 tsp lemon juice

salt

2 tbsp vegetable oil

4 small tomatoes, quartered

mint sprigs, to garnish

YOGURT DRESSING

150 ml/¼ pint/⅔ cup low-fat yogurt

5 cm/2 in piece cucumber, grated

2 tbsp chopped fresh mint

½ tsp toasted cumin seeds (optional)

1 Place the minced lamb in a bowl. Finely chop 1 onion and add to the bowl with the garlic and chilli (if using). Stir in the garam masala, mint and lemon juice and season well with salt. Mix well.

2 Divide the mixture in half, then divide each half into 10 equal portions and form each into a small ball. Roll balls in the oil to coat. Quarter the remaining onion half and separate into layers.

3 Thread 5 of the spicy meatballs, 4 tomato quarters and some of the onion layers on to each of 4 pre-soaked bamboo or metal skewers.

4 Brush the vegetables with the remaining oil and cook the koftas under a hot grill for about 10 minutes, turning frequently until they are browned all over and cooked through.

5 Meanwhile, prepare the yogurt dressing for the koftas. In a small bowl mix together the yogurt, grated cucumber, mint and toasted cumin seeds (if using).

6 Garnish the lamb and tomato koftas with mint sprigs and place on a large serving platter. Serve the koftas hot with the yogurt dressing.

Lamb with a Spice Crust

Lamb neck fillet is a tender cut that is not too thick and is, therefore, ideal for cooking on the barbecue (grill).

NUTRITIONAL INFORMATION

Calories 203   Sugars 9g
Protein ....16g   Fat 10g
Carbohydrate ...12g   Saturates 4g

 5 MINS   45 MINS

SERVES 4

INGREDIENTS

1 tbsp olive oil

2 tbsp light muscovado sugar

2 tbsp wholegrain mustard

1 tbsp horseradish sauce

1 tbsp plain (all-purpose) flour

350 g/12 oz neck fillet of lamb

salt and pepper

TO SERVE

coleslaw

slices of tomato

1 Combine the oil, sugar, mustard, horseradish sauce, flour and salt and pepper to taste in a shallow, non-metallic dish until they are well mixed.

2 Roll the lamb in the spice mixture until well coated.

COOK'S TIP

If preferred, the lamb can be completely removed from the kitchen foil for the second part of the cooking. Barbecue (grill) the lamb directly over the coals for a smokier barbecue (grill) flavour, basting with extra oil if necessary.

3 Lightly oil one or two pieces of foil or a large, double thickness of foil. Place the lamb on the foil and wrap it up so that the meat is completely enclosed.

4 Place the foil parcel over hot coals for 30 minutes, turning the parcel over occasionally.

5 Open the kitchen foil, spoon the cooking juices over the lamb and continue to barbecue (grill) for a further 10-15 minutes or until cooked through.

6 Placer the lamb on a platter and remove the foil. Cut into thick slices and serve with coleslaw and tomato slices.

Lamb with Rosemary

This is a pretty dish of pink tender lamb fillet (tenderloin) served on a light green bed of mashed leeks and potatoes.

NUTRITIONAL INFORMATION

Calories 388	Sugars 11g	
Protein 35g	Fat 12g	
Carbohydrate ...38g	Saturates 5g	

1¼ HOURS   55 MINS

SERVES 4

I N G R E D I E N T S

500 g/1 lb 2 oz lean lamb fillet (tenderloin)

4 tbsp redcurrant jelly

1 tbsp chopped fresh rosemary

1 garlic clove, crushed

450 g/1 lb potatoes, diced

450 g/1 lb leeks, sliced

150 ml/¼ pint/⅔ cup Fresh Vegetable Stock, (see page 8)

4 tsp low-fat natural fromage frais

salt and pepper

freshly steamed vegetables, to serve

TO GARNISH

chopped fresh rosemary

redcurrants

1 Put the lamb in a shallow baking tin (pan). Blend 2 tablespoons of the redcurrant jelly with the rosemary, garlic and seasoning. Brush over the lamb and cook in a preheated oven at 230°C/450°F/Gas Mark 8, brushing occasionally with any cooking juices, for 30 minutes.

2 Meanwhile, place the potatoes in a saucepan and cover with water. Bring to the boil, and cook for 8 minutes until softened. Drain well.

3 Put the leeks in a saucepan with the stock. Cover and simmer for 7–8 minutes or until soft. Drain, reserving the cooking liquid.

4 Place the potato and leeks in a bowl and mash with a potato masher. Season to taste and stir in the fromage frais. Pile on to a warmed platter and keep warm.

5 In a saucepan, melt the remaining redcurrant jelly and stir in the leek cooking liquid. Bring to the boil for 5 minutes.

6 Slice the lamb and arrange over the mash. Spoon the sauce over the top. Garnish the lamb with rosemary and redcurrants and serve with freshly steamed vegetables.

Aubergine (Eggplant) Cake

Layers of toasty-brown aubergine (eggplant), meat sauce and cheese-flavoured pasta make this a popular family supper dish.

NUTRITIONAL INFORMATION

Calories 859	Sugars 39g	
Protein 36g	Fat 58g	
Carbohydrate ...51g	Saturates 19g	

 1½ HOURS   1½ HOURS

SERVES 4

INGREDIENTS

1 aubergine (eggplant), thinly sliced

5 tbsp olive oil

225 g/8 oz/2 cups dried fusilli

600 ml/1 pint/2½ cups Béchamel Sauce (see page 6)

90 g/3 oz/¾ cup grated Cheddar cheese

butter, for greasing

25 g/1 oz/⅓ cup freshly grated Parmesan cheese

salt and pepper

LAMB SAUCE

2 tbsp olive oil

1 large onion, sliced

2 celery sticks (stalks), thinly sliced

450 g/1 lb minced (ground) lamb

3 tbsp tomato purée (paste)

150 g/5½ oz bottled sun-dried tomatoes, drained and chopped

1 tsp dried oregano

1 tbsp red wine vinegar

150 ml/¼ pint/⅔ cup chicken stock

salt and pepper

1 Put the aubergine (eggplant) slices in a colander, sprinkle with salt and set aside for 45 minutes.

2 To make the lamb sauce, heat the oil in a pan. Fry the onion and celery for 3–4 minutes. Add the lamb and fry, stirring frequently, until browned. Stir in the remaining sauce ingredients, bring to the boil and cook for 20 minutes.

3 Rinse the aubergine (eggplant) slices, drain and pat dry. Heat 4 tablespoons of the oil in a frying pan (skillet). Fry the aubergine (eggplant) slices for about 4 minutes on each side. Remove from the pan and drain well.

4 Bring a large pan of lightly salted water to the boil. Add the fusilli and

the remaining oil and cook for 8–10 minutes until almost tender, but still firm to the bite. Drain well.

5 Gently heat the Béchamel Sauce, stirring constantly. Stir in the Cheddar cheese. Stir half of the cheese sauce into the fusilli.

6 Make layers of fusilli, lamb sauce and aubergine (eggplant) slices in a greased dish. Spread the remaining cheese sauce over the top. Sprinkle over the Parmesan and bake in a preheated oven, at 190°C/375°F/Gas Mark 5, for 25 minutes. Serve hot or cold.

Lamb with Noodles

Lamb is quick fried, coated in a soy sauce and served on a bed of transparent noodles for a richly flavoured dish.

NUTRITIONAL INFORMATION

Calories 285   Sugars 1g
Protein ....27g   Fat 16g
Carbohydrate ...10g   Saturates 6g

5 MINS   15 MINS

SERVES 4

I N G R E D I E N T S

150 g/5½ oz cellophane noodles

2 tbsp peanut oil

450 g/1 lb lean lamb, thinly sliced

2 garlic cloves, crushed

2 leeks, sliced

3 tbsp dark soy sauce

250 ml/9 fl oz/1 cup lamb stock

dash of chilli sauce

red chilli strips, to garnish

1 Bring a large saucepan of water to the boil. Add the cellophane noodles and cook for 1 minute. Drain the noodles well, place in a sieve, rinse under cold running water and drain thoroughly again. Set aside until required.

2 Heat the peanut oil in a preheated wok or frying pan (skillet), swirling the oil around until it is really hot.

3 Add the lamb to the wok or frying pan (skillet) and stir-fry for about 2 minutes.

4 Add the crushed garlic and sliced leeks to the wok and stir-fry for a further 2 minutes.

5 Stir in the dark soy sauce, lamb stock and chilli sauce and cook for 3-4

minutes, stirring frequently, until the meat is cooked through.

6 Add the drained cellophane noodles to the wok or frying pan (skillet) and cook for about 1 minute, stirring, until heated through.

7 Transfer the lamb and cellophane noodles to serving plates, garnish with red chilli strips and serve.

COOK'S TIP

Transparent noodles are available in Chinese supermarkets. Use egg noodles instead if transparent noodles are unavailable, and cook them according to the instructions on the packet.

Lamb & Ginger Stir-fry

Slices of lamb cooked with garlic, ginger and shiitake mushrooms make a quick and easy supper. It is best served with Chinese egg noodles.

NUTRITIONAL INFORMATION

Calories 347	Sugars 2g
Protein 31g	Fat 21g
Carbohydrate 7g	Saturates 7g

 10 MINS 5 MINS

SERVES 4

I N G R E D I E N T S

500 g/1 lb 2 oz lamb fillet (tenderloin)

2 tbsp sunflower oil

1 tbsp chopped ginger root

2 garlic cloves, chopped

6 spring onions (scallions), white and
 green parts diagonally sliced

175 g/6 oz shiitake mushrooms, sliced

175 g/6 oz sugar snap peas

1 tsp cornflour (cornstarch)

2 tbsp dry sherry

1 tbsp light soy sauce

1 tsp sesame oil

1 tbsp sesame seeds, toasted

Chinese egg noodles to serve

1 Using a sharp knife or meat cleaver, cut the lamb into 5 mm/$\frac{1}{2}$ inch slices.

2 Heat the sunflower oil in a large preheated wok or frying pan (skillet).

3 Add the lamb to the wok or frying pan (skillet) and stir-fry for 2 minutes.

4 Add the chopped ginger root, chopped garlic cloves, sliced spring onions (scallions), mushrooms and sugar snap peas and stir-fry for 2 minutes.

5 Blend the cornflour (cornstarch) with the sherry and stir into the wok.

6 Add the light soy sauce and sesame oil and cook, stirring, for 1 minute until thickened.

7 Sprinkle over the sesame seeds, transfer the lamb and ginger stir-fry to a warm serving dish and serve the stir-fry with Chinese egg noodles.

COOK'S TIP

Shiitake mushrooms are much used in Chinese cooking. They have a slightly meaty flavour and can be bought both fresh and dried. Their powerful flavour will permeate more bland mushrooms. Cook them briefly or they begin to toughen.

Sweet Lamb Fillet

Lamb fillet, enhanced by a sweet and spicy glaze, is cooked on the barbecue (grill) in a kitchen foil parcel for deliciously moist results.

NUTRITIONAL INFORMATION

Calories 258	Sugars 13g
Protein 24g	Fat 13g
Carbohydrate ...13g	Saturates 5g

 5 MINS   1 HOUR

SERVES 4

I N G R E D I E N T S

2 fillets of neck of lean lamb, each 225 g/8 oz

1 tbsp olive oil

½ onion, chopped finely

1 clove garlic, crushed

2.5 cm/1 inch piece root (fresh) ginger, grated

5 tbsp apple juice

3 tbsp smooth apple sauce

1 tbsp light muscovado sugar

1 tbsp tomato ketchup (catsup)

½ tsp mild mustard

salt and pepper

green salad leaves, croûtons and fresh crusty bread, to serve

1 Place the lamb fillet on a large piece of double thickness kitchen foil. Season with salt and pepper to taste.

2 Heat the oil in a small pan and fry the onion and garlic for 2–3 minutes until softened but not browned. Stir in the grated ginger and cook for 1 minute, stirring occasionally.

3 Stir in the apple juice, apple sauce, sugar, ketchup (catsup) and mustard and bring to the boil. Boil rapidly for about 10 minutes until reduced by half.

Stir the mixture occasionally so that it does not burn and stick to the base of the pan.

4 Brush half of the sauce over the lamb, then wrap up the lamb in the kitchen foil to completely enclose it. Barbecue (grill)the lamb parcels over hot coals for about 25 minutes, turning the parcel over occasionally.

5 Open out the kitchen foil and brush the lamb with some of the sauce. Continue to barbecue (grill) for a further 15–20 minutes or until cooked through.

6 Place the lamb on a chopping board, remove the foil and cut into thick slices. Transfer to serving plates and spoon over the remaining sauce. Serve with green salad leaves, croûtons and fresh crusty bread.

Twice-cooked Lamb

Here lamb is first boiled and then fried with soy sauce, oyster sauce and spinach and finally tossed with noodles for a richly flavoured dish.

NUTRITIONAL INFORMATION

Calories 315   Sugars 5g
Protein . . . . .27g   Fat 16g
Carbohydrate . . .16g   Saturates 6g

 5 MINS   30 MINS

SERVES 4

INGREDIENTS

250 g/9 oz packet egg noodles

450 g/1 lb lamb loin fillet,
   thinly sliced

2 tbsp soy sauce

2 tbsp sunflower oil

2 cloves garlic, crushed

1 tbsp caster (superfine) sugar

2 tbsp oyster sauce

175 g/6 oz baby spinach

1 Place the egg noodles in a large bowl and cover with boiling water. Leave to soak for about 10 minutes.

2 Bring a large saucepan of water to the boil. Add the lamb and cook for 5 minutes. Drain thoroughly.

3 Place the slices of lamb in a bowl and mix with the soy sauce and 1 tablespoon of the sunflower oil.

4 Heat the remaining sunflower oil in a large preheated wok, swirling the oil around until it is really hot.

5 Add the marinated lamb and crushed garlic to the wok and stir-fry for about 5 minutes or until the meat is just beginning to brown.

6 Add the caster (superfine) sugar and oyster sauce to the wok and stir well to combine.

7 Drain the noodles thoroughly. Add the noodles to the wok and stir-fry for a further 5 minutes.

8 Add the spinach to the wok and cook for 1 minute or until the leaves just wilt. Transfer the lamb and noodles to serving bowls and serve hot.

COOK'S TIP

If using dried noodles, follow the instructions on the packet as they require less soaking.

Lamb Couscous

Couscous is a dish that originated among the Berbers of North Africa. When steamed, it is a delicious plump grain, ideal for serving with stews.

NUTRITIONAL INFORMATION

Calories 537	Sugars 11g
Protein 32g	Fat 14g
Carbohydrate ...73g	Saturates 4g

 15 MINS   35 MINS

SERVES 4

INGREDIENTS

2 medium red onions, sliced

juice of 1 lemon

1 large red (bell) pepper, deseeded and thickly sliced

1 large green (bell) pepper, deseeded and thickly sliced

1 large orange (bell) pepper, deseeded and thickly sliced

pinch of saffron strands

cinnamon stick, broken

1 tbsp clear honey

300 ml/½ pint/1¼ cups vegetable stock

2 tsp olive oil

350 g/12 oz lean lamb fillet, trimmed and sliced

1 tsp Harissa paste

200 g/7 oz can chopped tomatoes

425 g/15 oz can chick-peas (garbanzo beans), drained

350 g/12 oz precooked couscous

2 tsp ground cinnamon

salt and pepper

1 Toss the onions in the lemon juice and transfer to a saucepan. Mix in the (bell) peppers, saffron, cinnamon stick and honey. Pour in the stock, bring to the boil, cover and simmer for 5 minutes.

2 Meanwhile, heat the oil in a frying pan (skillet) and gently fry the lamb for 3–4 minutes until browned all over.

3 Using a slotted spoon, drain the lamb and transfer it to the pan with the onions and peppers. Season and stir in the Harissa paste, tomatoes and chick-peas (garbanzo beans). Mix well, bring back to the boil and simmer, uncovered, for 20 minutes.

4 Soak the couscous, following the packet instructions. Bring a saucepan of water to the boil. Put the couscous in a steamer or sieve (strainer) lined with muslin (cheese-cloth) over the pan of boiling water. Cover and steam.

5 Transfer the couscous to a serving platter and dust with ground cinnamon. Discard the cinnamon stick and spoon the stew over the couscous.

Lamb Meatballs

These small meatballs are made with minced (ground) lamb and flavoured with chilli, garlic, parsley and Chinese curry powder.

NUTRITIONAL INFORMATION

Calories	320	Sugars	.........1g
Protein	........28g	Fat	..........20g
Carbohydrate	....8g	Saturates	.......6g

 5 MINS   20 MINS

SERVES 4

INGREDIENTS

450 g/1 lb minced (ground) lamb

3 garlic cloves, crushed

2 spring onions (scallions), finely chopped

½ tsp chilli powder

1 tsp Chinese curry powder

1 tbsp chopped fresh parsley

25 g/1 oz/½ cup fresh white breadcrumbs

1 egg, beaten

3 tbsp vegetable oil

125 g/4½ oz Chinese leaves (cabbage), shredded

1 leek, sliced

1 tbsp cornflour (cornstarch)

2 tbsp water

300 ml/½ pint/1¼ cups lamb stock

1 tbsp dark soy sauce

shredded leek, to garnish

VARIATION

Use minced (ground) pork or beef instead of the lamb as an alternative.

1 Mix the lamb, garlic, spring onions (scallions), chilli powder, Chinese curry powder, parsley and breadcrumbs together in a bowl. Work the egg into the mixture, bringing it together to form a firm mixture. Roll into 16 small, even-sized balls.

2 Heat the oil in a preheated wok. Add the Chinese leaves (cabbage) and leek and stir-fry for 1 minute. Remove from the wok with a slotted spoon and set aside.

3 Add the meatballs to the wok and fry in batches, turning gently, for 3-4 minutes, or until golden brown all over.

4 Mix the cornflour (cornstarch) and water together to form a smooth paste and set aside. Pour the lamb stock and soy sauce into the wok and cook for 2–3 minutes. Stir in the cornflour (cornstarch) paste. Bring to the boil and cook, stirring constantly, until the sauce is thickened and clear.

5 Return the Chinese leaves (cabbage) and leek to the wok and cook for 1 minute, until heated through. Arrange the Chinese leaves (cabbage) and leek on a warm serving dish, top with the meatballs, garnish with shredded leek and serve immediately.

Liver with (Bell) Peppers

This is a richly flavoured dish which is great served with plain rice or noodles to soak up the delicious juices.

NUTRITIONAL INFORMATION

Calories 331	Sugars 5g
Protein 25g	Fat 17g
Carbohydrate . . .15g	Saturates 4g

 5 MINS   10 MINS

SERVES 4

I N G R E D I E N T S

450 g/1 lb lamb's liver

2 tbsp cornflour (cornstarch)

2 tbsp groundnut oil

1 onion, sliced

2 cloves garlic, crushed

2 green (bell) peppers, deseeded and sliced

2 tbsp tomato purée (paste)

3 tbsp dry sherry

1 tbsp cornflour (cornstarch)

2 tbsp soy sauce

1 Using a sharp knife, trim any excess fat from the lamb's liver. Slice the lamb's liver into thin strips.

2 Place the cornflour (cornstarch) in a large bowl.

3 Add the strips of lamb's liver to the cornflour (cornstarch) and toss well until coated evenly all over.

4 Heat the groundnut oil in a large preheated wok or heavy-based frying pan (skillet).

5 Add the lamb's liver, sliced onion, crushed garlic and sliced green (bell) peppers to the wok or frying pan (skillet) and stir-fry for 6–7 minutes, or until the

lamb's liver is just cooked through and the vegetables are tender.

6 Mix together the tomato purée (paste), sherry, cornflour (cornstarch) and soy sauce. Stir the mixture into the wok and cook for a further 2 minutes or until the juices have thickened.

7 Transfer to warm serving bowls and serve immediately.

COOK'S TIP

Use rice wine instead of the sherry for a really authentic Oriental flavour. Chinese rice wine is made from glutinous rice and is also known as 'yellow wine' because of its golden colour. The best variety, from south-east China, is called Shao Hsing or Shaoxing.

Pan-Fried Liver with Thyme

This elegant dish is very simple to make. You can use either calf's or lamb's liver for the main ingredient.

NUTRITIONAL INFORMATION

Calories 462	Sugars 1g	
Protein 27g	Fat 31g	
Carbohydrate ...14g	Saturates 6g	

5 MINS · 10 MINS

SERVES 1

INGREDIENTS

1 slice calf's liver, about 125 g/4½ oz, or
   2 smaller slices, or 2 slices lamb's liver

1 tbsp seasoned flour

2 tsp oil

15 g/½ oz/1 tbsp butter or margarine

2 tbsp white wine

½ tsp chopped fresh thyme or a large pinch
   of dried thyme

pinch of finely grated lime or lemon rind

2 tsp lemon juice

1 tsp capers

1–2 tbsp double (heavy) cream (optional)

salt and pepper

TO GARNISH

lemon or lime slices

fresh thyme or parsley

1 Trim the liver if necessary and toss in the seasoned flour until evenly coated.

2 Heat the oil and margarine in a frying pan (skillet). When foaming, add the liver and fry for 2–3 minutes on each side until well sealed and just cooked through. Take care not to overcook or the liver will become tough and hard. Transfer to a plate and keep warm.

3 Add the wine, 1 tablespoon of water, the thyme, citrus rind, lemon juice, capers and seasoning to the pan juices, and heat through gently until bubbling and syrupy. Add the cream (if using) to the sauce and reheat gently. Adjust the seasoning and spoon over the liver.

4 Serve the liver, garnished with lemon or lime slices and thyme or parsley, with new potatoes and a salad.

COOK'S TIP

Liver is traditionally served with bacon and onions. Grilled (broiled) bacon rolls and crisply fried onions can be used as an extra garnish, if desired.

Liver with Wine Sauce

Liver is popular in Italy and is served in many ways. Tender calf's liver is the best type to use for this recipe, but you could use lamb's liver.

NUTRITIONAL INFORMATION

Calories	435	Sugars	.........2g
Protein	........30g	Fat	..........31g
Carbohydrate	....4g	Saturates	......12g

25 MINS   20 MINS

SERVES 4

INGREDIENTS

4 slices calf's liver or 8 slices lamb's liver,
   about 500 g/1 lb 2 oz

flour, for coating

1 tbsp olive oil

25 g/1 oz/2 tbsp butter

1 garlic clove, crushed

125 g/4½ oz lean bacon rashers, rinded and
   cut into narrow strips

1 onion, chopped

1 celery stalk, sliced thinly

150 ml/¼ pint/⅔ cup red wine

150 ml/¼ pint/⅔ cup beef stock

good pinch of ground allspice

1 tsp Worcestershire sauce

1 tsp chopped fresh sage or ½ tsp
   dried sage

3–4 tomatoes, peeled, quartered and
   deseeded

salt and pepper

fresh sage leaves, to garnish

new potatoes or sauté potatoes, to serve

1 Wipe the liver with paper towels, season with salt and pepper to taste and then coat lightly in flour, shaking off any excess.

2 Heat the oil and butter in a pan and fry the liver until well sealed on both sides and just cooked through – take care not to overcook. Remove the liver from the pan, cover and keep warm, but do not allow to dry out.

3 Add the bacon to the fat left in the pan, with the onion and celery. Fry gently until soft.

4 Add the red wine, beef stock, allspice, Worcestershire sauce, sage and salt and pepper to taste. Bring to the boil and simmer for 3–4 minutes.

5 Cut each tomato segment in half. Add to the sauce and continue to cook for 2–3 minutes.

6 Serve the liver on a little of the sauce, with the remainder spooned over. Garnish with fresh sage leaves and serve with tiny new potatoes or sauté potatoes.

Pork with Fennel & Aniseed

Lean pork chops, stuffed with an aniseed and orange filling, are pan-cooked with fennel in an aniseed-flavoured sweet sauce.

NUTRITIONAL INFORMATION

Calories 298   Sugars 10g
Protein . . . . .30g   Fat 10g
Carbohydrate . . .18g   Saturates 3g

 20 MINS   35 MINS

SERVES 4

I N G R E D I E N T S

4 lean pork chops, 125 g/4½ oz each

60 g/2 oz/⅓ cup brown rice, cooked

1 tsp orange rind, grated

4 spring onions (scallions), trimmed and finely chopped

½ tsp aniseed

1 tbsp olive oil

1 fennel bulb, trimmed and thinly sliced

450 ml/16 fl oz/2 cups unsweetened orange juice

1 tbsp cornflour (cornstarch)

2 tbsp Pernod

salt and pepper

fennel fronds, to garnish

cooked vegetables, to serve

1 Trim away any excess fat from the pork chops. Using a small, sharp knife, make a slit in the centre of each chop to create a pocket.

2 Mix the rice, orange rind, spring onions (scallions), seasoning and aniseed together in a bowl.

3 Push the rice mixture into the pocket of each chop, then press gently to seal.

4 Heat the oil in a frying pan (skillet) and fry the pork chops on each side for 2–3 minutes until lightly browned.

5 Add the sliced fennel and orange juice to the pan, bring to the boil and simmer for 15–20 minutes until the meat is tender and cooked through. Remove the pork and fennel with a slotted spoon and transfer to a serving plate.

6 Blend the cornflour (cornstarch) and Pernod together in a small bowl. Add the cornflour (cornstarch) mixture to the pan and stir into the pan juices. Cook for 2–3 minutes, stirring, until the sauce thickens.

7 Pour the Pernod sauce over the pork chops, garnish with fennel fronds and serve with some cooked vegetables.

Pork Chow Mein

This is a basic recipe – the meat and/or vegetables can be varied as much as you like.

NUTRITIONAL INFORMATION

Calories 239	Sugars 1g	
Protein 17g	Fat 14g	
Carbohydrate ...12g	Saturates 2g	

 15 MINS 15 MINS

SERVES 4

I N G R E D I E N T S

250 g/9 oz egg noodles

4-5 tbsp vegetable oil

250 g/9 oz pork fillet, cooked

125g/4½ oz French (green) beans

2 tbsp light soy sauce

1 tsp salt

½ tsp sugar

1 tbsp Chinese rice wine or dry sherry

2 spring onions (scallions), finely shredded

a few drops sesame oil

chilli sauce, to serve (optional)

1 Cook the noodles in boiling water according to the instructions on the packet, then drain and rinse under cold water. Drain again then toss with 1 tablespoon of the oil.

2 Slice the pork into thin shreds and top and tail the beans.

3 Heat 3 tablespoons of oil in a preheated wok until hot. Add the noodles and stir-fry for 2-3 minutes with 1 tablespoon soy sauce, then remove to a serving dish. Keep warm.

4 Heat the remaining oil and stir-fry the beans and meat for 2 minutes. Add the salt, sugar, wine or sherry, the remaining soy sauce and about half the spring onions (scallions) to the wok.

5 Stir the mixture in the wok, adding a little stock if necessary, then pour on top of the noodles, and sprinkle with sesame oil and the remaining spring onions (scallions).

6 Serve the chow mein hot or cold with chilli sauce, if desired.

COOK'S TIP

Chow Mein literally means 'stir-fried noodles' and is highly popular in the West as well as in China. Almost any ingredient can be added, such as fish, meat, poultry or vegetables. It is very popular for lunch and makes a tasty salad served cold.

Sweet & Sour Pork

In this classic Chinese dish, tender pork pieces are fried and served in a crunchy sauce. This dish is perfect served with plain rice.

NUTRITIONAL INFORMATION

Calories 357	Sugars 25g	
Protein 28g	Fat 14g	
Carbohydrate ...30g	Saturates 4g	

10 MINS   20 MINS

SERVES 4

INGREDIENTS

450 g/1 lb pork tenderloin

2 tbsp sunflower oil

225 g/8 oz courgettes (zucchini)

1 red onion, cut into thin wedges

2 cloves garlic, crushed

225 g/8 oz carrots, cut into thin sticks

1 red (bell) pepper, deseeded and sliced

100 g/3½ oz/1 cup baby corn corbs

100 g/3½ oz button mushrooms, halved

175 g/6 oz/1¼ cups fresh pineapple, cubed

100 g/3½ oz/1 cup bean sprouts

150 ml/¼ pint/⅔ cup pineapple juice

1 tbsp cornflour (cornstarch)

2 tbsp soy sauce

3 tbsp tomato ketchup

1 tbsp white wine vinegar

1 tbsp clear honey

COOK'S TIP

If you prefer a crisper coating, toss the pork in a mixture of cornflour (cornstarch) and egg white and deep fry in the wok in step 2.

1 Using a sharp knife, thinly slice the pork tenderloin into even-size pieces.

2 Heat the sunflower oil in a large preheated wok. Add the pork to the wok and stir-fry for 10 minutes, or until the pork is completely cooked through and beginning to turn crispy at the edges.

3 Meanwhile, cut the courgettes (zucchini) into thin sticks.

4 Add the onion, garlic, carrots, courgettes (zucchini), (bell) pepper, corn cobs and mushrooms to the wok and stir-fry for a further 5 minutes.

5 Add the pineapple cubes and bean sprouts to the wok and stir-fry for 2 minutes.

6 Mix together the pineapple juice, cornflour (cornstarch), soy sauce, tomato ketchup, white wine vinegar and honey.

7 Pour the sweet and sour mixture into the wok and cook over a high heat, tossing frequently, until the juices thicken. Transfer the sweet and sour pork to serving bowls and serve hot.

Pork Chops with Sage

The fresh taste of sage is the perfect ingredient to counteract the richness of pork.

NUTRITIONAL INFORMATION

Calories	364	Sugars 5g
Protein	........34g	Fat 19g
Carbohydrate	...14g	Saturates 7g

10 MINS   15 MINS

SERVES 4

INGREDIENTS

2 tbsp flour

1 tbsp chopped fresh sage or 1 tsp dried

4 lean boneless pork chops, trimmed of
excess fat

2 tbsp olive oil

15 g/½ oz/1 tbsp butter

2 red onions, sliced into rings

1 tbsp lemon juice

2 tsp caster (superfine) sugar

4 plum tomatoes, quartered

salt and pepper

1 Mix the flour, sage and salt and pepper to taste on a plate. Lightly dust the pork chops on both sides with the seasoned flour.

2 Heat the oil and butter in a frying pan (skillet), add the chops and cook them for 6–7 minutes on each side until cooked through. Drain the chops, reserving the pan juices, and keep warm.

3 Toss the onion in the lemon juice and fry along with the sugar and tomatoes for 5 minutes until tender.

4 Serve the pork with the tomato and onion mixture and a green salad.

Spare Ribs with Chilli

For best results, chop the spare ribs into small bite-size pieces.

NUTRITIONAL INFORMATION

Calories 497   Sugars 3g
Protein . . . . .13g   Fat 47g
Carbohydrate . . . .4g   Saturates 11g

4 /₄ HOURS   20 MINS

SERVES 4

INGREDIENTS

500 g/1 lb 2 oz pork spare ribs

1 tsp sugar

1 tbsp light soy sauce

1 tsp rice wine or dry sherry

1 tsp cornflour (cornstarch)

about 600 ml/1pint/2½ cups vegetable oil

1 garlic clove, finely chopped

1 spring onion (scallion), cut into short
  sections

1 small hot chilli pepper (green or red),
  thinly sliced

2 tbsp black bean sauce

about 150 ml/¼ pint/⅔ cup Chinese Stock
  (see page 8) or water

1 small onion, diced

1 medium green (bell) pepper, cored,
  seeded and diced

COOK'S TIP

Be very careful when handling
and cutting chilli peppers as their
juice can cause irritation of the
skin. Be sure to wash your hands
after handling, and keep well away
from face and eyes. The seeds of the
chilli are the hottest part – remove
seeds if you want a milder dish.

1 Trim any excess fat from the ribs. Using a sharp knife
or meat cleaver, chop each rib into 3-4 bite-sized
piecess and place in a shallow dish.

2 Mix together the sugar, soy sauce, wine and cornflour
(cornstarch) and pour the mixture over the pork ribs.
Leave to marinate for 35-45 minutes.

3 Heat the vegetable oil in a large preheated wok or
frying pan (skillet).

4 Add the spare ribs to the wok and deep-fry for 2-3
minutes until light brown. Remove with a slotted
spoon and drain on absorbent kitchen paper (paper towels).

5 Pour off the oil, leaving about 1 tablespoon in the wok.
Add the garlic, spring onion (scallion), chilli pepper and
black bean sauce and stir-fry for 30-40 seconds.

6 Add the spare ribs, blend well, then add the stock or
water. Bring to the boil, then reduce the heat, cover
and braise for 8-10 minutes, stirring once or twice.

7 Add the onion and green (bell) pepper, increase the
heat to high, and stir uncovered for about 2 minutes to
reduce the sauce a little. Serve hot.

Chilli Pork Noodles

This is quite a spicy dish, with a delicious peanut flavour. Increase or reduce the amount of chilli to your liking.

NUTRITIONAL INFORMATION

Calories 421	Sugars 3g
Protein 27g	Fat 26g
Carbohydrate . . .20g	Saturates 6g

 35 MINS   10 MINS

SERVES 4

INGREDIENTS

350 g/12 oz minced (ground) pork

1 tbsp light soy sauce

1 tbsp dry sherry

350 g/12 oz egg noodles

2 tsp sesame oil

2 tbsp vegetable oil

2 garlic cloves, crushed

2 tsp grated fresh root ginger

2 fresh red chillies, sliced

1 red (bell) pepper, seeded and finely sliced

25 g/1 oz/¼ cup unsalted peanuts

3 tbsp peanut butter

3 tbsp dark soy sauce

dash of chilli oil

300 ml/½ pint/1¼ cups pork stock

1 Mix together the pork, light soy sauce and dry sherry in a large bowl. Cover and leave to marinate for 30 minutes.

2 Meanwhile, cook the noodles in a saucepan of boiling water for 4 minutes. Drain well, rinse in cold water and drain again. Toss the noodles in the sesame oil.

3 Heat the vegetable oil in a preheated wok and stir-fry the garlic, ginger, chillies and (bell) pepper for 30 seconds.

4 Add the pork to the mixture in the wok, together with the marinade. Continue cooking for about 1 minute, until the pork is sealed.

5 Add the peanuts, peanut butter, soy sauce, chilli oil and stock and cook for 2-3 minutes.

6 Toss the noodles in the mixture and serve at once.

VARIATION

Minced (ground) chicken or lamb would also be excellent in this recipe instead of the pork.

Pork with Ratatouille Sauce

Serve this delicious combination of meat and vegetables with baked potatoes for an appetizing supper dish.

NUTRITIONAL INFORMATION

Calories ....230 Sugars 8g
Protein ....29g Fat 9g
Carbohydrate ....8g Saturates 3g

10 MINS   35 MINS

SERVES 4

INGREDIENTS

4 lean, boneless pork chops, about
    125 g/4½ oz each

1 tsp dried mixed herbs

salt and pepper

baked potatoes, to serve

SAUCE

1 medium onion

1 garlic clove

1 small green (bell) pepper, deseeded

1 small yellow (bell) pepper, deseeded

1 medium courgette (zucchini), trimmed

100 g/3½ oz button mushrooms

400 g/14 oz can chopped tomatoes

2 tbsp tomato purée (paste)

1 tsp dried mixed herbs

1 tsp caster (superfine) sugar

COOK'S TIP

This vegetable sauce could be served with any other grilled (broiled) or baked meat or fish. It would also make an excellent alternative filling for savoury crêpes.

1 To make the sauce, peel and chop the onion and garlic. Dice the (bell) peppers. Dice the courgette (zucchini). Wipe and halve the mushrooms.

2 Place all of the vegetables in a saucepan and stir in the chopped tomatoes and tomato purée (paste). Add the dried herbs, sugar and plenty of seasoning. Bring to the boil, cover and simmer for 20 minutes.

3 Meanwhile, preheat the grill (broiler) to medium. Trim away any excess fat from the chops, then season on both sides and rub in the dried mixed herbs. Cook the chops for 5 minutes, then turn over and cook for a further 6–7 minutes or until cooked through.

4 Drain the chops on absorbent kitchen paper and serve accompanied with the sauce and baked potatoes.

Pork Stuffed with Prosciutto

This sophisticated roast with Mediterranean flavours is ideal served with a pungent olive paste.

NUTRITIONAL INFORMATION

Calories 427   Sugars 0g
Protein ....31g   Fat 34g
Carbohydrate ...0.2g   Saturates 7g

🥘 25 MINS   🕐 55 MINS

SERVES 4

I N G R E D I E N T S

500 g/1 lb 2 oz piece of lean pork fillet

small bunch fresh of basil leaves, washed

2 tbsp freshly grated Parmesan

2 tbsp sun-dried tomato paste

6 thin slices Parma ham (prosciutto)

1 tbsp olive oil

salt and pepper

O L I V E   P A S T E

125 g/4½ oz/⅔ cup pitted black olives

4 tbsp olive oil

2 garlic cloves, peeled

1 Trim away excess fat and membrane from the pork fillet. Slice the pork lengthways down the middle, taking care not to cut all the way through.

2 Open out the pork and season the inside. Lay the basil leaves down the centre. Mix the cheese and sun-dried tomato paste and spread over the basil.

3 Press the pork back together. Wrap the ham around the pork, overlapping, to cover. Place on a rack in a roasting tin (pan), seamside down, and brush with oil. Bake in a preheated oven,190°C/375°F/Gas Mark 5, for 30–40 minutes depending on thickness until cooked through. Allow to stand for 10 minutes.

4 For the olive paste, place all the ingredients in a blender or food processor and blend until smooth. Alternatively, for a coarser paste, finely chop the olives and garlic and mix with the oil.

5 Drain the cooked pork and slice thinly. Serve with the olive paste and a salad.

Fish-flavoured Pork

'Fish-flavoured' is a Szechuan cookery term meaning that the dish is prepared with seasonings normally used in fish dishes.

NUTRITIONAL INFORMATION

Calories 183	Sugars 0.2g	
Protein 14g	Fat 13g	
Carbohydrate 3g	Saturates 3g	

🧊 25 MINS   🕐 10 MINS

SERVES 4

I N G R E D I E N T S

about 2 tbsp dried wood ears

250-300 g/9-10½ oz pork fillet

1 tsp salt

2 tsp cornflour (cornstarch) paste
  (see page 6)

3 tbsp vegetable oil

1 garlic clove, finely chopped

½ tsp finely chopped ginger root

2 spring onions (scallions), finely chopped,
  with the white and green parts separated

2 celery stalks, thinly sliced

½ tsp sugar

1 tbsp light soy sauce

1 tbsp chilli bean sauce

2 tsp rice vinegar

1 tsp rice wine or dry sherry

a few drops of sesame oil

COOK'S TIP

Also known as cloud ears, this is a dried grey-black fungus widely used in Szechuan cooking. It is always soaked in warm water before using. Wood ears have a crunchy texture and a mild flavour.

1 Soak the wood ears in warm water for about 20 minutes, then rinse in cold water until the water is clear. Drain well, then cut into thin shreds.

2 Cut the pork into thin shreds, then mix in a bowl with a pinch of salt and about half the cornflour (cornstarch) paste until well coated.

3 Heat 1 tablespoon of vegetable oil in a preheated wok. Add the pork strips and stir-fry for about 1 minute, or until the colour changes, then remove with a slotted spoon and set aside until required.

4 Heat the remaining oil to the wok. Add the garlic, ginger, the white parts of the spring onions (scallions), the wood ears and celery and stir-fry for about 1 minute.

5 Return the pork strips together with the salt, sugar, soy sauce, chili bean sauce, vinegar and wine or sherry. Blend well and continue stirring for another minute.

6 Finally add the green parts of the spring onions (scallions) and blend in the remaining cornflour (cornstarch) paste and sesame oil. Stir until the sauce has thickened. Transfer the fish-flavoured pork to a warm serving dish and serve immediately.

Pork with (Bell) Peppers

This is a really simple yet colourful dish, the trio of (bell) peppers offsetting the pork and sauce wonderfully.

NUTRITIONAL INFORMATION

Calories 459	Sugars 5g	
Protein 19g	Fat 39g	
Carbohydrate 8g	Saturates 13g	

 30 MINS   25 MINS

SERVES 4

I N G R E D I E N T S

15 g/½ oz Chinese dried mushrooms

450 g/1 lb pork leg steaks

2 tbsp vegetable oil

1 onion, sliced

1 red (bell) pepper, deseeded and diced

1 green (bell) pepper, deseeded and diced

1 yellow (bell) pepper, deseeded and diced

4 tbsp oyster sauce

1 Place the mushrooms in a large bowl. Pour over enough boiling water to cover and leave to stand for 20 minutes.

2 Using a sharp knife, trim any excess fat from the pork steaks. Cut the pork into thin strips.

3 Bring a large saucepan of water to the boil. Add the pork to the boiling water and cook for 5 minutes.

4 Remove the pork from the pan with a slotted spoon and leave to drain thoroughly.

5 Heat the oil in a large preheated wok. Add the pork to the wok and stir-fry for about 5 minutes.

6 Remove the mushrooms from the water and leave to drain thoroughly. Roughly chop the mushrooms.

7 Add the mushrooms, onion and the (bell) peppers to the wok and stir-fry for 5 minutes.

8 Stir in the oyster sauce and cook for 2-3 minutes. Serve immediately.

COOK'S TIP

Use open-cap mushrooms, sliced, instead of Chinese mushrooms, if you prefer.

Pork with Plums

Plum sauce is often used in Chinese cooking with duck or rich, fattier meat to counteract the flavour

NUTRITIONAL INFORMATION

Calories	.281	Sugars	.6g
Protein	.25g	Fat	.14g
Carbohydrate	.10g	Saturates	.4g

35 MINS   25 MINS

SERVES 4

INGREDIENTS

450 g/1 lb pork fillet (tenderloin)

1 tbsp cornflour (cornstarch)

2 tbsp light soy sauce

2 tbsp Chinese rice wine

4 tsp light brown sugar

pinch of ground cinnamon

5 tsp vegetable oil

2 garlic cloves, crushed

2 spring onions (scallions), chopped

4 tbsp plum sauce

1 tbsp hoisin sauce

150 ml/¼ pint/⅔ cup water

dash of chilli sauce

fried plum quarters and spring onions
(scallions), to garnish

1 Cut the pork fillet (tenderloin) into thin slices.

2 Combine the cornflour (cornstarch), soy sauce, rice wine, sugar and cinnamon in a small bowl.

3 Place the pork in a shallow dish and pour the cornflour (cornstarch) mixture over it. Toss the meat in the marinade until it is completely coated. Cover and leave to marinate for at least 30 minutes.

4 Remove the pork from the dish, reserving the marinade.

5 Heat the oil in a preheated wok or large frying pan (skillet). Add the pork and stir-fry for 3–4 minutes, until a light golden colour.

6 Stir in the garlic, spring onions (scallions), plum sauce, hoisin sauce, water and chilli sauce. Bring the sauce to the boil. Reduce the heat, cover and leave to simmer for 8–10 minutes, or until the pork is cooked through and tender.

7 Stir in the reserved marinade and cook, stirring, for about 5 minutes.

8 Transfer the pork stir-fry to a warm serving dish and garnish with fried plum quarters and spring onions (scallions). Serve immediately.

Tangy Pork Fillet

Barbecued (grilled) in a parcel of kitchen foil, these tasty pork fillets are served with a tangy orange sauce.

NUTRITIONAL INFORMATION

Calories 230   Sugars 16g
Protein ....19g   Fat 9g
Carbohydrate ...20g   Saturates 3g

10 MINS   55 MINS

SERVES 4

INGREDIENTS

400 g/14 oz lean pork fillet

3 tbsp orange marmalade

grated rind and juice of 1 orange

1 tbsp white wine vinegar

dash of Tabasco sauce

salt and pepper

SAUCE

1 tbsp olive oil

1 small onion, chopped

1 small green (bell) pepper, deseeded and thinly sliced

1 tbsp cornflour (cornstarch)

150 ml/5 fl oz/⅔ cup orange juice

TO SERVE

cooked rice

mixed salad leaves

1 Place a large piece of double thickness foil in a shallow dish. Put the pork fillet in the centre of the foil and season.

2 Heat the marmalade, orange rind and juice, vinegar and Tabasco sauce in a small pan, stirring until the marmalade melts and the ingredients combine. Pour the mixture over the pork and wrap the meat in foil, making sure that the parcel is well sealed so that the juices cannot run out. Place over hot coals and barbecue (grill) for about 25 minutes, turning the parcel occasionally.

3 For the sauce, heat the oil and cook the onion for 2–3 minutes. Add the (bell) pepper and cook for 3–4 minutes.

4 Remove the pork from the kitchen foil and place on to the rack. Pour the juices into the pan with the sauce.

5 Barbecue (grill) the pork for a further 10–20 minutes, turning, until cooked through and golden on the outside.

6 In a small bowl, mix the cornflour (cornstarch) with a little orange juice to form a paste. Add to the sauce with the remaining cooking juices. Cook, stirring, until the sauce thickens. Slice the pork, spoon over the sauce and serve with rice and mixed salad leaves.

Pork Satay Stir-Fry

Satay sauce is easy to make and is one of the best known and loved sauces in Oriental cooking. It is perfect with beef, chicken or pork.

NUTRITIONAL INFORMATION

Calories 506	Sugars 11g	
Protein 31g	Fat 36g	
Carbohydrate ...15g	Saturates 8g	

10 MINS   15 MINS

SERVES 4

INGREDIENTS

150 g/5½ oz carrots

2 tbsp sunflower oil

350 g/12 oz pork neck fillet, thinly sliced

1 onion, sliced

2 cloves garlic, crushed

1 yellow (bell) pepper, deseeded and sliced

150 g/5½ oz/2⅓ cups mangetout (snow peas)

75 g/2¾ oz/1½ cups fine asparagus

chopped salted peanuts, to serve

SATAY SAUCE

6 tbsp crunchy peanut butter

6 tbsp coconut milk

1 tsp chilli flakes

1 clove garlic, crushed

1 tsp tomato purée (paste)

COOK'S TIP

Cook the sauce just before serving as it tends to thicken very quickly and will not be spoonable if you cook it too far in advance.

1 Using a sharp knife, slice the carrots into thin sticks.

2 Heat the oil in a large, preheated wok. Add the pork, onion and garlic and stir-fry for 5 minutes or until the lamb is cooked through.

3 Add the carrots, (bell) pepper, mangetout (snow peas) and asparagus to the wok and stir-fry for 5 minutes.

4 To make the satay sauce, place the peanut butter, coconut milk, chilli flakes, garlic and tomato purée (paste) in a small pan and heat gently, stirring, until well combined. Be careful not to let the sauce stick to the bottom of the pan.

5 Transfer the stir-fry to warm serving plates. Spoon the satay sauce over the stir-fry and scatter with chopped peanuts. Serve immediately.

Pork with Mooli

Pork and mooli (white radish) are a perfect combination, especially with the added heat of the sweet chilli sauce.

NUTRITIONAL INFORMATION

Calories 280	Sugars 1g
Protein 25g	Fat 19g
Carbohydrate 2g	Saturates 4g

 10 MINS   15 MINS

SERVES 4

INGREDIENTS

4 tbsp vegetable oil

450 g/1 lb pork tenderloin

1 aubergine (eggplant)

225 g/8 oz mooli (white radish)

2 cloves garlic, crushed

3 tbsp soy sauce

2 tbsp sweet chilli sauce

boiled rice or noodles, to serve

1 Heat 2 tablespoons of the vegetable oil in a large preheated wok or frying pan (skillet).

2 Using a sharp knife, thinly slice the pork into even-size pieces.

3 Add the slices of pork to the wok or frying pan (skillet) and stir-fry for about 5 minutes.

4 Using a sharp knife, trim and dice the aubergine (eggplant). Peel and slice the mooli (white radish).

5 Add the remaining vegetable oil to the wok.

6 Add the diced aubergine (eggplant) to the wok or frying pan (skillet) together with the garlic and stir-fry for 5 minutes.

7 Add the mooli (white radish) to the wok and stir-fry for about 2 minutes.

8 Stir the soy sauce and sweet chilli sauce into the mixture in the wok and cook until heated through.

9 Transfer the pork and mooli (white radish) to warm serving bowls and serve immediately with boiled rice or noodles.

COOK'S TIP

Mooli (white radish) are long white vegetables common in Chinese cooking. Usually grated, they have a milder flavour than red radish. They are generally available in most large supermarkets.

Pork with Vegetables

This is a basic 'meat and veg' recipe – the meat can be pork, chicken, beef or lamb, and the vegetables can be varied according to the season.

NUTRITIONAL INFORMATION

Calories 227   Sugars 4g
Protein ....15g   Fat 16g
Carbohydrate ....7g   Saturates 3g

3³/₄ HOURS   10 MINS

SERVES 4

INGREDIENTS

250 g/9 oz pork fillet

1 tsp sugar

1 tbsp light soy sauce

1 tsp rice wine or dry sherry

1 tsp cornflour (cornstarch) paste (see page 6)

1 small carrot

1 small green (bell) pepper, cored and seeded

about 175 g/6 oz Chinese leaves (cabbage)

4 tbsp vegetable oil

1 spring onion (scallion), cut into short sections

a few small slices of peeled ginger root

1 tsp salt

2-3 tbsp Chinese Stock (see page 8) or water

a few drops of sesame oil

VARIATION

This dish can be made with other meats, as mentioned in the introduction. If using chicken strips, reduce the initial cooking time in the wok.

1 Thinly slice the pork fillet into small pieces and place in a shallow dish.

2 In a small bowl, mix together half the sugar and the soy sauce, the wine or sherry and cornflour (cornstarch) paste. Pour the mixture over the pork, stir well to coat the meat and leave in the refrigerator to marinate for 10-15 minutes.

3 Cut the carrot, green (bell) pepper and Chinese leaves (cabbage) into thin slices roughly the same length and width as the pork pieces.

4 Heat the oil in a preheated wok and stir-fry the pork for about 1 minute to seal in the flavour. Remove with a slotted spoon and keep warm.

5 Add the carrot, (bell) pepper, Chinese leaves (cabbage), spring onion (scallion) and ginger and stir-fry for about 2 minutes.

6 Add the salt and remaining sugar, followed by the pork and remaining soy sauce, and the Chinese stock or water. Blend well and stir for another 1-2 minutes until hot. Sprinkle the stir-fry with the sesame oil and serve immediately.

Pork & Apple Skewers

Flavoured with mustard and served with a mustard sauce, these kebabs (kabobs) make an ideal lunch.

NUTRITIONAL INFORMATION

Calories	290	Sugars	........11g
Protein	........24g	Fat	..........17g
Carbohydrate	....11g	Saturates	......5g

10 MINS   15 MINS

SERVES 4

INGREDIENTS

450 g/1 lb pork fillet

2 (dessert) eating apples

a little lemon juice

1 lemon

2 tsp wholegrain mustard

2 tsp Dijon mustard

2 tbsp apple or orange juice

2 tbsp sunflower oil

crusty brown bread, to serve

MUSTARD SAUCE

1 tbsp wholegrain mustard

1 tsp Dijon mustard

6 tbsp single (light) cream

1 To make the mustard sauce, combine the wholegrain and Dijon mustards in a small bowl and slowly blend in the cream. Leave to stand until required.

2 Cut the pork fillet into bite-size pieces and set aside until required.

3 Core the apples, then cut them into thick wedges. Toss the apple wedges in a little lemon juice – this will prevent any discoloration. Slice the lemon.

4 Thread the pork, apple and lemon slices alternately on to 4 metal or pre-soaked wooden skewers.

5 Mix together the mustards, apple or orange juice and sunflower oil. Brush the mixture over the kebabs (kabobs) and barbecue (grill) over hot coals for 10–15 minutes, until cooked through, frequently turning and basting the kebabs (kabobs) with the mustard marinade.

6 Transfer the kebabs to warm serving plates and spoon over a little of the mustard sauce. Serve the kebabs (kabobs) with fresh, crusty brown bread.

Pork with Apple & Berries

We are accustomed to certain meat/fruit combinations, but this one really is a delicious dish of tender cooked meat with luscious juicy fruits.

NUTRITIONAL INFORMATION

Calories . . . . . . .298 Sugars 16g
Protein . . . . .27g Fat 11g
Carbohydrate . . .18g Saturates 3g

1 HOUR   20 MINS

SERVES 4

I N G R E D I E N T S

500 g/1 lb 2 oz piece lean pork fillet
   (tenderloin)

2 tsp sunflower oil

150 ml/¼ pint/⅔ cup Fresh Vegetable Stock
   (see page 8)

150 ml/¼ pint/⅔ cup dry rosé wine

1 tbsp chopped fresh thyme

1 tbsp clear honey

2 green-skinned dessert apples,
   cored and sliced, and tossed in
   1 tbsp lemon juice

175 g/6 oz/1¼ cups prepared fresh or
   frozen blackberries, or 213 g/7½ oz can
   blackberries in natural juice, drained

2 tsp cornflour (cornstarch) mixed with
   4 tsp cold water

salt and pepper

freshly cooked vegetables, to serve

VARIATION

This dish works very well with fresh
raspberries or even blueberries, but
frozen or canned berries in natural
juice make a suitable substitute.

1 Trim away any fat and silvery skin from the pork fillet and cut into 1 cm/½ inch thick slices, taking care to keep the slices a good shape.

2 Heat the oil in a non-stick frying pan (skillet), add the pork slices and fry for 4–5 minutes until browned all over. Using a perforated spoon, transfer the pork to paper towels. Reserve the pan juices.

3 Pour the stock and wine into the pan with the juices and add the thyme and honey. Mix well, bring to a simmer and add the pork and apples. Continue to simmer, uncovered, for 5 minutes.

4 Add the blackberries, season to taste and simmer for a further 5 minutes.

5 Stir in the cornflour (cornstarch) mixture until thickened. Serve with freshly cooked vegetables.

Pork Balls with Mint Sauce

Made with lean minced pork the balls are first stir-fried, then braised in the wok with stock and pickled walnuts to give a tangy flavour.

NUTRITIONAL INFORMATION

Calories 318   Sugars 2g
Protein . . . . .30g   Fat 20g
Carbohydrate . . . .6g   Saturates 5g

🍳 5 MINS   🕐 25 MINS

SERVES 4

I N G R E D I E N T S

500 g/1 lb 2 oz lean minced
   (ground) pork

40 g/1½ oz/¾ cup fine fresh white
   breadcrumbs

½ tsp ground allspice

1 garlic clove, crushed

2 tbsp freshly chopped mint

1 egg, beaten

2 tbsp sunflower oil

1 red (bell) pepper, cored, seeded
   and thinly sliced

250 ml/9 fl oz/1 cup chicken stock

4 pickled walnuts, sliced

salt and pepper

rice or Chinese noodles, to serve

fresh mint, to garnish

1 Mix together the minced (ground) pork, breadcrumbs, seasoning, allspice, garlic and half the chopped mint in a mixing bowl, then bind together with the beaten egg.

2 Shape the meat mixture into 20 small balls with your hands, damping your hands if it is easier for shaping.

3 Heat the sunflower oil in the a wok or heavy-based frying pan (skillet),

swirling the oil around until really hot, then stir-fry the pork balls for about 4-5 minutes, or until browned all over.

4 Remove the pork balls from the wok with a slotted spoon as they are ready and drain on absorbent kitchen paper (paper towels).

5 Pour off all but 1 tablespoon of fat and oil from the wok or frying pan (skillet) then add the red (bell) pepper slices and stir-fry for 2-3 minutes, or until they begin to soften, but not colour.

6 Add the chicken stock and bring to the boil. Season well with salt and pepper and return the pork balls to the wok, stirring well to coat in the sauce. Simmer for 7-10 minutes, turning the pork balls from time to time.

7 Add the remaining chopped mint and the pickled walnuts to the wok and continue to simmer for 2-3 minutes, turning the pork balls regularly to coat them in the sauce.

8 Adjust the seasoning and serve the pork balls with rice or Chinese noodles, or with a stir-fried vegetable dish, garnished with sprigs of fresh mint.

Pork Chops & Spicy Beans

A tasty and substantial dish, and the spicy bean mixture, served on its own, also makes a good accompaniment to other meat or chicken dishes.

NUTRITIONAL INFORMATION

Calories ....388 Sugars 5g
Protein ....20g Fat 27g
Carbohydrate ...17g Saturates 8g

 5 MINS   50 MINS

SERVES 4

INGREDIENTS

3 tbsp vegetable oil

4 lean pork chops, rind removed

2 onions, peeled and thinly sliced

2 garlic cloves, peeled and crushed

2 fresh green chillies, seeded and
   chopped or use 1-2 tsp minced
   chilli (from a jar)

2.5 cm/1 in piece ginger root, peeled and
   chopped

1½ tsp cumin seeds

1½ tsp ground coriander

600 ml/1 pint/2½ cups stock or water

2 tbsp tomato purée (paste)

½ aubergine (eggplant), trimmed and cut
   into 1 cm/½ inch dice

salt

1 x 400 g/14 oz can red kidney beans,
   drained

4 tbsp double (heavy) cream

sprigs of coriander (cilantro), to garnish

1 Heat the ghee or vegetable oil in a large frying pan (skillet), add the pork chops and fry until sealed and browned on both sides. Remove from the pan and set aside until required.

2 Add the sliced onions, garlic, chillies, ginger and spices and fry gently for 2 minutes. Stir in the stock or water, tomato purée (paste), diced aubergine (eggplant) and season with salt and pepper.

3 Bring the mixture to the boil, place the pork chops on top, then cover and simmer gently over medium heat for 30 minutes .

4 Remove the chops for a moment and stir the red kidney beans and double (heavy) cream into the mixture. Return the chops to the pan, cover and heat through gently for 5 minutes.

5 Taste and adjust the seasoning, if necessary. Serve hot, garnished with coriander (cilantro) sprigs.

Pork Fry with Vegetables

This is a very simple dish which lends itself to almost any combination of vegetables that you have to hand.

NUTRITIONAL INFORMATION

Calories	216	Sugars	.........3g
Protein	.........19g	Fat	...........12g
Carbohydrate	....5g	Saturates	.......3g

🍲 5 MINS   🕐 15 MINS

SERVES 4

I N G R E D I E N T S

350 g/12 oz lean pork fillet (tenderloin)

2 tbsp vegetable oil

2 garlic cloves, crushed

1-cm/½-inch piece fresh root ginger, cut into slivers

1 carrot, cut into thin strips

1 red (bell) pepper, seeded and diced

1 fennel bulb, sliced

25 g/1 oz water chestnuts, halved

75 g/2 ¾ oz bean sprouts

2 tbsp Chinese rice wine

300 ml/½ pint/1¼ cups pork or chicken stock

pinch of dark brown sugar

1 tsp cornflour (cornstarch)

2 tsp water

1 Cut the pork into thin slices. Heat the oil in a preheated wok. Add the garlic, ginger and pork and stir-fry for 1–2 minutes, until the meat is sealed.

2 Add the carrot, (bell) pepper, fennel and water chestnuts to the wok and stir-fry for about 2-3 minutes.

3 Add the bean sprouts and stir-fry for 1 minute. Remove the pork and vegetables from the wok and keep warm.

4 Add the Chinese rice wine, pork or chicken stock and sugar to the wok. Blend the cornflour (cornstarch) to a smooth paste with the water and stir it into the sauce. Bring to the boil, stirring constantly until thickened and clear.

5 Return the meat and vegetables to the wok and cook for 1–2 minutes, until heated through and coated with the sauce. Serve immediately.

VARIATION

Use dry sherry instead of the Chinese rice wine if you have difficulty obtaining it.

Pork Stroganoff

Tender, lean pork, cooked in a tasty, rich tomato sauce is flavoured with the extra tang of natural (unsweetened) yogurt.

NUTRITIONAL INFORMATION

Calories 223	Sugars 7g
Protein 22g	Fat 10g
Carbohydrate ...12g	Saturates 3g

2¼ HOURS   30 MINS

SERVES 4

I N G R E D I E N T S

350 g/12 oz lean pork fillet

1 tbsp vegetable oil

1 medium onion, chopped

2 garlic cloves, crushed

25 g/1 oz plain (all-purpose) flour

2 tbsp tomato purée (paste)

425 ml/15 fl oz/1¾ cups Fresh Chicken or
   Vegetable stock (see pages 8-9)

125 g/4½ oz button mushrooms, sliced

1 large green (bell) pepper, deseeded and
   diced

½ tsp ground nutmeg

4 tbsp low-fat natural (unsweetened)
   yogurt, plus extra to serve

salt and pepper

white rice, freshly boiled, to serve

ground nutmeg, to garnish

1   Trim away any excess fat and silver skin from the pork, then cut the meat into slices 1 cm/½ inch thick.

2   Heat the oil in a large saucepan and gently fry the pork, onion and garlic for 4–5 minutes until lightly browned.

3   Stir in the flour and tomato purée (paste), pour in the stock and stir to mix thoroughly.

4   Add the mushrooms, (bell) pepper, seasoning and nutmeg. Bring to the boil, cover and simmer for 20 minutes until the pork is tender and cooked through.

5   Remove the saucepan from the heat and stir in the yogurt.

6   Serve the pork and sauce on a bed of rice with an extra spoonful of yogurt, and garnish with a dusting of ground nutmeg.

COOK'S TIP

You can buy ready-made stock from leading supermarkets. Although more expensive, they are more nutritious than stock cubes, which are high in salt and artificial flavourings.

Pan-Cooked Pork Medallions

In this dish these lean and tender cuts of meat are perfectly complemented by the eating (dessert) apples and dry (hard) cider.

NUTRITIONAL INFORMATION

Calories ....256 Sugars 12g
Protein ....21g Fat 13g
Carbohydrate ...12g Saturates 3g

2¹⁄₂ HOURS   40 MINS

SERVES 4

INGREDIENTS

8 lean pork medallions, about 50 g/1¾ oz each

2 tsp vegetable oil

1 medium onion, finely sliced

1 tsp caster (superfine) sugar

1 tsp dried sage

150 ml/5 fl oz/⅔ cup dry (hard) cider

150 ml/5 fl oz/⅔ cup Fresh Chicken or Vegetable Stock (see pages 8-9)

1 green-skinned apple

1 red-skinned apple

1 tbsp lemon juice

salt and pepper

fresh sage leaves, to garnish

freshly cooked vegetables, to serve

1 Discard the string from the pork and trim away any excess fat. Re-tie with clean string and set aside until required.

2 Heat the oil in a frying pan (skillet) and gently fry the onion for 5 minutes until softened. Add the sugar and cook for 3–4 minutes until golden. Add the pork to the pan and cook for 2 minutes on each side until browned.

3 Add the sage, cider and stock. Bring to the boil and then simmer for 20 minutes.

4 Meanwhile, core and cut each apple into 8 wedges. Toss the apple wedges in lemon juice so that they do not turn brown.

5 Add the apples to the pork and mix gently. Season and cook for a further 3–4 minutes until tender.

6 Remove the string from the pork and serve immediately, garnished with fresh sage and accompanied with freshly cooked vegetables.

Stuffed Cannelloni

Cannelloni, the thick, round pasta tubes, make perfect containers for close-textured sauces of all kinds.

NUTRITIONAL INFORMATION

Calories	520	Sugars	.........5g
Protein	........21g	Fat	..........39g
Carbohydrate	...23g	Saturates	......18g

 30 MINS   1¹/₄ HOURS

SERVES 4

I N G R E D I E N T S

8 dried cannelloni tubes

1 tbsp olive oil

25 g/1 oz/¼ cup freshly grated
  Parmesan cheese

fresh herb sprigs, to garnish

F I L L I N G

25 g/1 oz/2 tbsp butter

300 g/10½ oz frozen spinach, thawed
  and chopped

115 g/4 oz/½ cup ricotta cheese

25 g/1 oz/¼ cup freshly grated
  Parmesan cheese

60 g/2 oz/¼ cup chopped ham

pinch of freshly grated nutmeg

2 tbsp double (heavy) cream

2 eggs, lightly beaten

salt and pepper

S A U C E

25 g/1 oz/2 tbsp butter

25 g/1 oz/¼ cup plain
  (all-purpose) flour

300 ml/½ pint/1¼ cups milk

2 bay leaves

pinch of freshly grated nutmeg

1 To make the filling, melt the butter in a pan and stir-fry the spinach for 2–3 minutes. Remove from the heat and stir in the ricotta and Parmesan cheeses and the ham. Season to taste with nutmeg, salt and pepper. Beat in the cream and eggs to make a thick paste.

2 Bring a pan of lightly salted water to the boil. Add the pasta and the oil and cook for 10–12 minutes, or until almost tender. Drain and set aside to cool.

3 To make the sauce, melt the butter in a pan. Stir in the flour and cook, stirring, for 1 minute. Gradually stir in the milk. Add the bay leaves and simmer, stirring, for 5 minutes. Add the nutmeg and salt and pepper to taste. Remove from the heat and discard the bay leaves.

4 Spoon the filling into a piping bag and fill the cannelloni.

5 Spoon a little sauce into the base of an ovenproof dish. Arrange the cannelloni in the dish in a single layer and pour over the remaining sauce. Sprinkle over the Parmesan cheese and bake in a preheated oven at 190°C/375°F/Gas Mark 5 for 40–45 minutes. Garnish with fresh herb sprigs and serve.

Garlic Pork & Noodles

This is a wonderful one-pot dish of stir-fried pork fillet with (small) shrimps and noodles that is made in minutes.

NUTRITIONAL INFORMATION

Calories 424	Sugars 1g	
Protein 33g	Fat 27g	
Carbohydrate . . .13g	Saturates 5g	

 5 MINS   15 MINS

SERVES 4

I N G R E D I E N T S

250 g/9 oz packet medium egg noodles

3 tbsp vegetable oil

2 garlic cloves, crushed

350 g/12 oz pork fillet, cut into strips

4 tbsp/⅓ cup dried (small) shrimps, or
   125 g/4½ oz peeled prawns (shrimp)

1 bunch spring onions (scallions), finely
   chopped

90 g/3 oz/¾ cup chopped roasted and
   shelled unsalted peanuts

3 tbsp fish sauce

1½ tsp palm or demerara (brown crystal)
   sugar

1-2 small red chillies, seeded and finely
   chopped (to taste)

3 tbsp lime juice

3 tbsp chopped fresh coriander (cilantro)

1 Place the noodles in a large pan of boiling water, then immediately remove from the heat. Cover and leave to stand for 6 minutes, stirring once halfway through the time. After 6 minutes the noodles will be perfectly cooked. Alternatively, follow the instructions on the packet. Drain and keep warm.

2 Heat the oil in a wok, add the garlic and pork and stir-fry until the pork strips are browned, about 2-3 minutes.

3 Add the dried (small) shrimps or shelled prawns (shrimp), spring onions (scallions), peanuts, fish sauce, palm or demerara (brown crystal) sugar, chillies to taste and lime juice. Stir-fry for a further 1 minute.

4 Add the cooked noodles and chopped fresh coriander (cilantro) and stir-fry until heated through, about 1 minute. Serve the stir-fry immediately.

COOK'S TIP

Fish sauce is made from pressed, salted fish and is widely available in super-markets and oriental stores. It is very salty, so no extra salt should be added.

Pork with Fennel & Juniper

The addition of juniper and fennel to the pork chops gives an unusual and delicate flavour to this dish.

NUTRITIONAL INFORMATION

Calories 277   Sugars 0.4g

Protein . . . . .32g   Fat 16g

Carbohydrate . . .0.4g   Saturates 5g

 2¼ HOURS   15 MINS

SERVES 4

INGREDIENTS

½ fennel bulb

1 tbsp juniper berries

about 2 tbsp olive oil

finely grated rind and juice of 1 orange

4 pork chops, each about 150 g/5½ oz

fresh bread and a crisp salad, to serve

1 Finely chop the fennel bulb, discarding the green parts.

2 Grind the juniper berries in a pestle and mortar. Mix the crushed juniper berries with the fennel flesh, olive oil and orange rind.

3 Using a sharp knife, score a few cuts all over each chop.

COOK'S TIP

Juniper berries are most commonly associated with gin, but they are often added to meat dishes in Italy for a delicate citrus flavour. They can be bought dried from most health food shops and some larger supermarkets.

4 Place the pork chops in a roasting tin (pan) or an ovenproof dish. Spoon the fennel and juniper mixture over the chops.

5 Pour the orange juice over the top of each chop, cover and marinate in the refrigerator for about 2 hours.

6 Cook the pork chops, under a preheated grill (broiler), for 10–15 minutes, depending on the thickness of the meat, or until the meat is tender and cooked through, turning occasionally.

7 Transfer the pork chops to serving plates and serve with a crisp, fresh salad and plenty of fresh bread to mop up the cooking juices.

Fruity Pork Skewers

Prunes and apricots bring colour and flavour to these tasty pork kebabs (kabobs). They are delicious eaten straight off the barbecue (grill).

NUTRITIONAL INFORMATION

Calories	205	Sugars	.........8g
Protein	........21g	Fat	..........10g
Carbohydrate	....8g	Saturates	......3g

1¼ HOURS   15 MINS

MAKES 4

I N G R E D I E N T S

4 boneless lean pork loin steaks

8 ready-to-eat prunes

8 ready-to-eat dried apricots

4 bay leaves

slices of orange and lemon, to garnish

M A R I N A D E

4 tbsp orange juice

2 tbsp olive oil

1 tsp ground bay leaves

salt and pepper

1 Trim the visible fat from the pork and then cut the meat into evenly-sized chunks.

2 Place the pork in a shallow, non-metallic dish and add the prunes and apricots.

3 To make the marinade, mix together the orange juice, oil and bay leaves in a bowl. Season with salt and pepper to taste.

4 Pour the marinade over the pork and fruit and toss until well coated. Leave to marinate in the refrigerator for at least 1 hour or preferably overnight.

5 Soak 4 wooden skewers in cold water to prevent them from catching alight on the barbecue (grill).

6 Remove the pork and fruit from the marinade, using a perforated spoon, reserving the marinade for basting. Thread the pork and fruit on to the skewers, alternating with the bay leaves.

7 Barbecue (grill) the skewers on an oiled rack over medium hot coals for 10–15 minutes, turning and frequently basting with the reserved marinade, or until the pork is cooked through.

8 Transfer the pork and fruit skewers to warm serving plates. Garnish with slices of orange and lemon and serve hot.

Red Roast Pork in Soy Sauce

In this traditional Chinese dish the pork turns 'red' during cooking because it is basted in dark soy sauce.

NUTRITIONAL INFORMATION

Calories 268   Sugars 20g
Protein . . . . .26g   Fat 8g
Carbohydrate . . .22g   Saturates 3g

 1¼ HOURS   1¼ HOURS

SERVES 4

I N G R E D I E N T S

450 g/1 lb lean pork fillets

6 tbsp dark soy sauce

2 tbsp dry sherry

1 tsp five-spice powder

2 garlic cloves, crushed

2.5 cm/1 inch piece root (fresh) ginger, finely chopped

1 large red (bell) pepper

1 large yellow (bell) pepper

1 large orange (bell) pepper

4 tbsp caster (superfine) sugar

2 tbsp red wine vinegar

TO GARNISH

spring onions (scallions), shredded

fresh chives, snipped

1 Trim away any excess fat and silver skin from the pork and place in a shallow dish.

2 Mix together the soy sauce, sherry, five-spice powder, garlic and ginger. Spoon over the pork, cover and marinate in the refrigerator for at least 1 hour or until required.

3 Preheat the oven to 190°C/375°F/Gas Mark 5. Drain the pork, reserving the marinade.

4 Place the pork on a roasting rack over a roasting pan. Cook in the oven, occasionally basting with the marinade, for 1 hour or until cooked through.

5 Meanwhile, halve and deseed the (bell) peppers. Cut each (bell) pepper half into 3 equal portions. Arrange them on a baking sheet (cookie sheet) and bake alongside the pork for the last 30 minutes of cooking time.

6 Place the caster (superfine) sugar and vinegar in a saucepan and heat gently until the sugar dissolves. Bring to the boil and simmer for 3–4 minutes, until syrupy.

7 When the pork is cooked, remove it from the oven and brush with the sugar syrup. Leave for about 5 minutes, then slice and arrange on a serving platter with the (bell) peppers, garnished with the spring onions (scallions) and chives.

8 Serve garnished with the spring onions (scallions) and freshly snipped chives.

Twice-cooked Pork

Twice-cooked is a popular way of cooking meat in China. The meat is first boiled to tenderize it, then cut into strips or slices and stir-fried.

NUTRITIONAL INFORMATION

Calories	199	Sugars	.........3g
Protein	........15g	Fat	..........13g
Carbohydrate	....4g	Saturates	.......3g

3¼ HOURS   30 MINS

SERVES 4

INGREDIENTS

250-300 g/9-10½ oz shoulder or leg of pork, in one piece

1 small green (bell) pepper, cored and seeded

1 small red (bell) pepper, cored and seeded

125 g/4½ oz canned sliced bamboo shoots, rinsed and drained

3 tbsp vegetable oil

1 spring onion (scallion), cut into short sections

1 tsp salt

½ tsp sugar

1 tbsp light soy sauce

1 tsp chilli bean sauce or freshly minced chilli

1 tsp rice wine or dry sherry

a few drops of sesame oil

1 Immerse the pork in a pot of boiling water to cover. Return to the boil and skim the surface. Reduce the heat, cover and simmer for 15-20 minutes. Turn off the heat and leave the pork in the water to cool for at least 2-3 hours.

2 Remove the pork and drain well. Trim off any excess fat, then cut into small, thin slices. Cut the (bell) peppers into pieces about the same size as the pork and the sliced bamboo shoots.

3 Heat the vegetable oil in a preheated wok and add the vegetables together with the spring onion (scallion). Stir-fry for about 1 minute.

4 Add the pork, followed by the salt, sugar, light soy sauce, chilli bean sauce and wine or sherry. Blend well and continue stirring for another minute. Transfer the stir-fry to a warm serving dish, sprinkle with sesame oil and serve.

COOK'S TIP

For ease of handling, buy a boned piece of meat, and roll into a compact shape. Tie securely with string before placing in the boiling water.

Spicy Pork Balls

These small meatballs are packed with flavour and cooked in a crunchy tomato sauce for a very quick dish.

NUTRITIONAL INFORMATION

Calories 299   Sugars 3g
Protein . . . . .28g   Fat 15g
Carbohydrate . . .14g   Saturates 4g

10 MINS   40 MINS

SERVES 4

I N G R E D I E N T S

450 g/1 lb minced (ground) pork

2 shallots, finely chopped

2 cloves garlic, crushed

1 tsp cumin seeds

½ tsp chilli powder

25 g/1 oz/½ cup wholemeal
    breadcrumbs

1 egg, beaten

2 tbsp sunflower oil

400 g/14 oz can chopped tomatoes,
    flavoured with chilli

2 tbsp soy sauce

200 g/7 oz can water chestnuts,
    drained

3 tbsp chopped fresh coriander (cilantro)

COOK'S TIP

Add a few teaspoons of chilli
sauce to a tin of chopped
tomatoes, if you can't find
the flavoured variety.

1 Place the minced (ground) pork in a large mixing bowl. Add the shallots, garlic, cumin seeds, chilli powder, breadcrumbs and beaten egg and mix together well.

2 Form the mixture into balls between the palms of your hands.

3 Heat the oil in a large preheated wok. Add the pork balls and stir-fry, in batches, over a high heat for about 5 minutes or until sealed on all sides.

4 Add the tomatoes, soy sauce and water chestnuts and bring to the boil. Return the pork balls to the wok, reduce the heat and leave to simmer for 15 minutes.

5 Scatter with chopped fresh coriander (cilantro) and serve hot.

Pork Ribs with Plum Sauce

Pork ribs are always very popular at barbecues (grills), and you can flavour them with a number of spicy bastes.

NUTRITIONAL INFORMATION

Calories . . . . . . .590 Sugars 1g
Protein . . . . .26g Fat 51g
Carbohydrate . . . .3g Saturates 17g

35 MINS   45 MINS

SERVES 4

I N G R E D I E N T S

900 g/2 lb pork spare ribs

2 tbsp sunflower oil

1 tsp sesame oil

2 cloves garlic, crushed

2.5 cm/1 inch piece root (fresh) ginger, grated

150 ml/¼ pint/⅔ cup plum sauce

2 tbsp dry sherry

2 tbsp hoisin sauce

2 tbsp soy sauce

4–6 spring onions (scallions), to garnish (optional)

1   To prepare the garnish, trim the spring onions (scallions) to about 7.5 cm/ 3 inches long. Slice both ends into thin strips, leaving the onion intact in the centre.

2   Put the spring onions (scallions) into a bowl of iced water for at least 30 minutes until the ends start to curl up. Leave them in the water and set aside until required.

3   If you buy the spare ribs in a single piece, cut them into individual ribs. Bring a large pan of water to the boil and add the ribs. Cook for 5 minutes, then drain thoroughly.

4   Heat the oils in a pan, add the garlic and ginger and cook gently for 1–2 minutes. Stir in the plum sauce, sherry, hoisin and soy sauce and heat through.

5   Brush the sauce over the pork ribs. Barbecue (grill) over hot coals for 5–10 minutes, then move to a cooler part of the barbecue (grill) for a further 15–20 minutes, basting with the remaining sauce. Garnish and serve hot.

COOK'S TIP

Par-cooking the ribs in boiling water removes excess fat, which helps prevent the ribs from spitting during cooking. Do not be put off by the large quantity – there is only a little meat on each, but they are quite cheap to buy.

Artichoke & Ham Salad

This elegant starter would make a good first course. Serve it with a little fresh bread for mopping up the juices.

NUTRITIONAL INFORMATION

Calories	124	Sugars	.........2g
Protein	.........2g	Fat	...........11g
Carbohydrate	....4g	Saturates	.......1g

25 MINS   0 MINS

SERVES 4

INGREDIENTS

275 g/9 ½ oz can artichoke hearts
    in oil, drained

4 small tomatoes

25 g/1 oz sun-dried tomatoes in oil

40 g/1 ½ oz Parma ham (prosciutto)

25 g/1 oz pitted black olives, halved

a few basil leaves

DRESSING

3 tbsp olive oil

1 tbsp white wine vinegar

1 clove garlic, crushed

½ tsp mild mustard

1 tsp clear honey

salt and pepper

COOK'S TIP

Use bottled artichokes in oil if you can find them as they have a better flavour. If only canned artichokes are available, rinse them carefully to remove the salty liquid.

1 Make sure the artichokes hearts are thoroughly drained, then cut them into quarters and place in a bowl.

2 Cut each fresh tomato into wedges. Slice the sun-dried tomatoes into thin strips. Cut the Parma ham (prosciutto) into thin strips and add to the bowl with the tomatoes and olive halves.

3 Keeping a few basil leaves whole for garnishing, tear the remainder of the leaves into small pieces and add to the bowl containing the other salad ingredients.

4 To make the dressing, put the oil, wine vinegar, garlic, mustard, honey and salt and pepper to taste in a screw-top jar and shake vigorously until the ingredients are well blended.

5 Pour the dressing over the salad and toss together.

6 Serve the salad garnished with a few whole basil leaves.

Fruity Stuffed Bacon Chops

This combination of green lentils, celery and apricots stuffed into bacon chops, served with a sweet sauce is a speedy dish for the microwave.

NUTRITIONAL INFORMATION

Calories 148	Sugars 5g
Protein 15g	Fat 6g
Carbohydrate 9g	Saturates 3g

20 MINS   30 MINS

SERVES 4

I N G R E D I E N T S

60 g/2 oz/¼ cup green lentils, washed

1 celery stick, sliced

2 spring onions (scallions), chopped

4 thick cut tendersweet lean bacon chops

1 tbsp chopped fresh sage

4 apricot halves canned in natural juice, drained and chopped

1 tsp cornflour (cornstarch)

4 tbsp natural juice from can of apricots

2 tbsp fresh orange juice

1 tsp grated orange rind

1 tbsp low-fat crème fraîche

salt and pepper

TO GARNISH

orange slices

sprigs of fresh sage

1 Place the lentils and celery in a bowl. Pour on boiling water to cover them. Cover and cook on HIGH power for 18–20 minutes until tender, adding extra water if necessary. Add the spring onions (scallions) for the last minute of cooking. Leave to stand, covered, for 10 minutes.

2 Using a sharp knife, slit the meaty end of each chop nearly through to the fat side, to form a pocket.

3 Drain the lentils and mix with half of the sage and the apricots. Season to taste.

4 Spoon the lentil stuffing into the pockets in the bacon chops. Arrange 2 on a plate. Cover with a paper towel. Cook on HIGH power for 4 minutes until cooked through. Transfer to warmed plates, cover and keep warm while cooking the remaining stuffed chops.

5 Mix the cornflour (cornstarch) with a little water in a bowl, then stir in the juice from the apricots, and the orange juice and rind. Cover and cook on HIGH power for 2 minutes, stirring every 30 seconds. Stir in the crème fraîche and remaining sage. Season and reheat on HIGH power for 30 seconds.

6 Serve the chops with the sauce. Garnish with orange slices and sage.

Sausage & Bean Casserole

In this traditional Tuscan dish, Italian sausages are cooked with cannellini beans and tomatoes.

NUTRITIONAL INFORMATION

Calories 609	Sugars 7g
Protein 27g	Fat 47g
Carbohydrate ...20g	Saturates 16g

15 MINS   35 MINS

SERVES 4

INGREDIENTS

8 Italian sausages

1 tbsp olive oil

1 large onion, chopped

2 garlic cloves, chopped

1 green (bell) pepper

225g/8 oz fresh tomatoes, skinned and chopped or 400 g/14 oz can tomatoes, chopped

2 tbsp sun-dried tomato paste

400 g/14 oz can cannellini beans

mashed potato or rice, to serve

1 Using a sharp knife, deseed the (bell) pepper and cut it into thin strips.

2 Prick the Italian sausages all over with a fork. Cook the sausages, under a preheated grill (broiler), for 10–12 minutes, turning occasionally, until brown all over. Set aside and keep warm.

3 Heat the oil in a large frying pan (skillet). Add the onion, garlic and (bell) pepper to the frying pan (skillet) and cook for 5 minutes, stirring occasionally, or until softened.

4 Add the tomatoes to the frying pan (skillet) and leave the mixture to simmer for about 5 minutes, stirring occasionally, or until slightly reduced and thickened.

5 Stir the sun-dried tomato paste, cannellini beans and Italian sausages into the mixture in the frying pan (skillet). Cook for 4–5 minutes or until the mixture is piping hot. Add 4–5 tablespoons of water, if the mixture becomes too dry during cooking.

6 Transfer the Italian sausage and bean casserole to serving plates and serve with mashed potato or cooked rice.

COOK'S TIP

Italian sausages are coarse in texture and have quite a strong flavour. They can be bought in specialist sausage shops, Italian delicatessens and some larger supermarkets. They are replaceable in this recipe only by game sausages.

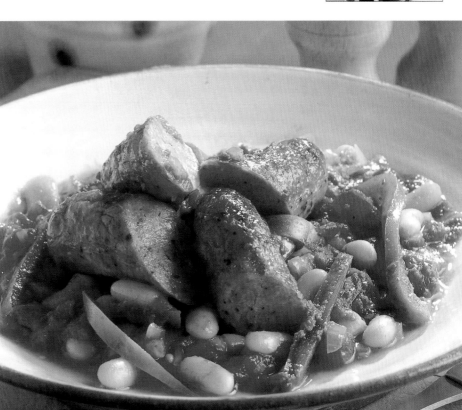

Escalopes & Italian Sausage

Anchovies are often used to enhance flavour, particularly in meat dishes. Either veal or turkey escalopes can be used for this pan-fried dish.

NUTRITIONAL INFORMATION

Calories 233	Sugars 1g	
Protein 28g	Fat 13g	
Carbohydrate 1g	Saturates 1g	

10 MINS　　20 MINS

SERVES 4

INGREDIENTS

1 tbsp olive oil

6 canned anchovy fillets, drained

1 tbsp capers, drained

1 tbsp fresh rosemary, stalks removed

finely grated rind and juice of 1 orange

75 g/2¾ oz Italian sausage, diced

3 tomatoes, skinned and chopped

4 turkey or veal escalopes, each about
　　125 g/4½ oz

salt and pepper

crusty bread or cooked polenta, to serve

1 Heat the oil in a large frying pan (skillet). Add the anchovies, capers, fresh rosemary, orange rind and juice, Italian sausage and tomatoes to the pan and cook for 5–6 minutes, stirring occasionally.

2 Meanwhile, place the turkey or veal escalopes between sheets of greasproof paper. Pound the meat with a meat mallet or the end of a rolling pin to flatten it.

3 Add the meat to the mixture in the frying pan (skillet). Season to taste with salt and pepper, cover and cook for 3–5 minutes on each side, slightly longer if the meat is thicker.

4 Transfer to serving plates and serve with fresh crusty bread or cooked polenta, if you prefer.

VARIATION

Try using 4-minute steaks, slightly flattened, instead of the turkey or veal. Cook them for 4–5 minutes on top of the sauce in the pan.

Saltimbocca

The Italian name for this dish, *saltimbocca*, means 'jump into the mouth'. The stuffed rolls are quick and easy to make and taste delicious.

NUTRITIONAL INFORMATION

Calories . . . . . . .303 Sugars 0.3g
Protein . . . . .29g Fat 17g
Carbohydrate . . . .1g Saturates 1g

15 MINS   20 MINS

SERVES 4

INGREDIENTS

4 turkey fillets or 4 veal escalopes, about
   450 g/1 lb in total

100 g/3½ oz Parma ham (prosciutto)

8 sage leaves

1 tbsp olive oil

1 onion, finely chopped

200 ml/7 fl oz/¾ cup white wine

200 ml/7 fl oz/¾ cup chicken stock

1 Place the turkey or veal between sheets of greaseproof paper. Pound the meat with a meat mallet or the end of a rolling pin to flatten it slightly. Cut each escalope in half.

2 Trim the Parma ham (prosciutto) to fit each piece of turkey or veal and place over the meat. Lay a sage leaf on top. Roll up the escalopes and secure with a cocktail stick (toothpick).

3 Heat the oil in a frying pan (skillet) and cook the onion for 3–4 minutes.

Add the turkey or veal rolls to the pan and cook for 5 minutes until browned all over.

4 Pour the white wine and chicken stock into the pan and leave to simmer for 15 minutes if using turkey, and 20 minutes if using veal, or until tender. Serve immediately.

VARIATION

Try a similar recipe called *bocconcini*, meaning 'little mouthfuls'. Follow the same method as given here, but replace the sage leaf with a piece of Gruyère cheese.

Veal in a Rose Petal Sauce

This truly spectacular dish is equally delicious whether you use veal or pork fillet. Make sure the roses are free of blemishes and pesticides.

NUTRITIONAL INFORMATION

Calories 810   Sugars 2g
Protein . . . . .31g   Fat 56g
Carbohydrate . . .49g   Saturates 28g

10 MINS   35 MINS

SERVES 4

INGREDIENTS

450 g/1 lb dried fettuccine

7 tbsp olive oil

1 tsp chopped fresh oregano

1 tsp chopped fresh marjoram

175 g/6 oz/¾ cup butter

450 g/1 lb veal fillet, thinly sliced

150 ml/¼ pint/⅔ cup rose petal vinegar
  (see Cook's Tip)

150 ml/¼ pint/⅔ cup fish stock

50 ml/2 fl oz/¼ cup grapefruit juice

50 ml/2 fl oz/¼ cup double
  (heavy) cream

salt

TO GARNISH

12 pink grapefruit segments

12 pink peppercorns

rose petals

fresh herb leaves

1 Bring a large saucepan of lightly salted water to the boil. Add the fettuccine and 1 tablespoon of the oil and cook for 8–10 minutes or until tender, but still firm to the bite. Drain and transfer to a warm serving dish, sprinkle over 2 tablespoons of the olive oil, the oregano and marjoram.

2 Heat 50 g/2 oz/4 tbsp of the butter with the remaining oil in a large frying pan (skillet). Add the veal and cook over a low heat for 6 minutes. Remove the veal from the pan and place on top of the pasta.

3 Add the vinegar and fish stock to the pan and bring to the boil. Boil vigorously until reduced by two thirds. Add the grapefruit juice and cream and simmer over a low heat for 4 minutes. Dice the remaining butter and add to the pan, one piece at a time, whisking constantly until it has been completely incorporated.

4 Pour the sauce around the veal, garnish with grapefruit segments, pink peppercorns, the rose petals (washed) and your favourite herb leaves.

COOK'S TIP

To make rose petal vinegar, infuse the petals of 8 pesticide-free roses in 150 ml/¼ pint/⅔ cup white wine vinegar for 48 hours. Prepare well in advance to reduce the preparation time.

Venison Meatballs

The sharp, citrusy flavour of kumqats is the perfect complement to these tasty steamed meatballs. Serve simply on a bed of pasta or noodles.

NUTRITIONAL INFORMATION

Calories 309	Sugars 5g	
Protein 40g	Fat 7g	
Carbohydrate ...15g	Saturates 0g	

 10 MINS   20 MINS

SERVES 4

INGREDIENTS

450 g/1 lb lean venison, minced (ground)

1 small leek, finely chopped

1 medium carrot, finely grated

½ tsp ground nutmeg

1 medium egg white, lightly beaten

salt and pepper

TO SERVE

freshly cooked pasta or noodles

freshly cooked vegetables

SAUCE

100 g/3½ oz kumquats

15 g/½ oz caster (superfine) sugar

150 ml/5 fl oz/⅔ cup water

4 tbsp dry sherry

1 tsp cornflour (cornstarch)

1 Place the venison in a mixing bowl together with the leek, carrot, seasoning and nutmeg. Add the egg white and bind the ingredients together with your hands until the mixture is well moulded and firm.

2 Divide the venison mixture into 16 equal portions. Wirh your hands and fingers, form each portion into a small round ball.

3 Bring a large saucepan of water to the boil. Arrange the meatballs on a layer of baking parchment in a steamer or large sieve (strainer) and place over the pan. Cover and steam for 10 minutes.

4 To make the sauce. Wash and thinly slice the kumquats. Place them in a saucepan with the sugar and water and bring to the boil. Simmer for 2–3 minutes.

5 Blend the sherry and cornflour (cornstarch) together and add to the pan. Heat through, stirring, until the sauce thickens. Season to taste with the salt and pepper.

6 Drain the meatballs and transfer to a serving plate. Spoon over the sauce and serve the meatballs with pasta or noodles and vegetables.

Char-Grilled Venison Steaks

Venison has a good strong flavour, which makes it an ideal meat to barbecue (grill). Marinate overnight to tenderize the meat.

NUTRITIONAL INFORMATION

Calories ....233 Sugars 2g
Protein ....35g Fat 6g
Carbohydrate ....3g Saturates 0g

12 HOURS   25 MINS

SERVES 4

I N G R E D I E N T S

4 venison steaks

150 ml/5 fl oz/⅔ cup red wine

2 tbsp sunflower oil

1 tbsp red wine vinegar

1 onion, chopped

few sprigs fresh parsley

2 sprigs fresh thyme

1 bay leaf

1 tsp caster (superfine) sugar

½ tsp mild mustard

salt and pepper

T O S E R V E

jacket potatoes

salad leaves and cherry tomatoes

1 Place the venison steaks in a shallow, non-metallic dish.

2 Combine the wine, oil, wine vinegar, onion, fresh parsley, thyme, bay leaf, sugar, mustard and salt and pepper to taste in a screw-top jar and shake vigorously until well combined. Alternatively, using a fork, whisk the ingredients together in a bowl.

3 Pour the marinade mixture over the venison, cover and leave to marinate in the refrigerator overnight. Turn the steaks over in the mixture occasionally so that the meat is well coated.

4 Barbecue (grill) the venison over hot coals, searing the meat over the hottest part of the barbecue (grill) for about 2 minutes on each side.

5 Move the meat to an area with slightly less intense heat and barbecue (grill) for a further 4–10 minutes on each side, depending on how well done you like your steaks.

6 Test if the meat is cooked by inserting the tip of a knife into the meat – the juices will run from red when the meat is still rare to clear as the meat becomes well cooked.

7 Serve with jacket potatoes, salad leaves and tomatoes.

Venison with Plums

The rich, slightly gamey flavour of venison is complemented by the sharpness of the plums. Add port and brandy for a delectable sauce.

NUTRITIONAL INFORMATION

Calories 311	Sugars 4g
Protein 35g	Fat 12g
Carbohydrate 8g	Saturates 1g

 5 MINS 10 MINS

SERVES 4

I N G R E D I E N T S

500 g/1 lb 2 oz venison fillet (tenderloin)

2 tbsp olive oil

4 plums, halved, pitted and sliced

1 tsp chopped fresh sage

6 spring onions (scallions), white
and green parts, cut into 2.5 cm/
1 inch lengths

1 tbsp cornflour (cornstarch)

2 tbsp orange juice

150 ml/¼ pint/⅔ cup stock

4 tbsp port

1 tbsp redcurrant jelly

1 tbsp brandy

salt and pepper

fresh purple sage sprigs, to garnish

creamed potatoes, to serve

1 Cut the venison into 1 cm/½ inch strips. Heat the oil in a heavy-based frying pan (skillet) and fry the venison over a high heat for about 2 minutes until browned. Remove from the pan with a perforated spoon.

2 Add the plums, sage and spring onions (scallions) to the pan and cook for 2 minutes, stirring occasionally.

3 Mix the cornflour (cornstarch) with the orange juice and add to the pan.

4 Add the stock, port and redcurrant jelly and heat, stirring, until thickened.

5 Return the venison to the pan, season to taste and pour in the brandy or port. Heat gently to warm through.

6 Garnish with purple sage and serve with creamed potatoes.

COOK'S TIP

If venison is eaten young it is very tender, and better cuts such as saddle or loin can be roasted, but do not overcook them – they should still be fairly pink inside.

Venison & Garlic Mash

Rich game is best served with a sweet fruit sauce. Here the venison steaks are cooked with sweet, juicy prunes and redcurrant jelly.

NUTRITIONAL INFORMATION

Calories 602	Sugars 18g	
Protein 51g	Fat 14g	
Carbohydrate . . .62g	Saturates 1g	

 10 MINS   35 MINS

SERVES 4

I N G R E D I E N T S

8 medallions of venison, 75 g/2¾ oz each

1 tbsp vegetable oil

1 red onion, chopped

150 ml/5 fl oz/⅔ cup Fresh Beef Stock (see page 9)

150 ml/5 fl oz/⅔ cup red wine

3 tbsp redcurrant jelly

100 g/3½ oz no-need-to-soak dried, pitted prunes

2 tsp cornflour (cornstarch)

2 tbsp brandy

salt and pepper

patty pans, to serve (optional)

G A R L I C   M A S H

900 g/2 lb potatoes, peeled and diced

½ tsp garlic purée (paste)

2 tbsp low-fat natural fromage frais (unsweetened yogurt)

4 tbsp fresh parsley, chopped

1 Trim off any excess fat from the meat and season with salt and pepper on both sides. Heat the oil in a frying pan (skillet) and fry the lamb with the onions for 2 minutes on each side until brown.

2 Lower the heat and pour in the stock and wine. Add the redcurrant jelly and prunes and stir until the jelly melts. Cover and simmer for 10 minutes.

3 Meanwhile, make the garlic mash. Place the potatoes in a saucepan and cover with water. Bring to the boil and cook for 8–10 minutes. Drain well and mash until smooth. Add the garlic purée (paste), fromage frais (yogurt) and parsley and blend thoroughly. Season, set aside and keep warm.

4 Remove the medallions from the frying pan (skillet) with a slotted spoon and keep warm.

5 Blend the cornflour (cornstarch) with the brandy in a small bowl and add to the pan juices. Heat, stirring, until thickened. Season with salt and pepper to taste. Serve the venison with the redcurrant and prune sauce, garlic mash and patty pans (if using).

Breast of Pheasant Lasagne

This scrumptious and unusual baked lasagne is virtually a meal in itself. It is served with baby onions and green peas.

NUTRITIONAL INFORMATION

Calories . . . . . . .1038 Sugars 13g
Protein . . . . .65g   Fat 64g
Carbohydrate . . .54g   Saturates 27g

40 MINS   1¼ HOURS

SERVES 4

I N G R E D I E N T S

butter, for greasing

14 sheets pre-cooked lasagne

850 ml/1½ pints/3¾ cups Béchamel Sauce
  (see page 6)

75 g/2¾ oz/¾ cup grated Mozzarella
  cheese

FILLING

225 g/8 oz pork fat, diced

60 g/2 oz/2 tbsp butter

16 small onions

8 large pheasant breasts, thinly sliced

25 g/1 oz/¼ cup plain (all-purpose) flour

600 ml/1 pint/2½ cups chicken stock

bouquet garni

450 g/1 lb fresh peas, shelled

salt and pepper

1 To make the filling, put the pork fat into a saucepan of boiling, salted water and simmer for 3 minutes, then drain and pat dry.

2 Melt the butter in a large frying pan (skillet). Add the pork fat and onions to the pan and cook for about 3 minutes, or until lightly browned.

3 Remove the pork fat and onions from the pan and set aside. Add the slices of pheasant and cook over a low heat for 12 minutes, until browned all over. Transfer to an ovenproof dish.

4 Stir the flour into the pan and cook until just brown, then blend in the stock. Pour the mixture over the pheasant, add the bouquet garni and cook in a preheated oven, at 200°C/400°F/Gas Mark 6, for 5 minutes. Remove the bouquet

garni. Add the onions, pork fat and peas and return to the oven for 10 minutes.

5 Put the pheasant and pork in a food processor and mince (grind) finely.

6 Lower the oven temperature to 190°C/375°F/Gas Mark 5. Grease an ovenproof dish with butter. Make layers of lasagne, pheasant sauce and Béchamel Sauce in the dish, ending with Béchamel Sauce. Sprinkle over the cheese and bake for 30 minutes.

Pesto Baked Partridge

Partridge has a more delicate flavour than many game birds and this subtle sauce perfectly complements it.

NUTRITIONAL INFORMATION

Calories	895	Sugars 5g
Protein	........79g	Fat 45g
Carbohydrate	...45g	Saturates 18g

 15 MINS   🕐 40 MINS

SERVES 4

I N G R E D I E N T S

8 partridge pieces (about 115 g/4 oz each)

60 g/2 oz/4 tbsp butter, melted

4 tbsp Dijon mustard

2 tbsp lime juice

1 tbsp brown sugar

6 tbsp pesto

450 g/1 lb dried rigatoni

1 tbsp olive oil

115 g/4 oz/1⅓ cups freshly grated
   Parmesan cheese

salt and pepper

1 Arrange the partridge pieces, smooth side down, in a single layer in a large, ovenproof dish.

2 Mix together the butter, Dijon mustard, lime juice and brown sugar in a bowl. Season to taste. Brush this mixture over the partridge pieces and bake in a preheated oven at 200°C/400°F/Gas Mark 6 for 15 minutes.

3 Remove the dish from the oven and coat the partridge pieces with 3 tbsp of the Pesto Sauce. Return to the oven and bake for a further 12 minutes.

4 Remove the dish from the oven and carefully turn over the partridge pieces. Coat the top of the partridges with the remaining mustard mixture and return to the oven for a further 10 minutes.

5 Meanwhile, bring a large pan of lightly salted water to the boil. Add the rigatoni and olive oil and cook for 8–10 minutes until tender, but still firm to the bite. Drain and transfer to a serving dish. Toss the pasta with the remaining Pesto Sauce and the Parmesan cheese.

6 Serve the partridge with the pasta, pouring over the cooking juices.

VARIATION

You could also prepare young pheasant in the same way.

Fish & Seafood

Naturally low in fat, yet rich in minerals and proteins, white fish and shellfish are important ingredients in a low-fat diet. The different varieties of fish vary enormously in texture and flavour and therefore lend themselves to assorted cooking methods. Grilling (broiling) and steaming, two of the most popular methods for cooking fish, are also low in fat, thereby providing a mouthwatering yet also healthy meal. Whenever you serve fish, remember that it must always be fresh – try to cook it within 24 hours, and always store it in the refrigerator. As well as fish, this chapter also includes an exciting selection of seafood dishes from around the world, including Provençale-style Mussels, Seared Scallops with Butter Sauce and Squid & Macaroni Stew. Whatever the occasion, you are sure to find a dish to tempt your guests.

Sea Bass with Olive Sauce

A favourite fish for chefs, the delicious sea bass is now becoming increasingly common in supermarkets and fish stores for family meals.

NUTRITIONAL INFORMATION

Calories	.877	Sugars	.3g
Protein	.50g	Fat	.47g
Carbohydrate	.67g	Saturates	.26g

 10 MINS · 30 MINS

SERVES 4

INGREDIENTS

450 g/1 lb dried macaroni

1 tbsp olive oil

8 x 115 g/4 oz sea bass medallions

SAUCE

25 g/1 oz/2 tbsp butter

4 shallots, chopped

2 tbsp capers

175 g/6 oz/1 ½ cups stoned (pitted) green
   olives, chopped

4 tbsp balsamic vinegar

300 ml/ ½ pint/1 ¼ cups fish stock

300 ml/ ½ pint/1 ¼ cups double
   (heavy) cream

juice of 1 lemon

salt and pepper

TO GARNISH

lemon slices

shredded leek

shredded carrot

1 To make the sauce, melt the butter in a frying pan (skillet). Add the shallots and cook over a low heat for 4 minutes. Add the capers and olives and cook for a further 3 minutes.

2 Stir in the balsamic vinegar and fish stock, bring to the boil and reduce by half. Add the cream, stirring, and reduce again by half. Season to taste with salt and pepper and stir in the lemon juice. Remove the pan from the heat, set aside and keep warm.

3 Bring a large pan of lightly salted water to the boil. Add the pasta and olive oil and cook for about 12 minutes, until tender but still firm to the bite.

4 Meanwhile, lightly grill (broil) the sea bass medallions for 3–4 minutes on each side, until cooked through, but still moist and delicate.

5 Drain the pasta thoroughly and transfer to large individual serving dishes. Top the pasta with the fish medallions and pour over the olive sauce. Garnish with lemon slices, shredded leek and shredded carrot and serve immediately.

Salmon Yakitori

The Japanese sauce used here combines well with salmon, although it is usually served with chicken.

NUTRITIONAL INFORMATION

Calories	247	Sugars	........10g
Protein	.........19g	Fat	...........11g
Carbohydrate	...12g	Saturates	......2g

 20 MINS 15 MINS

SERVES 4

I N G R E D I E N T S

350 g/12 oz chunky salmon fillet

8 baby leeks

Y A K I T O R I   S A U C E

5 tbsp light soy sauce

5 tbsp fish stock

2 tbsp caster (superfine) sugar

5 tbsp dry white wine

3 tbsp sweet sherry

1 clove garlic, crushed

1 Skin the salmon and cut the flesh into 5 cm/2 inch chunks. Trim the leeks and cut them into 5 cm/2 inch lengths.

2 Thread the salmon and leeks alternately on to 8 pre-soaked wooden skewers. Leave to chill in the refrigerator until required.

3 To make the sauce, place all of the ingredients in a small pan and heat gently, stirring, until the sugar has dissolved.

4 Bring to the boil, then reduce the heat and simmer for 2 minutes. Strain the sauce through a fine seive (strainer) and leave to cool until it is required.

5 Pour about one-third of the sauce into a small dish and set aside to serve with the kebabs.

6 Brush plenty of the remaining sauce over the skewers and cook directly on the rack.

7 If preferred, place a sheet of oiled kitchen foil on the rack and cook the salmon on that.

8 Barbecue (grill) the salmon and leek kebabs over hot coals for about 10 minutes or until cooked though, turning once.

9 Use a brush to baste frequently during cooking with the remaining sauce in order to prevent the fish and vegetables from drying out. Transfer the kebabs to a large serving platter and serve with a small bowl of the reserved sauce for dipping.

Stir-fried Salmon with Leeks

Salmon is marinated in a deliciously rich, sweet sauce, stir-fried and served on a bed of crispy leeks.

NUTRITIONAL INFORMATION

Calories . . . . . . .360 Sugars 9g
Protein . . . . .24g Fat 25
Carbohydrate . . . .11g Saturates 4g

35 MINS   15 MINS

SERVES 4

INGREDIENTS

450 g/1 lb salmon fillet, skinned

2 tbsp sweet soy sauce

2 tbsp tomato ketchup

1 tsp rice wine vinegar

1 tbsp demerara (brown crystal)
   sugar

1 clove garlic, crushed

4 tbsp corn oil

450 g/1 lb leeks, thinly shredded

finely chopped red chillies,
   to garnish

1 Using a sharp knife, cut the salmon into slices. Place the slices of salmon in a shallow non-metallic dish.

2 Mix together the soy sauce, tomato ketchup, rice wine vinegar, sugar and garlic.

3 Pour the mixture over the salmon, toss well and leave to marinate for about 30 minutes.

4 Meanwhile, heat 3 tablespoons of the corn oil in a large preheated wok.

5 Add the leeks to the wok and stir-fry over a medium-high heat for about 10 minutes, or until the leeks become crispy and tender.

6 Using a slotted spoon, carefully remove the leeks from the wok and transfer to warmed serving plates.

7 Add the remaining oil to the wok. Add the salmon and the marinade to the wok and cook for 2 minutes.

8 Remove the salmon from the wok and spoon over the leeks, garnish with finely chopped red chillies and serve immediately.

VARIATION

You can use a fillet of beef instead of the salmon, if you prefer.

Grilled (Broiled) Stuffed Sole

A delicious stuffing of sun-dried tomatoes and fresh lemon thyme are used to stuff whole sole.

NUTRITIONAL INFORMATION

Calories	207	Sugars	.......0.2g
Protein	........24g	Fat	..........10g
Carbohydrate	....8g	Saturates	.......4g

 25 MINS   20 MINS

SERVES 4

INGREDIENTS

1 tbsp olive oil

25 g/1 oz/2 tbsp butter

1 small onion, finely chopped

1 garlic clove, chopped

3 sun-dried tomatoes, chopped

2 tbsp lemon thyme

50 g/1¾ oz breadcrumbs

1 tbsp lemon juice

4 small whole sole, gutted and cleaned

salt and pepper

lemon wedges, to garnish

fresh green salad leaves, to serve

1 Heat the oil and butter in a frying pan (skillet) until it just begins to froth.

2 Add the onion and garlic to the frying pan (skillet) and cook, stirring, for 5 minutes until just softened.

3 To make the stuffing, mix the tomatoes, thyme, breadcrumbs and lemon juice in a bowl, and season.

4 Add the stuffing mixture to the pan, and stir to mix.

5 Using a sharp knife, pare the skin from the bone inside the gut hole of the fish to make a pocket. Spoon the tomato and herb stuffing into the pocket.

6 Cook the fish, under a preheated grill (broiler), for 6 minutes on each side or until golden brown.

7 Transfer the stuffed fish to serving plates and garnish with lemon wedges. Serve immediately with fresh green salad leaves.

COOK'S TIP

Lemon thyme (*Thymus* x *citriodorus*) has a delicate lemon scent and flavour. Ordinary thyme can be used instead, but mix it with 1 teaspoon of lemon rind to add extra flavour.

Pineapple & Fish Curry

This is a fiery hot Thai curry dish all the better for serving with refreshing (and cooling) fresh pineapple pieces.

NUTRITIONAL INFORMATION

Calories . . . . . . .249 Sugars 4g
Protein . . . . .29g Fat 9g
Carbohydrate . . .15g Saturates 1g

  15 MINS   15 MINS

SERVES 4

I N G R E D I E N T S

2 pineapples

7 cm/3 inch piece galangal, sliced

2 blades of lemon grass, bruised then chopped

5 sprigs fresh basil

450 g/1 lb firm white fish fillets (monkfish, halibut or cod, for example), cubed

125 g/4½ oz peeled prawns (shrimp)

2 tbsp vegetable oil

2 tbsp Red Curry Paste (see page 30)

125 ml/4 fl oz/½ cup thick coconut milk or cream

2 tbsp fish sauce

2 tsp palm or demarara sugar

2-3 red chillies, seeded and cut into thin julienne strips

about 6 kaffir lime leaves, torn into pieces

coriander sprigs, to garnish

COOK'S TIP

Monkfish, like sole, goes well with a many different types of sauces – cream, tomato or hollandaise – and is delicious served cold with fresh mayonnaise.

1 Cut the pineapples in half lengthways. Remove the flesh, reserving the shells if using (see right). Remove the core from the pineapple flesh then dice into bite-sized pieces.

2 Place the galangal in a large shallow pan with the lemon grass and basil. Add the fish cubes and just enough water to cover. Bring to the boil, reduce the heat and simmer for about 2 minutes.

3 Add the prawns (shrimp) and cook for a further 1 minute or until the fish is just cooked. Remove from the flavoured stock with a slotted spoon and keep warm.

4 Heat the oil in a heavy-based pan or wok. Add the curry paste and cook for 1 minute. Stir in the coconut milk or cream, fish sauce, brown sugar, chillies and lime leaves.

5 Add the pineapple and cook until just heated through. Add the cooked fish and mix gently to combine.

6 Spoon into the reserved pineapple shells, if liked, and serve immediately, garnished with sprigs of coriander.

Trout in Red Wine

This recipe from Trentino is best when the fish are freshly caught,
but it is a good way to cook any trout, giving it an interesting flavour.

NUTRITIONAL INFORMATION

Calories 489	Sugars 0.6g
Protein 48g	Fat 27g
Carbohydrate . . .0.6g	Saturates 14g

🐟 20 MINS   🕐 45 MINS

SERVES 4

INGREDIENTS

4 fresh trout, about 300 g/10 oz each

250 ml/9 fl oz/1 cup red or
   white wine vinegar

300 ml/½ pint/1¼ cups red or
   dry white wine

150 ml/¼ pint/⅔ cup water

1 carrot, sliced

2–4 bay leaves

thinly pared rind of 1 lemon

1 small onion, sliced very thinly

4 sprigs fresh parsley

4 sprigs fresh thyme

1 tsp black peppercorns

6–8 whole cloves

90 g/3 oz/6 tbsp butter

1 tbsp chopped fresh mixed herbs

salt and pepper

TO GARNISH

sprigs of herbs

lemon slices

1 Gut the trout but leave their heads on. Dry on paper towels and lay the fish head to tail in a shallow container or baking tin (pan) large enough to hold them.

2 Bring the wine vinegar to the boil and pour slowly all over the fish. Leave the fish to marinate in the refrigerator for about 20 minutes.

3 Meanwhile, put the wine, water, carrot, bay leaves, lemon rind, onion, herbs, peppercorns and cloves into a pan with a good pinch of sea salt and heat gently.

4 Drain the fish thoroughly, discarding the vinegar. Place the fish in a fish kettle or large frying pan (skillet) so they touch. When the wine mixture boils, strain gently over the fish so they are about half covered. Cover the pan and simmer very gently for 15 minutes.

5 Carefully remove the fish from the pan, draining off as much of the liquid as possible, and arrange on a serving dish. Keep warm.

6 Boil the cooking liquid until reduced to about 4–6 tablespoons. Melt the butter in a pan and strain in the cooking liquor. Season and spoon the sauce over the fish. Garnish and serve.

Indonesian-Style Spicy Cod

A delicious aromatic coating makes this dish rather special. Serve it with a crisp salad and crusty bread.

NUTRITIONAL INFORMATION

Calories ....146 Sugars 2g
Protein ....19g Fat 7g
Carbohydrate ....2g Saturates 4g

 10 MINS 15 MINS

SERVES 4

I N G R E D I E N T S

4 cod steaks

1 stalk lemon grass

1 small red onion, chopped

3 cloves garlic, chopped

2 fresh red chillies, deseeded and chopped

1 tsp grated root (fresh) ginger

¼ tsp turmeric

2 tbsp butter, cut into small cubes

8 tbsp canned coconut milk

2 tbsp lemon juice

salt and pepper

red chillies, to garnish (optional)

1 Rinse the cod steaks and pat them dry on absorbent kitchen paper (paper towels).

2 Remove and discard the outer leaves from the lemon grass and thinly slice the inner section.

3 Place the lemon grass, onion, garlic, chillies, ginger and turmeric in a food processor and blend until the ingredients are finely chopped. Season with salt and pepper to taste.

4 With the processor running, add the butter, coconut milk and lemon juice and process until well blended.

5 Place the fish in a shallow, non-metallic dish. Pour over the coconut mixture and turn the fish until well coated.

6 If you have one, place the fish steaks in a hinged basket, which will make them easier to turn. Barbecue (grill) over hot coals for 15 minutes or until the fish is cooked through, turning once. Serve garnished with red chillies (if using).

COOK'S TIP

If you prefer a milder flavour, omit the chillies altogether. For a hotter flavour do not remove the seeds from the chillies.

Celery & Salt Cod Casserole

Salt cod is dried and salted in order to preserve it. It has an unusual flavour, which goes particularly well with celery in this dish.

NUTRITIONAL INFORMATION

Calories	....	173
Sugars	....	3g
Protein	....	14g
Fat	....	12g
Carbohydrate	....3g	Saturates	.......1g

 25 MINS   25 MINS

SERVES 4

I N G R E D I E N T S

250 g/9 oz salt cod, soaked overnight

1 tbsp oil

4 shallots, finely chopped

2 garlic cloves, chopped

3 celery sticks, chopped

1 x 400g/14 oz can tomatoes, chopped

150 ml/¼ pint/⅔ cup fish stock

50 g/1¾ oz pine nuts

2 tbsp roughly chopped tarragon

2 tbsp capers

crusty bread or mashed potato, to serve

1 Drain the salt cod, rinse it under plenty of running water and drain again thoroughly. Remove and discard any skin and bones. Pat the fish dry with paper towels and cut it into chunks.

2 Heat the oil in a large frying pan (skillet). Add the shallots and garlic and cook for 2–3 minutes. Add the celery and cook for a further 2 minutes, then add the tomatoes and stock.

3 Bring the mixture to the boil, reduce the heat and leave to simmer for about 5 minutes.

4 Add the fish and cook for 10 minutes or until tender.

5 Meanwhile, place the pine nuts on a baking tray (cookie sheet). Place under a preheated grill (broiler) and toast for 2–3 minutes or until golden.

6 Stir the tarragon, capers and pine nuts into the fish casserole and heat gently to warm through.

7 Transfer to serving plates and serve with lots of fresh crusty bread or mashed potato.

COOK'S TIP

Salt cod is a useful ingredient to keep in the storecupboard and, once soaked, can be used in the same way as any other fish. It does, however, have a stronger, salty flavour than normal. It can be found in fishmongers, larger supermarkets and delicatessens.

Sesame Salmon with Cream

Salmon fillet holds its shape when tossed in sesame seeds and stir-fried. It is served in a creamy sauce of diced courgettes (zucchini).

NUTRITIONAL INFORMATION

Calories 550   Sugars 1g
Protein . . . . .35g   Fat 45g
Carbohydrate . . . .2g   Saturates 12g

 5 MINS   10 MINS

SERVES 4

INGREDIENTS

625-750 g/1 lb 6 oz– 1 lb 10 oz salmon or pink trout fillets

2 tbsp light soy sauce

3 tbsp sesame seeds

3 tbsp sunflower oil

4 spring onions (scallions), thinly sliced diagonally

2 large courgettes (zucchini), diced, or 2.5-cm/5-inch piece cucumber, diced

grated rind of ½ lemon

1 tbsp lemon juice

½ tsp turmeric

6 tbsp fish stock or water

3 tbsp double (heavy) cream or fromage frais

salt and pepper

curly endive, to garnish

1 Skin the fish and cut into strips about 4 x 2 cm/1½ x ¾ inch. Pat dry on kitchen paper (paper towels). Season lightly, then brush with soy sauce and sprinkle all over with sesame seeds.

2 Heat 2 tablespoons of oil in the wok. Add the pieces of fish and stir-fry for 3-4 minutes until lightly browned all over. Remove with a fish slice, drain on kitchen paper (paper towels) and keep warm.

3 Heat the remaining oil to the wok and add the spring onions (scallions) and courgettes (zucchini) or cucumber and stir-fry for 1-2 minutes. Add the lemon rind and juice, turmeric, stock and seasoning and bring to the boil for 1 minute. Stir in the cream or fromage frais.

4 Return the fish pieces to the wok and toss gently in the sauce until they are really hot. Garnish and serve.

COOK'S TIP

Lay the fillet skin-side down. Insert a sharp, flexible knife at one end between the flesh and the skin. Hold the skin tightly at the end and push the knife along, keeping the knife blade as flat as possible against the skin.

Fish with Ginger Butter

Whole mackerel or trout are stuffed with herbs, wrapped in foil, baked and then drizzled with a fresh ginger butter.

NUTRITIONAL INFORMATION

Calories ....328 Sugar 0g
Protein ....24g Fat 25g
Carbohydrate ....1g Saturates 13g

10 MINS   30 MINS

SERVES 4

INGREDIENTS

4 x 250 g/9 oz whole trout or mackerel, gutted

4 tbsp chopped fresh coriander (cilantro)

5 garlic cloves, crushed

2 tsp grated lemon or lime zest

2 tsp vegetable oil

banana leaves, for wrapping (optional)

90 g/3 oz/6 tbsp butter

1 tbsp grated ginger root

1 tbsp light soy sauce

salt and pepper

coriander (cilantro) sprigs and lemon or lime wedges, to garnish

1 Wash and dry the fish. Mix the coriander (cilantro) with the garlic, lemon or lime zest and salt and pepper to taste. Spoon into the fish cavities.

2 Brush the fish with a little oil, season well and place each fish on a double thickness sheet of baking parchment or foil and wrap up well to enclose. Alternatively, wrap in banana leaves (see right).

3 Place on a baking tray (cookie sheet) and bake in a preheated oven for about 25 minutes or until the flesh will flake easily.

4 Meanwhile, melt the butter in a small pan. Add the ginger and mix well.

5 Stir the light soy sauce into the saucepan.

6 To serve, unwrap the fish parcels, drizzle over the ginger butter and garnish with coriander (cilantro) and lemon or lime wedges.

COOK'S TIP

For a really authentic touch, wrap the fish in banana leaves, which can be ordered from specialist oriental supermarkets. They are not edible, but impart a delicate flavour to the fish.

Poached Salmon

Salmon steaks, poached in a well-flavoured stock and served with a piquant sauce, make a delicious summer lunch or supper dish.

NUTRITIONAL INFORMATION

Calories . . . . .712 Sugars 5g
Protein . . . . .66g Fat 47g
Carbohydrate . . . .6g Saturates 9g

10 MINS   30 MINS

SERVES 4

I N G R E D I E N T S

1 small onion, sliced

1 small carrot, sliced

1 stick celery, sliced

1 bay leaf

pared rind and juice of ½ orange

a few stalks of parsley

salt

5-6 black peppercorns

700 ml/1¼ pints/3 cups water

4 salmon steaks, about 350 g/12 oz each

salad leaves, to serve

lemon twists, to garnish

S A U C E

1 large avocado, peeled, halved and stoned

125 ml/4 fl oz/½ cup low-fat natural yogurt

grated zest and juice of ½ orange

black pepper

a few drops of hot red pepper sauce

1 Put the onion, carrot, celery, bay leaf, orange rind, orange juice, parsley stalks, salt and peppercorns in a pan just large enough to take the salmon steaks in a single layer. Pour on the water, cover the pan and bring to the boil. Simmer the stock for 20 minutes.

2 Arrange the salmon steaks in the pan, return the stock to the boil and simmer for 3 minutes. Cover the pan, remove from the heat and leave the salmon to cool in the stock.

3 Roughly chop the avocado and place it in a blender or food processor with the yogurt, orange zest and orange juice. Process until smooth, then season to taste with salt, pepper and hot pepper sauce.

4 Remove the salmon steaks from the stock (reserve it to make fish soup or a sauce), skin them and pat dry with kitchen paper (paper towels).

5 Cover the serving dish with salad leaves, arrange the salmon steaks on top and spoon a little of the sauce into the centre of each one. Garnish the fish with lemon twists, and serve the remaining sauce separately.

Steamed Stuffed Snapper

Red mullet may be used instead of the snapper, although they are a little more difficult to stuff because of their size. Use one mullet per person.

NUTRITIONAL INFORMATION

Calories 406	Sugar 4g	
Protein 68g	Fat 9g	
Carbohydrate 9g	Saturates 0g	

20 MINS   10 MINS

SERVES 4

I N G R E D I E N T S

1.4 kg/3 lb whole snapper, cleaned and scaled

175 g/6 oz spinach

orange slices and shredded spring onion (scallion), to garnish

S T U F F I N G

60 g/2 oz/2 cups cooked long-grain rice

1 tsp grated fresh root ginger

2 spring onions (scallions), finely chopped

2 tsp light soy sauce

1 tsp sesame oil

½ tsp ground star anise

1 orange, segmented and chopped

1 Rinse the fish inside and out under cold running water and pat dry with kitchen paper (paper towels).

2 Blanch the spinach for 40 seconds, rinse in cold water and drain well, pressing out as much moisture as possible.

3 Arrange the spinach on a heatproof plate and place the fish on top.

4 To make the stuffing, mix together the cooked rice, grated ginger, spring onions (scallions), soy sauce, sesame oil, star anise and orange in a bowl.

5 Spoon the stuffing into the body cavity of the fish, pressing it in well with a spoon.

6 Cover the plate and cook in a steamer for 10 minutes, or until the fish is cooked through.

7 Transfer the fish to a warmed serving dish, garnish with orange slices and shredded spring onion (scallion) and serve.

COOK'S TIP

The name snapper covers a family of tropical and subtropical fish that vary in colour. They may be red, orange, pink, grey or blue-green. Some are striped or spotted and they range in size from about 15 cm/ 6 inches to 90 cm/3 ft.

Sole Fillets in Marsala

A rich wine and cream sauce makes this an excellent dinner party dish.
Make the stock the day before to cut down on the preparation time.

NUTRITIONAL INFORMATION

Calories	474	Sugars	. . . . .3g
Protein	. . . . .47g	Fat	. . . . .28g
Carbohydrate	. . . .3g	Saturates	. . . . . .14g

 1¼ HOURS   1½ HOURS

SERVES 4

INGREDIENTS

1 tbsp peppercorns, lightly crushed

8 sole fillets

100 ml/3½ fl oz/⅓ cup Marsala

150 ml/¼ pint/⅔ cup double (heavy) cream

STOCK

600 ml/1 pint/2½ cups water

bones and skin from the sole fillets

1 onion, peeled and halved

1 carrot, peeled and halved

3 fresh bay leaves

SAUCE

1 tbsp olive oil

15 g/½ oz/1 tbsp butter

4 shallots, finely chopped

100 g/ 3½ oz baby button mushrooms,
    wiped and halved

1 To make the stock, place the water, fish bones and skin, onion, carrot and bay leaves in a large saucepan and bring to the boil.

2 Reduce the heat and leave the mixture to simmer for 1 hour or until the stock has reduced to about 150 ml/¼ pint/⅔ cup. Drain the stock through a fine sieve, discarding the bones and vegetables, and set aside.

3 To make the sauce, heat the oil and butter in a frying pan (skillet). Add the shallots and cook, stirring, for 2–3 minutes or until just softened.

4 Add the mushrooms to the frying pan (skillet) and cook, stirring, for a further 2–3 minutes or until they are just beginning to brown.

5 Add the peppercorns and sole fillets to the frying pan (skillet) in batches. Fry the sole fillets for 3–4 minutes on each side or until golden brown. Remove the

fish with a perforated spoon, set aside and keep warm while you cook the remainder.

6 Pour the wine and stock over the last fillet and leave to simmer for 3 minutes. Remove the fish with a fish slice or a perforated spoon, set aside and keep warm. Increase the heat and boil the mixture in the pan for about 5 minutes or until the sauce has reduced and thickened.

7 Pour in the cream and heat through. Pour the sauce over the fish and serve with the cooked vegetables of your choice.

Tuna & Vegetable Stir-Fry

Fresh tuna is a dark, meaty fish and is now widely available at fresh fish counters. It lends itself perfectly to the rich flavours in this recipe.

NUTRITIONAL INFORMATION

Calories 245   Sugars 11g
Protein ....30g   Fat 7g
Carbohydrate ...14g   Saturates 1g

10 MINS   10 MINS

SERVES 4

INGREDIENTS

225 g/8 oz carrots

1 onion

175 g/6 oz/1¾ cups baby corn cobs

2 tbsp corn oil

175 g/6 oz/2½ cups mangetout (snow peas)

450 g/1 lb fresh tuna

2 tbsp fish sauce

15 g/½ oz/1 tbsp palm sugar

finely grated zest and juice of 1 orange

2 tbsp sherry

1 tsp cornflour (cornstarch)

rice or noodles, to serve

1 Using a sharp knife, cut the carrots into thin sticks, slice the onion and halve the baby corn cobs.

2 Heat the corn oil in a large preheated wok or frying pan (skillet).

3 Add the onion, carrots, mangetout (snow peas) and baby corn cobs to the wok or frying pan (skillet) and stir-fry for 5 minutes.

4 Using a sharp knife, thinly slice the fresh tuna.

5 Add the tuna slices to the wok or frying pan (skillet) and stir-fry for about 2–3 minutes, or until the tuna turns opaque.

6 Mix together the fish sauce, palm sugar, orange zest and juice, sherry and cornflour (cornstarch).

7 Pour the mixture over the tuna and vegetables and cook for 2 minutes, or until the juices thicken. Serve the stir-fry with rice or noodles.

VARIATION

Try using swordfish steaks instead of the tuna. Swordfish steaks are now widely available and are similar in texture to tuna

Stir-Fried Cod with Mango

Fish and fruit are a classic combination, and in this recipe a tropical flavour is added which gives a great scented taste to the dish.

NUTRITIONAL INFORMATION

Calories 200	Sugars 12g
Protein 21g	Fat 7g
Carbohydrate ...14g	Saturates 1g

  10 MINS   15 MINS

SERVES 4

INGREDIENTS

175 g/6 oz carrots

2 tbsp vegetable oil

1 red onion, sliced

1 red (bell) pepper, deseeded and sliced

1 green (bell) pepper, deseeded and sliced

450 g/1 lb skinless cod fillet

1 ripe mango

1 tsp cornflour (cornstarch)

1 tbsp soy sauce

100 ml/3½ fl oz/1⅓ cups tropical fruit juice

1 tbsp lime juice

1 tbsp chopped fresh coriander (cilantro), to garnish

VARIATION

You can use paw-paw (papaya) as an alternative to the mango, if you prefer.

1 Using a sharp knife, slice the carrots into thin sticks.

2 Heat the oil in a preheated wok and stir-fry the onion, carrots and (bell) peppers for 5 minutes.

3 Using a sharp knife, cut the cod into small cubes. Peel the mango, then carefully remove the flesh from the centre stone. Cut the flesh into thin slices.

4 Add the cod and mango to the wok and stir-fry for a further 4–5 minutes, or until the fish is cooked through. Be careful not to break the fish up.

5 Mix together the cornflour (cornstarch), soy sauce, fruit juice and lime juice. Pour the mixture into the wok and stir until the mixture bubbles and the juices thicken. Scatter with coriander (cilantro) and serve immediately.

Crab-Stuffed Red Snapper

This popular fish is pinkish-red in colour and has moist, tender flesh. For this recipe it is steamed, but it can also be baked or braised.

NUTRITIONAL INFORMATION

Calories 205	Sugars 0.1g
Protein 36g	Fat 6g
Carbohydrate . . .0.1g	Saturates 1g

10 MINS   25 MINS

SERVES 4

INGREDIENTS

4 red snappers, cleaned and scaled, about 175 g/6 oz each

2 tbsp dry sherry

salt and pepper

wedges of lime, to garnish

red chilli strips, to garnish

stir-fried shredded vegetables, to serve

STUFFING

1 small red chilli

1 garlic clove

1 spring onion (scallion)

½ tsp finely grated lime rind

1 tbsp lime juice

100 g/3½ oz white crab meat, flaked

1 Rinse the fish and pat dry on kitchen paper (paper towels). Season inside and out and place in a shallow dish. Spoon over the sherry and set aside.

2 Meanwhile, make the stuffing. Carefully halve, deseed and finely chop the chilli. Place in a small bowl.

3 Peel and finely chop the garlic. Trim and finely chop the spring onion (scallion). Add to the chilli together with the grated lime rind, lime juice and the flaked crab meat.

4 Season with salt and pepper to taste and combine.

5 Spoon some of the stuffing into the cavity of each fish.

6 Bring a large saucepan of water to the boil. Arrange the fish in a steamer lined with baking parchment or in a large sieve (strainer) and place over the boiling water.

7 Cover and steam for 10 minutes. Turn the fish over and steam for a further 10 minutes or until the fish is completely cooked through.

8 Drain the fish and transfer to warm serving plates.

9 Garnish with wedges of lime and strips of chill, and serve the fish on a bed of stir-fried vegetables.

Mullet with Ginger

Ginger is used widely in Chinese cooking for its strong, pungent flavour. Although fresh ginger is best, ground ginger may be used instead.

NUTRITIONAL INFORMATION

Calories 195	Sugars 6g
Protein 31g	Fat 3g
Carbohydrate 9g	Saturates 0g

10 MINS   15 MINS

SERVES 4

INGREDIENTS

1 whole mullet, cleaned and scaled

2 spring onions (scallions), chopped

1 tsp grated fresh root ginger

125 ml/4 fl oz/½ cup garlic wine vinegar

125 ml/4 fl oz/½ cup light soy sauce

3 tsp caster (superfine) sugar

dash of chilli sauce

125 ml/4 fl oz/½ cup fish stock

1 green (bell) pepper, seeded and thinly sliced

1 large tomato, skinned, seeded and cut into thin strips

salt and pepper

sliced tomato, to garnish

1 Rinse the fish inside and out and pat dry with kitchen paper (paper towels).

2 Make 3 diagonal slits in the flesh on each side of the fish. Season the fish with salt and pepper inside and out, according to taste.

3 Place the fish on a heatproof plate and scatter the chopped spring onions (scallions) and grated ginger over the top. Cover and steam for 10 minutes, or until the fish is cooked through.

4 Meanwhile, place the garlic wine vinegar, light soy sauce, caster (superfine) sugar, chilli sauce, fish stock, (bell) pepper and tomato in a saucepan and bring to the boil, stirring occasionally.

5 Cook the sauce over a high heat until the sauce has slightly reduced and thickened.

6 Remove the fish from the steamer and transfer to a warm serving dish. Pour the sauce over the fish, garnish with tomato slices and serve immediately.

VARIATION

Use fillets of fish for this recipe if preferred, and reduce the cooking time to 5–7 minutes.

Baked Sea Bass

Sea bass is a delicious white-fleshed fish. If cooking two small fish, they can be grilled (broiled); if cooking one large fish, bake it in the oven.

NUTRITIONAL INFORMATION

Calories 378	Sugars 0g	
Protein 62g	Fat 14g	
Carbohydrate 0g	Saturates 2g	

 15-20 MINS   20-55 MINS

SERVES 4

I N G R E D I E N T S

1.4 kg/3 lb fresh sea bass or

   2 x 750 g/1 lb 10 oz sea bass, gutted

2–4 sprigs fresh rosemary

½ lemon, sliced thinly

2 tbsp olive oil

bay leaves and lemon wedges, to garnish

G A R L I C   S A U C E

2 tsp coarse sea salt

2 tsp capers

2 garlic cloves, crushed

4 tbsp water

2 fresh bay leaves

1 tsp lemon juice or wine vinegar

2 tbsp olive oil

pepper

1 Scrape off the scales from the fish and cut off the sharp fins. Make diagonal cuts along both sides. Wash and dry thoroughly. Place a sprig of rosemary in the cavity of each of the smaller fish with half the lemon slices; or two sprigs and all the lemon in the large fish.

2 To grill (broil), place in a foil-lined pan, brush with 1–2 tablespoons oil and grill (broil) under a moderate heat for 5 minutes each side, until cooked through.

3 To bake: place the fish in a foil-lined dish or roasting tin (pan) brushed with oil, and brush the fish with the rest of the oil. Cook in a preheated oven, 190°C/375°F/Gas Mark 5, for 30 minutes for the small fish or 45–50 minutes for the large fish, until the thickest part of the fish is opaque.

4 For the sauce: crush the salt and capers with the garlic in a pestle and mortar and then work in the water. Or, work in a food processor or blender until smooth.

5 Bruise the bay leaves and remaining sprigs of rosemary and put in a bowl. Add the garlic mixture, lemon juice or vinegar and oil and pound together until the flavours are released. Season with pepper to taste.

6 Place the fish on a serving dish and, if liked, remove the skin. Spoon some of the sauce over the fish and serve the rest separately. Garnish with fresh bay leaves and lemon wedges.

Oriental Monkfish Tail

Use a two-layered steamer for this recipe and cook the fish in one layer and the vegetables in the other.

NUTRITIONAL INFORMATION

Calories ....255 Sugars 9g
Protein ....44g Fat 4g
Carbohydrate ....11g Saturates 1g

1 HOUR   30 MINS

SERVES 6

INGREDIENTS

750 g/1 lb 10 oz monkfish tail

175 g/6 oz peeled prawns (shrimp), defrosted if frozen

4 spring onions (scallions), chopped

1 fresh red chilli, seeded and finely chopped

2 tbsp oyster sauce

175 g/6 oz/6 slices lean rindless back bacon

SWEET & SOUR VEGETABLES

225 g/8 oz/2 courgettes (zucchini), trimmed

225 g/8 oz/2–3 carrots, peeled

1 red (bell) pepper, deseeded

125 g/4½ oz/1⅓ cups mangetout (snow peas), prepared

½ tsp grated lemon rind

SAUCE

300 ml/½ pint/1¼ cups Fresh Fish Stock (see page 8)

4 tbsp white wine vinegar

1 tbsp caster (superfine) sugar

2 tbsp tomato purée (paste)

2 tbsp light soy sauce

2 tsp cornflour (cornstarch) mixed with 4 tsp cold water

1 Strip away the skin and membrane from the monkfish. Slice in half by cutting along the sides of the central bone.

2 Lay the fish between 2 layers of baking parchment and flatten to 1 cm/½ inch thick with a rolling pin. Mix the remaining ingredients, except the bacon, to form a stuffing.

3 Press stuffing on to one half of the fish and top with the other piece. Lay 5 slices of bacon on baking parchment and place the fish on top. Fold the bacon over the fish and cover with the remaining bacon slice. Secure with string. Place the fish into one compartment of a large steamer. Bring a wok of water to the boil and put the steamer on top. Cover and steam for 20 minutes.

4 Meanwhile slice the vegetables except the mangetout. Place in the second steaming compartment with the mangetout and lemon rind. Turn the fish over and place the vegetable compartment on top. Steam for 10 minutes until cooked.

5 To make sauce, put the ingredients into a pan. Bring to the boil, stirring, and simmer for 5 minutes. Slice fish and serve with vegetables and sauce.

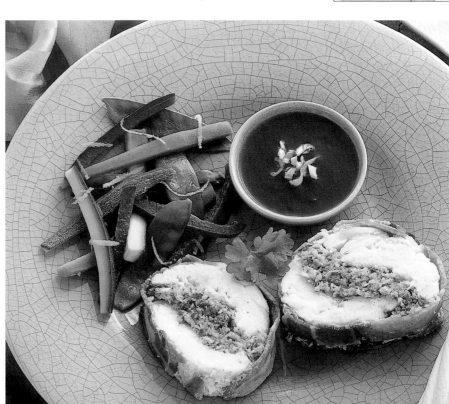

Red Mullet & Amaretto Sauce

This succulent fish and pasta dish is ideal for serving on a warm, summer's evening – preferably *al fresco*.

NUTRITIONAL INFORMATION

Calories 806   Sugars 6g
Protein . . . . .64g   Fat 34g
Carbohydrate . . .64g   Saturates 16g

15 MINS   25 MINS

SERVES 4

I N G R E D I E N T S

90 g/3 oz/3¾ cup plain (all-purpose) flour

8 red mullet fillets

25 g/1 oz/2 tbsp butter

150 ml/¼ pint/⅔ cup fish stock

1 tbsp crushed almonds

1 tsp pink peppercorns

1 orange, peeled and cut into segments

1 tbsp orange liqueur

grated rind of 1 orange

450 g/1 lb dried orecchiette

1 tbsp olive oil

150 ml/¼ pint/⅔ cup double
   (heavy) cream

4 tbsp amaretto

salt and pepper

T O   G A R N I S H

2 tbsp snipped fresh chives

1 tbsp toasted almonds

1 Season the flour with salt and pepper and sprinkle into a shallow bowl. Press the fish fillets into the flour to coat. Melt the butter in a frying pan (skillet). Add the fish and fry over a low heat for 3 minutes, until browned.

2 Add the fish stock to the pan and cook for 4 minutes. Carefully remove the fish, cover with foil and keep warm.

3 Add the almonds, pink peppercorns, half the orange, the orange liqueur and orange rind to the pan. Simmer until the liquid has reduced by half.

4 Meanwhile, bring a large pan of lightly salted water to the boil. Add the orecchiette and oil and cook for 15 minutes, until tender but still firm to the bite.

5 Meanwhile, season the sauce with salt and pepper and stir in the cream and amaretto. Cook for 2 minutes. Return the fish to the pan to coat with the sauce.

6 Drain the pasta and transfer to a serving dish. Top with the fish fillets and their sauce. Garnish with the remaining orange segments, the chives and toasted almonds. Serve immediately.

Szechuan White Fish

Szechuan pepper is quite hot and should be used sparingly to avoid making the dish unbearably spicy.

NUTRITIONAL INFORMATION

Calories 225   Sugars 3g
Protein ....20g   Fat 8g
Carbohydrate ...17g   Saturates 1g

5 MINS   20 MINS

SERVES 4

INGREDIENTS

350 g/12 oz white fish fillets

1 small egg, beaten

3 tbsp plain (all-purpose) flour

4 tbsp dry white wine

3 tbsp light soy sauce

vegetable oil, for frying

1 garlic clove, cut into slivers

1-cm/½-inch piece fresh root ginger, finely chopped

1 onion, finely chopped

1 celery stick, chopped

1 fresh red chilli, chopped

3 spring onions (scallions), chopped

1 tsp rice wine vinegar

½ tsp ground Szechuan pepper

175 ml/6 fl oz/¾ cup fish stock

1 tsp caster (superfine) sugar

1 tsp cornflour (cornstarch)

2 tsp water

1 Cut the fish into 4-cm/1½-inch cubes. Beat together the egg, flour, wine and 1 tablespoon of soy sauce to make a batter. Dip the cubes of fish into the batter to coat well.

2 Heat the oil in a wok, reduce the heat slightly and cook the fish, in batches, for 2–3 minutes, until golden brown. Remove with a slotted spoon, drain on kitchen paper (paper towels), set aside and keep warm.

3 Pour all but 1 tablespoon of oil from the wok and return to the heat. Add the garlic, ginger, onion, celery, chilli and spring onions (scallions) and stir-fry for 1–2 minutes. Stir in the remaining soy sauce and the vinegar.

4 Add the Szechuan pepper, fish stock and caster (superfine) sugar to the wok. Mix the cornflour (cornstarch) with the water to form a smooth paste and stir it into the stock. Bring to the boil and cook, stirring, for 1 minute, until the sauce thickens and clears.

5 Return the fish cubes to the wok and cook for 1–2 minutes. Serve immediately.

Trout with Pineapple

Pineapple is widely used in Chinese cooking. The tartness of fresh pineapple complements fish particularly well.

NUTRITIONAL INFORMATION

Calories 243	Sugars 4g
Protein 30g	Fat 11g
Carbohydrate 6g	Saturates 2g

5 MINS   15 MINS

SERVES 4

INGREDIENTS

4 trout fillets, skinned

2 tbsp vegetable oil

2 garlic cloves, cut into slivers

4 slices fresh pineapple, peeled and diced

1 celery stick, sliced

1 tbsp light soy sauce

50 ml/2 fl oz/¼ cup fresh or unsweetened
   pineapple juice

150 ml/¼ pint/⅔ cup fish stock

1 tsp cornflour (cornstarch)

2 tsp water

shredded celery leaves and fresh red chilli
   slices, to garnish

1 Cut the trout fillets into strips. Heat 1 tablespoon of the vegetable oil in a preheated wok until almost smoking. Reduce the heat slightly, add the fish and sauté for 2 minutes. Remove from the wok and set aside.

2 Add the remaining oil to the wok, reduce the heat and add the garlic, diced pineapple and celery. Stir-fry for 1–2 minutes.

3 Add the soy sauce, pineapple juice and fish stock to the wok. Bring to the boil and cook, stirring, for 2–3 minutes, or until the sauce has reduced.

4 Blend the cornflour (cornstarch) with the water to form a paste and stir it into the wok. Bring the sauce to the boil and cook, stirring constantly, until the sauce thickens and clears.

5 Return the fish to the wok, and cook, stirring gently, until heated through. Transfer to a warmed serving dish and serve, garnished with shredded celery leaves and red chilli slices.

VARIATION

Use canned pineapple instead of fresh pineapple if you wish, choosing slices in unsweetened, natural juice in preference to a syrup.

Smoky Fish Pie

This flavoursome and colourful fish pie is perfect for a light supper. The addition of smoked salmon gives it a touch of luxury.

NUTRITIONAL INFORMATION

Calories	523	Sugars	........15g	
Protein	........58g	Fat	..........6g	
Carbohydrate	...63g	Saturates	......2g	

15 MINS   1 HOUR

SERVES 4

INGREDIENTS

900 g/2 lb smoked haddock or
   cod fillets

600 ml/1 pint/2½ cups skimmed milk

2 bay leaves

115 g/4 oz button mushrooms, quartered

115 g/4 oz frozen peas

115 g/4 oz frozen sweetcorn kernels

675 g/1½ lb potatoes, diced

5 tbsp low-fat natural (unsweetened)
   yogurt

4 tbsp chopped fresh parsley

60 g/2 oz smoked salmon, sliced into
   thin strips

3 tbsp cornflour (cornstarch)

25 g/1 oz smoked cheese, grated

salt and pepper

COOK'S TIP

If possible, use smoked haddock or cod that has not been dyed bright yellow or artificially flavoured to give the illusion of having been smoked.

1 Preheat the oven to 200°C/400°F/Gas Mark 6. Place the fish in a pan and add the milk and bay leaves. Bring to the boil, cover and then simmer for 5 minutes.

2 Add the mushrooms, peas and sweetcorn, bring back to a simmer, cover and cook for 5–7 minutes. Leave to cool.

3 Place the potatoes in a saucepan, cover with water, boil and cook for 8 minutes. Drain well and mash with a fork or a potato masher. Stir in the yogurt, parsley and seasoning. Set aside.

4 Using a slotted spoon, remove the fish from the pan. Flake the cooked fish away from the skin and place in an ovenproof gratin dish. Reserve the cooking liquid.

5 Drain the vegetables, reserving the cooking liquid, and gently stir into the fish with the salmon strips.

6 Blend a little cooking liquid into the cornflour (cornstarch) to make a paste. Transfer the rest of the liquid to a saucepan and add the paste. Heat through, stirring, until thickened. Discard the bay leaves and season to taste. Pour the sauce over the fish and vegetables and mix. Spoon over the mashed potato so that the fish is covered, sprinkle with cheese and bake for 25–30 minutes.

Salmon Fillet with Herbs

This is a great party dish, as the salmon is cooked in one piece. The combination of the herbs and barbecue (grill) give a great flavour.

NUTRITIONAL INFORMATION

Calories 507   Sugars 0.4g
Protein . . . . .46g   Fat 35g
Carbohydrate . . .0.5g   Saturates 6g

5 MINS   30 MINS

SERVES 4

INGREDIENTS

½ large bunch dried thyme

5 fresh rosemary branches, 15–20 cm/
  6–8 inches long

8 bay leaves

1 kg/2 lb salmon fillet

1 bulb fennel, cut into 8 pieces

2 tbsp lemon juice

2 tbsp olive oil

TO SERVE

crusty bread

green salad

1 Make a base on a hot barbecue (grill) with the dried thyme, rosemary branches and bay leaves, overlapping them so that they cover a slightly bigger area than the salmon.

2 Carefully place the salmon on top of the herbs.

3 Arrange the fennel around the edge of the fish.

4 Combine the lemon juice and oil and brush the salmon with it.

5 Cover the salmon loosely with a piece of foil, to keep it moist.

6 Cook for about 20–30 minutes, basting frequently with the lemon juice mixture.

7 Remove the salmon from the barbecue, cut it into slices and serve with the fennel.

8 Serve with slices of crusty bread and a green salad.

VARIATION

Use whatever combination of herbs you may have to hand – but avoid the stronger tasting herbs, such as sage and marjoram, which are unsuitable for fish.

Yucatan Fish

Herbs, onion, green (bell) pepper and pumpkin seeds are used to flavour this baked fish dish, which is first marinated in lime juice.

NUTRITIONAL INFORMATION

Calories 248   Sugars 2g
Protein . . . . .33g   Fat 11g
Carbohydrate . . . .3g   Saturates 1g

40 MINS   35 MINS

SERVES 4

I N G R E D I E N T S

4 cod cutlets or steaks or hake cutlets
   (about 175 g/6 oz each)

2 tbsp lime juice

salt and pepper

1 green (bell) pepper

1 tbsp olive oil

1 onion, chopped finely

1–2 garlic cloves, crushed

40 g/1½ oz green pumpkin seeds

grated rind of ½ lime

1 tbsp chopped fresh coriander (cilantro)
   or parsley

1 tbsp chopped fresh mixed herbs

60 g/2 oz button mushrooms,
   sliced thinly

2–3 tbsp fresh orange juice or
   white wine

TO GARNISH

lime wedges

fresh mixed herbs

1 Wipe the fish, place in a shallow ovenproof dish and pour the lime juice over. Turn the fish in the juice, season with salt and pepper, cover and leave in a cool place for 15–30 minutes.

2 Halve the (bell) pepper, remove the seeds and place under a preheated moderate grill, skin-side upwards, until the skin burns and splits. Leave to cool slightly, then peel off the skin and chop the flesh.

3 Heat the oil in a pan and fry the onion, garlic, (bell) pepper and pumpkin seeds gently for a few minutes until the onion is soft.

4 Stir in the lime rind, coriander (cilantro) or parsley, mixed herbs, mushrooms and seasoning, and spoon over the fish.

5 Spoon or pour the orange juice or wine over the fish, cover with foil or a lid and place in a preheated oven at 180°C/350°F/Gas Mark 4 for about 30 minutes, or until the fish is just tender.

6 Garnish the fish with lime wedges and fresh herbs and serve.

Herrings with Lemon

Cook these fish in foil parcels for a wonderfully moist texture. Serve with lots of fresh bread to soak up the delicious juices.

NUTRITIONAL INFORMATION

Calories 355	Sugars 0g
Protein 19g	Fat 31g
Carbohydrate 0g	Saturates 13g

10 MINS　　　20 MINS

SERVES 4

I N G R E D I E N T S

4 herrings, cleaned

salt

4 bay leaves

1 lemon, sliced

50 g/1¾ oz unsalted butter

2 tbsp chopped fresh parsley

½ tsp lemon pepper

fresh crusty bread, to serve

1 Season the prepared herrings inside and out with freshly ground salt to taste.

2 Place a bay leaf inside the cavity of each fish.

3 Place 4 squares of kitchen foil on the work surface and divide the lemon slices evenly among them. Place a fish on top of the lemon slices.

4 Beat the butter until softened, then mix in the parsley and lemon pepper. Dot the flavoured butter liberally all over the fish.

5 Wrap the fish tightly in the kitchen foil and barbecue (grill) over medium hot coals for 15-20 minutes or until the fish is cooked through – the flesh should be white in colour and firm to the touch

(unwrap the foil to check, then wrap up the fish again).

6 Transfer the wrapped fish parcels to individual, warm serving plates.

7 Unwrap the foil parcels before serving.

8 Serve the fish with fresh, crusty bread to mop up the cooking juices.

COOK'S TIP

For a main course use trout instead of herring. Cook for 20–30 minutes until the flesh is firm to the touch and opaque in colour.

Spaghetti alla Bucaniera

Brill was once known as poor man's turbot, an unfair description as it is a delicately flavoured and delicious fish in its own right.

NUTRITIONAL INFORMATION

Calories	588	Sugars	........5g
Protein	........36g	Fat	..........18g
Carbohydrate	...68g	Saturates	.......9g

 25 MINS   50 MINS

SERVES 4

I N G R E D I E N T S

90 g/3 oz/¾ cup plain (all-purpose) flour

450 g/1 lb brill or sole fillets,
    skinned and chopped

450 g/1 lb hake fillets,
    skinned and chopped

90 g/3 oz/6 tbsp butter

4 shallots, finely chopped

2 garlic cloves, crushed

1 carrot, diced

1 leek, finely chopped

300 ml/½ pint/1¼ cups
    dry (hard) cider

300 ml/½ pint/1¼ cups
    medium sweet cider

2 tsp anchovy essence (extract)

1 tbsp tarragon vinegar

450 g/1 lb dried spaghetti

1 tbsp olive oil

salt and pepper

chopped fresh parsley, to garnish

crusty brown bread, to serve

1 Season the flour with salt and pepper. Sprinkle 25 g/ 1 oz/¼ cup of the seasoned flour on to a shallow plate. Press the fish pieces into the seasoned flour to coat thoroughly.

2 Melt the butter in a flameproof casserole. Add the fish fillets, shallots, garlic, carrot and leek and cook over a low heat, stirring frequently, for about 10 minutes.

3 Sprinkle over the remaining seasoned flour and cook, stirring constantly, for 2 minutes. Gradually stir in the cider, anchovy essence (extract) and tarragon vinegar. Bring to the boil and simmer over a low heat for 35 minutes. Alternatively, bake in a preheated oven at 180°C/350°F/Gas 4 for 30 minutes.

4 About 15 minutes before the end of the cooking time, bring a large pan of lightly salted water to the boil. Add the spaghetti and olive oil and cook for about 12 minutes, until tender but still firm to the bite. Drain the pasta thoroughly and transfer to a large serving dish.

5 Arrange the fish on top of the spaghetti and pour over the sauce. Garnish with chopped parsley and serve immediately with warm, crusty brown bread.

Salmon with Pineapple

Presentation plays a major part in Chinese cooking and this dish demonstrates this perfectly with the wonderful combination of colours.

NUTRITIONAL INFORMATION

Calories ....347 Sugars 12g
Protein ....24g Fat 20g
Carbohydrate ...16g Saturates 3g

10 MINS   15 MINS

SERVES 4

I N G R E D I E N T S

2 tbsp sunflower oil

1 red onion, sliced

1 orange (bell) pepper, deseeded and sliced

1 green (bell) pepper, deseeded and sliced

100 g/3½ oz/1 cup baby corn cobs, halved

450 g/1 lb salmon fillet, skin removed

1 tbsp paprika

225 g/8 oz can cubed pineapple, drained

100 g/3½ oz/1 cup bean sprouts

2 tbsp tomato ketchup

2 tbsp soy sauce

2 tbsp medium sherry

1 tsp cornflour (cornstarch)

1 Heat the sunflower oil in a large preheated wok. Add the onion, (bell) peppers and baby corn cobs to the wok and stir-fry for 5 minutes.

3 Rinse the salmon fillet under cold running water and pat dry with absorbent kitchen paper (paper towels).

4 Cut the salmon flesh into thin strips and place in a large bowl. Sprinkle with the paprika and toss well to coat.

5 Add the salmon to the wok together with the pineapple and stir-fry for a

further 2–3 minutes or until the fish is tender.

6 Add the bean sprouts to the wok and toss well.

7 Mix together the tomato ketchup, soy sauce, sherry and cornflour (cornstarch). Add to the wok and cook until the juices start to thicken. Transfer to warm serving plates and serve immediately.

VARIATION

You can use trout fillets instead of the salmon as an alternative, if you prefer.

Trout with Smoked Bacon

Most trout available nowadays is farmed rainbow trout, however, if you can, buy wild brown trout for this recipe.

NUTRITIONAL INFORMATION

Calories 802   Sugars 8g
Protein . . . . .68g   Fat 36g
Carbohydrate . . .54g   Saturates 10g

 35 MINS   25 MINS

SERVES 4

INGREDIENTS

butter, for greasing

4 x 275 g/9½ oz trout, gutted and cleaned

12 anchovies in oil, drained and chopped

2 apples, peeled, cored and sliced

4 fresh mint sprigs

juice of 1 lemon

12 slices rindless smoked fatty bacon

450 g/1 lb dried tagliatelle

1 tbsp olive oil

salt and pepper

TO GARNISH

2 apples, cored and sliced

4 fresh mint sprigs

1 Grease a deep baking tray (cookie sheet) with butter.

2 Open up the cavities of each trout and rinse with warm salt water.

3 Season each cavity with salt and pepper. Divide the anchovies, sliced apples and mint sprigs between each of the cavities. Sprinkle the lemon juice into each cavity.

4 Carefully cover the whole of each trout, except the head and tail, with three slices of smoked bacon in a spiral.

5 Arrange the trout on the baking tray (cookie sheet) with the loose ends of bacon tucked underneath. Season with pepper and bake in a preheated oven at 200°C/400°F/Gas Mark 6 for 20 minutes, turning the trout over after 10 minutes.

6 Meanwhile, bring a large pan of lightly salted water to the boil. Add the tagliatelle and olive oil and cook for about 12 minutes, until tender but still firm to the bite. Drain the pasta and transfer to a large, warm serving dish.

7 Remove the trout from the oven and arrange on the tagliatelle. Garnish with sliced apples and fresh mint sprigs and serve immediately.

Fish in Szechuan Hot Sauce

This is a classic Szechuan recipe. When served in a restaurant, the fish head and tail are removed before cooking.

NUTRITIONAL INFORMATION

Calories . . . . .470 Sugar 3g
Protein . . . . .45g Fat 29g
Carbohydrate . . . .7g Saturates 4g

 3³/₄ HOURS   15 MINS

SERVES 4

INGREDIENTS

1 carp, bream, sea bass, trout,
   grouper or grey mullet, about
   750g/1 lb 10 oz, gutted

1 tbsp light soy sauce

1 tbsp Chinese rice wine or dry sherry

vegetable oil, for deep-frying

flat-leaf parsley or coriander (cilatnro)
   sprigs, to garnish

SAUCE

2 garlic cloves, finely chopped

2-3 spring onions (scallions),
   finely chopped

1 tsp finely chopped ginger root

2 tbsp chilli bean sauce

1 tbsp tomato purée (paste)

2 tsp sugar

1 tbsp rice vinegar

125 ml/4 fl oz/½ cup Chinese Stock
   (see page 8) or water

1 tbsp cornflour (cornstarch) paste
   (see page 6)

½ tsp sesame oil

1 Wash the fish and dry well on kitchen paper absorbent (paper towels).

2 Score both sides of the fish to the bone with a sharp knife, making diagonal cuts at intervals of 2.5 cm/1 inch.

3 Rub the fish with the soy sauce and rice wine or sherry on both sides. Transfer the fish to a plate, cover with cling film (plastic wrap) and leave to marinate in the refrigerator for 10-15 minutes.

4 Heat the oil in a preheated wok or large frying pan (skillet) until smoking.

5 Deep-fry the fish in the hot oil for about 3-4 minutes on both sides, or until golden brown.

6 Pour off the oil, leaving about 1 tablespoon in the wok. Push the fish to one side of the wok and add the garlic, white parts of the spring onions (scallions), ginger, chilli bean sauce, tomato purée (paste), sugar, vinegar and Chinese stock or water.

7 Bring the mixture in the wok to the boil and braise the fish in the sauce for 4-5 minutes, turning it over once.

8 Add the green parts of the spring onions (scallions) and stir in the cornflour (cornstarch) paste to thicken the sauce.

9 Sprinkle with sesame oil and serve immediately, garnished with fresh parsley or coriander (cilantro).

Monkfish with Coconut

This is a tasty kebab with a mild marinade. Allow the skewers to marinate for at least an hour before cooking.

NUTRITIONAL INFORMATION

Calories	193	Sugars	.........2g
Protein	........39g	Fat	..........3g
Carbohydrate	....2g	Saturates	......1g

4 HOURS   30 MINS

SERVES 4

INGREDIENTS

450 g/1 lb monkfish tails

225 g/8 oz uncooked peeled prawns (shrimp)

desiccated (shredded) coconut, toasted, to garnish (optional)

MARINADE

1 tsp sunflower oil

½ small onion, finely grated

1 tsp root (fresh) ginger, grated

150 ml/5 fl oz/⅔ cup canned coconut milk

2 tbsp chopped, fresh coriander (cilantro)

1 To make the marinade, heat the oil in a wok or saucepan and fry the onion and ginger for 5 minutes until just softened but not browned.

COOK'S TIP

Look out for uncooked prawns (shrimp) in the freezer cabinet in large supermarkets. If you cannot obtain them, you can use cooked prawns (shrimp), but remember they only need heating through.

2 Add the coconut milk to the pan and bring to the boil. Boil rapidly for about 5 minutes or until reduced to the consistency of single (light) cream.

3 Remove the pan from the heat and allow to cool completely.

4 When cooled, stir the coriander (cilantro) into the coconut milk and pour into a shallow dish.

5 Cut the fish into bite-sized chunks and stir gently into the coconut mixture together with the prawns (shrimp). Leave to chill for 1–4 hours.

6 Thread the fish and prawns (shrimp) on to skewers and discard any remaining marinade. Barbecue (grill) the skewers over hot coals for 10–15 minutes, turning frequently. Garnish with toasted coconut (if using).

Smoked Fish Lasagne

Use smoked cod or haddock in this delicious lasagne.
It's a great way to make a little go a long way.

NUTRITIONAL INFORMATION

Calories 483   Sugars 8g
Protein ....36g   Fat 24g
Carbohydrate ...32g   Saturates 12g

20 MINS   1¹/₄ HOURS

SERVES 4

INGREDIENTS

2 tsp olive or vegetable oil

1 garlic clove, crushed

1 small onion, chopped finely

125 g/4½ oz mushrooms, sliced

400 g/14 oz can chopped tomatoes

1 small courgette (zucchini), sliced

150 ml/¼ pint/⅔ cup vegetable stock
   or water

25 g/1 oz/2 tbsp butter or margarine

300 ml/½ pint/1¼ cups skimmed milk

25 g/1 oz/¼ cup plain (all-purpose) flour

125 g/4 oz/1 cup grated mature (sharp)
   Cheddar cheese

1 tbsp chopped fresh parsley

125 g/4½ oz (6 sheets) pre-cooked lasagne

350 g/12 oz skinned and boned smoked
   cod or haddock, cut into chunks

salt and pepper

fresh parsley sprigs to garnish

1 Heat the oil in a saucepan and fry the garlic and onion for about 5 minutes. Add the mushrooms and cook for 3 minutes, stirring.

2 Add the tomatoes, courgette (zucchini) and stock or water and simmer, uncovered, for 15–20 minutes until the vegetables are soft. Season.

3 Put the butter or margarine, milk and flour into a small saucepan and heat, whisking constantly, until the sauce boils and thickens. Remove from the heat and add half of the cheese and all of the parsley. Stir gently to melt the cheese and season to taste.

4 Spoon the tomato sauce mixture into a large, shallow ovenproof dish and top with half of the lasagne sheets. Scatter the chunks of fish evenly over the top, then pour over half of the cheese sauce. Top with the remaining lasagne sheets and then spread the rest of the cheese sauce on top. Sprinkle with the remaining cheese.

5 Bake in a preheated oven at 190°C/375°F/Gas Mark 5 for 40 minutes, until the top is golden brown and bubbling. Garnish with parsley sprigs and serve hot.

Lemon Sole & Haddock Ravioli

This delicate-tasting dish is surprisingly satisfying for even the hungriest appetites. Prepare the Italian Red Wine Sauce well in advance.

NUTRITIONAL INFORMATION

Calories 977   Sugars 7g
Protein . . . . .67g   Fat 40g
Carbohydrate . . .93g   Saturates 17g

9³/₄ HOURS   25 MINS

SERVES 4

INGREDIENTS

450 g/1 lb lemon sole fillets, skinned

450 g/1 lb haddock fillets, skinned

3 eggs beaten

450 g/1 lb cooked potato gnocchi

175 g/6 oz/3 cups fresh breadcrumbs

50 ml/2 fl oz/¼ cup double
    (heavy) cream

450 g/1 lb Basic Pasta Dough
    (see page 6)

300 ml/½ pint/1¼ cups Italian Red Wine
    Sauce (see page 7)

60 g/2 oz/⅔ cup freshly grated
    Parmesan cheese

salt and pepper

1 Flake the lemon sole and haddock fillets with a fork and transfer the flesh to a large mixing bowl.

2 Mix the eggs, cooked potato gnocchi, breadcrumbs and cream in a bowl until thoroughly combined. Add the fish to the bowl containing the gnocchi and season the mixture with salt and pepper to taste.

3 Roll out the pasta dough on to a lightly floured surface and cut out 7.5 cm/3 inch rounds using a plain cutter.

4 Place a spoonful of the fish stuffing on each round. Dampen the edges slightly and fold the pasta rounds over, pressing together to seal.

5 Bring a large saucepan of lightly salted water to the boil. Add the ravioli and cook for 15 minutes.

6 Drain the ravioli, using a slotted spoon, and transfer to a large serving dish. Pour over the Italian Red Wine Sauce, sprinkle over the Parmesan cheese and serve immediately.

COOK'S TIP

For square ravioli, divide the dough in two. Wrap half in cling film; thinly roll out the other half. Cover; roll out the remaining dough. Pipe the filling at regular intervals and brush the spaces in between with water or beaten egg. Lift the second sheet of dough into position with a rolling pin and press between the filling to seal. Cut with a ravioli cutter or a knife.

Fillets of Red Mullet & Pasta

This simple recipe perfectly complements the sweet flavour and delicate texture of the fish.

NUTRITIONAL INFORMATION

Calories ....457 Sugars 3g
Protein ....39g Fat 12g
Carbohydrate ...44g Saturates 5g

15 MINS   1 HOUR

SERVES 4

INGREDIENTS

1 kg/2 lb 4 oz red mullet fillets

300 ml/½ pint/1¼ cups dry white wine

4 shallots, finely chopped

1 garlic clove, crushed

3 tbsp finely chopped mixed fresh herbs

finely grated rind and juice of 1 lemon

pinch of freshly grated nutmeg

3 anchovy fillets, roughly chopped

2 tbsp double (heavy) cream

1 tsp cornflour (cornstarch)

450 g/1 lb dried vermicelli

1 tbsp olive oil

salt and pepper

TO GARNISH

1 fresh mint sprig

lemon slices

lemon rind

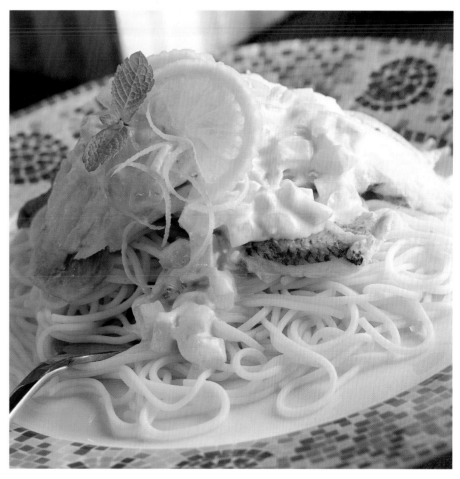

1 Put the red mullet fillets in a large casserole. Pour over the wine and add the shallots, garlic, herbs, lemon rind and juice, nutmeg and anchovies. Season. Cover and bake in a preheated oven at 180°C/350°F/Gas Mark 4 for 35 minutes.

2 Transfer the mullet to a warm dish. Set aside and keep warm.

3 Pour the cooking liquid into a pan and bring to the boil. Simmer for 25 minutes, until reduced by half. Mix the cream and cornflour (cornstarch) and stir into the sauce to thicken.

4 Meanwhile, bring a pan of lightly salted water to the boil. Add the vermicelli and oil and cook for 8–10 minutes, until tender but still firm to the bite. Drain the pasta and transfer to a warm serving dish.

5 Arrange the red mullet fillets on top of the vermicelli and pour over the sauce. Garnish with a fresh mint sprig, slices of lemon and strips of lemon rind and serve immediately.

Italian Cod

Cod roasted with herbs and topped with a lemon and rosemary crust is a delicious main course.

NUTRITIONAL INFORMATION

Calories 313   Sugars 0.4g
Protein . . . . .29g   Fat 20g
Carbohydrate . . . .6g   Saturates 5g

10 MINS   35 MINS

SERVES 4

INGREDIENTS

25 g/1 oz/2 tbsp butter

50 g/1¾ oz wholemeal breadcrumbs

25 g/1 oz chopped walnuts

grated rind and juice of 2 lemons

2 sprigs rosemary, stalks removed

2 tbsp chopped parsley

4 cod fillets, each about 150 g/5½ oz

1 garlic clove, crushed

3 tbsp walnut oil

1 small red chilli, diced

salad leaves, to serve

1 Melt the butter in a large saucepan, stirring.

2 Remove the pan from the heat and add the breadcrumbs, walnuts, the rind and juice of 1 lemon, half of the rosemary and half of the parsley.

3 Press the breadcrumb mixture over the top of the cod fillets. Place the cod fillets in a shallow, foil-lined roasting tin (pan).

4 Bake in a preheated oven at 200°C/400°F/Gas Mark 6 for 25–30 minutes.

5 Mix the garlic, the remaining lemon rind and juice, rosemary, parsley and chilli in a bowl. Beat in the walnut oil and mix to combine. Drizzle the dressing over the cod steaks as soon as they are cooked.

6 Transfer to serving plates and serve immediately.

VARIATION

If preferred, the walnuts may be omitted from the crust. In addition, extra virgin olive oil can be used instead of walnut oil, if you prefer.

Fish & Ginger Stir-fry

This delicious and spicy recipe is a really quick fish dish, ideal for mid-week family meals or light lunches at weekends.

NUTRITIONAL INFORMATION

Calories ...... .280   Sugars 2g
Protein ....31g   Fat .... .10g
Carbohydrate ...17g   Saturates 2g

 5 MINS   15 MINS

SERVES 4

INGREDIENTS

4 tbsp cornflour (cornstarch)

½ tsp ground ginger

675 g/1½ lb firm white fish fillets, skinned and cubed

3 tbsp peanut oil

2.5-cm/1-inch fresh ginger root, grated

1 leek, thinly sliced

1 tbsp white wine vinegar

2 tbsp Chinese rice wine or dry sherry

3 tbsp dark soy sauce

1 tsp caster (superfine) sugar

2 tbsp lemon juice

finely shredded leek, to garnish

1 Mix the cornflour (cornstarch) and ground ginger in a bowl.

2 Add the cubes of fish, in batches, to the cornflour (cornstarch) mixture, turning to coat the fish thoroughly in the mixture.

3 Heat the peanut oil in a preheated wok or large, heavy-based frying pan (skillet), swirling the oil around the base of the wok until it is really hot.

4 Add the grated fresh ginger and sliced leek to the wok or frying pan (skillet) and stir-fry for 1 minute.

5 Add the coated fish to the wok and cook for a further 5 minutes, until browned, stirring to prevent the fish from sticking to the base of the wok.

6 Add the remaining ingredients and cook over a low heat for 3–4 minutes, until the fish is cooked through.

7 Transfer the fish and ginger stir-fry to a serving dish and serve immediately.

VARIATION

Use any firm white fish which will hold its shape, such as cod, haddock or monkfish.

Piquant Fish Cakes

The combination of pink- and white-fleshed fish, with a tasty tomato sauce, transforms the humble fish into something a bit special.

NUTRITIONAL INFORMATION

Calories 334   Sugars 7g
Protein . . . . . . .31g   Fat 7g
Carbohydrate . . .37g   Saturates 1g

 2 HOURS   55 MINS

SERVES 4

INGREDIENTS

450 g/1 lb potatoes, diced

225 g/8 oz each trout and haddock fillet

1 bay leaf

425 ml/15 fl oz/1¾ cups Fresh Fish Stock (see page 9)

2 tbsp low-fat natural fromage frais (unsweetened yogurt)

4 tbsp fresh snipped chives

75 g/2¾ oz dry white breadcrumbs

1 tbsp sunflower oil

salt and pepper

freshly snipped chives, to garnish

lemon wedges and salad leaves, to serve

PIQUANT TOMATO SAUCE

200 ml/7 fl oz/¾ cup passata (sieved tomatoes)

4 tbsp dry white wine

4 tbsp low-fat natural (unsweetened) yogurt

chilli powder

1 Place the potatoes in a saucepan and cover with water. Bring to the boil and cook for about 10 minutes or until the potatoes are tender. Drain well and mash.

2 Meanwhile, place the fish in a pan with the bay leaf and fish stock. Bring to the boil and simmer for 7–8 minutes until tender.

3 Remove the fish with a slotted spoon and flake the flesh away from the skin. Gently mix the cooked fish with the potato, fromage frais (unsweetened yogurt), chives and seasoning. Leave to cool, then cover and leave to chill for 1 hour.

4 Sprinkle the breadcrumbs on to a plate. Divide the fish mixture into 8 and form each portion into a patty, about 7.5 cm/3 inches in diameter. Press each fish cake into the breadcrumbs, coating all over.

5 Brush a frying pan (skillet) with oil and fry the fish cakes for 6 minutes. Turn the fish cakes over and cook for a further 5–6 minutes until golden. Drain on kitchen paper (paper towels) and keep warm.

6 To make the sauce, heat the passata (sieved tomatoes) and wine. Season, remove from the heat and stir in the yogurt. Return briefly to the heat then transfer to a small serving bowl and sprinkle with chilli powder. Garnish the fish cakes with chives and serve with lemon wedges, salad leaves and the sauce.

Fish with Coconut & Basil

Fish curries are sensational and this is no exception. Red curry and coconut are fantastic flavours with the fried fish.

NUTRITIONAL INFORMATION

Calories 209	Sugars 10g	
Protein 21g	Fat 8g	
Carbohydrate ...15g	Saturates 1g	

5 MINS

15 MINS

SERVES 4

INGREDIENTS

2 tbsp vegetable oil

450 g/1 lb skinless cod fillet

25 g/1 oz/¼ cup seasoned flour

1 clove garlic, crushed

2 tbsp red curry paste

1 tbsp fish sauce

300 ml/½ pint/1¼ cups coconut milk

175 g/6 oz cherry tomatoes, halved

20 fresh basil leaves

fragrant rice, to serve

1 Heat the vegetable oil in a large preheated wok.

2 Using a sharp knife, cut the fish into large cubes, removing any bones with a pair of clean tweezers.

3 Place the seasoned flour in a bowl. Add the cubes of fish and mix until well coated.

4 Add the coated fish to the wok and stir-fry over a high heat for 3–4 minutes, or until the fish just begins to brown at the edges.

5 Mix together the garlic, curry paste, fish sauce and coconut milk. Pour the mixture over the fish and bring to the boil.

6 Add the tomatoes to the mixture in the wok and leave to simmer for 5 minutes.

7 Roughly chop or tear the fresh basil leaves. Add the basil to the wok, stir carefully to combine, taking care not to break up the cubes of fish.

8 Transfer to serving plates and serve hot with fragrant rice.

COOK'S TIP

Take care not to overcook the dish once the tomatoes are added, otherwise they will break down and the skins will come away.

Pasta Pudding

A tasty mixture of creamy fish and pasta cooked in a bowl, unmoulded and drizzled with tomato sauce presents macaroni in a new guise.

NUTRITIONAL INFORMATION

Calories ... 536	Sugars ... 4g	
Protein ... 35g	Fat ... 35g	
Carbohydrate ... 21g	Saturates ... 17g	

35 MINS   2 HOURS

SERVES 4

INGREDIENTS

125 g/4½ oz short-cut macaroni

1 tbsp olive oil

15 g/½ oz/1 tbsp butter, plus extra
    for greasing

500 g/1 lb 2 oz white fish fillets, such as
    cod or coley, or for luxury, monkfish

a few parsley stalks

6 black peppercorns

125 ml/4 fl oz/½ cup double (heavy) cream

2 eggs, separated

2 tbsp chopped parsley

pinch of grated nutmeg

60 g/2 oz/½ cup Parmesan, grated

Basic Tomato Sauce (see page 6), to serve

pepper

parsley sprigs, to garnish

1 Cook the pasta in a pan of salted boiling water, adding the oil, for 8–10 minutes. Drain, return to the pan, add the butter and cover. Keep warm.

2 Place the fish in a frying pan (skillet) with the parsley stalks and peppercorns and pour on just enough water to cover. Bring to the boil, cover, and simmer for 10 minutes. Lift out the fish with a fish slice,

reserving the liquor. When the fish is cool enough to handle, skin and remove any bones. Cut into bite-sized pieces.

3 Transfer the pasta to a large bowl and stir in the cream, egg yolks and dill. Stir in the fish, taking care not to break it up, and enough liquor to make a moist but firm mixture. It should fall easily from a spoon, but not be too runny. Whisk the egg whites until stiff but not dry, then fold into the mixture.

4 Grease a heatproof bowl or pudding basin and spoon in the mixture to within 4 cm/1½ inch of the rim. Cover the

top with greased greaseproof paper and a cloth, or with foil, and tie firmly around the rim. Do not use foil if you cook the pudding in a microwave.

5 Stand the pudding on a trivet in a large pan of boiling water to come halfway up the sides. Cover and steam for 1½ hours, topping up the boiling water as needed, or cook in a microwave on maximum power for 7 minutes.

6 Run a knife around the inside of the bowl and invert on to a warm serving dish. Pour some tomato sauce over the top; serve the rest separately. Garnish and serve.

Japanese Plaice (Flounder)

The marinade for this dish has a distinctly Japanese flavour. Its subtle flavour goes well with any white fish.

NUTRITIONAL INFORMATION

Calories 207   Sugars 9g
Protein . . . . .22g   Fat 8g
Carbohydrate . . .10g   Saturates 1g

6 HOURS   10 MINS

SERVES 4

INGREDIENTS

4 small plaice (flounders)

6 tbsp soy sauce

2 tbsp sake or dry white wine

2 tbsp sesame oil

1 tbsp lemon juice

2 tbsp light muscovado sugar

1 tsp root (fresh) ginger, grated

1 clove garlic, crushed

TO GARNISH

1 small carrot

4 spring onions (scallion)

1 Rinse the fish and pat them dry on kitchen paper (paper towels).

2 Cut a few slashes into the sides of the fish so that they absorb the marinade.

3 Mix together the soy sauce, sake or wine, oil, lemon juice, sugar, ginger and garlic in a large, shallow dish.

4 Place the fish in the marinade and turn them over so that they are well coated on both sides. Leave to stand in the refrigerator for 1–6 hours.

5 Meanwhile, prepare the garnish. Cut the carrot into evenly-sized thin sticks and clean and shred the spring onions (scallions).

6 Barbecue (grill) the fish over hot coals for about 10 minutes, turning once.

7 Scatter the chopped spring onions (scallions) and carrot over the fish and transfer the fish to a serving dish. Serve immediately.

VARIATION

Use sole instead of the plaice (flounders) and scatter over some toasted sesame seeds instead of the carrot and spring onions (scallions), if you prefer.

Sole & Smoked Salmon Rolls

In this elegant dish, the delicate flavour of sole and salmon blend together perfectly with a light, citrus filling.

NUTRITIONAL INFORMATION

Calories .... Sugars ....
Protein .... Fat ....
Carbohydrate ...... Saturates ....

 1 HOUR ⏱ 20 MINS

SERVES 4

INGREDIENTS

60 g/2 oz/1 cup fresh wholemeal (whole wheat) breadcrumbs

½ tsp grated lime rind

1 tbsp lime juice

60 g/2 oz/¼ cup low-fat soft cheese

4 × 125 g/4½ oz sole fillets

60 g/2 oz smoked salmon

150 ml/¼ pint/⅔ cup Fresh Fish Stock (see page 8)

150 ml/¼ pint/⅔ cup low-fat natural yogurt

1 tbsp chopped fresh chervil

salt and pepper

fresh chervil, to garnish

TO SERVE

selection of freshly steamed vegetables

lime wedges

COOK'S TIP

When buying fresh fish, choose fish with a bright eye and red gills. The fish should be firm to the touch, with just a slight 'fishy' smell.

1 In a mixing bowl, combine the breadcrumbs, lime rind and juice, soft cheese and seasoning, to form a soft stuffing mixture.

2 Skin the sole fillets by inserting a sharp knife in between the skin and flesh at the tail end. Holding the skin in your fingers and keeping it taut, strip the flesh away from the skin.

3 Halve the sole fillets lengthways. Place strips of smoked salmon over the skinned side of each fillet, trimming the salmon as necessary.

4 Spoon one-eighth of the stuffing on to each fish fillet and press down along the fish with the back of a spoon. Carefully roll up from the head to the tail end. Place, seam-side down, in an ovenproof dish and pour in the stock. Bake in a preheated oven at 190°C/ 375°F/Gas Mark 5 for 15 minutes.

5 Using a fish slice, transfer the fish to a warm serving plate, cover and keep warm. Pour the cooking juices into a saucepan and add the yogurt and chopped chervil. Season to taste and heat gently without boiling. Garnish the fish rolls with chervil and serve with the yogurt sauce, and the steamed vegetables and lime wedges.

Herrings with Tarragon

The fish are filled with an orange-flavoured stuffing and are wrapped in kitchen foil before being baked on the barbecue (grill).

NUTRITIONAL INFORMATION

Calories 332   Sugars 4g
Protein ....21g   Fat 24g
Carbohydrate ....9g   Saturates 6g

15 MINS   35 MINS

SERVES 4

INGREDIENTS

1 orange

4 spring onions (scallions)

50 g/1¾ oz fresh wholemeal breadcrumbs

1 tbsp fresh tarragon, chopped

4 herrings, cleaned and gutted

salt and pepper

green salad, to serve

TO GARNISH

2 oranges

1 tbsp light brown sugar

1 tbsp olive oil

sprigs of fresh tarragon

1 To make the stuffing, grate the rind from half of the orange, using a zester.

2 Peel and chop all of the orange flesh on a plate in order to catch all of the juice.

3 Mix together the orange flesh, juice, rind, spring onions (scallions), breadcrumbs and tarragon in a bowl. Season with salt and pepper to taste.

4 Divide the stuffing into 4 equal portions and use it to fill the body cavities of the fish.

5 Place each fish on to a square of lightly greased kitchen foil and wrap the foil around the fish so that it is completely enclosed. Barbecue (grill) over hot coals for 20–30 minutes until the fish are cooked through – the flesh should be white and firm to the touch.

6 Meanwhile make the garnish. Peel and thickly slice the 2 oranges and sprinkle over the sugar.

7 Just before the fish is cooked, drizzle a little oil over the orange slices and place them on the barbecue for about 5 minutes to heat through.

8 Transfer the fish to serving plates and garnish with the barbecued (grilled) orange slices and sprigs of fresh tarragon.

9 Serve the fish with fresh green salad leaves.

Mediterranean Fish Stew

Popular in fishing ports around Europe, gentle stewing is an excellent way to maintain the flavour and succulent texture of fish and shellfish.

NUTRITIONAL INFORMATION

Calories	533	Sugars	........11g
Protein	........71g	Fat	..........10g
Carbohydrate	...30g	Saturates	......2g

1¼ HOURS   25 MINS

SERVES 4

INGREDIENTS

2 tsp olive oil

2 red onions, sliced

2 garlic cloves, crushed

2 tbsp red wine vinegar

2 tsp caster (superfine) sugar

300 ml/½ pint/1¼ cups Fresh Fish Stock (see page 78)

300 ml/½ pint/1¼ cups dry red wine

2 × 400 g/14 oz cans chopped tomatoes

225 g/8 oz baby aubergines (eggplant), quartered

225 g/8 oz yellow courgettes (zucchini), quartered or sliced

1 green (bell) pepper, sliced

1 tbsp chopped fresh rosemary

500 g/1 lb 2 oz halibut fillet, skinned and cut into 2.5 cm/1 inch cubes

750 g/1 lb 10 oz fresh mussels, prepared

225 g/8 oz baby squid, cleaned, trimmed and sliced into rings

225 g/8 oz fresh tiger prawns (shrimp), peeled and deveined

salt and pepper

4 slices toasted French bread rubbed with a cut garlic clove

lemon wedges, to serve

1 Heat the oil in a large non-stick saucepan and fry the onions and garlic gently for 3 minutes.

2 Stir in the vinegar and sugar and cook for a further 2 minutes.

3 Stir in the stock, wine, canned tomatoes, aubergines (eggplant) courgettes (zucchini), (bell) pepper and rosemary. Bring to the boil and simmer, uncovered, for 10 minutes.

4 Add the halibut, mussels and squid. Mix well and simmer, covered, for 5 minutes until the fish is opaque.

5 Stir in the prawns (shrimp) and continue to simmer, covered, for a further 2–3 minutes until the prawns (shrimp) are pink and cooked through.

6 Discard any mussels which haven't opened and season to taste.

7 To serve, put a slice of the prepared garlic bread in the base of each warmed serving bowl and ladle the stew over the top. Serve with lemon wedges.

Monkfish with Caper Sauce

Monkfish is a very meaty-textured fish. It cooks very well as it doesn't flake like most other fish.

25 MINS   10 MINS

SERVES 4

INGREDIENTS

750 g/1 lb 10 oz monkfish tail

finely grated rind and juice 1 small lemon

2 tbsp olive oil

a small bunch of fresh bay leaves

1 small lemon, cut into wedges

SAUCE

6 tbsp olive oil

1 garlic clove, chopped finely

finely grated rind and juice 1 small lemon

1 tbsp chopped fresh parsley

2 tbsp capers, drained and chopped

3 anchovy fillets, chopped finely

pepper

1 Wash and pat dry the monkfish using paper towels. Carefully trim away the pinky grey membrane and slice either side of the central bone to give 2 thick fillets.

2 Cut the monkfish into 2.5 cm/1 inch cubes and place in a shallow dish. Toss in the lemon rind and juice and the olive oil.

3 Drain the fish, reserving the juices, and thread on to four bamboo skewers, threading a few bay leaves and wedges of lemon in between the fish cubes.

4 Preheat a grill (broiler) to medium. Place the skewers on a rack and cover the ends of the skewers with foil to prevent burning. Brush with some of the reserved juices and cook for 3 minutes. Turn over, brush again and cook for a further 3–4 minutes until tender and cooked through.

5 Meanwhile, mix together all the ingredients for the caper sauce and set aside.

6 Drain the skewers and transfer to warmed serving plates. Serve with the sauce and a green salad.

Pasta & Fish Pudding

This is a great recipe to cook mid-week when you want something satisfying and delicious, yet not too heavy.

NUTRITIONAL INFORMATION

Calories 454	Sugars 1g
Protein 30g	Fat 30g
Carbohydrate ...17g	Saturates 16g

 10 MINS   2 HOURS

SERVES 4

INGREDIENTS

115 g/4 oz/1 cup dried short-cut
   macaroni or penne

1 tbsp olive oil

15 g/½ oz/1 tbsp butter,
   plus extra for greasing

450 g/1 lb haddock fillets

2–3 fresh parsley sprigs

6 black peppercorns

125 ml/4 fl oz/½ cup double (heavy) cream

2 eggs, separated

2 tbsp chopped fresh dill

pinch of freshly grated nutmeg

60 g/2 oz/⅔ cup freshly grated
   Peccorino cheese

salt and pepper

fresh dill sprigs, to garnish

1 Bring a pan of salted water to the boil. Add the pasta and oil and cook for 8–10 minutes until tender, but still firm to the bite. Drain the pasta and return to the pan. Add the butter, cover and keep warm.

2 Place the fish in a frying pan (skillet). Add the parsley sprigs, peppercorns and enough water to cover. Bring to the boil, cover and simmer for 10 minutes. Lift out the fish and set aside to cool. Reserve the cooking liquid.

3 Skin the fish carefully and then cut into bite-size pieces. Put the pasta in a bowl. Mix the cream, egg yolks, chopped dill, nutmeg and Peccorino cheese together. Pour this mixture into the pasta and mix. Spoon in the fish without breaking it. Add enough of the reserved cooking liquid to make a moist, but firm mixture. Whisk the egg whites until stiff, then fold them into the mixture.

4 Grease a heatproof bowl and spoon in the fish mixture to within 4 cm/1½ inches of the rim. Cover with greased greaseproof (baking) paper and foil and tie securely with string.

5 Stand the bowl on a trivet in a saucepan. Add boiling water to reach halfway up the sides. Cover and steam for 1½ hours.

6 Invert the pudding carefully onto a serving plate. Garnish and serve immediately with a tomato relish or tartare sauce.

Ocean Pie

A tasty fish pie combining a mixture of fish and shellfish. You can use a wide variety of fish – whatever is available.

NUTRITIONAL INFORMATION

Calories	.599	Sugars	.8g
Protein	.45g	Fat	.21g
Carbohydrate	.58g	Saturates	.4g

15 MINS   1 HOUR

SERVES 4

INGREDIENTS

500 g/1 lb 2 oz cod or haddock fillet, skinned

225 g/8 oz salmon steak

425 ml/¾ pint/scant 2 cups skimmed milk

1 bay leaf

1 kg/2 lb potatoes

60 g/2 oz/⅓ cup peeled prawns (shrimp), thawed if frozen

60 g/2 oz/¼ cup margarine

25 g/1 oz/4 tbsp plain (all-purpose) flour

2–4 tbsp white wine

1 tsp chopped fresh dill or ½ tsp dried dill

2 tbsp drained capers

salt and pepper

few whole prawns (shrimp) in their shells, to garnish

1 Put the fish into a saucepan with 300 ml/½ pint/1¼ cups of the milk, the bay leaf and seasoning. Bring to the boil, cover and simmer gently for 10–15 minutes until tender.

2 Coarsely chop the potatoes and cook in boiling salted water until tender.

3 Drain the fish, reserving 300 ml/½ pint/1¼ cups of the cooking liquid (make up with more milk if necessary).

Flake the fish, discarding any bones and place in a shallow ovenproof dish. Add the prawns (shrimp).

4 Melt half the margarine in a saucepan, add the flour and cook, stirring, for a minute or so. Gradually stir in the reserved stock and the wine and bring to the boil. Add the dill, capers and seasoning to taste and simmer until thickened. Pour over the fish and mix well.

5 Drain the potatoes and mash, adding the remaining margarine, seasoning and sufficient milk to give a piping consistency.

6 Put the mashed potato into a piping bag. Use a large star nozzle (tip) and pipe over the fish. Cook in a preheated oven at 200°C/400°F/Gas Mark 6 for about 25 minutes until piping hot and browned. Serve garnished with prawns (shrimp).

Smoked Haddock Casserole

This quick, easy and inexpensive dish would be ideal for a mid-week family supper.

NUTRITIONAL INFORMATION

Calories	525	Sugars	.........8g
Protein	........41g	Fat	..........18g
Carbohydrate	...53g	Saturates	......10g

20 MINS   45 MINS

SERVES 4

INGREDIENTS

25 g/1 oz/2 tbsp butter, plus extra

   for greasing

450 g/1 lb smoked haddock fillets,

   cut into 4 slices

600 ml/1 pint/2½ cups milk

25 g/1 oz/¼ cup plain (all purpose) flour

pinch of freshly grated nutmeg

3 tbsp double (heavy) cream

1 tbsp chopped fresh parsley

2 eggs, hard boiled (hard cooked) and

   mashed to a pulp

450 g/1 lb/4 cups dried fusilli

1 tbsp lemon juice

salt and pepper

boiled new potatoes and beetroot (beet),

   to serve

1 Thoroughly grease a casserole with butter. Put the haddock in the casserole and pour over the milk. Bake in a preheated oven at 200°C/400°F/Gas Mark 6 for about 15 minutes. Carefully pour the cooking liquid into a jug (pitcher) without breaking up the fish.

2 Melt the butter in a saucepan and stir in the flour. Gradually whisk in the reserved cooking liquid. Season to taste with salt, pepper and nutmeg. Stir in the cream, parsley and mashed egg and cook, stirring constantly, for 2 minutes.

3 Meanwhile, bring a large saucepan of lightly salted water to the boil. Add the fusilli and lemon juice and cook for 8–10 minutes until tender, but still firm to the bite.

4 Drain the pasta and spoon or tip it over the fish. Top with the egg sauce and return the casserole to the oven for 10 minutes.

5 Serve the casserole with boiled new potatoes and beetroot (beet).

VARIATION

You can use any type of dried pasta for this casserole. Try penne, conchiglie or rigatoni.

Sardine & Potato Bake

Fresh sardines are now readily available, so this traditional dish from Liguria can be enjoyed by all.

NUTRITIONAL INFORMATION

Calories	626	Sugars	.........6g
Protein	........45g	Fat	..........29g
Carbohydrate	...43g	Saturates	.......8g

🍲 20 MINS   🕐 1 HOUR

SERVES 4

INGREDIENTS

1 kg/2 lb 4 oz potatoes

1 kg/2 lb 4 oz sardines, defrosted if frozen

1 tbsp olive oil, plus extra for oiling

1 onion, chopped

2–3 garlic cloves, crushed

2 tbsp chopped fresh parsley

350 g/12 oz ripe tomatoes, peeled and
   sliced or 400 g/14 oz can peeled
   tomatoes, partly drained and chopped

1–2 tbsp chopped fresh Italian herbs, such
   as oregano, thyme, rosemary, marjoram

150 ml/¼ pint/⅔ cup dry white wine

salt and pepper

1 Put the potatoes in a pan of salted water, bring to the boil, cover and simmer for 10 minutes, then drain. When cool enough to handle, cut into slices about 5 mm/¼ inch thick.

2 Gut and clean the sardines: cut off their heads and tails and then slit open the length of the belly. Turn the fish over so the skin is facing upwards and press firmly along the backbone to loosen the bones. Turn over again and carefully remove the backbone. Wash the fish in cold water, drain well and dry them on paper towels.

3 Heat the oil in a pan and fry the onion and garlic until soft, but not coloured.

4 Arrange the potatoes in a well-oiled ovenproof dish and sprinkle with the onions, parsley and plenty of salt and pepper to taste.

5 Lay the open sardines over the potatoes, skin-side down, then cover with the tomatoes and the rest of the herbs. Pour on the wine and season with salt and pepper.

6 Cook uncovered in a preheated oven, 190°C/180°F/Gas Mark 5, for about 40 minutes until the fish is tender. If the casserole seems to be drying out, add another couple of tablespoons of wine. Serve hot.

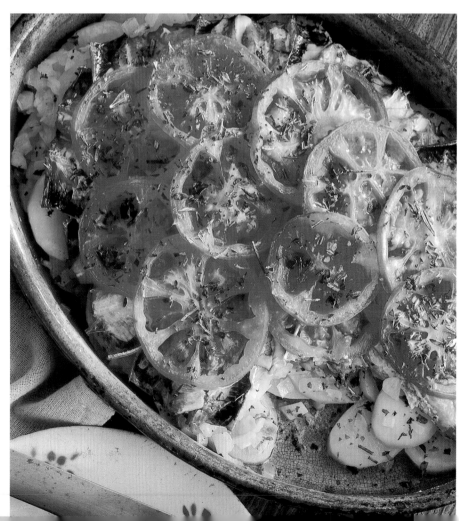

Salmon with Caper Sauce

The richness of salmon is beautifully balanced by the tangy capers in this creamy herb sauce.

NUTRITIONAL INFORMATION

Calories 302   Sugars 0g
Protein ....21g   Fat 24g
Carbohydrate ....1g   Saturates 9g

5 MINS   25 MINS

SERVES 4

INGREDIENTS

4 salmon fillets, skinned

1 fresh bay leaf

few black peppercorns

1 tsp white wine vinegar

150 ml/¼ pint/⅔ cup fish stock

3 tbsp double (heavy) cream

1 tbsp capers

1 tbsp chopped fresh dill

1 tbsp chopped fresh chives

1 tsp cornflour (cornstarch)

2 tbsp skimmed milk

salt and pepper

new potatoes, to serve

TO GARNISH

fresh dill sprigs

chive flowers

1 Lay the salmon fillets in a shallow ovenproof dish. Add the bay leaf, peppercorns, vinegar and stock.

2 Cover with foil and bake in a preheated oven at 180°C/350°F/ Gas Mark 4 for 15–20 minutes until the flesh is opaque and flakes easily when tested with a fork.

3 Transfer the fish to warmed serving plates, cover and keep warm.

4 Strain the cooking liquid into a saucepan. Stir in the cream, capers, dill and chives and seasoning to taste.

5 Blend the cornflour (cornstarch) with the milk. Add to the saucepan and heat, stirring, until thickened slightly. Boil for 1 minute.

6 Spoon the sauce over the salmon, garnish with dill sprigs and chive flowers.

7 Serve with new potatoes.

COOK'S TIP

Ask the fishmonger to skin the fillets for you. The cooking time for the salmon will depend on the thickness of the fish: the thin tail end of the salmon takes the least time to cook.

Soused Trout

In this recipe, fillets of trout are gently poached in a spiced vinegar, left to marinate for 24 hours and served cold with a potato salad.

NUTRITIONAL INFORMATION

Calories 521	Sugars 3g	
Protein 61g	Fat 20g	
Carbohydrate . . .27g	Saturates 4g	

5 HOURS   35 MINS

SERVES 4

I N G R E D I E N T S

4 trout, about 225–350 g/8–12 oz each, filleted

1 onion, sliced very thinly

2 bay leaves, preferably fresh

sprigs of fresh parsley and dill, or other fresh herbs

10–12 black peppercorns

4–6 cloves

good pinch of salt

150 ml/¼ pint/⅔ cup red wine vinegar

salad leaves, to garnish

P O T A T O   S A L A D

500 g/1 lb 2 oz small new potatoes

2 tbsp French dressing

4 tbsp thick low-fat mayonnaise

3–4 spring onions (scallions), sliced

1 Trim the trout fillets, cutting off any pieces of fin. If preferred, remove the skin – use a sharp knife and, beginning at the tail end, carefully cut the flesh from the skin, pressing the knife down firmly as you go.

2 Lightly grease a shallow ovenproof dish and lay the fillets in it, packing them fairly tightly together but keeping them in a single layer. Arrange the sliced onion, bay leaves and herbs over the fish.

3 Put the peppercorns, cloves, salt and vinegar into a saucepan and bring almost to the boil. Remove from the heat and pour evenly over the fish. Cover with foil and cook in a preheated oven at 160°C/325°F/ Gas Mark 3 for 15 minutes. Leave until cold, and then chill thoroughly.

4 Cook the potatoes in boiling salted water for 10–15 minutes until just tender. Drain. While still warm, cut into large dice and place in a bowl. Combine the French dressing and mayonnaise, add to the potatoes while warm and toss evenly. Leave until cold, then sprinkle the potato salad with chopped spring onions (scallions).

5 Pour a little of the juices over each portion of fish. Garnish with salad leaves and serve with the potato salad.

Baked Trout Mexican-Style

Make this dish as hot or as mild as you like by adjusting the amount of red chilli. The green chillies are milder and add a pungency to the dish.

NUTRITIONAL INFORMATION

Calories 329	Sugars 5g
Protein 53g	Fat 10g
Carbohydrate 6g	Saturates 2g

 10 MINS   30 MINS

SERVES 4

INGREDIENTS

4 trout, 225 g/8 oz each

1 small bunch fresh coriander (cilantro)

4 shallots, shredded finely

1 small yellow (bell) pepper, deseeded and very finely chopped

1 small red (bell) pepper, deseeded and very finely chopped

2 green chillies, deseeded and finely chopped

1–2 red chillies, deseeded and finely chopped

1 tbsp lemon juice

1 tbsp white wine vinegar

2 tsp caster (superfine) sugar

salt and pepper

fresh coriander (cilantro), to garnish

salad leaves, to serve

1 Preheat the oven to 180°C/350°F/Gas Mark 4. Wash the trout and pat dry with kitchen paper (paper towels). Season and stuff with coriander (cilantro) leaves.

2 Place the fish side by side in a shallow ovenproof dish. Sprinkle over the shallots, (bell) peppers and chillies.

3 Mix together the lemon juice, vinegar and sugar in a bowl. Spoon over the trout and season with salt and pepper. Cover the dish and bake for 30 minutes or until the fish is tender and the flesh is opaque.

4 Remove the the fish with a fish slice and drain. Transfer to warm serving plates and spoon the cooking juices over the fish. Garnish with fresh coriander (cilantro) and serve with salad and chilli bean rice (see Cook's Tip).

COOK'S TIP

For the chilli bean rice, cook 225 g/8 oz/1¼ cup long-grain white rice. Drain and rinse a 400 g/14 oz can kidney beans and stir into the rice with 1 tsp each of ground cumin and coriander. Stir in 4 tbsp chopped fresh coriander (cilantro) and season.

Bajan Fish

Bajan seasoning comes from Barbados and can be used with all kinds of meat, fish, poultry and game. Add more chilli if you like it really hot.

NUTRITIONAL INFORMATION

Calories	247	Sugars	.........4g
Protein	........27g	Fat	..........12g
Carbohydrate	....5g	Saturates	.......1g

45 MINS   15 MINS

SERVES 4

INGREDIENTS

500-625 g /1 lb 2 oz-1 lb 6 oz monkfish tails, boned and cubed

2 large carrots

175-225 g/6-8 oz baby sweetcorn

3 tbsp sunflower oil

1 yellow (bell) pepper, cored, seeded and thinly sliced

1 tbsp wine vinegar

150 ml/¼ pint/⅔ cup fish or vegetable stock

1 tbsp lemon juice

2 tbsp sherry

1 tsp cornflour (cornstarch)

salt and pepper

fresh herbs and lemon slices, to garnish

BAJAN SEASONING

1 small onion, quartered

2 shallots

3-4 garlic cloves, crushed

4-6 large spring onions (scallions), sliced

small handful of fresh parsley

2-3 sprigs of fresh thyme

small strip of green chilli peper, seeds removed, or ½-¼ tsp chilli powder

½ tsp salt

¼ tsp freshly ground black pepper

2 tbsp brown rum or red wine vinegar

1 Process the ingredients for the Bajan seasoning very finely. Put the fish in a dish, spread with the seasoning to coat evenly. Cover and chill for 30 minutes.

2 Cut the carrots into narrow 4 cm/ 1½ inch slices. Slice the baby sweetcorn diagonally. Heat 2 tablespoons of oil in the wok, swirling it around until really hot. Add the fish and stir-fry for 3-4 minutes. Remove to a bowl and keep warm.

3 Add the remaining oil and stir-fry the carrots and corn for 2 minutes. Add the (bell) pepper and stir-fry for another minute. Return the fish and juices to the wok and stir-fry for 1-2 minutes.

4 Blend the vinegar, stock, lemon juice, sherry and seasoning with the cornflour (cornstarch). Stir into the wok and boil until thickened. Serve garnished with herbs and lemon.

Smoky Fish Skewers

The combination of fresh and smoked fish gives these kebabs a special flavour. Choose thick fish fillets to get good-sized pieces.

NUTRITIONAL INFORMATION

Calories	221	Sugars	.........0g
Protein	........33g	Fat	..........10g
Carbohydrate	....0g	Saturates	.......1g

4 HOURS   10 MINS

SERVES 4

INGREDIENTS

350 g/12 oz smoked cod fillet

350 g/12 oz cod fillet

8 large raw prawns (shrimp)

8 bay leaves

fresh dill, to garnish (optional)

MARINADE

4 tbsp sunflower oil, plus a little for
   brushing

2 tbsp lemon or lime juice

rind of ½ lemon or lime, grated

¼ tsp dried dill

salt and pepper

1 Skin both types of cod and cut the flesh into bite-size pieces. Peel the prawns (shrimp), leaving just the tail.

2 To make the marinade, combine the oil, lemon or lime juice and rind, dill and salt and pepper to taste in a shallow, non-metallic dish.

3 Place the prepared fish in the marinade and stir together until the fish is well coated on all sides. Leave the fish to marinate for 1–4 hours.

4 Thread the fish on to 4 skewers, alternating the 2 types of cod with the prawns (shrimp) and bay leaves.

5 Cover the rack with lightly oiled kitchen foil and place the fish skewers on top of the foil.

6 Barbecue (grill) the fish skewers over hot coals for 5-10 minutes, basting with any remaining marinade, turning once.

7 Garnish the skewers with fresh dill (if using) and serve immediately.

COOK'S TIP

Cod fillet can be rather flaky, so choose the thicker end which is easier to cut into chunky pieces. Cook the fish on kitchen foil rather directly on the rack, so that if the fish breaks away from the skewer, it is not wasted.

Citrus Fish Kebabs

Use your favourite fish for this dish as long as it is firm enough to thread on to skewer. The tang of orange makes this a refreshing meal.

NUTRITIONAL INFORMATION

Calories	333	Sugars	........10g
Protein	........41g	Fat	..........14g
Carbohydrate	...10g	Saturates	.......3g

2¹/₂ HOURS   10 MINS

SERVES 4

INGREDIENTS

450 g/1 lb firm white fish fillets (such as cod or monkfish)

450 g/1 lb thick salmon fillet

2 large oranges

1 pink grapefruit

1 bunch fresh bay leaves

1 tsp finely grated lemon rind

3 tbsp lemon juice

2 tsp clear honey

2 garlic cloves, crushed

salt and pepper

TO SERVE

crusty bread

mixed salad

1 Skin the white fish and the salmon, rinse and pat dry on kitchen paper (paper towels). Cut each fillet into 16 pieces.

2 Using a sharp knife, remove the skin and pith from the oranges and grapefruit. Cut out the segments of flesh, removing all remaining traces of the pith and dividing membrane.

3 Thread the pieces of fish alternately with the orange and grapefruit segments and the bay leaves onto 8 skewers. Place the kebabs in a shallow dish.

4 In a small bowl, mix together the lemon rind and juice, the honey and garlic.

5 Pour over the fish kebabs and then season well. Cover and chill for 2 hours, turning occasionally.

6 Preheat the grill (broiler) to medium. Remove the fish kebabs from the marinade and place on the rack.

7 Cook for 7–8 minutes, turning once, until cooked through.

8 Drain, transfer to serving plates and serve with crusty bread and a fresh mixed salad.

Fragrant Tuna Steaks

Fresh tuna steaks are very meaty – they have a firm texture, yet the flesh is succulent. Steaks from the belly are best of all.

NUTRITIONAL INFORMATION

Calories ....239 Sugars 0.1g
Protein ....42g Fat 8g
Carbohydrate ...0.5g Saturates 2g

15 MINS   15 MINS

SERVES 4

INGREDIENTS

4 tuna steaks, 175 g/6 oz each

½ tsp finely grated lime rind

1 garlic clove, crushed

2 tsp olive oil

1 tsp ground cumin

1 tsp ground coriander

pepper

1 tbsp lime juice

fresh coriander (cilantro), to garnish

TO SERVE

avocado relish (see Cook's Tip, below)

lime wedges

tomato wedges

COOK'S TIP

For the avocado relish, peel and chop a small ripe avocado. Mix in 1 tbsp lime juice, 1 tbsp freshly chopped coriander (cilantro), 1 small finely chopped red onion and some chopped fresh mango or tomato. Season to taste.

1 Trim the skin from the tuna steaks, rinse and pat dry on absorbent kitchen paper (paper towels).

2 In a small bowl, mix together the lime rind, garlic, olive oil, cumin, ground coriander and pepper to make a paste.

3 Spread the paste thinly on both sides of the tuna. Heat a non-stick, ridged frying pan (skillet) until hot and press the

tuna steaks into the pan to seal them. Lower the heat and cook for 5 minutes. Turn the fish over and cook for a further 4–5 minutes until the fish is cooked through. Drain on kitchen paper (paper towels) and transfer to a serving plate.

4 Sprinkle the lime juice and chopped coriander (cilantro) over the fish. Serve with avocado relish (see Cook's Tip), and tomato and lime wedges.

Sole Paupiettes

A delicate dish of sole fillets rolled up with spinach and prawns, (shrimp), and served in a creamy ginger sauce.

NUTRITIONAL INFORMATION

Calories 253   Sugars 7g
Protein . . . . .24g   Fat 14g
Carbohydrate . . . .9g   Saturates 5g

10 MINS   45 MINS

SERVES 4

INGREDIENTS

125 g/4½ oz fresh young spinach leaves

2 Dover soles or large lemon soles or plaice, filleted

125 g/4½ oz peeled prawns (shrimp), defrosted if frozen

2 tsp sunflower oil

2-4 spring onions (scallions), finely sliced diagonally

2 thin slices ginger root, finely chopped

150 ml/¼ pint/⅔ cup fish stock or water

2 tsp cornflour (cornstarch)

4 tbsp single cream

6 tbsp low-fat natural yogurt

salt and pepper

whole prawns (shrimp), to garnish (optional)

1 Strip the stalks off the spinach, wash and dry on kitchen paper (paper towels). Divide the spinach between the seasoned fish fillets, laying the leaves on the skin side. Divide half the prawns (shrimp) between them. Roll up the fillets from head to tail and secure with wooden cocktail sticks. Arrange the rolls on a plate in the base of a bamboo steamer.

2 Stand a low metal trivet in the wok and add enough water to come almost to the top of it. Bring to the boil.

Place the bamboo steamer on the trivet, cover with the steamer lid and then the wok lid, or cover tightly with a domed piece of foil. Steam gently for 30 minutes until the fish is tender and cooked through.

3 Remove the fish rolls and keep warm. Empty the wok and wipe dry with kitchen paper (paper towels). Heat the oil in the wok, swirling it around until really hot. Add the spring onions (scallions) and ginger and stir-fry for 1-2 minutes.

4 Add the stock to the wok and bring to the boil. Blend the cornflour (cornstarch) with the cream. Add the yogurt and remaining prawns (shrimp) to the wok and heat gently until boiling. Add a little sauce to the blended cream and return it all to the wok. Heat gently until thickened and season to taste. Serve the paupiettes with the sauce spooned over and garnished with whole prawns (shrimp), if using.

Char-grilled Mackerel

The sharpness of the apricot glaze complements the oiliness of the fish and has a delicious hint of ginger.

NUTRITIONAL INFORMATION

Calories 343   Sugars 21g
Protein ....23g   Fat 18g
Carbohydrate ...22g   Saturates 4g

 5 MINS   10 MINS

SERVES 4

INGREDIENTS

4 mackerel, about 225 g/8 oz each

400 g/14 oz can apricots in natural juice

3 tbsp dark muscovado sugar

3 tbsp Worcestershire sauce

3 tbsp soy sauce

2 tbsp tomato purée (paste)

1 tsp ground ginger

dash Tabasco sauce

1 clove garlic, crushed (optional)

salt and pepper

1 Clean and gut the mackerel, removing the heads if preferred. Place the fish in a shallow dish.

2 Drain the apricots, reserving the juice. Roughly chop half of the apricots and set aside. Place the remaining apricots in a food processor with the sugar, Worcestershire sauce, soy sauce, tomato purée (paste), ginger, Tabasco sauce and garlic (if using) and process until smooth. Alternatively, chop the apricots and mix with the other ingredients. Season to taste.

3 Pour the sauce over the fish, turning them so that they are well coated on both sides. Leave to chill in the refrigerator until required.

4 Transfer the mackerel to the barbecue (grill) either directly on the rack or on a piece of greased kitchen foil. Barbecue (grill) the mackerel over hot coals for 5–7 minutes, turning once.

5 Spoon any remaining marinade into a saucepan. Add the reserved chopped apricots and about half of the reserved apricot juice and bring to the boil. Reduce the heat and simmer for 2 minutes. Transfer the mackerel to a serving plate and serve with the apricot sauce.

COOK'S TIP

Use a hinged rack if you have one as it will make it much easier to turn the fish during barbecueing (grilling).

Fish with Black Bean Sauce

Any firm and delicate fish steaks such as salmon or salmon trout can be cooked by the same method.

NUTRITIONAL INFORMATION

Calories ....194 Sugars 0.2g
Protein ....27g Fat 9g
Carbohydrate ....1g Saturates 2g

  5 MINS   20 MINS

SERVES 6

INGREDIENTS

1 sea bass, trout or turbot, weighing about 700g/1 lb 9 oz, cleaned

1 tsp salt

1 tbsp sesame oil

2-3 spring onions (scallions), cut in half lengthways

1 tbsp light soy sauce

1 tbsp Chinese rice wine or dry sherry

1 tbsp finely shredded ginger root

1 tbsp oil

2 tbsp crushed black bean sauce

2 finely shredded spring onions (scallions)

fresh coriander leaves, to garnish (optional)

lemon slices, to garnish

1 Score both sides of the fish with diagonal cuts at 2.5 cm (1 inch) intervals. Rub both the inside and outside of the fish with salt and sesame oil.

2 Place the fish on top of the spring onions (scallions) on a heat-proof platter. Blend the soy sauce and wine with the ginger shreds and pour evenly all over the fish.

3 Place the fish on the platter in a very hot steamer (or inside a wok on a rack), cover and steam vigorously for 12-15 minutes.

4 Heat the oil until hot, then blend in the black bean sauce. Remove the fish from the steamer and place on a serving dish.

5 Pour the hot black bean sauce over the whole length of the fish and place the shredded spring onions (scallions) on top. Place the fish on a platter and serve garnished with coriander leaves (if using) and lemon slices.

COOK'S TIP

If using fish steaks, rub them with the salt and sesame oil, but do not score with a knife. The fish may require less cooking, depending on the thickness of the steaks – test with a skewer after about 8 minutes to check whether they are done.

Monkfish Kebabs (Kabobs)

A simple basting sauce is brushed over these tasty kebabs (kabobs), which make a perfect light meal on their own.

NUTRITIONAL INFORMATION

Calories 209   Sugars 1g
Protein . . . . .20g   Fat 14g
Carbohydrate . . . .1g   Saturates 2g

20 MINS   15 MINS

SERVES 4

INGREDIENTS

450 g/1 lb monkfish tail

2 courgettes (zucchini)

1 lemon

12 cherry tomatoes

8 bay leaves

SAUCE

4 tbsp olive oil

2 tbsp lemon juice

1 tsp chopped, fresh thyme

½ tsp lemon pepper

salt

TO SERVE

green salad leaves

fresh, crusty bread

VARIATION

Use plaice (flounder) fillets instead of the monkfish, if you prefer. Allow two fillets per person, and skin and cut each fillet lengthwise into two. Roll up each piece and thread them on to the skewers.

1 Cut the monkfish into 5 cm/2 inch chunks. Cut the courgettes (zucchini) into thick slices and the lemon into wedges.

2 Thread the monkfish, courgettes (zucchini), lemon, tomatoes and bay leaves on to 4 skewers.

3 To make the basting sauce, combine the oil, lemon juice, thyme, lemon pepper and salt to taste in a small bowl.

4 Brush the basting sauce liberally all over the fish, lemon, tomatoes and bay leaves.

5 Cook the kebabs (kabobs) on the barbecue (grill) for about 15 minutes, basting frequently with the sauce, until the fish is cooked through.

6 Serve the kebabs (kabobs) with green salad leaves and lots of warm, fresh crusty bread.

Baked Red Snapper

You can substitute other whole fish for the snapper, or use cutlets of cod or halibut.

NUTRITIONAL INFORMATION

Calories . . . . .519 Sugars 12g
Protein . . . . .61g Fat 23g
Carbohydrate . . .18g Saturates 3g

20 MINS   50 MINS

SERVES 4

INGREDIENTS

1 red snapper, about 1.25 kg/2 lb 12 oz, cleaned

juice of 2 limes, or 1 lemon

4-5 sprigs of thyme or parsley

3 tbsp olive oil

1 large onion, chopped

2 garlic cloves, finely chopped

1 x 425 g/15 oz can chopped tomatoes

2 tbsp tomato purée (paste)

2 tbsp red wine vinegar

5 tbsp low-fat yogurt

2 tbsp chopped parsley

2 tsp dried oregano

6 tbsp dry breadcrumbs

60 g/2 oz/¼ cup feta cheese, crumbled

salt and pepper

SALAD

1 small lettuce, thickly sliced

10-12 young spinach leaves, torn

½ small cucumber, sliced and quartered

4 spring onions (scallions), thickly sliced

3 tbsp chopped parsley

2 tbsp olive oil

2 tbsp plain low-fat yogurt

1 tbsp red wine vinegar

1 Sprinkle the lime or lemon juice inside and over the fish and season. Place the herbs inside the fish.

2 Heat the oil in a pan and fry the onion until translucent. Stir in the garlic and cook for 1 minute, then add the chopped tomatoes, tomato purée (paste) and vinegar. Simmer, uncovered, for 5 minutes. Allow the sauce to cool, then stir in the yogurt, parsley and oregano.

3 Pour half the sauce into an ovenproof dish just large enough for the fish. Add the fish an then pour the remainder of the sauce over it, and sprinkle with breadcrumbs. Bake uncovered for 30-35 minutes. Sprinkle the cheese over the fish and serve with lime wedges and dill sprigs.

4 Arrange the salad ingredients in a bowl. Whisk the oil, yogurt and vinegar and pour over the salad.

Salmon Lasagne Rolls

Sheets of green lasagne are filled with a mixture of fresh salmon and oyster mushrooms. This recipe has been adapted for the microwave.

NUTRITIONAL INFORMATION

Calories 352	Sugars 5g	
Protein 19g	Fat 19g	
Carbohydrate ...25g	Saturates 9g	

20 MINS   35 MINS

SERVES 4

INGREDIENTS

8 sheets green lasagne

1 onion, sliced

15 g/½ oz/1 tbsp butter

½ red (bell) pepper, chopped

1 courgette (zucchini), diced

1 tsp chopped ginger root

125 g/4½ oz oyster mushrooms, preferably yellow, chopped coarsely

225 g/8 oz fresh salmon fillet, skinned, and cut into chunks

2 tbsp dry sherry

2 tsp cornflour (cornstarch)

20 g/¾ oz/3 tbsp plain (all-purpose) flour

20 g/¾ oz/1½ tbsp butter

300 ml/½ pint/1¼ cups milk

25 g/1 oz/¼ cup Cheddar cheese, grated

15 g/½ oz/¼ cup fresh white breadcrumbs

salt and pepper

salad leaves, to serve

1 Place the lasagne sheets in a large shallow dish. Cover with plenty of boiling water. Cook on HIGH power for 5 minutes. Leave to stand, covered, for a few minutes before draining. Rinse in cold water and lay the sheets out on a clean work surface.

2 Put the onion and butter into a bowl. Cover and cook on HIGH power for 2 minutes. Add the (bell) pepper, courgette (zucchini) and ginger root. Cover and cook on HIGH power for 3 minutes.

3 Add the mushrooms and salmon to the bowl. Mix the sherry into the cornflour (cornstarch) then stir into the bowl. Cover and cook on HIGH power for 4 minutes until the fish flakes when tested with a fork. Season to taste.

4 Whisk the flour, butter and milk in a bowl. Cook on HIGH power for 3–4 minutes, whisking every minute, to give a sauce of coating consistency. Stir in half the cheese and season with salt and pepper to taste.

5 Spoon the salmon filling in equal quantities along the shorter side of each lasagne sheet. Roll up to enclose the filling. Arrange in a lightly oiled large rectangular dish. Pour over the sauce and sprinkle over the remaining cheese and the breadcrumbs.

6 Cook on HIGH power for 3 minutes until heated through. If possible, lightly brown under a preheated grill (broiler) before serving. Serve with salad.

Baked Seabass

Seabass is often paired with subtle oriental flavours. For a special occasion, you may like to bone the fish.

NUTRITIONAL INFORMATION

Calories	140	Sugars	.......0.1g
Protein	........29g	Fat	...........1g
Carbohydrate	...0.1g	Saturates	.....0.2g

 10 MINS   15 MINS

SERVES 4–6

INGREDIENTS

2 seabass, about 1 kg/2 lb 4 oz each, cleaned and scaled

2 spring onions (scallions), green part only, cut into strips

5 cm/2 inch piece ginger, peeled and cut into strips

2 garlic cloves, unpeeled, crushed lightly

2 tbsp mirin or dry sherry

salt and pepper

TO SERVE

pickled sushi ginger (optional)

soy sauce

1 For each fish lay out a double thickness of foil and oil the top piece well, or lay a piece of silicon paper over the foil.

2 Place the fish in the middle and expose the cavity.

3 Divide the spring onion (scallion) and ginger between each cavity. Put a garlic clove in each cavity.

4 Pour over the mirin or dry sherry. Season the fish well.

5 Close the cavities and lay each fish on its side. Bring over the foil and fold

the edges together to seal securely. Fold each end neatly.

6 Cook over a medium barbecue (grill) for 15 minutes, turning once.

7 To serve, remove the foil and cut each fish into 2 or 3 pieces.

8 Serve with the pickled ginger (if using) accompanied by soy sauce.

COOK'S TIP

Fresh seabass is just as delicious when cooked very simply. Stuff the fish with garlic and chopped herbs, brush with olive oil and bake in the oven.

Five-Spice Salmon

Five-spice powder is a blend of star anise, fennel, cinamon, cloves and Szechwan peppercorns (fagara) that is often used in Chinese dishes.

NUTRITIONAL INFORMATION

Calories	267	Sugars	.........3g
Protein	........24g	Fat	..........17g
Carbohydrate	....4g	Saturates	.......3g

15 MINS   15 MINS

SERVES 4

INGREDIENTS

4 salmon fillets, skinned, 125 g/4½ oz
  each

2 tsp five-spice powder

1 large leek

1 large carrot

115 g/4 oz mangetout (snow peas)

2.5 cm/1 inch piece root (fresh) ginger

2 tbsp ginger wine

2 tbsp light soy sauce

1 tbsp vegetable oil

salt and pepper

TO GARNISH

shredded leek

root (fresh) ginger, shredded

carrot, shredded

1 Wash the salmon and pat dry on kitchen paper (paper towels). Rub the five-spice powder into both sides of the fish and season with salt and pepper. Set aside until required.

2 Trim the leek, slice it down the centre and rinse under cold water to remove any dirt. Finely shred the leek. Peel the carrot and cut it into very thin strips. Top and tail the mangetout (snow peas) and cut them into shreds. Peel the ginger and slice thinly into strips.

3 Place all of the vegetables into a large bowl and toss in the ginger wine and 1 tablespoon soy sauce.

4 Preheat the grill (broiler) to medium. Place the salmon fillets on the rack and brush with the remaining soy sauce. Cook for 2–3 minutes on each side until cooked through.

5 While the salmon is cooking, heat the oil in a non-stick wok or large frying pan (skillet) and stir-fry the vegetables for 5 minutes until just tender. Take care that you do not overcook the vegetables – they should still have bite. Transfer to serving plates. Drain the salmon on kitchen paper and serve on a bed of stir-fried vegetables. Garnish with shredded leek, ginger and carrot.

COOK'S TIP

Five-spice powder is strong and pungent and should be used sparingly.

Spaghetti, Tuna & Parsley

This is a recipe to look forward to when parsley is at its most prolific, in the growing season.

NUTRITIONAL INFORMATION

Calories 970   Sugars 2g
Protein . . . . .23g   Fat 80g
Carbohydrate . . .42g   Saturates 18g

10 MINS   15 MINS

SERVES 4

I N G R E D I E N T S

500 g/1 lb 2 oz spaghetti

1 tbsp olive oil

25 g/1 oz/2 tbsp butter

black olives, to serve (optional)

S A U C E

200 g/7 oz can tuna, drained

60 g/2 oz can anchovies, drained

250 ml/9 fl oz/1 cup olive oil

250 ml/9 fl oz/1 cup roughly chopped fresh,
 flat-leaf parsley

150 ml/¼ pint/⅔ cup crème fraîche

salt and pepper

1 Cook the spaghetti in a large saucepan of salted boiling water, adding the olive oil, for 8–10 minutes or until tender. Drain the spaghetti in a colander and return to the pan. Add the butter, toss thoroughly to coat and keep warm until required.

2 Remove any bones from the tuna and flake into smaller pieces, using 2 forks. Put the tuna in a blender or food processor with the anchovies, olive oil and parsley and process until the sauce is smooth. Pour in the crème fraîche and process for a few seconds to blend. Taste the sauce and season with salt and pepper.

3 Warm 4 plates. Shake the saucepan of spaghetti over a medium heat for a few minutes or until it is thoroughly warmed through.

4 Pour the sauce over the spaghetti and toss quickly, using 2 forks. Serve immediately with a small dish of black olives, if liked.

Macaroni & Tuna Fish Layer

A layer of tuna fish with garlic, mushroom and red (bell) pepper is sandwiched between two layers of macaroni with a crunchy topping.

NUTRITIONAL INFORMATION

Calories 691   Sugars 10g
Protein . . . . .41g   Fat 33g
Carbohydrate . . .62g   Saturates 15g

20 MINS   50 MINS

SERVES 2

INGREDIENTS

125–150 g/4½–5½ oz/1¼ cup dried
macaroni

2 tbsp oil

1 garlic clove, crushed

60 g/2 oz/¾ cup button mushrooms, sliced

½ red (bell) pepper, thinly sliced

200 g/7 oz can of tuna fish in brine,
drained and flaked

½ tsp dried oregano

salt and pepper

SAUCE

25 g/1 oz/2 tbsp butter or margarine

1 tbsp plain (all-purpose) flour

250 ml/9 fl oz/1 cup milk

2 tomatoes, sliced

2 tbsp dried breadcrumbs

25 g/1 oz/¼ cup mature (sharp) Cheddar or
Parmesan cheese, grated

VARIATION

Replace the tuna fish with
chopped cooked chicken, beef,
pork or ham or with 3–4 sliced
hard-boiled (hard-cooked) eggs.

1 Cook the macaroni in boiling salted water, with 1 tablespoon of the oil added, for 10–12 minutes or until tender. Drain, rinse and drain thoroughly.

2 Heat the remaining oil in a saucepan or frying pan (skillet) and fry the garlic, mushrooms and (bell) pepper until soft. Add the tuna fish, oregano and seasoning, and heat through.

3 Grease an ovenproof dish (about 1 litre/1¾ pint/4 cup capacity), and add half of the cooked macaroni. Cover with the tuna mixture and then add the remaining macaroni.

4 To make the sauce, melt the butter or margarine in a saucepan, stir in the flour and cook for 1 minute. Add the milk gradually and bring to the boil. Simmer for 1–2 minutes, stirring continuously, until thickened. Season to taste. Pour the sauce over the macaroni.

5 Lay the sliced tomatoes over the sauce and sprinkle with the breadcrumbs and cheese.

6 Place in a preheated oven, at 200°C/400°F/Gas Mark 6, for about 25 minutes, or until piping hot and the top is well browned.

Cannelloni Filetti di Sogliola

This is a lighter dish than the better-known cannelloni stuffed with minced beef.

NUTRITIONAL INFORMATION

Calories	555	Sugars	. . . . .4g
Protein	. . . . .53g	Fat	. . . . .21g
Carbohydrate	. . .36g	Saturates	. . . . . .12g

20 MINS   45 MINS

SERVES 6

I N G R E D I E N T S

12 small **fillets** of sole (115 g/4 oz each)

150 ml/¼ **pint**/⅝ cup red wine

90 g/3 oz/**6 tbsp** butter

115 g/4 oz/3 ⅞ cups sliced button
　mushrooms

4 shallots, **finely** chopped

115 g/4 oz tomatoes, chopped

2 tbsp **tomato** purée (paste)

60 g/2 oz/ ½ **cup** plain (all purpose)
　flour, **sifted**

150 ml/¼ **pint**/⅝ cup warm milk

2 tbsp **double** (heavy) cream

6 dried **cannelloni** tubes

175 g/6 oz **cooked**, peeled prawns (shrimp),
　preferably freshwater

salt and **pepper**

1 fresh **fennel** sprig, to garnish

1 Brush the fillets with a little wine, season with salt and pepper and roll them up, skin side inwards. Secure with a skewer or cocktail stick (toothpick).

2 Arrange the fish rolls in a single layer in a large frying pan (skillet), add the remaining red wine and poach for 4 minutes. Remove from the pan; reserve the liquid.

3 Melt the butter in another pan. Fry the mushrooms and shallots for 2 minutes, then add the tomatoes and tomato purée (paste). Season the flour and stir it into the pan. Stir in the reserved cooking liquid and half the milk. Cook over a low heat, stirring, for 4 minutes. Remove from the heat and stir in the cream.

4 Bring a large saucepan of lightly salted water to the boil. Add the cannelloni and cook for about 8 minutes, until tender but still firm to the bite. Drain and set aside to cool.

5 Remove the skewers or cocktail sticks (toothpicks) from the fish rolls. Put 2 sole fillets into each cannelloni tube with 2–3 prawns (shrimp) and a little red wine sauce. Arrange the cannelloni in an ovenproof dish, pour over the sauce and bake in a preheated oven at 200°C/400°F/Gas 6 for 20 minutes.

6 Serve the cannelloni with the red wine sauce, garnished with the remaining prawns (shrimp) and a fresh sprig of fennel.

Seafood in Red Curry Sauce

For something very quick and simple that sets your tastebuds alight, try this inspired dish of prawns (shrimp) in a wonderfully spicy sauce.

NUTRITIONAL INFORMATION

Calories	175	Sugars	.........3g
Protein	........29g	Fat	...........5g
Carbohydrate	....3g	Saturates	......1g

10 MINS   10 MINS

SERVES 4

INGREDIENTS

1 tbsp vegetable oil

6 spring onions (scallions), trimmed and sliced

1 stalk lemon grass

1 cm/½ inch piece of fresh ginger root

250 ml/9 fl oz/1 cup coconut milk

2 tbsp Thai red curry paste

1 tbsp fish sauce

500 g/1 lb 2 oz/3 cups uncooked king prawns (jumbo shrimp)

1 tbsp chopped fresh coriander (cilantro)

fresh chillies, to garnish

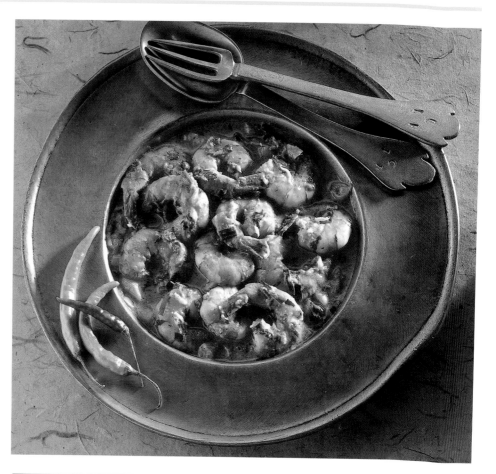

1 Heat the vegetable oil in a wok or large frying pan (skillet) and fry the spring onions (scallions) gently until softened, about 2 minutes.

VARIATION

Try this recipe using Thai green curry sauce instead of red. Both varieties are obtainable from many supermarkets – look for them in the oriental foods section.

2 Bruise the stalk of lemon grass using a meat mallet or rolling pin.

3 Peel and finely grate the piece of fresh ginger root.

4 Add the bruised lemon grass and grated ginger root to the wok or frying pan (skillet) with the coconut milk, Thai red curry paste and fish sauce. Heat the coconut milk until almost boiling.

5 Peel the prawns (shrimp), leaving the tails intact. Remove the black vein along the back of each prawn (shrimp).

6 Add the prawns (shrimp) to the wok or frying pan (skillet) with the chopped coriander (cilantro) and cook gently for 5 minutes.

7 Serve the prawns (shrimp) with the sauce, garnished with fresh chillies.

Caribbean Prawns (Shrimp)

This is an ideal recipe for cooks who have difficulty in finding raw prawns (shrimp).

NUTRITIONAL INFORMATION

Calories . . . . .110 Sugars 15g
Protein . . . . .5g Fat 4g
Carbohydrate . . .15g Saturates 3g

 40 MINS   15 MINS

SERVES 4

I N G R E D I E N T S

16 cooked king (tiger) prawns (shrimp)

1 small pineapple

flaked coconut, to garnish (optional)

M A R I N A D E

150 ml/5 fl oz/⅔ cup pineapple juice

2 tbsp white wine vinegar

2 tbsp dark muscovado sugar

2 tbsp desiccated (shredded) coconut

1 If they are unpeeled, peel the prawns (shrimp), leaving the tails attached if preferred.

2 Peel the pineapple and cut it in half lengthways. Cut one pineapple half into wedges then into chunks.

3 To make the marinade, mix together half of the pineapple juice and the vinegar, sugar and coconut in a shallow, non-metallic dish. Add the peeled prawns (shrimp) and pineapple chunks and toss until well coated. Leave the prawns and pineapple to marinate for at least 30 minutes.

4 Remove the pineapple and prawns (shrimp) from the marinade and thread them on to skewers. Reserve the marinade.

5 Strain the marinade and place in a food processor. Roughly chop the remaining pineapple and add to the processor with the remaining pineapple juice. Process the pineapple for a few seconds to produce a thick sauce.

6 Pour the sauce into a small saucepan. Bring to the boil then simmer for about 5 minutes. If you prefer, you can heat up the sauce by the side of the barbecue (grill).

7 Transfer the kebabs to the barbecue (grill) and brush with some of the sauce. Barbecue (grill) for about 5 minutes until the kebabs are piping hot. Turn the kebabs, brushing occasionally with the sauce. Serve the kebabs with extra sauce, sprinkled with flaked coconut (if using).

Prawn (Shrimp) Omelette

This really is a meal in minutes, combining many Chinese ingredients for a truly tasty dish.

NUTRITIONAL INFORMATION

Calories 270   Sugars 1g
Protein . . . . .30g   Fat 15g
Carbohydrate . . . .3g   Saturates 3g

5 MINS   10 MINS

SERVES 4

INGREDIENTS

2 tbsp sunflower oil

4 spring onions (scallions)

350 g/12 oz peeled prawns (shrimp)

100 g/3½ oz/1 cup bean sprouts

1 tsp cornflour (cornstarch)

1 tbsp light soy sauce

6 eggs

3 tbsp cold water

1 Heat the sunflower oil in a large preheated wok or frying pan (skillet).

2 Using a sharp knife, trim the spring onions (scallions) and cut into slices.

3 Add the prawns (shrimp), spring onions (scallions) and bean sprouts to the wok and stir-fry for 2 minutes.

4 In a small bowl, mix together the cornflour (cornstarch) and soy sauce until well combined.

5 In a separate bowl, beat the eggs with the water, using a metal fork, and then blend with the cornflour (cornstarch) and soy mixture.

6 Add the egg mixture to the wok and cook for 5–6 minutes, or until the mixture sets.

7 Transfer the omelette to a warm serving plate and cut into quarters to serve.

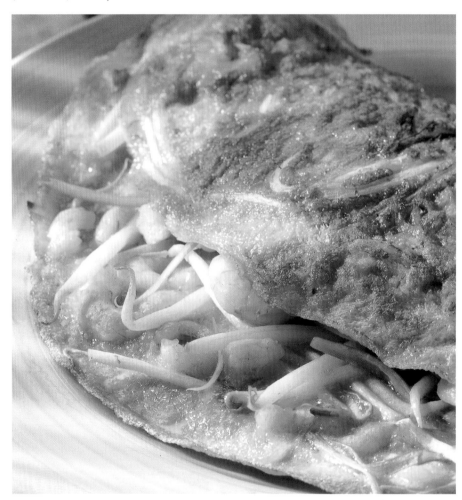

COOK'S TIP

It is important to use fresh bean sprouts for this dish as the canned ones don't have the crunchy texture necessary.

Prawn (Shrimp) Biryani

The flavours in this recipe are quite subtle, so it is a lighter dish and therefore suitable for every day.

NUTRITIONAL INFORMATION

Calories ....177 Sugars 6g
Protein ....15g Fat 6g
Carbohydrate ...18g Saturates 0.5g

2½ HOURS   45 MINS

SERVES 8

INGREDIENTS

1 tsp saffron strands

50 ml/2 fl oz/4 tbsp tepid water

2 shallots, chopped coarsely

3 garlic cloves, crushed

1 tsp chopped ginger root

2 tsp coriander seeds

½ tsp black peppercorns

2 cloves

2 green cardamom pods

2.5 cm/1 inch piece cinnamon stick

1 tsp ground turmeric

1 fresh green chilli, chopped

½ tsp salt

2 tbsp ghee

1 tsp whole black mustard seeds

500 g/1 lb 2 oz uncooked tiger prawns (shrimp) in their shells, or 400 g/14 oz uncooked and peeled

300 ml/½ pint/1¼ cups coconut milk

300 ml/½ pint/1¼ cups low-fat natural yogurt

225 g/8 oz/generous 1 cup basmati rice, soaked for 2 hours and drained

1 tbsp sultanas (golden raisins)

flaked (slivered) almonds, toasted and 1 spring onion (scallion), sliced, to garnish

1 Soak the saffron in the tepid water for 10 minutes. Put the shallots, garlic, spices and salt into a spice grinder or pestle and mortar and grind to a paste.

2 Heat the ghee in a saucepan and add the mustard seeds. When they start to pop, add the prawns (shrimp) and stir over a high heat for 1 minute. Stir in the spice mix, then the coconut milk and yogurt. Simmer for 20 minutes.

3 Bring a large saucepan of salted water to the boil. Add the rice to the pan. Boil for 12 minutes. Drain. Pile the rice on the prawns. Spoon over the sultanas (golden raisins) and trickle the saffron water over the rice in lines. Cover the pan with a clean cloth and put the lid on tightly. Remove the pan from heat and leave to stand for 5 minutes. Serve, garnished with the almonds and spring onion (scallion).

Prawn (Shrimp) Dansak

The spicy lentil purée sauce in this recipe is of Parsi origin and is popular throughout the Indian continent.

NUTRITIONAL INFORMATION

Calories 379	Sugars 5g
Protein 45g	Fat 12g
Carbohydrate . . .25g	Saturates 2g

1¼ HOURS   1¼ HOURS

SERVES 4

I N G R E D I E N T S

700 g/1 lb 9 oz uncooked tiger prawns (shrimp) in their shells or 650 g/1 lb 7 oz peeled tiger prawns (shrimp), or cooked, peeled Atlantic prawns (shrimp)

1 tsp salt

1 dried bay leaf

3 garlic cloves, crushed

90 g/3 oz/⅓ cup split yellow peas, soaked for 1 hour in cold water and drained

60 g/2 oz/¼ cup red lentils

1 carrot, chopped

1 potato, cut into large dice

3 tbsp drained canned sweetcorn

3 tbsp oil

2 onions, chopped

½ tsp yellow mustard seeds

1½ tsp coriander seeds, ground

½ tsp cumin seeds, ground

½ tsp fenugreek seeds, ground

1h½ tsp ground turmeric

1 dried red chilli

425 g/15 oz can tomatoes

½ tsp garam masala

3 tbsp chopped fresh coriander (cilantro)

2 tbsp chopped fresh mint

1 Reserve 4 prawns (shrimp) for garnish and peel the rest. Cook those for the garnish in boiling water for 3–5 minutes.

2 Fill a pan with water and add the salt, bay leaf, ⅓ of the garlic and the split peas. Bring to the boil and cook for 15 minutes. Add the lentils, carrot and potato and cook for a further 15 minutes. Drain, discarding the garlic and bay leaf, and blend with the sweetcorn until smooth.

3 Heat the oil in a large saucepan and cook the remaining garlic and onion for 3–4 minutes. Add the mustard seeds and when they start to pop, stir in the other spices. Add the peeled prawns (shrimp) and stir for 1–2 minutes. Add the tomatoes and lentil purée, and simmer, uncovered, for 30–40 minutes. Stir in the garam masala and season. Serve sprinkled with coriander (cilantro) and mint and garnished with the prawns (shrimp).

Sweet & Sour Noodles

This delicious dish combines sweet and sour flavours with the addition of egg, rice noodles, king prawns (shrimp) and vegetables for a real treat.

NUTRITIONAL INFORMATION

Calories 352   Sugars 14g
Protein . . . . .23g   Fat 17g
Carbohydrate . . .29g   Saturates 3g

10 MINS   10 MINS

SERVES 4

INGREDIENTS

3 tbsp fish sauce

2 tbsp distilled white vinegar

2 tbsp caster (superfine) or palm sugar

2 tbsp tomato purée (paste)

2 tbsp sunflower oil

3 cloves garlic, crushed

350 g/12 oz rice noodles, soaked in boiling water for 5 minutes

8 spring onions (scallions), sliced

175 g/6 oz carrot, grated

150 g/5½ oz/1¼ cups bean sprouts

2 eggs, beaten

225 g/8 oz peeled king prawns (shrimp)

50 g/1¾ oz/½ cup chopped peanuts

1 tsp chilli flakes, to garnish

1 Mix together the fish sauce, vinegar, sugar and tomato purée (paste).

2 Heat the sunflower oil in a large preheated wok.

3 Add the garlic to the wok and stir-fry for 30 seconds.

4 Drain the noodles thoroughly and add them to the wok together with the fish sauce and tomato purée (paste) mixture. Mix well to combine.

5 Add the spring onions (scallions), carrot and bean sprouts to the wok and stir-fry for 2–3 minutes.

6 Move the contents of the wok to one side, add the beaten eggs to the empty part of the wok and cook until the egg sets. Add the noodles, prawns (shrimp) and peanuts to the wok and mix well. Transfer to warm serving dishes and garnish with chilli flakes. Serve hot.

COOK'S TIP

Chilli flakes may be found in the spice section of large supermarkets.

Stir-fried Prawns (Shrimp)

The (bell) peppers in this dish can be replaced by either mangetout (snow peas), or broccoli to maintain the attractive pink-green contrast.

NUTRITIONAL INFORMATION

Calories 116   Sugars 1g
Protein . . . . .10g   Fat 6g
Carbohydrate . . . .4g   Saturates 1g

  5 MINS   10 MINS

SERVES 4

I N G R E D I E N T S

170 g/6 oz raw prawns (shrimp), peeled

1 tsp salt

¼ tsp egg white

2 tsp cornflour (cornstarch) paste (see page 6)

300 ml/½ pint/1¼ cups vegetable oil

1 spring onion (scallion), cut into short sections

2.5-cm/1-inch piece ginger root, thinly sliced

1 small green (bell) pepper, cored, seeded and cubed

½ tsp sugar

1 tbsp light soy sauce

1 tsp rice wine or dry sherry

a few drops sesame oil

VARIATION

1-2 small green or red hot chillies, sliced, can be added with the green (bell) pepper to create a more spicy dish. Leave the chillies unseeded for a very hot dish.

1 Mix the prawns (shrimp) with a pinch of the salt, the egg white and cornflour (cornstarch) paste until well coated.

2 Heat the oil in a preheated wok and stir-fry the prawns (shrimp) for 30-40 seconds only. Remove and drain on kitchen paper (paper towels).

3 Pour off the oil, leaving about 1 tablespoon in the wok. Add the spring onion (scallion) and ginger to flavour the oil for a few seconds, then add the green (bell) pepper and stir-fry for about 1 minute.

4 Add the remaining salt and the sugar followed by the prawns (shrimp). Continue stirring for another minute or so, then add the soy sauce and wine and blend well. Sprinkle with sesame oil and serve immediately.

Sweet & Sour Prawns

Use raw prawns (shrimp) if possible. Omit steps 1 and 2 if ready-cooked ones are used.

NUTRITIONAL INFORMATION

Calories 373   Sugars 11g
Protein ....13g   Fat 26g
Carbohydrate ...19g   Saturates 3g

3¹/₂ HOURS   10 MINS

SERVES 4

INGREDIENTS

175-250 g/6-9 oz peeled raw tiger prawns

pinch of salt

1 tsp egg white

1 tsp cornflour (cornstarch) paste (see page 6)

300 ml/½ pint/1¼ cups vegetable oil

SAUCE

1 tbsp vegetable oil

½ small green (bell) pepper, cored, seeded and thinly sliced

½ small carrot, thinly sliced

125 g/4½ oz canned water chestnuts, drained and sliced

½ tsp salt

1 tbsp light soy sauce

2 tbsp sugar

3 tbsp rice or sherry vinegar

1 tsp rice wine or dry sherry

1 tbsp tomato sauce

½ tsp chilli sauce

3-4 tbsp Chinese Stock (see page 8) or water

2 tsp cornflour (cornstarch) paste (see page 6)

a few drops sesame oil

1 Mix together the prawns (shrimp) with the salt, egg white and cornflour (cornstarch) paste.

2 Heat the oil in a preheated wok and stir-fry the prawns (shrimp) for 30-40 seconds only. Remove and drain on kitchen paper (paper towels).

3 Pour off the oil and wipe the wok clean with kitchen paper (paper towels). To make the sauce, first heat the tablespoon of oil. Add the vegetables and stir-fry for about 1 minute, then add the seasonings with the stock or water and bring to the boil.

4 Add the prawns (shrimp) and stir until blended well. Thicken the sauce with the cornflour (cornstarch) paste and stir until smooth. Sprinkle with sesame oil and serve hot.

Vegetable & Egg Prawns

In this recipe, a light Chinese omelette is shredded and tossed back into the dish before serving.

NUTRITIONAL INFORMATION

Calories 258   Sugars 7g
Protein ....21g   Fat 15g
Carbohydrate ...10g   Saturates 3g

  10 MINS   15 MINS

SERVES 4

INGREDIENTS

225 g/8 oz courgettes (zucchini)

3 tbsp vegetable oil

2 eggs

2 tbsp cold water

225 g/8 oz carrots, grated

1 onion, sliced

150 g/5½ oz/1½ cups bean sprouts

225 g/8 oz peeled prawns (shrimp)

2 tbsp soy sauce

pinch of Chinese five-spice powder

25 g/1 oz/¼ cup peanuts, chopped

2 tbsp fresh chopped coriander (cilantro)

1 Finely grate the courgettes (zucchini).

2 Heat 1 tablespoon of the vegetable oil in a large preheated wok.

3 Beat the eggs with the water and pour the mixture into the wok and cook for 2–3 minutes or until the egg sets.

4 Remove the omelette from the wok and transfer to a clean board. Fold the omelette, cut it into thin strips and set aside until required.

5 Add the remaining oil to the wok. Add the carrots, onion and courgettes (zucchini) and stir-fry for 5 minutes.

6 Add the bean sprouts and prawns (shrimp) to the wok and cook for a further 2 minutes, or until the prawns (shrimp) are heated through.

7 Add the soy sauce, Chinese five-spice powder and peanuts to the wok, together with the strips of omelette and heat through. Garnish with chopped fresh coriander (cilantro) and serve.

COOK'S TIP

The water is mixed with the egg in step 3 for a lighter, less rubbery omelette.

Pork Sesame Toasts

This classic Chinese appetizer is also a great nibble for serving at parties – but be sure to make plenty!

NUTRITIONAL INFORMATION

Calories . . . . .674 Sugars 2g
Protein . . . . .33g Fat 46g
Carbohydrate . . .33g Saturates 7g

 5 MINS   35 MINS

SERVES 4

I N G R E D I E N T S

250 g/9 oz lean pork

250 g/9 oz/⅔ cup uncooked peeled prawns (shrimp), deveined

4 spring onions (scallions), trimmed

1 garlic clove, crushed

1 tbsp chopped fresh coriander (cilantro) leaves and stems

1 tbsp fish sauce

1 egg

8–10 slices of thick-cut white bread

3 tbsp sesame seeds

150 ml/¼ pint/⅔ cup vegetable oil

salt and pepper

TO GARNISH

sprigs of fresh coriander (cilantro)

red (bell) pepper, sliced finely

1 Put the pork, prawns (shrimp), spring onions (scallions), garlic, coriander (cilantro), fish sauce, egg and seasoning into a food processor or blender. Process for a few seconds until the ingredients are finely chopped. Transfer the mixture to a bowl. Alternatively, chop the pork, prawns (shrimp) and spring onions (scallions) very finely, and mix with the garlic, coriander (cilantro), fish sauce, beaten egg and seasoning until all the ingredients are well combined.

2 Spread the pork and prawn (shrimp) mixture thickly over the bread so that it reaches right up to the edges. Cut off the crusts and slice each piece of bread into 4 squares or triangles.

3 Sprinkle the topping liberally with sesame seeds.

4 Heat the oil in a wok or frying pan (skillet). Fry a few pieces of the bread, topping side down first so that it sets the egg, for about 2 minutes or until golden brown. Turn the pieces over to cook on the other side, about 1 minute.

5 Drain the pork and prawn (shrimp) toasts and place them on kitchen paper (paper towels). Fry the remaining pieces. Serve garnished with sprigs of fresh coriander (cilantro) and strips of red (bell) pepper.

Hot & Sweet Prawns (Shrimp)

Uncooked prawns (shrimp) are speared on skewers, brushed with a sesame oil, lime juice and coriander (cilantro) baste and then grilled.

NUTRITIONAL INFORMATION

Calories 239	Sugars 8g
Protein 28g	Fat 11g
Carbohydrate 8g	Saturates 2g

1 HOUR   10 MINS

SERVES 4

INGREDIENTS

wooden skewers soaked in warm water for 20 minutes

500 g/1 lb 2 oz/2½ cups uncooked prawns (shrimp)

3 tbsp sesame oil

2 tbsp lime juice

1 tbsp chopped fresh coriander (cilantro)

SAUCE

4 tbsp light malt vinegar

2 tbsp fish sauce or light soy sauce

2 tbsp water

2 tbsp light muscovado sugar

2 garlic cloves, crushed

2 tsp grated fresh ginger root

1 red chilli, deseeded and chopped finely

2 tbsp chopped fresh coriander (cilantro)

salt

1 Peel the prawns (shrimp), leaving the tails intact. Remove the black vein that runs along the back of each one, then skewer the prawns (shrimp) on to the wooden skewers.

2 Mix together the sesame oil, lime juice and chopped coriander (cilantro) in a shallow bowl. Lay the skewered prawns (shrimp) in this mixture. Cover and chill in the refrigerator for 30 minutes,

turning once, so that the prawns (shrimp) absorb the marinade.

3 Meanwhile, make the sauce. Heat the vinegar, fish sauce or soy sauce, water, sugar and salt to taste until boiling. Remove from the heat and leave to cool.

4 Mix together the crushed garlic, grated ginger, red chilli and coriander (cilantro) in a small serving bowl. Add

the cooled vinegar mixture and stir until well combined.

5 Place the prawns (shrimp) on a foil-lined grill (broiler) pan under a preheated grill (broiler) for about 6 minutes, turning once and basting often with the marinade, until cooked.

6 Transfer to a warmed serving platter and serve with the dipping sauce.

Shrimp & Sweetcorn Patties

Chopped (small) shrimps and sweetcorn are combined in a light batter, which is dropped in spoonfuls into hot fat to make these tasty patties.

NUTRITIONAL INFORMATION

Calories 250	Sugars 1g	
Protein 17g	Fat 9g	
Carbohydrate ...26g	Saturates 2g	

 35 MINS   20 MINS

SERVES 4

INGREDIENTS

125 g/4½ oz/1 cup plain (all-purpose) flour

1½ tsp baking powder

2 eggs

about 250 ml/9 fl oz/1 cup cold water

1 garlic clove, very finely chopped

3 spring onions (scallions), trimmed and very finely chopped

250 g/9 oz/1 cup peeled (small) shrimps, chopped

125 g/4½ oz/½ cup canned sweetcorn, drained

vegetable oil for frying

salt and pepper

TO GARNISH

spring onion (scallion) brushes (see Cook's Tip, right)

lime slices

1 chilli flower

1 Sift the flour, baking powder and ½ tsp salt into a bowl. Add the eggs and half the water and beat to make a smooth batter, adding extra water to give the consistency of double (heavy) cream. Add the garlic and spring onions (scallions). Cover and leave for 30 minutes.

2 Stir the (small) shrimps and corn into the batter. Season with pepper.

3 Heat 2–3 tablespoons of oil in a wok. Drop tablespoonfuls of the batter into the wok and cook over a medium heat until bubbles rise and the surface just sets. Flip the patties over and cook the other side until golden brown. Drain on kitchen paper (paper towels).

4 Cook the remaining batter in the same way, adding more oil to the wok if required. Garnish and serve at once.

COOK'S TIP

Make a spring onion (scallion) brush by trimming off the tips of the leaves and making several fine cuts from the leaf tips to the top of the bulb. Place in iced water to make the leaves curl.

Shrimp Curry & Fruit Sauce

Serve this lightly-spiced dish as part of a buffet meal, or as a refreshingly different lunch dish, with a bowl of rice.

NUTRITIONAL INFORMATION

Calories	538	Sugars	.......28g
Protein	........40g	Fat	.........28g
Carbohydrate	...33g	Saturates	......15g

  30 MINS 20 MINS

SERVES 4

INGREDIENTS

2 tbsp vegetable oil

25 g/1 oz/2 tbsp butter

2 onions, finely chopped

2 garlic cloves, finely chopped

1 tsp cumin seeds, lightly crushed

1 tsp ground turmeric

1 tsp paprika

½ tsp chilli powder, or to taste

60 g/2 oz creamed coconut

1 x 400g/14 oz can chopped tomatoes

1 tbsp tomato purée (paste)

500 g/1 lb 2 oz frozen cooked shrimps, defrosted

½ cucumber, thinly diced

150 ml/¼ pint/⅔ cup low-fat yogurt

2 hard-boiled eggs, quartered

salt

coriander and onion rings, to garnish

FRUIT SAUCE

300 ml/½ pint/1¼ cups low-fat natural yogurt

¼ tsp salt

1 garlic clove, crushed

2 tbsp chopped mint

4 tbsp seedless raisins

1 small pomegranate

1 Heat the oil and butter in a frying pan. Add the chopped onions and fry until translucent. Add the garlic and fry for a further minute, until softened but not browned.

2 Stir in the spices and cook for 2 minutes, stirring. Stir in the creamed coconut, chopped tomatoes and tomato purée (paste) and bring to the boil. Simmer for 10 minutes, or until the sauce has thickened slightly. It should not be at all runny.

3 Remove the pan from the heat and set aside to cool. Stir in the shrimps, cucumber and yogurt. Taste the sauce and adjust the seasoning if necessary. Cover and chill until ready to serve.

4 To make the fruit sauce, place everything except the pomegrantes into a bowl. Cut the pomegranate in half, scoop out the seeds, discarding the white membrane, and stir into the fruit mixture, reserving a few for garnish.

5 Transfer the curry to a serving dish and arrange the hard-boiled egg, coriander and onion rings on top. Serve the sauce separately, sprinkled with the reserved pomegranate seeds.

Prawns (Shrimp) with Ginger

Crispy ginger is a wonderful garnish which offsets the spicy prawns (shrimp) both visually and in flavour.

NUTRITIONAL INFORMATION

Calories 229	Sugars 7g	
Protein 29g	Fat 8g	
Carbohydrate . . .10g	Saturates 1g	

10 MINS   15 MINS

SERVES 4

INGREDIENTS

5 cm/2 inch piece fresh root ginger

oil, for frying

1 onion, diced

225 g/8 oz carrots, diced

100 g/3½ oz/½ cup frozen peas

100 g/3½ oz/1 cup bean sprouts

450 g/1 lb peeled king prawns (shrimp)

1 tsp Chinese five-spice powder

1 tbsp tomato purée (paste)

1 tbsp soy sauce

1 Using a sharp knife, peel the ginger and slice it into very thin sticks.

2 Heat about 2.5 cm/1 inch of oil in a large preheated wok. Add the ginger and stir-fry for 1 minute or until the ginger is crispy. Remove the ginger with a slotted spoon and leave to drain on absorbent kitchen paper (paper towels).

3 Drain all of the oil from the wok except for about 2 tablespoons. Add the onions and carrots to the wok and stir-fry for 5 minutes. Add the peas and bean sprouts and stir-fry for 2 minutes.

4 Rinse the prawns (shrimp) under cold running water and pat dry with absorbent kitchen paper (paper towels).

5 Combine the five-spice, tomato purée (paste) and soy sauce. Brush the mixture over the prawns (shrimp).

6 Add the prawns (shrimp) to the wok and stir-fry for a further 2 minutes, or until the prawns (shrimp) are completely cooked through. Transfer the prawn (shrimp) mixture to a warm serving bowl and top with the reserved crispy ginger. Serve immediately.

VARIATION

Use slices of white fish instead of the prawns (shrimp) as an alternative, if you wish.

Szechuan Prawns (Shrimp)

Raw prawns (shrimp) should be used if possible, otherwise add the ready-cooked prawns (shrimp) at the beginning of step 3.

NUTRITIONAL INFORMATION

Calories 315	Sugars 1g
Protein 16g	Fat 27g
Carbohydrate 3g	Saturates 3g

3¹/₂ HOURS   10 MINS

SERVES 4

INGREDIENTS

250-300 g/9-10½ oz raw tiger prawns (jumbo shrimp)

pinch of salt

½ egg white, lightly beaten

1 tsp cornflour (cornstarch) paste (see page 6)

600 ml/1 pint/2½ cups vegetable oil

fresh coriander (cilantro) leaves, to garnish

SAUCE

1 tsp finely chopped ginger root

2 spring onions (scallions), finely chopped

1 garlic clove, finely chopped

3-4 small dried red chillies, seeded and chopped

1 tbsp light soy sauce

1 tsp rice wine or dry sherry

1 tbsp tomato purée (paste)

1 tbsp oyster sauce

2-3 tbsp Chinese Stock (see page 8) or water

a few drops sesame oil

1 Peel the raw prawns (shrimp), then mix with the salt, egg white and cornflour (cornstarch) paste until the prawns (shrimp) are well coated.

2 Heat the oil in a preheated wok or large frying pan (skillet) until it is smoking, then deep-fry the prawns (shrimp) in hot oil for about 1 minute. Remove with a slotted spoon and drain on kitchen paper (paper towels).

3 Pour off the oil, leaving about 1 tablespoon in the wok. Add all the ingredients for the sauce, in the order listed, bring to the boil and stir until smooth and well blended.

4 Add the prawns (shrimp) to the sauce and stir until blended well.

5 Serve the prawns (shrimp) garnished with fresh coriander (cilantro) leaves.

Spiced Balti Seafood

Although prawns (shrimp) are not a traditional ingredient of Balti cooking, they work will with Balti spices and cooking methods.

NUTRITIONAL INFORMATION

Calories 194   Sugars 2g
Protein ....29g   Fat 8g
Carbohydrate ....2g   Saturates 1g

2¼ HOURS   15 MINS

SERVES 4

INGREDIENTS

1 garlic clove, crushed

2 tsp freshly grated ginger root

2 tsp ground coriander

2 tsp ground cumin

½ tsp ground cardamom

¼ tsp chilli powder

2 tbsp tomato purée (paste)

5 tbsp water

3 tbsp chopped fresh coriander (cilantro)

500 g/1 lb peeled cooked king prawns (jumbo shrimp)

2 tbsp oil

2 small onions, sliced

1 fresh green chilli, chopped

salt

1 Put the garlic, ginger, ground coriander, cumin, cardamom, chilli powder, tomato purée (paste), 4 tablespoons of the water and 2 tablespoons of the fresh coriander (cilantro) into a bowl. Mix all the ingredients together.

2 Add the prawns (shrimp) to the bowl and leave to marinate for 2 hours.

3 Heat the oil in a karahi or wok, add the onions and stir-fry until golden brown.

4 Add the prawns (shrimp), marinade and the chilli and stir-fry over a medium heat for 5 minutes. Add salt, and the remaining tablespoon of water if the mixture is very dry. Stir-fry over a medium heat for a further 5 minutes.

5 Serve the prawns (shrimp) immediately, garnished with the remaining fresh chopped coriander (cilantro).

COOK'S TIP

Prawns (shrimp) lose less flavour if they are put without water in a tightly covered pan and set over a high heat to cook in their own juice.

Pan-Fried Prawns (Shrimp)

A luxurious dish which makes an impressive starter or light meal. Prawns (shrimp) and garlic are a winning combination.

NUTRITIONAL INFORMATION

Calories 455   Sugars 0g
Protein ....6g   Fat 37g
Carbohydrate ....0g   Saturates 18g

 10 MINS   5 MINS

SERVES 4

INGREDIENTS

4 garlic cloves

20–24 unshelled large raw prawns (shrimp)

125 g/4½ oz/8 tbsp butter

4 tbsp olive oil

6 tbsp brandy

salt and pepper

2 tbsp chopped fresh parsley

TO SERVE

lemon wedges

ciabatta bread

1 Using a sharp knife, peel and slice the garlic.

2 Wash the prawns (shrimp) and pat dry using paper towels.

3 Melt the butter with the oil in a large frying pan (skillet), add the garlic and prawns (shrimp), and fry over a high heat, stirring, for 3–4 minutes until the prawns (shrimp) are pink.

4 Sprinkle with brandy and season with salt and pepper to taste. Sprinkle with parsley and serve immediately with lemon wedges and ciabatta bread, if liked.

Cantonese Prawns (Shrimp)

This prawn (shrimp) dish is very simple and is ideal for supper or lunch when time is short.

10 MINS   20 MINS

SERVES 4

I N G R E D I E N T S

5 tbsp vegetable oil

4 garlic cloves, crushed

675 g/1½ lb raw prawns (shrimp), shelled and deveined

5-cm/2-inch piece fresh root ginger, chopped

175 g/6 oz lean pork, diced

1 leek, sliced

3 eggs, beaten

shredded leek and red (bell) pepper matchsticks, to garnish

rice, to serve

S A U C E

2 tbsp Chinese rice wine or dry sherry

2 tbsp light soy sauce

2 tsp caster (superfine) sugar

150 ml/¼ pint/⅔ cup fish stock

4½ tsp cornflour (cornstarch)

3 tbsp water

1 Heat 2 tablespoons of the vegetable oil in a preheated wok.

2 Add the garlic to the wok and stir-fry for 30 seconds.

3 Add the prawns (shrimp) to the wok and stir-fry for 5 minutes, or until they change colour. Remove the prawns (shrimp) from the wok or frying pan (skillet) with a slotted spoon, set aside and keep warm.

4 Add the remaining oil to the wok and heat, swirling the oil around the base of the wok until it is really hot.

5 Add the ginger, diced pork and leek to the wok and stir-fry over a medium heat for 4-5 minutes, or until the pork is lightly coloured and sealed.

6 To make the sauce, add the rice wine or sherry, soy sauce, caster (superfine) sugar and fish stock to the wok and stir to blend.

7 In a small bowl, blend the cornflour (cornstarch) with the water to form a smooth paste and stir it into the wok. Cook, stirring, until the sauce thickens and clears.

8 Return the prawns (shrimp) to the wok and add the beaten eggs. Cook for 5-6 minutes, gently stirring occasionally, until the eggs set.

9 Transfer to a warm serving dish, garnish with shredded leek and (bell) pepper matchsticks and serve immediately with rice.

Chilli Prawns (Shrimp)

Large prawns (shrimp) are marinated in a chilli mixture then stir-fried with cashews. Serve with a fluffy rice and braised vegetables.

NUTRITIONAL INFORMATION

Calories	435	Sugars 2g
Protein	. . . . .4.2g	Fat 23
Carbohydrate	. . .10g	Saturates 4g

2¹/₄ HOURS   5 MINS

SERVES 4

INGREDIENTS

5 tbsp soy sauce

5 tbsp dry sherry

3 dried red chillies, seeded and chopped

2 garlic cloves, crushed

2 tsp grated ginger root

5 tbsp water

625 g/1 lb 6 oz shelled tiger prawns (jumbo shrimp)

1 large bunch spring onions (scallions), chopped

90 g/3 oz/⅔ cup salted cashew nuts

3 tbsp vegetable oil

2 tsp cornflour (cornstarch)

1 Mix the soy sauce, sherry, chillies, garlic, ginger and water in a bowl.

2 Add the tiger prawns (jumbo shrimp), spring onions (scallions) and cashews and mix well. Cover tightly and leave to marinate for at least 2 hours, stirring occasionally.

3 Heat the oil in a large wok. Remove the prawns (shrimp), spring onions

(scallions) and cashews from the marinade with a slotted spoon and add to the wok, reserving the marinade. Stir-fry over a high heat for 1-2 minutes.

4 Mix the reserved marinade with the cornflour (cornstarch), add to the wok and stir-fry for about 30 seconds, until the marinade forms a slightly thickened shiny glaze over the prawn (shrimp) mixture. Serve immediately.

COOK'S TIP

For an attractive presentation serve this dish on mixed wild rice and basmati rice. Start cooking the wild rice in boiling water. After 10 minutes, add the basmati rice or other rice and continue boiling until all grains are tender. Drain well and adjust the seasoning.

Macaroni & Seafood Bake

This adaptation of an eighteenth-century Italian dish is baked until it is golden brown and sizzling, then cut into wedges like a cake.

NUTRITIONAL INFORMATION

Calories ....478 Sugars 6g
Protein ....27g Fat 17g
Carbohydrate ...57g Saturates 7g

 30 MINS   50 MINS

SERVES 4

INGREDIENTS

350 g/12 oz/3 cups dried
   short-cut macaroni

1 tbsp olive oil, plus extra for brushing

90 g/3 oz/6 tbsp butter, plus extra
   for greasing

2 small fennel bulbs, thinly sliced and
   fronds reserved

175 g/6 oz mushrooms, thinly sliced

175 g/6 oz peeled, cooked prawns (shrimp)

pinch of cayenne pepper

300 ml/½ pint/1¼ cups Béchamel Sauce
   (see page 6)

60 g/2 oz/⅔ cup freshly grated
   Parmesan cheese

2 large tomatoes, sliced

1 tsp dried oregano

salt and pepper

1 Bring a saucepan of salted water to the boil. Add the pasta and oil and cook for 8–10 minutes until tender, but still firm to the bite. Drain the pasta and return to the pan.

2 Add 25 g/1 oz/2 tbsp of the butter to the pasta, cover, shake the pan and keep warm.

3 Melt the remaining butter in a saucepan. Fry the fennel for 3–4 minutes. Stir in the mushrooms and fry for a further 2 minutes.

4 Stir in the prawns (shrimp), then remove the pan from the heat.

5 Stir the cayenne pepper and prawn (shrimp) mixture into the Béchamel Sauce, stirring.

6 Pour into a greased ovenproof dish and spread evenly. Sprinkle over the Parmesan cheese and arrange the tomato slices in a ring around the edge. Brush the tomatoes with olive oil and then sprinkle over the oregano.

7 Bake in a preheated oven at 180°C/ 350°F/Gas Mark 4 for 25 minutes, until golden brown. Serve immediately.

(Small) Shrimp Fu Yong

The classic ingredients of this popular dish are eggs, carrots and (small) shrimps. Add extra ingredients such as peas or crabmeat, if desired.

NUTRITIONAL INFORMATION

Calories 240	Sugars 1g
Protein 22g	Fat 16g
Carbohydrate 1g	Saturates 3g

 5 MINS   10 MINS

SERVES 4

I N G R E D I E N T S

2 tbsp vegetable oil

1 carrot, grated

5 eggs, beaten

225 g/8 oz raw (small) shrimp, peeled

1 tbsp light soy sauce

pinch of Chinese five-spice powder

2 spring onions (scallions), chopped

2 tsp sesame seeds

1 tsp sesame oil

COOK'S TIP

If only cooked prawns (shrimp) are available, add them just before the end of cooking, but make sure they are fully incorporated into the fu yong. They require only heating through. Overcooking will make them chewy and tasteless.

1 Heat the vegetable oil in a preheated wok or frying pan (skillet), swirling it around until the oil is really hot.

2 Add the grated carrot and stir-fry for 1–2 minutes.

3 Push the carrot to one side of the wok or frying pan (skillet) and add the beaten eggs. Cook, stirring gently, for 1–2 minutes.

4 Stir the (small) shrimp, light soy sauce and five-spice powder into the mixture in the wok. Stir-fry the mixture for 2–3 minutes, or until the (small) shrimps change colour and the mixture is almost dry.

5 Turn the (small) shrimp fu yong out on to a warm plate and sprinkle the spring onions (scallions), sesame seeds and sesame oil on top. Serve immediately.

Pasta & Prawn (Shrimp) Parcels

This is the ideal dish when you have unexpected guests because the parcels can be prepared in minutes, then put in the oven when you are ready to eat.

NUTRITIONAL INFORMATION

Calories	640	Sugars	.........1g
Protein	........50g	Fat	..........29g
Carbohydrate	...42g	Saturates	.......4g

 15 MINS   30 MINS

SERVES 4

I N G R E D I E N T S

450 g/1 lb dried fettuccine

150 ml/¼ pint/⅝ cup pesto sauce

4 tsp extra virgin olive oil

750 g/1 lb 10 oz large raw prawns (shrimp), peeled and deveined

2 garlic cloves, crushed

125 ml/4 fl oz/½ cup dry white wine

salt and pepper

1 Cut out 4 x 30 cm/12 inch squares of greaseproof paper.

2 Bring a large saucepan of lightly salted water to the boil. Add the fettuccine and cook for 2–3 minutes, until just softened. Drain and set aside.

3 Mix together the fettuccine and half of the pesto sauce. Spread out the paper squares and put 1 teaspoon olive oil in the middle of each. Divide the fettuccine between the squares, then divide the prawns (shrimp) and place on top of the fettuccine.

4 Mix together the remaining pesto sauce and the garlic and spoon it over the prawns (shrimp). Season each parcel with salt and black pepper and sprinkle with the white wine.

5 Dampen the edges of the greaseproof paper and wrap the parcels loosely, twisting the edges to seal.

6 Place the parcels on a baking tray (cookie sheet) and bake in a preheated oven at 200°C/400°F/Gas Mark 6 for 10–15 minutes. Transfer the parcels to 4 individual serving plates and serve.

COOK'S TIP

Traditionally, these parcels are designed to look like money bags. The resemblance is more effective with greaseproof paper than with foil.

Prawn (Shrimp) Bhuna

This is a fiery recipe with subtle undertones. As the flavour of the prawns should be noticeable, the spices should not take over this dish.

NUTRITIONAL INFORMATION

Calories 141   Sugars 0.4g
Protein . . . . .19g   Fat 7g
Carbohydrate . . . .1g   Saturates 1g

15 MINS   20 MINS

SERVES 4–6

INGREDIENTS

2 dried red chillies, deseeded if liked

3 fresh green chillies, finely chopped

1 tsp ground turmeric

3 garlic cloves, crushed

½ tsp pepper

1 tsp paprika

2 tsp white wine vinegar

½ tsp salt

500 g/1 lb 2 oz uncooked peeled king prawns (shrimp)

3 tbsp oil

1 onion, chopped very finely

175 ml/6 fl oz/¾ cup water

2 tbsp lemon juice

2 tsp garam masala

sprigs of fresh coriander (cilantro), to garnish

COOK'S TIP

Garam masala should be used sparingly and is generally added to foods towards the end of their cooking time. It is also used sprinkled over cooked meats, vegetabls and pulses as a garnish.

1 Combine the chillies, spices, vinegar and salt in a non-metallic bowl. Stir in the prawns and leave for 10 minutes.

2 Heat the oil in a large frying pan (skillet) or wok, add the onion and fry for 3–4 minutes until soft.

3 Add the prawns (shrimp) and the contents of the bowl to the pan and stir-fry over a high heat for 2 minutes. Reduce the heat, add the water and boil

for 10 minutes, stirring occasionally, until the water is evaporated and the curry is fragrant.

4 Stir in the lemon juice and garam masala then transfer the mixture to a warm serving dish and garnish with fresh coriander (cilantro) sprigs.

5 Serve garnished with sprigs of fresh coriander (cilantro).

Spicy Prawns (Shrimp)

Basil and tomatoes are ideal flavourings for prawn (shrimp), spiced with cumin seeds and garlic.

NUTRITIONAL INFORMATION

Calories 208	Sugars 8g	
Protein 27g	Fat 8g	
Carbohydrate 8g	Saturates 1g	

5 MINS   20 MINS

SERVES 4

INGREDIENTS

2 tbsp corn oil

1 onion

2 cloves garlic, crushed

1 tsp cumin seeds

1 tbsp demerara sugar

400 g/14 oz can chopped tomatoes

1 tbsp sundried tomato purée (paste)

1 tbsp chopped fresh basil

450 g/1 lb peeled king prawns (shrimp)

salt and pepper

1 Heat the corn oil in a large preheated wok.

2 Using a sharp knife, finely chop the onion. Add the onion and crushed garlic to the wok and stir-fry for 2–3 minutes, or until softened.

3 Stir in the cumin seeds and stir-fry for 1 minute.

4 Add the sugar, chopped tomatoes and tomato purée (paste) to the wok.

5 Bring the mixture to the boil, then reduce the heat and leave the sauce to simmer for 10 minutes.

6 Add the basil and prawns (shrimp) to the mixture in the wok. Season to taste with salt and pepper.

7 Increase the heat and cook for a further 2–3 minutes or until the prawns (shrimp) are completely cooked through. Transfer to a warm serving dish and serve immediately.

COOK'S TIP

Sundried tomato purée (paste) has a much more intense flavour than that of normal tomato purée (paste). It adds a distinctive intensity to any tomato-based dish.

Noodles with Chilli & Prawn

This is a simple dish to prepare and is packed with flavour, making it an ideal choice for special occasions.

NUTRITIONAL INFORMATION

Calories 259   Sugars 9g
Protein . . . . .28g   Fat 8g
Carbohydrate . . .20g   Saturates 1g

10 MINS   5 MINS

SERVES 4

I N G R E D I E N T S

250 g/9 oz thin glass noodles

2 tbsp sunflower oil

1 onion, sliced

2 red chillies, deseeded and very finely chopped

4 lime leaves, thinly shredded

1 tbsp fresh coriander (cilantro)

2 tbsp palm or caster (superfine) sugar

2 tbsp fish sauce

450 g/1 lb raw tiger prawns (jumbo shrimp), peeled

1 Place the noodles in a large bowl. Pour over enough boiling water to cover the noodles and leave to stand for 5 minutes. Drain thoroughly and set aside until required.

COOK'S TIP

If you cannot buy raw tiger prawns (jumbo shrimp), use cooked prawns (shrimp) instead and cook them with the noodles for 1 minute only, just to heat through.

2 Heat the sunflower oil in a large preheated wok or frying pan (skillet) until it is really hot.

3 Add the onion, red chillies and lime leaves to the wok and stir-fry for 1 minute.

4 Add the coriander (cilantro), palm or caster (superfine) sugar, fish sauce and prawns (shrimp) to the wok or frying

apn (skillet) and stir-fry for a further 2 minutes or until the prawns (shrimp) turn pink.

5 Add the drained noodles to the wok, toss to mix well, and stir-fry for 1–2 minutes or until heated through.

6 Transfer the noodles and prawns (shrimp) to warm serving bowls and serve immediately.

Special Noodles

This dish combines meat, vegetables, prawns (shrimp) and noodles in a curried coconut sauce. Serve as a main meal or as an accompaniment.

NUTRITIONAL INFORMATION

Calories 409	Sugars 12g
Protein 24g	Fat 23g
Carbohydrate . . .28g	Saturates 8g

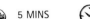

5 MINS   25 MINS

SERVES 4

INGREDIENTS

250 g/9 oz thin rice noodles

4 tbsp groundnut oil

2 cloves garlic, crushed

2 red chillies, deseeded and very finely chopped

1 tsp grated fresh ginger

2 tbsp Madras curry paste

2 tbsp rice wine vinegar

1 tbsp caster (superfine) sugar

225 g/8 oz cooked ham, finely shredded

100 g/3½ oz/1¼ cups canned water chestnuts, sliced

100 g/3½ oz mushrooms, sliced

100 g/3½ oz/¾ cup peas

1 red (bell) pepper, deseeded and thinly sliced

100 g/3½ oz peeled prawns (shrimp)

2 large eggs

4 tbsp coconut milk

25 g/1 oz/¼ cup desiccated (shredded) coconut

2 tbsp chopped fresh coriander (cilantro)

1 Place the rice noodles in a large bowl, cover with boiling water and leave to soak for about 10 minutes. Drain the noodles thoroughly, then toss with 2 tablespoons of groundnut oil.

2 Heat the remaining groundnut oil in a large preheated wok until the oil is really hot.

3 Add the garlic, chillies, ginger, curry paste, rice wine vinegar and caster (superfine) sugar to the wok and stir-fry for 1 minute.

4 Add the ham, water chestnuts, mushrooms, peas and red (bell) pepper to the wok and stir-fry for 5 minutes.

5 Add the noodles and prawns (shrimps) to the wok and stir-fry for 2 minutes.

6 In a small bowl, beat together the eggs and coconut milk. Drizzle over the mixture into the wok and stir-fry until the egg sets.

7 Add the desiccated (shredded) coconut and chopped fresh coriander (cilantro) to the wok and toss to combine. Transfer the noodles to warm serving dishes and serve immediately.

Prawns with Vegetables

This colourful and delicious dish is cooked with vegetables: vary them according to seasonal availability.

NUTRITIONAL INFORMATION

Calories 298   Sugars 1g
Protein . . . . .13g   Fat 26g
Carbohydrate . . . .3g   Saturates 3g

5 MINS   10 MINS

SERVES 4

I N G R E D I E N T S

60 g/2 oz mangetout (snow peas)

½ small carrot

60 g/2 oz baby sweetcorn

60 g/2 oz straw mushrooms

175–250 g/6–9 oz raw tiger prawns
    (jumbo shrimp), peeled

1 tsp salt

½ egg white, lightly beaten

1 tsp cornflour (cornstarch) paste
    (see page 6)

about 300 ml/½ pint/1¼ cups
    vegetable oil

1 spring onion (scallion), cut into
    short sections

4 slices ginger root, peeled and finely
    chopped

½ tsp sugar

1 tbsp light soy sauce

1 tsp Chinese rice wine or dry sherry

a few drops sesame oil

lemon slices and chopped fresh chives,
    to garnish

COOK'S TIP

The water is mixed with
the egg in step 3 for a lighter,
less rubbery omelete.

1 Using a sharp knife, top and tail the mangetout (snow peas); cut the carrot into the same size as the mangetout (snow peas); halve the baby sweetcorn and straw mushrooms.

2 Mix the prawns (shrimp) with a pinch of the salt, the egg white and cornflour (cornstarch) paste until the prawns (shrimp) are evenly coated.

3 Preheat a wok over a high heat for 2–3 minutes, then add the vegetable oil and heat to medium-hot.

4 Add the prawns (shrimp) to the wok, stirring to separate them. Remove the prawns (shrimp) with a slotted spoon as soon as the colour changes.

5 Pour off the oil, leaving about 1 tablespoon in the wok. Add the mangetout (snow peas), carrot, sweetcorn, mushrooms and spring onions (scallions).

6 Add the prawns (shrimp) together with the ginger, sugar, soy sauce and wine or sherry, blending well.

7 Sprinkle with the sesame oil and serve hot, garnished with lemon slices and chopped fresh chives.

Fried Rice with Prawns

Use either large peeled prawns (shrimp) or tiger prawns (jumbo shrimp) for this rice dish.

NUTRITIONAL INFORMATION

Calories	599	Sugars 0g
Protein	........26g	Fat 16g
Carbohydrate	...94g	Saturates 3g

5 MINS   35 MINS

SERVES 4

I N G R E D I E N T S

300 g/10½ oz/1½ cups long-grain rice

2 eggs

4 tsp cold water

salt and pepper

3 tbsp sunflower oil

4 spring onions (scallions), thinly sliced diagonally

1 garlic clove, crushed

125 g/4½ oz closed-cup or button mushrooms, thinly sliced

2 tbsp oyster or anchovy sauce

1 x 200 g/7 oz can water chestnuts, drained and sliced

250 g/9 oz peeled prawns (shrimp), defrosted if frozen

½ bunch watercress, roughly chopped

watercress sprigs, to garnish (optional)

1 Cook the rice in boiling salted water and keep warm.

2 Beat each egg separately with 2 teaspoons of cold water and salt and pepper.

3 Heat 2 teaspoons of sunflower oil in a wok or large frying pan (skillet), swirling it around until really hot. Pour in the first egg, swirl it around and leave

to cook undisturbed until set. Remove to a plate or board and repeat with the second egg. Cut the omelettes into 2.5 cm/1 inch squares.

4 Heat the remaining oil in the wok and when really hot add the spring onions (scallions) and garlic and stir-fry for 1 minute. Add the mushrooms and continue to cook for a further 2 minutes.

5 Stir in the oyster or anchovy sauce and seasoning and add the water chestnuts and prawns (shrimp); stir-fry for 2 minutes.

6 Stir in the cooked rice and stir-fry for 1 minute, then add the watercress and omelette squares and stir-fry for a further 1-2 minutes until piping hot. Serve at once garnished with sprigs of watercress, if liked.

Coconut Prawns (Shrimp)

Fan-tail prawns (shrimp) make any meal a special occasion, especially when cooked in such a delicious crispy coating.

NUTRITIONAL INFORMATION

Calories	236	Sugars	.........1g
Protein	........27g	Fat	..........13g
Carbohydrate	....3g	Saturates	.......7g

 5 MINS 10 MINS

SERVES 4

INGREDIENTS

50 g/1¾ oz/½ cup desiccated (shredded) coconut

25 g/1 oz/½ cup fresh white breadcrumbs

1 tsp Chinese five-spice powder

½ tsp salt

finely grated zest of 1 lime

1 egg white

450 g/1 lb fan-tail prawns (shrimp)

sunflower or corn oil, for frying

lemon wedges, to garnish

soy or chilli sauce, to serve

1 Mix together the dessicated (shredded) coconut, white breadcrumbs, Chinese five-spice powder, salt and finely grated lime zest in a bowl.

2 Lightly whisk the egg white in a separate bowl.

3 Rinse the prawns (shrimp) under cold running water, and pat dry with kitchen paper (paper towels).

4 Dip the prawns (shrimp) into the egg white then into the coconut and breadcrumb mixture, so that they are evenly coated.

5 Heat about 5 cm/2 inches of sunflower or corn oil in a large preheated wok.

6 Add the prawns (shrimp) to the wok and stir-fry for about 5 minutes or until golden and crispy.

7 Remove the prawns (shrimp) with a slotted spoon and leave to drain on kitchen paper (paper towels).

8 Transfer the coconut prawns (shrimp) to warm serving dishes and garnish with lemon wedges. Serve immediately with a soy or chilli sauce.

COOK'S TIP

Chinese five-spice powder is a mixture of star anise, fennel seeds, cloves, cinnamon bark and Szechuan pepper. It is very pungent, so should be used sparingly. It will keep indefinitely in an airtight container.

Chilli (Small) Shrimp Noodles

Cellophane or 'glass' noodles are made from mung beans. They are sold dried, so they need soaking before use.

NUTRITIONAL INFORMATION

Calories ....152 Sugars 2g
Protein ....11g Fat 8g
Carbohydrate ...10g Saturates 1g

 🦀 🦀 🦀

🥘 25 MINS   🕐 10 MINS

SERVES 4

INGREDIENTS

2 tbsp light soy sauce

1 tbsp lime or lemon juice

1 tbsp fish sauce

125 g/4½ oz firm tofu (bean curd), cut into chunks

125 g/4½ oz cellophane noodles

2 tbsp sesame oil

4 shallots, sliced finely

2 garlic cloves, crushed

1 small red chilli, deseeded and chopped finely

2 celery sticks, sliced finely

2 carrots, sliced finely

125 g/4½ oz/⅔ cup cooked, peeled (small) shrimps

60 g/2 oz/1 cup bean sprouts

TO GARNISH

celery leaves

fresh chillies

1 Mix together the light soy sauce, lime or lemon juice and fish sauce in a small bowl. Add the tofu (bean curd) cubes and toss them until coated in the mixture. Cover and set aside for 15 minutes.

2 Put the noodles into a large bowl and cover with warm water. Leave them to soak for about 5 minutes, and then drain them well.

3 Heat the sesame oil in a wok or large frying pan (skillet). Add the shallots, garlic and red chilli, and stir-fry for 1 minute.

4 Add the sliced celery and carrots to the wok or pan and stir-fry for a further 2–3 minutes.

5 Tip the drained noodles into the wok or frying pan (skillet) and cook, stirring, for 2 minutes, then add the (small) shrimps, bean sprouts and tofu (bean curd), with the soy sauce mixture. Cook over a medium high heat for 2–3 minutes until heated through.

6 Transfer the mixture in the wok to a serving dish and garnish with celery leaves and chillies.

Fried Squid Flowers

The addition of green (bell) pepper and black bean sauce to the squid makes a colourful and delicious dish from the Cantonese school.

NUTRITIONAL INFORMATION

Calories 172   Sugars 1g
Protein . . . . .13g   Fat 13g
Carbohydrate . . . .2g   Saturates 1g

 10 MINS   5 MINS

SERVES 4

I N G R E D I E N T S

350-400 g/12-14 oz prepared and cleaned squid (see Cook's Tip, below)

1 medium green (bell) pepper, cored and seeded

3-4 tbsp vegetable oil

1 garlic clove, finely chopped

¼ tsp finely chopped ginger root

2 tsp finely chopped spring onions (scallions)

½ tsp salt

2 tbsp crushed black bean sauce

1 tsp Chinese rice wine or dry sherry

a few drops sesame oil

boiled rice, to serve

1 If ready-prepared squid is not available, prepare as instructed in the Cook's Tip, below.

2 Open up the squid and, using a meat cleaver or sharp knife, score the inside of the flesh in a criss-cross pattern.

3 Cut the squid into pieces about the size of an oblong postage stamp.

4 Blanch the squid pieces in a bowl of boiling water for a few seconds. Remove and drain; dry well on absorbent kitchen paper (paper towels).

5 Cut the (bell) pepper into small triangular pieces. Heat the oil in a preheated wok or large frying pan (skillet) and stir-fry the (bell) pepper for about 1 minute.

6 Add the garlic, ginger, spring onion (scallion), salt and squid. Continue stirring for another minute.

7 Finally add the black bean sauce and Chinese rice wine or dry sherry, and blend well.

8 Transfer the squid flowers to a serving dish, sprinkle with sesame oil and serve with boiled rice.

COOK'S TIP

Clean the squid by first cutting off the head. Cut off the tentacles and reserve. Remove the small soft bone at the base of the tentacles and the transparent backbone, as well as the ink bag. Peel off the thin skin, then wash and dry well.

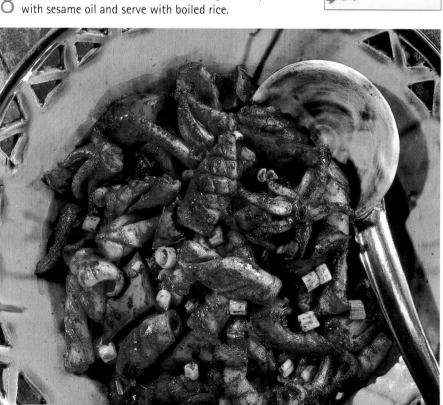

Oriental Shellfish Kebabs

These shellfish and vegetable kebabs are ideal for serving at parties. They are quick and easy to prepare and take next to no time to cook.

NUTRITIONAL INFORMATION

Calories ....93 Sugars 1g
Protein ....15g Fat 2g
Carbohydrate ....2g Saturates 0.3g

2¹/₂ HOURS   5 MINS

MAKES 12

INGREDIENTS

350 g/12 oz raw tiger prawns (jumbo shrimp), peeled leaving tails intact

350 g/12 oz scallops, cleaned, trimmed and halved (quartered if large)

1 bunch spring onions (scallions), sliced into 2.5 cm/1 inch pieces

1 medium red (bell) pepper, deseeded and cubed

100 g/3½ oz baby corn cobs, trimmed and sliced into 1 cm/½ inch pieces

3 tbsp dark soy sauce

½ tsp hot chilli powder

½ tsp ground ginger

1 tbsp sunflower oil

1 red chilli, deseeded and sliced, to garnish

DIP

4 tbsp dark soy sauce

4 tbsp dry sherry

2 tsp clear honey

2.5 cm/1 inch piece root (fresh) ginger, peeled and grated

1 spring onion (scallion), trimmed and sliced very finely

1 Divide the prawns (shrimp), scallops, spring onions (scallions), (bell) pepper and baby corn into 12 portions and thread on to the skewers (soaked for 10 minutes in water to prevent them from burning). Cover the ends with foil so that they do not burn and place in a shallow dish.

2 Mix the soy sauce, chilli powder and ground ginger and coat the kebabs. Cover and chill for about 2 hours.

3 Preheat the grill (broiler) to hot. Arrange the kebabs on the rack, brush with oil and cook for 2–3 minutes on each side until the prawns (shrimp) turn pink, the scallops become opaque and the vegetables soften.

4 Mix together the dip ingredients.

5 Remove the foil and transfer the kebabs to a warm serving platter. Garnish with sliced chilli and serve with the dip.

Squid Casserole

Squid is often served fried in Italy, but here it is casseroled with tomatoes and (bell) peppers to give a rich sauce.

NUTRITIONAL INFORMATION

Calories 281   Sugars 8g
Protein . . . . .31g   Fat 10g
Carbohydrate . . . .9g   Saturates 1g

 25 MINS   1½ HOURS

SERVES 4

I N G R E D I E N T S

1 kg/2 lb 4 oz whole squid, cleaned or
750 g/1 lb 10 oz squid rings, defrosted if
frozen

3 tbsp olive oil

1 large onion, sliced thinly

2 garlic cloves, crushed

1 red (bell) pepper, cored,
deseeded and sliced

1–2 sprigs fresh rosemary

150 ml/1/4 pint/⅔ cup dry white wine and
250 ml/8 fl oz/1 cup water, or 350 ml/
12 fl oz/1½ cups water or fish stock

400 g/14 oz can chopped tomatoes

2 tbsp tomato purée (paste)

1 tsp paprika

salt and pepper

fresh sprigs of rosemary or parsley,
to garnish

1 Cut the squid pouch into 1 cm/½ inch slices; cut the tentacles into lengths of about 5 cm/2 inches. If using frozen squid rings, make sure they are fully defrosted and well drained.

2 Heat the oil in a flameproof casserole and fry the onion and garlic gently until soft. Add the squid, increase the heat and continue to cook for about 10 minutes until sealed and beginning to colour lightly. Add the red (bell) pepper, rosemary, wine (if using) and water or stock and bring up to the boil. Cover and simmer gently for 45 minutes.

3 Discard the sprigs of rosemary (but don't take out any leaves that have come off). Add the tomatoes, tomato purée (paste), seasonings and paprika. Continue to simmer gently for 45–60 minutes, or cover the casserole tightly and cook in a moderate oven, 180°C/350°F/Gas Mark 4, for 45–60 minutes until tender.

4 Give the sauce a good stir, season and serve with fresh, crusty bread.

Fried Prawns with Cashews

Cashew nuts are delicious as part of a stir-fry with almost any other ingredient. Use the unsalted variety in cooking.

NUTRITIONAL INFORMATION

Calories . . . . . . .406 Sugar 3g
Protein . . . . .31g Fat 25g
Carbohydrate . . .13g Saturates 4g

5 MINS   5 MINS

SERVES 4

INGREDIENTS

2 garlic cloves, crushed

1 tbsp cornflour (cornstarch)

pinch of caster (superfine) sugar

450 g/1 lb raw tiger prawns
   (jumbo shrimp)

4 tbsp vegetable oil

1 leek, sliced

125 g/4½ oz broccoli florets

1 orange (bell) pepper, seeded
   and diced

75 g/2 ¾ oz/¾ cup unsalted
   cashew nuts

SAUCE

175 ml/6 fl oz/¾ cup fish stock

1 tbsp cornflour (cornstarch)

dash of chilli sauce

2 tsp sesame oil

1 tbsp Chinese rice wine

1 Mix together the garlic, cornflour (cornstarch) and sugar in a bowl.

2 Peel and devein the prawns (shrimp). Stir the prawns (shrimp) into the mixture to coat thoroughly.

3 Heat the vegetable oil in a preheated wok and add the prawn (shrimp) mixture. Stir-fry over a high heat for 20–30 seconds until the prawns (shrimp) turn pink. Remove the prawns (shrimp) from the wok with a slotted spoon, drain on absorbent kitchen paper (paper towels) and set aside until required.

4 Add the leek, broccoli and (bell) pepper to the wok and stir-fry for 2 minutes.

5 To make the sauce, place the fish stock, cornflour (cornstarch), chilli sauce to taste, the sesame oil and Chinese rice wine in a small bowl. Mix until thoroughly

6 Add the sauce to the wok, together with the cashew nuts. Return the prawns (shrimp) to the wok and cook for 1 minute to heat through.

7 Transfer the prawn (shrimp) stir-fry to a warm serving dish and serve immediately.

Squid & Macaroni Stew

This scrumptious seafood dish is quick and easy to make, yet deliciously satisfying to eat.

NUTRITIONAL INFORMATION

Calories . . . . . . .292 Sugars 3g
Protein . . . . .13g Fat 14g
Carbohydrate . . .24g Saturates 2g

15 MINS   35 MINS

SERVES 6

INGREDIENTS

225 g/8 oz/2 cups dried short-cut macaroni
  or other small pasta shapes

7 tbsp olive oil

2 onions, sliced

350 g/12 oz prepared squid, cut into
  4 cm/1½ inch strips

225 ml/8 fl oz/1 cup fish stock

150 ml/¼ pint/⅝ cup red wine

350 g/12 oz tomatoes, skinned and
  thinly sliced

2 tbsp tomato purée (paste)

1 tsp dried oregano

2 bay leaves

2 tbsp chopped fresh parsley

salt and pepper

crusty bread, to serve

COOK'S TIP

To prepare squid, peel off the skin, then cut off the head and tentacles. Discard the transparent flat oval bone from the body. Remove the sac of black ink, then turn the body sac inside out. Wash in cold water. Cut off the tentacles; discard the rest. Rinse.

1 Bring a large saucepan of lightly salted water to the boil. Add the pasta and 1 tablespoon of the olive oil and cook for 3 minutes. Drain, return to the pan, cover and keep warm.

2 Heat the remaining oil in a pan over a medium heat. Add the onions and fry until they are translucent. Add the squid and stock and simmer for 5 minutes. Pour in the wine and add the tomatoes, tomato purée (paste), oregano and bay leaves. Bring the sauce to the boil, season to taste and cook for 5 minutes.

3 Stir the pasta into the pan, cover and simmer for about 10 minutes, or until the squid and macaroni are tender and the sauce has thickened. If the sauce remains too liquid, uncover the pan and continue cooking for a few minutes longer.

4 Remove and discard the bay leaves. Reserve a little parsley and stir the remainder into the pan. Transfer to a warm serving dish and sprinkle over the remaining parsley. Serve with crusty bread to soak up the sauce.

Squid with Oyster Sauce

Squid is a delicious fish, which if prepared and cooked correctly, is a quick cooking, attractive and tasty ingredient.

NUTRITIONAL INFORMATION

Calories 320   Sugars 1g
Protein . . . . .18g   Fat 26g
Carbohydrate . . . .2g   Saturates 3g

5 MINS   15 MINS

SERVES 4

INGREDIENTS

450 g/1 lb squid

150 ml/¼ pint/⅔ cup vegetable oil

1-cm/½-inch piece fresh root ginger, grated

60 g/2 oz mangetout (snow peas)

5 tbsp hot fish stock

red (bell) pepper triangles, to garnish

SAUCE

1 tbsp oyster sauce

1 tbsp light soy sauce

pinch of caster (superfine) sugar

1 garlic clove, crushed

1 To prepare the squid, cut down the centre of the body lengthways. Flatten the squid out, inside uppermost, and score a lattice design deep into the flesh, using a sharp knife.

2 To make the sauce, combine the oyster sauce, soy sauce, sugar and garlic in a small bowl. Stir to dissolve the sugar and set aside until required.

3 Heat the oil in a preheated wok until almost smoking. Lower the heat slightly, add the squid and stir-fry until they curl up. Remove with a slotted spoon and drain thoroughly on kitchen paper (paper towels).

4 Pour off all but 2 tablespoons of the oil and return the wok to the heat. Add the ginger and mangetout (snow peas) and stir-fry for 1 minute.

5 Return the squid to the wok and pour in the sauce and hot fish stock. Leave to simmer for 3 minutes until thickened. Transfer to a warm serving dish, garnish with (bell) pepper triangles and serve immediately.

COOK'S TIP

Take care not to overcook the squid, otherwise it will be rubbery and unappetizing.

Baked Scallops & Pasta

This is another tempting seafood dish where the eye is delighted as much as the tastebuds.

NUTRITIONAL INFORMATION

Calories 725   Sugars 2g
Protein ....38g   Fat 48g
Carbohydrate ...38g   Saturates 25g

 20 MINS   30 MINS

SERVES 4

I N G R E D I E N T S

12 scallops

3 tbsp olive oil

350 g/12 oz/3 cups small, dried wholemeal
   (whole-wheat) pasta shells

150 ml/¼ pint/⅔ cup fish stock

1 onion, chopped

juice and finely grated rind of 2 lemons

150 ml/¼ pint/⅔ cup double (heavy) cream

225 g/8 oz/2 cups grated Cheddar cheese

salt and pepper

crusty brown bread, to serve

1 Remove the scallops from their shells. Scrape off the skirt and the black intestinal thread. Reserve the white part (the flesh) and the orange part (the coral or roe). Very carefully ease the flesh and coral from the shell with a short, but very strong knife.

2 Wash the shells thoroughly and dry them well. Put the shells on a baking tray (cookie sheet), sprinkle lightly with two thirds of the olive oil and set aside.

3 Meanwhile, bring a large saucepan of lightly salted water to the boil. Add the pasta shells and remaining olive oil and cook for 8–10 minutes or until tender, but still firm to the bite. Drain well and

spoon about 25 g/1 oz of pasta into each scallop shell.

4 Put the scallops, fish stock and onion in an ovenproof dish and season to taste with pepper. Cover with foil and bake in a preheated oven at 180°C/ 350°F/Gas Mark 4 for 8 minutes.

5 Remove the dish from the oven. Remove the foil and, using a slotted spoon, transfer the scallops to the shells.

Add 1 tablespoon of the cooking liquid to each shell, together with a drizzle of lemon juice and a little cream, and top with the grated cheese.

6 Increase the oven temperature to 230°C/450°F/Gas Mark 8 and return the scallops to the oven for a further 4 minutes.

7 Serve the scallops in their shells with crusty brown bread and butter.

Mussels with Tomato Sauce

This recipe for Mediterranean-style baked mussels, topped with a fresh tomato sauce and breadcrumbs, has been adapted for the microwave.

NUTRITIONAL INFORMATION

Calories	254	Sugars	.........1g
Protein	........37g	Fat	..........10g
Carbohydrate	....4g	Saturates	.......3g

20 MINS   15 MINS

SERVES 4

INGREDIENTS

½ small onion, chopped

1 garlic clove, crushed

1 tbsp olive oil

3 tomatoes

1 tbsp chopped fresh parsley

900 g/2 lb live mussels

1 tbsp freshly grated Parmesan cheese

1 tbsp fresh white breadcrumbs

salt and pepper

chopped fresh parsley, to garnish

1 Place the onion, garlic and oil in a bowl. Cover and cook on HIGH power for 3 minutes.

2 Cut a cross in the base of each tomato and place them in a small bowl. Pour on boiling water and leave for about 45 seconds. Drain and then plunge into cold water. The skins will slide off easily. Chop the tomatoes, removing any hard cores.

3 Add the tomatoes to the onion mixture, cover and cook on HIGH power for 3 minutes. Stir in the parsley and season to taste.

4 Scrub the mussels well in several changes of cold water. Remove the beards and discard any open mussels and those which do not close when tapped sharply with the back of a knife.

5 Place the mussels in a large bowl. Add enough boiling water to cover them. Cover and cook on HIGH power for 2 minutes, stirring halfway through, until the mussels open. Drain well and remove the empty half of each shell. Arrange the mussels in 1 layer on a plate.

6 Spoon the tomato sauce over each mussel. Mix the Parmesan cheese with the breadcrumbs and sprinkle on top.

Cook, uncovered, on HIGH power for 2 minutes. Garnish with parsley and serve.

COOK'S TIP

Dry out the breadcrumbs in the microwave for an extra crunchy topping. Spread them on a plate and cook on HIGH power for 2 minutes, stirring once. Leave to stand, uncovered.

Saffron Mussel Tagliatelle

Saffron is the most expensive spice in the world, but you only ever need a small quantity. Saffron threads or powdered saffron may be used.

NUTRITIONAL INFORMATION

Calories 854	Sugars 3g
Protein 43g	Fat 49g
Carbohydrate ...57g	Saturates 28g

 15 MINS 35 MINS

SERVES 4

INGREDIENTS

1 kg/2 lb 4 oz mussels

150 ml/¼ pint/⅔ cup white wine

1 medium onion, finely chopped

25 g/1 oz/2 tbsp butter

2 garlic cloves, crushed

2 tsp cornflour (cornstarch)

300 ml/½ pint/1¼ cups double
  (heavy) cream

pinch of saffron threads or saffron powder

juice of ½ lemon

1 egg yolk

450 g/1 lb dried tagliatelle

1 tbsp olive oil

salt and pepper

3 tbsp chopped fresh parsley, to garnish

1 Scrub and debeard the mussels under cold running water. Discard any that do not close when sharply tapped. Put the mussels in a pan with the wine and onion. Cover and cook over a high heat, shaking the pan, for 5–8 minutes, until the shells open.

2 Drain and reserve the cooking liquid. Discard any mussels that are still closed. Reserve a few mussels for the garnish and remove the remainder from their shells.

3 Strain the cooking liquid into a pan. Bring to the boil and reduce by about half. Remove the pan from the heat.

4 Melt the butter in a saucepan. Add the garlic and cook, stirring frequently, for 2 minutes, until golden brown. Stir in the cornflour (cornstarch) and cook, stirring, for 1 minute. Gradually stir in the cooking liquid and the cream. Crush the saffron threads and add to the pan. Season with salt and pepper to taste and simmer over a low heat for 2–3 minutes, until thickened.

5 Stir in the egg yolk, lemon juice and shelled mussels. Do not allow the mixture to boil.

6 Meanwhile, bring a pan of salted water to the boil. Add the pasta and oil and cook for 8–10 minutes until tender, but still firm to the bite. Drain and transfer to a serving dish. Add the mussel sauce and toss. Garnish with the parsley and reserved mussels and serve.

Penne with Fried Mussels

This is quick and simple, but one of the nicest of Italian fried fish dishes, served with penne.

NUTRITIONAL INFORMATION

Calories	537	Sugars	.........2g
Protein	........22g	Fat	..........24g
Carbohydrate	...62g	Saturates	.......3g

10 MINS   25 MINS

SERVES 6

INGREDIENTS

400 g/14 oz/3 ½ cups dried penne

125 ml/4 fl oz/ ½ cup olive oil

450 g/1 lb mussels, cooked and shelled

1 tsp sea salt

90 g/3 oz/ ⅔ cup flour

100 g/3 ½ oz sun-dried tomatoes, sliced

2 tbsp chopped fresh basil leaves

salt and pepper

1 lemon, thinly sliced, to garnish

1 Bring a large saucepan of lightly salted water to the boil. Add the penne and 1 tablespoon of the olive oil and cook for 8–10 minutes or until the pasta is just tender, but still firm to the bite.

2 Drain the pasta thoroughly and place in a large, warm serving dish. Set aside and keep warm while you cook the mussels.

3 Lightly sprinkle the mussels with the sea salt. Season the flour with salt and pepper to taste, sprinkle into a bowl and toss the mussels in the flour until well coated.

4 Heat the remaining oil in a large frying pan (skillet). Add the mussels and fry, stirring frequently, until a golden brown colour.

5 Toss the mussels with the penne and sprinkle with the sun-dried tomatoes and basil leaves. Garnish with slices of lemon and serve immediately.

COOK'S TIP

Sun-dried tomatoes, used in Italy for a long time, have become popular elsewhere only quite recently. They are dried and then preserved in oil. They have a concentrated, roasted flavour and a dense texture. They should be drained and chopped or sliced before using.

Thai Potato Crab Cakes

These small crab cakes are based on a traditional Thai recipe. They make a delicious snack when served with this sweet and sour cucumber sauce.

NUTRITIONAL INFORMATION

Calories 254   Sugars 9g
Protein ....12g   Fat 6g
Carbohydrate ...40g   Saturates 1g

  10 MINS   30 MINS

SERVES 4

INGREDIENTS

450 g/1 lb floury (mealy) potatoes, diced

175 g/6 oz white crab meat, drained if canned

4 spring onions (scallions), chopped

1 tsp light soy sauce

½ tsp sesame oil

1 tsp chopped lemon grass

1 tsp lime juice

3 tbsp plain (all-purpose) flour

2 tbsp vegetable oil

salt and pepper

SAUCE

4 tbsp finely chopped cucumber

2 tbsp clear honey

1 tbsp garlic wine vinegar

½ tsp light soy sauce

1 chopped red chilli

TO GARNISH

1 red chilli, sliced

cucumber slices

1 Cook the diced potatoes in a saucepan of boiling water for 10 minutes until cooked through. Drain well and mash.

2 Mix the crab meat into the potato with the spring onions (scallions), soy sauce, sesame oil, lemon grass, lime juice and flour. Season with salt and pepper.

3 Divide the potato mixture into 8 portions of equal size and shape them into small rounds, using floured hands.

4 Heat the oil in a wok or frying pan (skillet) and cook the cakes, 4 at a time, for 5-7 minutes, turning once. Keep warm and repeat with the remaining crab cakes.

5 Meanwhile, make the sauce. In a small serving bowl, mix the cucumber, honey, vinegar, soy sauce and chopped red chilli.

6 Garnish the cakes with the sliced red chilli and cucumber slices and serve with the sauce.

Spiced Scallops

Scallops are available both fresh and frozen. Make sure they are completely defrosted before cooking.

NUTRITIONAL INFORMATION

Calories 276   Sugar 6g
Protein . . . . .25g   Fat 15g
Carbohydrate . . . .8g   Saturates 2g

 10 MINS   10 MINS

SERVES 4

INGREDIENTS

12 large scallops with coral attached,
   defrosted if frozen, or 350 g/
   12 oz small scallops without
   coral, defrosted

4 tbsp sunflower oil

4-6 spring onions (scallions), thinly sliced
   diagonally

1 garlic clove, crushed

2.5 cm/1 inch ginger root,
   finely chopped

250 g/9 oz mangetout (snow peas)

125 g/4½ oz button or closed cup
   mushrooms, sliced

2 tbsp sherry

2 tbsp soy sauce

1 tbsp clear honey

¼ tsp ground allspice

salt and pepper

1 tbsp sesame seeds, toasted

1 Wash and dry the scallops, discarding any black pieces and detach the corals, if using.

2 Slice each scallop into 3-4 pieces and if the corals are large halve them.

3 Heat 2 tablespoons of the sunflower oil in a preheated wok or large, heavy-based frying pan (skillet), swirling it around until really hot.

4 Add the spring onions (scallions), garlic and ginger to the wok or frying pan (skillet) and stir-fry for about 1 minute.

5 Add the mangetout (snow peas) to the wok and continue to cook for a further 2-3 minutes, stirring continuously. Remove to a bowl and set aside.

6 Add the remaining sunflower oil to the wok and when really hot add the scallops and corals and stir-fry for a couple of minutes.

7 Add the mushrooms and continue to cook for a further minute or so.

8 Add the sherry, soy sauce, honey and allspice to the wok, with salt and pepper to taste. Mix thoroughly, then return the mangetout (snow peas) mixture to the wok.

9 Season well with salt and pepper and toss together over a high heat for a minute or so until piping hot. Serve the scallops and vegetables immediately, sprinkled with sesame seeds.

Balti Scallops

This is a wonderful recipe for a special occasion dish. Cooked with coriander (cilantro) and tomatoes, the scallops have a spicy flavour.

NUTRITIONAL INFORMATION

Calories 258	Sugars 2g
Protein 44g	Fat 8g
Carbohydrate 3g	Saturates 1g

 1¼ HOURS 🕐 15 MINS

SERVES 4

INGREDIENTS

750 g/1 lb 10 oz shelled scallops

2 tbsp oil

2 onions, chopped

3 tomatoes, quartered

2 fresh green chillies, sliced

4 lime wedges, to garnish

MARINADE

3 tbsp chopped fresh coriander (cilantro)

2.5 cm/1 inch piece ginger root, grated

1 tsp ground coriander

3 tbsp lemon juice

grated rind of 1 lemon

¼ tsp ground black pepper

½ tsp salt

½ tsp ground cumin

1 garlic clove, crushed

1 To make the marinade, mix all the ingredients together in a bowl.

2 Put the scallops into a bowl. Add the marinade and turn the scallops until they are well coated.

3 Then cover and leave to marinate for 1 hour or overnight in the fridge.

4 Heat the oil in a Balti pan or wok, add the onions and stir-fry until softened.

5 Add the tomatoes and chillies and stir-fry for 1 minute.

6 Add the scallops and stir-fry for 6–8 minutes until the scallops are cooked through, but still succulent inside.

7 Serve garnished with lime wedges.

COOK'S TIP

It is best to buy the scallops fresh in the shell with the roe – you will need 1.5 kg/3 lb 5 oz – a fishmonger will clean them and remove the shell for you.

Provençale-Style Mussels

These delicious large mussels are served hot with a tasty tomato and vegetable sauce. Mop up the delicious sauce with some crusty bread.

NUTRITIONAL INFORMATION

Calories ....253 Sugars 8g
Protein ....31g Fat 8g
Carbohydrate ....9g Saturates 1g

  5 MINS   50 MINS

SERVES 4

INGREDIENTS

1 tbsp olive oil

1 large onion, finely chopped

1 garlic clove, finely chopped

1 small red (bell) pepper, deseeded and finely chopped

sprig of rosemary

2 bay leaves

400 g/14 oz can chopped tomatoes

150 ml/5 fl oz/⅔ cup white wine

1 courgette (zucchini), diced finely

2 tbsp tomato purée (paste)

1 tsp caster (superfine) sugar

50 g/1¾ oz pitted black olives in brine, drained and chopped

675 g/1½ lb cooked New Zealand mussels in their shells

1 tsp orange rind

salt and pepper

crusty bread, to serve

2 tbsp chopped, fresh parsley, to garnish

1 Heat the oil in a large saucepan and gently fry the onion, garlic and (bell) pepper for 3–4 minutes until just softened.

2 Add the sprig of rosemary and the bay leaves to the saucepan with the tomatoes and 100 ml/3½ fl oz/⅓ cup wine. Season with salt and pepper to taste, then bring to the boil and simmer for 15 minutes.

3 Stir in the courgette (zucchini), tomato purée (paste), sugar and olives. Simmer for 10 minutes.

4 Meanwhile, bring a pan of water to the boil. Arrange the mussels in a steamer or a large sieve (strainer) and place over the water. Sprinkle with the remaining wine and the orange rind. Cover and steam until the mussels open (discard any that remain closed).

5 Remove the mussels with a slotted spoon and arrange on a serving plate. Discard the herbs and spoon the sauce over the mussels. Garnish with chopped parsley and serve with crusty bread.

Curried Crab

If you can buy fresh crab, clean the shell and brush lightly with oil and use as a container for the crab meat.

NUTRITIONAL INFORMATION

Calories	272	Sugars	.........5g
Protein	........27g	Fat	..........16g
Carbohydrate	....5g	Saturates	.......2g

5 MINS   15 MINS

SERVES 4

I N G R E D I E N T S

2 tbsp mustard oil

1 tbsp ghee

1 onion, chopped finely

5 cm/2 inch piece ginger root, grated

2 garlic cloves, peeled but left whole

1 tsp ground turmeric

1 tsp salt

1 tsp chilli powder

2 fresh green chillies, chopped

1 tsp paprika

125 g/4½ oz/½ cup brown crab meat

350 g/12 oz/1½ cups white crab meat

250 ml/9 fl oz /1 cup low-fat natural yogurt

1 tsp garam masala

basmati rice, to serve

fresh coriander (cilantro), to garnish

1 Heat the mustard oil in a large, preferably non-stick, frying pan (skillet), wok or saucepan.

2 When it starts to smoke, add the ghee and onion. Stir for 3 minutes over a medium heat until the onion is soft.

3 Stir in the ginger and whole garlic cloves.

4 Add the turmeric, salt, chilli powder, chillies and paprika. Mix thoroughly.

5 Increase the heat and add the crab meat and yogurt. Simmer, stirring occasionally, for 10 minutes until the sauce is thickened slightly.

6 Add garam masala to taste.

7 Serve hot, over plain basmati rice, with the fresh coriander (cilantro) either chopped or in sprigs.

COOK'S TIP

For an unusual combination of flavours, mix the crab meat with segments of grapefruit in a mayonnaise. Sprinkle with slivers of almonds.

Crab with Chinese Leaves

The delicate flavour of Chinese leaves (cabbage) and crab meat are enhanced by the coconut milk in this recipe.

NUTRITIONAL INFORMATION

Calories 109   Sugars 1g
Protein . . . . .11g   Fat 6g
Carbohydrate . . . .2g   Saturates 1g

5 MINS   10 MINS

SERVES 4

INGREDIENTS

225 g/8 oz shiitake mushrooms

2 tbsp vegetable oil

2 cloves garlic, crushed

6 spring onions (scallions), sliced

1 head Chinese leaves (cabbage), shredded

1 tbsp mild curry paste

6 tbsp coconut milk

200 g/7 oz can white crab meat, drained

1 tsp chilli flakes

1 Using a sharp knife, cut the the mushrooms into slices.

2 Heat the vegetable oil in a large preheated wok or heavy-based frying pan (skillet).

3 Add the mushrooms and garlic to the wok or frying pan (skillet) and stir-fry for 3 minutes or until the mushrooms have softened.

4 Add the spring onions (scallions) and shredded Chinese leaves (cabbage) to the wok and stir-fry until the leaves have wilted.

5 Mix together the mild curry paste and coconut milk in a small bowl.

6 Add the curry paste and coconut milk mixture to the wok, together with the crab meat and chilli flakes. Mix together until well combined.

7 Heat the mixture in the wok until the juices start to bubble.

8 Transfer the crab and vegetable stir-fry to warm serving bowls and serve immediately.

COOK'S TIP

Shiitake mushrooms are now readily available in the fresh vegetable section of most large supermarkets.

Crab in Ginger Sauce

In this recipe, the crabs are served in the shell for ease and visual effect and coated in a glossy ginger sauce.

NUTRITIONAL INFORMATION

Calories 125   Sugars 2g
Protein . . . . .8g   Fat 8g
Carbohydrate . . . .5g   Saturates 1g

 10 MINS   10 MINS

SERVES 4

INGREDIENTS

2 small cooked crabs

2 tbsp vegetable oil

9-cm/3-inch piece fresh root ginger, grated

2 garlic cloves, thinly sliced

1 green (bell) pepper, seeded and cut into thin strips

6 spring onions (scallions), cut into 2.5-cm/1-inch lengths

2 tbsp dry sherry

½ tsp sesame oil

150 ml/¼ pint/⅔ cup fish stock

1 tsp light brown sugar

2 tsp cornflour (cornstarch)

150 ml/¼ pint/⅔ cup water

VARIATION

If preferred, remove the crab-meat from the shells prior to stir-frying and add to the wok with the (bell) pepper.

1 Rinse the crabs and gently loosen around the shell at the top. Using a sharp knife, cut away the grey tissue and discard. Rinse the crabs again.

2 Twist off the legs and claws from the crabs. Using a pair of crab claw crackers or a cleaver, gently crack the claws to break through the shell to expose the flesh. Remove and discard any loose pieces of shell.

3 Separate the body and discard the inedible lungs and sac. Cut down the centre of each crab to separate the body into two pieces and then cut each of these in half again.

4 Heat the oil in a preheated wok. Add the ginger and garlic and stir-fry for 1 minute. Add the crab pieces and stir-fry for a further minute.

5 Stir in the (bell) pepper, spring onions (scallions), sherry, sesame oil, stock and sugar. Bring to the boil, reduce the heat, cover and simmer for 3–4 minutes.

6 Blend the cornflour (cornstarch) with the water and stir into the wok. Bring to the boil, stirring, until the sauce is thickened and clear. Transfer to a warm serving dish and serve immediately.

Crab Fried Rice

Canned crabmeat is used in this recipe for convenience, but fresh white crabmeat could be used - quite deliciously - in its place.

NUTRITIONAL INFORMATION

Calories 225   Sugars 1g
Protein ....12g   Fat 11g
Carbohydrate ...20g   Saturates 2g

 5 MINS   25 MINS

SERVES 4

INGREDIENTS

150 g/5½ oz/⅔ cup long-grain rice

2 tbsp peanut oil

125 g/4½ oz canned white crabmeat, drained

1 leek, sliced

150 g/5½ oz/⅔ cup bean sprouts

2 eggs, beaten

1 tbsp light soy sauce

2 tsp lime juice

1 tsp sesame oil

salt

sliced lime, to garnish

1 Cook the rice in a saucepan of boiling salted water for 15 minutes. Drain well, rinse under cold running water and drain again thoroughly.

2 Heat the peanut oil in a preheated wok until it is really hot.

3 Add the crabmeat, leek and bean sprouts to the wok and stir-fry for 2-3 minutes. Remove the mixture from the wok with a slotted spoon and set aside until required.

4 Add the eggs to the wok and cook, stirring occasionally, for 2-3 minutes, until they begin to set.

5 Stir the rice and the crabmeat, leek and bean sprout mixture into the eggs in the wok.

6 Add the soy sauce and lime juice to the mixture in the wok. Cook for 1 minute, stirring to combine, and sprinkle with the sesame oil.

7 Transfer the crab fried rice to a serving dish, garnish with the sliced lime and serve immediately.

VARIATION

Cooked lobster may be used instead of the crab for a really special dish.

Seafood Stir Fry

This combination of assorted seafood and tender vegetables flavoured with ginger makes an ideal light meal served with thread noodles.

NUTRITIONAL INFORMATION

Calories 226	Sugars 5g
Protein 35g	Fat 7g
Carbohydrate 6g	Saturates 1g

5 MINS   15 MINS

SERVES 4

INGREDIENTS

100 g/3½ oz small, thin asparagus spears, trimmed

1 tbsp sunflower oil

2.5 cm/1 inch piece root (fresh) ginger, cut into thin strips

1 medium leek, shredded

2 medium carrots, julienned

100 g/3½ oz baby sweetcorn cobs, quartered lengthwise

2 tbsp light soy sauce

1 tbsp oyster sauce

1 tsp clear honey

450 g/1 lb cooked, assorted shellfish, thawed if frozen

freshly cooked egg noodles, to serve

TO GARNISH

4 large cooked prawns

small bunch fresh chives, freshly snipped

1 Bring a small saucepan of water to the boil and blanch the asparagus for 1–2 minutes.

2 Drain the asparagus, set aside and keep warm.

3 Heat the oil in a wok or large frying pan (skillet) and stir-fry the ginger,

leek, carrot and sweetcorn for about 3 minutes. Do not allow the vegetables to brown.

4 Add the soy sauce, oyster sauce and honey to the wok or frying pan (skillet).

5 Stir in the cooked shellfish and continue to stir-fry for 2–3 minutes until the vegetables are just tender and the shellfish are thoroughly heated

through. Add the blanched asparagus and stir-fry for about 2 minutes.

6 To serve, pile the cooked noodles on to 4 warm serving plates and spoon the seafood and vegetable stir fry over them.

7 Garnish with the cooked prawns and freshly snipped chives and serve immediately. Serve garnished with a large prawn and freshly snipped chives.

Crab Meat Cakes

Make these tasty crab-meat cakes to serve as a snack or starter, or as an accompaniment to a main meal.

NUTRITIONAL INFORMATION

Calories 262   Sugars 4g
Protein . . . . .13g   Fat 17g
Carbohydrate . . .14g   Saturates 3g

 20 MINS   55 MINS

SERVES 4

I N G R E D I E N T S

90 g/3 oz/generous 1 cup long-grain rice

1 tbsp sesame oil

1 small onion, chopped finely

1 large garlic clove, crushed

2 tbsp chopped fresh coriander (cilantro)

200 g/7 oz can of crab meat, drained

1 tbsp fish sauce or light soy sauce

250 ml/9 fl oz/1 cup coconut milk

2 eggs

4 tbsp vegetable oil

salt and pepper

sliced spring onions (scallions), to garnish

1 Cook the rice in plenty of boiling, lightly salted water until just tender, about 12 minutes. Rinse with cold water and drain well.

2 Heat the sesame oil in a small frying pan (skillet) and fry the onion and garlic gently for about 5 minutes, until softened and golden brown.

3 Combine the rice, onion, garlic, coriander (cilantro), crab meat, fish sauce or soy sauce and coconut milk. Season. Beat the eggs and add to the mixture. Divide the mixture between 8 greased ramekin dishes or teacups and place them in a baking dish or roasting tin (pan) with enough warm water to come halfway up their sides. Place in a preheated oven at 180°C/ 350°F/Gas Mark 4 for 25 minutes, until set. Leave to cool.

4 Turn the crab cakes out of the ramekin dishes . Heat the oil in a wok or frying pan (skillet) and fry the crab cakes in the oil until golden brown. Drain on kitchen paper (paper towels), garnish and serve.

COOK'S TIP

If you want, you can prepare these crab cakes up to the point where they have been baked. Cool them, then cover and chill, ready for frying when needed.

Vermicelli with Clams

A quickly-cooked recipe that transforms store-cupboard ingredients into a dish with style.

NUTRITIONAL INFORMATION

Calories 520	Sugars 2g	
Protein 26g	Fat 13g	
Carbohydrate 71g	Saturates 4g	

🍴 10 MINS   🕐 25 MINS

SERVES 4

INGREDIENTS

400 g/14 oz dried vermicelli, spaghetti or
    other long pasta

2 tbsp olive oil

25 g/1 oz/2 tbsp butter

2 onions, chopped

2 garlic cloves, chopped

2 x 200 g/7 oz jars clams in brine

125 ml/4 fl oz/½ cup white wine

4 tbsp chopped fresh parsley

½ tsp dried oregano

pinch of freshly grated nutmeg

salt and pepper

TO GARNISH

2 tbsp Parmesan cheese shavings

fresh basil sprigs

1 Bring a large pan of lightly salted water to the boil. Add the pasta and half of the olive oil and cook for 8–10 minutes until tender, but still firm to the bite. Drain, return to the pan and add the butter. Cover the pan, shake well and keep warm.

2 Heat the remaining oil in a pan over a medium heat. Add the onions and fry until they are translucent. Stir in the garlic and cook for 1 minute.

3 Strain the liquid from 1 jar of clams and add the liquid to the pan, with the wine. Stir, bring to simmering point and simmer for 3 minutes. Drain the second jar of clams and discard the liquid.

4 Add the clams, parsley and oregano to the pan and season with pepper and nutmeg. Lower the heat and cook until the sauce is heated through.

5 Transfer the pasta to a warm serving dish and pour over the sauce. Sprinkle with the Parmesan cheese, garnish with the basil and serve immediately.

COOK'S TIP

There are many different types of clams found along almost every coast in the world. Those traditionally used in this dish are the tiny ones – only 2.5-5 cm/1-2 inches across – known in Italy as vongole.

Farfallini Buttered Lobster

This is one of those dishes that looks almost too lovely to eat – but you should!

NUTRITIONAL INFORMATION

Calories 686   Sugars 1g
Protein ....45g   Fat 36g
Carbohydrate ...44g   Saturates 19g

  30 MINS   25 MINS

SERVES 4

INGREDIENTS

2 x 700 g/1 lb 9 oz lobsters, split into halves

juice and grated rind of 1 lemon

115 g/4 oz/½ cup butter

4 tbsp fresh white breadcrumbs

2 tbsp brandy

5 tbsp double (heavy) cream or crème fraîche

450 g/1 lb dried farfallini

1 tbsp olive oil

60 g/2 oz/⅔ cup freshly grated Parmesan cheese

salt and pepper

TO GARNISH

1 kiwi fruit, sliced

4 unpeeled, cooked king prawns (shrimp)

fresh dill sprigs

1 Carefully discard the stomach sac, vein and gills from each lobster. Remove all the meat from the tail and chop. Crack the claws and legs, remove the meat and chop. Transfer the meat to a bowl and add the lemon juice and grated lemon rind.

2 Clean the shells thoroughly and place in a warm oven at 170°C/325°/Gas Mark 3 to dry out.

3 Melt 25 g/1 oz/2 tbsp of the butter in a frying pan (skillet). Add the breadcrumbs and fry for about 3 minutes, until crisp and golden brown.

4 Melt the remaining butter in a saucepan. Add the lobster meat and heat through gently. Add the brandy and cook for a further 3 minutes, then add the cream or crème fraîche and season to taste with salt and pepper.

5 Meanwhile, bring a large pan of lightly salted water to the boil. Add the farfallini and olive oil and cook for 8–10 minutes, until tender but still firm to the bite. Drain and spoon the pasta into the clean lobster shells.

6 Top with the buttered lobster and sprinkle with a little grated Parmesan cheese and the breadcrumbs. Grill (broil) for 2–3 minutes, until golden brown.

7 Transfer the lobster shells to a warm serving dish, garnish with the lemon slices, kiwi fruit, king prawns (shrimp) and dill sprigs and serve immediately.

Seafood Medley

Use any combination of fish and seafood in this delicious dish of coated fish served in a wine sauce.

NUTRITIONAL INFORMATION

Calories ....168 Sugars 2g
Protein ....29g Fat 3g
Carbohydrate ....4g Saturates 1g

5 MINS   15 MINS

SERVES 4

INGREDIENTS

2 tbsp dry white wine

1 egg white, lightly beaten

½ tsp Chinese five-spice powder

1 tsp cornflour (cornstarch)

300 g/10½ oz raw prawns (shrimp),
   peeled and deveined

125 g/4½ oz prepared squid,
   cut into rings

125 g/4½ oz white fish fillets,
   cut into strips

vegetable oil, for deep-frying

1 green (bell) pepper, seeded and
   cut into thin strips

1 carrot, cut into thin strips

4 baby corn cobs, halved lengthways

1 Mix the wine, egg white, five-spice powder and cornflour (cornstarch) in a large bowl. Add the prawns (shrimp), squid rings and fish fillets and stir to coat evenly. Remove the fish and seafood with a slotted spoon, reserving any leftover cornflour (cornstarch) mixture.

2 Heat the oil in a preheated wok and deep-fry the prawns (shrimp), squid and fish for 2–3 minutes. Remove the

seafood mixture from the wok with a slotted spoon and set aside.

3 Pour off all but 1 tablespoon of oil from the wok and return to the heat. Add the (bell) pepper, carrot and corn cobs and stir-fry for 4–5 minutes.

4 Return the seafood to the wok with any remaining cornflour (cornstarch) mixture. Heat through, stirring, and serve.

COOK'S TIP

Open up the squid rings and using a sharp knife, score a lattice pattern on the flesh to make them look attractive.

Seafood Pizza

Make a change from the standard pizza toppings – this dish is piled high with seafood baked with a red (bell) pepper and tomato sauce.

NUTRITIONAL INFORMATION

Calories	248	Sugars 7g
Protein	........27g	Fat 6g
Carbohydrate	...22g	Saturates 2g

 25 MINS   55 MINS

SERVES 4

INGREDIENTS

145 g/5 oz standard pizza base mix

4 tbsp chopped fresh dill or 2 tbsp dried dill

fresh dill, to garnish

SAUCE

1 large red (bell) pepper

400 g/14 oz can chopped tomatoes with onion and herbs

3 tbsp tomato purée (paste)

salt and pepper

TOPPING

350 g/12 oz assorted cooked seafood, thawed if frozen

1 tbsp capers in brine, drained

25 g/1 oz pitted black olives in brine, drained

25 g/1 oz low-fat Mozzarella cheese, grated

1 tbsp grated, fresh Parmesan cheese

1 Preheat the oven to 200°C/400°F/Gas Mark 6. Place the pizza base mix in a bowl and stir in the dill. Make the dough according to the instructions on the packet.

2 Press the dough into a round measuring 25.5 cm/10 inches across on a baking sheet lined with baking parchment. Set aside to prove (rise).

3 Preheat the grill (broiler) to hot. To make the sauce, halve and deseed the (bell) pepper and arrange on a grill (broiler) rack. Cook for 8–10 minutes until softened and charred. Leave to cool slightly, peel off the skin and chop the flesh.

4 Place the tomatoes and (bell) pepper in a saucepan. Bring to the boil and simmer for 10 minutes. Stir in the tomato purée (paste) and season to taste.

5 Spread the sauce over the pizza base and top with the seafood. Sprinkle over the capers and olives, top with the cheeses and bake for 25–30 minutes.

6 Garnish with sprigs of dill and serve hot.

Marinara

This pizza is topped with a cocktail of mixed seafood, such as prawns (shrimp), mussels, cockles and squid rings.

NUTRITIONAL INFORMATION

Calories 359   Sugars 9g
Protein ....19g   Fat 14g
Carbohydrate ...42g   Saturates 4g

3¹/₄ HOURS   20 MINS

SERVES 4

INGREDIENTS

Basic Pizza Dough (see page 861)

Basic Tomato Sauce (see page 6)

200 g/7 oz frozen seafood cocktail, defrosted

1 tbsp capers

1 small yellow (bell) pepper, chopped

1 tbsp chopped fresh marjoram

½ tsp dried oregano

60 g/2 oz Mozzarella, grated

15 g/½ oz Parmesan, grated

12 black olives

olive oil, for drizzling

salt and pepper

sprig of fresh marjoram or oregano, to garnish

1 Roll out or press out the pizza dough, using a rolling pin or your hands, into a 25 cm/10 inch circle on a lightly floured work surface.

2 Place the dough on a large greased baking tray (cookie sheet) or pizza pan and push up the edge a little with your fingers to form a rim.

3 Spread the tomato sauce evenly over the base almost to the edge.

4 Arrange the seafood cocktail, capers and yellow (bell) pepper on top of the tomato sauce.

5 Sprinkle over the herbs and cheeses. Arrange the olives on top. Drizzle over a little olive oil and season with salt and pepper to taste.

6 Bake in a preheated oven, at 200°C/400°F/Gas Mark 6, for 18–20 minutes or until the edge of the pizza is crisp and golden brown.

7 Transfer to a warmed serving plate, garnish with a sprig of marjoram or oregano and serve immediately.

Genoese Seafood Risotto

This is cooked in a different way from any of the other risottos. First, you cook the rice, then you prepare a sauce, then you mix the two together.

NUTRITIONAL INFORMATION

Calories ....424 Sugars 0g
Protein ....23g Fat 17g
Carbohydrate ...46g Saturates 10g

10 MINS   25 MINS

SERVES 4

INGREDIENTS

1.2 litres/2 pints/5 cups hot fish or
  chicken stock

350 g/12 oz arborio (risotto) rice, washed

50 g/1¾ oz/3 tbsp butter

2 garlic cloves, chopped

250 g/9 oz mixed seafood, preferably raw,
  such as prawns (shrimp), squid, mussels,
  clams and (small) shrimps

2 tbsp chopped oregano, plus extra
  for garnishing

50 g/1¾ oz pecorino or Parmesan
  cheese, grated

1 In a large saucepan, bring the stock to the boil. Add the rice and cook for about 12 minutes, stirring, or until the rice is tender. Drain thoroughly, reserving any excess liquid.

2 Heat the butter in a large frying pan (skillet) and add the garlic, stirring.

3 Add the raw mixed seafood to the pan (skillet) and cook for 5 minutes. If you are using cooked seafood, fry for 2–3 minutes.

4 Stir the oregano into the seafood mixture in the frying pan (skillet).

5 Add the cooked rice to the pan and cook for 2–3 minutes, stirring, or until hot. Add the reserved stock if the mixture gets too sticky.

6 Add the pecorino or Parmesan cheese and mix well.

7 Transfer the risotto to warm serving dishes and serve immediately.

COOK'S TIP

The Genoese are excellent cooks, and they make particularly delicious fish dishes flavoured with the local olive oil.

Seafood Omelette

This delicious omelette is filled with a mixture of fresh vegetables, sliced squid and prawns (shrimp).

NUTRITIONAL INFORMATION

Calories 216	Sugars 2g
Protein 20g	Fat 13g
Carbohydrate 4g	Saturates 4g

 5 MINS   10 MINS

SERVES 4

INGREDIENTS

4 eggs

3 tbsp milk

1 tbsp fish sauce or light soy sauce

1 tbsp sesame oil

3 shallots, sliced finely

1 small red (bell) pepper, cored, deseeded and sliced very finely

1 small leek, trimmed and cut into matchstick pieces

125 g/4½ oz squid rings

125 g/4½ oz/⅔ cup cooked peeled prawns (shrimp)

1 tbsp chopped fresh basil

15 g/½ oz/1 tbsp butter

salt and pepper

sprigs of fresh basil, to garnish

1 Beat the eggs, milk and fish sauce or soy sauce together.

2 Heat the sesame oil in a wok or large frying pan (skillet) and add the shallots, (bell) pepper and leek. Stir-fry briskly for 2–3 minutes.

3 Add the squid rings, prawns (shrimp) and chopped basil to the wok or frying pan (skillet). Stir-fry for a further 2–3 minutes, until the squid looks opaque.

4 Season the mixture in the wok with salt and pepper to taste. Transfer to a warmed plate and keep warm until required.

5 Melt the butter in a large omelette pan or frying pan (skillet) and add the beaten egg mixture. Cook over a medium-high heat until just set.

6 Spoon the vegetable and seafood mixture in a line down the middle of the omelette, then fold each side of the omelette over.

7 Transfer the omelette to a warmed serving dish and cut into 4 portions. Garnish with sprigs of fresh basil and serve at once.

VARIATION

Chopped, cooked chicken makes a delicious alternative to the squid.

Use fresh coriander (cilantro) instead of the basil, if desired.

Prawn (Shrimp) Stir-fry

A very quick and tasty stir-fry using prawns (shrimp) and cucumber, cooked with lemon grass, chilli and ginger.

NUTRITIONAL INFORMATION

Calories	178	Sugars	.........1g
Protein	........22g	Fat	...........7g
Carbohydrate	....3g	Saturates	.......1g

 5 MINS 5 MINS

SERVES 4

INGREDIENTS

½ cucumber

2 tbsp sunflower oil

6 spring onions (scallions), halved lengthways and cut into 4 cm/ 1½ inch lengths

1 stalk lemon grass, sliced thinly

1 garlic clove, chopped

1 tsp chopped fresh red chilli

125 g/4½ oz oyster mushrooms

1 tsp chopped ginger root

350 g/12 oz cooked peeled prawns (shrimp)

2 tsp cornflour (cornstarch)

2 tbsp water

1 tbsp dark soy sauce

½ tsp fish sauce

2 tbsp dry sherry or rice wine

boiled rice, to serve

1 Cut the cucumber into strips about 5 mm x 4 cm/¼ x 1¾ inches.

2 Heat the sunflower oil in a wok or large frying pan (skillet).

3 Add the spring onions (scallions), cucumber, lemon grass, garlic, chilli, oyster mushrooms and ginger to the wok or frying pan (skillet) and stir-fry for 2 minutes.

4 Add the prawns (shrimp) and stir-fry for a further minute.

5 Mix together the cornflour (cornstarch), water, soy sauce and fish sauce until smooth.

6 Stir the cornflour (cornstarch) mixture and sherry or wine into the wok and heat through, stirring, until the sauce has thickened. Serve with rice.

COOK'S TIP

The white part of the lemon grass stem can be thinly sliced and left in the cooked dish. If using the whole stem, remove it before serving. You can buy lemon grass chopped and dried, or preserved in jars, but neither has the fragrance or delicacy of the fresh variety.

A Seafood Medley

You can use almost any kind of sea fish in this recipe. Red sea bream is an especially good choice.

NUTRITIONAL INFORMATION

Calories	699	Sugars	.........4g
Protein	........56g	Fat	..........35g
Carbohydrate	...35g	Saturates	......20g

 20 MINS 30 MINS

SERVES 4

I N G R E D I E N T S

12 raw tiger prawns (shrimp)

12 raw (small) shrimp

450 g/1 lb fillet of sea bream

60 g/2 oz/4 tbsp butter

12 scallops, shelled

125 g/4½ oz freshwater prawns (shrimp)

juice and finely grated rind of 1 lemon

pinch of saffron powder or threads

1 litre/1¾ pints/4 cups vegetable stock

150 ml/¼ pint/⅔ cup rose petal vinegar

450 g/1 lb dried farfalle

1 tbsp olive oil

150 ml/¼ pint/⅔ cup white wine

1 tbsp pink peppercorns

115 g/4 oz baby carrots

150 ml/¼ pint/⅔ cup double (heavy) cream
or fromage frais

salt and pepper

1 Peel and devein the prawns (shrimp) and (small) shrimp. Thinly slice the sea bream. Melt the butter in a frying pan (skillet), add the sea bream, scallops, prawns (shrimp) and (small) shrimp and cook for 1–2 minutes.

2 Season with pepper to taste. Add the lemon juice and grated rind. Very carefully add a pinch of saffron powder or a few strands of saffron to the cooking juices (not to the seafood).

3 Remove the seafood from the pan, set aside and keep warm.

4 Return the pan to the heat and add the stock. Bring to the boil and reduce by one third. Add the rose petal vinegar and cook for 4 minutes, until reduced.

5 Bring a pan of salted water to the boil. Add the farfalle and oil and cook for 8–10 minutes until tender, but still firm to the bite. Drain the pasta, transfer to a serving plate and top with the seafood.

6 Add the wine, peppercorns, and carrots to the pan and reduce the sauce for 6 minutes. Add the cream or fromage frais and simmer for 2 minutes.

7 Pour the sauce over the seafood and pasta and serve immediately.

Seafood Pasta

This attractive seafood salad platter is full of different flavours, textures and colours.

NUTRITIONAL INFORMATION

Calories ....188 Sugars 2g
Protein ....16g Fat 7g
Carbohydrate ...13g Saturates 1g

 30 MINS   30 MINS

SERVES 8

I N G R E D I E N T S

175 g/6 oz/1½ cups dried pasta shapes

1 tbsp oil

4 tbsp Italian dressing

2 garlic cloves, crushed

6 tbsp white wine

125 g/4½ oz baby button
    mushrooms, trimmed

3 carrots

600 ml/1 pint/2½ cups fresh mussels in
    shells

125–175 g/4½–6 oz frozen squid or
    octopus rings, thawed

175 g/6 oz/1 cup peeled tiger prawns
    (shrimp), thawed if frozen

6 sun-dried tomatoes, drained and sliced

3 tbsp chives, cut into 2.5 cm/1 inch pieces

salt and pepper

TO GARNISH

24 mangetout (snow peas), trimmed

12 baby corn

12 prawns (shrimp) in shells

1 Cook the pasta in a pan of boiling salted water, with the oil added, for 8–10 minutes or until just tender. Drain the pasta thoroughly.

2 Combine the dressing, garlic and 2 tablespoons of wine. Mix in the mushrooms and leave to marinate.

3 Slice the carrots about 1 cm/½ inch thick and using a cocktail cutter, cut each slice into shapes. Blanch for 3–4 minutes, drain and add to the mushrooms.

4 Scrub the mussels, discarding any that are open or do not close when sharply tapped. Put into a saucepan with 150 ml/ ¼ pint/⅔ cup water and the remaining wine. Bring to the boil, cover and simmer for 3–4 minutes or until they open. Drain, discarding any that are still closed. Reserve 12 mussels for garnish, leaving them on the half shell; remove the other mussels from the shells and add to the mushroom mixture with the squid or octopus rings and prawns (shrimp).

5 Add the sun-dried tomatoes, pasta and chives to the salad. Toss to mix and turn on to a large platter.

6 Blanch the mangetout (snow peas) for 1 minute and baby corn for 3 minutes, rinse under cold water and drain. Arrange around the edge of the salad, alternating with the mussels on shells and whole prawns (shrimp). Cover with cling film (plastic wrap) and leave to chill until ready to serve.

Aromatic Seafood Rice

One of those easy, delicious meals where the rice and fish are cooked together in one pan. Remove the whole spices before serving

NUTRITIONAL INFORMATION

Calories 380	Sugar 2g	
Protein 40g	Fats 13g	
Carbohydrates . . .26g	Saturates 5g	

   20 MINS 25 MINS

SERVES 4

INGREDIENTS

225 g/8 oz/1¼ cups basmati rice

2 tbsp ghee or vegetable oil

1 onion, peeled and chopped

1 garlic clove, peeled and crushed

1 tsp cumin seeds

½-1 tsp chilli powder

4 cloves

1 cinnamon stick or a piece of cassia bark

2 tsp curry paste

225 g/8 oz peeled prawns (shrimp)

500g/1 lb 2 oz white fish fillets (such as monkfish, cod or haddock), skinned and boned and cut into bite-sized pieces

salt and freshly ground black pepper

600 ml/1 pint/2½ cups boiling water

60 g/2 oz/⅓ cup frozen peas

60 g/2 oz/⅓ cup frozen sweetcorn kernels

1-2 tbsp lime juice

2 tbsp toasted desiccated (shredded) coconut

coriander (cilantro) sprigs and lime slices, to garnish

1 Place the rice in a sieve and wash well under cold running water until the water runs clear, then drain well.

2 Heat the ghee or oil in a saucepan, add the onion, garlic, spices and curry paste and fry very gently for 1 minute.

3 Stir in the rice and mix well until coated in the spiced oil. Add the prawns (shrimp) and white fish and season well with salt and pepper. Stir lightly, then pour in the boiling water.

4 Cover and cook gently for 10 minutes, without uncovering the pan. Add the peas and corn, cover and continue cooking for a further 8 minutes. Remove from the heat and allow to stand for 10 minutes.

5 Uncover the pan, fluff up the rice with a fork and transfer to a warm serving platter.

6 Sprinkle the dish with the lime juice and toasted coconut, and serve garnished with coriander (cilantro) sprigs and lime slices.

Spaghetti & Seafood Sauce

Peeled prawns (shrimp) from the freezer can become the star ingredient in this colourful and tasty dish.

NUTRITIONAL INFORMATION

Calories	498	Sugars	.........5g
Protein	........32g	Fat	..........23g
Carbohydrate	...43g	Saturates	......11g

30 MINS   35 MINS

SERVES 4

INGREDIENTS

225 g/8 oz dried spaghetti, broken into
   15 cm/6 inch lengths

2 tbsp olive oil

300 ml/½ pint/1¼ cups chicken stock

1 tsp lemon juice

1 small cauliflower, cut into florets

2 carrots, thinly sliced

115 g/4 oz mangetout (snow peas)

60 g/2 oz/4 tbsp butter

1 onion, sliced

225 g/8 oz courgettes (zucchini), sliced

1 garlic clove, chopped

350 g/12 oz frozen, cooked, peeled prawns
   (shrimp), defrosted

2 tbsp chopped fresh parsley

25 g/1 oz/⅓ cup freshly grated
   Parmesan cheese

½ tsp paprika

salt and pepper

4 unpeeled, cooked prawns (shrimp),
   to garnish

1 Bring a pan of lightly salted water to the boil. Add the spaghetti and 1 tbsp of the olive oil and cook for 8–10 minutes until tender, but still firm to the bite. Drain the spaghetti and return to the pan. Toss with the remaining olive oil, cover and keep warm.

2 Bring the chicken stock and lemon juice to the boil. Add the cauliflower and carrots and cook for 3–4 minutes. Remove from the pan and set aside. Add the mangetout (snow peas) to the pan and cook for 1–2 minutes. Set aside with the other vegetables.

3 Melt half of the butter in a frying pan (skillet) over a medium heat. Add the onion and courgettes (zucchini) and fry for about 3 minutes. Add the garlic and prawns (shrimp) and cook for a further 2–3 minutes, until thoroughly heated through.

4 Stir in the reserved vegetables and heat through. Season to taste and stir in the remaining butter.

5 Transfer the spaghetti to a warm serving dish. Pour over the sauce and add the chopped parsley. Toss well with 2 forks until coated. Sprinkle over the Parmesan cheese and paprika, garnish with the unpeeled prawns (shrimp) and serve immediately.

Vegetables & Salads

Anyone with more than a passing interest in their health can be unaware of the importance of fresh fruit and vegetables in the diet. We should, according to recent studies, be eating at least five portions a day. Elsewhere in the world, particularly China and India, vegetables play a larger role in the diet. This is due to both economic and religious reasons. The recipes in this chapter offer a sumptuous range of vegetable and vegetarian dishes, as well as salads, from India, China, Italy, Turkey, France, and many other countries to show you how easy it is to incorporate fruit and vegetables into your diet. Original and inventive ways to cook vegetables so that you do not even miss the meat include Vegetable Lasagne, Mexican Chilli Corn Pie, or Broccoli, (Bell) Pepper & Almond Salad.

Baked Aubergines (Eggplants)

This delicious recipe is from Parma. Ensure that you simmer the tomato sauce gently to reduce it slightly before using.

NUTRITIONAL INFORMATION

Calories	578	Sugars	........22g
Protein	........17g	Fat	..........43g
Carbohydrate	...25g	Saturates	......13g

15 MINS   1¼ HOURS

SERVES 4

INGREDIENTS

4 aubergines (eggplants), trimmed

3 tbsp olive oil

2 x 150g/5½ oz packets Mozzarella, thinly sliced

4 slices Parma ham (prosciutto), shredded

1 tbsp chopped fresh marjoram

1 tbsp chopped fresh basil

½ quantity Béchamel Sauce (see page 6)

25 g/1 oz/¼ cup Parmesan, grated

salt and pepper

TOMATO SAUCE

4 tbsp olive oil

1 large onion, sliced

4 garlic cloves, crushed

400 g/14 oz can chopped tomatoes

450 g/1 lb fresh tomatoes, peeled and chopped

4 tbsp chopped fresh parsley

600 ml/1 pint/2½ cups hot vegetable stock

1 tbsp sugar

2 tbsp lemon juice

150 ml/¼ pint/⅔ cup dry white wine

salt and pepper

1 To make the Tomato Sauce, heat the oil in a large pan. Fry the onion and garlic until just beginning to soften. Add the canned and fresh tomatoes, parsley, stock, sugar and lemon juice. Cover and simmer for 15 minutes. Stir in the wine and season.

2 Slice the aubergines (eggplant) thinly lengthways. Bring a large saucepan of water to the boil and cook the aubergine (eggplant) slices for 5 minutes. Drain the aubergine (eggplant) slices on paper towels and pat dry.

3 Pour half of the fresh tomato sauce into a large, greased ovenproof dish. Cover with half of the cooked aubergines (eggplants) and drizzle with a little oil. Cover with half of the Mozzarella, Parma ham (prosciutto) and herbs. Season with salt and pepper to taste.

4 Repeat the layers and cover with the Béchamel Sauce. Sprinkle with the Parmesan. Bake in a preheated oven, 190°C/375°F/Gas Mark 5, for 35–40 minutes until golden on top. Serve.

Vegetable Jalousie

This is a really easy dish to make, but looks impressive. The mixture of vegetables gives the dish a wonderful colour and flavour.

NUTRITIONAL INFORMATION

Calories 660   Sugars 7g
Protein . . . . .11g   Fat 45g
Carbohydrate . . .53g   Saturates 15g

25 MINS   45 MINS

SERVES 4

I N G R E D I E N T S

500 g/1 lb 2 oz puff pastry

1 egg, beaten

F I L L I N G

2 tbsp butter or margarine

1 leek, shredded

2 garlic cloves, crushed

1 red (bell) pepper, seeded and sliced

1 yellow (bell) pepper, seeded and sliced

50 g/1¾ oz/½ cup sliced mushrooms

75 g/2¾ oz small asparagus spears

2 tbsp plain (all-purpose) flour

6 tbsp vegetable stock

6 tbsp milk

4 tbsp dry white wine

1 tbsp chopped oregano

salt and pepper

1 Melt the butter or margarine in a frying pan (skillet) and sauté the leek and garlic, stirring frequently, for 2 minutes. Add the remaining vegetables and cook, stirring, for 3–4 minutes.

2 Add the flour and cook for 1 minute. Remove the pan from the heat and stir in the vegetable stock, milk and white wine. Return the pan to the heat and bring to the boil, stirring, until thickened.

Stir in the oregano and season with salt and pepper to taste.

3 Roll out half of the pastry on a lightly floured surface to form a rectangle 38 x 15 cm/15 x 6 inches.

4 Roll out the other half of the pastry to the same shape, but a little larger all round. Put the smaller rectangle on a baking tray (cookie sheet) lined with dampened baking parchment.

5 Spoon the filling evenly on top of the smaller rectangle, leaving a 1 cm/½ inch clear margin around the edges.

6 Using a sharp knife, cut parallel diagonal slits across the larger rectangle to within 2.5 cm/1 inch of each of the long edges.

7 Brush the edges of the smaller rectangle with beaten egg and place the larger rectangle on top, pressing the edges firmly together to seal.

8 Brush the whole jalousie with egg to glaze and bake in a preheated oven, 200°C/400°F/Gas Mark 6, for about 30–35 minutes, until risen and golden. Transfer to a warmed serving dish and serve immediately.

Potato & Cheese Soufflé

This soufflé is very simple to make, yet it has a delicious flavour and melts in the mouth. Choose three alternative cheeses, if preferred.

NUTRITIONAL INFORMATION

Calories	447	Sugars	.........1g
Protein	........22g	Fat	..........23g
Carbohydrate	...41g	Saturates	......11g

10 MINS   55 MINS

SERVES 4

INGREDIENTS

25 g/1 oz/2 tbsp butter

2 tsp plain (all-purpose) flour

900 g/2 lb floury (mealy) potatoes

8 eggs, separated

25 g/1 oz/¼ cup grated Gruyère (Swiss) cheese

25 g/1 oz/¼ cup crumbled blue cheese

25 g/1 oz/¼ cup grated mature (sharp) Cheddar cheese

salt and pepper

1 Butter a 2.4 litre/4 pint/10 cup soufflé dish and dust with the flour. Set aside.

2 Cook the potatoes in a saucepan of boiling water until tender. Mash until very smooth and then transfer to a mixing bowl to cool.

3 Beat the egg yolks into the potato and stir in the Gruyère (Swiss) cheese, blue cheese and Cheddar, mixing well. Season to taste with salt and pepper.

4 Whisk the egg whites until standing in peaks, then gently fold them into the potato mixture with a metal spoon until fully incorporated.

5 Spoon the potato mixture into the prepared soufflé dish.

6 Cook in a preheated oven, 220°C/ 425°F/Gas Mark 7, for 35–40 minutes, until risen and set. Serve immediately.

COOK'S TIP

Insert a fine skewer into the centre of the soufflé; it should come out clean when the soufflé is fully cooked through.

Kidney Bean Kiev

This is a vegetarian version of chicken Kiev – the bean patties are topped with garlic and herb butter and coated in breadcrumbs.

NUTRITIONAL INFORMATION

Calories 688	Sugars 8g
Protein 17g	Fat 49g
Carbohydrate ...49g	Saturates 20g

25 MINS   20 MINS

SERVES 4

INGREDIENTS

GARLIC BUTTER

100 g/3½ oz/ 7 tbsp butter

3 garlic cloves, crushed

1 tbsp chopped parsley

BEAN PATTIES

675 g/1½ lb canned red kidney beans

150 g/5½ oz/1¼ cups fresh
    white breadcrumbs

25 g/1 oz/2 tbsp butter

1 leek, chopped

1 celery stick, chopped

1 tbsp chopped parsley

1 egg, beaten

salt and pepper

vegetable oil, for shallow frying

1 To make the garlic butter, put the butter, garlic and parsley in a bowl and blend together with a wooden spoon. Place the garlic butter on to a sheet of baking parchment, roll into a cigar shape and wrap in the baking parchment. Chill in the refrigerator until required.

2 Using a potato masher, mash the red kidney beans in a mixing bowl and stir in 75 g/ 2¾ oz/¾ cup of the breadcrumbs until thoroughly blended.

3 Melt the butter in a heavy-based frying pan (skillet). Add the leek and celery and sauté over a low heat, stirring constantly, for 3–4 minutes.

4 Add the bean mixture to the pan, together with the parsley, season with salt and pepper to taste and mix thoroughly. Remove the pan from the heat and set aside to cool slightly.

5 Divide the kidney bean mixture into 4 equal portions and shape them into ovals.

6 Slice the garlic butter into 4 pieces and place a slice in the centre of each bean patty. With your hands, mould the bean mixture around the garlic butter to encase it completely.

7 Dip each bean patty into the beaten egg to coat and then roll in the remaining breadcrumbs.

8 Heat a little oil in a frying pan (skillet) and fry the patties, turning once, for 7–10 minutes. or until golden brown. Serve immediately.

Turkish Kebabs (Kabobs)

A spicy chickpea (garbanzo bean) sauce is served with barbecued (grilled) colourful vegetable kebabs (kabobs).

NUTRITIONAL INFORMATION

Calories	303	Sugars	........13g
Protein	........13g	Fat	..........15g
Carbohydrate	...30g	Saturates	.......2g

20 MINS   20 MINS

SERVES 4

INGREDIENTS

SAUCE

4 tbsp olive oil

3 garlic cloves, crushed

1 small onion, finely chopped

425 g/15 oz can chickpeas
   (garbanzo beans), rinsed and drained

300 ml/½ pint/1¼ cups natural

(unsweetened) yogurt

1 tsp ground cumin

½ tsp chilli powder

lemon juice

salt and pepper

KEBABS (KABOBS)

1 aubergine (eggplant)

1 red (bell) pepper, seeded

1 green (bell) pepper, seeded

4 plum tomatoes

1 lemon, cut into wedges

8 small fresh bay leaves

olive oil, for brushing

1 To make the sauce, heat the olive oil in a small frying pan (skillet). Add the garlic and onion and fry over a medium heat, stirring occasionally, for about 5 minutes, until the onion is softened and golden brown.

2 Put the chickpeas (garbanzo beans) and yogurt into a blender or food processor and add the cumin, chilli powder and onion mixture. Process for about 15 seconds, until smooth. Alternatively, mash the chickpeas (garbanzo beans) with a potato masher and stir in the yogurt, ground cumin, chilli powder and onion.

3 Place the puréed mixture in a bowl and season to taste with lemon juice, salt and pepper. Cover and chill until ready to serve.

4 To prepare the kebabs (kabobs), cut the vegetables into large chunks and thread them on to 4 skewers, placing a bay leaf and lemon wedge at both ends of each kebab (kabob).

5 Brush the kebabs (kabobs) with olive oil and cook them over the barbecue (grill), turning frequently, for 5–8 minutes. Heat the chickpea (garbanzo bean) sauce and serve with the kebabs (kabobs).

Vegetable Toad-in-the-hole

This dish can be cooked in a single large dish or in four individual Yorkshire pudding tins (pans).

NUTRITIONAL INFORMATION

Calories 313   Sugars 9g
Protein . . . . .9g   Fat 18g
Carbohydrate . . .31g   Saturates 7g

 15 MINS   55 MINS

SERVES 4

INGREDIENTS

BATTER

100 g/3½ oz/¾ cup plain (all-purpose) flour

2 eggs, beaten

200 ml/7 fl oz/scant 1 cup milk

2 tbsp wholegrain mustard

2 tbsp vegetable oil

FILLING

25 g/1 oz/2 tbsp butter

2 garlic cloves, crushed

1 onion, cut into eight

75 g/2¾ oz baby carrots, halved lengthways

50 g/1¾ oz French (green) beans

50 g/1¾ oz/⅓ cup canned sweetcorn, (corn) drained

2 tomatoes, seeded and cut into chunks

1 tsp wholegrain mustard

1 tbsp chopped mixed herbs

salt and pepper

1 To make the batter, sift the flour and a pinch of salt into a bowl. Beat in the eggs and milk to make a batter. Stir in the mustard and leave to stand.

2 Pour the oil into a shallow ovenproof dish and heat in a preheated oven, 200°C/400°F/ Gas Mark 6, for 10 minutes.

3 To make the filling, melt the butter in a frying pan (skillet) and sauté the garlic and onion, stirring constantly, for 2 minutes. Cook the carrots and beans in a saucepan of boiling water for 7 minutes, or until tender. Drain well.

4 Add the sweetcorn (corn) and tomatoes to the frying pan (skillet) with the mustard and herbs. Season well and add the carrots and beans.

5 Remove the dish from the oven and pour in the batter. Spoon the vegetables into the centre, return to the oven and cook for 30–35 minutes, until the batter has risen and set. Serve the vegetable toad-in-the-hole immediately.

Red Bean Stew & Dumplings

There's nothing better on a cold day than a hearty dish topped with dumplings. This recipe is quick and easy to prepare.

NUTRITIONAL INFORMATION

Calories 508	Sugars 15g	
Protein 22g	Fat 12g	
Carbohydrate . . .83g	Saturates 4g	

1¼ HOURS   35 MINS

SERVES 4

I N G R E D I E N T S

1 tbsp vegetable oil

1 red onion, sliced

2 celery stalks, chopped

850 ml/1½ pints/3½ cups Fresh Vegetable Stock (see page 8)

225 g/8 oz carrots, diced

225 g/8 oz potatoes, diced

225 g/8 oz courgettes (zucchini), diced

4 tomatoes, peeled and chopped

125 g/4½ oz/½ cup red lentils

400 g/14 oz can kidney beans, rinsed and drained

1 tsp paprika

salt and pepper

D U M P L I N G S

125 g/4½ oz/1 cup plain (all-purpose) flour

½ tsp salt

2 tsp baking powder

1 tsp paprika

1 tsp dried mixed herbs

25 g/1 oz/2 tbsp vegetable suet

7 tbsp water

sprigs of fresh flat-leaf parsley, to garnish

1 Heat the oil in a flameproof casserole or a large saucepan and gently fry the onion and celery for 3–4 minutes until just softened. Pour in the stock and stir in the carrots and potatoes. Bring to the boil, cover and cook for 5 minutes.

2 Stir in the courgettes (zucchini), tomatoes, lentils, kidney beans, paprika and seasoning. Bring to the boil, cover and cook for 5 minutes.

3 To make the dumplings, sift the flour, salt, baking powder and paprika into a bowl. Stir in the herbs and suet. Bind together with the water to form a soft dough. Divide into eight and roll into balls.

4 Add the dumplings to the stew, pushing them slightly into the stew. Cover and simmer for 15 minutes until the dumplings have risen and are cooked through. Garnish with flat-leaf parsley.

Butternut Squash Stir-fry

Butternut squash is as its name suggests, deliciously buttery and nutty in flavour. If the squash is not in season, use sweet potatoes instead.

NUTRITIONAL INFORMATION

Calories . . . . .301 Sugars 4g
Protein . . . . .9g Fat 22g
Carbohydrate . . .19g Saturates 4g

 5 MINS   25 MINS

SERVES 4

INGREDIENTS

1 kg/2 lb 4 oz butternut squash, peeled

3 tbsp groundnut oil

1 onion, sliced

2 cloves garlic, crushed

1 tsp coriander seeds

1 tsp cumin seeds

2 tbsp chopped coriander (cilantro)

150 ml/¼ pint/⅔ cup coconut milk

100 ml/3½ fl oz/½ cup water

100 g/3½ oz/⅓ cup salted cashew nuts

TO GARNISH

freshly grated lime zest

fresh coriander (cilantro)

lime wedges

1 Using a sharp knife, slice the butternut squash into small, bite-sized cubes.

2 Heat the groundnut oil in a large preheated wok.

3 Add the butternut squash, onion and garlic to the wok and stir-fry for 5 minutes.

4 Stir in the coriander seeds, cumin seeds and fresh coriander (cilantro) and stir-fry for 1 minute.

5 Add the coconut milk and water to the wok and bring to the boil. Cover the wok and leave to simmer for 10–15 minutes, or until the squash is tender.

6 Add the cashew nuts and stir to combine.

7 Transfer to warm serving dishes and garnish with freshly grated lime zest, fresh coriander (cilantro) and lime wedges. Serve hot.

COOK'S TIP

If you do not have coconut milk, grate some creamed coconut into the dish with the water in step 5.

Lentil Roast

The perfect dish to serve for Sunday lunch. Roast vegetables make a succulent accompaniment.

NUTRITIONAL INFORMATION

Calories	400	Sugars	.........2g
Protein	........26g	Fat	..........20g
Carbohydrate	...32g	Saturates	......10g

 15 MINS   🕐 1 HR 20 MINS

SERVES 6

INGREDIENTS

225 g/8 oz/1 cup red lentils

450 ml/16 fl oz/2 cups vegetable stock

1 bay leaf

15 g/½ oz/1 tbsp butter or
    margarine, softened

2 tbsp dried wholemeal
    (whole wheat) breadcrumbs

225 g/8 oz/2 cups grated mature
    (sharp) Cheddar cheese

1 leek, finely chopped

125 g/4½ oz button mushrooms,
    finely chopped

90 g/3 oz/1½ cups fresh wholemeal
    (whole wheat) breadcrumbs

2 tbsp chopped parsley

1 tbsp lemon juice

2 eggs, lightly beaten

salt and pepper

flat leaf parsley sprigs, to garnish

mixed roast vegetables, to serve

1 Put the lentils, stock and bay leaf in a saucepan. Bring to the boil, cover and simmer gently for 15–20 minutes, until all the liquid is absorbed and the lentils have softened. Discard the bay leaf.

2 Base-line a 1 kg/2 lb 4 oz loaf tin (pan) with baking parchment. Grease with the butter or margarine and sprinkle with the dried breadcrumbs.

3 Stir the cheese, leek, mushrooms, fresh breadcrumbs and parsley into the lentils.

4 Bind the mixture together with the lemon juice and eggs. Season with salt and pepper. Spoon into the prepared loaf tin (pan) and smooth the top.

5 Bake in a preheated oven, 190°C/ 375°F/Gas Mark 5, for about 1 hour, until golden.

6 Loosen the loaf with a palette knife (spatula) and turn on to a warmed serving plate. Garnish with parsley and serve sliced, with roast vegetables.

Aubergine (Eggplant) & Pasta

Prepare the marinated aubergines well in advance so that all you have to do is cook the pasta.

NUTRITIONAL INFORMATION

Calories	378	Sugars	.........3g
Protein	........12g	Fat	..........30g
Carbohydrate	...16g	Saturates	.......3g

12¼ HOURS   15 MINS

SERVES 4

INGREDIENTS

150 ml/¼ pint/⅝ cup vegetable stock

150 ml/¼ pint/⅝ cup white wine vinegar

2 tsp balsamic vinegar

3 tbsp olive oil

fresh oregano sprig

450 g/1 lb aubergine (eggplant), peeled and thinly sliced

400 g/14 oz dried linguine

MARINADE

2 tbsp extra virgin oil

2 garlic cloves, crushed

2 tbsp chopped fresh oregano

2 tbsp finely chopped roasted almonds

2 tbsp diced red (bell) pepper

2 tbsp lime juice

grated rind and juice of 1 orange

salt and pepper

1 Put the vegetable stock, wine vinegar and balsamic vinegar into a saucepan and bring to the boil over a low heat. Add 2 teaspoons of the olive oil and the sprig of oregano and simmer gently for about 1 minute.

2 Add the aubergine (eggplant) slices to the pan, remove from the heat and set aside for 10 minutes.

3 Meanwhile make the marinade. Combine the oil, garlic, fresh oregano, almonds, (bell) pepper, lime juice, orange rind and juice together in a large bowl and season to taste.

4 Carefully remove the aubergine (eggplant) from the saucepan with a slotted spoon, and drain well. Add the aubergine (eggplant) slices to the marinade, mixing well, and set aside in the refrigerator for about 12 hours.

5 Bring a large pan of lightly salted water to the boil. Add half of the remaining oil and the linguine and cook for 8–10 minutes until just tender. Drain the pasta thoroughly and toss with the remaining oil while still warm. Arrange the pasta on a serving plate with the aubergine (eggplant) slices and the marinade and serve.

Braised Vegetables with Tofu

Also known Buddha's Delight, the original recipe calls for 18 different vegetables to represent the 18 Buddhas – but 6-8 are quite acceptable!

NUTRITIONAL INFORMATION

Calories ....300 Sugars 2g
Protein ....8g Fat 28g
Carbohydrate ....6g Saturates 3g

3³/₄ HOURS   10 MINS

SERVES 4

INGREDIENTS

5 g/¼ oz dried wood ears

1 cake tofu (bean curd)

60 g/2 oz mangetout (snow peas)

125 g/4½ oz Chinese leaves (cabbage)

1 small carrot

90 g/3 oz canned baby sweetcorn, drained

90 g/3 oz canned straw mushrooms, drained

60 g/2 oz canned water chestnuts, drained

300 ml/½ pint/1¼ cups vegetable oil

1 tsp salt

½ tsp sugar

1 tbsp light soy sauce or oyster sauce

2-3 tbsp Chinese Stock (see page 8) or water

a few drops sesame oil

1 Soak the wood ears in warm water for 15-20 minutes, then rinse and drain, discarding any hard bits, and dry on kitchen paper (paper towels).

2 Cut the cake of tofu into about 18 small pieces.

3 Top and tail the mangetout (snow peas). Cut the Chinese leaves (cabbage) and the carrot into slices roughly the same size and shape as the mangetout (snow peas). Cut the baby sweetcorn, the straw mushrooms and the water chestnuts in half.

4 Heat the oil in a preheated wok. Add the tofu (bean curd) and deep-fry for about 2 minutes until it turns slightly golden. Remove and drain.

5 Pour off the oil, leaving about 2 tablespoons in the wok. Add the carrot, Chinese leaves (cabbage) and mangetout (snow peas) and stir-fry for about 1 minute.

6 Add the sweetcorn, mushrooms and water chestnuts. Stir gently for 2 more minutes, then add the salt, sugar, soy sauce or oyster sauce and Chinese stock or water. Bring to the boil and stir-fry for 1 more minute. Sprinkle with sesame oil and serve hot or cold.

Green Curry with Tempeh

Green curry paste will keep for up to three weeks in the refrigerator. Serve the curry over rice or noodles.

NUTRITIONAL INFORMATION

Calories ....237 Sugars 4g
Protein ....16g Fat 17g
Carbohydrate ....5g Saturates 3g

 20 MINS   15–20 MINS

SERVES 4

INGREDIENTS

1 tbsp sunflower oil

175 g/6 oz marinated or plain tempeh, cut into diamonds

6 spring onions (scallions), cut into 2.5 cm/1 inch pieces

150 ml/¼ pint/⅔ cup coconut milk

grated rind of 1 lime

15 g/½ oz/¼ cup fresh basil leaves

¼ tsp liquid seasoning, such as Maggi

GREEN CURRY PASTE

2 tsp coriander seeds

1 tsp cumin seeds

1 tsp black peppercorns

4 large green chillies, seeded

2 shallots, quartered

2 garlic cloves,

2 tbsp chopped coriander (cilantro)

grated rind of 1 lime

1 tbsp roughly chopped galangal

1 tsp ground turmeric

salt

2 tbsp oil

TO GARNISH

coriander (cilantro) leaves

2 green chillies, thinly sliced

1 To make the green curry paste, grind together the coriander and cumin seeds and the peppercorns in a food processor or in a mortar with a pestle.

2 Blend the remaining ingredients together and add the ground spice mixture. Store in a clean, dry jar for up to 3 weeks in the refrigerator, or freeze in a suitable container.

3 Heat the oil in a wok or large, heavy frying pan (skillet). Add the tempeh and stir over a high heat for about 2 minutes until sealed on all sides. Add the spring onions (scallions) and stir-fry for 1 minute. Remove the tempeh and spring onions (scallions) and reserve.

4 Put half the coconut milk into the wok or pan (skillet) and bring to the boil. Add 6 tablespoons of the curry paste and the lime rind, and cook for 1 minute, until fragrant. Add the reserved tempeh and spring onions (scallions).

5 Add the remaining coconut milk and simmer for 7–8 minutes. Stir in the basil leaves and liquid seasoning. Leave to simmer for 1 minute before serving, garnished with coriander (cilantro) leaves and chillies.

Indian Curry Feast

This vegetable curry is quick and easy to prepare and it tastes superb.
A colourful Indian salad and mint raita make perfect accompaniments.

NUTRITIONAL INFORMATION

Calories ....473 Sugars 18g
Protein ....19g Fat 9g
Carbohydrate ...84g Saturates 1g

25-30 MINS   55 MINS

SERVES 4

INGREDIENTS

1 tbsp vegetable oil

2 garlic cloves, crushed

1 onion, chopped

3 celery sticks, sliced

1 apple, cored and chopped

1 tbsp medium-strength curry powder

1 tsp ground ginger

400 g/14 oz can chickpeas
  (garbanzo beans)

125 g/4½ oz dwarf green beans (thin
  beans), sliced

225 g/8 oz cauliflower, broken into florets

225 g/8 oz potatoes, cut into cubes

175 g/6 oz/2 cups sliced mushrooms

600 ml/1 pint/2½ cups vegetable stock

1 tbsp tomato purée (paste)

25 g/1 oz sultanas (golden raisins)

175 g/6 oz/scant 1 cup basmati rice

1 tbsp garam masala

MINT RAITA

150 ml/¼ pint/⅔ cup natural
  (unsweetened) yogurt

1 tbsp chopped mint

1 Heat the oil in a large saucepan. Add the garlic, onion, celery and apple and fry over a medium heat, stirring frequently, for 3–4 minutes. Add the curry powder and ginger, and cook gently for 1 more minute.

2 Drain the chickpeas (garbanzo beans) and add to the onion mixture, together with the dwarf green beans (thin beans), cauliflower, potatoes, mushrooms, stock, tomato purée (paste) and sultanas (golden raisins). Bring to the boil, then reduce the heat. Cover and simmer for 35–40 minutes.

3 Meanwhile, make the raita. Mix the yogurt and mint together. Transfer to a small serving bowl, then cover and chill in the refrigerator.

4 Cook the rice in a large saucepan of boiling, lightly salted water for about 12 minutes, or until just tender. Drain, rinse with boiling water and drain again.

5 Just before serving, stir the garam masala into the curry. Divide between four warmed serving plates and serve with the rice. Garnish the raita with fresh mint and hand the bowl separately.

Vegetable Pasta Stir-Fry

East meets West in this delicious dish. Prepare all the vegetables and cook the pasta in advance, then the dish can be cooked in a few minutes.

NUTRITIONAL INFORMATION

Calories	383	Sugars	........18g
Protein	........14g	Fat	..........23g
Carbohydrate	...32g	Saturates	.......8g

🍲 20 MINS ⏱ 30 MINS

SERVES 4

I N G R E D I E N T S

400 g/14 oz/4⅔ cups dried wholewheat
    pasta shells, or other short pasta shapes

1 tbsp olive oil

2 carrots, thinly sliced

115 g/4 oz baby corn cobs

3 tbsp peanut oil

2.5-cm/1-inch piece fresh ginger root,
    thinly sliced

1 large onion, thinly sliced

1 garlic clove, thinly sliced

3 celery sticks, thinly sliced

1 small red (bell) pepper, seeded and sliced
    into matchstick strips

1 small green (bell) pepper,
    seeded and sliced into matchstick strips

salt

steamed mangetouts (snow peas),
    to serve

S A U C E

1 tsp cornflour (cornstarch)

2 tbsp water

3 tbsp soy sauce

3 tbsp dry sherry

1 tsp clear honey

dash of hot pepper sauce (optional)

1 Cook the pasta in a large pan of boiling lightly salted water, adding the tablespoon of olive oil. When tender, but still firm to the bite, drain the pasta in a colander, return to the pan, cover and keep warm.

2 Cook the carrots and baby corn cobs in boiling, salted water for 2 minutes. Drain in a colander, plunge into cold water to prevent further cooking and drain again.

3 Heat the peanut oil in a large frying pan (skillet) over medium heat. Add the ginger and stir-fry for 1 minute, to flavour the oil. Remove with a slotted spoon and discard.

4 Add the onion, garlic, celery and (bell) peppers to the oil and stir-fry over a medium heat for 2 minutes. Add the carrots and baby corn cobs, and stir-fry for a further 2 minutes, then stir in the reserved pasta.

5 Put the cornflour (cornstarch) in a small bowl and mix to a smooth paste with the water. Stir in the soy sauce, sherry and honey.

6 Pour the sauce into the pan, stir well and cook for 2 minutes, stirring once or twice. Taste the sauce and season with hot pepper sauce if wished. Serve with a steamed green vegetable, such as mangetouts (snow peas).

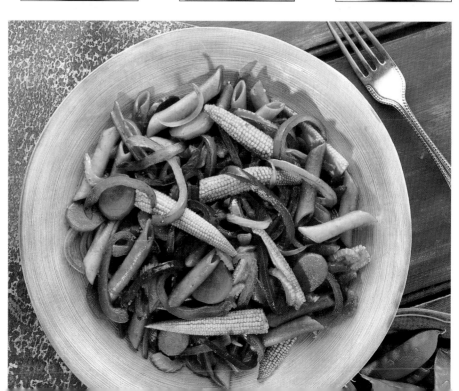

Tagliatelle with Pumpkin

This unusual pasta dish comes from the Emilia Romagna region of Italy.

NUTRITIONAL INFORMATION

Calories 454   Sugars 4g
Protein ....9g   Fat 33g
Carbohydrate ...33g   Saturates 12g

 15 MINS   35 MINS

SERVES 4

I N G R E D I E N T S

500 g/1 lb 2 oz pumpkin or butternut
    squash

2 tbsp olive oil

1 onion, chopped finely

2 garlic cloves, crushed

4–6 tbsp chopped fresh parsley

good pinch of ground or freshly grated
    nutmeg

about 250 ml/9 fl oz/1 cup chicken or
    vegetable stock

125 g/4½ oz Parma ham (prosciutto), cut
    into narrow strips

275 g/9 oz tagliatelle, green or white (fresh
    or dried)

150 ml/¼ pint/⅔ cup double (heavy) cream

salt and pepper

freshly grated Parmesan, to serve

1 Peel the pumpkin or squash and scoop out the seeds and membrane. Cut the flesh into 1 cm/½ inch dice.

2 Heat the olive oil in a pan and gently fry the onion and garlic until softened. Add half of the parsley and fry for 1–2 minutes.

3 Add the pumpkin or squash and continue to cook for 2–3 minutes. Season well with salt, pepper and nutmeg.

4 Add half of the stock, bring to the boil, cover and simmer for about 10 minutes or until the pumpkin is tender, adding more stock as necessary. Add the Parma ham (prosciutto) and continue to cook for 2 minutes, stirring frequently.

5 Meanwhile, cook the tagliatelle in a large saucepan of boiling salted water, allowing 3–4 minutes for fresh pasta or 8–10 minutes for dried. Drain thoroughly and turn into a warmed dish.

6 Add the cream to the ham mixture and heat gently. Season and spoon over the pasta. Sprinkle with the remaining parsley and grated Parmesan separately.

Tofu (Bean Curd), Corn & Peas

Chunks of tofu (bean curd) marinated in ginger and soy sauce impart something of an oriental flavour to this pizza.

NUTRITIONAL INFORMATION

Calories 596	Sugars 17g
Protein 33g	Fat 23g
Carbohydrate . . .66g	Saturates 9g

🍖 1 HOUR   🕐 35 MINS

SERVES 4

I N G R E D I E N T S

1 litre/1¾ pints milk

1 tsp salt

225 g/8 oz semolina

1 tbsp soy sauce

1 tbsp dry sherry

½ tsp grated fresh ginger root

250 g/9 oz tofu (bean curd), cut into chunks

2 eggs

60 g/2 oz Parmesan, grated

Basic Tomato Sauce (see page 6)

25 g/1 oz baby sweetcorn, cut into 4

25 g/1 oz mangetout (snow peas), trimmed and cut into 4

4 spring onions (scallions), trimmed and cut into 2.5 cm/1 inch strips

60 g/2 oz Mozzarella, sliced thinly

2 tsp sesame oil

salt and pepper

1 Bring the milk to the boil with the salt. Sprinkle the semolina over the surface, stirring all the time. Cook for 10 minutes over a low heat, stirring occasionally, taking care not to let it burn. Remove from the heat and leave to cool until tepid.

2 Mix the soy sauce, sherry and ginger together in a bowl, add the tofu (bean curd) and stir gently to coat. Leave to marinate in a cool place for 20 minutes.

3 Beat the eggs with a little pepper. Add to the semolina with the Parmesan and mix well. Place on a large greased baking tray (cookie sheet) or pizza pan and pat into a 25 cm/10 inch round, using the back of a metal spoon. Spread the tomato sauce almost to the edge.

4 Blanch the sweetcorn and mangetout (snow peas) in a saucepan of boiling water for 1 minute, drain and place on the pizza with the drained tofu (bean curd). Top with the spring onions (scallions) and slices of cheese. Drizzle over the sesame oil and season with salt and pepper.

5 Bake in a preheated oven, at 200°C/400°F/Gas Mark 6, for 18–20 minutes, or until the edge is crisp and golden. Serve immediately.

Ratatouille & Lentil Pizza

Ratatouille and lentils on a wholemeal bread base are topped with cheese and sunflower seeds. The lentils need to be soaked so prepare in advance.

NUTRITIONAL INFORMATION

Calories 377	Sugars 6g
Protein 11g	Fat 19g
Carbohydrate ...44g	Saturates 5g

2½ HOURS   55 MINS

SERVES 4

INGREDIENTS

60 g/2 oz green lentils

½ small aubergine (eggplant), diced

1 small onion, sliced

1 garlic clove, crushed

3 tbsp olive oil

½ courgette (zucchini), sliced

½ red (bell) pepper, sliced

½ green (bell) pepper, sliced

200 g/7 oz can chopped tomatoes

1 tbsp chopped fresh oregano or 1 tsp dried

Basic Pizza Dough (see page 861), made
   with wholemeal flour

60 g/2 oz Cheddar, sliced thinly

1 tbsp sunflower seeds

olive oil, for drizzling

salt and pepper

1 Soak the lentils in hot water for 30 minutes. Drain and rinse; then cover with fresh water and simmer over a low heat for 10 minutes.

2 Place the aubergine (eggplant) in a colander, sprinkle with a little salt and leave the bitter juices to drain for about 20 minutes. Rinse well and pat dry with paper towels.

3 Fry the onion and garlic gently in the oil for 3 minutes. Add the courgette (zucchini), (bell) peppers and aubergine (eggplant). Cover and leave to cook over a low heat for about 5 minutes.

4 Add the tomatoes, drained lentils, oregano, 2 tablespoons of water and seasoning. Cover and simmer for 15 minutes, stirring occasionally, adding more water if necessary.

5 Roll out or press the dough, using a rolling pin or your hands, into a 25 cm/10 inch circle on a lightly floured work surface. Place on a large greased baking tray (cookie sheet) or pizza pan and push up the edge slightly. Cover and leave the dough to rise slightly for 10 minutes in a warm place.

6 Spread the ratatouille over the dough base almost to the edge. Arrange the cheese slices on top and sprinkle over the sunflower seeds. Drizzle with a little olive oil and season with a little salt and pepper to taste.

7 Bake in a preheated oven, at 200°C/400°F/Gas Mark 6, for 18–20 minutes, or until the edge is crisp and golden brown. Serve immediately.

Creamy Baked Fennel

Fennel tastes fabulous in this creamy sauce, flavoured with caraway seeds. A crunchy breadcrumb topping gives an interesting texture.

NUTRITIONAL INFORMATION

Calories	292	Sugars	.........5g
Protein	........10g	Fat	..........23g
Carbohydrate	...12g	Saturates	......14g

10 MINS   45 MINS

SERVES 4

INGREDIENTS

2 tbsp lemon juice

2 fennel bulbs, thinly sliced

60 g/2 oz/¼ cup butter, plus extra
    for greasing

125 g/4½ oz/¼ cup low-fat soft cheese

150 ml/¼ pint/⅔ cup single (light) cream

150 ml/¼ pint/⅔ cup milk

1 egg, beaten

2 tsp caraway seeds

60 g/2 oz/1 cup fresh white breadcrumbs

salt and pepper

parsley sprigs, to garnish

1 Bring a saucepan of water to the boil and add the lemon juice and fennel. Cook for 2–3 minutes to blanch, drain and place in a greased ovenproof dish.

2 Beat the soft cheese in a bowl until smooth. Add the cream, milk and beaten egg, and whisk together until combined. Season with salt and pepper and pour the mixture over the fennel.

3 Melt 15 g/½ oz/1 tbsp of the butter in a small frying pan (skillet) and fry the caraway seeds gently for 1–2 minutes, until they release their aroma. Sprinkle them over the fennel.

4 Melt the remaining butter in a frying pan (skillet). Add the breadcrumbs and fry over a low heat, stirring frequently, until lightly browned. Sprinkle them evenly over the surface of the fennel.

5 Place in a preheated oven, 180°C/ 350°F/Gas Mark 4, and bake for 25–30 minutes, or until the fennel is tender. Serve immediately, garnished with sprigs of parsley.

Chilli & (Bell) Pepper Pasta

This roasted (bell) pepper and chilli sauce is sweet and spicy – the perfect combination!

NUTRITIONAL INFORMATION

Calories	423	Sugars	.........5g
Protein	.........9g	Fat	..........27g
Carbohydrate	...38g	Saturates	.......4g

25 MINS   30 MINS

SERVES 4

INGREDIENTS

2 red (bell) peppers, halved and deseeded

1 small red chilli

4 tomatoes, halved

2 garlic cloves

50 g/1¾ oz ground almonds

7 tbsp olive oil

675 g/1½ lb fresh pasta or 350 g/12 oz
   dried pasta

fresh oregano leaves, to garnish

1 Place the (bell) peppers, skin-side up, on a baking tray (cookie sheet) with the chilli and tomatoes. Cook under a preheated grill (broiler) for 15 minutes or until charred. After 10 minutes turn the tomatoes skin-side up. Place the (bell) peppers and chillies in a polythene bag and leave to sweat for 10 minutes.

2 Remove the skin from the (bell) peppers and chillies and slice the flesh into strips, using a sharp knife.

3 Peel the garlic, and peel and deseed the tomatoes.

4 Place the almonds on a baking tray (cookie sheet) and place under the grill (broiler) for 2–3 minutes until golden.

5 Using a food processor, blend the (bell) pepper, chilli, garlic and tomatoes to make a purée. Keep the motor running and slowly add the olive oil to form a thick sauce. Alternatively, mash the

mixture with a fork and beat in the olive oil, drop by drop.

6 Stir the toasted ground almonds into the mixture.

7 Warm the sauce in a saucepan until it is heated through.

8 Cook the pasta in a saucepan of boiling water for 8–10 minutes if using dried, or 3–5 minutes if using fresh. Drain the pasta thoroughly and transfer to a serving dish. Pour over the sauce and toss to mix. Garnish with the fresh oregano leaves.

VARIATION

Add 2 tablespoons of red wine vinegar to the sauce and use as a dressing for a cold pasta salad, if you wish.

Red Curry with Cashews

This is a wonderfully quick dish to prepare. If you don't time to prepare the curry paste, it can be bought ready-made.

NUTRITIONAL INFORMATION

Calories . . . . . . .274 Sugars 5g
Protein . . . . .10g Fat 10g
Carbohydrate . . .38g Saturates 3g

 25 MINS   🕐 15 MINS

SERVES 4

I N G R E D I E N T S

250 ml/9 fl oz/1 cup coconut milk

1 kaffir lime leaf

¼ tsp light soy sauce

60 g/2 oz/4 baby corn cobs,
    halved lengthways

125 g/4½ oz/1¼ cups broccoli florets

125 g/4½ oz French (green) beans, cut into
    5 cm/2 inch pieces

25 g/1 oz/¼ cup cashew nuts

15 fresh basil leaves

1 tbsp chopped coriander (cilantro)

1 tbsp chopped roast peanuts, to garnish

R E D   C U R R Y   P A S T E

7 fresh red chillies, halved, seeded
    and blanched

2 tsp cumin seeds

2 tsp coriander seeds

2.5 cm/1 inch piece galangal, chopped

½ stalk lemon grass, chopped

1 tsp salt

grated rind of 1 lime

4 garlic cloves, chopped

3 shallots, chopped

2 kaffir lime leaves, shredded

1 tbsp vegetable oil

1 To make the curry paste, grind all the ingredients together in a large mortar with a pestle or a grinder. Alternatively, process briefly in a food processor. The quantity of red curry paste is more than required for this recipe. However, it will keep for up to 3 weeks in a sealed container in the refrigerator.

2 Put a wok or large, heavy-based frying pan (skillet) over a high heat, add 3 tablespoons of the red curry paste and stir until it gives off its aroma. Reduce the heat to medium.

3 Add the coconut milk, kaffir lime leaf, light soy sauce, baby corn cobs, broccoli florets, French (green) beans and cashew nuts. Bring to the boil and simmer for about 10 minutes, until the vegetables are cooked, but still firm and crunchy.

4 Remove and discard the lime leaf and stir in the basil leaves and coriander (cilantro). Transfer to a warmed serving dish, garnish with peanuts and serve immediately.

Lentil & Vegetable Shells

These stuffed aubergines (eggplants) are delicious served hot or cold, topped with natural (unsweetened) yogurt or cucumber raita.

NUTRITIONAL INFORMATION

Calories 386   Sugars 9g
Protein . . . . .14g   Fat 24g
Carbohydrate . . .30g   Saturates 3g

25 MINS   1 HOUR

SERVES 6

INGREDIENTS

225 g/8 oz/1⅓ cup continental lentils

850 ml/1½ pints/3¾ cups water

2 garlic cloves, crushed

3 well-shaped aubergines (eggplants)

150 ml/¼ pint/⅔ cup vegetable oil, plus
   extra for brushing

2 onions, chopped

4 tomatoes, chopped

2 tsp cumin seeds

1 tsp ground cinnamon

2 tbsp mild curry paste

1 tsp minced chilli

2 tbsp chopped mint

salt and pepper

natural (unsweetened) yogurt and
   mint sprigs, to serve

1 Rinse the lentils under cold running water. Drain and place in a saucepan with the water and garlic. Cover and simmer for 30 minutes.

2 Cook the aubergines (eggplants) in a saucepan of boiling water for 5 minutes. Drain, then plunge into cold water for 5 minutes. Drain again, then cut the aubergines (eggplants) in half lengthways and scoop out most of the flesh and reserve, leaving a 1 cm/½ inch thick border to form a shell.

3 Place the aubergine (eggplant) shells in a shallow greased ovenproof dish, brush with a little oil and sprinkle with salt and pepper. Cook in a preheated oven, 190°C/375°F/Gas Mark 5, for 10 minutes. Meanwhile, heat half the remaining oil in a frying pan, add the onions and tomatoes and fry gently for 5 minutes. Chop the reserved aubergine (eggplant) flesh, add to the pan with the spices and cook gently for 5 minutes. Season with salt.

4 Stir in the lentils, most of the remaining oil, reserving a little for later, and the mint. Spoon the mixture into the shells. Drizzle with remaining oil and bake for 15 minutes. Serve hot or cold, topped with a spoonful of natural (unsweetened) yogurt and mint sprigs.

COOK'S TIP

Choose nice plump aubergines (eggplants), rather than thin tapering ones, as they retain their shape better when filled and baked with a stuffing.

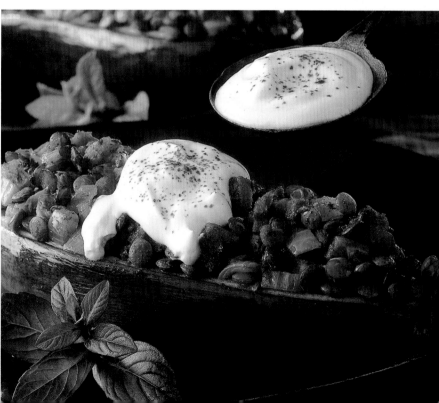

Vegetable Stir-Fry

A range of delicious flavours are captured in this simple recipe which is ideal if you are in a hurry.

NUTRITIONAL INFORMATION

Calories ....127 Sugars 7g
Protein ....4g Fat 9g
Carbohydrate ....8g Saturates 1g

5 MINS   25 MINS

SERVES 4

INGREDIENTS

3 tbsp vegetable oil

8 baby onions, halved

1 aubergine (eggplant), cubed

225 g/8 oz courgettes (zucchini), sliced

225 g/8 oz open-cap mushrooms, halved

2 cloves garlic, crushed

400 g/14 oz can chopped tomatoes

2 tbsp sundried tomato purée (paste)

2 tbsp soy sauce

1 tsp sesame oil

1 tbsp Chinese rice wine or dry sherry

freshly ground black pepper

fresh basil leaves, to garnish

1 Heat the vegetable oil in a large preheated wok or frying pan (skillet).

2 Add the baby onions and aubergine (eggplant) to the wok or frying pan (skillet) and stir-fry for 5 minutes, or until the vegetables are golden and just beginning to soften.

3 Add the sliced courgettes (zucchini), mushrooms, garlic, chopped tomatoes and tomato purée (paste) to the wok and stir-fry for about 5 minutes. Reduce the

heat and leave to simmer for 10 minutes, or until the vegetables are tender.

4 Add the soy sauce, sesame oil and rice wine or sherry to the wok, bring back to the boil and cook for 1 minute.

5 Season the vegetable stir-fry with freshly ground black pepper and scatter with fresh basil leaves. Serve immediately.

COOK'S TIP

Basil has a very strong flavour which is perfect with vegetables and Chinese flavourings. Instead of using basil simply as a garnish in this dish, try adding a handful of fresh basil leaves to the stir-fry in step 4.

Deep South Rice & Beans

Cajun spices add a flavour of the American Deep South to this colourful rice and red kidney bean salad.

NUTRITIONAL INFORMATION

Calories 336   Sugars 8g
Protein . . . . .7g   Fat 13g
Carbohydrate . . .51g   Saturates 2g

 10 MINS   15 MINS

SERVES 4

INGREDIENTS

175 g/6 oz/scant 1 cup long grain rice

4 tbsp olive oil

1 small green (bell) pepper, seeded
   and chopped

1 small red (bell) pepper, seeded
   and chopped

1 onion, finely chopped

1 small red or green chilli, seeded and
   finely chopped

2 tomatoes, chopped

125 g/4½ oz/½ cup canned red kidney
   beans, rinsed and drained

1 tbsp chopped fresh basil

2 tsp chopped fresh thyme

1 tsp Cajun spice

salt and pepper

fresh basil leaves, to garnish

1 Cook the rice in plenty of boiling, lightly salted water for about 12 minutes, until just tender. Rinse with cold water and drain well.

2 Meanwhile, heat the olive oil in a frying pan (skillet) and fry the green and red (bell) peppers and onion gently for about 5 minutes, until softened.

3 Add the chilli and tomatoes, and cook for a further 2 minutes.

4 Add the vegetable mixture and red kidney beans to the rice. Stir well to combine thoroughly.

5 Stir the chopped herbs and Cajun spice into the rice mixture. Season to taste with salt and pepper, and serve, garnished with basil leaves.

Eight Jewel Vegetables

This recipe, as the title suggests, is a colourful mixture of eight vegetables, cooked in a black bean and soy sauce.

NUTRITIONAL INFORMATION

Calories 110   Sugars 3g
Protein . . . . .4g   Fat 8g
Carbohydrate . . . .7g   Saturates 1g

 5 MINS   10 MINS

SERVES 4

INGREDIENTS

2 tbsp peanut oil

6 spring onions (scallions), sliced

3 garlic cloves, crushed

1 green (bell) pepper, seeded
and diced

1 red (bell) pepper, seeded and diced

1 fresh red chilli, sliced

2 tbsp chopped water chestnuts

1 courgette (zucchini), chopped

125 g/4½ oz oyster mushrooms

3 tbsp black bean sauce

2 tsp Chinese rice wine or dry sherry

4 tbsp dark soy sauce

1 tsp dark brown sugar

2 tbsp water

1 tsp sesame oil

1 Heat the peanut oil in a preheated wok or large frying pan (skillet) until it is almost smoking.

2 Lower the heat slightly, add the spring onions (scallions) and garlic and stir-fry for about 30 seconds.

3 Add the red and green (bell) peppers, fresh red chilli, water chestnuts and courgette (zucchini) to the wok or frying pan (skillet) and stir-fry for 2–3 minutes,

or until the vegetables are just beginning to soften.

4 Add the oyster mushrooms, black bean sauce, Chinese rice wine or dry sherry, dark soy sauce, dark brown sugar and water to the wok and stir-fry for a further 4 minutes.

5 Sprinkle the stir-fry with sesame oil and serve immediately.

COOK'S TIP

Eight jewels or treasures form a traditional part of the Chinese New Year celebrations, which start in the last week of the old year. The Kitchen God, an important figure, is sent to give a report to heaven, returning on New Year's Eve in time for the feasting.

Stuffed Vegetables

You can fill your favourite vegetables with this nutty-tasting combination of cracked wheat, tomatoes and cucumber.

NUTRITIONAL INFORMATION

Calories	194	Sugars	.........7g
Protein	.........5g	Fat	...........4g
Carbohydrate	...36g	Saturates	.....0.5g

40 MINS · 25 MINS

SERVES 4

INGREDIENTS

4 large beefsteak tomatoes

4 medium courgettes (zucchini)

2 orange (bell) peppers

salt and pepper

FILLING

225 g/8 oz/1¼ cups cracked wheat

¼ cucumber

1 medium red onion

2 tbsp lemon juice

2 tbsp chopped fresh coriander (cilantro)

2 tbsp chopped fresh mint

1 tbsp olive oil

2 tsp cumin seeds

TO SERVE

warm pitta bread and low-fat hummus

1 Preheat the oven to 200°C/400°F/Gas Mark 6. Cut off the tops of the tomatoes and reserve. Using a teaspoon, scoop out the tomato pulp, chop and place in a bowl. Season the tomato shells, then turn them upside down on absorbent kitchen paper.

2 Trim the courgettes (zucchini) and cut a V-shaped groove lengthwise down each one. Finely chop the cut-out courgette (zucchini) flesh and add to the tomato pulp. Season the courgettes (zucchini) shells and set aside. Halve the (bell) peppers. Leaving the stalks intact, cut out the seeds and discard. Season the (bell) pepper shells and set aside.

3 To make the filling, soak the cracked wheat according to the instructions on the packet. Finely chop the cucumber and add to the reserved tomato pulp and courgette (zucchini) mixture. Finely chop the red onion, and add to the vegetable mixture with the lemon juice, herbs, olive oil, cumin and seasoning and mix together well.

4 When the wheat has soaked, mix with the vegetables and stuff into the tomato, courgette (zucchini) and (bell) pepper shells. Place the tops on the tomatoes, transfer to a roasting tin (pan) and bake for 20–25 minutes until cooked through. Drain and serve pitta bread and hummus.

COOK'S TIP

It is a good idea to blanch vegetables (except for tomatoes) before stuffing. Blanch (bell) peppers, courgettes (zucchini) and aubergine (eggplant) for 5 minutes.

Italian Stuffed (Bell) Peppers

Halved (bell) peppers are stuffed with the flavours of Italy in this sunshine-bright dish.

NUTRITIONAL INFORMATION

Calories 193   Sugars 8g
Protein ....2g   Fat 17g
Carbohydrate ....9g   Saturates 2g

20 MINS   25 MINS

SERVES 4

I N G R E D I E N T S

1 red (bell) pepper

1 green (bell) pepper

1 yellow (bell) pepper

1 orange (bell) pepper

6 tbsp olive oil

1 small red onion, sliced

1 small aubergine (eggplant),
    chopped roughly

125 g/4½ oz button mushrooms, wiped

125 g/4½ oz/1 cup cherry tomatoes, halved

few drops of mushroom ketchup

handful of fresh basil leaves,
    torn into pieces

2 tbsp lemon juice

salt and pepper

sprigs of fresh basil, to garnish

lemon wedges, to serve

1 Halve the (bell) peppers, remove the cores and deseed them. Sprinkle over a few drops of olive oil and season.

2 Heat the remaining olive oil in a frying pan (skillet). Add the onion, aubergine (eggplant) and mushrooms, and fry for 3–4 minutes, stirring frequently. Remove from the heat and transfer to a mixing bowl.

3 Add the cherry tomatoes, mushroom ketchup, basil leaves and lemon juice to the aubergine (eggplant) mixture. Season well with salt and pepper.

4 Spoon the aubergine (eggplant) mixture into the (bell) pepper halves. Enclose in foil parcels (packages) and barbecue (grill) over the hot coals for about 15–20 minutes, turning once.

5 Unwrap carefully and serve garnished with sprigs of fresh basil. Serve with lemon wedges.

VARIATION

Dried herbs can be used instead of fresh ones if they are unavailable. Substitute 1 tsp dried basil or use mixed dried Italian herbs as an alternative. If you wish, top these stuffed (bell) peppers with grated Mozzarella or Cheddar cheese – 75 g/3 oz/¼ cup will be sufficient.

Ratatouille Vegetable Grill

Ratatouille is a classic dish of vegetables cooked in a tomato and herb sauce. Here it is topped with diced potatoes and cheese.

NUTRITIONAL INFORMATION

Calories ....287 Sugars 13g
Protein ....14g Fat 4g
Carbohydrate ...53g Saturates 2g

15 MINS   45 MINS

SERVES 4

I N G R E D I E N T S

2 medium onions

1 garlic clove

1 medium red (bell) pepper

1 medium green (bell) pepper

1 medium aubergine (eggplant)

2 medium courgettes (zucchini)

2 x 400 g/14 oz cans chopped tomatoes

1 bouquet garni

2 tbsp tomato purée (paste)

900 g/2 lb potatoes

75 g/2¾ oz reduced-fat mature (sharp)
  Cheddar cheese, grated

salt and pepper

2 tbsp snipped fresh chives, to garnish

VARIATION

You can vary the vegetables in this dish depending on seasonal availability and personal preference. Try broccoli, carrots or sweetcorn, if you prefer.

1 Peel and finely chop the onions and garlic. Rinse, deseed and slice the (bell) peppers. Rinse, trim and cut the aubergine (eggplant) into small dice. Rinse, trim and thinly slice the courgettes (zucchini).

2 Place the onion, garlic and (bell) peppers into a large saucepan. Add the tomatoes, and stir in the bouquet garni, tomato purée (paste) and salt and pepper to taste. Bring to the boil, cover and simmer for 10 minutes, stirring half-way through. Stir in the prepared aubergine (eggplant) and courgettes (zucchini) and cook, uncovered, for a further 10 minutes, stirring occasionally.

3 Meanwhile, peel the potatoes and cut into 2.5 cm/ 1 inch cubes. Place the potatoes into another saucepan and cover with water. Bring to the boil and cook for 10–12 minutes until tender. Drain and set aside.

4 Transfer the vegetables to a heatproof gratin dish. Arrange the cooked potato evenly over the vegetables.

5 Preheat the grill (broiler) to medium. Sprinkle grated cheese over the potatoes and place under the grill for 5 minutes until golden, bubbling and hot. Serve garnished with snipped chives.

Char-Grilled Kebabs

This medley of (bell) peppers, courgettes (zucchini), aubergine (eggplant) and red onion can be served on its own or as an unusual side dish.

NUTRITIONAL INFORMATION

Calories 66   Sugars 7g
Protein ....2g   Fat 3g
Carbohydrate ....7g   Saturates 0.5g

15 MINS   15 MINS

SERVES 4

INGREDIENTS

1 large red (bell) pepper

1 large green (bell) pepper

1 large orange (bell) pepper

1 large courgette (zucchini)

4 baby aubergines (eggplant)

2 medium red onions

2 tbsp lemon juice

1 tbsp olive oil

1 garlic clove, crushed

1 tbsp chopped, fresh rosemary or 1 tsp dried rosemary

salt and pepper

TO SERVE

cracked wheat, cooked

tomato and olive relish

1 Halve and deseed the (bell) peppers and cut into even sized pieces, about 2.5 cm/1 inch wide.

2 Trim the courgettes (zucchini), cut in half lengthways and slice into 2.5 cm/1 inch pieces. Place the (bell) peppers and courgettes (zucchini) in a large bowl.

3 Trim the aubergines (eggplant) and quarter them lengthways. Peel both the onions, then cut each one into 8 even-sized wedges.

4 Add the pieces of aubergine (eggplant) and onions to the bowl containing the wedges of (bell) peppers and courgettes (zucchini).

5 In a small bowl, whisk together the lemon juice, olive oil, garlic, rosemary and seasoning.

6 Pour the mixture over the vegetables and stir to coat evenly.

7 Preheat the grill (broiler) to medium. Thread the vegetables on to 8 metal or pre-soaked wooden skewers. Arrange the kebabs on the rack and cook for 10–12 minutes, turning frequently until the vegetables are lightly charred and just softened.

8 Drain the vegetable kebabs and serve on a bed of cracked wheat accompanied with a tomato and olive relish.

Homemade Noodles

These noodles are simple to make; you do not need a pasta-making machine as they are rolled out by hand.

NUTRITIONAL INFORMATION

Calories 294	Sugars 3g
Protein 7g	Fat 15g
Carbohydrate ...35g	Saturates 2g

🍲 20 MINS   🕐 15 MINS

SERVES 2–4

I N G R E D I E N T S

N O O D L E S

125 g/4½ oz/1 cup plain (all-purpose) flour

2 tbsp cornflour (cornstarch)

½ tsp salt

125 ml/4 fl oz/½ cup boiling water

5 tbsp vegetable oil

S T I R - F R Y

1 courgette (zucchini), cut into thin sticks

1 celery stick, cut into thin sticks

1 carrot, cut into thin sticks

125 g/4½ oz open-cup mushrooms, sliced

125 g/4½ oz broccoli florets and stalks, peeled and thinly sliced

1 leek, sliced

125 g/4½ oz/2 cups bean sprouts

1 tbsp soy sauce

2 tsp rice wine vinegar

½ tsp sugar

1 To prepare the noodles, sift the flour, cornflour (cornstarch) and salt into a bowl. Make a well in the centre and pour in the boiling water and 1 teaspoon of oil. Mix quickly to make a soft dough. Cover and leave for 5–6 minutes.

2 Make the noodles by breaking off small pieces of dough and rolling into balls. Roll each ball across a very lightly oiled work surface (counter) with the palm of your hand to form thin noodles. Do not worry if some of the noodles break into shorter lengths. Set the noodles aside.

3 Heat 3 tablespoons of oil in a wok. Add the noodles in batches and fry over a high heat for 1 minute. Reduce the heat and cook for a further 2 minutes. Remove and drain on kitchen paper (paper towels). Set aside.

4 Heat the remaining oil in the pan. Add the courgette (zucchini), celery and carrot, and stir-fry for 1 minute. Add the mushrooms, broccoli and leek, and stir-fry for a further minute. Stir in the remaining ingredients and mix well until thoroughly heated.

5 Add the noodles and cook over a high heat, tossing to mix the ingredients. Serve immediately.

Layered Vegetable Gratin

In this tasty recipe an assortment of vegetables are cooked in a light nutmeg sauce with a potato and cheese topping.

NUTRITIONAL INFORMATION

Calories 236	Sugars 9g
Protein 9g	Fat 9g
Carbohydrate . . .31g	Saturates 3g

 25 MINS   1½ HOURS

SERVES 6

I N G R E D I E N T S

225 g/8 oz/2 large carrots

225 g/8 oz baby parsnips

1 fennel bulb

500 g/1 lb 2 oz/3 potatoes

90 g/3 oz/⅓ cup low-fat spread

25 g/1 oz/¼ cup plain (all-purpose) flour

300 ml/½ pint/1¼ cups skimmed milk

½ tsp ground nutmeg

1 egg, beaten

25 g/1 oz/¼ cup freshly grated Parmesan cheese

salt and pepper

TO SERVE

crusty bread

tomato salad

1 Cut the carrots and parsnips into thin strips lengthways. Cook in boiling water for 5 minutes. Drain well and transfer to an ovenproof baking dish.

2 Thinly slice the fennel and cook in boiling water for 2–3 minutes. Drain well and add to the carrots and parsnips. Season.

3 Peel and dice the potatoes into 2 cm/¾ inch cubes. Cook in boiling water for 6 minutes. Drain well.

4 Gently melt half the low-fat spread and stir in the flour. Remove from the heat and gradually mix in the milk.

5 Return to the heat and stir until thickened. Season and stir in the nutmeg. Cool for 10 minutes.

6 Beat in the egg and spoon over the vegetables. Arrange the potatoes on top and sprinkle over the cheese.

7 Dot the potatoes with the remaining low-fat spread. Bake in a preheated oven at 180°C/350°F/Gas Mark 4 for 1 hour until the vegetables are tender.

8 Serve the vegetable gratin as a light meal with wedges of crusty bread and a tomato salad, or as an accompaniment to a light main course.

Stuffed Globe Artichokes

This imaginative and attractive recipe for artichokes stuffed with nuts, tomatoes, olives and mushrooms, has been adapted for the microwave.

NUTRITIONAL INFORMATION

Calories 248	Sugars 8g
Protein 5g	Fat 19g
Carbohydrate ...16g	Saturates 2g

30 MINS   25 MINS

SERVES 4

INGREDIENTS

4 globe artichokes

8 tbsp water

4 tbsp lemon juice

1 onion, chopped

1 garlic clove, crushed

2 tbsp olive oil

225 g/8 oz/2 cups button
    mushrooms, chopped

40 g/1½ oz/½ cup pitted black
    olives, sliced

60 g/2 oz/¼ cup sun-dried tomatoes in oil,
    drained and chopped

1 tbsp chopped fresh basil

60 g/2 oz/1 cup fresh
    white breadcrumbs

25 g/1 oz/¼ cup pine nuts, toasted

oil from the jar of sun-dried tomatoes
    for drizzling

salt and pepper

1 Cut the stalks and lower leaves off the artichokes. Snip off the leaf tips with scissors. Place 2 artichokes in a large bowl with half the water and half the lemon juice. Cover and cook on HIGH power for 10 minutes, turning the artichokes over halfway through, until a leaf pulls away easily from the base. Leave to stand, covered, for 3 minutes before draining. Turn the artichokes upside down and leave to cool. Repeat to cook the remaining artichokes.

2 Place the onion, garlic and oil in a bowl. Cover and cook on HIGH power for 2 minutes, stirring once. Add the mushrooms, olives and sun-dried tomatoes. Cover and cook on HIGH power for 2 minutes.

3 Stir in the basil, breadcrumbs and pine nuts. Season to taste with salt and pepper.

4 Turn the artichokes the right way up and carefully pull the leaves apart. Remove the purple-tipped central leaves. Using a teaspoon, scrape out the hairy choke and discard.

5 Divide the stuffing into 4 equal portions and spoon into the centre of each artichoke. Push the leaves back around the stuffing.

6 Arrange in a shallow dish and drizzle over a little oil from the jar of sun-dried tomatoes. Cook on HIGH power for 7–8 minutes to reheat, turning the artichokes around halfway through.

Potato Hash

This is a variation of the American dish, beef hash, which was made with salt beef and leftovers, and served to seagoing New Englanders.

NUTRITIONAL INFORMATION

Calories	302	Sugars	........05g
Protein	.........15g	Fat	..........10g
Carbohydrate	...40g	Saturates	......4g

 5 MINS   30 MINS

SERVES 4

INGREDIENTS

25 g/1 oz/2 tbsp butter

1 red onion, halved and sliced

1 carrot, diced

25 g/1 oz French (green) beans, halved

3 large waxy potatoes, diced

2 tbsp plain (all purpose) flour

600 ml/1 pint/1¼ cups vegetable stock

225 g/8 oz tofu (bean curd), diced

salt and pepper

chopped fresh parsley, to garnish

1 Melt the butter in a frying pan (skillet).

2 Add the onion, carrot, French (green) beans and potatoes and fry gently, stirring, for 5-7 minutes or until the vegetables begin to brown.

3 Add the flour to the frying pan (skillet) and cook for 1 minute, stirring constantly.

4 Gradually pour in the stock.

5 Reduce the heat and leave the mixture to simmer for 15 minutes or until the potatoes are tender.

6 Add the diced tofu (bean curd) to the mixture and cook for a further 5 minutes.

7 Season to taste with salt and pepper.

8 Sprinkle the chopped parsley over the top of the potato hash to garnish, then serve hot from the pan (skillet).

COOK'S TIP

Hash is an American term meaning to chop food into small pieces. Therefore a traditional hash dish is made from chopped fresh ingredients, such as roast beef or corned beef, (bell) peppers, onion and celery, often served with gravy.

Colourful Kebabs (Kabobs)

Brighten up a barbecue (grill) meal with these colourful vegetable kebabs (kabobs). They are basted with an aromatic flavoured oil.

NUTRITIONAL INFORMATION

Calories 131   Sugars 7g
Protein . . . . .2g   Fat 11g
Carbohydrate . . . .8g   Saturates 2g

 15 MINS   15 MINS

SERVES 4

I N G R E D I E N T S

1 red (bell) pepper, seeded

1 yellow (bell) pepper, seeded

1 green (bell) pepper, seeded

1 small onion

8 cherry tomatoes

100 g/3½ oz wild mushrooms

S E A S O N E D   O I L

6 tbsp olive oil

1 garlic clove, crushed

½ tsp mixed dried herbs or
    herbes de Provence

1 Cut the (bell) peppers into 2.5 cm/ 1 inch pieces.

2 Peel the onion and cut it into wedges, leaving the root end just intact to help keep the wedges together.

3 Thread the (bell) peppers, onion wedges, tomatoes and mushrooms on to skewers, alternating the colours of the (bell) peppers.

4 To make the seasoned oil, mix together the olive oil, garlic and mixed herbs or herbes de Provence in a a small bowl. Brush the mixture liberally over the kebabs (kabobs).

5 Barbecue (grill) the kebabs (kabobs) over medium hot coals for 10–15 minutes, brushing with the seasoned oil and turning the skewers frequently.

6 Transfer the vegetable kebabs (kabobs) to warm serving plates. Serve the kebabs (kabobs) immediately with walnut sauce (see Cook's Tip, below), if you wish.

COOK'S TIP

To make walnut sauce, process 125 g/4½ oz/1 cup walnuts in a food processor to a smooth paste. With the machine running, add 150 ml/¼ pint/²⁄₃ cup double (heavy) cream and 1 tbsp olive oil. Season to taste with salt and pepper.

Oriental Vegetable Noodles

This dish has a mild, nutty flavour from the peanut butter and dry-roasted peanuts.

NUTRITIONAL INFORMATION

Calories 193   Sugars 5g
Protein ....7g   Fat 12g
Carbohydrate ...14g   Saturates 2g

 10 MINS   15 MINS

SERVES 4

I N G R E D I E N T S

175 g/6 oz/1½ cups green thread noodles or multi-coloured spaghetti

1 tsp sesame oil

2 tbsp crunchy peanut butter

2 tbsp light soy sauce

1 tbsp white wine vinegar

1 tsp clear honey

125 g/4½ oz daikon (mooli), grated

125 g/4½ oz/1 large carrot, grated

125 g/4½ oz cucumber, shredded finely

1 bunch spring onions (scallions), shredded finely

1 tbsp dry-roasted peanuts, crushed

TO GARNISH

carrot flowers

spring onion (scallion) tassels

1 Bring a large saucepan of water to the boil, add the noodles or spaghetti and cook according to the packet instructions. Drain well and rinse in cold water. Leave in a bowl of cold water until required.

2 To make the peanut butter sauce, put the sesame oil, peanut butter, soy sauce, vinegar, honey and seasoning into a small screw-top jar. Seal and shake well to mix thoroughly.

3 Drain the noodles or spaghetti well, place in a large serving bowl and mix in half the peanut sauce.

4 Using 2 forks, toss in the daikon (mooli), carrot, cucumber and spring onions (scallions). Sprinkle with crushed peanuts and garnish with carrot flowers and spring onion (scallion) tassels. Serve the noodles with the remaining peanut sauce.

COOK'S TIP

There are many varieties of oriental noodles available from oriental markets, delicatessens and supermarkets. Try rice noodles, which contain very little fat and require little cooking; usually soaking in boiling water is sufficient.

Basil & Tomato Pasta

Roasting the tomatoes gives a sweeter flavour to this sauce. Buy Italian tomatoes, such as plum or flavia, as these have a better flavour and colour.

NUTRITIONAL INFORMATION

Calories 177   Sugars 4g
Protein . . . . .5g   Fat 4g
Carbohydrate . . .31g   Saturates 1g

 15 MINS   35 MINS

SERVES 4

INGREDIENTS

1 tbsp olive oil

2 sprigs rosemary

2 cloves garlic

450 g/1 lb tomatoes, halved

1 tbsp sun-dried tomato paste

12 fresh basil leaves, plus extra to garnish

salt and pepper

675 g/1½ lb fresh farfalle or 350 g/12 oz
    dried farfalle

1 Place the oil, rosemary, garlic and tomatoes, skin side up, in a shallow roasting tin (pan).

2 Drizzle with a little oil and cook under a preheated grill (broiler) for 20 minutes or until the tomato skins are slightly charred.

COOK'S TIP

This sauce tastes just as good when served cold in a pasta salad.

3 Peel the skin from the tomatoes. Roughly chop the tomato flesh and place in a pan.

4 Squeeze the pulp from the garlic cloves and mix with the tomato flesh and sun-dried tomato paste.

5 Roughly tear the fresh basil leaves into smaller pieces and then stir them into the sauce. Season with a little salt and pepper to taste. Set aside.

6 Cook the farfalle in a saucepan of boiling water for 8–10 minutes or until it is cooked through, but still has 'bite'. Drain well.

7 Gently re-heat the tomato and basil sauce, stirring.

8 Transfer the farfalle to serving plates and pour over the basil and tomato sauce. Serve at once.

Pasta Provençale

A Mediterranean mixture of red (bell) peppers, garlic and courgettes (zucchini) cooked in olive oil and tossed with pasta.

NUTRITIONAL INFORMATION

Calories	487	Sugars	........14g
Protein	........17g	Fat	..........24g
Carbohydrate	...53g	Saturates	.......8g

5 MINS   20 MINS

SERVES 4

INGREDIENTS

3 tbsp olive oil

1 onion, sliced

2 garlic cloves, chopped

3 red (bell) peppers, seeded
 and cut into strips

3 courgettes (zucchini), sliced

400 g/14 oz can chopped tomatoes

3 tbsp sun-dried tomato paste

2 tbsp chopped fresh basil

225 g/8 oz fresh pasta spirals

125 g/4½ oz/1 cup grated Gruyère cheese

salt and pepper

fresh basil sprigs, to garnish

1 Heat the oil in a heavy-based saucepan or flameproof casserole. Add the onion and garlic and cook, stirring occasionally, until softened. Add the (bell) peppers and courgettes (zucchini) and fry, stirring occasionally, for 5 minutes.

2 Add the tomatoes, sun-dried tomato paste and basil and season to taste with salt and pepper. Cover and cook for a further 5 minutes.

3 Meanwhile, bring a large saucepan of salted water to the boil and add the pasta. Stir and bring back to the boil.

Reduce the heat slightly and cook, uncovered, for 3 minutes, until just tender. Drain thoroughly and add to the vegetables. Toss gently to mix well.

4 Transfer to a shallow flameproof dish and sprinkle with the cheese.

5 Cook under a preheated grill (broiler) for 5 minutes, until the cheese is golden brown and bubbling. Garnish with basil sprigs and serve immediately.

Vegetable Lasagne

This rich, baked pasta dish is packed full of vegetables, tomatoes and Italian Mozzarella cheese.

NUTRITIONAL INFORMATION

Calories . . . . .510 Sugars 14g
Protein . . . . .17g Fat 38g
Carbohydrate . . .28g Saturates 14g

50 MINS   50 MINS

SERVES 6

I N G R E D I E N T S

1 kg/2 lb 4 oz aubergines (eggplant)

8 tbsp olive oil

25 g/1/ oz/2 tbsp garlic and herb butter

450 g/1 lb courgettes (zucchini), sliced

225 g/8 oz/2 cups grated
    Mozzarella cheese

600 ml/1 pint/2½ cups passata (sieved
    tomatoes)

6 sheets pre-cooked green lasagne

600 ml/1 pint/2½ cups Béchamel Sauce
    (see page 6)

60 g/2 oz/⅔ cup freshly grated
    Parmesan cheese

1 tsp dried oregano

salt and pepper

1 Thinly slice the aubergines (eggplant) and place in a colander. Sprinkle with salt and set aside for 20 minutes. Rinse and pat dry with kitchen paper.

2 Heat 4 tablespoons of the oil in a large frying pan (skillet). Fry half of the aubergine (eggplant) slices over a low heat for 6–7 minutes, or until golden. Drain thoroughly on kitchen paper. Repeat with the remaining oil and aubergine (eggplant) slices.

3 Melt the garlic and herb butter in the frying pan (skillet). Add the courgettes (zucchini) and fry for 5–6 minutes, until golden brown all over. Drain thoroughly on kitchen paper.

4 Place half of the aubergine (eggplant) and courgette (zucchini) slices in a large ovenproof dish. Season with pepper and sprinkle over half of the Mozzarella cheese. Spoon over half of the passata

(sieved tomatoes) and top with 3 sheets of lasagne. Repeat the process, ending with a layer of lasagne.

5 Spoon over the Béchamel Sauce and sprinkle over the Parmesan cheese and oregano. Put the dish on a baking tray (cookie sheet) and bake in a preheated oven, at 220°C/425°F/Gas Mark 7, for 30–35 minutes, or until golden brown. Serve immediately.

Spaghetti & Mushroom Sauce

This easy vegetarian dish is ideal for busy people with little time, but good taste!

NUTRITIONAL INFORMATION

Calories	604	Sugars	.........5g
Protein	........11g	Fat	..........39g
Carbohydrate	...54g	Saturates	......21g

 20 MINS   35 MINS

SERVES 4

I N G R E D I E N T S

60 g/2 oz/4 tbsp butter

2 tbsp olive oil

6 shallots, sliced

450 g/1 lb/6 cups sliced button mushrooms

1 tsp plain (all-purpose) flour

150 ml/¼ pint/⅔ cup double (heavy) cream

2 tbsp port

115 g/4 oz sun-dried tomatoes, chopped

freshly grated nutmeg

450g /1 lb dried spaghetti

1 tbsp freshly chopped parsley

salt and pepper

6 triangles of fried white bread, to serve

1 Heat the butter and 1 tbsp of the oil in a large pan. Add the shallots and cook over a medium heat for 3 minutes. Add the mushrooms and cook over a low heat for 2 minutes. Season with salt and pepper, sprinkle over the flour and cook, stirring constantly, for 1 minute.

2 Gradually stir in the cream and port, add the sun-dried tomatoes and a pinch of grated nutmeg and cook over a low heat for 8 minutes.

3 Meanwhile, bring a large saucepan of lightly salted water to the boil. Add

the spaghetti and remaining olive oil and cook for 12–14 minutes, until tender but still firm to the bite.

4 Drain the spaghetti and return to the pan. Pour over the mushroom sauce and cook for 3 minutes. Transfer the spaghetti and mushroom sauce to a large serving plate and sprinkle over the chopped parsley. Serve with crispy triangles of fried bread.

VARIATION

Non-vegetarians could add 115 g/4 oz Parma ham (prosciutto), cut into thin strips and heated gently in 25 g/1 oz/ 2 tbsp butter, to the pasta along with the mushroom sauce.

Tomato Sauce & (Bell) Peppers

This pizza is made with a pastry base flavoured with cheese and topped with a delicious tomato sauce and roasted (bell) peppers.

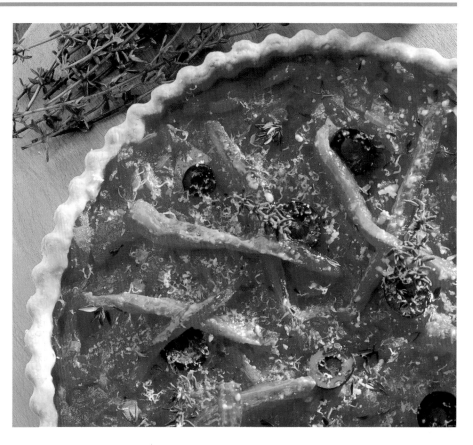

NUTRITIONAL INFORMATION

Calories 611	Sugars 8g
Protein 14g	Fat 38g
Carbohydrate . . .56g	Saturates 21g

1½ HOURS   55 MINS

SERVES 4

INGREDIENTS

225 g/8 oz plain (all-purpose) flour

125 g/4½ oz butter, diced

½ tsp salt

2 tbsp dried Parmesan cheese

1 egg, beaten

2 tbsp cold water

2 tbsp olive oil

1 large onion, finely chopped

1 garlic clove, chopped

400 g/14 oz can chopped tomatoes

4 tbsp concentrated tomato purée (paste)

1 red (bell) pepper, halved

5 sprigs of thyme, stalks removed

6 black olives, pitted and halved

25 g/1 oz Parmesan cheese, grated

1 Sift the flour and rub in the butter to make breadcrumbs. Stir in the salt and dried Parmesan. Add the egg and 1 tablespoon of the water and mix with a round-bladed knife. Add more water if necessary to make a soft dough. Cover with cling film (plastic wrap) and chill for 30 minutes.

2 Meanwhile, heat the oil in a frying pan (skillet) and cook the onions and garlic for about 5 minutes or until golden.

Add the tomatoes and cook for 8–10 minutes. Stir in the tomato purée (paste).

3 Place the (bell) peppers, skin-side up, on a baking tray (cookie sheet) and cook under a preheated grill (broiler) for 15 minutes until charred. Place in a plastic bag and leave to sweat for 10 minutes. Peel off the skin and slice the flesh into thin strips.

4 Roll out the dough to fit a 23 cm/ 9 inch loose base fluted flan tin (pan).

Line with foil and bake in a preheated oven, at 200°C/400°F/Gas Mark 6, for 10 minutes or until just set. Remove the foil and bake for a further 5 minutes until lightly golden. Leave to cool slightly.

5 Spoon the tomato sauce over the pastry base and top with the (bell) peppers, thyme, olives and fresh Parmesan. Return to the oven for 15 minutes or until the pastry is crisp. Serve warm or cold.

Spinach & Ricotta Pie

This puff pastry pie looks impressive, but it is actually fairly easy and quite quick to make. Serve it hot or cold.

NUTRITIONAL INFORMATION

Calories 545   Sugars 3g
Protein . . . . .19g   Fat 42g
Carbohydrate . . .25g   Saturates 13g

25 mins   50 mins

SERVES 4

INGREDIENTS

225 g/8 oz spinach

25 g/1 oz pine kernels

100 g/3½ oz ricotta cheese

2 large eggs, beaten

50 g/1¾ oz ground almonds

40 g/1½ oz Parmesan cheese,
   freshly grated

250 g/9 oz puff pastry, defrosted if frozen

1 small egg, beaten

1 Rinse the spinach, place in a large pan and cook with just the water clinging to the leaves for 4–5 minutes until wilted. Drain thoroughly. When the spinach is cool enough to handle, squeeze out the excess liquid.

2 Place the pine kernels on a baking tray and lightly toast under a preheated grill for 2–3 minutes or until golden brown.

3 Place the ricotta, spinach and eggs in a bowl and mix together. Add the pine kernels, beat well, then stir in the ground almonds and Parmesan cheese.

4 Roll out the puff pastry and make 2 squares, 20 cm/8 inches wide. Trim the edges, reserving the pastry trimmings.

5 Place 1 pastry square on a baking tray. Spoon over the spinach mixture to within 1 cm/½ inch of the edge of the pastry. Brush the edges with beaten egg and place the second square over the top.

6 Using a round-bladed knife, press the pastry edges together by tapping along the sealed edge. Use the pastry trimmings to make a few leaves to decorate the pie.

7 Brush the pie with the beaten egg and bake in a preheated oven, 220°C/

425°F/Gas Mark 8, for 10 minutes. Reduce the oven temperature to 190°C/375°F/Gas Mark 5 and bake for a further 25–30 minutes. Serve hot.

COOK'S TIP
Spinach must be washed very thoroughly in several changes of water to get rid of the grit and soil that can be trapped in it. Cut off any thick central ribs.

Green Risotto

A simple rice dish cooked with green vegetables and herbs. This recipe has been adapted for the microwave.

NUTRITIONAL INFORMATION

Calories 344   Sugars 4g
Protein . . . . .13g   Fat 10g
Carbohydrate . . .54g   Saturates 4g

 15 MINS   20 MINS

SERVES 4

INGREDIENTS

1 onion, chopped

2 tbsp olive oil

225 g/8 oz/generous 1 cup risotto rice

700 ml/1¼ pints/3 cups hot
vegetable stock

350 g/12 oz mixed green vegetables, such
as asparagus, thin green beans,
mangetout (snow peas), courgettes
(zucchini), broccoli florets, frozen peas

2 tbsp chopped fresh parsley

60 g/2 oz/¼ cup fresh Parmesan cheese,
shaved thinly

salt and pepper

1 Place the onion and oil in a large bowl. Cover and cook on HIGH power for 2 minutes.

2 Add the rice and stir until thoroughly coated in the oil. Pour in about 75 ml/ 3 fl oz/⅓ cup of the hot stock. Cook, uncovered, for 2 minutes, until the liquid has been absorbed. Pour in another 75 ml/ 3 fl oz/⅓ cup of the stock and cook, uncovered, on HIGH power for 2 minutes. Repeat once more.

3 Chop or slice the vegetables into even-sized pieces. Stir into the rice with the remaining stock. Cover and cook on HIGH power for 8 minutes, stirring occasionally, until most of the liquid has been absorbed and the rice is just tender.

4 Stir in the parsley and season generously. Leave to stand, covered, for almost 5 minutes. The rice should be tender and creamy.

5 Scatter the Parmesan cheese over the risotto before serving.

COOK'S TIP

For extra texture, stir in a few toasted pine kernels (nuts) or coarsely chopped cashew nuts at the end of the cooking time.

Green Vegetable Gougère

A tasty, simple supper dish of choux pastry and crisp green vegetables.
The choux pastry ring can be filled with all kinds of vegetables.

NUTRITIONAL INFORMATION

Calories	672	Sugars	.........6g
Protein	........19g	Fat	..........51g
Carbohydrate	...36g	Saturates	......14g

30 MINS   40 MINS

SERVES 4

INGREDIENTS

150 g/5½ oz/1¼ cups plain (all-purpose)
   flour

125 g/4½ oz/½ cup butter

300 ml/½ pint/1¼ cups water

4 eggs, beaten

90 g/3 oz/¾ cup grated Gruyère
   (Swiss) cheese

1 tbsp milk

salt and pepper

FILLING

2 tbsp garlic and herb butter or margarine

2 tsp olive oil

2 leeks, shredded

225 g/8 oz green cabbage, finely shredded

125 g/4½ oz/2 cups beansprouts

½ tsp grated lime rind

1 tbsp lime juice

celery salt and pepper

lime slices, to garnish

1 Sift the flour on to a piece of baking parchment. Cut the butter into dice and put in a saucepan with the water. Heat until the butter has melted.

2 Bring the butter and water to the boil, then tip in the flour all at once. Beat until the mixture becomes thick. Remove from the heat and beat until the mixture is glossy and comes away from the sides of the saucepan.

3 Transfer to a mixing bowl and cool for 10 minutes. Gradually beat in the eggs, a little at a time, making sure they are thoroughly incorporated after each addition. Stir in 60 g/2 oz/½ cup of the cheese and season with salt and pepper.

4 Place spoonfuls of the mixture in a 23 cm/9 inch circle on a dampened baking tray (cookie sheet). Brush with milk and sprinkle with the remaining cheese. Bake in a preheated oven, 220°C/425°F/Gas Mark 7, for 30–35 minutes, until golden and crisp. Transfer to a warmed serving plate.

5 Meanwhile, make the filling. Heat the butter or margarine and the oil in a large frying pan (skillet) and stir-fry the leeks and cabbage for 2 minutes. Add the beansprouts, lime rind and juice and stir-fry for 1 minute. Season to taste.

6 Pile into the centre of the pastry ring. Garnish with lime slices and serve.

Cauliflower & Broccoli Flan

This really is a tasty flan, the pastry case for which may be made in advance and frozen until required.

NUTRITIONAL INFORMATION

Calories 252	Sugars 3g
Protein 7g	Fat 16g
Carbohydrate . . .22g	Saturates 5g

🍲 15 MINS   🕐 50 MINS

SERVES 8

I N G R E D I E N T S

PASTRY

175 g/6 oz/1½ cups plain (all-purpose) flour

pinch of salt

½ tsp paprika

1 tsp dried thyme

75 g/2¾ oz/6 tbsp margarine

3 tbsp water

FILLING

100 g/3½ oz cauliflower florets

100 g/3½ oz broccoli florets

1 onion, cut into eight

25 g/1 oz/2 tbsp butter or margarine

1 tbsp plain (all-purpose) flour

6 tbsp vegetable stock

125 ml/4 fl oz/½ cup milk

75 g/2¾ oz/¾ cup grated Cheddar cheese,

salt and pepper

paprika, to garnish

1 To make the pastry, sift the flour and salt into a bowl. Add the paprika and thyme and rub in the margarine. Stir in the water and bind to form a dough.

2 Roll out the pastry on a floured surface and use to line an 18 cm/7 inch loose-based flan tin (pan). Prick the base with a fork and line with baking parchment. Fill with baking beans and bake in a preheated oven, 190°C/375°F/ Gas Mark 5, for 15 minutes. Remove the parchment and beans and return the pastry case to the oven for 5 minutes.

3 To make the filling, cook the vegetables in a pan of lightly salted boiling water for 10–12 minutes, until tender. Drain and reserve.

4 Melt the butter in a pan. Add the flour and cook, stirring constantly, for 1 minute. Remove from the heat, stir in the stock and milk and return to the heat. Bring to the boil, stirring, and add 50 g/1¾ oz/½ cup of the cheese. Season to taste with salt and pepper.

5 Spoon the cauliflower, broccoli and onion into the pastry case. Pour over the sauce and sprinkle with the cheese. Return to the oven for 10 minutes, until the cheese is bubbling. Dust with paprika, garnish and serve.

Mushroom & Nut Crumble

A filling, tasty dish that is ideal for a warming family supper. The crunchy topping is flavoured with three different types of nuts.

NUTRITIONAL INFORMATION

Calories 779	Sugars 5g	
Protein 16g	Fat 59g	
Carbohydrate ...48g	Saturates 14g	

20 MINS   55 MINS

SERVES 4

INGREDIENTS

350 g/12 oz/5 cups sliced open-
cup mushrooms

350 g/12 oz/5 cups sliced chestnut
(crimini) mushrooms, sliced

400 ml/14 fl oz/1¾ cups vegetable stock

60 g/2 oz/¼ cup butter or margarine

1 large onion, finely chopped

1 garlic clove, crushed

60 g/2 oz/½ cup plain (all-purpose) flour

4 tbsp double (heavy) cream

2 tbsp chopped parsley

salt and pepper

herbs, to garnish

CRUMBLE TOPPING

90 g/3 oz/¾ cup medium oatmeal

90 g/3 oz/¾ cup wholemeal
(whole wheat) flour

25 g/1 oz/¼ cup ground almonds

25 g/1 oz/¼ cup finely chopped walnuts

60 g/2 oz/½ cup finely chopped unsalted
shelled pistachio nuts

1 tsp dried thyme

90 g/3 oz/⅓ cup butter or
margarine, softened

1 tbsp fennel seeds

1 Put the mushrooms and stock in a large saucepan, bring to the boil, cover and simmer for 15 minutes, until tender. Drain, reserving the stock.

2 In another saucepan, melt the butter or margarine and fry the onion and garlic for 2–3 minutes, until just soft. Stir in the flour and cook for 1 minute.

3 Remove from the heat and gradually stir in the reserved mushroom stock. Return to the heat and cook, stirring, until thickened. Stir in the mushrooms, seasoning, cream and parsley and spoon into a shallow ovenproof dish.

4 To make the topping, in a bowl, mix together the oatmeal, flour, nuts, thyme and plenty of salt and pepper to taste.

5 Using a fork, mix in the butter or margarine until the topping resembles coarse breadcrumbs.

6 Sprinkle the topping mixture evenly over the mushrooms and then sprinkle with the fennel seeds. Bake in a preheated oven, at 190°C/375°F/Gas Mark 5, for about 25–30 minutes, or until the topping is golden and crisp. Garnish with fresh herbs and serve immediately.

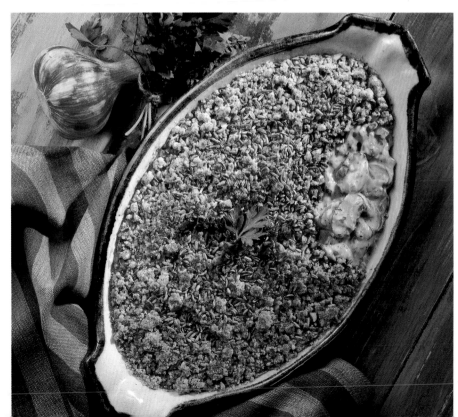

Vegetable Couscous

Couscous is a semolina grain which is very quick and easy to cook, and it makes a pleasant change from rice or pasta.

NUTRITIONAL INFORMATION

Calories 280	Sugars 13g
Protein 10g	Fat 7g
Carbohydrate . . .47g	Saturates 1g

  20 MINS   40 MINS

SERVES 4

I N G R E D I E N T S

2 tbsp vegetable oil

1 large onion, coarsely chopped

1 carrot, chopped

1 turnip, chopped

600 ml/1 pint/2½ cups vegetable stock

175 g/6 oz/1 cup couscous

2 tomatoes, peeled and quartered

2 courgettes (zucchini), chopped

1 red (bell) pepper, seeded and chopped

125 g/4½ oz French (green) beans, chopped

grated rind of 1 lemon

pinch of ground turmeric (optional)

1 tbsp finely chopped fresh coriander
   (cilantro) or parsley

salt and pepper

fresh flat leaf parsley sprigs,
   to garnish

1 Heat the oil in a large saucepan and fry the onion, carrot and turnip for 3–4 minutes. Add the stock, bring to the boil, cover and simmer for 20 minutes.

2 Meanwhile, put the couscous in a bowl and moisten with a little boiling water, stirring, until the grains have swollen and separated.

3 Add the tomatoes, courgettes (zucchini), (bell) pepper and French (green) beans to the saucepan.

4 Stir the lemon rind into the couscous and add the turmeric, if using, the and mix thoroughly. Put the couscous in a steamer and position it over the saucepan of vegetables. Simmer the vegetables so

that the couscous steams for about 8–10 minutes.

5 Pile the couscous on to warmed serving plates. Ladle the vegetables and some of the liquid over the top. Scatter with the coriander (cilantro) or parsley and serve at once, garnished with parsley sprigs.

Risotto-stuffed (Bell) Peppers

Sweet roasted (bell) peppers are delightful containers for a creamy risotto and especially good topped with Mozzarella cheese.

NUTRITIONAL INFORMATION

Calories 613	Sugars 7g
Protein 17g	Fat 32g
Carbohydrate . . .61g	Saturates 15g

  15 MINS   35 MINS

SERVES 4

INGREDIENTS

4 red or orange (bell) peppers

1 tbsp olive oil

1 large onion, finely chopped

350 g/12 oz arborio (risotto) rice, washed

about 15 strands of saffron

150 ml/¼ pint/⅔ cup white wine

850 ml/1½ pints hot vegetable or
    chicken stock

50 g/1¾ oz/3 tbsp butter

50 g/1¾ oz pecorino cheese, grated

50 g/1¾ oz Italian sausage, such as
    felino salame or other coarse Italian
    salame, chopped

200 g/7 oz Mozzarella cheese, sliced

1 Cut the (bell) peppers in half, retaining some of the stalk. Remove the seeds.

2 Place the (bell) peppers, cut side up, under a preheated grill (broiler) for 12–15 minutes or until softened and charred.

3 Meanwhile, heat the oil in a large frying pan (skillet). Add the onion and cook for 3–4 minutes or until softened. Add the rice and saffron, stirring to coat in the oil, and cook for 1 minute.

4 Add the wine and stock slowly, a ladleful at a time, making sure that all of the liquid is absorbed before adding the next ladleful of liquid. When all of the liquid is absorbed, the rice should be cooked. Test by tasting a grain – if it is still crunchy add a little more water and continue cooking. It should take at least 15 minutes to cook.

5 Stir in the butter, pecorino cheese and the chopped Italian sausage.

6 Spoon the risotto into the (bell) peppers. Top with a slice of Mozzarella and grill (broil) for 4–5 minutes or until the cheese is bubbling. Serve hot.

VARIATION

Use tomatoes instead of the (bell) peppers, if you prefer. Halve 4 large tomatoes and scoop out the seeds. Follow steps 3–6 as there is no need to roast them.

Tofu with Mushrooms

Chunks of cucumber and smoked tofu (beancurd) stir-fried with straw mushrooms, mangetout (snow peas) and corn in a yellow bean sauce.

NUTRITIONAL INFORMATION

Calories	130	Sugars	........2g
Protein	.........9g	Fat	..........9g
Carbohydrate	....3g	Saturates	.......1g

 15 MINS   10 MINS

SERVES 4

INGREDIENTS

1 large cucumber

1 tsp salt

225 g/8 oz smoked tofu (bean curd)

2 tbsp vegetable oil

60 g/2 oz mangetout (snow peas)

125 g/4½ oz/8 baby corn

1 celery stick, sliced diagonally

425 g/15 oz can straw mushrooms, drained

2 spring onions (scallions), cut into strips

1 cm/½ inch piece ginger root, chopped

1 tbsp yellow bean sauce

1 tbsp light soy sauce

1 tbsp dry sherry

COOK'S TIP

Straw mushrooms are available in cans from oriental suppliers and some supermarkets. If unavailable, substitute 250 g/ 9 oz baby button mushrooms.

1 Halve the cucumber lengthways and remove the seeds, using a teaspoon or melon baller.

2 Cut the cucumber into cubes, place in a colander and sprinkle over the salt. Leave to drain for 10 minutes. Rinse thoroughly in cold water to remove the salt and drain thoroughly on absorbent kitchen paper (paper towels).

3 Cut the tofu (bean curd) into cubes.

4 Heat the vegetable oil in a wok or large frying pan (skillet) until smoking.

5 Add the tofu (bean curd), mangetout (snow peas), baby corn and celery to the wok. Stir until the tofu (bean curd) is lightly browned.

6 Add the straw mushrooms, spring onions (scallions) and ginger, and stir-fry for a further minute.

7 Stir in the cucumber, yellow bean sauce, light soy sauce, dry sherry and 2 tablespoons of water. Stir-fry for 1 minute and ensure that all the vegetables are coated in the sauces before serving.

Vegetable Fried Rice

This dish can be served as part of a substantial meal for a number of people or as a vegetarian meal in itself for four.

NUTRITIONAL INFORMATION

Calories ....175 Sugars 3g
Protein ....3g Fat 10g
Carbohydrate ...20g Saturates 2g

10 MINS   20 MINS

SERVES 4

INGREDIENTS

125 g/4½ oz/⅔ cup long-grain white rice

3 tbsp peanut oil

2 garlic cloves, crushed

½ tsp Chinese five-spice powder

60 g/2 oz/⅓ cup green beans

1 green (bell) pepper, seeded and chopped

4 baby corn cobs, sliced

25 g/1 oz bamboo shoots, chopped

3 tomatoes, skinned, seeded and chopped

60 g/2 oz/½ cup cooked peas

1 tsp sesame oil

1 Bring a large saucepan of water to the boil.

2 Add the long-grain white rice to the saucepan and cook for about 15 minutes. Drain the rice well, rinse under cold running water and drain thoroughly again.

3 Heat the peanut oil in a preheated wok or large frying pan (skillet). Add the garlic and Chinese five-spice and stir-fry for 30 seconds.

4 Add the green beans, chopped green (bell) pepper and sliced corn cobs and stir-fry the ingredients in the wok for 2 minutes.

5 Stir the bamboo shoots, tomatoes, peas and rice into the mixture in the wok and stir-fry for 1 further minute.

6 Sprinkle with sesame oil and transfer to serving dishes. Serve immediately.

VARIATION

Use a selection of vegetables of in this recipe, cutting them to a similar size to ensure that they cook in the same amount of time.

Tofu Casserole

Tofu (bean curd) is ideal for absorbing all the other flavours in this dish.
If marinated tofu (bean curd) is used, it will add a flavour of its own.

NUTRITIONAL INFORMATION

Calories ....228 Sugars 3g
Protein ....16g Fat 15g
Carbohydrate ....7g Saturates 2g

5 MINS   15 MINS

SERVES 4

INGREDIENTS

450 g/1 lb tofu (bean curd)

2 tbsp peanut oil

8 spring onions (scallions), cut
   into batons

2 celery sticks, sliced

125 g/4½ oz broccoli florets

125 g/4½ oz courgettes
   (zucchini), sliced

2 garlic cloves, thinly sliced

450 g/1 lb baby spinach

rice, to serve

SAUCE

425 ml/¾ pint/2 cups vegetable stock

2 tbsp light soy sauce

3 tbsp hoisin sauce

½ tsp chilli powder

1 tbsp sesame oil

VARIATION

This recipe has a green
vegetable theme, but alter the
colour and flavour by adding
your favourite vegetables.
Add 75 g/2¾ oz fresh or canned
and drained straw mushrooms
with the vegetables in step 2.

1 Cut the tofu (bean curd) into 2.5-cm/1-inch cubes and
   set aside until required.

2 Heat the peanut oil in a preheated wok or large frying
   pan (skillet).

3 Add the spring onions (scallions), celery, broccoli,
   courgettes (zucchini), garlic, spinach and tofu (bean
   curd) to the wok or frying pan (skillet) and stir-fry for
   3–4 minutes.

4 To make the sauce, mix together the vegetable stock,
   soy sauce, hoisin sauce, chilli powder and sesame oil in
   a flameproof casserole and bring to the boil.

5 Add the stir-fried vegetables and tofu (bean curd) to
   the saucepan, reduce the heat, cover and simmer for
   10 minutes.

6 Transfer the tofu (bean curd) and vegetables to a warm
   serving dish and serve with rice.

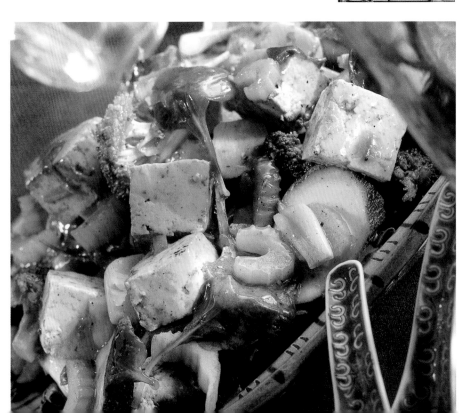

Satay Noodles

Rice noodles and vegetables are tossed in a crunchy peanut and chilli sauce for a quick satay-flavoured recipe.

NUTRITIONAL INFORMATION

Calories 281   Sugars 7g
Protein . . . . .9g   Fat 20g
Carbohydrate . . .18g   Saturates 4g

 5 MINS   20 MINS

SERVES 4

INGREDIENTS

275 g/9½ oz rice sticks (wide, flat rice
    noodles)

3 tbsp groundnut oil

2 cloves garlic, crushed

2 shallots, sliced

225 g/8 oz green beans, sliced

100 g/3¾ oz cherry tomatoes, halved

1 tsp chilli flakes

4 tbsp crunchy peanut butter

150 ml/¼ pint/⅔ cup coconut milk

1 tbsp tomato purée (paste)

sliced spring onions (scallions),
    to garnish

1 Place the rice sticks (wide, flat rice noodles) in a large bowl and pour over enough boiling water to cover. Leave to stand for 10 minutes.

2 Heat the groundnut oil in a large preheated wok or heavy-based frying pan (skillet).

3 Add the crushed garlic and sliced shallots to the wok or frying pan (skillet) and stir-fry for 1 minute.

4 Drain the rice sticks (wide, flat rice noodles) thoroughly. Add the green beans and drained noodles to the wok or frying pan (skillet) and stir-fry for about 5 minutes.

5 Add the cherry tomatoes to the wok and mix well.

6 Mix together the chilli flakes, peanut butter, coconut milk and tomato purée (paste).

7 Pour the chilli mixture over the noodles, toss well until all the ingredients are thoroughly combined and heat through.

8 Transfer the satay noodles to warm serving dishes and garnish with spring onion (scallion) slices and serve immediately.

Fried Vegetable Noodles

In this recipe, noodles are first boiled and then deep-fried for a crisply textured dish, and tossed with fried vegetables.

NUTRITIONAL INFORMATION

Calories ......229 Sugars 4g
Protein ....5g Fat 15g
Carbohydrate ...20g Saturates 2g

5 MINS   25 MINS

SERVES 4

INGREDIENTS

350 g/12 oz/3 cups dried egg noodles

2 tbsp peanut oil

2 garlic cloves, crushed

½ tsp ground star anise

1 carrot, cut into matchsticks

1 green (bell) pepper, cut into matchsticks

1 onion, quartered and sliced

125 g/4½ oz broccoli florets

75 g/2¾ oz bamboo shoots

1 celery stick, sliced

1 tbsp light soy sauce

150 ml/¼ pint/⅔ cup vegetable stock

oil, for deep-frying

1 tsp cornflour (cornstarch)

2 tsp water

1 Cook the noodles in a saucepan of boiling water for 1-2 minutes. Drain well and rinse under cold running water. Leave the noodles to drain thoroughly in a colander until required.

2 Heat the peanut oil in a preheated wok until smoking. Reduce the heat, add the crushed garlic and ground star anise and stir-fry for 30 seconds. Add the remaining vegetables and stir-fry for 1-2 minutes.

3 Add the soy sauce and vegetable stock to the wok and cook over a low heat for 5 minutes.

4 Heat the oil for deep-frying to 180°C/350°F, or until a cube of bread browns in 30 seconds.

5 Using a fork, twist the drained noodles and form them into rounds. Deep-fry them in batches until crisp, turning once. Leave to drain on kitchen paper (paper towels).

6 Blend the cornflour (cornstarch) with the water to form a paste and stir into the wok. Bring to the boil, stirring until the sauce is thickened and clear.

7 Arrange the noodles on a warm serving plate, spoon the vegetables on top and serve immediately.

Mushroom Pizza

Juicy mushrooms and stringy Mozzarella top this tomato-based pizza.
Use wild mushrooms or a combination of wild and cultivated mushrooms.

NUTRITIONAL INFORMATION

Calories ....302 Sugars 7g
Protein ....10g Fat 12g
Carbohydrate ...41g Saturates 4g

1¼ HOURS   45 MINS

SERVES 4

INGREDIENTS

1 portion Basic Pizza Dough (see page 861)

TOPPING

400g/14 oz can chopped tomatoes

2 garlic cloves, crushed

1 tsp dried basil

1 tbsp olive oil

2 tbsp tomato purée (paste)

200 g/7 oz mushrooms

150 g/5½ oz Mozzarella cheese, grated

salt and pepper

basil leaves, to garnish

1 Place the yeast and sugar in a measuring jug and mix with 50 ml/2 fl oz/4 tbsp of the water. Leave the yeast mixture in a warm place for 15 minutes or until frothy.

2 Mix the flour with the salt and make a well in the centre. Add the oil, the yeast mixture and the remaining water. Using a wooden spoon, mix to form a smooth dough.

3 Turn the dough out on to a floured surface and knead for 4–5 minutes or until smooth. Return the dough to the bowl, cover with an oiled sheet of cling film (plastic wrap) and leave to rise for 30 minutes or until doubled in size.

4 Remove the dough from the bowl. Knead the dough for 2 minutes. Using a rolling pin, roll out the dough to form an oval or a circular shape, then place it on an oiled baking tray (cookie sheet), pushing out the edges until even. The dough should be no more than 6 mm/¼ inch thick because it will rise during cooking.

5 Using a sharp knife, chop the mushrooms into slices.

6 To make the topping, place the tomatoes, garlic, dried basil, olive oil and salt and pepper in a large pan and simmer for 20 minutes or until the sauce has thickened. Stir in the tomato purée (paste) and leave to cool slightly.

7 Spread the sauce over the base of the pizza, top with the mushrooms and scatter over the Mozzarella. Bake in a preheated oven, at 200°C/400°F/Gas Mark 6, for 25 minutes. Garnish with basil leaves.

Baked Potatoes with Pesto

This is an easy, but very filling meal. The potatoes are baked until fluffy, then they are mixed with a tasty pesto filling and baked again.

NUTRITIONAL INFORMATION

Calories	444	Sugars 3g
Protein	........10g	Fat 28g
Carbohydrate	...40g	Saturates 13g

10 MINS   1½ HOURS

SERVES 4

INGREDIENTS

4 baking potatoes, about 225 g/8 oz each

150 ml/¼ pint/⅔ cup double (heavy) cream

75 ml/3 fl oz/⅓ cup vegetable stock

1 tbsp lemon juice

2 garlic cloves, crushed

3 tbsp chopped basil

2 tbsp pine nuts

2 tbsp grated Parmesan cheese

salt and pepper

1 Scrub the potatoes well and prick the skins with a fork. Rub a little salt into the skins and place on a baking tray (cookie sheet).

2 Cook in a preheated oven, 190°C/ 375°F/Gas Mark 5, for 1 hour, or until the potatoes are cooked through and the skins are crisp.

3 Remove the potatoes from the oven and cut them in half lengthways. Using a spoon, scoop the potato flesh into a mixing bowl, leaving a thin shell of potato inside the skins. Mash the potato flesh with a fork.

4 Meanwhile, mix the cream and stock in a saucepan and simmer over a low heat for about 8-10 minutes, or until reduced by half.

5 Stir in the lemon juice, garlic and chopped basil and season to taste with salt and pepper. Stir the mixture into the mashed potato flesh, together with the pine nuts.

6 Spoon the mixture back into the potato shells and sprinkle the Parmesan cheese on top. Return the potatoes to the oven for 10 minutes, or until the cheese has browned. Serve.

VARIATION

Add full-fat soft cheese or thinly sliced mushrooms to the mashed potato flesh in step 5, if you prefer.

Cabbage & Walnut Stir-Fry

This is a really quick, one-pan dish using white and red cabbage for both colour and flavour.

NUTRITIONAL INFORMATION

Calories ....422 Sugars 9g
Protein ....13g Fat 37g
Carbohydrate ...10g Saturates 5g

 10 MINS   10 MINS

SERVES 4

I N G R E D I E N T S

350 g/12 oz white cabbage

350 g/12 oz red cabbage

4 tbsp peanut oil

1 tbsp walnut oil

2 garlic cloves, crushed

8 spring onions (scallions)

225 g/8 oz firm tofu (bean curd), cubed

2 tbsp lemon juice

100 g/3½ oz walnut halves

2 tsp Dijon mustard

2 tsp poppy seeds

salt and pepper

1 Using a sharp knife, shred the white and red cabbages thinly and set aside until required.

2 Heat the peanut and walnut oils in a preheated wok or heavy-based frying pan (skillet). Add the garlic, cabbage, spring onions (scallions) and tofu (bean curd) and cook, stirring constantly, for 5 minutes.

3 Add the lemon juice, walnuts and Dijon mustard, season to taste with salt and pepper and cook for a further 5 minutes, or until the cabbage is tender.

4 Transfer the stir-fry to a warm serving bowl, sprinkle with poppy seeds and serve immediately.

COOK'S TIP

As well as adding protein, vitamins and useful fats to the diet, nuts and seeds add flavour and texture to vegetarian meals. Keep a good supply of them in your store-cupboard as they can be used in a great variety of dishes – salads, bakes, stir-fries to name but a few.

Sauté of Summer Vegetables

The freshness of lightly cooked summer vegetables is enhanced by the aromatic flavour of a tarragon and white wine dressing.

NUTRITIONAL INFORMATION

Calories 217   Sugars 8g
Protein . . . . .2g   Fat 18g
Carbohydrate . . . .9g   Saturates 9g

 10 MINS   10–15 MINS

SERVES 4

INGREDIENTS

225 g/8 oz baby carrots, scrubbed

125 g/4½ oz runner (string) beans

2 courgettes (zucchini), trimmed

1 bunch large spring onions (scallions)

1 bunch radishes

60 g/2 oz/½ cup butter

2 tbsp light olive oil

2 tbsp white wine vinegar

4 tbsp dry white wine

1 tsp caster (superfine) sugar

1 tbsp chopped tarragon

salt and pepper

tarragon sprigs, to garnish

1 Cut the carrots in half lengthways, slice the beans and courgettes (zucchini), and halve the spring onions (scallions) and radishes, so that all the vegetables are cut to even-size pieces.

2 Melt the butter in a large, heavy-based frying pan (skillet) or wok. Add all the vegetables and fry them over a medium heat, stirring frequently, until they are tender, but still crisp and firm to the bite.

3 Heat the olive oil, vinegar, white wine and sugar in a small saucepan over a low heat, stirring until the sugar has dissolved. Remove from the heat and add the chopped tarragon.

4 When the vegetables are just cooked, pour over the 'dressing'. Stir through, tossing the vegetables well to coat, and then transfer to a warmed serving dish. Garnish with sprigs of fresh tarragon and serve at once.

Carrots with Coconut

Sliced carrots and chunks of parsnip are cooked in a creamy coconut sauce with ground almonds and served on a bed of spinach.

NUTRITIONAL INFORMATION

Calories 386   Sugars 14g
Protein ....6g   Fat 32g
Carbohydrate ...20g   Saturates 15g

10 MINS   35 MINS

SERVES 4

INGREDIENTS

90 g/3 oz/⅓ cup creamed coconut

300 ml/½ pint/1¼ cups hot water

15 g/½ oz/2 tbsp flaked (slivered) almonds

4 tbsp vegetable oil

5 cardamom pods

4 thin slices ginger root

350 g/12 oz/2½ cups carrots, sliced

350 g/12 oz/2½ cups parsnips, cut into small chunks

¼ tsp five-spice powder

15 g/½ oz/2 tbsp ground almonds

200 g/7 oz/4 cups young spinach leaves

½ red onion, sliced thinly

1 garlic clove, sliced

salt

1 Crumble the creamed coconut into a bowl or jug, add the hot water and stir until dissolved.

2 Heat a saucepan and dry-fry the flaked (slivered) almonds until golden. Remove from the pan and set aside until required.

3 Heat half the oil in the saucepan. Lightly crush the cardamom pods (this helps to release their flavour) and add to the saucepan with the ginger root.

Fry for 30 seconds to flavour the oil. Add the chopped carrots and parsnips. Stir-fry for 2–3 minutes.

4 Stir in the five-spice powder and ground almonds, and pour in the coconut liquid. Bring to the boil and season with salt to taste. Cover and simmer for 12–15 minutes until the vegetables are tender. Stir occasionally, adding extra water if necessary.

5 Wash and drain the spinach. Remove any stalks. Heat the remaining oil in a wok and stir-fry the onion and garlic for 2 minutes. Add the spinach and stir-fry until it has just wilted. Drain off any excess liquid and season with salt.

6 Remove the cardamom pods and ginger from the carrots and parsnips, and adjust the seasoning. Serve on a bed of the spinach sprinkled with the almonds.

Mooli (White Radish) Curry

This is rather an unusual recipe for a vegetarian curry. The dish is good served hot with chapatis

NUTRITIONAL INFORMATION

Calories 384	Sugars 4g
Protein 3g	Fat 38g
Carbohydrate 9g	Saturates 4g

 10 MINS 20 MINS

SERVES 4

I N G R E D I E N T S

500 g/1 lb 2 oz mooli (white radish),
    preferably with leaves

1 tbsp moong dhal

600 ml/1 pint/2½ cups water

150 ml/¼ pint/⅔cup vegetable oil

1 medium onion, thinly sliced

1 tsp crushed garlic

1 tsp crushed dried red chillies

1 tsp salt

1 Rinse, peel and roughly slice the mooli (white radish), together with its leaves, if using.

2 Place the mooli (white radish), the leaves, if using, and the moong dhal in a large saucepan and pour over the water. Bring to the boil and cook over a medium heat until the mooli (white radish) has softened enough to handle.

3 Drain the mooli (white radish) thoroughly and squeeze out any excess water, using your hands.

4 Heat the vegetable oil in a heavy-based saucepan. Add the onion, garlic, crushed red chillies and salt and fry over a medium heat, stirring from time to time, for about 5–7 minutes, until the onions have softened and turned light golden brown in colour.

5 Stir the mooli (white radish) mixture into the spiced onion mixture and combine well. Reduce the heat and continue cooking, stirring frequently, for about 3–5 minutes.

6 Transfer the mooli (white radish) curry to individual serving plates and serve hot with chapatis

COOK'S TIP

The vegetable used in this recipe, mooli (white radish), looks a bit like a parsnip without the tapering end and is now sold in most supermarkets, as well as in Indian grocers.

Pasta & Bean Casserole

A satisfying winter dish, this is a slow-cooked, one-pot meal. The haricot (navy) beans need to be soaked overnight, so prepare well in advance.

NUTRITIONAL INFORMATION

Calories 323	Sugars 5g
Protein 13g	Fat 12g
Carbohydrate . . .41g	Saturates 2g

 25 MINS   3¹/₂ HOURS

SERVES 6

INGREDIENTS

225 g/8 oz/generous 1 cup dried haricot
   (navy) beans, soaked overnight and
   drained

225 g/8 oz penne,
   or other short pasta shapes

6 tbsp olive oil

850 ml/1½ pints/3½ cups vegetable stock

2 large onions, sliced

2 cloves garlic, chopped

2 bay leaves

1 tsp dried oregano

1 tsp dried thyme

5 tbsp red wine

2 tbsp tomato purée (paste)

2 celery stalks, sliced

1 fennel bulb, sliced

125 g/4½ oz mushrooms, sliced

225 g/8 oz tomatoes, sliced

1 tsp dark muscovado sugar

4 tbsp dry white breadcrumbs

salt and pepper

TO SERVE

salad leaves

crusty bread

1 Put the beans in a large pan, cover them with water and bring to the boil. Boil the beans rapidly for 20 minutes, then drain them.

2 Cook the pasta for only 3 minutes in a large pan of boiling salted water, adding 1 tablespoon of the oil. Drain in a colander and set aside.

3 Put the beans in a large flameproof casserole, pour on the vegetable stock and stir in the remaining olive oil, the onions, garlic, bay leaves, herbs, wine and tomato purée (paste).

4 Bring to the boil, cover the casserole and cook in a preheated oven, 180°C/350°F/Gas Mark 4, for 2 hours.

5 Add the reserved pasta, the celery, fennel, mushrooms and tomatoes, and season with salt and pepper.

6 Stir in the sugar and sprinkle on the breadcrumbs. Cover the casserole and continue cooking for 1 hour. Serve hot, with salad leaves and crusty bread.

Giardiniera

As the name implies, this colourful pizza should be topped with fresh vegetables from the garden, especially in the summer months.

 3¹/₂ HOURS   20 MINS

SERVES 4

INGREDIENTS

6 spinach leaves

Basic Pizza Dough (see page 861)

Basic Tomato Sauce (see page 6)

1 tomato, sliced

1 celery stalk, sliced thinly

½ green (bell) pepper, sliced thinly

1 baby courgette (zucchini), sliced

25 g/1 oz asparagus tips

25 g/1 oz sweetcorn, defrosted if frozen

25 g/1 oz peas, defrosted if frozen

4 spring onions (scallions), trimmed and
   chopped

1 tbsp chopped fresh mixed herbs

60 g/2 oz Mozzarella, grated

2 tbsp freshly grated Parmesan

1 artichoke heart

olive oil, for drizzling

salt and pepper

1 Remove any tough stalks from the spinach and wash the leaves in cold water. Pat dry with paper towels.

2 Roll out or press the pizza dough, using a rolling pin or your hands, into a large 25 cm/10 inch circle on a lightly floured work surface. Place the round on a large greased baking tray (cookie sheet) or pizza pan and push up the edge a little. Spread with the tomato sauce.

3 Arrange the spinach leaves on the sauce, followed by the tomato slices. Top with the remaining vegetables and the herbs.

4 Mix together the cheeses and sprinkle over. Place the artichoke heart in the centre. Drizzle the pizza with a little olive oil and season.

5 Bake in a preheated oven, at 200°C/400°F/Gas Mark 6, for 18–20 minutes, or until the edges are crisp and golden brown. Serve immediately.

Couscous Royale

Serve this stunning dish as a centrepiece for a North African-style feast; it will prove to be a truly memorable meal.

NUTRITIONAL INFORMATION

Calories	329	Sugars	........31g
Protein	.........6g	Fat	..........13g
Carbohydrate	...50g	Saturates	.......6g

25 MINS   45 MINS

SERVES 6

INGREDIENTS

3 carrots

3 courgettes (zucchini)

350 g/12 oz pumpkin or squash

1.25 litres/2¼ pints/5 cups vegetable stock

2 cinnamon sticks, broken in half

2 tsp ground cumin

1 tsp ground coriander

pinch of saffron strands

2 tbsp olive oil

pared rind and juice of 1 lemon

2 tbsp clear honey

500 g/1 lb 2 oz/2¾ cups pre-
    cooked couscous

60 g/2 oz/¼ cup butter or, softened

175 g/6 oz/1 cup large
    seedless raisins

salt and pepper

coriander (cilantro), to garnish

1 Cut the carrots and courgettes (zucchini) into 7 cm/3 inch pieces and cut in half lengthways.

2 Trim the pumpkin or squash and discard the seeds. Peel and cut into pieces the same size as the carrots and courgettes (zucchini).

3 Put the stock, spices, saffron and carrots in a large saucepan. Bring to the boil, skim off any scum and add the olive oil. Simmer for 15 minutes.

4 Add the lemon rind and juice to the pan, together with the honey, courgettes (zucchini) and pumpkin or squash. Season well. Bring back to the boil and simmer for a further 10 minutes.

5 Meanwhile, soak the couscous according to the packet instructions. Transfer to a steamer or large strainer lined with muslin (cheesecloth) and place over the vegetable pan. Cover and steam as directed. Stir in the butter.

6 Pile the couscous on to a warmed serving plate. Drain the vegetables, reserving the stock, lemon rind and cinnamon. Arrange the vegetables on top of the couscous. Put the raisins on top and spoon over 6 tablespoons of the reserved stock. Keep warm.

7 Return the remaining stock to the heat and boil for 5 minutes to reduce slightly. Discard the lemon rind and cinnamon. Garnish with sprigs of coriander (cilantro) and serve immediately, handing the sauce separately.

Aubergine (Eggplant) Cake

This dish would make a stunning dinner party dish, yet it contains simple ingredients and is easy to make.

NUTRITIONAL INFORMATION

Calories 201   Sugars 4g
Protein . . . . .14g   Fat 7g
Carbohydrate . . .22g   Saturates 4g

 55 MINS   35 MINS

SERVES 4

INGREDIENTS

1 medium aubergine (eggplant)

300 g/10½ oz tricolour pasta shapes

125 g/4½ oz low-fat soft cheese with garlic and herbs

350ml/12 fl oz/1⅓ cups passata (sieved tomatoes)

4 tbsp grated Parmesan cheese

1½ tsp dried oregano

2 tbsp dry white breadcrumbs

salt and pepper

1 Preheat the oven to 190°C/375°F/Gas Mark 5. Grease and line a 20.5 cm/ 8 inch round spring-form cake tin (pan).

2 Trim the aubergine (eggplant) and slice lengthwise into slices about 5 mm/¼ inch thick. Place in a bowl, sprinkle with salt, and set aside for 30 minutes to remove any bitter juices. Rinse well under cold running water and drain.

3 Bring a saucepan of water to the boil and blanch the aubergine (eggplant) slices for 1 minute. Drain and pat dry with kitchen paper (paper towels). Set aside.

4 Cook the pasta shapes according to the instructions on the packet; for best results, the pasta should be slightly undercooked. Drain well and return to the

saucepan. Add the soft cheese and allow it to melt over the pasta.

5 Stir in the passata (sieved tomatoes), Parmesan cheese, oregano and salt and pepper. Set aside.

6 Arrange the aubergine (eggplant) over the base and sides of the tin, overlapping the slices and making sure there are no gaps.

7 Pile the pasta mixture into the tin (pan), packing down well, and sprinkle with the breadcrumbs. Bake for 20 minutes and leave to stand for 15 minutes.

8 Loosen the cake round the edge with a palette knife (spatula) and release from the tin. Turn out the pasta cake, aubergine (eggplant)-side uppermost, and serve hot.

Vegetable Biryani

The Biryani originated in the North of India, and was a dish reserved for festivals. The vegetables are marinated in a yogurt-based marinade.

NUTRITIONAL INFORMATION

Calories ....449 Sugars 18g
Protein ....12g Fat 12g
Carbohydrate ...79g Saturates 6g

2¼ HOURS   1 HR 5 MINS

SERVES 4

INGREDIENTS

1 large potato, cubed

100 g/3½ oz baby carrots

50 g/1¾ oz okra, thickly sliced

2 celery sticks, sliced

75 g/2¾ oz baby button mushrooms, halved

1 aubergine (eggplant), halved and sliced

300 ml/½ pint/1¼ cups natural
   (unsweetened) yogurt

1 tbsp grated root ginger

2 large onions, grated

4 garlic cloves, crushed

1 tsp turmeric

1 tbsp curry powder

25 g/1 oz/2 tbsp butter

2 onions, sliced

225 g/8 oz/1¼ cups basmati rice

chopped coriander (cilantro),
   to garnish

1 Cook the potato cubes, carrots and okra in a pan of boiling salted water for 7–8 minutes. Drain well and place in a large bowl. Mix with the celery, mushrooms and aubergine (eggplant).

2 Mix the natural (unsweetened) yogurt, ginger, grated onions, garlic, turmeric and curry powder and spoon over the vegetables. Set aside in a cool place to marinate for at least 2 hours.

3 Heat the butter in a heavy-based frying pan (skillet). Add the sliced onions and cook over a medium heat for 5–6 minutes, until golden brown. Remove a few onions from the pan and reserve for the garnish.

4 Cook the rice in a large pan of boiling water for 7 minutes. Drain thoroughly and set aside.

5 Add the marinated vegetables to the onions and cook for 10 minutes.

6 Put half of the rice in a 2 litre/ 3½ pint/8¾ cup casserole dish. Spoon the vegetables on top and cover with the remaining rice. Cover and cook in a preheated oven, 190°C/375°F/Gas Mark 5, for 20–25 minutes, or until the rice is tender.

7 Spoon the biryani on to a serving plate, garnish with the reserved onions and coriander (cilantro) and serve.

Chatuchak Fried Rice

An excellent way to use up leftover rice. Pop it in the freezer as soon as it is cool, and it will be ready to reheat at any time.

NUTRITIONAL INFORMATION

Calories 241	Sugars 5g
Protein 7g	Fat 5g
Carbohydrate . . .46g	Saturates 1g

25 MINS   15 MINS

SERVES 4

I N G R E D I E N T S

1 tbsp sunflower oil

3 shallots, chopped finely

2 garlic cloves, crushed

1 red chilli, deseeded and chopped finely

2.5-cm/1-inch piece ginger root, shredded finely

½ green (bell) pepper, deseeded and sliced finely

150 g/5½ oz/2-3 baby aubergines (eggplants), quartered

90 g/3 oz sugar snap peas or mangetout (snow peas), trimmed and blanched

90 g/3 oz/6 baby sweetcorn, halved lengthways and blanched

1 tomato, cut into 8 pieces

90 g/3 oz/1½ cups bean sprouts

500 g/1 lb 2 oz/3 cups cooked jasmine rice

2 tbsp tomato ketchup

2 tbsp light soy sauce

T O   G A R N I S H

fresh coriander (cilantro) leaves

lime wedges

1 Heat the sunflower oil in a wok or large, heavy frying pan (skillet) over a high heat.

2 Add the shallots, garlic, chilli and ginger to the wok or frying pan (skillet). Stir until the shallots have softened.

3 Add the green (bell) pepper and baby aubergines (eggplants) and stir well.

4 Add the sugar snap peas or mangetout (snow peas), baby sweetcorn, tomato and bean sprouts. Stir-fry for 3 minutes.

5 Add the cooked jasmine rice to the wok, and lift and stir with two spoons for 4–5 minutes, until no more steam is released.

6 Stir the tomato ketchup and soy sauce into the mixture in the wok.

7 Serve the Chatuchak fried rice immediately, garnished with coriander (cilantro) leaves and lime wedges to squeeze over.

Chilled Noodles & Peppers

This is a convenient dish to serve when you are arriving home just before family or friends. Quick to prepare and assemble, it is ready in minutes.

NUTRITIONAL INFORMATION

Calories ....260 Sugars 4g
Protein ....4g Fat 21g
Carbohydrate ...15g Saturates 4g

 5 MINS 🕐 15 MINS

SERVES 4-6

I N G R E D I E N T S

250 g/9 oz ribbon noodles, or Chinese egg noodles

1 tbsp sesame oil

1 red (bell) pepper

1 yellow (bell) pepper

1 green (bell) pepper

6 spring onions (scallions), cut into matchstick strips

salt

D R E S S I N G

5 tbsp sesame oil

2 tbsp light soy sauce

1 tbsp tahini (sesame seed paste)

4-5 drops hot pepper sauce

1 Preheat the grill (broiler) to medium. Cook the noodles in a large pan of boiling, salted water until they are almost tender. Drain them in a colander, run cold water through them and drain thoroughly. Tip the noodles into a bowl, stir in the sesame oil, cover and chill.

2 Cook the (bell) peppers under the grill (broiler), turning them frequently, until they are blackened on all sides. Plunge into cold water, then skin them. Cut in half, remove the core and seeds and cut the flesh into thick strips. Set aside in a covered container.

3 To make the dressing, mix together the sesame oil, light soy sauce, tahini (sesame seed paste) and hot pepper sauce until well combined.

4 Pour the dressing on the noodles, reserving 1 tablespoon, and toss well. Turn the noodles into a serving dish, arrange the grilled (bell) peppers over the noodles and spoon on the reserved dressing. Scatter on the spring onion (scallion) strips.

COOK'S TIP

If you have time, another way of skinning (bell) peppers is to first grill (broil) them, then place in a plastic bag, seal and leave for about 20 minutes. The skin will then peel off easily.

Green Rice

Based on the Mexican dish *Arroz Verde*, this recipe is perfect for (bell) pepper and chilli lovers. Serve with iced lemonade to quell the fire!

NUTRITIONAL INFORMATION

Calories	445	Sugars	.........6g
Protein	........13g	Fat	..........12g
Carbohydrate	...76g	Saturates	.......2g

25 MINS   30 MINS

SERVES 4

I N G R E D I E N T S

2 large green (bell) peppers

2 fresh green chillies

2 tbsp, plus 1 tsp vegetable oil

1 large onion, finely chopped

1 garlic clove, crushed

1 tbsp ground coriander

300 g/10½ oz/1½ cups long grain rice

700 ml/1¼ pints/3 cups Vegetable stock

225 g/8 oz/2 cups frozen peas

6 tbsp chopped coriander (cilantro)

1 egg, beaten

salt and pepper

coriander (cilantro), to garnish

TO SERVE

tortilla chips

lime wedges

COOK'S TIP

There are hundreds of varieties of chillies, many of them very similar in appearance, so it is not always easy to tell how hot they are. As a general rule, small, pointed chillies are hotter than larger, more rounded ones, but this is not invariable.

1 Halve, core and seed the (bell) peppers. Cut the flesh into small cubes. Seed and finely chop the chillies.

2 Heat 2 tablespoons of the oil in a saucepan and fry the onion, garlic, (bell) peppers and chillies for 5–6 minutes, until softened, but not browned.

3 Stir in the ground coriander, rice, and stock. Bring to the boil, cover and simmer for 10 minutes. Add the peas, bring back to the boil, cover and simmer for a further 5 minutes, until the rice is tender. Remove from the heat and leave to stand, covered, for 10 minutes.

4 Season to taste with salt and pepper and mix in the fresh coriander (cilantro). Pile into a warmed serving dish and keep warm.

5 Heat the remaining oil in a small omelette pan. Pour in the egg and cook over a medium heat for 1–2 minutes on each side, until set. Slide the omelette on to a plate, roll up loosely and slice into thin rounds.

6 Arrange the omelette strips on top of the rice. Garnish with coriander (cilantro) and serve immediately with tortilla chips and lime wedges.

Vegetable & Lentil Koftas

A mixture of vegetables, nuts and lentils is shaped into small balls and baked in the oven with a sprinkling of aromatic garam masala.

NUTRITIONAL INFORMATION

Calories	679	Sugars	........20g
Protein	........29g	Fat	..........33g
Carbohydrate	...73g	Saturates	.......5g

🍲 30 MINS   🕐 50 MINS

SERVES 4

I N G R E D I E N T S

6 tbsp vegetable ghee or oil

1 onion, finely chopped

2 carrots, finely chopped

2 celery sticks, finely chopped

2 garlic cloves, crushed

1 fresh green chilli, seeded and
  finely chopped

4½ tsp curry powder or paste

225 g/8 oz/1¼ cups split red lentils

600 ml/1 pint/2½ cups vegetable stock

2 tbsp tomato purée (paste)

125 g/4½ oz/2 cups fresh wholemeal
  (whole wheat) breadcrumbs

90 g/3 oz/¾ cup unsalted cashews,
  finely chopped

2 tbsp chopped coriander (cilantro)

1 egg, beaten

salt and pepper

garam masala, for sprinkling

Y O G U R T   D R E S S I N G

250 ml/9 fl oz/1 cup natural
  (unsweetened) yogurt

1-2 tbsp chopped coriander

1-2 tbsp mango chutney,
  chopped if necessary

1 Heat 4 tablespoons of ghee or oil in a large saucepan and gently fry the onion, carrots, celery, garlic and chilli, stirring frequently, for 5 minutes. Add the curry powder or paste and the lentils and cook, stirring constantly, for 1 minute.

2 Add the stock and tomato purée (paste) and bring to the boil. Reduce the heat, cover and simmer for 20 minutes, or until the lentils are tender and all the liquid is absorbed.

3 Remove from the heat and cool slightly. Add the breadcrumbs, nuts, coriander (cilantro), egg and seasoning to taste. Mix well and leave to cool. Shape into rounds about the size of golf balls (use 2 spoons to help shape the rounds).

4 Place the balls on a greased baking tray (cookie sheet), drizzle with the remaining oil and sprinkle with a little garam masala, to taste. Cook in a preheated oven, at 180°C/350°F/Gas Mark 4, for 15-20 minutes, or until piping hot and lightly golden in colour.

5 Meanwhile, make the yogurt dressing. Mix all the ingredients together in a bowl. Serve the koftas hot with the yogurt dressing.

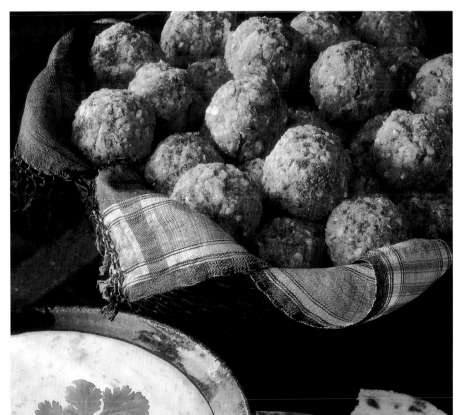

Potato Fritters with Relish

These are incredibly simple to make and sure to be popular served as a tempting snack or as an accompaniment to almost any Indian meal.

NUTRITIONAL INFORMATION

Calories 294	Sugars 4g
Protein 4g	Fat 24g
Carbohydrate ...18g	Saturates 3g

🍲 40 MINS   🕐 15 MINS

SERVES 8

INGREDIENTS

60 g/2 oz/½ cup plain wholemeal (whole wheat) flour

½ tsp ground coriander

½ tsp cumin seeds

¼ tsp chilli powder

½ tsp ground turmeric

¼ tsp salt

1 egg

3 tbsp milk

350 g/12 oz potatoes, peeled

1-2 garlic cloves, crushed

4 spring onions (scallions), chopped

60 g/2 oz corn kernels

vegetable oil, for shallow frying

ONION & TOMATO RELISH

1 onion, peeled

225 g/8 oz tomatoes

2 tbsp chopped coriander (cilantro)

2 tbsp chopped mint

2 tbsp lemon juice

½ tsp roasted cumin seeds

¼ tsp salt

pinch of cayenne pepper

1 First make the relish. Cut the onion and tomatoes into small dice and place in a bowl with the remaining ingredients. Mix together well and leave to stand for at least 15 minutes before serving to allow time for the flavours to blend.

2 Place the flour in a bowl, stir in the spices and salt and make a well in the centre. Add the egg and milk and mix to form a fairly thick batter.

3 Coarsely grate the potatoes, place in a sieve and rinse well under cold running water. Drain and squeeze dry, then stir into the batter with the garlic, spring onions (scallions)and corn.

4 Heat about 5 mm/¼ inches vegetable oil in a large frying pan and add a few tablespoonfuls of the mixture at a time, flattening each one to form a thin cake. Fry over a low heat, turning frequently, for 2-3 minutes, or until golden brown and cooked through.

5 Drain on kitchen paper (paper towels) and keep hot while frying the remaining mixture in the same way. Serve hot with onion and tomato relish.

Spinach & Nut Pilau

Fragrant basmati rice is cooked with porcini (cep) mushrooms, spinach and pistachio nuts in this easy microwave recipe.

NUTRITIONAL INFORMATION

Calories 403	Sugars 7g	
Protein 10g	Fat 15g	
Carbohydrate . . .62g	Saturates 2g	

55 MINS   15–20 MINS

SERVES 4

INGREDIENTS

10 g/⅓ oz dried porcini

  (cep) mushrooms

300 ml/½ pint/1¼ cups hot water

1 onion, chopped

1 garlic clove, crushed

1 tsp grated root ginger

½ fresh green chilli, seeded

  and chopped

2 tbsp oil

225 g/8 oz/generous 1 cup basmati rice

1 large carrot, grated

175 ml/6 fl oz/¾ cup vegetable stock

½ tsp ground cinnamon

4 cloves

½ tsp saffron strands

225 g/8 oz/6 cups fresh spinach, long

  stalks removed

60 g/2 oz/½ cup pistachio nuts

1 tbsp chopped coriander (cilantro)

salt and pepper

coriander (cilantro) leaves

  to garnish

1 Place the porcini (cep) mushrooms in a small bowl. Pour over the hot water and leave to soak for 30 minutes.

2 Place the onion, garlic, ginger, chilli and oil in a large bowl. Cover and cook on HIGH power for 2 minutes. Rinse the rice, then stir it into the bowl, together with the carrot. Cover and cook on HIGH power for 1 minute.

3 Strain and coarsely chop the mushrooms. Add the mushroom soaking liquid to the stock to make 425 ml/¾ pint/scant 2 cups. Pour on to the rice. Stir in the mushrooms, cinnamon,

cloves, saffron and ½ teaspoon salt. Cover and cook on HIGH power for 10 minutes, stirring once. Leave to stand, covered, for 10 minutes.

4 Place the spinach in a large bowl. Cover and cook on HIGH power for 3½ minutes, stirring once. Drain well and chop coarsely.

5 Stir the spinach, pistachio nuts and chopped coriander (cilantro) into the rice. Season to taste with salt and pepper and garnish with coriander (cilantro) leaves. Serve immediately.

Stir-Fried Japanese Noodles

This quick dish is an ideal lunchtime meal, packed with whatever mixture of mushrooms you like in a sweet sauce.

NUTRITIONAL INFORMATION

Calories 379   Sugars 8g
Protein ....12g   Fat 13g
Carbohydrate ...53g   Saturates 3g

 15 MINS   🕐 15 MINS

SERVES 4

I N G R E D I E N T S

225 g/8 oz Japanese egg noodles

2 tbsp sunflower oil

1 red onion, sliced

1 garlic clove, crushed

500 g/1 lb 2 oz mixed mushrooms, such as
    shiitake, oyster, brown cap

350 g/12 oz pak choi

2 tbsp sweet sherry

6 tbsp soy sauce

4 spring onions (scallions), sliced

1 tbsp toasted sesame seeds

1 Place the egg noodles in a large bowl. Pour over enough boiling water to cover and leave to soak for 10 minutes.

2 Heat the sunflower oil in a large preheated wok.

3 Add the red onion and garlic to the wok and stir-fry for 2–3 minutes, or until softened.

4 Add the mushrooms to the wok and stir-fry for about 5 minutes, or until the mushrooms have softened.

5 Drain the Japanese egg noodles thoroughly and set aside.

6 Add the the pak choi, noodles, sweet sherry and soy sauce to the wok. Toss all of the ingredients together to mix well and stir-fry for 2–3 minutes, or until the liquid is just bubbling.

7 Transfer the mushroom noodles to warm serving bowls and scatter with sliced spring onions (scallions) and toasted sesame seeds. Serve immediately.

COOK'S TIP

The variety of mushrooms in supermarkets has greatly improved and a good mixture should be easily obtainable. If not, use the more common button and flat mushrooms.

Bean & Tomato Casserole

This quick and easy casserole can be eaten as a healthy supper dish or as a side dish to accompany sausages or grilled fish.

NUTRITIONAL INFORMATION

Calories 273   Sugars 8g
Protein ....15g   Fat 7g
Carbohydrate ...40g   Saturates 1g

10 MINS   15 MINS

SERVES 4

I N G R E D I E N T S

400g/14 oz can cannellini beans

400g/14 oz can borlotti beans

2 tbsp olive oil

1 stick celery

2 garlic cloves, chopped

175 g/6 oz baby onions, halved

450 g/1 lb tomatoes

75 g/2¾ oz rocket (arugula)

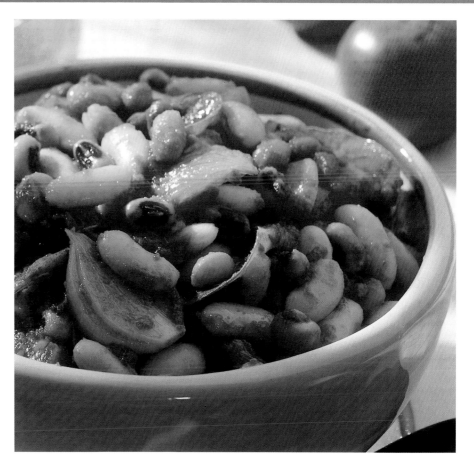

1 Drain both cans of beans and reserve 6 tablespoons of the liquid.

2 Heat the oil in a large pan. Add the celery, garlic and onions and sauté for 5 minutes or until the onions are golden.

3 Cut a cross in the base of each tomato and plunge them into a bowl of boiling water for 30 seconds until the skins split. Remove the tomatoes with a perforated spoon and leave until cool enough to handle. Peel off the skin and chop the flesh.

4 Add the tomato flesh and the reserved bean liquid to the pan and cook for 5 minutes.

5 Add the beans to the pan and cook for a further 3–4 minutes or until the beans are hot.

6 Stir in the rocket (arugula) and allow to wilt slightly before serving. Serve hot.

VARIATION

For a spicier tasting dish, add 1–2 teaspoons of hot pepper sauce with the cannellini and borlotti beans in step 5.

Bubble & Squeak

Bubble and squeak is best known as mashed potato and leftover greens cooked in meat fat in a pan and served as an accompaniment.

NUTRITIONAL INFORMATION

Calories 301   Sugars 5g
Protein . . . . .11g   Fat 18g
Carbohydrate . . .24g   Saturates 2g

15 MINS   40 MINS

SERVES 4

I N G R E D I E N T S

450 g/1 lb floury (mealy) potatoes, diced

225 g/8 oz Savoy cabbage, shredded

5 tbsp vegetable oil

2 leeks, chopped

1 garlic clove, crushed

225 g/8 oz smoked tofu (bean curd), cubed

salt and pepper

shredded cooked leek, to garnish

1 Cook the diced potatoes in a saucepan of lightly salted boiling water for 10 minutes, until tender. Drain and mash the potatoes.

2 Meanwhile, in a separate saucepan, blanch the cabbage in boiling water for 5 minutes. Drain well and add to the potato.

COOK'S TIP

This vegetarian version is a perfect main meal, as the smoked tofu (bean curd) cubes added to the basic bubble and squeak mixture make it very substantial and nourishing.

3 Heat the oil in a heavy-based frying pan (skillet). Add the leeks and garlic and fry gently for 2-3 minutes. Stir into the potato and cabbage mixture.

4 Add the smoked tofu (bean curd) and season well with salt and pepper. Cook over a moderate heat for 10 minutes.

5 Carefully turn the whole mixture over and continue to cook over a moderate heat for a further 5-7 minutes, until crispy underneath. Serve immediately, garnished with shredded leek.

Pasta with Nuts & Cheese

Simple and inexpensive, this tasty pasta dish can be prepared fairly quickly.

NUTRITIONAL INFORMATION

Calories 531	Sugars 4g
Protein 20g	Fat 35g
Carbohydrate . . .35g	Saturates 16g

10 MINS   30 MINS

SERVES 4

INGREDIENTS

60 g/2 oz/1 cup pine kernels (nuts)

350 g/12 oz dried pasta shapes

2 courgettes (zucchini), sliced

125 g/4½ oz/1¼ cups broccoli, broken into florets

200 g/7 oz/1 cup full-fat soft cheese

150 ml/¼ pint/⅔ cup milk

1 tbsp chopped fresh basil

125 g/4½ oz button mushrooms, sliced

90 g/3 oz blue cheese, crumbled

salt and pepper

sprigs of fresh basil, to garnish

green salad, to serve

1 Scatter the pine kernels (nuts) on to a baking tray (cookie sheet) and grill (broil), turning occasionally, until lightly browned all over. Set aside.

2 Cook the pasta in plenty of boiling salted water for 8–10 minutes or until just tender.

3 Meanwhile, cook the courgettes (zucchini) and broccoli in a small amount of boiling, lightly salted water for about 5 minutes or until just tender.

4 Put the soft cheese into a pan and heat gently, stirring constantly. Add the milk and stir to mix. Add the basil and mushrooms and cook gently for 2–3 minutes. Stir in the blue cheese and season to taste.

5 Drain the pasta and the vegetables and mix together. Pour over the cheese and mushroom sauce and add the pine kernels (nuts). Toss gently to mix. Garnish with basil sprigs and serve with a green salad.

Stuffed Rice Pancakes

Dosas (pancakes) are widely eaten in southern India. The rice and urid dhal need to soak and ferment, so prepare well in advance.

NUTRITIONAL INFORMATION

Calories 748   Sugars 1g
Protein . . . . .10g   Fat 47g
Carbohydrate . . .76g   Saturates 5g

6¼ HOURS   40–45 MINS

SERVES 4

I N G R E D I E N T S

200 g/7 oz/1 cup rice and 50 g/1¾ oz/
  ¼ cup urid dhal, or 200 g/7 oz/1¾ cups
  ground rice and 50 g/1¾ oz/7 tbsp urid
  dhal flour (ata)

425–600 ml/¾–1 pint/2–2½ cups water

1 tsp salt

4 tbsp vegetable oil

F I L L I N G

4 medium potatoes, diced

3 fresh green chillies, chopped

½ tsp turmeric

1 tsp salt

150 ml/¼ pint/⅔ cup oil

1 tsp mixed mustard and onion seeds

3 dried chillies

4 curry leaves

2 tbsp lemon juice

1 To make the dosas (pancakes), soak the rice and urid dhal for 3 hours. Grind the rice and urid dhal to a smooth consistency, adding water if necessary. Set aside for a further 3 hours to ferment. Alternatively, if you are using ground rice and urid dhal flour (ata), mix together in a bowl. Add the water and salt and stir until a batter is formed.

2 Heat about 1 tablespoon of oil in a large, non-stick, frying-pan (skillet). Using a ladle, spoon the batter into the frying-pan (skillet). Tilt the frying-pan (skillet) to spread the mixture over the base. Cover and cook over a medium heat for about 2 minutes. Remove the lid and turn the dosa over very carefully. Pour a little oil around the edge, cover and cook for a further 2 minutes. Repeat with the remaining batter.

3 To make the filling, cook the potatoes in a pan of boiling water. Add the chillies, turmeric and salt and cook until the potatoes are just soft. Drain and mash lightly with a fork.

4 Heat the oil in a saucepan and fry the mustard and onion seeds, dried red chillies and curry leaves, stirring constantly, for about 1 minute. Pour the spice mixture over the mashed potatoes, then sprinkle over the lemon juice and mix well. Spoon the potato filling on one half of each of the dosas (pancakes) and fold the other half over it. Transfer to a warmed serving dish and serve hot.

Vegetable & Goat's Cheese

Wonderfully colourful vegetables are roasted in olive oil with thyme and garlic. The goat's cheese adds a nutty, piquant flavour.

NUTRITIONAL INFORMATION

Calories 387	Sugars 9g	
Protein 10g	Fat 21g	
Carbohydrate ...42g	Saturates 5g	

 2¹/₂ HOURS   40 MINS

SERVES 4

I N G R E D I E N T S

2 baby courgettes (zucchini), halved
  lengthways

2 baby aubergines (eggplant), quartered
  lengthways

½ red (bell) pepper, cut into 4 strips

½ yellow (bell) pepper, cut into 4 strips

1 small red onion, cut into wedges

2 garlic cloves, unpeeled

4 tbsp olive oil

1 tbsp red wine vinegar

1 tbsp chopped fresh thyme

Basic Pizza Dough (see page 861)

Basic Tomato Sauce (see page 6)

90 g/3 oz goat's cheese

salt and pepper

fresh basil leaves, to garnish

1 Place all of the prepared vegetables in a large roasting tin (pan). Mix together the olive oil, vinegar, thyme and plenty of seasoning and pour over, coating well.

2 Roast the vegetables in a preheated oven, at 200°C/400°F/Gas Mark 6, for 15–20 minutes or until the skins have started to blacken in places, turning half-way through. Leave to rest for 5 minutes after roasting.

3 Carefully peel off the skins from the roast (bell) peppers and the garlic cloves. Slice the garlic.

4 Roll out or press the dough, using a rolling pin or your hands, into a 25 cm/ 10 inch circle on a lightly floured work surface. Place on a large greased baking tray (cookie sheet) or pizza pan and raise the edge a little. Cover and leave for 10 minutes to rise slightly in a warm place. Spread with the tomato sauce almost to the edge.

5 Arrange the roasted vegetables on top and dot with the cheese. Drizzle the oil and juices from the roasting tin (pan) over the pizza and season.

6 Bake in a preheated oven, at 200°C/ 400°F/Gas Mark 6, for 18–20 minutes, or until the edge is crisp and golden. Serve immediately, garnished with basil leaves.

Vegetable Jambalaya

This dish traditionally contains spicy sausage, but it is equally delicious filled with vegetables in this spicy vegetarian version.

NUTRITIONAL INFORMATION

Calories 181   Sugars 8g
Protein . . . . .6g   Fat 7g
Carbohydrate . . .25g   Saturates 1g

10 MINS   55 MINS

SERVES 4

INGREDIENTS

75 g/2¾ oz/½ cup brown rice

2 tbsp olive oil

2 garlic cloves, crushed

1 red onion, cut into eight

1 aubergine (eggplant), diced

1 green (bell) pepper, diced

50 g/1¾ oz baby corn cobs,
    halved lengthways

50 g/1¾ oz/½ cup frozen peas

100 g/3½ oz small broccoli florets

150 ml/¼ pint/⅔ cup vegetable stock

225 g/8 oz can chopped tomatoes

1 tbsp tomato purée (paste)

1 tsp creole seasoning

½ tsp chilli flakes

salt and pepper

COOK'S TIP

Use a mixture of different kinds of rice, such as wild or red rice, for colour and texture. Cook the rice in advance for a speedier recipe.

1 Cook the rice in a large saucepan of salted boiling water for 20 minutes, or until cooked through. Drain, rinse with boiling water, drain again and set aside.

2 Heat the oil in a heavy-based frying pan (skillet) and cook the garlic and onion, stirring constantly, for 2–3 minutes.

3 Add the aubergine (eggplant), (bell) pepper, corn, peas and broccoli to the pan and cook, stirring occasionally, for 2–3 minutes.

4 Stir in the vegetable stock and canned tomatoes, tomato purée (paste), creole seasoning and chilli flakes.

5 Season to taste and cook over a low heat for 15–20 minutes, or until the vegetables are tender.

6 Stir the brown rice into the vegetable mixture and cook, mixing well, for 3–4 minutes, or until hot. Transfer the vegetable jambalaya to a warm serving dish and serve immediately.

Yellow Split Pea Casserole

If ever there was a winter warmer, this is it – an intensely satisfying dish, ideal for serving with rice or fresh naan bread.

NUTRITIONAL INFORMATION

Calories 358	Sugars 10g	
Protein 19g	Fat 12g	
Carbohydrate . . .45g	Saturates 1g	

2¹/₄ HOURS   1¹/₂ HOURS

SERVES 4

INGREDIENTS

2 tbsp ghee

1 tsp black mustard seeds

1 onion, chopped finely

2 garlic cloves, crushed

1 carrot, grated

2.5 cm/1 inch piece ginger root, grated

1 green chilli, deseeded and chopped finely

1 tbsp tomato purée (paste)

250 g/9 oz/1 cup yellow split peas, soaked in water for 2 hours

400 g/14 oz can chopped tomatoes

500 ml/18 fl oz/2 cups vegetable stock

225 g/8 oz/1½ cups pumpkin, cubed

225 g/8 oz cauliflower, cut into florets

2 tbsp oil

1 large aubergine (eggplant), cubed

1 tbsp chopped fresh coriander (cilantro)

1 tsp garam masala

salt and pepper

1 Melt the ghee over a medium heat in a large pan. Add the mustard seeds, and when they start to splutter, add the onion, garlic, carrot, and ginger.

2 Cook until soft, about 5 minutes. Add the green chilli and stir in the tomato purée (paste). Stir in the split peas.

3 Add the tomatoes and stock, and bring to the boil. Season well.

4 Simmer for 40 minutes, stirring occasionally. Add the pumpkin cubes and cauliflower florets, and simmer for a further 30 minutes, covered, until the split peas are soft.

5 Meanwhile, heat the oil in a frying pan (skillet) over a high heat. Add the aubergine (eggplant), and stir until sealed

on all sides; remove and drain on kitchen paper (paper towels).

6 Stir the aubergine (eggplant) into the split pea mixture with the coriander (cilantro) and garam masala. Check for seasoning.

7 Transfer to a serving dish and serve immediately.

Sweet Potato & Leek Patties

Sweet potatoes have very dense flesh and a delicious, sweet, earthy taste, which contrasts well with the pungent flavour of the ginger.

NUTRITIONAL INFORMATION

Calories 403   Sugars 34g
Protein . . . . .8g   Fat 12g
Carbohydrate . . .67g   Saturates 2g

2 HOURS   40 MINS

SERVES 4

I N G R E D I E N T S

900 g/2 lb sweet potato

4 tsp sunflower oil

2 medium leeks, trimmed and finely chopped

1 garlic clove, crushed

2.5 cm/1 inch piece root (fresh) ginger, finely chopped

200 g/7 oz can sweetcorn kernels, drained

2 tbsp low-fat natural fromage frais (unsweetened yogurt)

60 g/2 oz wholemeal (whole wheat) flour

salt and pepper

G I N G E R   S A U C E

2 tbsp white wine vinegar

2 tsp caster (superfine) sugar

1 red chilli, deseeded and chopped

2.5 cm/1 inch piece root (fresh) ginger, cut into thin strips

2 tbsp ginger wine

4 tbsp Fresh Vegetable Stock (see page 8)

1 tsp cornflour (cornstarch)

T O   S E R V E

lettuce leaves

spring onions (scallions), shredded

1 Peel the potatoes, cut into thick cubes and boil for 10–15 minutes. Drain well and mash. Leave to cool.

2 Fry the leeks, garlic and ginger for 2–3 minutes in 2 teaspoons of oil. Stir into the potato with the sweetcorn, seasoning and fromage frais (unsweetened yogurt). Form into 8 patties and toss in flour. Chill for 30 minutes. Place the patties on a preheated grill (broiler) rack and lightly brush with oil. Grill (broil) for 5 minutes, then turn over, brush with oil and grill (broil) for a further 5 minutes.

3 Place the vinegar, sugar, chilli and ginger in a pan and simmer for 5 minutes. Stir in the wine. Blend the stock and cornflour (cornstarch) and add to the sauce, stirring, until thickened. Serve the patties with lettuce and spring onions (scallions), and the sauce.

Vegetable & Tofu Strudels

These strudels look really impressive and are perfect if friends are coming round or for a more formal dinner party dish.

NUTRITIONAL INFORMATION

Calories 485	Sugars 5g	
Protein 16g	Fat 27g	
Carbohydrate ...47g	Saturates 5g	

 25 MINS   🕐 30 MINS

SERVES 4

I N G R E D I E N T S

F I L L I N G

2 tbsp vegetable oil

2 tbsp butter

150 g/5½ oz/⅓ cup potatoes, finely diced

1 leek, shredded

2 garlic cloves, crushed

1 tsp garam masala

½ tsp chilli powder

½ tsp turmeric

50 g/1¾ oz okra, sliced

100 g/3½ oz/1¼ cups sliced button mushrooms

2 tomatoes, diced

225 g/8 oz firm tofu (bean curd), diced

12 sheets filo pastry

2 tbsp butter, melted

salt and pepper

1 To make the filling, heat the oil and butter in a frying pan (skillet). Add the potatoes and leek and fry, stirring constantly, for 2–3 minutes. Add the garlic and spices, okra, mushrooms, tomatoes, and tofu (bean curd) and season to taste with salt and pepper. Cook, stirring, for 5–7 minutes, or until tender.

2 Lay the pastry out on a chopping board and brush each individual sheet with melted butter. Place 3 sheets on top of one another; repeat to make 4 stacks.

3 Spoon a quarter of the filling along the centre of each stack and brush the edges with melted butter. Fold the short edges in and roll up lengthways to form a cigar shape. Brush the outside with melted butter. Place the strudels on a greased baking tray (cookie sheet).

4 Cook in a preheated oven, 190°C/ 375°F/Gas Mark 5, for 20 minutes, or until golden brown and crisp. Transfer to a warm serving dish and serve immediately.

Filled Jacket Potatoes

Cook these potatoes conventionally, wrap them in foil and keep warm at the edge of the barbecue (grill), ready to fill with inspired mixtures.

NUTRITIONAL INFORMATION

Calories 564   Sugars 14g
Protein . . . . .21g   Fat 29g
Carbohydrate . . .58g   Saturates 18g

15 MINS   1 HR 5 MINS

SERVES 4

I N G R E D I E N T S

4 large or 8 medium baking potatoes

paprika or chilli powder, or chopped herbs,
    to garnish

MEXICAN RELISH

225 g/8 oz can sweetcorn (corn), drained

½ red (bell) pepper, seeded and chopped

5 cm/2 inch piece of cucumber,
    finely chopped

½ tsp chilli powder

salt and pepper

CHEESE & CHIVES

125 g/4½ oz/½ cup full-fat soft cheese

125 g/4½ oz/½ cup natural fromage frais

125 g/4½ oz blue cheese, cut into cubes

1 celery stick, finely chopped

2 tsp snipped chives

celery salt and pepper

SPICY MUSHROOMS

25 g/1 oz/2 tbsp butter or margarine

225 g/8 oz button mushrooms

150 g/5½ oz/⅔ cup natural
    (unsweetened) yogurt

1 tbsp tomato purée (paste)

2 tsp mild curry powder

salt and pepper

1 Scrub the potatoes and prick them with a fork. Bake in a preheated oven, 200°C/400°F/Gas Mark 6, for about 1 hour, until just tender.

2 To make the Mexican Relish, put half the sweetcorn (corn) into a bowl. Process the remainder into a blender or food processor for 10–15 seconds, or chop and mash roughly by hand. Add the puréed corn to the corn kernels with the (bell) pepper, cucumber and chilli powder. Season to taste with salt and pepper.

3 To make the Cheese & Chives filling, mix the soft cheese and fromage frais together until smooth. Add the blue cheese, celery and chives. Season with celery salt and pepper.

4 To make the Spicy Mushrooms, melt the butter or margarine in a small frying pan (skillet). Add the mushrooms and cook gently for 3–4 minutes. Remove from the heat and stir in the yogurt, tomato purée (paste) and curry powder. Season to taste with salt and pepper.

5 Wrap the cooked potatoes in foil and keep warm at the edge of the barbecue. Serve the fillings sprinkled with paprika or chilli powder or herbs.

Spicy Fried Noodles

This is a simple idea to add an extra kick to noodles, which accompany many main course dishes in Thailand.

NUTRITIONAL INFORMATION

Calories	568	Sugars	.........3g
Protein	........16g	Fat	..........19g
Carbohydrate	...90g	Saturates	.......4g

15 MINS   3-5 MINS

SERVES 4

INGREDIENTS

500 g/1 lb 2 oz medium egg noodles

60 g/2 oz/1 cup bean sprouts

15 g/½ oz chives

3 tbsp sunflower oil

1 garlic clove, crushed

4 fresh green chillies, seeded, sliced and
    soaked in 2 tbsp rice vinegar

salt

1 Place the noodles in a bowl, cover with boiling water and soak for 10 minutes. Drain and set aside.

2 Pick over the bean sprouts and soak in cold water while you cut the chives into 2.5 cm/1 inch pieces. Set a few chives aside for the garnish. Drain the bean sprouts thoroughly.

3 Heat the oil in a preheated wok or large, heavy-based frying pan (skillet). Add the crushed garlic and stir; then add the chillies and stir-fry for about 1 minute, until fragrant.

4 Add the bean sprouts, stir and then add the noodles. Stir in salt to taste and add the chives. Using 2 spoons or a wok scoop, lift and toss the noodles for 1 minute.

5 Transfer the noodles to a warm serving dish, garnish the with the reserved chives and serve immediately.

COOK'S TIP
Soaking a chilli in rice vinegar has the effect of distributing the hot chilli flavour throughout the dish. To reduce the heat, you can slice the chilli more thickly before soaking.

Roast (Bell) Pepper Tart

This tastes truly delicious, the flavour of roasted vegetables being entirely different from that of boiled or fried.

NUTRITIONAL INFORMATION

Calories 237   Sugars 3g
Protein . . . . .6g   Fat 15g
Carbohydrate . . .20g   Saturates 4g

 25 MINS   40 MINS

SERVES 8

I N G R E D I E N T S

PASTRY

175 g/6 oz/1½ cups plain
   (all-purpose) flour

pinch of salt

75 g/2¾ oz/6 tbsp butter
   or margarine

2 tbsp green pitted olives,
   finely chopped

3 tbsp cold water

FILLING

1 red (bell) pepper

1 green (bell) pepper

1 yellow (bell) pepper

2 garlic cloves, crushed

2 tbsp olive oil

100 g/3½ oz/1 cup grated
   mozzarella cheese

2 eggs

150 ml/¼ pint/⅔ cup milk

1 tbsp chopped basil

salt and pepper

1 To make the pastry, sift the flour and salt into a bowl. Rub in the butter or margarine until the mixture resembles breadcrumbs. Add the olives and cold water, bringing the mixture together to form a dough.

2 Roll the dough out on a floured surface and use to line a 20 cm/8 inch loose-based flan tin (pan). Prick the base with a fork and leave to chill.

3 Cut all the (bell) peppers in half lengthways, seed and place them, skin side uppermost, on a baking tray (cookie sheet). Mix the garlic and oil and brush over the (bell) peppers. Cook in a preheated oven, 200°C/400°F/Gas Mark 6, for 20 minutes, or until beginning to char slightly. Let the (bell) peppers cool slightly and thinly slice. Arrange in the base of the pastry case, layering with the mozzarella.

4 Beat the egg and milk and add the basil. Season and pour over the (bell) peppers. Put the tart on a baking tray (cookie sheet) and return to the oven for 20 minutes, or until set. Serve hot or cold.

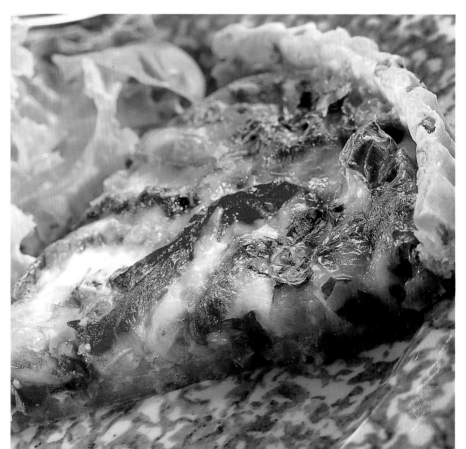

Potato & Spinach Gnocchi

These small potato dumplings are flavoured with spinach, cooked in boiling water and served with a simple tomato sauce.

NUTRITIONAL INFORMATION

Calories 315	Sugars 7g	
Protein 8g	Fat 8g	
Carbohydrate ...56g	Saturates 1g	

20 MINS   30 MINS

SERVES 4

I N G R E D I E N T S

300 g/10½ oz floury (mealy) potatoes, diced

175 g/6 oz spinach

1 egg yolk

1 tsp olive oil

125 g/4½ oz/1 cup plain (all-purpose) flour

salt and pepper

spinach leaves, to garnish

S A U C E

1 tbsp olive oil

2 shallots, chopped

1 garlic clove, crushed

300 ml/½ pint/1¼ cups passata (sieved tomatoes)

2 tsp soft light brown sugar

1 Cook the diced potatoes in a saucepan of boiling water for 10 minutes or until cooked through. Drain and mash the potatoes.

2 Meanwhile, in a separate pan, blanch the spinach in a little boiling water for 1-2 minutes. Drain the spinach and shred the leaves.

3 Transfer the mashed potato to a lightly floured chopping board and make a well in the centre. Add the egg yolk, olive oil, spinach and a little of the flour and quickly mix the ingredients into the potato, adding more flour as you go, until you have a firm dough. Divide the mixture into very small dumplings.

4 Cook the gnocchi, in batches, in a saucepan of boiling salted water for about 5 minutes or until they rise to the surface.

5 Meanwhile, make the sauce. Put the oil, shallots, garlic, passata (sieved tomatoes) and sugar into a saucepan and cook over a low heat for 10-15 minutes or until the sauce has thickened.

6 Drain the gnocchi using a perforated spoon and transfer to warm serving dishes. Spoon the sauce over the gnocchi and garnish with the fresh spinach leaves.

VARIATION

Add chopped fresh herbs and cheese to the gnocchi dough instead of the spinach, if you prefer.

Vegetable Crêpes

Crêpes or pancakes are ideal for filling with your favourite ingredients. In this recipe they are packed with a spicy vegetable filling.

NUTRITIONAL INFORMATION

Calories	509	Sugars	........10g
Protein	........17g	Fat	..........34g
Carbohydrate	...36g	Saturates	.......9g

15 MINS   45 MINS

SERVES 4

I N G R E D I E N T S

C R E P E S

100 g/3½ oz/¾ cup plain (all-purpose) flour

pinch of salt

1 egg, beaten

300 ml/½ pint/1¼ cups milk

vegetable oil, for frying

F I L L I N G

2 tbsp vegetable oil

1 leek, shredded

½ tsp chilli powder

½ tsp ground cumin

50 g/1¾ oz mangetout (snow peas)

100 g/3½ oz button mushrooms,

1 red (bell) pepper, sliced

25 g/1 oz/¼ cup cashew nuts, chopped

S A U C E

25 g/1 oz/2 tbsp margarine

25 g/1 oz/3 tbsp plain (all-purpose) flour

150 ml/¼ pint/⅔ cup vegetable stock

150 ml/¼ pint/⅔ cup milk

1 tsp Dijon mustard

75 g/2¾ oz/¾ cup grated
   Cheddar cheese

2 tbsp chopped coriander (cilantro)

1 For the crêpes, sift the flour and salt into a bowl. Beat in the egg and milk to make a batter.

2 For the filling, heat the oil and sauté the leek for 2–3 minutes. Add the remaining ingredients and cook, stirring, for 5 minutes.

3 For the sauce, melt the margarine in a pan and add the flour. Cook, stirring, for 1 minute. Remove from the heat, stir in the stock and milk and return to the heat. Bring to the boil, stirring until thick.

Add the mustard, half the cheese and the coriander (cilantro); cook for 1 minute.

4 Heat 1 tablespoon of oil in a small frying pan (skillet). Pour off the oil and add an eighth of the batter. Tilt to cover the base. Cook for 2 minutes, turn and cook the other side for 1 minute. Repeat with the remaining batter. Spoon a little of the filling along the centre of each crêpe and roll up. Place in a flameproof dish and pour the sauce on top. Top with cheese and heat under a hot grill (broiler) for 3–5 minutes or until the cheese melts.

Stuffed Mushrooms

Large mushrooms have more flavour than the smaller button mushrooms. Serve these mushrooms as a side vegetable or appetizer.

NUTRITIONAL INFORMATION

Calories 148   Sugars 1g
Protein . . . . .11g   Fat 7g
Carbohydrate . . . .11g   Saturates 3g

10 MINS   15 MINS

SERVES 4

INGREDIENTS

12 open-cap mushrooms

4 spring onions (scallions), chopped

4 tsp olive oil

100 g/3½ oz fresh brown breadcrumbs

1 tsp fresh oregano, chopped

100 g/3½ oz low-fat mature (sharp)
   Cheddar cheese

1 Wash the mushrooms and pat dry with kitchen paper (paper towels). Remove the stalks and chop the stalks finely.

2 Sauté the mushroom stalks and spring onions (scallions) in half of the oil.

3 In a large bowl, mix together the mushroom stalks and spring onions (scallions).

4 Add the breadcrumbs and oregano to the mushrooms and spring onions (scallions), mix and set aside.

5 Crumble the cheese into small pieces in a small bowl. Add the cheese to the breadcrumb mixture and mix well. Spoon the stuffing mixture into the mushroom caps.

6 Drizzle the remaining oil over the mushrooms. Barbecue (grill) on an oiled rack over medium hot coals for 10 minutes or until cooked through.

7 Transfer the mushrooms to serving plates and serve hot.

VARIATION

For a change replace the cheese with finely-chopped chorizo sausage (remove the skin first), chopped hard-boiled eggs, chopped olives or chopped anchovy fillets. Mop up the juices with some crusty bread.

Parmesan Potatoes

This is a very simple way to jazz up roast potatoes. Serve them in the same way as roast potatoes with roasted meats or fish.

NUTRITIONAL INFORMATION

Calories 307   Sugars 2g
Protein . . . . .11g   Fat 14g
Carbohydrate . . .37g   Saturates 6g

15 MINS   1 HR 5 MINS

SERVES 4

INGREDIENTS

6 potatoes

50 g/1 ¾ oz Parmesan cheese, grated

pinch of grated nutmeg

1 tbsp chopped fresh parsley

4 smoked bacon slices, cut into strips

oil, for roasting

salt

1 Cut the potatoes in half lengthways and cook them in a saucepan of boiling salted water for 10 minutes. Drain thoroughly.

2 Mix the grated Parmesan cheese, nutmeg and parsley together in a shallow bowl.

3 Roll the potato pieces in the cheese mixture to coat them completely. Shake off any excess.

4 Pour a little oil into a roasting tin (pan) and heat it in a preheated oven, 200°C/400°F/Gas Mark 6, for 10 minutes. Remove from the oven and place the potatoes into the tin (pan). Return the tin (pan) to the oven and cook for 30 minutes, turning once.

5 Remove from the oven and sprinkle the bacon on top of the potatoes. Return to the oven for 15 minutes or until the potatoes and bacon are cooked. Drain off any excess fat and serve.

VARIATION

If you prefer, use slices of salami or Parma ham (prosciutto) instead of the bacon, adding it to the dish 5 minutes before the end of the cooking time.

Tofu with (Bell) Peppers

Tofu (bean curd) is perfect for marinating as it readily absorbs flavours for a great tasting main dish.

NUTRITIONAL INFORMATION

Calories	267	Sugars	........2g
Protein	.........9g	Fat	.........23g
Carbohydrate	....5g	Saturates	.......3g

25 MINS   15 MINS

SERVES 4

INGREDIENTS

350 g/12 oz tofu (bean curd)

2 cloves garlic, crushed

4 tbsp soy sauce

1 tbsp sweet chilli sauce

6 tbsp sunflower oil

1 onion, sliced

1 green (bell) pepper, deseeded
   and diced

1 tbsp sesame oil

1 Using a sharp knife, cut the tofu (bean curd) into bite-sized pieces. Place the tofu (bean curd) in a shallow non-metallic dish.

2 Mix together the garlic, soy sauce and sweet chilli sauce and drizzle over the tofu (bean curd). Toss well to coat and leave to marinate for about 20 minutes.

3 Meanwhile, heat the sunflower oil in a large preheated wok.

4 Add the onion to the wok and stir-fry over a high heat until brown and crispy. Remove the onion with a slotted spoon and leave to drain on absorbent kitchen paper (paper towels).

5 Add the tofu (bean curd) to the hot oil and stir-fry for about 5 minutes.

6 Remove all but 1 tablespoon of the sunflower oil from the wok. Add the (bell) pepper to the wok and stir-fry for 2–3 minutes, or until softened.

7 Return the tofu (bean curd) and onions to the wok and heat through, stirring occasionally.

8 Drizzle with sesame oil. Transfer to serving plates and serve immediately.

COOK'S TIP

If you are in a real hurry, buy ready-marinated tofu (bean curd) from your supermarket.

Filled Aubergines (Eggplants)

An aubergine (eggplant) is halved and filled with a risotto mixture, topped with cheese and baked to make a snack or quick meal for two.

NUTRITIONAL INFORMATION

Calories ....435 Sugars 17g
Protein ....13g Fat 23g
Carbohydrate ...48g Saturates 8g

20 MINS   1 HOUR

SERVES 2

I N G R E D I E N T S

60 g/2 oz/¼ cup mixed long-grain and
   wild rice

1 aubergine (eggplant), about 350 g/12 oz

1 tbsp olive oil

1 small onion, chopped finely

1 garlic clove, crushed

½ small red (bell) pepper, cored, deseeded
   and chopped

2 tbsp water

25 g/1 oz/3 tbsp raisins

25 g/1 oz/¼ cup cashew nuts,
   chopped roughly

½ tsp dried oregano

45 g/1½ oz/⅓ cup mature (sharp) Cheddar
   or Parmesan cheese, grated

salt and pepper

fresh oregano or parsley, to garnish

1 Cook the rice in a pan of boiling salted water for 15 minutes or until tender. Drain, rinse and drain again.

2 Bring a large pan of water to the boil. Cut the stem off the aubergine (eggplant) and then cut in half lengthwise. Cut out the flesh from the centre, leaving a 1.5 cm/½ inch shell. Blanch the shells in the boiling water for 3–4 minutes. Drain.

3 Chop the aubergine (eggplant) flesh finely.

4 Heat the oil in a pan and fry the onion and garlic gently until just beginning to soften. Add the (bell) pepper and aubergine (eggplant) flesh and continue cooking for 2 minutes. Add the water and cook for 2–3 minutes.

5 Stir the raisins, cashew nuts, oregano and rice into the aubergine (eggplant) mixture and season with salt and pepper to taste.

6 Lay the aubergine (eggplant) shells in an ovenproof dish and spoon in the rice mixture, piling it up well. Cover and place in a preheated oven, at 190°C/375°F/Gas Mark 5, for 20 minutes.

7 Remove the lid and sprinkle the cheese over the rice. Place under a preheated moderate grill (broiler) for 3–4 minutes or until golden brown. Serve hot garnished with oregano or parsley.

Vegetable-filled Ravioli

These small parcels are very easy to make and have the advantage of being filled with your favourite mixture of succulent mushrooms.

NUTRITIONAL INFORMATION

Calories	333	Sugars	.........1g
Protein	.........7g	Fat	..........30g
Carbohydrate	...10g	Saturates	......13g

 20 MINS   20 MINS

SERVES 4

INGREDIENTS

FILLING

25 g/1 oz/3 tbsp butter or margarine

2 garlic cloves, crushed

1 small leek, chopped

2 celery sticks, chopped

200 g/7 oz/2⅓ cups open-cap
　mushrooms, chopped

1 egg, beaten

2 tbsp grated Parmesan cheese

salt and pepper

RAVIOLI

4 sheets filo pastry

25 g/1 oz/3 tbsp margarine

oil, for deep-frying

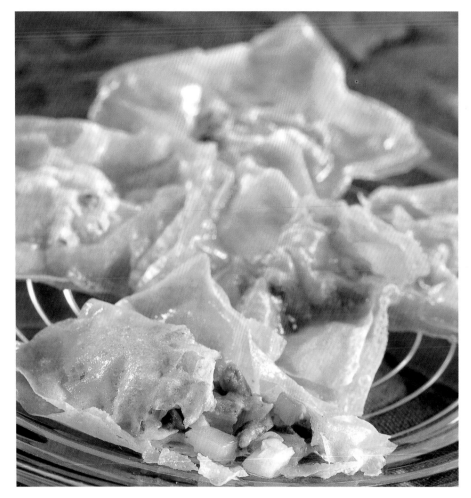

1 To make the filling, melt the butter or margarine in a frying pan (skillet) and sauté the garlic and leek for 2–3 minutes until softened.

2 Add the celery and mushrooms and cook for a further 4–5 minutes until all of the vegetables are tender.

3 Turn off the heat and stir in the egg and grated Parmesan cheese. Season with salt and pepper to taste.

4 Lay the pastry sheets on a chopping board and cut each into nine squares.

5 Spoon a little of the filling into the centre half of the squares and brush the edges of the pastry with butter or margarine. Lay another square on top and seal the edges to make a parcel.

6 Heat the oil for deep-frying to 180°C/350°F or until a cube of bread browns in 30 seconds. Fry the ravioli, in batches, for 2–3 minutes or until golden brown. Remove from the oil with a slotted spoon and pat dry on absorbent paper towels. Transfer to a warm serving plate and serve.

Baked Potatoes with Salsa

This is a great way to eat a baked potato! Once cooked, the flesh is flavoured with avocado and served with a hot tomato salsa.

NUTRITIONAL INFORMATION

Calories	274	Sugars	.........4g
Protein	110	Fat	...........8g
Carbohydrate	...43g	Saturates	......2g

 15 MINS — 1 HOUR

SERVES 4

INGREDIENTS

4 baking potatoes, about 225 g/8 oz each

1 large ripe avocado

1 tsp lemon juice

175 g/6 oz smoked tofu (bean curd), diced

2 garlic cloves, crushed

1 onion, chopped finely

1 tomato, chopped finely

125 g/4½ oz mixed salad leaves

fresh coriander (cilantro) sprigs, to garnish

SALSA

2 ripe tomatoes, seeded and diced

1 tbsp chopped coriander (cilantro)

1 shallot, diced finely

1 green chilli, diced

1 tbsp lemon juice

salt and pepper

1 Scrub the potatoes and prick the skins with a fork. Rub a little salt into the skins and place them on a baking tray (cookie sheet).

2 Cook in a preheated oven, 190°C/ 375°F/Gas Mark 5, for 1 hour or until cooked through and the skins are crisp.

3 Cut the potatoes in half lengthways and scoop the flesh into a bowl, leaving a thin layer of potato inside the shells.

4 Halve and stone the avocado. Using a spoon, scoop out the avocado flesh and add to the bowl containing the potato. Stir in the lemon juice and mash the mixture together with a fork. Mix in the tofu (bean curd), garlic, onion and tomato. Spoon the mixture into one half of the potato shells.

5 Arrange the mixed salad leaves on top of the guacamole mixture and place the other half of the potato shell on top.

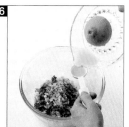

Cheese & Artichoke Pizza

Sliced artichokes combined with mature (sharp) Cheddar, Parmesan and blue cheese give a really delicious topping to this pizza.

NUTRITIONAL INFORMATION

Calories 424   Sugars 9g
Protein ....16g   Fat 20g
Carbohydrate ...47g   Saturates 8g

1¾ HOURS   20 MINS

SERVES 4

INGREDIENTS

Basic Pizza Dough (see page 861)

Basic Tomato Sauce (see page 6)

60 g/2 oz blue cheese, sliced

125 g/4½ oz artichoke hearts in oil, sliced

½ small red onion, chopped

45 g/1½ oz mature (sharp) cheese, grated

2 tbsp freshly grated Parmesan

1 tbsp chopped fresh thyme

oil from artichokes for drizzling

salt and pepper

TO SERVE

salad leaves

cherry tomatoes, halved

1 Roll out or press the dough, using a rolling pin or your hands, to form a 25 cm/10 inch circle on a lightly floured work surface.

2 Place the pizza base on a large greased baking tray (cookie sheet) or pizza pan and push up the edge slightly. Cover and leave to rise for 10 minutes in a warm place.

3 Spread the tomato sauce almost to the edge of the base. Arrange the blue cheese on top of the tomato sauce, followed by the artichoke hearts and red onion.

4 Mix the Cheddar and Parmesan cheeses together with the thyme and sprinkle the mixture over the pizza. Drizzle a little of the oil from the jar of artichokes over the pizza and season to taste.

5 Bake in a preheated oven, at 200°C/ 400°F/Gas Mark 6, for 18–20 minutes, or until the edge is crisp and golden and the cheese is bubbling.

6 Mix the fresh salad leaves and cherry tomato halves together and serve with the pizza, cut into slices.

Neapolitan Seafood Salad

This delicious mix of seafood, salad leaves (greens) and ripe tomatoes conjures up all the warmth and sunshine of Naples.

NUTRITIONAL INFORMATION

Calories 1152	Sugars 3g	
Protein 67g	Fat 81g	
Carbohydrate . . .35g	Saturates 12g	

6 ½ HOURS   25 MINS

SERVES 4

I N G R E D I E N T S

450 g/1 lb prepared squid,
  cut into strips

750 g/1 lb 10 oz cooked mussels

450 g/1 lb cooked cockles in brine

150 ml/¼ pint/⅔ cup white wine

300 ml/½ pint/1¼ cups olive oil

225 g/8 oz/2 cups dried campanelle or
  other small pasta shapes

juice of 1 lemon

1 bunch chives, snipped

1 bunch fresh parsley,
finely chopped

4 large tomatoes

mixed salad leaves (greens)

salt and pepper

sprig of fresh basil, to garnish

VARIATION

You can substitute cooked scallops for the mussels and clams in brine for the cockles, if you prefer. The seafood needs to be marinated for 6 hours, so prepare well in advance.

1 Put all of the seafood into a large bowl, pour over the wine and half of the olive oil, and set aside for 6 hours.

2 Put the seafood mixture into a saucepan and simmer over a low heat for 10 minutes. Set aside to cool.

3 Bring a large saucepan of lightly salted water to the boil. Add the pasta and 1 tablespoon of the remaining olive oil and cook for 8–10 minutes or until tender, but still firm to the bite. Drain thoroughly and refresh in cold water.

4 Strain off about half of the cooking liquid from the seafood and discard the rest. Mix in the lemon juice, chives, parsley and the remaining olive oil. Season to taste with salt and pepper. Drain the pasta and add to the seafood.

5 Cut the tomatoes into quarters. Shred the salad leaves (greens) and arrange them at the base of a salad bowl. Spoon in the seafood salad and garnish with the tomatoes and a sprig of basil. Serve.

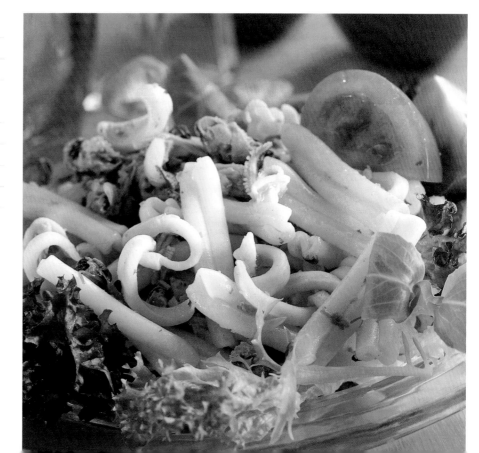

Tabbouleh Salad

This kind of salad is eaten widely throughout the Middle East. The flavour improves as it is kept, so it tastes even better on the second day.

NUTRITIONAL INFORMATION

Calories 637   Sugars 8g
Protein . . . . .20g   Fat 41g
Carbohydrate . . .50g   Saturates 11g

🥗 1½ HOURS   🕐 5-10 MINS

SERVES 2

I N G R E D I E N T S

125 g/4½ oz/1 cup bulgar wheat

600 ml/1 pint/2½ cups boiling water

1 red (bell) pepper, seeded and halved

3 tbsp olive oil

1 garlic clove, crushed

grated rind of ½ lime

about 1 tbsp lime juice

1 tbsp chopped mint

1 tbsp chopped parsley

3–4 spring onions (scallions), trimmed and
    thinly sliced

8 pitted black olives, halved

40 g/1½ oz/⅓ cup large salted peanuts or
    cashew nuts

1–2 tsp lemon juice

60–90 g/2–3 oz Gruyère cheese

salt and pepper

mint sprigs, to garnish

warm pitta (pocket) bread or crusty rolls,
    to serve

1 Put the bulgar wheat into a bowl and cover with the boiling water to reach about 2.5 cm/1 inch above the bulgar. Set aside to soak for up to 1 hour, until most of the water is absorbed and is cold.

2 Meanwhile, put the halved red (bell) pepper, skin side upwards, on a grill (broiler) rack and cook under a preheated moderate grill (broiler) until the skin is thoroughly charred and blistered. Leave to cool slightly.

3 When cool enough to handle, peel off the skin and discard the seeds. Cut the (bell) pepper flesh into narrow strips.

4 Whisk together the oil, garlic and lime rind and juice. Season to taste and whisk until thoroughly blended. Add 4½ teaspoons of the dressing to the (bell) peppers and mix lightly.

5 Drain the soaked bulgar wheat thoroughly, squeezing it in a dry cloth to make it even drier, then place in a bowl.

6 Add the chopped herbs, spring onions (scallions), olives and peanuts or cashew nuts to the bulgar and toss . Add the lemon juice to the remaining dressing, and stir through the salad. Spoon the salad on to 2 serving plates.

7 Cut the cheese into narrow strips and mix with the (bell) pepper strips. Spoon alongside the bulgar salad. Garnish with mint sprigs and serve with warm pitta (pocket) bread or crusty rolls.

Provençale Pasta Salad

A combination of Italian vegetables tossed in a tomato dressing, served on a bed of assorted salad leaves, makes an appetizing meal.

NUTRITIONAL INFORMATION

Calories	197	Sugars 5g
Protein	. . . . .10g	Fat 5g
Carbohydrate	. . .30g	Saturates 1g

10 MINS   15 MINS

SERVES 4

I N G R E D I E N T S

225 g/8 oz penne (quills)

1 tbsp olive oil

25 g/1 oz pitted black olives, drained and chopped

25 g/1 oz dry-pack sun-dried tomatoes, soaked, drained and chopped

400 g/14 oz can artichoke hearts, drained and halved

115 g/4 oz baby courgettes (zucchini), trimmed and sliced

115 g/4 oz baby plum tomatoes, halved

100 g/3½ oz assorted baby salad leaves

salt and pepper

shredded basil leaves, to garnish

D R E S S I N G

4 tbsp passata (sieved tomatoes)

2 tbsp low-fat natural fromage frais (unsweetened yogurt)

1 tbsp unsweetened orange juice

1 small bunch fresh basil, shredded

1 Cook the penne (quills) according to the instructions on the packet. Do not overcook the pasta – it should still have 'bite'. Drain well and return to the pan.

2 Stir in the olive oil, salt and pepper, olives and sun-dried tomatoes. Leave to cool.

3 Gently mix the artichokes, courgettes (zucchini) and plum tomatoes into the cooked pasta. Arrange the salad leaves in a serving bowl.

4 To make the dressing, mix all the ingredients together and toss into the vegetables and pasta.

5 Spoon the mixture on top of the salad leaves and garnish with shredded basil leaves.

Moroccan Salad

Couscous is a type of semolina made from durum wheat. It is wonderful in salads, as it readily takes up the flavour of the dressing.

NUTRITIONAL INFORMATION

Calories	195	Sugars	........15g
Protein	.........8g	Fat	...........2g
Carbohydrate	...40g	Saturates	.....0.3g

30-35 MINS   0 MINS

SERVES 6

INGREDIENTS

175 g/6 oz/2 cups couscous

1 bunch spring onions (scallions),
   finely chopped

1 small green (bell) pepper, seeded
   and chopped

10 cm/4 inch piece of cucumber, chopped

175 g/6 oz can chickpeas (garbanzo
   beans), rinsed and drained

60 g/2 oz/⅔ cup sultanas (golden raisins)
   or raisins

2 oranges

salt and pepper

mint sprigs, to garnish

lettuce leaves, to serve

DRESSING

finely grated rind of 1 orange

1 tbsp chopped fresh mint

150 ml/¼ pint/⅔ cup natural yogurt

1 Put the couscous into a bowl and cover with boiling water. Leave it to soak for about 15 minutes to swell the grains, then stir gently with a fork to separate them.

2 Add the spring onions (scallions), green (bell) pepper, cucumber,

chickpeas (garbanzo beans) and sultanas (golden raisins) or raisins to the couscous, stirring to combine. Season well with salt and pepper.

3 To make the dressing, place the orange rind, mint and yogurt in a bowl and mix together until well combined. Pour over the couscous mixture and stir to mix well.

4 Using a sharp serrated knife, remove the peel and pith from the oranges. Cut the flesh into segments, removing all the membrane.

5 Arrange the lettuce leaves on 4 serving plates. Divide the couscous mixture between the plates and arrange the orange segments on top. Garnish with sprigs of fresh mint and serve.

Three-Way Potato Salad

Small new potatoes, served warm in a delicious dressing. The nutritional information is for the potato salad with the curry dressing only.

NUTRITIONAL INFORMATION

Calories 310	Sugars 12g
Protein 6g	Fat 19g
Carbohydrate . . .31g	Saturates 4g

 15-20 MINS   20 MINS

SERVES 4

INGREDIENTS

500 g/1 lb 2 oz new potatoes (for each
   dressing)

herbs, to garnish

LIGHT CURRY DRESSING

1 tbsp vegetable oil

1 tbsp medium curry paste

1 small onion, chopped

1 tbsp mango chutney, chopped

6 tbsp natural (unsweetened) yogurt

3 tbsp single (light) cream

2 tbsp mayonnaise

salt and pepper

1 tbsp single (light) cream, to garnish

VINAIGRETTE DRESSING

6 tbsp hazelnut oil

3 tbsp cider vinegar

1 tsp wholegrain mustard

1 tsp caster (superfine) sugar

few basil leaves, torn

PARSLEY CREAM

150 ml/¼ pint/⅔ cup soured cream

3 tbsp light mayonnaise

4 spring onions (scallions), finely chopped

1 tbsp chopped fresh parsley

1 To make the Light Curry Dressing, heat the vegetable oil in a saucepan, add the curry paste and onion and fry, stirring frequently, until the onion is soft. Remove from the heat and set aside to cool slightly.

2 Mix together the mango chutney, yogurt, cream and mayonnaise. Add the curry mixture and blend together. Season with salt and pepper.

3 To make the Vinaigrette Dressing, whisk the oil, vinegar, mustard, sugar and basil together in a small jug or bowl. Season with salt and pepper.

4 To make the Parsley Cream, combine the mayonnaise, soured cream, spring onions (scallions) and parsley, mixing well. Season with salt and pepper.

5 Cook the potatoes in lightly salted boiling water until just tender. Drain well and set aside to cool for 5 minutes, then add the chosen dressing, tossing to coat. Serve, garnished with fresh herbs, spooning a little single (light) cream on to the potatoes if you have used the curry dressing.

Italian Potato Salad

Potato salad is always a favourite, but it is even more delicious with the addition of sun-dried tomatoes and fresh parsley.

NUTRITIONAL INFORMATION

Calories . . . . . . .425 Sugars 6g
Protein . . . . .6g Fat 27g
Carbohydrate . . .43g Saturates 5g

 40 MINS   15 MINS

SERVES 4

INGREDIENTS

450 g/1 lb baby potatoes, unpeeled, or
   larger potatoes, halved

4 tbsp natural yogurt

4 tbsp mayonnaise

8 sun-dried tomatoes

2 tbsp flat leaf parsley, chopped

salt and pepper

1 Rinse and clean the potatoes and place them in a large pan of water. Bring to the boil and cook for 8–12 minutes or until just tender. (The cooking time will vary according to the size of the potatoes.)

2 Using a sharp knife, cut the sun-dried tomatoes into thin slices.

3 To make the dressing, mix together the yogurt and mayonnaise in a bowl and season to taste with a little salt and pepper. Stir in the sun-dried tomato slices and the chopped flat leaf parsley.

4 Remove the potatoes with a perforated spoon, drain them thoroughly and then set them aside to cool. If you are using larger potatoes, cut them into 5 cm/2 inch chunks.

5 Pour the dressing over the potatoes and toss to mix.

6 Leave the potato salad to chill in the refrigerator for about 20 minutes, then serve as a starter or as an accompaniment.

COOK'S TIP

It is easier to cut the larger potatoes once they are cooked. Although smaller pieces of potato will cook more quickly, they tend to disintegrate and become mushy.

Potato, Apple & Bean Salad

Use any mixture of beans you have to hand in this recipe, but the wider the variety, the more colourful the salad.

NUTRITIONAL INFORMATION

Calories ....183 Sugars 8g
Protein ....6g Fat 7g
Carbohydrate ...26g Saturates 1g

 10 MINS   15 MINS

SERVES 4

INGREDIENTS

225 g/8 oz new potatoes, scrubbed and quartered

225 g/8 oz mixed canned beans, such as red kidney beans, flageolet and borlotti beans, drained and rinsed

1 red dessert apple, diced and tossed in 1 tbsp lemon juice

1 small yellow (bell) pepper, diced

1 shallot, sliced

½ head fennel, sliced

oak leaf lettuce leaves

DRESSING

1 tbsp red wine vinegar

2 tbsp olive oil

½ tbsp American mustard

1 garlic clove, crushed

2 tsp chopped fresh thyme

1 Cook the quartered potatoes in a saucepan of boiling water for 15 minutes until tender. Drain and transfer to a mixing bowl.

2 Add the potatoes to the mixed beans with the diced apple and yellow (bell) pepper, and the sliced shallots and fennel. Mix well, taking care not to break up the cooked potatoes.

3 In a bowl, whisk all the dressing ingredients together.

4 Pour the dressing over the potato salad.

5 Line a plate or salad bowl with the oak leaf and spoon the potato mixture into the centre. Serve the salad immediately.

COOK'S TIP

Canned beans are used here for convenience, but dried beans may be used instead. Soak for 8 hours or overnight, drain and place in a saucepan. Cover with water, bring to the boil and boil for 10 minutes, then simmer until tender.

Potato & Radish Salad

The radishes and the herb and mustard dressing give this colourful salad a mild mustard flavour which complements the potatoes perfectly.

NUTRITIONAL INFORMATION

Calories 140	Sugars 3g
Protein 3g	Fat 6g
Carbohydrate ...20g	Saturates 1g

1³/₄ HOURS   20 MINS

SERVES 4

INGREDIENTS

450 g/1 lb new potatoes, scrubbed and halved

½ cucumber, sliced thinly

2 tsp salt

1 bunch radishes, sliced thinly

DRESSING

1 tbsp Dijon mustard

2 tbsp olive oil

1 tbsp white wine vinegar

2 tbsp mixed chopped herbs

1 Cook the potatoes in a saucepan of boiling water for 10-15 minutes or until tender. Drain and leave to cool.

2 Spread out the cucumber slices on a plate and sprinkle with the salt. Leave to stand for 30 minutes, then rinse under cold running water and pat dry with kitchen paper (paper towels).

3 Arrange the cucumber and radish slices on a serving plate in a decorative pattern

4 Pile the cooked potatoes in the centre of the cucumber and radish slices.

5 Pour all the dressing ingredients in a screw-top jar and shake vigorously to combine all the ingredients. Pour the dressing over the salad, tossing well to coat all of the salad ingredients.

6 Leave the salad to chill in the refrigerator before serving.

COOK'S TIP

Dijon mustard has a mild clean taste which is perfect for this salad as it does not overpower the other flavours. If unavailable, use another mild mustard – English mustard is too strong for this salad.

Green & White Salad

This potato, rocket (arugula) and apple salad is flavoured with creamy, salty goat's cheese – perfect with salad leaves (greens).

NUTRITIONAL INFORMATION

Calories 282   Sugars 10g
Protein ....8g   Fat 17g
Carbohydrate ...26g   Saturates 5g

 15 MINS   20 MINS

SERVES 4

INGREDIENTS

2 large potatoes, unpeeled and sliced

2 green eating apples, diced

1 tsp lemon juice

25 g/1 oz/¼ cup walnut pieces

125 g/4½ oz goat's cheese, cubed

150 g/5½ oz/2–3 bunches rocket
   (arugula) leaves

salt and pepper

DRESSING

2 tbsp olive oil

1 tbsp red wine vinegar

1 tsp clear honey

1 tsp fennel seeds

COOK'S TIP

Serve this salad immediately to prevent the apple from discolouring. Alternatively, prepare all of the other ingredients in advance and add the apple at the last minute.

1 Cook the potatoes in a pan of boiling water for 15 minutes, until tender. Drain and set aside to cool. Transfer the cooled potatoes to a serving bowl.

2 Toss the diced apples in the lemon juice, drain and stir them into the cold potatoes.

3 Add the walnut pieces, cheese cubes and rocket (arugula) leaves, then toss the salad to mix.

4 In a small bowl, whisk the dressing ingredients together until well combined and pour the dressing over the salad. Serve immediately.

Chinese Salad Nests

Crisp fried potato nests are perfect as an edible salad bowl and delicious when filled with a colourful Chinese-style salad of vegetables and fruit.

NUTRITIONAL INFORMATION

Calories 272   Sugars 11g
Protein . . . . .4g   Fat 4g
Carbohydrate . . .59g   Saturates 0.4g

🧊 15 MINS   🕐 15 MINS

SERVES 4

I N G R E D I E N T S

POTATO NESTS

450 g/1 lb floury (mealy) potatoes, grated

125 g/4½ oz/1 cup cornflour (cornstarch)

vegetable oil, for frying

fresh chives, to garnish

SALAD

125 g/4½ oz pineapple, cubed

1 green (bell) pepper, cut into strips

1 carrot, cut into thin strips

50 g/1¾ oz mangetout (snowpeas), sliced
   thickly

4 baby sweetcorn cobs, halved lengthways

25 g/1 oz beansprouts

2 spring onions (scallions), sliced

DRESSING

1 tbsp clear honey

1 tsp light soy sauce

1 garlic clove, crushed

1 tsp lemon juice

 To make the nests, rinse the potatoes several times in cold water. Drain well on kitchen paper (paper towels) so they are completely dry. This is to prevent the potatoes spitting when they are cooked in the fat. Place the potatoes in a mixing bowl. Add the cornflour (cornstarch), mixing well to coat the potatoes.

2 Half fill a wok with vegetable oil and heat until smoking. Line a 15 cm/ 6 inch diameter wire sieve with a quarter of the potato mixture and press another sieve of the same size on top.

3 Lower the sieves into the oil and cook for 2 minutes until the potato nest is golden brown and crisp. Remove from the wok, allowing the excess oil to drain off.

4 Repeat 3 more times to use up all of the mixture and make a total of 4 nests. Leave to cool.

5 Mix the salad ingredients together then spoon into the potato baskets.

6 Mix the dressing ingredients together in a bowl. Pour the dressing over the salad, garnish with chives and serve immediately.

Potato & Tuna Salad

This colourful dish is a variation of the classic Salade Niçoise. Packed with tuna and vegetables, it is both filling and delicious.

NUTRITIONAL INFORMATION

Calories 225	Sugars 5g
Protein 21g	Fat 5g
Carbohydrate . . .27g	Saturates 2g

 40 MINS   20 MINS

SERVES 4

INGREDIENTS

450 g/1 lb new potatoes, scrubbed and quartered

1 green (bell) pepper, sliced

50 g/1¾ oz canned sweetcorn, drained

1 red onion, sliced

300 g/10½ oz canned tuna in brine, drained and flaked

2 tbsp chopped stoned (pitted) black olives

salt and pepper

lime wedges, to garnish

DRESSING

2 tbsp low-fat mayonnaise

2 tbsp soured cream

1 tbsp lime juice

2 garlic cloves, crushed

finely grated rind of 1 lime

1 Cook the potatoes in a saucepan of boiling water for 15 minutes until tender. Drain and leave to cool in a mixing bowl.

2 Gently stir in the sliced green (bell) pepper, sweetcorn and sliced red onion.

3 Spoon the potato mixture into a large serving bowl and arrange the flaked tuna and chopped black olives over the top.

4 Season the salad generously with salt and pepper.

5 To make the dressing, mix together the mayonnaise, soured cream, lime juice, garlic and lime rind in a bowl.

6 Spoon the dressing over the tuna and olives, garnish with lime wedges and serve.

COOK'S TIP

Green beans and hard-boiled (hard-cooked) egg slices can be added to the salad for a more traditional Salade Niçoise.

Waldorf Chicken Salad

This colourful and healthy dish is a variation of a classic salad. You can use a selection of mixed salad leaves, if preferred.

NUTRITIONAL INFORMATION

Calories 471   Sugars 19g
Protein . . . . .38g   Fat 27g
Carbohydrate . . .20g   Saturates 4g

30 MINS   0 MINS

SERVES 4

I N G R E D I E N T S

500 g/1 lb 2 oz red apples, diced

3 tbsp fresh lemon juice

150 ml/¼ pint/⅔ cup low-fat mayonnaise

1 head of celery

4 shallots, sliced

1 garlic clove, crushed

90 g/3 oz/¾ cup walnuts, chopped

500 g/1 lb 2 oz lean cooked chicken, cubed

1 cos (romaine) lettuce

pepper

sliced apple and walnuts, to garnish

1 Place the apples in a bowl with the lemon juice and 1 tablespoon of mayonnaise. Leave for 40 minutes or until required.

2 Slice the celery very thinly. Add the celery with the shallots, garlic and walnuts to the apple, mix and then add the remaining mayonnaise and blend thoroughly.

3 Add the chicken and mix with the other ingredients.

4 Lline a glass salad bowl or serving dish with the lettuce.

5 Pile the chicken salad into the centre, sprinkle with pepper and garnish with apple slices and walnuts.

VARIATION

Instead of the shallots, use spring onions (scallions) for a milder flavour. Trim the spring onions (scallions) and slice finely.

(Bell) Peppers & Rosemary

The flavour of grilled (broiled) or roasted (bell) peppers is very different from when they are eaten raw, so do try them cooked in this way.

NUTRITIONAL INFORMATION

Calories 201   Sugars 6g
Protein . . . . .2g   Fat 19g
Carbohydrate . . . .6g   Saturates 2g

20 MINS   10 MINS

SERVES 4

INGREDIENTS

4 tbsp olive oil

finely grated rind of 1 lemon

4 tbsp lemon juice

1 tbsp balsamic vinegar

1 tbsp crushed fresh rosemary, or 1 tsp
dried rosemary

2 red (bell) peppers, halved, cored
and deseeded

2 yellow (bell) peppers, halved, cored
and deseeded

2 tbsp pine kernels (nuts)

salt and pepper

sprigs of fresh rosemary, to garnish

1 Mix together the olive oil, lemon rind, lemon juice, vinegar and rosemary. Season with salt and pepper.

2 Place the (bell) peppers, skin-side uppermost, on the rack of a grill (broiler) pan, lined with foil. Brush the olive oil mixture over them.

3 Grill (broil) the (bell) peppers for 3–4 minutes or until the skin begins to char, basting frequently with the lemon juice mixture. Remove from the heat, cover with foil to trap the steam and leave for 5 minutes.

4 Meanwhile, scatter the pine kernels (nuts) on to the grill (broiler) rack and toast them lightly for 2–3 minutes. Keep a close eye on the pine kernels (nuts) as they tend to burn very quickly.

5 Peel the (bell) peppers, slice them into strips and place them in a warmed serving dish. Sprinkle with the pine kernels and drizzle any remaining lemon juice mixture over them. Garnish with sprigs of fresh rosemary and serve at once.

Bean Sprouts & Vegetables

This dish is served cold as a salad or appetizer and is very easy to make. It is a form of cold *chop suey*.

NUTRITIONAL INFORMATION

Calories . . . . .56 Sugars 5g
Protein . . . . .4g Fat 1g
Carbohydrate . . . .9g Saturates 0.2g

 3¹⁄₄ HOURS   0 MINS

SERVES 4

INGREDIENTS

450 g/1 lb bean sprouts

2 fresh red chillies, seeded and finely chopped

1 red (bell) pepper, seeded and thinly sliced

1 green (bell) pepper, seeded and thinly sliced

60 g/2 oz water chestnuts, quartered

1 celery stick, sliced

Chinese roasted meats and noodles, to serve

MARINADE

3 tbsp rice wine vinegar

2 tbsp light soy sauce

2 tbsp chopped chives

1 garlic clove, crushed

pinch of Chinese curry powder

1 Place the bean sprouts, chopped red chillies, red and green (bell) peppers, water chestnuts and celery in a large bowl and mix well to combine all the ingredients.

2 To make the marinade, mix together the rice wine vinegar, light soy sauce, chopped chives, crushed garlic and Chinese curry powder in a bowl.

3 Pour the marinade over the prepared vegetables. Toss to mix the vegetables thoroughly in the marinade.

4 Cover the salad with cling film (plastic wrap) and leave to chill in the refrigerator for at least 3 hours.

5 Drain the vegetables thoroughly, transfer to a serving dish and serve with Chinese roasted meats or noodles.

COOK'S TIP

There are hundreds of varieties of chillies and it is not always possible to tell how hot they are going to be. As a general rule, dark green chillies are hotter than light green and red chillies. Thin, pointed chillies are usually hotter than fatter, blunter chillies.

Potato & Sausage Salad

Sliced Italian sausage blends well with the other Mediterranean flavours of sun-dried tomato and basil in this salad.

NUTRITIONAL INFORMATION

Calories	450	Sugars	.........6g
Protein	........13g	Fat	..........28g
Carbohydrate	...38g	Saturates	.......1g

 25 MINS   25 MINS

SERVES 4

INGREDIENTS

450 g/1 lb waxy potatoes

1 raddichio or lollo rosso lettuce

1 green (bell) pepper, sliced

175 g/6 oz Italian sausage, sliced

1 red onion, halved and sliced

125 g/4½ oz sun-dried tomatoes, sliced

2 tbsp shredded fresh basil

DRESSING

1 tbsp balsamic vinegar

1 tsp tomato purée (paste)

2 tbsp olive oil

salt and pepper

COOK'S TIP

Any sliced Italian sausage or salami can be used in this salad. Italy is home of the salami and there are numerous varieties to choose from – those from the south tend to be more highly spiced than those from the north of the country.

1 Cook the potatoes in a saucepan of boiling water for 20 minutes or until cooked through. Drain and leave to cool.

2 Line a large serving platter with the radicchio or lollo rosso lettuce leaves.

3 Slice the cooled potatoes and arrange them in layers on the lettuce-lined serving platter together with the sliced green (bell) pepper, sliced Italian sausage, red onion, sun-dried tomatoes and shredded fresh basil.

4 In a small bowl, whisk the balsamic vinegar, tomato purée (paste) and olive oil together and season to taste with salt and pepper. Pour the dressing over the potato salad and serve immediately.

Mexican Potato Salad

The flavours of Mexico are echoed in this dish where potato slices are topped with tomatoes, chillies and ham, and served with guacamole.

NUTRITIONAL INFORMATION

Calories	260	Sugars 6g
Protein	.........6g	Fat 9g
Carbohydrate	...41g	Saturates 2g

20 MINS   20 MINS

SERVES 4

INGREDIENTS

4 large waxy potatoes, sliced

1 ripe avocado

1 tsp olive oil

1 tsp lemon juice

1 garlic clove, crushed

1 onion, chopped

2 large tomatoes, sliced

1 green chilli, chopped

1 yellow (bell) pepper, seeded and sliced

2 tbsp chopped coriander (cilantro)

salt and pepper

lemon wedges, to garnish

1 Cook the potato slices in a saucepan of boiling water for 10–15 minutes, or until tender. Drain and set aside to cool.

2 Meanwhile, cut the avocado in half and remove the stone (pit). Mash the avocado flesh with a fork (you could also scoop the avocado flesh from the 2 halves using a spoon and then mash it).

3 Add the olive oil, lemon juice, garlic and chopped onion to the avocado flesh and stir to mix. Cover the bowl with clear film (plastic wrap), to minimize discolouration, and set aside.

4 Mix the tomatoes, chilli and yellow (bell) pepper together and transfer to a salad bowl with the potato slices.

5 Arrange the avocado mixture on top of the salad and sprinkle with the coriander (cilantro). Season to taste with salt and pepper and serve garnished with lemon wedges.

VARIATION

You can omit the green chilli from this salad if you do not like hot dishes.

Chicken & Paw-paw Salad

Try this recipe with peaches or nectarines instead of paw-paw (papaya), for an equally tasty salad.

NUTRITIONAL INFORMATION

Calories	408	Sugars	.........8g
Protein	........30g	Fat	..........28g
Carbohydrate	...10g	Saturates	.......5g

5 MINS   15 MINS

SERVES 4

INGREDIENTS

4 skinless, boneless chicken breasts

1 red chilli, deseeded and chopped

30 ml/1 fl oz/1⅞ tbsp red wine vinegar

75 ml/3 fl oz/⅓ cup olive oil

1 paw-paw (papaya), peeled

1 avocado, peeled

125 g/4½ oz alfalfa sprouts

125 g/4½ oz bean sprouts

salt and pepper

TO GARNISH

diced red (bell) pepper

diced cucumber

1 Poach the chicken breasts in boiling water for about 15 minutes or until cooked through.

2 Remove the chicken with a slotted spoon and set aside to cool.

3 To make the dressing, combine the chilli, red wine vinegar and olive oil, season well with salt and pepper and set aside.

4 Place the chicken breasts on a chopping board. Using a very sharp knife, cut the chicken breasts across the grain into thin diagonal slices. Set aside.

5 Slice the paw-paw (papaya) and avocado to the same thickness as the chicken.

6 Arrange the slices of paw-paw (papaya) and avocado, together with the chicken, in an alternating pattern on four serving plates.

7 Arrange the alfalfa sprouts and bean sprouts on the serving plates and garnish with the diced red (bell) pepper and cucumber. Serve the salad with the dressing.

VARIATION

Try this recipe with peaches or nectarines instead of paw-paw (papaya).

Green Sesame Salad

A very elegant and light salad which will complement rice and noodle dishes beautifully.

NUTRITIONAL INFORMATION

Calories ....78 Sugars 8g
Protein ....3g Fat 3g
Carbohydrate ....3g Saturates 0.5g

 10 MINS   0 MINS

SERVES 4

INGREDIENTS

125 g/4½ oz/2 cups bean sprouts

1½ tbsp chopped fresh coriander (cilantro)

3 tbsp fresh lime juice

½ tsp mild chilli powder

1 tsp sugar

½ tsp salt

3 celery sticks

1 large green (bell) pepper, deseeded

1 large Granny Smith apple

2 tbsp toasted sesame seeds, to garnish

1 Rinse the bean sprouts and drain thoroughly.

2 Pick over the bean sprouts, removing any that seem a little brown or limp – it is essential that they are fresh and crunchy for this recipe.

3 To make the dressing, combine the coriander (cilantro), lime juice, chilli powder, sugar and salt in a small bowl and mix thoroughly.

4 Using a sharp knife, cut the celery into 2.5 cm/1 inch pieces. Cut the (bell) pepper into small pieces and the Granny Smith apple into small chunks.

5 Place the chopped celery, (bell) pepper and apple into a large mixing bowl and stir gently to mix.

6 Just before serving, pour the dressing over the salad, tossing well to mix.

7 Garnish the green sesame salad with the toasted sesame seeds and serve with rice or noodle dishes.

COOK'S TIP

Keeping each ingredient as fresh and crunchy as possible will make all the difference to the appearance and taste of this elegant salad. To prevent the apples from going brown, soak the slices briefly in a little lemon juice and water as soon as you have cut them.

Prawn (Shrimp) Salad

Noodles and bean sprouts form the basis of this refreshing salad which combines the flavours of fruit and prawns (shrimp).

NUTRITIONAL INFORMATION

Calories . . . . . . .359 Sugars 4g
Protein . . . . .31g Fat 15g
Carbohydrate . . .25g Saturates 2g

 15 MINS   5 MINS

SERVES 4

I N G R E D I E N T S

250 g/9 oz fine egg noodles

3 tbsp sunflower oil

1 tbsp sesame oil

1 tbsp sesame seeds

150 g/5½ oz/1½ cups bean sprouts

1 ripe mango, sliced

6 spring onions (scallions), sliced

75 g/2¾ oz radish, sliced

350 g/12 oz peeled cooked prawns (shrimp)

2 tbsp light soy sauce

1 tbsp sherry

1 Place the egg noodles in a large bowl and pour over enough boiling water to cover. Leave to stand for 10 minutes.

2 Drain the noodles thoroughly and pat dry with kitchen paper (paper towels).

COOK'S TIP

If fresh mango is unavailable, use canned mango slices, rinsed and drained, instead.

3 Heat the sunflower oil in a large wok or frying pan (skillet) and stir-fry the noodles for 5 minutes, tossing frequently.

4 Remove the wok from the heat and add the sesame oil, sesame seeds and bean sprouts, tossing to mix well.

5 In a separate bowl, mix together the sliced mango, spring onions (scallions), radish and prawns (shrimp). Stir in the light soy sauce and sherry and mix until thoroughly combined.

6 Toss the prawn (shrimp) mixture with the noodles and transfer to a serving dish. Alternatively, arrange the noodles around the edge of a serving plate and pile the prawn (shrimp) mixture into the centre. Serve immediately as this salad is best eaten warm.

Gado Gado

This is a well-known and very popular Indonesian salad of mixed vegetables with a peanut dressing.

NUTRITIONAL INFORMATION

Calories . . . . . . .392 Sugars 8g
Protein . . . . .9g Fat 35g
Carbohydrate . . . .11g Saturates 5g

10 MINS   25 MINS

SERVES 4

I N G R E D I E N T S

100 g/3½ oz/1 cup shredded
   white cabbage

100 g/3½ oz French (green) beans,
   cut into three

100 g/3½ oz carrots, cut into matchsticks

100 g/3½ oz cauliflower florets

100 g/3½ oz bean sprouts

D R E S S I N G

100 ml/3½ fl oz/½ cup vegetable oil

100 g/3½ oz/1 cup unsalted peanuts

2 garlic cloves, crushed

1 small onion, finely chopped

½ tsp chilli powder

½ tsp light brown sugar

425 ml/¾ pint/2 cups water

juice of ½ lemon

salt

sliced spring onions (scallions),
   to garnish

1 Cook the vegetables separately in a saucepan of salted boiling water for 4–5 minutes, drain well and chill.

2 To make the dressing, heat the oil in a frying pan (skillet) and fry the peanuts, tossing frequently, for 3–4 minutes.

3 Remove from the pan with a slotted spoon and drain on absorbent kitchen paper (paper towels). Process the peanuts in a food processor or crush with a rolling pin until a fine mixture is formed.

4 Pour all but 1 tablespoon of the oil from the pan and fry the garlic and onion for 1 minute. Add the chilli powder, sugar, a pinch of salt and the water and bring to the boil.

5 Stir in the peanuts. Reduce the heat and simmer for 4–5 minutes. until the sauce thickens. Add the lemon juice and set aside to cool.

6 Arrange the vegetables in a serving dish and spoon the peanut dressing into the centre. Garnish and serve.

Beetroot & Orange Salad

Use freshly cooked beetroot in this unusual combination of colours and flavours, as beetroot soaked in vinegar will spoil the delicate balance.

NUTRITIONAL INFORMATION

Calories	240	Sugars	........29g
Protein	........10g	Fat	...........2g
Carbohydrate	...49g	Saturates	.....0.3g

2¼ HOURS   1 HOUR

SERVES 4

INGREDIENTS

225 g/8 oz/1⅓ cups long-grain and wild rices

4 large oranges

450 g/1 lb cooked beetroot, peeled and drained (if necessary)

2 heads of chicory

salt and pepper

fresh snipped chives, to garnish

DRESSING

4 tbsp low-fat natural fromage frais (unsweetened yogurt)

1 garlic clove, crushed

1 tbsp wholegrain mustard

½ tsp finely grated orange rind

2 tsp clear honey

1 Cook the rices according to the packet instructions. Drain and set aside to cool.

2 Meanwhile, slice the top and bottom off each orange. Using a sharp knife, remove the skin and pith. Holding the orange over a bowl to catch the juice, carefully slice between each segment. Place the segments in a separate bowl. Cover the juice and leave to chill.

3 Dice the beetroot into small cubes. Mix with the orange segments, cover and chill.

4 When the rice has cooled, mix in the reserved orange juice until thoroughly incorporated and season with salt and pepper to taste.

5 Line 4 bowls or plates with the chicory leaves. Spoon over the rice and top with the beetroot and orange.

6 Mix all the dressing ingredients together and spoon over the salad, or serve separately in a bowl, if preferred. Garnish with fresh snipped chives.

Broccoli & Almond Salad

This is a colourful, crunchy salad with a delicious dressing. It is better left overnight if possible for the flavours to mingle.

NUTRITIONAL INFORMATION

Calories 181   Sugars 7g
Protein . . . . .9g   Fat 12g
Carbohydrate . . . .9g   Saturates 2g

4¹/₂ HOURS   10 MINS

SERVES 4

I N G R E D I E N T S

450 g/1 lb small broccoli florets

50 g/1¾ oz baby corn cobs, halved, lengthways

1 red (bell) pepper, seeded and cut into thin strips

50 g/1¾ oz blanched almonds

D R E S S I N G

1 tbsp sesame seeds

1 tbsp peanut oil

2 garlic cloves, crushed

2 tbsp light soy sauce

1 tbsp clear honey

2 tsp lemon juice

pepper

lemon zest, to garnish (optional)

1 Blanch the broccoli and baby corn cobs in boiling water for 5 minutes. Drain well, rinse and drain again.

2 Transfer the broccoli and baby corn cobs to a large mixing bowl and add the (bell) pepper and almonds.

3 To make the dressing, heat a wok and add the sesame seeds. Dry-fry, stirring constantly, for about 1 minute, or until the sesame seeds are lightly browned and are giving off a delicious aroma.

4 Mix the peanut oil, garlic, soy sauce, honey, lemon juice and pepper to taste. Add the sesame seeds and mix well.

5 Pour the dressing over the salad, cover and set aside in the refrigerator for a minimum of 4 hours and preferably overnight.

6 Garnish the salad with lemon zest (if using) and serve.

COOK'S TIP

Take care when browning the sesame seeds, as they will quickly burn. Dry-fry over a low heat and stir constantly.

Chicory (Endive) Salad

The contrast of the pink grapefruit, creamy chicory (endive) and bright green lamb's lettuce (corn salad) make this a stunning accompaniment.

NUTRITIONAL INFORMATION

Calories	137	Sugars	.........4g
Protein	.........1g	Fat	..........13g
Carbohydrate	....4g	Saturates	......2g

10 MINS   0 MINS

SERVES 4

I N G R E D I E N T S

1 pink grapefruit

1 avocado

1 packet lamb's lettuce (corn salad), washed thoroughly

2 heads chicory (endive), sliced diagonally

1 tbsp chopped fresh mint

FRENCH DRESSING

3 tbsp olive oil

1 tbsp wine vinegar

1 small garlic clove, crushed

½ tsp Dijon or Meaux mustard

1 tsp clear honey

salt and pepper

1 Peel the grapefruit with a serrated-edge knife.

2 Cut the grapefruit into segments by cutting between the membranes.

3 To make the French dressing, put all the ingredients into a screw-top jar and shake vigorously.

4 Halve the avocado and remove the stone (pit) by stabbing the stone (pit) with a sharp knife and twisting to loosen. Remove the skin.

5 Cut the avocado into small slices, put into a bowl and toss in the French dressing.

6 Remove any stalks from the lamb's lettuce (corn salad) and put into a bowl with the grapefruit, chicory (endive) and mint.

7 Add the avocado and 2 tablespoons of the French dressing. Toss well and transfer to serving plates.

COOK'S TIP

Lamb's lettuce is so called because the shape of its dark green leaves resembles a lamb's tongue. It is also known as corn salad and the French call it mâche. It is easy to grow in the garden and will withstand the frost.

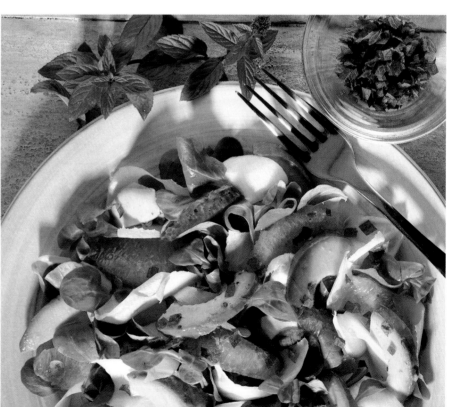

Paw-paw (Papaya) Salad

Choose firm paw-paws – or papayas as they are sometimes called – for this delicious salad.

NUTRITIONAL INFORMATION

Calories 193	Sugars 11g	
Protein 3g	Fat 15g	
Carbohydrate . . .12g	Saturates 2g	

10 MINS   0 MINS

SERVES 4

I N G R E D I E N T S

D R E S S I N G

4 tbsp olive oil

1 tbsp fish sauce or light soy sauce

2 tbsp lime or lemon juice

1 tbsp dark muscovado sugar

1 tsp finely chopped fresh red or green chilli

S A L A D

1 crisp lettuce

¼ small white cabbage

2 paw-paws (papayas)

2 tomatoes

25 g/1 oz/¼ cup roasted peanuts, chopped roughly

4 spring onions (scallions), trimmed and sliced thinly

basil leaves, to garnish

1 To make the dressing, whisk together the oil, fish sauce or soy sauce, lime or lemon juice, sugar and chilli. Set aside, stirring occasionally to dissolve the sugar.

2 Shred the lettuce and white cabbage, then toss together and arrange on a large serving plate.

3 Peel the paw-paws (papayas) and slice them in half. Scoop out the seeds, then slice the flesh thinly. Arrange on top of the lettuce and cabbage.

4 Soak the tomatoes in a bowl of boiling water for 1 minute, then lift out and peel. Remove the seeds and chop the flesh. Arrange on the salad leaves.

5 Scatter the peanuts and spring onions (scallions) over the top. Whisk the dressing and pour over the salad. Garnish with basil leaves and serve at once.

COOK'S TIP

Choose plain, unsalted peanuts and toast them under the grill (broiler) until golden to get the best flavour. Take care not to burn them, as they brown very quickly.

Tomato Salsa

This salad is used extensively in Mexican cooking and served as a dip or a relish, and is eaten as an accompaniment to almost any dish.

NUTRITIONAL INFORMATION

Calories 10	Sugars 2g	
Protein 0.4g	Fat 0.1g	
Carbohydrate 2g	Saturates 0g	

10 MINS   0 MINS

SERVES 4

INGREDIENTS

4 ripe red tomatoes

1 medium red onion or 6 spring onions (scallions)

1–2 garlic cloves, crushed (optional)

2 tbsp chopped fresh coriander (cilantro)

½ red or green chilli (optional)

finely grated rind of ½–1 lemon or lime

1–2 tbsp lemon or lime juice

pepper

1 Chop the tomatoes fairly finely and evenly, and put into a bowl. They must be firm and a good strong red colour for the best results, but if preferred, they may be peeled by placing them in boiling water for about 20 seconds and then plunging into cold water. The skins should then slip off easily when they are nicked with a knife.

2 Peel and slice the red onion thinly, or trim the spring onions (scallions) and cut into thin slanting slices; add to the tomatoes with the garlic and coriander (cilantro) and mix lightly.

3 Remove the seeds from the red or green chilli (if using) chop the flesh very finely and add to the salad. Treat the chillies with care; do not touch your eyes or face after handling them until you have washed your hands thoroughly. Chilli juices can burn.

4 Add the lemon or lime rind and juice to the salsa, and mix well. Transfer to a serving bowl and sprinkle with pepper.

COOK'S TIP

If you don't like the distinctive flavour of fresh coriander (cilantro), you can replace it with flat-leaf parsley instead.

Green Salad

Herb-flavoured croûtons are topped with peppery rocket (arugula), red chard, green olives and pistachios to make an elegant combination.

NUTRITIONAL INFORMATION

Calories 256	Sugars 3g	
Protein 4g	Fat 17g	
Carbohydrate ...23g	Saturates 3g	

25 MINS 10 MINS

SERVES 4

INGREDIENTS

25 g/1 oz pistachio nuts

5 tbsp extra virgin olive oil

1 tbsp rosemary, chopped

2 garlic cloves, chopped

4 slices rustic bread

1 tbsp red wine vinegar

1 tsp wholegrain mustard

1 tsp sugar

25 g/1 oz rocket (arugula)

25 g/1 oz red chard

50 g/1¾ oz green olives, pitted

2 tbsp fresh basil, shredded

1 Shell the pistachios and roughly chop them, using a sharp knife.

2 Place 2 tablespoons of the extra virgin olive oil in a frying pan (skillet). Add the rosemary and garlic and cook for 2 minutes.

3 Add the slices of bread to the pan and fry for 2–3 minutes on both sides until golden. Remove the bread from the pan and drain on absorbent kitchen paper.

4 To make the dressing, mix together the remaining olive oil with the red wine vinegar, mustard and sugar.

5 Place a slice of bread on to a serving plate and top with the rocket (arugula) and red chard. Sprinkle with the olives.

6 Drizzle the dressing over the top of the salad leaves. Sprinkle with the chopped pistachios and shredded basil leaves and serve the salad immediately.

COOK'S TIP

If you cannot find red chard, try slicing a tomato into very thin wedges to add a splash of vibrant red colour to the salad.

Potato & Chicken Salad

The spicy peanut dressing served with this salad may be prepared in advance and left to chill a day before required.

NUTRITIONAL INFORMATION

Calories 802   Sugars 15g
Protein ....35g   Fat 55g
Carbohydrate ...45g   Saturates 10g

  5 MINS   15 MINS

SERVES 4

INGREDIENTS

4 large waxy potatoes

300 g/10½ oz fresh pineapple, diced

2 carrots, grated

175 g/6 oz bean sprouts

1 bunch spring onions (scallions), sliced

1 large courgette (zucchini), cut into matchsticks

3 celery sticks, cut into matchsticks

175 g/6 oz unsalted peanuts

2 cooked chicken breast fillets, about 125 g/4½ oz each, sliced

DRESSING

6 tbsp crunchy peanut butter

6 tbsp olive oil

2 tbsp light soy sauce

1 red chilli, chopped

2 tsp sesame oil

4 tsp lime juice

COOK'S TIP

Unsweetened canned pineapple may be used in place of the fresh pineapple for convenience. If only sweetened canned pineapple is available, drain it and rinse under cold running water before using.

1 Using a sharp knife, cut the potatoes into small dice. Bring a saucepan of water to the boil.

2 Cook the diced potatoes in a saucepan of boiling water for 10 minutes or until tender. Drain and leave to cool until required.

3 Transfer the cooled potatoes to a salad bowl.

4 Add the pineapple, carrots, bean sprouts, spring onions (scallions), courgette (zucchini), celery, peanuts and sliced chicken to the potatoes. Toss well to mix all the salad ingredients together.

5 To make the dressing, put the peanut butter in a small mixing bowl and gradually whisk in the olive oil and light soy sauce.

6 Stir in the chopped red chilli, sesame oil and lime juice. Mix until well combined.

7 Pour the spicy dressing over the salad and toss lightly to coat all of the ingredients. Serve the potato and chicken salad immediately.

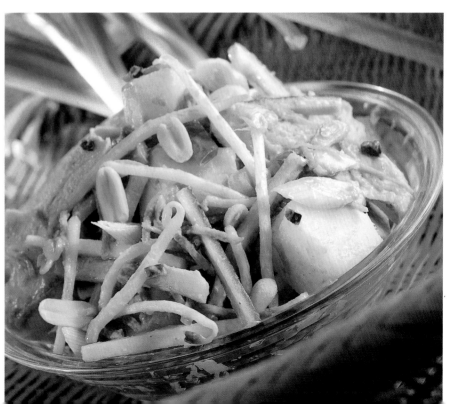

Pasta & Garlic Mayo Salad

This crisp salad would make an excellent accompaniment to grilled (broiled) meat and is ideal for summer barbecues (grills).

NUTRITIONAL INFORMATION

Calories 858   Sugars 35g
Protein ....11g   Fat 64g
Carbohydrate ...64g   Saturates 8g

1½ HOURS   10 MINS

SERVES 4

INGREDIENTS

2 large lettuces

260 g/9 oz dried penne

1 tbsp olive oil

8 red eating apples

juice of 4 lemons

1 head of celery, sliced

115 g/4 oz/¾ cup shelled, halved walnuts

250 ml/9 fl oz/1⅛ cups fresh garlic mayonnaise (see Cook's Tip)

salt

1 Wash, drain and pat dry the lettuce leaves with kitchen paper. Transfer them to the refrigerator for 1 hour or until crisp.

2 Meanwhile, bring a large saucepan of lightly salted water to the boil. Add the pasta and olive oil and cook for 8–10 minutes or until tender, but still firm to the bite. Drain the pasta and refresh under cold running water. Drain thoroughly again and set aside.

3 Core and dice the apples, place them in a small bowl and sprinkle with the lemon juice.

4 Mix together the pasta, celery, apples and walnuts and toss the mixture in the garlic mayonnaise (see Cook's Tip, right). Add more mayonnaise, if liked.

5 Line a salad bowl with the lettuce leaves and spoon the pasta salad into the lined bowl. Serve when required.

COOK'S TIP

To make garlic mayo, beat 2 egg yolks with a pinch of salt and 6 crushed garlic cloves. Start beating in 350ml/12 fl oz/1½ cups oil, 1–2 tsp at a time. When ¼ of the oil has been incorporated, beat in 1–2 tbsp white wine vinegar. Continue beating in the oil. Stir in 1 tsp Dijon mustard and season.

Mango Salad

This is an unusual combination but works well as long as the mango is very unripe. Paw-paw (papaya) can be used instead, if you prefer.

NUTRITIONAL INFORMATION

Calories 26   Sugars 3g
Protein ....1g   Fat 0.2g
Carbohydrate ....6g   Saturates 0g

10 MINS   0 MINS

SERVES 4

INGREDIENTS

1 large unripe mango, peeled and
   cut into long thin shreds

1 small red chilli, deseeded and
   chopped finely

2 shallots, chopped finely

2 tbsp lemon juice

1 tbsp light soy sauce

6 roasted canned chestnuts,
   quartered

1 melon, to serve

1 lollo biondo lettuce, or any crunchy
   lettuce

15 g/½ oz coriander (cilantro) leaves

1 Soak the mango briefly in cold water, in order to remove any syrup. Meanwhile, combine the chilli, shallots, lemon juice and soy sauce. Drain the mango and combine with the chestnuts.

2 To make the melon basket, stand the watermelon on one end on a level surface. Holding a knife level and in one place, turn the watermelon on its axis so that the knife marks an even line all around the middle. Mark a 2.5 cm/ 1 inch wide handle across the top and through the centre stem, joining the middle line at either end. (If you prefer a zigzag finish, mark the shape to be cut at this point before any cuts are made, to ensure even zigzags.)

3 Take a sharp knife and, following the marks made for the handle, make the first vertical cut. Then cut down the other side of the handle. Now follow the middle line and make your straight or zigzag cut, taking care that the knife is always pointing towards the centre of the watermelon, and is level with the work surface (counter), as this ensures that when you reach the handle cuts, the cut out piece of melon will pull away cleanly.

4 Hollow out the flesh with a spoon, leaving a clean edge and line with the lettuce and coriander (cilantro). Fill with the salad, pour over the dressing and serve.

COOK'S TIP

A relative of the onion, though less pungent, shallots come in round and elongated varieties. When buying shallots, choose firm, dry-skinned ones which show no signs of wrinkling. Fresh shallots can be stored in the refrigerator for up to a week.

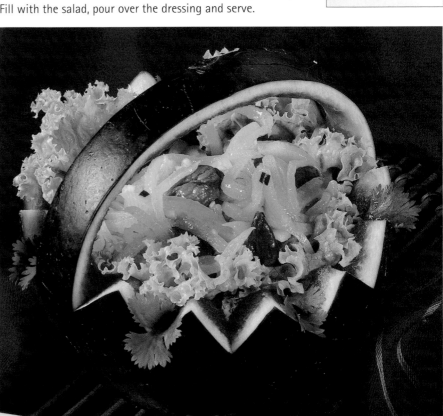

Quick Bean Salad

This attractive-looking salad served with meat from the barbecue (grill) makes a delicious light meal in summer.

NUTRITIONAL INFORMATION

Calories	139	Sugars 5g
Protein	.........8g	Fat 3g
Carbohydrate	...21g	Saturates 0.4g

 10 MINS   0 MINS

SERVES 4

I N G R E D I E N T S

400 g/14 oz can chick-peas (garbanzo beans)

4 carrots

1 bunch spring onions (scallions)

1 medium cucumber

½ tsp salt

½ tsp pepper

3 tbsp lemon juice

1 red (bell) pepper

1 Drain the chick-peas (garbanzo beans) and place in a salad bowl.

2 Using a sharp knife, peel and slice the carrots.

3 Cut the spring onions (scallions) into small pieces.

4 Cut the cucumber into thick quarters.

5 Add the carrots, spring onions (scallions) and cucumber to the chick-peas (garbanzo beans) and mix. Season with the salt and pepper and sprinkle with the lemon juice.

6 Toss the salad ingredients together gently using 2 serving spoons.

7 Using a sharp knife, slice the red (bell) pepper thinly.

8 Arrange the slices of red (bell) pepper on top of the chick-pea (garbanzo bean) salad.

9 Serve the salad immediately or leave to chill in the refrigerator and serve when required.

COOK'S TIP

Using canned chick-peas (garbanzo beans) rather than the dried ones speeds up the cooking time.

Sweet & Sour Fish Salad

This refreshing blend of pink and white fish mixed with fresh pineapple and (bell) peppers makesan interesting starter or a light meal.

NUTRITIONAL INFORMATION

Calories ....168 Sugars 5g
Protein ....24g Fat 6g
Carbohydrate ....5g Saturates 1g

35 MINS   10 MINS

SERVES 4

INGREDIENTS

225 g/8 oz trout fillets

225 g/8 oz white fish fillets (such as haddock or cod)

300 ml/½ pint/1¼ cups water

1 stalk lemon grass

2 lime leaves

1 large red chilli

1 bunch spring onions (scallions), trimmed and shredded

115 g/4 oz fresh pineapple flesh, diced

1 small red (bell) pepper, deseeded and diced

1 bunch watercress, washed and trimmed

fresh snipped chives, to garnish

DRESSING

1 tbsp sunflower oil

1 tbsp rice wine vinegar

pinch of chilli powder

1 tsp clear honey

salt and pepper

1 Rinse the fish, place in a frying pan (skillet) and pour over the water. Bend the lemon grass in half to bruise it and add to the pan with the lime leaves. Prick the chilli with a fork and add to the pan. Bring to the boil and simmer for 7–8 minutes. Let cool.

2 Drain the fish fillet thoroughly, flake the flesh away from the skin and place in a bowl. Gently stir in the spring onions (scallions), pineapple and (bell) pepper.

3 Arrange the washed watercress on 4 serving plates and spoon the cooked fish mixture on top.

4 To make the dressing, mix all the ingredients together and season well. Spoon over the fish and serve garnished

Pasta & Chicken Medley

Strips of cooked chicken are tossed with coloured pasta, grapes and carrot sticks in a pesto-flavoured dressing.

NUTRITIONAL INFORMATION

Calories 609   Sugars 11g
Protein . . . . .26g   Fat 38g
Carbohydrate . . .45g   Saturates 6g

 30 MINS   10 MINS

SERVES 2

INGREDIENTS

125–150 g/4½–5½ oz dried pasta shapes,
   such as twists or bows

1 tbsp oil

2 tbsp mayonnaise

2 tsp bottled pesto sauce

1 tbsp soured cream or natural
   fromage frais

175 g/6 oz cooked skinless, boneless
   chicken meat

1–2 celery stalks

125 g/4½ oz/1 cup black grapes
   (preferably seedless)

1 large carrot, trimmed

salt and pepper

celery leaves, to garnish

FRENCH DRESSING

1 tbsp wine vinegar

3 tbsp extra-virgin olive oil

salt and pepper

1 To make the French dressing, whisk all the ingredients together until smooth.

2 Cook the pasta with the oil for 8–10 minutes in plenty of boiling salted water until just tender. Drain thoroughly, rinse and drain again. Transfer to a bowl and mix in 1 tablespoon of the French dressing while hot; set aside until cold.

3 Combine the mayonnaise, pesto sauce and soured cream or fromage frais in a bowl, and season to taste.

4 Cut the chicken into narrow strips. Cut the celery diagonally into narrow slices. Reserve a few grapes for garnish, halve the rest and remove any pips (seeds). Cut the carrot into narrow julienne strips.

5 Add the chicken, the celery, the halved grapes, the carrot and the mayonnaise mixture to the pasta, and toss thoroughly. Check the seasoning, adding more salt and pepper if necessary.

6 Arrange the pasta mixture on two plates and garnish with the reserved black grapes and the celery leaves.

Hot Rice Salad

Nutty brown rice combines well with peanuts and a sweet and sour mixture of fruit and vegetables in this tangy combination.

NUTRITIONAL INFORMATION

Calories 464	Sugars 17g
Protein 15g	Fat 24g
Carbohydrate . . .52g	Saturates 4g

5 MINS   30 MINS

SERVES 4

INGREDIENTS

300 g/10½ oz/1½ cups brown rice

1 bunch spring onions (scallions)

1 red (bell) pepper

125 g/4½ oz radishes

425 g/15 oz can pineapple pieces in natural juice, drained

125 g/4½ oz/2 cups bean sprouts

90 g/3 oz/¾ cup dry-roasted peanuts

DRESSING

2 tbsp crunchy peanut butter

1 tbsp groundnut oil

2 tbsp light soy sauce

2 tbsp white wine vinegar

2 tsp clear honey

1 tsp chilli powder

½ tsp garlic salt

pepper

1 Put the rice in a pan and cover with water. Bring to the boil, then cover and simmer for 30 minutes until tender.

2 Meanwhile, chop the spring onions (scallions), using a sharp knife. Deseed and chop the red (bell) pepper and thinly slice the radishes.

3 To make the dressing. Place the crunchy peanut butter, groundnut oil, light soy sauce, white wine vinegar, honey, chilli powder, garlic salt and pepper in a small bowl and whisk for a few seconds until well combined.

4 Drain the rice thoroughly and place in a heatproof bowl.

5 Heat the dressing in a small saucepan for 1 minute and then toss into the rice and mix well.

6 Working quickly, stir the pineapple pieces, spring onions (scallions), (bell) pepper, bean sprouts and peanuts into the mixture in the bowl.

7 Pile the hot rice salad into a warmed serving dish.

8 Arrange the radish slices around the outside of the salad and serve immediately.

(Bell) Pepper Salad

Colourful marinated Mediterranean vegetables make a tasty starter.
Serve with fresh bread or Tomato Toasts (see below).

NUTRITIONAL INFORMATION

Calories 234   Sugars 4g
Protein ....6g   Fat 17g
Carbohydrate ...15g   Saturates 2g

5–10 MINS   35 MINS

SERVES 4

INGREDIENTS

1 onion

2 red (bell) peppers

2 yellow (bell) peppers

3 tbsp olive oil

2 large courgettes (zucchini), sliced

2 garlic cloves, sliced

1 tbsp balsamic vinegar

50 g/1¾ oz anchovy fillets, chopped

25 g/1 oz/¼ cup black olives,
   halved and pitted

1 tbsp chopped fresh basil

salt and pepper

TOMATO TOASTS

small stick of French bread

1 garlic clove, crushed

1 tomato, peeled and chopped

2 tbsp olive oil

1 Cut the onion into wedges. Core and deseed the (bell) peppers and cut into thick slices.

2 Heat the oil in a large heavy-based frying pan (skillet). Add the onion, (bell) peppers, courgettes (zucchini) and garlic and fry gently for 20 minutes, stirring occasionally.

3 Add the vinegar, anchovies, olives and seasoning to taste, mix thoroughly and leave to cool.

4 Spoon on to individual plates and sprinkle with the basil.

5 To make the tomato toasts, cut the French bread diagonally into 1 cm/ ½ inch slices.

6 Mix the garlic, tomato, oil and seasoning together, and spread thinly over each slice of bread.

7 Place the bread on a baking tray (cookie sheet), drizzle with the olive oil and bake in a preheated oven, 220°C/425°F/Gas Mark 7, for 5–10 minutes until crisp. Serve the Tomato Toasts with the (Bell) Pepper Salad.

Light Meals & Side Dishes

In the busy lives we lead today, quick meals are becoming great favourites. But care must be taken to ensure 'food on the move' is properly prepared and cooked, well-balanced and not just 'junk' food. The recipes for light meals offer something for every taste – vegetables, cheese, meat and pasta. Pizza, everyone's favourite snack food, is also seen in many inventive guises, for example, Hawaiian Pizza, Mexican-style Pizzas or American Hot Chilli Beef Pizza. There is also a selection of side dishes in this chapter which are a welcome departure from boiled potatoes and soggy beans. Try Pommes Anna, Fragrant Rice in Lotus Leaves or Greek Green Beans – they all taste delicious.

Vegetable Medley

Serve this as a crisp and colourful vegetarian dish, with pitta bread, chapatis or naan, or as an accompaniment to roast or grilled meats.

NUTRITIONAL INFORMATION

Calories ......190 Sugars 17g
Protein ....7g Fat 7g
Carbohydrate ...27g Saturates 1g

10 MINS   20 MINS

SERVES 4

INGREDIENTS

150 g/5½ oz young, tender green beans

8 baby carrots

6 baby turnips

½ small cauliflower

2 tbsp vegetable oil

2 large onions, sliced

2 garlic cloves, finely chopped

300 ml/½ pint/1¼ cups low-fat
    (unsweetened) natural yogurt

1 tbsp cornflour (cornstarch)

2 tbsp tomato purée (paste)

large pinch of chilli powder

salt

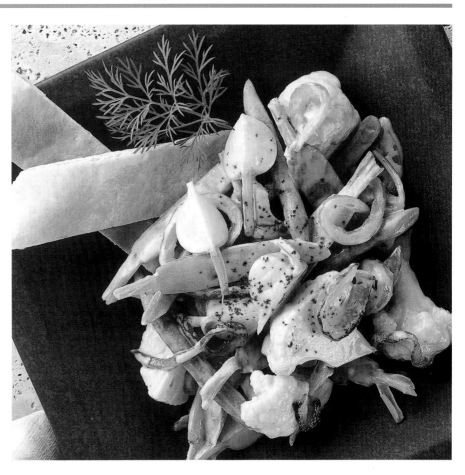

1 Top and tail the beans and snap them in half. Cut the carrots in half and the turnips in quarters. Divide the cauliflower into florets, discarding the thickest part of the stalk. Steam the vegetables over boiling, salted water for 3 minutes, then turn them into a colander and plunge them at once in a large bowl of cold water to prevent further cooking.

2 Heat the vegetable oil in a frying pan (skillet) and fry the onions until they

are translucent. Stir in the garlic and cook for 1 further minute.

3 Mix together the yogurt, cornflour (cornstarch) and tomato purée (paste) to form a smooth paste. Stir this paste into the onions in the pan and cook for 1–2 minutes until the sauce is well blended.

4 Drain the vegetables well, then gradually stir them into the sauce, taking care not to break them up. Season with salt and chilli powder to taste, cover and simmer gently for 5 minutes, until the vegetables are just tender. Taste and adjust the seasoning if necessary. Serve immediately.

Pancetta & Pecorino Cakes

This makes an excellent light meal when served with a topping of pesto or anchovy sauce.

NUTRITIONAL INFORMATION

Calories 619   Sugars 4g
Protein . . . . .22g   Fat 29g
Carbohydrate . . . .71g   Saturates 8g

🍞 20 MINS   🕐 25 MINS

SERVES 4

I N G R E D I E N T S

25 g/1 oz/2 tbsp butter, plus extra for
   greasing

100 g/3½ oz pancetta, rind removed

225 g/8 oz/2 cups self-raising
   (self-rising) flour

75 g/2¾ oz/⅞ cup grated pecorino cheese

150 ml/¼ pint/⅝ cup milk, plus extra
   for glazing

1 tbsp tomato ketchup

1 tsp Worcestershire sauce

400 g/14 oz/3½ cups dried farfalle

1 tbsp olive oil

salt and pepper

3 tbsp Pesto (see page 19) or anchovy
   sauce (optional)

green salad, to serve

1 Grease a baking tray (cookie sheet) with butter. Grill (broil) the pancetta until it is cooked. Allow the pancetta to cool, then chop finely.

2 Sift together the flour and a pinch of salt into a mixing bowl. Add the butter and rub in with your fingertips. When the butter and flour have been thoroughly incorporated, add the pancetta and one-third of the grated cheese.

3 Mix together the milk, tomato ketchup and Worcestershire sauce and add to the dry ingredients, mixing to make a soft dough.

4 Roll out the dough on a lightly floured board to make an 18 cm/7 inch round. Brush with a little milk to glaze and cut into 8 wedges.

5 Arrange the dough wedges on the prepared baking tray (cookie sheet)

and sprinkle over the remaining cheese. Bake in a preheated oven at 200°C/ 400°F/Gas Mark 6 for 20 minutes.

6 Meanwhile, bring a saucepan of lightly salted water to the boil. Add the farfalle and the oil and cook for 8–10 minutes until just tender, but still firm to the bite. Drain and transfer to a large serving dish. Top with the pancetta and pecorino cakes. Serve with the sauce of your choice and a green salad.

Pasta & Sicilian Sauce

This Sicilian recipe of anchovies mixed with pine nuts and sultanas in a tomato sauce is delicious with all types of pasta.

NUTRITIONAL INFORMATION

Calories ....286 Sugars 14g
Protein ....11g Fat 8g
Carbohydrate ...46g Saturates 1g

25 MINS   30 MINS

SERVES 4

INGREDIENTS

450 g/1 lb tomatoes, halved

25 g/1 oz pine nuts

50 g/1¾ oz sultanas

50 g/1¾ oz can anchovies, drained and
   halved lengthways

2 tbsp concentrated tomato purée (paste)

675 g/1½ lb fresh or
   350 g/12 oz dried penne

1 Cook the tomatoes under a preheated grill (broiler) for about 10 minutes. Leave to cool slightly, then once cool enough to handle, peel off the skin and dice the flesh.

2 Place the pine nuts on a baking tray (cookie sheet) and lightly toast under the grill (broiler) for 2–3 minutes or until golden brown.

VARIATION

Add 100 g/3½ oz bacon, grilled (broiled) for 5 minutes until crispy, then chopped, instead of the anchovies, if you prefer.

3 Soak the sultanas in a bowl of warm water for about 20 minutes. Drain the sultanas thoroughly.

4 Place the tomatoes, pine nuts and sultanas in a small saucepan and gently heat.

5 Add the anchovies and tomato purée, heating the sauce for a further 2–3 minutes or until hot.

6 Cook the pasta in a saucepan of boiling water for 8–10 minutes or until it is cooked through, but still has 'bite'. Drain thoroughly.

7 Transfer the pasta to a serving plate and serve with the hot Sicilian sauce.

Harlequin Chicken

This colourful dish will tempt the appetites of all the family – it is ideal for toddlers, who enjoy the fun shapes of the multi-coloured (bell) peppers.

NUTRITIONAL INFORMATION

Calories	183	Sugar	.........8g
Protein	........24g	Fats	...........6g
Carbohydrates	....8g	Saturates	......1g

5 MINS   25 MINS

SERVES 4

INGREDIENTS

10 skinless, boneless chicken thighs

1 medium onion

1 each medium red, green and yellow (bell) peppers

1 tbsp sunflower oil

400 g/14 oz can chopped tomatoes

2 tbsp chopped fresh parsley

pepper

wholemeal bread and salad, to serve

1 Using a sharp knife, cut the chicken thighs into bite-sized pieces.

2 Peel and thinly slice the onion. Halve and deseed the (bell) peppers and cut into small diamond shapes.

3 Heat the sunflower oil in a shallow pan then quickly fry the chicken and onion until golden.

4 Add the (bell) peppers, cook for 2–3 minutes, then stir in the tomatoes and chopped fresh parsley and season with pepper.

5 Cover tightly and simmer for about 15 minutes, until the chicken and vegetables are tender. Serve hot with wholemeal (whole wheat) bread and a green salad.

COOK'S TIP

If you are making this dish for small children, the chicken can be finely chopped or minced (ground) first.

Pasta Carbonara

Lightly cooked eggs and pancetta are combined with cheese to make this rich, classic sauce.

NUTRITIONAL INFORMATION

Calories	547	Sugars 1g
Protein	........21g	Fat 31g
Carbohydrate	...49g	Saturates 14g

15 MINS   20 MINS

SERVES 4

INGREDIENTS

1 tbsp olive oil

40 g/1½ oz/3 tbsp butter

100 g/3½ oz pancetta or
  unsmoked bacon, diced

3 eggs, beaten

2 tbsp milk

1 tbsp thyme, stalks removed

675 g/1½ lb fresh or 350 g/12 oz dried
  conchigoni rigati

50 g/1¾ oz Parmesan cheese, grated

salt and pepper

1 Heat the oil and butter in a frying pan (skillet) until the mixture is just beginning to froth.

2 Add the pancetta or bacon to the pan and cook for 5 minutes or until browned all over.

3 Mix together the eggs and milk in a small bowl. Stir in the thyme and season to taste with salt and pepper.

4 Cook the pasta in a saucepan of boiling water for 8–10 minutes until tender, but still has 'bite'. Drain thoroughly.

5 Add the cooked, drained pasta to the frying pan (skillet) with the eggs and cook over a high heat for about 30 seconds or until the eggs just begin to cook and set. Do not overcook the eggs or they will become rubbery.

6 Add half of the grated Parmesan cheese, stirring to combine.

7 Transfer the pasta to a serving plate, pour over the sauce and toss to mix well.

8 Sprinkle the rest of the grated Parmesan over the top and serve immediately.

VARIATION

For an extra rich Carbonara sauce, stir in 4 tablespoons of double (heavy) cream with the eggs and milk in step 3. Follow exactly the same cooking method.

Skewered Chicken Spirals

These unusual chicken kebabs (kabobs) have a wonderful Italian flavour, and the bacon helps keep them moist during cooking.

NUTRITIONAL INFORMATION

Calories 231   Sugars 1g
Protein . . . . .29g   Fat 13g
Carbohydrate . . . .1g   Saturates 5g

15 MINS   10 MINS

SERVES 4

INGREDIENTS

4 skinless, boneless chicken breasts

1 garlic clove, crushed

2 tbsp tomato purée (paste)

4 slices smoked back bacon

large handful of fresh basil leaves

oil for brushing

salt and pepper

1 Spread out a piece of chicken between two sheets of cling film (plastic wrap) and beat firmly with a rolling pin to flatten the chicken to an even thickness. Repeat with the remaining chicken breasts.

2 Mix the garlic and tomato purée (paste) and spread over the chicken. Lay a bacon slice over each, then scatter with the basil. Season with salt and pepper.

3 Roll up each piece of chicken firmly, then cut into thick slices.

4 Thread the slices on to 4 skewers, making sure the skewer holds the chicken in a spiral shape.

5 Brush lightly with oil and cook on a preheated hot barbecue (grill) or grill (broiler) for about 10 minutes, turning once. Serve hot with a green salad.

Rice-Stuffed Mushrooms

Flat mushrooms are ideal for baking. They are filled with more strongly-flavoured wild mushrooms although you can use the ordinary varieties.

NUTRITIONAL INFORMATION

Calories 168   Sugars 1g
Protein ....7g   Fat 3g
Carbohydrate ...23g   Saturates 1g

 25 MINS   35 MINS

SERVES 4

INGREDIENTS

4 large flat mushrooms

100 g/3½ oz assorted wild mushrooms, sliced

4 dry-pack, sun-dried tomatoes, shredded

150 ml/5 fl oz/⅔ cup dry red wine

4 spring onions (scallions), trimmed and finely chopped

75 g/2¾ oz/1½ cups cooked red rice

2 tbsp freshly grated Parmesan cheese

4 thick slices granary bread

salt and pepper

spring onion (scallion), shredded, to garnish

1 Preheat the oven to 190°C/375°F/Gas Mark 5. Peel the flat mushrooms, pull out the stalks and set aside. Finely chop the stalks and place in a saucepan.

2 Add the wild mushrooms to the saucepan along with the tomatoes and red wine.

3 Bring to the boil, cover and gently simmer the tomatoes and mushrooms for 2–3 minutes until just tender. Drain, reserving the cooking liquid, and place in a small bowl.

4 Gently stir in the chopped spring onions (scallions) and cooked rice.

Season well and spoon into the flat mushrooms, pressing the mixture down gently. Sprinkle with the grated Parmesan.

5 Arrange the mushrooms in an ovenproof baking dish and pour the reserved cooking juices around them. Bake in the oven for 20–25 minutes until they are just cooked.

6 Meanwhile, preheat the grill (broiler) to hot. Trim the crusts from the bread and toast on each side until lightly browned.

7 Drain the mushrooms and place each one on to a piece of toasted bread. Garnish with spring onions (scallions) and serve.

Pasta with Chicken Sauce

Spinach ribbon noodles, topped with a rich tomato sauce and creamy chicken, make a very appetizing dish.

NUTRITIONAL INFORMATION

Calories	995	Sugars	.....8g
Protein	.....36g	Fat	.....74g
Carbohydrate	...50g	Saturates	.....34g

 15 MINS   45 MINS

SERVES 4

INGREDIENTS

250 g/9 oz fresh green tagliatelle

1 tbsp olive oil

salt

fresh basil leaves, to garnish

TOMATO SAUCE

2 tbsp olive oil

1 small onion, chopped

1 garlic clove, chopped

400 g/14 oz can chopped tomatoes

2 tbsp chopped fresh parsley

1 tsp dried oregano

2 bay leaves

2 tbsp tomato purée (paste)

1 tsp sugar

salt and pepper

CHICKEN SAUCE

60 g/2 oz/4 tbsp unsalted butter

400 g/14 oz boned chicken breasts,
   skinned and cut into thin strips

90 g/3 oz/¾ cup blanched almonds

300 ml/½ pint/1¼ cups double
   (heavy) cream

salt and pepper

1 To make the tomato sauce, heat the oil in a pan over a medium heat. Add the onion and fry until translucent. Add the garlic and fry for 1 minute. Stir in the tomatoes, parsley, oregano, bay leaves, tomato purée (paste), sugar and salt and pepper to taste, bring to the boil and simmer, uncovered, for 15–20 minutes, until reduced by half. Remove the pan from the heat and discard the bay leaves.

2 To make the chicken sauce, melt the butter in a frying pan (skillet) over a medium heat. Add the chicken and almonds and stir-fry for 5–6 minutes, or until the chicken is cooked through.

3 Meanwhile, bring the cream to the boil in a small pan over a low heat and boil for about 10 minutes, until reduced by almost half. Pour the cream over the chicken and almonds, stir and season to taste with salt and pepper. Set aside and keep warm.

4 Bring a large pan of lightly salted water to the boil. Add the tagliatelle and olive oil and cook for 8–10 minutes until tender, but still firm to the bite. Drain and transfer to a warm serving dish. Spoon over the tomato sauce and arrange the chicken sauce down the centre. Garnish with the basil leaves and serve immediately.

Italian Chicken Parcels

This cooking method makes the chicken aromatic and succulent, and reduces the oil needed as the chicken and vegetables cook in their own juices.

NUTRITIONAL INFORMATION

Calories 234	Sugars 5g
Protein 28g	Fat 12g
Carbohydrate 5g	Saturates 5g

 25 MINS   30 MINS

SERVES 6

INGREDIENTS

1 tbsp olive oil

6 skinless chicken breast fillets

250 g/9 oz/2 cups Mozzarella cheese

500 g/1 lb 2 oz/3½ cups courgettes
(zucchini), sliced

6 large tomatoes, sliced

1 small bunch fresh basil or oregano

pepper

rice or pasta, to serve

1 Cut 6 pieces of foil, each measuring about 25 cm/10 inches square. Brush the foil squares lightly with oil and set aside until required.

2 With a sharp knife, slash each chicken breast at regular intervals. Slice the Mozzarella cheese and place between the cuts in the chicken.

COOK'S TIP

To aid cooking, place the vegetables and chicken on the shiny side of the foil so that once the parcel is wrapped up the dull surface of the foil is facing outwards. This ensures that the heat is absorbed into the parcel and not reflected away from it.

3 Divide the courgettes (zucchini) and tomatoes between the pieces of foil and sprinkle with pepper to taste. Tear or roughly chop the basil or oregano and scatter over the vegetables in each parcel.

4 Place the chicken on top of each pile of vegetables then wrap in the foil to enclose the chicken and vegetables, tucking in the ends.

5 Place on a baking tray (cookie sheet) and bake in a preheated oven, 200°C/400°C/Gas Mark 6, for about 30 minutes.

6 To serve, unwrap each foil parcel and serve with rice or pasta.

Potato Stir-Fry

In this sweet and sour dish, tender vegetables are simply stir-fried with spices and coconut milk, and flavoured with lime.

NUTRITIONAL INFORMATION

Calories ....138 Sugars 5g
Protein ....2g Fat 6g
Carbohydrate ...20g Saturates 1g

10 MINS   20 MINS

SERVES 4

INGREDIENTS

4 waxy potatoes

2 tbsp vegetable oil

1 yellow (bell) pepper, diced

1 red (bell) pepper, diced

1 carrot, cut into matchstick strips

1 courgette (zucchini), cut into matchstick strips

2 garlic cloves, crushed

1 red chilli, sliced

1 bunch spring onions (scallions), halved lengthways

8 tbsp coconut milk

1 tsp chopped lemon grass

2 tsp lime juice

finely grated rind of 1 lime

1 tbsp chopped fresh coriander (cilantro)

1 Using a sharp knife, cut the potatoes into small dice.

2 Bring a large saucepan of water to the boil and cook the diced potatoes for 5 minutes. Drain thoroughly.

3 Heat the vegetable oil in a wok or large frying pan (skillet), swirling the oil around the base of the wok until it is really hot.

4 Add the potatoes, diced (bell) peppers, carrot, courgette (zucchini), garlic and chilli to the wok and stir-fry the vegetables for 2-3 minutes.

5 Stir in the spring onions, (scallions), coconut milk, chopped lemon grass and lime juice and stir-fry the mixture for a further 5 minutes.

6 Add the lime rind and coriander (cilantro) and stir-fry for 1 minute. Serve hot.

COOK'S TIP

Check that the potatoes are not overcooked in step 2, otherwise the potato pieces will disintegrate when they are stir-fried in the wok.

Two-in-One Chicken

Cook four chicken pieces and serve two hot, topped with a crunchy herb mixture. Serve the remainder as a salad in a delicious curry sauce.

NUTRITIONAL INFORMATION

Calories 421	Sugars 20g
Protein 31g	Fat 18g
Carbohydrate . . .34g	Saturates 4g

🎣 2¹/₂ HOURS 🕐 45 MINS

SERVES 2

INGREDIENTS

4 lean chicken thighs

oil for brushing

garlic powder

½ dessert (eating) apple, grated coarsely

1½ tbsp dry parsley and thyme stuffing mix

salt and pepper

pasta shapes, to serve

SAUCE

15 g/½ oz/1 tbsp butter or margarine

2 tsp plain (all-purpose) flour

5 tbsp skimmed milk

2 tbsp dry white wine or stock

½ tsp dried mustard powder

1 tsp capers or chopped gherkins

SPICED CHICKEN SALAD

½ small onion, chopped finely

1 tbsp oil

1 tsp tomato purée (paste)

½ tsp curry powder

1 tsp apricot jam

1 tsp lemon juice

2 tbsp low-fat mayonnaise

1 tbsp low-fat natural fromage frais

90 g/3 oz/¾ cup seedless grapes, halved

60 g/2 oz ¼ cup white long-grain rice, cooked, to serve

1 Place the chicken in a shallow ovenproof dish. Brush with oil, sprinkle with garlic powder and season with salt and pepper. Place in a preheated oven, 200°C/400°F/Gas Mark 6, for 25 minutes, or until almost cooked through. Combine the apple with the stuffing mix. Baste the chicken, then spoon the mixture over two of the pieces. Return all the chicken pieces to the oven for about 10 minutes until the chicken is cooked.

2 To make the sauce, melt the magarine in a pan, stir in the flour and cook for 1–2 minutes. Add the milk gradually, then the wine or stock, and bring to the boil. Stir in the mustard, capers or gherkins, and seasoning. Simmer for 1 minute. Serve the two crunchy-topped pieces of chicken with the sauce and pasta shapes.

3 For the salad, fry the onion gently in the oil until barely coloured. Add the tomato purée (paste), curry powder and jam, and cook for 1 minute. Leave the mixture to cool. Blend the mixture in a food processor, or press through a sieve (strainer). Beat in the lemon juice, mayonnaise and fromage frais. Season to taste with salt and pepper.

4 Cut the chicken into strips and add to the sauce with the grapes. Mix well, and chill. Serve with the rice.

Pasta with Bacon & Tomatoes

As this dish cooks, the mouth-watering aroma of bacon, sweet tomatoes and oregano is a feast in itself.

NUTRITIONAL INFORMATION

Calories 431	Sugars 8g
Protein 10g	Fat 29g
Carbohydrate . . .34g	Saturates 14g

10 MINS   35 MINS

SERVES 4

I N G R E D I E N T S

900 g/2 lb small, sweet tomatoes

6 slices rindless smoked bacon

60 g/2 oz/4 tbsp butter

1 onion, chopped

1 garlic clove, crushed

4 fresh oregano sprigs, finely chopped

450 g/1 lb/4 cups dried orecchiette

1 tbsp olive oil

salt and pepper

freshly grated Pecorino cheese, to serve

1 Blanch the tomatoes in boiling water. Drain, skin and seed the tomatoes, then roughly chop the flesh.

2 Using a sharp knife, chop the bacon into small dice.

3 Melt the butter in a saucepan. Add the bacon and fry until it is golden.

4 Add the onion and garlic and fry over a medium heat for 5-7 minutes, until just softened.

5 Add the tomatoes and oregano to the pan and then season to taste with salt and pepper. Lower the heat and simmer for 10-12 minutes.

6 Bring a large pan of lightly salted water to the boil. Add the orecchiette and oil and cook for 12 minutes, until just tender, but still firm to the bite. Drain the pasta and transfer to a warm serving dish or bowl.

7 Spoon the bacon and tomato sauce over the pasta, toss to coat and serve with the cheese.

COOK'S TIP

For an authentic Italian flavour use pancetta, rather than ordinary bacon. This kind of bacon is streaked with fat and adds rich undertones of flavour to many traditional dishes. It is available both smoked and unsmoked from large supermarkets and Italian delicatessens.

Sticky Chicken Drumsticks

These drumsticks are always popular – provide plenty of napkins for wiping sticky fingers or provide finger bowls with a slice of lemon.

NUTRITIONAL INFORMATION

Calories . . . . .213 Sugars 14g
Protein . . . . .27g Fat 6g
Carbohydrate . . .14g Saturates 2g

5 MINS   30 MINS

SERVES 4

INGREDIENTS

10 chicken drumsticks

4 tbsp fine-cut orange marmalade

1 tbsp Worcestershire sauce

grated rind and juice of ½ orange

salt and pepper

TO SERVE

cherry tomatoes

salad leaves

1 Using a sharp knife, make 2–3 slashes in the flesh of each chicken drumstick.

2 Bring a large saucepan of water to the boil and add the chicken drumsticks. Cover the pan, return to the boil and cook for 5–10 minutes. Remove the chicken and drain thoroughly.

3 Meanwhile, make the baste. Place the orange marmalade, Worcestershire sauce, orange rind and juice and salt and pepper to taste in a small saucepan. Heat gently, stirring continuously, until the marmalade melts and all of the ingredients are well combined.

4 Brush the baste over the par-cooked chicken drumsticks and transfer them to the barbecue (grill) to complete cooking. Barbecue (grill) over hot coals for about 10 minutes, turning and basting frequently with the remaining baste.

5 Carefully thread 3 cherry tomatoes on to a skewer and transfer to the barbecue (grill) for 1–2 minutes.

6 Transfer the chicken drumsticks to serving plates. Serve with the cherry tomato skewers and a selection of fresh salad leaves.

COOK'S TIP

Par-cooking the chicken is an ideal way of making sure that it is cooked through without becoming overcooked and burned on the outside.

Vegetable Enchiladas

This Mexican dish uses prepared tortillas which are readily available in supermarkets, which are then filled with a spicy vegetable mixture.

NUTRITIONAL INFORMATION

Calories 309   Sugars 14g
Protein ....12g   Fat 19g
Carbohydrate ...23g   Saturates 8g

    20 MINS   🕐 55 MINS

SERVES 4

I N G R E D I E N T S

4 flour tortillas

75 g/2¾ oz/¾ cup grated

  Cheddar cheese

F I L L I N G

75 g/2¾ oz spinach

2 tbsp olive oil

8 baby corn cobs, sliced

25 g/1 oz/1 tbsp frozen peas, thawed

1 red (bell) pepper, seeded and diced

1 carrot, diced

1 leek, sliced

2 garlic cloves, crushed

1 red chilli, chopped

salt and pepper

S A U C E

300 ml/½ pint/1¼ cups passata

  (sieved tomatoes)

2 shallots, chopped

1 garlic clove, crushed

300 ml/½ pint/1¼ cups vegetable stock

1 tsp caster (superfine) sugar

1 tsp chilli powder

1 To make the filling, blanch the spinach in a pan of boiling water for 2 minutes. Drain well, pressing out as much excess moisture as possible, and chop.

2 Heat the oil in a frying pan (skillet) over a medium heat. Add the baby corn cobs, peas, (bell) pepper, carrot, leek, garlic and chilli and sauté, stirring briskly, for 3–4 minutes. Stir in the spinach and season well with salt and pepper to taste.

3 Put all the sauce ingredients in a heavy-based saucepan and bring to the boil, stirring constantly. Cook over a high heat, stirring constantly, for 20 minutes, until thickened and reduced by a third.

4 Spoon a quarter of the filling along the centre of each tortilla. Roll the tortillas around the filling and place, seam side down, in a single layer in an ovenproof dish.

5 Pour the sauce over the tortillas and sprinkle the cheese on top. Cook in a preheated oven, 180°C/350°F/Gas Mark 4, for 20 minutes, or until the cheese has melted and browned. Serve immediately.

Potato & Tuna Quiche

The base for this quiche is made from mashed potato instead of pastry, giving a softer textured case (shell) for the tasty tuna filling.

NUTRITIONAL INFORMATION

Calories 383   Sugars 5g
Protein ....25g   Fat 15g
Carbohydrate ...40g   Saturates 6g

20 MINS   1 HOUR

SERVES 4

INGREDIENTS

450 g/1 lb floury (mealy) potatoes, diced

25 g/1 oz/2 tbsp butter

6 tbsp plain (all-purpose) flour

FILLING

1 tbsp vegetable oil

1 shallot, chopped

1 garlic clove, crushed

1 red (bell) pepper, diced

175g/6 oz can tuna in brine, drained

50 g/1¾ oz canned sweetcorn, drained

150 ml/¼ pint/⅔ cup skimmed milk

3 eggs, beaten

1 tbsp chopped fresh dill

50 g/1¾ oz mature (sharp) low-fat cheese, grated

salt and pepper

TO GARNISH

fresh dill sprigs

lemon wedges

1 Cook the potatoes in a pan of boiling water for 10 minutes or until tender. Drain and mash the potatoes. Add the butter and flour and mix to form a dough.

2 Knead the potato dough on a floured surface and press the mixture into a 20 cm/8 inch flan tin (pan). Prick the base with a fork. Line with baking parchment and baking beans and bake blind in a preheated oven, 200°C/400°F/Gas Mark 6, for 20 minutes.

3 Heat the oil in a frying pan (skillet), add the shallot, garlic and (bell) pepper and fry gently for 5 minutes. Drain well and spoon the mixture into the flan case (shell). Flake the tuna and arrange it over the top with the sweetcorn.

4 In a bowl, mix the milk, eggs and chopped dill and season.

5 Pour the egg and dill mixture into the flan case (shell) and sprinkle the grated cheese on top.

6 Bake in the oven for 20 minutes or until the filling has set. Garnish the quiche with fresh dill and lemon wedges. Serve with mixed vegetables or salad.

Chicken Tortellini

Tortellini were said to have been created in the image of the goddess Venus's navel. Whatever the story, they are a delicious blend of Italian flavours.

NUTRITIONAL INFORMATION

Calories	635	Sugars	.........4g
Protein	........31g	Fat	..........36g
Carbohydrate	...50g	Saturates	......16g

1 HOUR   35 MINS

SERVES 4

INGREDIENTS

115 g/4 oz boned chicken breast, skinned

60 g/2 oz Parma ham (prosciutto)

40 g/1½ oz cooked spinach, well drained

1 tbsp finely chopped onion

2 tbsp freshly grated Parmesan cheese

pinch of ground allspice

1 egg, beaten

450 g/1 lb Basic Pasta Dough (see page 6)

salt and pepper

2 tbsp chopped fresh parsley, to garnish

SAUCE

300 ml/½ pint/1¼ cups single (light) cream

2 garlic cloves, crushed

115 g/4 oz button mushrooms, thinly sliced

4 tbsp freshly grated Parmesan cheese

1 Bring a saucepan of seasoned water to the boil. Add the chicken and poach for about 10 minutes. Leave to cool slightly, then put in a food processor with the Parma ham (prosciutto), spinach and onion and process until finely chopped. Stir in the Parmesan cheese, allspice and egg and season with salt and pepper to taste.

2 Thinly roll out the pasta dough and cut into 4–5 cm/1½–2 inch rounds.

3 Place ½ teaspoon of the filling in the centre of each round. Fold the pieces in half and press the edges to seal. Then wrap each piece around your index finger, cross over the ends and curl the rest of the dough backwards to make a navel shape. Re-roll the trimmings and repeat until all of the dough is used up.

4 Bring a saucepan of salted water to the boil. Add the tortellini, in batches, bring back to the boil and cook for

5 minutes. Drain well and transfer to a serving dish.

5 To make the sauce, bring the cream and garlic to the boil in a small pan, then simmer for 3 minutes. Add the mushrooms and half of the cheese, season with salt and pepper to taste and simmer for 2–3 minutes. Pour the sauce over the chicken tortellini. Sprinkle over the remaining Parmesan cheese, garnish with the parsley and serve.

Buck Rarebit

This substantial version of cheese on toast – a creamy cheese sauce topped with a poached egg – makes a tasty, filling snack.

NUTRITIONAL INFORMATION

Calories 478   Sugars 2g
Protein . . . . .29g   Fat 34g
Carbohydrate . . .14g   Saturates 20g

X MINS   X MINS

SERVES 4

INGREDIENTS

350 g/12 oz mature (sharp) Cheddar

125 g/4 oz Gouda (Dutch), Gruyère or
   Emmenthal (Swiss) cheese

1 tsp mustard powder

1 tsp wholegrain mustard

2-4 tbsp brown ale, cider or milk

½ tsp Worcestershire sauce

4 thick slices white or brown bread

4 eggs

salt and pepper

TO GARNISH

tomato wedges

watercress sprigs

1 Grate the cheeses and place in a non-stick saucepan.

2 Add the mustards, seasoning, brown ale, cider or milk and Worcestershire sauce and mix well.

VARIATION

For a change, you can use part or all Stilton or other blue cheese; the appearance is not so attractive but the flavour is very good.

3 Heat the cheese mixture gently, stirring until it has melted and is completely thick and creamy. Remove from the heat and leave to cool a little.

4 Toast the slices of bread on each side under a preheated grill (broiler) then spread the rarebit mixture evenly over each piece. Put under a moderate grill (broiler) until golden brown and bubbling.

5 Meanwhile, poach the eggs. If using a poacher, grease the cups, heat the

water in the pan and, when just boiling, break the eggs into the cups. Cover and simmer for 4-5 minutes until just set. Alternatively, bring about 4cm/1½ inches of water to the boil in a frying pan (skillet) or large saucepan and for each egg quickly swirl the water with a knife and drop the egg into the "hole" created. Cook for about 4 minutes until just set.

6 Top the rarebits with a poached egg and serve garnished with tomato wedges and sprigs of watercress.

Tagliatelle with Garlic Butter

Pasta is not difficult to make yourself, just a little time consuming. The resulting pasta only takes a couple of minutes to cook and tastes wonderful.

NUTRITIONAL INFORMATION

Calories	642	Sugars	.........2g
Protein	........16g	Fat	..........29g
Carbohydrate	...84g	Saturates	......13g

 45 MINS   5 MINS

SERVES 4

INGREDIENTS

450 g/1 lb strong white flour,
   plus extra for dredging

2 tsp salt

4 eggs, beaten

3 tbsp olive oil

75 g/2¾ oz/5 tbsp butter, melted

3 garlic cloves, finely chopped

2 tbsp chopped, fresh parsley

pepper

1 Sift the flour into a large bowl and stir in the salt.

2 Make a well in the middle of the dry ingredients and add the eggs and 2 tablespoons of oil. Using a wooden spoon, stir in the eggs, gradually drawing in the flour. After a few minutes the dough will be too stiff to use a spoon and you will need to use your fingers.

3 Once all of the flour has been incorporated, turn the dough out on to a floured surface and knead for about 5 minutes, or until smooth and elastic. If you find the dough is too wet, add a little more flour and continue kneading. Cover with cling film (plastic wrap) and leave to rest for at least 15 minutes.

4 The basic dough is now ready; roll out the pasta thinly and create the pasta shapes required. This can be done by hand or using a pasta machine. Results from a machine are usually neater and thinner, but not necessarily better.

5 To make the tagliatelle by hand, fold the thinly rolled pasta sheets into 3 and cut out long, thin stips, about 1 cm/ ½ inch wide.

6 To cook, bring a pan of water to the boil, add 1 tbsp of oil and the pasta. It will take 2–3 minutes to cook, and the texture should have a slight bite to it. Drain.

7 Mix together the butter, garlic and parsley. Stir into the pasta, season with a little pepper to taste and serve immediately.

COOK'S TIP

Generally allow about 150 g/5½ oz fresh pasta or about 100 g/3½ oz dried pasta per person.

Cheese & Onion Rosti

These grated potato cakes are also known as straw cakes, as they resemble a straw mat! Serve them with a tomato sauce or salad.

NUTRITIONAL INFORMATION

Calories 307	Sugars 4g
Protein 8g	Fat 13g
Carbohydrate . . .42g	Saturates 6g

 10 MINS 40 MINS

SERVES 4

INGREDIENTS

900 g/2 lb potatoes

1 onion, grated

50 g/1¾ oz/½ cup grated Gruyère cheese

2 tbsp chopped parsley

1 tbsp olive oil

25 g/1 oz/2 tbsp butter

salt and pepper

TO GARNISH

shredded spring onion (scallion)

1 small tomato, quartered

1 Parboil the potatoes in a pan of lightly salted boiling water for 10 minutes and leave to cool. Peel the potatoes and grate with a coarse grater. Place the grated potatoes in a large mixing bowl.

COOK'S TIP

The potato cakes should be flattened as much as possible during cooking, otherwise the outside will be cooked before the centre.

2 Stir in the onion, cheese and parsley. Season well with salt and pepper. Divide the potato mixture into 4 portions of equal size and form them into cakes.

3 Heat half of the olive oil and butter in a frying pan (skillet) and cook 2 of the potato cakes over a high heat for 1 minute, then reduce the heat and cook

for 5 minutes, until they are golden underneath. Turn them over and cook for a further 5 minutes.

4 Repeat with the other half of the oil and the remaining butter to cook the remaining 2 cakes. Transfer to warm individual serving plates, garnish and serve immediately.

Tofu (Bean Curd) Burgers

Flavoured with spices and served with a tahini-flavoured relish, these delicious burgers are perfect for vegetarians.

 15 MINS   20 MINS

SERVES 4

INGREDIENTS

1 small red onion, chopped finely

1 garlic clove, crushed

1 tsp ground cumin

1 tsp ground coriander

2 tbsp lemon juice

400 g/14 oz can chickpeas (garbanzo beans), drained and rinsed

75 g/2¾ oz soft silken tofu (bean curd), drained

115 g/4 oz cooked potato, diced

4 tbsp freshly chopped coriander (cilantro)

75 g/2¾ oz dry brown breadcrumbs

1 tbsp vegetable oil

burger buns

2 medium tomatoes, sliced

1 large carrot, grated

salt and pepper

RELISH

1 tsp tahini (sesame seed) paste

4 tbsp low-fat natural fromage frais (unsweetened yogurt)

2.5 cm/1 inch piece cucumber, finely chopped

1 tbsp chopped, fresh coriander (cilantro)

garlic salt, to season

1 Place the onion, garlic, spices and lemon juice in a pan, bring to the boil, cover and simmer for 5 minutes until softened.

2 Place the chickpeas (garbanzo beans), tofu (bean curd) and potato in a bowl and mash well. Stir in the onion mixture, coriander (cilantro) and seasoning, and mix together. Divide into 4 and form into patties 10 cm/4 inch across. Sprinkle the breadcrumbs on to a plate and press the burgers into the crumbs to coat both sides.

3 Heat the oil in a large frying pan (skillet) and fry the burgers for 5 minutes on each side until golden. Mix the relish ingredients together in a bowl and leave to chill. Place sliced tomato and grated carrot on the buns and top with a burger. Serve with the relish.

Parma-wrapped Chicken

Stuffed with ricotta, nutmeg and spinach, then wrapped with wafer thin slices of Parma ham (prosciutto) and gently cooked in white wine.

NUTRITIONAL INFORMATION

Calories 426	Sugars 4g
Protein 44g	Fat 21g
Carbohydrate 9g	Saturates 8g

 30 MINS   45 MINS

SERVES 4

INGREDIENTS

125 g/4½ oz/½ cup frozen spinach, defrosted

125 g/4½ oz/½ cup ricotta cheese

pinch of grated nutmeg

4 skinless, boneless chicken breasts, each weighing 175 g/6 oz

4 Parma ham (prosciutto) slices

25 g/1 oz/2 tbsp butter

1 tbsp olive oil

12 small onions or shallots

125 g/4½ oz/1½ cups button mushrooms, sliced

1 tbsp plain (all-purpose) flour

150 ml/¼ pint/⅔ cup dry white or red wine

300 ml/½ pint/1¼ cups chicken stock

salt and pepper

1 Put the spinach into a sieve (strainer) and press out the water with a spoon. Mix with the ricotta and nutmeg and season with salt and pepper to taste.

2 Using a sharp knife, slit each chicken breast through the side and enlarge each cut to form a pocket. Fill with the spinach mixture, reshape the chicken breasts, wrap each breast tightly in a slice of ham and secure with cocktail sticks. Cover and chill in the refrigerator.

3 Heat the butter and oil in a frying pan (skillet) and brown the chicken breasts for 2 minutes on each side. Transfer the chicken to a large, shallow ovenproof dish and keep warm until required.

4 Fry the onions and mushrooms for 2–3 minutes until lightly browned. Stir in the plain (all-purpose) flour, then gradually add the wine and stock. Bring to the boil, stirring constantly. Season with salt and pepper and spoon the mixture around the chicken.

5 Cook the chicken uncovered in a preheated oven, 200°C/400°F/Gas Mark 6, for 20 minutes. Turn the breasts over and cook for a further 10 minutes. Remove the cocktail sticks and serve with the sauce, together with carrot purée and green beans, if wished.

Leek & Tomato Timbales

Angel-hair pasta, known as cappellini, is mixed with fried leeks, sun-dried tomatoes, fresh oregano and beaten eggs, and baked in ramekins.

NUTRITIONAL INFORMATION

Calories 331	Sugars 10g	
Protein 10g	Fat 21g	
Carbohydrate . . .26g	Saturates 9g	

 5–10 MINS 50 MINS

SERVES 4

INGREDIENTS

90 g/3 oz angel-hair pasta (cappellini)

25 g/1 oz/2 tbsp butter

1 tbsp olive oil

1 large leek, sliced finely

60 g/2 oz/½ cup sun-dried tomatoes in oil,
    drained and chopped

1 tbsp chopped fresh oregano
    or 1 tsp dried oregano

2 eggs, beaten

100 ml/3½ fl oz/generous ⅓ cup
    single (light) cream

1 tbsp freshly grated Parmesan

salt and pepper

sprigs of oregano, to garnish

lettuce leaves, to serve

SAUCE

1 small onion, chopped finely

1 small garlic clove, crushed

350 g/12 oz tomatoes, peeled and chopped

1 tsp mixed dried Italian herbs

4 tbsp dry white wine

1 Cook the pasta in plenty of boiling salted water for about 3 minutes until 'al dente' (just tender). Drain and rinse with cold water to cool quickly.

2 Meanwhile, heat the butter and oil in a frying pan (skillet). Gently fry the leek until softened, about 5–6 minutes. Add the sun-dried tomatoes and oregano, and cook for a further 2 minutes. Remove from the heat.

3 Add the leek mixture to the pasta. Stir in the beaten eggs, cream and Parmesan. Season with salt and pepper. Divide between 4 greased ramekin dishes or dariole moulds (molds).

4 Place the dishes in a roasting tin (pan) with enough warm water to come halfway up their sides. Bake in a preheated oven, 180°C/350°F/Gas Mark 4, for about 30 minutes, until set.

5 Meanwhile, make the tomato sauce. Fry the onion and garlic in the remaining butter and oil until softened. Add the tomatoes, herbs and wine. Cover and cook gently for about 20 minutes until pulpy. Blend in a food processor until smooth, or press through a sieve.

6 Run a knife or small spatula around the edge of the ramekins, then turn out the timbales on to 4 warm serving plates. Pour over a little sauce and garnish with oregano. Serve with the lettuce leaves.

Sticky Chicken Wings

These need to be eaten with your fingers so serve them at an informal supper.

NUTRITIONAL INFORMATION

Calories ....165 Sugars 12g
Protein ....14g Fat 7g
Carbohydrate ...12g Saturates 1g

3¼ HOURS   1 HOUR

SERVES 4–6

INGREDIENTS

2 tbsp olive oil

1 small onion, finely chopped

2 garlic cloves, crushed

425 ml/¾ pint passata (sieved tomatoes)

2 tsp dried thyme

1 tsp dried oregano

pinch fennel seeds

3 tbsp red wine vinegar

2 tbsp Dijon mustard

pinch ground cinnamon

2 tbsp brown sugar

1 tsp chilli flakes

2 tbsp black treacle

16 chicken wings

salt and pepper

TO GARNISH

celery stalks

cherry tomatoes

1 Heat the olive oil in a large frying pan (skillet) and fry the onion and garlic for about 10 minutes.

2 Add the passata (sieved tomatoes), dried herbs, fennel, red wine vinegar, mustard and cinnamon to the frying pan (skillet) along with the sugar, chilli flakes, treacle, and salt and pepper. Bring to the boil, then reduce the heat and simmer gently for about 15 minutes, until the sauce is slightly reduced.

3 Put the chicken wings in a large dish, and coat liberally with the sauce. Leave to marinate for 3 hours or as long as possible, turning the wings over often in the marinade.

4 Transfer the wings to a clean baking sheet (cookie sheet), and roast in a preheated oven, 220°C/425°F/ Gas Mark 7, for 10 minutes. Reduce the heat to 190°C/375°F/Gas Mark 5 and cook for 20 minutes, basting often.

5 Serve the wings piping hot, garnished with celery stalks and cherry tomatoes.

Stuffed Tomatoes

These barbecued (grilled) tomato cups are filled with a delicious Greek-style combination of herbs, nuts and raisins.

NUTRITIONAL INFORMATION

Calories	156	Sugars	........10g
Protein	.........3g	Fat	...........7g
Carbohydrate	...22g	Saturates	.....0.7g

25 MINS   10 MINS

SERVES 4

I N G R E D I E N T S

4 beefsteak tomatoes

300 g/10½ oz /4½ cups cooked rice

8 spring onions (scallions), chopped

3 tbsp chopped, fresh mint

2 tbsp chopped, fresh parsley

3 tbsp pine nuts

3 tbsp raisins

2 tsp olive oil

salt and pepper

1 Cut the tomatoes in half, then scoop out the seeds and discard.

2 Stand the tomatoes upside down on absorbent kitchen paper (paper towels) for a few moments in order for the juices to drain out.

3 Turn the tomatoes the right way up and sprinkle the insides with salt and pepper.

4 Mix together the rice, spring onions (scallions), mint, parsley, pine nuts and raisins.

5 Spoon the mixture into the tomato cups.

6 Drizzle over a little olive oil, then barbecue (grill) the tomatoes on an oiled rack over medium hot coals for about 10 minutes until they are tender and cooked through.

7 Transfer the tomatoes to serving plates and serve immediately while still hot.

COOK'S TIP

Tomatoes are a popular barbecue (grill) vegetable. Try grilling (broiling) slices of beefsteak tomato and slices of onion, brushed with a little oil and topped with sprigs of fresh herbs. Or thread cherry tomatoes on to skewers and barbecue (grill) for 5–10 minutes.

Vegballs with Chilli Sauce

These tasty, nutty morsels are delicious served with a fiery, tangy sauce that counteracts the richness of the peanuts.

NUTRITIONAL INFORMATION

Calories . . . . .615 Sugars 13g
Protein . . . . .23g Fat 43g
Carbohydrate . . .37g Saturates 8g

25 MINS   30 MINS

SERVES 4

INGREDIENTS

3 tbsp groundnut oil

1 onion, finely chopped

1 celery stalk, chopped

1 tsp dried mixed herbs

225 g/8 oz/2 cups roasted unsalted
   peanuts, ground

175 g/6 oz/1 cup canned chickpeas
   (garbanzo beans), drained and mashed

1 tsp yeast extract

60 g/2 oz/1 cup fresh wholemeal
   (whole wheat) breadcrumbs

1 egg yolk

25 g/1 oz/¼ cup plain (all-purpose) flour

strips of fresh red chilli, to garnish

HOT CHILLI SAUCE

2 tsp groundnut oil

1 large red chilli, seeded and finely chopped

2 spring onions (scallions), finely chopped

2 tbsp red wine vinegar

200 g/7 oz can chopped tomatoes

2 tbsp tomato purée (paste)

2 tsp caster (superfine) sugar

salt and pepper

rice and green salad (salad greens),
   to serve

1 Heat 1 tablespoon of the oil in a frying pan (skillet) and gently fry the onion and celery for 3–4 minutes, until softened, but not browned.

2 Place all the other ingredients, except the remaining oil and the flour, in a mixing bowl and add the onion and celery. Mix well.

3 Divide the mixture into 12 portions and roll into small balls. Coat all over with the flour.

4 Heat the remaining oil in a frying pan (skillet). Add the chickpea (garbanzo bean) balls and cook over a medium heat, turning frequently, for 15 minutes, until cooked through and golden. Drain on kitchen paper (paper towels).

5 Meanwhile, make the hot chilli sauce. Heat the oil in a small frying pan (skillet) and gently fry the chilli and spring onions (scallions) for 2–3 minutes. Stir in the remaining ingredients and season. Bring to the boil and simmer for 5 minutes.

6 Serve the chickpea (garbanzo bean) and peanut balls with the hot chilli sauce, rice and a salad.

Egg & Lentil Curry

A nutritious meal that is easy and relatively quick to make. The curried lentil sauce would also be delicious served with cooked vegetables.

NUTRITIONAL INFORMATION

Calories 298   Sugars 6g
Protein ....17g   Fat 17g
Carbohydrate ...20g   Saturates 4g

 10 MINS   35 MINS

SERVES 4

INGREDIENTS

3 tbsp vegetable ghee or oil

1 large onion, chopped

2 garlic cloves, chopped

2.5 cm/1 inch piece of root,
    ginger chopped

½ tsp minced chilli or chilli powder

1 tsp ground coriander

1 tsp ground cumin

1 tsp paprika

90 g/3 oz/⅓ cup split red lentils

425 ml/¾ pint/1¾ cups vegetable stock

225 g/8 oz can chopped tomatoes

6 eggs

50 ml/2 fl oz/¼ cup coconut milk

salt

2 tomatoes, cut into wedges,
    and coriander (cilantro) sprigs, to garnish

parathas, chapatis or naan bread,
    to serve

1 Heat the ghee or oil in a saucepan, add the onion and fry gently for 3 minutes. Stir in the garlic, ginger, chilli and spices and cook gently, stirring frequently, for 1 minute. Stir in the lentils, stock and chopped tomatoes and bring to the boil. Reduce the heat, cover and simmer, stirring occasionally, for 30 minutes, until the lentils are tender.

2 Meanwhile, place the eggs in a saucepan of cold water and bring to the boil. Reduce the heat and simmer for 10 minutes. Drain and cover immediately with cold water.

3 Stir the coconut milk into the lentil mixture and season well with salt to taste. Process the mixture in a blender or food processor until smooth. Return to the pan and heat through.

4 Shell the hard-boiled (hard-cooked) eggs and cut in half lengthways. Arrange 3 halves, in a petal design, on each serving plate. Spoon the hot lentil sauce over the eggs, adding enough to flood the plate. Arrange a tomato wedge and a coriander (cilantro) sprig between each halved egg. Serve hot with parathas, chapatis or naan bread.

Spinach & Ricotta Shells

This is a classic combination in which the smooth, creamy cheese balances the sharper taste of the spinach.

NUTRITIONAL INFORMATION

Calories 672   Sugars 10g
Protein . . . . .23g   Fat 26g
Carbohydrate . . .93g   Saturates 8g

5 MINS   40 MINS

SERVES 4

INGREDIENTS

400 g/14 oz dried lumache rigate grande

5 tbsp olive oil

60 g/2 oz/1 cup fresh white breadcrumbs

125 ml/4 fl oz/½ cup milk

300 g/10½ oz frozen spinach, thawed
   and drained

225 g/8 oz/1 cup ricotta cheese

pinch of freshly grated nutmeg

400 g/14 oz can chopped tomatoes, drained

1 garlic clove, crushed

salt and pepper

1 Bring a large saucepan of lightly salted water to the boil. Add the lumache and 1 tbsp of the olive oil and cook for 8–10 minutes until just tender, but still firm to the bite. Drain the pasta, refresh under cold water and set aside until required.

2 Put the breadcrumbs, milk and 3 tbsp of the remaining olive oil in a food processor and work to combine.

3 Add the spinach and ricotta cheese to the food processor and work to a smooth mixture. Transfer to a bowl, stir in the nutmeg, and season with salt and pepper to taste.

4 Mix together the tomatoes, garlic and remaining oil and spoon the mixture into the base of a large ovenproof dish.

5 Using a teaspoon, fill the lumache with the spinach and ricotta mixture and arrange on top of the tomato mixture in the dish. Cover and bake in a preheated oven at 180°C/350°F/Gas 4 for 20 minutes. Serve hot.

COOK'S TIP

Ricotta is a creamy Italian cheese traditionally made from ewes' milk whey. It is soft and white, with a smooth texture and a slightly sweet flavour. It should be used within 2–3 days of purchase.

Baked Stuffed Onions

Spanish onions are ideal for this recipe, as they have a milder, sweeter flavour that is not too overpowering.

NUTRITIONAL INFORMATION

Calories 182   Sugars 6g
Protein . . . . .10g   Fat 9g
Carbohydrate . . .18g   Saturates 5g

 15 MINS   2¼ HOURS

SERVES 4

I N G R E D I E N T S

4 large Spanish onions

2 slices streaky bacon, diced

½ red (bell) pepper, deseeded and diced

125 g/4½ oz lean minced (ground) beef

1 tbsp chopped mixed fresh herbs
    such as parsley, thyme and rosemary
    or 1 tsp dried mixed herbs

25 g/1 oz/½ cup fresh white breadcrumbs

300 ml/½ pint/1¼ cups beef stock

salt and pepper

chopped fresh parsley to garnish

long grain rice to serve

G R A V Y

25 g/1 oz/2 tbsp butter

125 g/4½ oz mushrooms, chopped finely

300 ml/½ pint/1¼ cups beef stock

2 tbsp cornflour (cornstarch)

2 tbsp water

1 Put the onions in a saucepan of lightly salted water. Bring to the boil, then simmer for 15 minutes until tender.

2 Remove the onions from the pan, drain and cool slightly, then hollow out the centres and finely chop.

3 Heat a frying pan (skillet) and cook the bacon until the fat runs. Add the chopped onion and (bell) pepper and cook for 5–7 minutes, stirring frequently.

4 Add the beef to the frying pan (skillet) and cook, stirring, for 3 minutes, until browned. Remove from the heat and stir in the herbs, breadcrumbs and seasoning.

5 Grease an ovenproof dish and stand the whole onions in it. Pack the beef mixture into the centres and pour the stock around them.

6 Bake the stuffed onions in a preheated oven at 180°C/350°F/Gas Mark 4 for 1–1½ hours or until tender.

7 To make the gravy, heat the butter in a small saucepan and fry the mushrooms for 3–4 minutes. Strain the liquid from the onions and add to the pan with the stock. Cook for 2–3 minutes.

8 Mix the cornflour (cornstarch) with the water then stir into the gravy and heat, stirring, until thickened and smooth. Season with salt and pepper to taste. Serve the onions with the gravy and rice, garnished with chopped fresh parsley.

Vegetable Calzone

These pizza base parcels are great for making in advance and freezing – they can be defrosted when required for a quick snack.

NUTRITIONAL INFORMATION

Calories 499   Sugars 7g
Protein . . . . .16g   Fat 9g
Carbohydrate . . .95g   Saturates 2g

1¹/₂ HOURS   40 MINS

SERVES 4

INGREDIENTS

DOUGH

450 g/1 lb/3¹/₂ cups strong white flour

2 tsp easy-blend dried yeast

1 tsp caster (superfine) sugar

150 ml/¹/₄ pint/³/₄ cup vegetable stock

150 ml/¹/₄ pint/³/₄ cup passata (sieved
   tomatoes)

beaten egg

FILLING

1 tbsp vegetable oil

1 onion, chopped

1 garlic clove, crushed

2 tbsp chopped sun-dried tomatoes

100 g/3¹/₂ oz spinach, chopped

3 tbsp canned and drained sweetcorn

25 g/1 oz/¹/₄ cup French (green) beans, cut
   into 3

1 tbsp tomato purée (paste)

1 tbsp chopped oregano

50 g/1³/₄ oz Mozzarella cheese, sliced

salt and pepper

1 Sieve the flour into a bowl. Add the
   yeast and sugar and beat in the stock
and passata (sieved tomatoes) to make a
smooth dough.

2 Knead the dough on a lightly floured
   surface for 10 minutes, then place in a
clean, lightly oiled bowl and leave to rise
in a warm place for 1 hour.

3 Heat the oil in a frying pan (skillet)
   and sauté the onion for 2–3 minutes.

4 Stir in the garlic, tomatoes, spinach,
   corn and beans and cook for 3–4
minutes. Add the tomato purée (paste)
and oregano and season with salt and
pepper to taste.

5 Divide the risen dough into 4 equal
   portions and roll each on to a floured
surface to form an 18 cm/7 inch circle.

6 Spoon a quarter of the filling on to
   one half of each circle and top with
cheese. Fold the dough over to encase the
filling, sealing the edge with a fork. Glaze
with beaten egg. Put the calzone on a
lightly greased baking tray (cookie sheet)
and cook in a preheated oven, at 220°C/
425°F/Gas Mark 7, for 25–30 minutes
until risen and golden. Serve warm.

Kofta Kebabs (Kabobs)

Traditionally, koftas are made from a spicy meat mixture, but this bean and wheat version makes a tasty vegetarian alternative.

NUTRITIONAL INFORMATION

Calories	598	Sugars	.........7g
Protein	........26g	Fat	..........17g
Carbohydrate	...90g	Saturates	.......3g

 1 HR 20 MINS 1½ HOURS

SERVES 4

INGREDIENTS

175 g/6 oz/1 cup aduki beans

175 g/6 oz/1 cup bulgur wheat

450 ml/16 fl oz/scant 2 cups vegetable
    stock

3 tbsp olive oil

1 onion, finely chopped

2 garlic cloves, crushed

1 tsp ground coriander

1 tsp ground cumin

2 tbsp chopped fresh coriander (cilantro)

3 eggs, beaten

125 g/4½ oz/¾ cup dried breadcrumbs

salt and pepper

TABBOULEH

175 g/6 oz/1 cup bulgur wheat

2 tbsp lemon juice

1 tbsp olive oil

6 tbsp chopped parsley

4 spring onions (scallions), finely chopped

60 g/2 oz cucumber, finely chopped

3 tbsp chopped mint

1 extra-large tomato, finely chopped

TO SERVE

black olives

pitta (pocket bread)

1 Cook the aduki beans in boiling water for 40 minutes, until tender. Drain, rinse and leave to cool. Cook the bulgur wheat in the stock for 10 minutes, until the stock is absorbed. Set aside.

2 Heat 1 tablespoon of the oil in a frying pan (skillet) and fry the onion, garlic and spices for 4–5 minutes.

3 Transfer to a bowl, together with the beans, coriander (cilantro), seasoning and eggs and mash with a potato masher or fork. Add the breadcrumbs and bulgur wheat and stir well. Cover and chill for 1 hour, until firm.

4 To make the tabbouleh, soak the bulgur wheat in 450 ml/¾ pint/scant 2 cups of boiling water for 15 minutes. Combine with the remaining ingredients. Cover and chill.

5 With wet hands, mould the kofta mixture into 32 oval shapes.

6 Press on to skewers, brush with oil and grill (broil) for 5–6 minutes. until golden. Turn, brush with oil again and cook for 5–6 minutes. Drain on kitchen paper (paper towels). Garnish and serve with the tabbouleh, black olives and pitta (pocket) bread.

Pancakes with Smoked Fish

These are delicious as a starter or light supper dish and you can vary the filling with whichever fish you prefer.

NUTRITIONAL INFORMATION

Calories 399   Sugars 6g
Protein . . . . .36g   Fat 18g
Carbohydrate . . .25g   Saturates 10g

 15 MINS   1 HR 20 MINS

Makes 12 pancakes

I N G R E D I E N T S

PANCAKES

100 g/3 ½ oz flour

½ tsp salt

1 egg, beaten

300 ml/ ½ pint/1 ¼ cups milk

1 tbsp oil, for frying

SAUCE

450 g/1 lb smoked haddock, skinned

300 ml/ ½ pint/1 ¼ cups milk

40 g/1 ½ oz/3 tbsp butter or margarine

40 g/1 ½ oz flour

300 ml/ ½ pint/1 ¼ cups fish stock

75 g/2 ¾ oz Parmesan cheese, grated

100 g/3 ½ oz frozen peas, defrosted

100 g/3 ½ oz prawns (shrimp), cooked and peeled

50 g/1 ¾ oz Gruyère cheese, grated

salt and pepper

1 To make the pancake batter, sift the flour and salt into a large bowl and make a well in the centre. Add the egg and, using a wooden spoon, begin to draw in the flour. Slowly add the milk and beat together to form a smooth batter. Set aside until required.

2 Place the fish in a large frying pan (skillet), add the milk and bring to the boil. Simmer for 10 minutes or until the fish begins to flake. Drain thoroughly, reserving the milk.

3 Melt the butter in a saucepan. Add the flour, mix to a paste and cook for 2–3 minutes. Remove the pan from the heat and add the reserved milk a little at a time, stirring to make a smooth sauce. Repeat with the fish stock. Return to the heat and bring to the boil, stirring. Stir in the Parmesan and season with salt and pepper to taste.

4 Grease a frying pan (skillet) with oil. Add 2 tablespoons of the pancake batter, swirling it around the pan and cook for 2–3 minutes. Loosen the sides with a palette knife (spatula) and flip over the pancake. Cook for 2–3 minutes until golden; repeat. Stack the pancakes with sheets of baking parchment between them and keep warm in the oven.

5 Stir the flaked fish, peas and prawns (shrimp) into half of the sauce and use to fill each pancake. Pour over the remaining sauce, top with the Gruyère and bake for 20 minutes until golden.

Potato Fritters

Chunks of cooked potato are coated first in Parmesan cheese, then in a light batter before being fried until golden for a delicious hot snack.

NUTRITIONAL INFORMATION

Calories 599	Sugars 9g
Protein 22g	Fat 39g
Carbohydrate ...42g	Saturates 13g

20 MINS   20-25 MINS

SERVES 4

INGREDIENTS

500 g/1 lb 2 oz waxy potatoes, cut into

   large cubes

125 g/4½ oz/1¼ cups grated

   Parmesan cheese

oil, for deep-frying

SAUCE

25 g/1 oz/2 tbsp butter

1 onion, halved and sliced

2 garlic cloves, crushed

25 g/1 oz/¼ cup plain (all-

   purpose) flour

300 ml/½ pint/1¼ cups milk

1 tbsp chopped parsley

BATTER

50 g/1¾ oz/½ cup plain (all-purpose) flour

1 small egg

150 ml/¼ pint/⅔ cup milk

1 To make the sauce, melt the butter in a saucepan and cook the sliced onion and garlic over a low heat, stirring frequently, for 2-3 minutes. Add the flour and cook, stirring constantly, for 1 minute.

2 Remove from the heat and stir in the milk and parsley. Return to the heat and bring to the boil. Keep warm.

3 Meanwhile, cook the cubed potatoes in a saucepan of boiling water for 5-10 minutes, until just firm. Do not overcook or they will fall apart.

4 Drain the potatoes and toss them in the Parmesan cheese. If the potatoes are still slightly wet, the cheese sticks to them and coats them well.

5 To make the batter, place the flour in a mixing bowl and gradually beat in the egg and milk until smooth. Dip the potato cubes into the batter to coat them.

6 In a large saucepan or deep-fryer, heat the oil to 180°C/350°F or until a cube of bread browns in 30 seconds. Add the fritters and cook for 3-4 minutes, or until golden.

7 Remove the fritters with a slotted spoon and drain well. Transfer them to a warm serving bowl and serve immediately with the garlic sauce.

Pasta & Lamb Loaf

Any dried pasta shape can be used for this delicious recipe. It has been adapted for microwave cooking for convenience.

NUTRITIONAL INFORMATION

Calories 245	Sugars 2g
Protein 15g	Fat 18g
Carbohydrate 6g	Saturates 7g

35 MINS · 35 MINS

SERVES 4

INGREDIENTS

15 g/½ oz/1 tbsp butter

½ small aubergine (eggplant), diced

60 g/2 oz multi-coloured fusilli

2 tsp olive oil

225 g/8 oz/1 cup minced (ground) lamb

½ small onion, chopped

½ red (bell) pepper, chopped

1 garlic clove, crushed

1 tsp dried mixed herbs

2 eggs, beaten

2 tbsp single (light) cream

salt and pepper

TO SERVE

salad

pasta sauce of your choice

1 Place the butter in a 500 g/1 lb 2 oz loaf dish. Cook on HIGH power for 30 seconds until melted. Brush over the base and sides of the dish.

2 Sprinkle the aubergine (eggplant) with salt, put in a colander and leave for 20 minutes. Rinse the aubergine (eggplant) well and pat dry with paper towels.

3 Place the pasta in a bowl, add a little salt and enough boiling water to cover by 2.5 cm/1 inch. Cover and cook on HIGH power for 8 minutes, stirring halfway through. Leave to stand, covered, for a few minutes.

4 Place the oil, lamb and onion in a bowl. Cover and cook on HIGH power for 2 minutes.

5 Break up any lumps of meat using a fork. Add the (bell) pepper, garlic, herbs and aubergine (eggplant). Cover and cook on HIGH power for 5 minutes, stirring halfway through.

6 Drain the pasta and add to the lamb with the eggs and cream. Season well. Turn into the loaf dish and pat down using the back of a spoon.

7 Cook on MEDIUM power for 10 minutes until firm to the touch. Leave to stand for 5 minutes before turning out. Serve in slices with a salad and a pasta sauce.

Minty Lamb Burgers

A tasty alternative to traditional hamburgers, these lamb burgers are flavoured with mint and are accompanied with a smooth minty dressing.

NUTRITIONAL INFORMATION

Calories 320   Sugars 11g
Protein . . . . .28g   Fat 10g
Carbohydrate . . .33g   Saturates 4g

40 MINS   20 MINS

SERVES 4

INGREDIENTS

350 g/12 oz lean lamb, minced (ground)

1 medium onion, finely chopped

4 tbsp dry wholemeal breadcrumbs

2 tbsp mint jelly

salt and pepper

TO SERVE

4 wholemeal baps, split

2 large tomatoes, sliced

small piece of cucumber, sliced

lettuce leaves

RELISH

4 tbsp low-fat natural fromage frais
   (unsweetened yogurt)

1 tbsp mint jelly, softened

5 cm/2 inch piece cucumber, finely diced

1 tbsp chopped fresh mint

1 Place the lamb in a large bowl and mix in the onion, breadcrumbs and mint jelly. Season well, then mould the ingredients together with your hands to form a firm mixture.

2 Divide the mixture into 4 and shape each portion into a round measuring 10 cm/4 inches across. Place the rounds on a plate lined with baking parchment and leave to chill for 30 minutes.

3 Preheat the grill (broiler) to medium. Line a grill rack with baking parchment, securing the ends under the rack, and place the burgers on top. Cook for 8 minutes, then turn over the burgers and cook for a further 7 minutes or until cooked through.

4 Meanwhile, make the relish. In a small bowl, mix together the fromage frais (unsweetened yogurt), mint jelly, cucumber and freshly chopped mint. Cover the relish with cling film (plastic wrap) and leave to chill in the refrigerator for an hour or until required.

5 Drain the burgers on absorbent kitchen paper (paper towels). Serve the burgers inside the baps with sliced tomatoes, cucumber, lettuce and relish.

Polenta Kebabs (Kabobs)

Here, skewers of thyme-flavoured polenta, wrapped in Parma ham (prosciutto), are grilled (broiled) or barbecued (grilled).

NUTRITIONAL INFORMATION

Calories 212   Sugars 0g
Protein . . . . .8g   Fat 6g
Carbohydrate . . .32g   Saturates 1g

🍲 20 MINS   🕐 45 MINS

SERVES 4

INGREDIENTS

175 g/6 oz instant polenta

750 ml/1 pint/scant 3¾ cups water

2 tbsp fresh thyme, stalks removed

8 slices Parma ham (prosciutto)
   (about 75 g/2¾ oz)

1 tbsp olive oil

salt and pepper

fresh green salad, to serve

1 Cook the polenta, using 750 ml/1 pint 7 fl oz/3¼ cups of water to 175 g/6 oz polenta, stirring occasionally, for 30–35 minutes. Alternatively, follow the instructions on the packet.

2 Add the fresh thyme to the polenta mixture and season to taste with salt and pepper.

COOK'S TIP

Try flavouring the polenta with chopped oregano, basil or marjoram instead of the thyme, if you prefer. You should use 3 tablespoons of chopped herbs to every 350 g/12 oz instant polenta.

3 Spread out the polenta, about 2.5 cm/ 1 inch thick, on to a board. Set aside to cool.

4 Using a sharp knife, cut the cooled polenta into 2.5 cm/1 inch cubes.

5 Cut the Parma ham (prosciutto) slices into 2 pieces lengthways. Wrap the Parma ham (prosciutto) around the polenta cubes.

6 Thread the Parma ham (prosciutto) wrapped polenta cubes on to skewers.

7 Brush the kebabs (kabobs) with a little oil and cook under a preheated grill (broiler), turning frequently, for 7–8 minutes. Alternatively, barbecue (grill) the kebabs (kabobs) until golden. Transfer to serving plates and serve with a salad.

Kibbeh

This Lebanese barbeque dish is similar to the Turkish kofte and the Indian kofta, but the spices used to flavour the meat are quite different.

NUTRITIONAL INFORMATION

Calories	232	Sugars	........3g
Protein	........19g	Fat	..........13g
Carbohydrate	....9g	Saturates	......4g

 1 HOUR   15 MINS

SERVES 4

INGREDIENTS

75 g/2¾ oz couscous

1 small onion

350 g/12 oz lean minced lamb

½ tsp ground cinnamon

¼ tsp cayenne

4 tsp ground allspice

green salad and onion rings, to serve

BASTE

2 tbsp tomato ketchup (catsup)

2 tbsp sunflower oil

1 Place the couscous in a large bowl, cover with cold water and leave to stand for 30 minutes or until the couscous has swelled and softened. Alternatively, soak the couscous according to the instructions on the packet.

2 Drain the couscous through a sieve and squeeze out as much moisture as you can.

3 If you have a food processor, add the onion and chop finely. Add the lamb and process briefly to chop the mince further. If you do not have a processor, grate the onion then add to the lamb.

4 Combine the couscous, lamb and spices and mix well together. Divide the mixture into 8 equal sized portions. Press and shape the mixture around 8 skewers, pressing the mixture together firmly so that it holds it shape. Leave to chill for at least 30 minutes or until required.

5 To make the baste, combine the oil and ketchup (catsup).

6 Barbecue (grill) the kibbeh over hot coals for 10–15 minutes, turning and basting frequently. Serve with barbecued (grilled) onion rings and green salad leaves, if wished.

Spinach & Ricotta Gnocchi

Try not to handle the mixture too much when making gnocchi, as this will make the dough a little heavy.

NUTRITIONAL INFORMATION

Calories 712   Sugars 15g
Protein . . . . .29g   Fat 59g
Carbohydrate . . .16g   Saturates 33g

 20 MINS   15 MINS

SERVES 4

INGREDIENTS

1 kg/2 lb 4 oz spinach

350 g/12 oz/1½ cups Ricotta

125 g/4½ oz/1 cup Pecorino, grated

3 eggs, beaten

¼ tsp freshly grated nutmeg

plain (all-purpose) flour, to mix

125 g/4½ oz/½ cup unsalted butter

25 g/1 oz/¼ cup pine kernels (nuts)

50 g/2 oz/⅓ cup raisins

salt and pepper

1 Wash and drain the spinach well and cook in a covered saucepan without any extra liquid until softened, about 8 minutes. Place the spinach in a colander and press well to remove as much juice as possible. Either rub the spinach through a sieve (strainer) or purée in a blender.

2 Combine the spinach purée with the Ricotta, half of the Pecorino, the eggs, nutmeg and seasoning to taste, mixing lightly but thoroughly. Work in enough flour, lightly and quickly, to make the mixture easy to handle.

3 Shape the dough quickly into small lozenge shapes, and dust lightly with a little flour.

4 Add a dash of oil to a large saucepan of salted water and bring to the boil. Add the gnocchi carefully and boil for about 2 minutes or until they float to the surface. Using a perforated spoon, transfer the gnocchi to a buttered ovenproof dish. Keep warm.

5 Melt the butter in a frying pan (skillet). Add the pine kernels (nuts) and raisins and fry until the nuts start to brown slightly, but do not allow the butter to burn. Pour the mixture over the gnocchi and serve sprinkled with the remaining grated Pecorino.

Potato Noodles

Potatoes are used to make a 'pasta' dough which is cut into thin noodles and boiled. The noodles are served with a bacon and mushroom sauce.

NUTRITIONAL INFORMATION

Calories 810   Sugars 5g
Protein . . . . .21g   Fat 47g
Carbohydrate . . .81g   Saturates 26g

30 MINS   25 MINS

SERVES 4

INGREDIENTS

450 g/1 lb floury (mealy) potatoes, diced

225 g/8 oz/2 cups plain (all-purpose) flour

1 egg, beaten

1 tbsp milk

salt and pepper

parsley sprig, to garnish

SAUCE

1 tbsp vegetable oil

1 onion, chopped

1 garlic clove, crushed

125 g/4½ oz open-capped
   mushrooms, sliced

3 smoked bacon slices, chopped

50 g/1¾ oz Parmesan cheese, grated

300 ml/½ pint/1¼ cups double
   (heavy) cream

2 tbsp chopped fresh parsley

1 Cook the diced potatoes in a saucepan of boiling water for 10 minutes or until cooked through. Drain well. Mash the potatoes until smooth, then beat in the flour, egg and milk. Season with salt and pepper to taste and bring together to form a stiff paste.

2 On a lightly floured surface, roll out the paste to form a thin sausage shape. Cut the sausage into 2.5 cm/1 inch lengths. Bring a large pan of salted water to the boil, drop in the dough pieces and cook for 3-4 minutes. They will rise to the surface when cooked.

3 To make the sauce, heat the oil in a pan and sauté the onion and garlic for 2 minutes. Add the mushrooms and bacon and cook for 5 minutes. Stir in the cheese, cream and parsley, and season.

4 Drain the noodles and transfer to a warm pasta bowl. Spoon the sauce over the top and toss to mix. Garnish with a parsley sprig and serve.

COOK'S TIP

Make the dough in advance, then wrap and store the noodles in the refrigerator for up to 24 hours.

Spicy Meatball Pizza

Small minced (ground) beef meatballs, spiced with chillies and cumin seeds, are baked on a scone (biscuit) base.

NUTRITIONAL INFORMATION

Calories 568   Sugars 5g
Protein . . . . .24g   Fat 37g
Carbohydrate . . .38g   Saturates 15g

 2¼ HOURS   25 MINS

SERVES 4

INGREDIENTS

225 g/8 oz minced (ground) lean beef

25 g/1 oz jalapeño chillies in brine, chopped

1 tsp cumin seeds

1 tbsp chopped fresh parsley

1 tbsp beaten egg

3 tbsp olive oil

Basic Pizza Dough (see page 861)

Basic Tomato Sauce (see page 6)

25 g/1 oz canned pimiento, sliced

2 rashers streaky bacon, cut into strips

60 g/2 oz mature (sharp) Cheddar, grated

olive oil, for drizzling

salt and pepper

chopped fresh parsley, to garnish

1 Mix the beef, chillies, cumin seeds, parsley and egg together in a bowl and season. Form into 12 small meatballs. Cover and chill for 1 hour.

2 Heat the oil in a large frying pan (skillet). Add the meatballs and brown all over. Remove with a perforated spoon or fish slice and drain on paper towels.

3 Roll out or press the dough into a 25 cm/ 10 inch circle on a lightly floured work surface. Place on a greased baking tray (cookie sheet) or pizza pan and push up the edge slightly to form a rim. Spread with the tomato sauce, almost to the edge.

4 Arrange the meatballs on the pizza with the pimiento and bacon. Sprinkle over the cheese and drizzle with a little olive oil. Season with salt and pepper.

5 Bake in a preheated oven, at 200°C/ 400°F/Gas Mark 6, for 18–20 minutes, or until the edge is crisp and a golden brown colour.

6 Serve immediately, garnished with chopped parsley.

Deep-fried Pork Fritters

Small pieces of pork are coated in a light batter and deep-fried in this recipe – they are delicious dipped in a soy and honey sauce.

NUTRITIONAL INFORMATION

Calories 528	Sugars 12g
Protein 32g	Fat 22g
Carbohydrate ...52g	Saturates 6g

10 MINS   15 MINS

SERVES 4

INGREDIENTS

450 g/1 lb pork fillet (tenderloin)

2 tbsp peanut oil

200 g/7 oz/1¾ cups plain (all-purpose) flour

2 tsp baking powder

1 egg, beaten

225 ml/8 fl oz/1 cup milk

pinch of chilli powder

vegetable oil, for deep-frying

SAUCE

2 tbsp dark soy sauce

3 tbsp clear honey

1 tbsp wine vinegar

1 tbsp chopped chives

1 tbsp tomato purée (paste)

chives, to garnish

1 Using a sharp knife, cut the pork into 2.5-cm/1-inch cubes.

2 Heat the peanut oil in a preheated wok. Add the pork to the wok and stir-fry for 2-3 minutes, until sealed.

3 Remove the pork with a slotted spoon and set aside until required.

4 Sift the flour and baking powder into a mixing bowl and make a well in the centre. Gradually beat in the egg, milk and chilli powder to make a thick batter.

5 Heat the oil for deep-frying in a wok until almost smoking, then reduce the heat slightly.

6 Toss the pork pieces in the batter to coat thoroughly. Add the pork to the wok and deep-fry until golden brown and cooked through. Remove with a slotted spoon and drain well on absorbent kitchen paper (paper towels).

7 Meanwhile, mix together the soy sauce, honey, wine vinegar, chives and tomato purée (paste) and spoon into a small serving bowl.

8 Transfer the pork fritters to serving dishes, garnish with chives and serve with the sauce.

Tagliarini with Gorgonzola

This simple, creamy pasta sauce is a classic Italian recipe. You could use Danish blue cheese instead of the Gorgonzola, if you prefer.

NUTRITIONAL INFORMATION

Calories ....904 Sugars 4g
Protein ....27g Fat 53g
Carbohydrate ...83g Saturates 36g

 5 MINS   20 MINS

SERVES 4

I N G R E D I E N T S

25 g/1 oz/2 tbsp butter

225 g/8 oz Gorgonzola cheese, roughly crumbled

150 ml/¼ pint/⅝ cup double (heavy) cream

30 ml/2 tbsp dry white wine

1 tsp cornflour (cornstarch)

4 fresh sage sprigs, finely chopped

400 g/14 oz dried tagliarini

2 tbsp olive oil

salt and white pepper

1 Melt the butter in a heavy-based pan. Stir in 175 g/6 oz of the cheese and melt, over a low heat, for about 2 minutes.

2 Add the cream, wine and cornflour (cornstarch) and beat with a whisk until fully incorporated.

COOK'S TIP

Gorgonzola is one of the world's oldest veined cheeses and, arguably, its finest. When buying, always check that it is creamy yellow with delicate green veining. Avoid hard or discoloured cheese. It should have a rich, piquant aroma, not a bitter smell.

3 Stir in the sage and season to taste with salt and white pepper. Bring to the boil over a low heat, whisking constantly, until the sauce thickens. Remove from the heat and set aside while you cook the pasta.

4 Bring a large saucepan of lightly salted water to the boil. Add the tagliarini and 1 tbsp of the olive oil. Cook the pasta for 8–10 minutes or until just tender, drain thoroughly and toss in the remaining olive oil. Transfer the pasta to a serving dish and keep warm.

5 Reheat the sauce over a low heat, whisking constantly. Spoon the Gorgonzola sauce over the tagliarini, generously sprinkle over the remaining cheese and serve immediately.

White Nut Filo Parcels

These crisp, buttery parcels, filled with nuts and pesto, would make an interesting break with tradition for Sunday lunch.

NUTRITIONAL INFORMATION

Calories 1100   Sugars 9g
Protein . . . . .29g   Fat 80g
Carbohydrate . . .73g   Saturates 15g

 15 MINS   25 MINS

SERVES 4

INGREDIENTS

40 g/1½ oz/3 tbsp butter or margarine

1 large onion, finely chopped

275 g/9½ oz/2¼ cups mixed white nuts,
    such as pine nuts, unsalted cashew nuts,
    blanched almonds, unsalted peanuts,
    finely chopped

90 g/3 oz/1½ cups fresh white
    breadcrumbs

½ tsp ground mace

1 egg, beaten

1 egg yolk

3 tbsp pesto sauce

2 tbsp chopped basil

125 g/4½ oz/½ cup butter or
    margarine, melted

16 sheets filo pastry

salt and pepper

basil sprigs to garnish

TO SERVE

cranberry sauce

steamed vegetables

1 Melt the butter or margarine in a frying pan (skillet) and gently fry the onion for 2–3 minutes, until just softened but not browned.

2 Remove from the heat and stir in the nuts, two-thirds of the breadcrumbs, the mace and beaten egg. Season to taste with salt and pepper. Set aside.

3 Place the remaining breadcrumbs in a bowl and stir in the egg yolk, pesto sauce, basil, and 1 tablespoon of the melted butter or margarine. Mix well.

4 Brush 1 sheet of filo with melted butter or margarine. Fold in half and brush again. Repeat with a second sheet and lay it on top of the first one so that it forms a cross.

5 Put one-eighth of the nut mixture in the centre of the pastry. Top with one-eighth of the pesto mixture. Fold over the edges, brushing with more butter or margarine, to form a parcel. Brush the top with butter or margarine and transfer to a baking tray (cookie sheet). Make eight parcels in the same way and brush with the remaining butter or margarine..

6 Bake in a preheated oven at 220°C/ 425°F/Gas Mark 7 for 15–20 minutes, until golden. Transfer to serving plates, garnish with basil sprigs and serve with cranberry sauce and steamed vegetables.

Three-Cheese Fondue

A hot cheese dip made from three different cheeses can be prepared easily and with guaranteed success in the microwave oven.

NUTRITIONAL INFORMATION

Calories 565   Sugars 1g
Protein . . . . .29g   Fat 38g
Carbohydrate . . .15g   Saturates 24g

 15 MINS   10 MINS

SERVES 4

INGREDIENTS

1 garlic clove

300 ml/½ pint/1¼ cups dry white wine

250 g/8 oz/2 cups grated mild
    Cheddar cheese

125 g/4½ oz/1 cup grated Gruyère
    (Swiss) cheese

125 g/4½ oz/1 cup grated mozzarella
    cheese

2 tbsp cornflour (cornstarch)

pepper

TO SERVE

French bread

vegetables, such as courgettes
    (zucchini), mushrooms, baby corn cobs
    and cauliflower

COOK'S TIP

Make sure you add the
cheese to the wine gradually,
mixing well in between each
addition, otherwise the mixture
might curdle.

1 Bruise the garlic by placing the flat side of a knife on top and pressing down with the heel of your hand.

2 Rub the garlic around the inside of a large bowl. Discard the garlic.

3 Pour the wine into the bowl and heat, uncovered, on HIGH power for 3–4 minutes, until hot but not boiling.

4 Gradually add the Cheddar and Gruyère (Swiss) cheeses, stirring well after each addition, then add the mozzarella. Stir until completely melted.

5 Mix the cornflour (cornstarch) with a little water to a smooth paste and stir into the cheese mixture. Season to taste with pepper.

6 Cover and cook on MEDIUM power for 6 minutes, stirring twice during cooking, until the sauce is smooth.

7 Cut the French bread into cubes and the vegetables into batons, slices or florets. To serve, keep the fondue warm over a spirit lamp or reheat as necessary in the microwave oven. Dip in cubes of French bread and batons, slices or florets of vegetables.

Falafel

These are a very tasty, well-known Middle Eastern dish of small chickpea (garbanzo bean) based balls, spiced and deep-fried.

NUTRITIONAL INFORMATION

Calories	.491	Sugars	.3g
Protein	.15g	Fat	.30g
Carbohydrate	...43g	Saturates	.3g

25 MINS   10–15 MINS

SERVES 4

I N G R E D I E N T S

675 g/1½ lb/6 cups canned chickpeas
    (garbanzo beans), drained

1 red onion, chopped

3 garlic cloves, crushed

100 g/3½ oz wholemeal (whole
    wheat) bread

2 small fresh red chillies

1 tsp ground cumin

1 tsp ground coriander

½ tsp turmeric

1 tbsp chopped coriander (cilantro), plus
    extra to garnish

1 egg, beaten

100 g/3½ oz/1 cup wholemeal (whole
    wheat) breadcrumbs

vegetable oil, for
    deep-frying

salt and pepper

tomato and cucumber salad
    and lemon wedges, to serve

1 Put the chickpeas (garbanzo beans), onion, garlic, bread, chillies, spices and coriander (cilantro) in a food processor and process for 30 seconds. Stir and season to taste with salt and pepper.

2 Remove the mixture from the food processor and shape into walnut-sized balls.

3 Place the beaten egg in a shallow bowl and place the wholemeal (whole wheat) breadcrumbs on a plate. Dip the balls first into the egg to coat and then roll them in the breadcrumbs, shaking off any excess.

4 Heat the oil for deep-frying to 180°C/350°F or until a cube of bread browns in 30 seconds. Fry the falafel, in batches if necessary, for 2–3 minutes, until crisp and browned. Remove from the oil with a slotted spoon and dry on absorbent kitchen paper (paper towels). Garnish with coriander (cilantro) and serve with a tomato and cucumber salad and lemon wedges.

Potatoes Lyonnaise

In this classic French recipe, sliced potatoes are cooked with onions to make a delicious accompaniment to a main meal.

NUTRITIONAL INFORMATION

Calories 277	Sugars 4g	
Protein 5g	Fat 12g	
Carbohydrate . . .40g	Saturates 4g	

 10 MINS 25 MINS

SERVES 6

INGREDIENTS

1.25 kg/2 lb 12 oz potatoes

4 tbsp olive oil

25 g/1 oz/2 tbsp butter

2 onions, sliced

2–3 garlic cloves, crushed (optional)

salt and pepper

chopped parsley, to garnish

1 Slice the potatoes into 5 mm/¼ inch slices. Put in a large saucepan of lightly salted water and bring to the boil. Cover and simmer gently for about 10–12 minutes, until just tender. Avoid boiling too rapidly or the potatoes will break up and lose their shape. When cooked, drain well.

COOK'S TIP

If the potatoes blacken slightly as they are boiling, add a spoonful of lemon juice to the cooking water.

2 While the potatoes are cooking, heat the oil and butter in a very large frying pan (skillet). Add the onions and garlic, if using, and fry over a medium heat, stirring frequently, until the onions are softened.

3 Add the cooked potato slices to the frying pan (skillet) and cook with the onions, carefully stirring occasionally, for about 5–8 minutes until the potatoes are well browned.

4 Season to taste with salt and pepper. Sprinkle over the chopped parsley to serve. If wished, transfer the potatoes and onions to a large ovenproof dish and keep warm in a low oven until ready to serve.

Spicy Chicken Tortillas

The chicken filling for these easy-to-prepare tortillas has a mild, mellow spicy heat and a fresh salad makes a perfect accompaniment.

NUTRITIONAL INFORMATION

Calories . . . . .650 Sugars 15g
Protein . . . . .48g Fat 31g
Carbohydrate . . .47g Saturates 10g

10 MINS   35 MINS

SERVES 4

I N G R E D I E N T S

2 tbsp oil

8 skinless, boneless chicken thighs, sliced

1 onion, chopped

2 garlic cloves, chopped

1 tsp cumin seeds, roughly crushed

2 large dried chillies, sliced

400 g/14 oz can tomatoes

400 g/14 oz can red kidney beans, drained

150 ml/¼ pint/⅔ cup chicken stock

2 tsp sugar

salt and pepper

lime wedges, to garnish

TO SERVE

1 large ripe avocado

1 lime

8 soft tortillas

225 ml/8 fl oz/1 cup thick yogurt

1 Heat the oil in a large frying pan or wok, add the chicken and fry for 3 minutes.

2 Add the chopped onion and fry for 5 minutes, stirring until browned.

3 Add the chopped garlic, cumin and chillies, with their seeds, and cook for about 1 minute.

4 Add the tomatoes, kidney beans, stock, sugar and salt and pepper. Bring to the boil, breaking up the tomatoes. Cover and simmer for 15 minutes. Remove the lid and cook for 5 minutes, stirring occasionally until the sauce has thickened.

5 Halve the avocado, discard the stone and scoop out the flesh onto a plate. Mash the avocado with a fork.

6 Cut half of the lime into 8 thin wedges. Now squeeze the juice from the remaining lime over the mashed avocado.

7 Warm the tortillas according to the directions on the pack. Put two tortillas on each serving plate, fill with the chicken mixture and top with spoonfuls of avocado and yogurt. Garnish the tortillas with lime wedges.

Curry Pasties

These pasties, which are suitable for vegans, are a delicious combination of vegetables and spices. They can be eaten either hot or cold.

NUTRITIONAL INFORMATION

Calories . . . . . . .455 Sugars 5g
Protein . . . . .8g Fat 27g
Carbohydrate . . .48g Saturates 5g

1 HOUR   1 HOUR

SERVES 4

INGREDIENTS

225 g/8 oz/2 cups plain (all-purpose)
  wholemeal (whole wheat) flour

100 g/3½ oz/ ⅓ cup margarine,
  cut into small pieces

4 tbsp water

2 tbsp oil

225 g/8 oz diced root vegetables, such as
  potatoes, carrots and parsnips

1 small onion, chopped

2 garlic cloves, finely chopped

½ tsp curry powder

½ tsp ground turmeric

½ tsp ground cumin

½ tsp wholegrain mustard

5 tbsp vegetable stock

soya milk, to glaze

1 Place the flour in a mixing bowl and rub in the margarine with your fingertips until the mixture resembles breadcrumbs. Stir in the water and bring together to form a soft dough. Wrap and set aside to chill in the refrigerator for 30 minutes.

2 To make the filling, heat the oil in a large saucepan. Add the diced root vegetables, chopped onion and garlic and fry, stirring occasionally, for 2 minutes. Stir in all of the spices, turning the vegetables to coat them thoroughly. Fry the vegetables, stirring constantly, for a further 1 minute.

3 Add the stock to the pan and bring to the boil. Cover and simmer, stirring occasionally, for about 20 minutes, until the vegetables are tender and the liquid has been absorbed. Leave to cool.

4 Divide the pastry (pie dough) into 4 portions. Roll each portion into a 15 cm/6 inch round. Place the filling on one half of each round.

5 Brush the edges of each round with soya milk, then fold over and press the edges together to seal. Place on a baking tray (cookie sheet). Bake in a preheated oven, 200°C/ 400°F/Gas Mark 6, for 25–30 minutes until golden brown.

Chilli Tofu (Bean Curd)

A tasty Mexican-style dish with a melt-in-the-mouth combination of tofu (bean curd) and avocado served with a tangy tomato sauce.

NUTRITIONAL INFORMATION

Calories	806	Sugars	........20g
Protein	........37g	Fat	..........54g
Carbohydrate	...45g	Saturates	......19g

 30 MINS   35 MINS

SERVES 4

I N G R E D I E N T S

½ tsp chilli powder

1 tsp paprika

2 tbsp plain (all-purpose) flour

225 g/8 oz tofu (bean curd),
    cut into 1 cm/½ inch pieces

2 tbsp vegetable oil

1 onion, finely chopped

1 garlic clove, crushed

1 large red (bell) pepper, seeded and
    finely chopped

1 large ripe avocado

1 tbsp lime juice

4 tomatoes, peeled, seeded and chopped

125 g/4½ oz/1 cup grated Cheddar cheese

8 soft flour tortillas

150 ml/¼ pint/⅔ cup soured cream

salt and pepper

coriander (cilantro) sprigs
    to garnish

pickled green jalapeño chillies, to serve

S A U C E

850 ml/1½ pints/3¾ cups sugocasa

3 tbsp chopped parsley

3 tbsp chopped coriander (cilantro)

1 Mix the chilli powder, paprika, flour and salt and pepper on a plate and coat the tofu (bean curd) pieces.

2 Heat the oil in a frying pan (skillet) and gently fry the tofu (bean curd) for 3–4 minutes, until golden. Remove with a slotted spoon, drain on kitchen paper (paper towels) and set aside.

3 Add the onion, garlic and (bell) pepper to the oil and fry for 2–3 minutes, until just softened. Drain and set aside.

4 Halve the avocado, peel and remove the stone (pit). Slice lengthways, put in a bowl with the lime juice and toss to coat.

5 Add the tofu (bean curd) and onion mixture and gently stir in the tomatoes and half the cheese. Spoon one-eighth of the filling down the centre of each tortilla, top with soured cream and roll up. Arrange the tortillas in a shallow ovenproof dish in a single layer.

6 To make the sauce, mix together all the ingredients. Spoon the sauce over the tortillas, sprinkle with the remaining grated cheese and bake in a preheated oven, 190°C/375°F/Gas Mark 5, for 25 minutes, until golden and bubbling. Garnish with coriander (cilantro) sprigs and serve immediately with pickled jalapeño chillies.

Calabrian Pizza

Traditionally, this pizza has a double layer of dough to make it robust and filling. Alternatively, it can be made as a single pizza (as shown here).

NUTRITIONAL INFORMATION

Calories . . . . . . .574 Sugars 6g
Protein . . . . .20g Fat 30g
Carbohydrate . . .60g Saturates 7g

 2½ HOURS   55 MINS

SERVES 6

I N G R E D I E N T S

400 g/14 oz/3½ cups plain (all-purpose) flour

½ tsp salt

1 sachet easy-blend yeast

2 tbsp olive oil

about 275 ml/9 fl oz/generous 1 cup warm water

F I L L I N G

2 tbsp olive oil

2 garlic cloves, crushed

1 red (bell) pepper, cored, deseeded and sliced

1 yellow (bell) pepper, cored, deseeded and sliced

125 g/4½ oz Ricotta

175 g/6 oz jar sun-dried tomatoes, drained

3 hard-boiled (hard-cooked) eggs, sliced thinly

1 tbsp chopped fresh mixed herbs

125 g/4½ oz salami, cut into strips

150–175 g/5½–6 oz Mozzarella, grated

a little milk, to glaze

salt and pepper

1 Sift the flour and salt into a bowl and mix in the easy-blend yeast.

2 Add the olive oil and enough warm water to mix to a smooth, pliable dough. Knead for 10–15 minutes by hand, or process for 5 minutes in a mixer.

3 Shape the dough into a ball, place in a lightly oiled polythene bag and put in a warm place for 1–1½ hours or until doubled in size.

4 To make the filling, heat the oil in a frying pan (skillet) and fry the garlic and (bell) peppers slowly in the oil until softened.

5 Knock back the dough and roll out half to fit the base of a 30 x 25 cm/ 12 x 10 inch oiled roasting tin (pan).

6 Season the dough and spread with the Ricotta, then cover with sun-dried tomatoes, hard-boiled (hard-cooked) eggs, herbs and the (bell) pepper mixture. Arrange the salami strips on top and sprinkle with the grated cheese.

7 Roll out the remaining dough and place over the filling, sealing the edges well, or use to make a second pizza. Leave to rise for 1 hour in a warm place. An uncovered pizza will only take about 30–40 minutes to rise.

8 Prick the double pizza with a fork about 20 times, brush the top with milk and cook in a preheated oven, at 180°C/350°F/Gas Mark 4, for about 50 minutes or until lightly browned. The uncovered pizza will take only 35–40 minutes. Serve hot.

Muffin Pizzas

Toasted muffins are topped with pineapple and Parma ham (prosciutto). Plain, wholemeal or cheese muffins will all make great pizza bases.

NUTRITIONAL INFORMATION

Calories 259   Sugars 7g
Protein ....9g   Fat 15g
Carbohydrate ...24g   Saturates 3g

  45 MINS   5 MINS

SERVES 4

INGREDIENTS

4 muffins

1 quantity Basic Tomato Sauce (see page 6)

2 sun-dried tomatoes in oil, chopped

60 g/2 oz Parma ham (prosciutto)

2 rings canned pineapple, chopped

½ green (bell) pepper, chopped

125 g/4½ oz Mozzarella cheese, sliced thinly

olive oil, for drizzling

salt and pepper

fresh basil leaves, to garnish

1 Cut the muffins in half and toast the cut side lightly.

2 Spread the tomato sauce evenly over the muffins.

3 Sprinkle the sun-dried tomatoes on top of the tomato sauce.

4 Cut the ham into thin strips and place on the muffins with the pineapple and green (bell) pepper.

5 Carefully arrange the Mozzarella slices on top.

6 Drizzle a little olive oil over each pizza, and season.

7 Place under a preheated medium grill (broiler) and cook until the cheese melts and bubbles.

8 Serve immediately garnished with small basil leaves.

COOK'S TIP

You don't have to use plain muffins for your base; wholemeal or cheese muffins will also make ideal pizza bases. Muffins freeze well, so always keep some in the freezer for an instant pizza.

(Bell) Peppers & Red Onion

The vibrant colours of the (bell) peppers and onion make this a delightful pizza. Served cut into fingers, it is ideal for a party or buffet.

NUTRITIONAL INFORMATION

Calories ......380 Sugars 19g
Protein ....7g Fat 17g
Carbohydrate ...53g Saturates 2g

2½ HOURS   25 MINS

SERVES 8

I N G R E D I E N T S

Basic Pizza Dough (see page 861)

2 tbsp olive oil

½ each red, green and yellow (bell) pepper, sliced thinly

1 small red onion, sliced thinly

1 garlic clove, crushed

Basic Tomato Sauce (see page 6)

3 tbsp raisins

25 g/1 oz pine kernels (nuts)

1 tbsp chopped fresh thyme

olive oil, for drizzling

salt and pepper

1 Roll out or press the dough, using a rolling pin or your hands, on a lightly floured work surface to fit a 30 x 18 cm/12 x 7 inch greased Swiss roll tin (pan). Place in the tin (pan) and push up the edges slightly.

2 Cover and leave the dough to rise slightly in a warm place for about 10 minutes.

3 Heat the oil in a large frying pan (skillet). Add the (bell) peppers, onion and garlic, and fry gently for 5 minutes until they have softened but not browned. Leave to cool.

4 Spread the tomato sauce over the base of the pizza almost to the edge.

5 Sprinkle over the raisins and top with the cooled (bell) pepper mixture. Add the pine kernels (nuts) and thyme. Drizzle with a little olive oil and season well.

6 Bake in a preheated oven, at 200°C/ 400°F/Gas Mark 6, for 18–20 minutes, or until the edges are crisp and golden. Cut into fingers and serve immediately.

Gnocchi with Herb Sauce

These little potato dumplings are a traditional Italian appetizer but, served with a salad and bread, they make a substantial main course.

NUTRITIONAL INFORMATION

Calories	.619	Sugars	.3g
Protein	.11g	Fat	.30g
Carbohydrate	.81g	Saturates	.9g

30 MINS   30 MINS

SERVES 6

INGREDIENTS

1 kg/2 lb 4 oz old potatoes, cut into

   1 cm/½ inch pieces

60 g/2 oz/¼ cup butter or margarine

1 egg, beaten

300 g/10½ oz/2½ cups plain

   (all-purpose) flour

salt

SAUCE

125 ml/4 fl oz/½ cup olive oil

2 garlic cloves, very finely chopped

1 tbsp chopped fresh oregano

1 tbsp chopped fresh basil

salt and pepper

TO SERVE

freshly grated Parmesan (optional)

mixed salad (greens)

warm ciabatta

1 Cook the potatoes in a saucepan of boiling salted water for about 10 minutes or until tender. Drain well.

2 Press the hot potatoes through a sieve (strainer) into a large bowl. Add 1 teaspoon of salt, the butter or margarine, egg and 150 g/5½ oz/1¼ cups of the flour. Mix well to bind together.

3 Turn on to a lightly floured surface and knead, gradually adding the remaining flour, until a smooth, soft, slightly sticky dough is formed.

4 Flour the hands and roll the dough into 2 cm/¾ inch thick rolls. Cut into 1 cm/½ inch pieces. Press the top of each piece with the floured prongs of a fork and spread out on a floured tea towel (dish cloth).

5 Bring a large saucepan of salted water to a simmer. Add the gnocchi and cook in batches for 2–3 minutes or until they rise to the surface.

6 Remove the gnocchi with a perforated spoon and put in a warmed, greased serving dish. Cover and keep warm.

7 To make the sauce, put the oil, garlic and seasoning in a pan and cook, stirring, for 3–4 minutes until the garlic is golden. Remove from the heat and stir in the herbs. Pour over the gnocchi and serve, sprinkled with Parmesan, and accompanied by salad and warm ciabatta.

Avocado & Ham Pizza

A smoked ham and avocado salad is served on a pizza with a base enriched with chopped sun-dried tomatoes and black olives.

NUTRITIONAL INFORMATION

Calories	397	Sugars	.........9g
Protein	........10g	Fat	..........22g
Carbohydrate	...43g	Saturates	.......5g

2³/₄ HOURS   20 MINS

SERVES 4

INGREDIENTS

Basic Pizza Dough Base (see page 861)

4 sun-dried tomatoes, chopped

25 g/1 oz black olives, chopped

Basic Tomato Sauce (see page 6)

4 small chicory (endive) leaves, shredded

4 small radicchio leaves, shredded

1 avocado, peeled, pitted and sliced

60 g/2 oz wafer-thin smoked ham

60 g/2 oz blue cheese, cut into small pieces

olive oil, for drizzling

salt and pepper

chopped fresh chervil, to garnish

1 Make the dough according to the instructions on page 861. Knead the dough gently with the sun-dried tomatoes and olives until well mixed.

2 Roll out or press the dough, using a rolling pin or your hands, into a 25 cm/10 inch circle on a lightly floured work surface. Place on a greased baking tray (cookie sheet) or pizza pan (tin) and push up the edge a little to form a rim.

3 Cover the dough and leave to rise slightly in a warm place for 10 minutes. Spread the tomato sauce almost to the edge of the pizza base.

4 Top the pizza with shredded lettuce leaves and avocado slices. Scrunch up the ham and add together with the blue cheese.

5 Drizzle with a little olive oil and season with salt and pepper to taste.

6 Bake in a preheated oven, at 200°C/400°F/Gas Mark 6, for 18–20 minutes, or until the edge is crisp and a golden brown colour.

7 Sprinkle with chervil to garnish and serve immediately.

Chicken & Peanut Pizza

This pizza is topped with chicken which has been marinated in a delicious peanut sauce.

NUTRITIONAL INFORMATION

Calories . . . . .418 Sugars 7g
Protein . . . . .22g Fat 19g
Carbohydrate . . .43g Saturates 5g

2³/₄ HOURS   20 MINS

SERVES 4

INGREDIENTS

2 tbsp crunchy peanut butter

1 tbsp lime juice

1 tbsp soy sauce

3 tbsp milk

1 red chilli, deseeded and chopped

1 garlic clove, crushed

175 g/6 oz cooked chicken, diced

1 quantity Basic Pizza Dough (see
     page 861)

1 quantity Basic Tomato Sauce (see
     page 6)

4 spring onions (scallions), trimmed and
     chopped

60 g/2 oz Mozzarella cheese, grated

olive oil, for drizzling

salt and pepper

1 Mix together the peanut butter, lime juice, soy sauce, milk, chilli and garlic in a bowl to form a sauce. Season well.

2 Add the chicken to the peanut sauce and stir until well coated. Cover and leave to marinate in a cool place for about 20 minutes.

3 Roll out or press the dough, using a rolling pin or your hands, into a 25 cm/

10 inch circle on a lightly floured work surface. Place on a large greased baking tray (cookie sheet) or pizza pan (tin) and push up the edge a little. Cover and leave to rise slightly for 10 minutes in a warm place.

4 When the dough has risen, spread the tomato sauce over the base, almost to the edge.

5 Top with the spring onions (scallions) and chicken pieces, spooning over the peanut sauce.

6 Sprinkle over the cheese. Drizzle with a little olive oil and season well. Bake in a preheated oven, at 200°C/400°F/Gas Mark 6, for 18–20 minutes, or until the crust is golden. Serve.

Spicy Tomato Tagliatelle

A deliciously fresh and slightly spicy tomato sauce which is excellent for lunch or a light supper.

NUTRITIONAL INFORMATION

Calories	306	Sugars	.........7g
Protein	.........8g	Fat	..........12g
Carbohydrate	...45g	Saturates	.......7g

15 MINS   35 MINS

SERVES 4

INGREDIENTS

50 g/1¾ oz/3 tbsp butter

1 onion, finely chopped

1 garlic clove, crushed

2 small red chillies,
    deseeded and diced

450 g/1 lb fresh tomatoes, skinned,
    deseeded and diced

200 ml/7 fl oz/¾ cup vegetable stock

2 tbsp tomato purée (paste)

1 tsp sugar

salt and pepper

675 g/1½ lb fresh green and white
    tagliatelle, or 350 g/12 oz dried

VARIATION

Try topping your pasta dish with 50 g/1¾ oz pancetta or unsmoked bacon, diced and dry-fried for 5 minutes until crispy.

1 Melt the butter in a large saucepan. Add the onion and garlic and cook for 3–4 minutes or until softened.

2 Add the chillies to the pan and continue cooking for about 2 minutes.

3 Add the tomatoes and stock, reduce the heat and leave to simmer for 10 minutes, stirring.

4 Pour the sauce into a food processor and blend for 1 minute until smooth.

Alternatively, push the sauce through a sieve.

5 Return the sauce to the pan and add the tomato purée (paste) sugar, and salt and pepper to taste. Gently reheat over a low heat, until piping hot.

6 Cook the tagliatelle in a pan of boiling water for 8–10 minutes or until it is tender, but still has 'bite'. Drain the tagliatelle, transfer to serving plates and serve with the tomato sauce.

Four Seasons Pizza

This is a traditional pizza on which the toppings are divided into four sections, each of which is supposed to depict a season of the year.

NUTRITIONAL INFORMATION

Calories 313   Sugars 8g
Protein . . . . .8g   Fat 13g
Carbohydrate . . .44g   Saturates 3g

 2³/₄ HOURS   20 MINS

SERVES 4

INGREDIENTS

Basic Pizza Dough (see page 861)

Basic Tomato Sauce (see page 6)

25 g/1 oz chorizo sausage, sliced thinly

25 g/1 oz button mushrooms, wiped and
   sliced thinly

45 g/1½ oz artichoke hearts, sliced thinly

25 g/1 oz Mozzarella, sliced thinly

3 anchovies, halved lengthways

2 tsp capers

4 pitted black olives, sliced

4 fresh basil leaves, shredded

olive oil, for drizzling

salt and pepper

1 Roll out or press the dough, using a rolling pin or your hands, into a 25 cm/10 inch circle on a lightly floured surface. Place on a large greased baking tray (cookie sheet) or pizza pan and push up the edge a little.

2 Cover and leave to rise slightly for 10 minutes in a warm place. Spread the tomato sauce over the pizza base, almost to the edge.

3 Put the sliced chorizo on to one quarter of the pizza, the sliced mushrooms on another, the artichoke hearts on a third, and the Mozzarella and anchovies on the fourth.

4 Dot with the capers, olives and basil leaves. Drizzle with a little olive oil and season. Do not put any salt on the anchovy section as the fish are very salty.

5 Bake in a preheated oven, at 200°C/ 400°F/Gas Mark 6, for 18–20 minutes, or until the crust is golden and crisp. Serve immediately.

Spicy Mushrooms

A mixture of mushrooms, common in Western cooking, have been used in this recipe for a richly flavoured dish.

NUTRITIONAL INFORMATION

Calories 103	Sugars 4g
Protein 3g	Fat 8g
Carbohydrate 5g	Saturates 2g

 5 MINS   10 MINS

SERVES 4

INGREDIENTS

2 tbsp peanut oil

2 garlic cloves, crushed

3 spring onions (scallions), chopped

300 g/10½ oz button mushrooms

2 large open-cap mushrooms, sliced

125 g/4½ oz oyster mushrooms

1 tsp chilli sauce

1 tbsp dark soy sauce

1 tbsp hoisin sauce

1 tbsp wine vinegar

½ tsp ground Szechuan pepper

1 tbsp dark brown sugar

1 tsp sesame oil

chopped parsley, to garnish

1 Heat the peanut oil in a preheated wok or large frying pan (skillet) until almost smoking.

2 Reduce the heat slightly, add the garlic and spring onions (scallions) to the wok or frying pan (skillet) and stir-fry for 30 seconds.

3 Add all the mushrooms to the wok, together with the chilli sauce, dark soy sauce, hoisin sauce, wine vinegar, ground Szechuan pepper and dark brown sugar and stir-fry for 4–5 minutes, or until the mushrooms are cooked through. Stir constantly to prevent the mixture sticking to the base of the wok.

4 Sprinkle the sesame oil on top of the mixture in the wok. Transfer to a warm serving dish, garnish with parsley and serve immediately.

COOK'S TIP

If Chinese dried mushrooms are available, add a small quantity to this dish for texture. Wood (tree) ears are widely used and are available dried from Chinese food stores. They should be rinsed, soaked in warm water for 20 minutes and rinsed again before use.

Onion & Anchovy Pizza

This tasty onion pizza is topped with a lattice pattern of anchovies and black olives. Cut the pizza into squares to serve.

NUTRITIONAL INFORMATION

Calories	373	Sugars	.........5g
Protein	........12g	Fat	..........20g
Carbohydrate	...39g	Saturates	.......4g

 1³/₄ HOURS   30 MINS

MAKES 6

INGREDIENTS

4 tbsp olive oil

3 onions, sliced thinly

1 garlic clove, crushed

1 tsp soft brown sugar

½ tsp crushed fresh rosemary

200 g/7 oz can chopped tomatoes

Basic Pizza Dough (see page 861)

2 tbsp freshly grated Parmesan

50 g/1¾ oz can anchovies

12–14 black olives

salt and pepper

1 Heat 3 tablespoons of the oil in a large saucepan and add the onions, garlic, sugar and rosemary. Cover and fry gently, stirring occasionally, for 10 minutes or until the onions are soft but not brown.

2 Add the tomatoes to the pan, stir and season with salt and pepper to taste. Leave to cool slightly.

3 Roll out or press the dough, using a rolling pin or your hands, on a lightly floured work surface to fit a 30 x 18 cm/ 12 x 7 inch greased Swiss roll tin (pan). Place in the tin (pan) and push up the edges slightly to form a rim.

4 Brush the remaining oil over the dough and sprinkle with the cheese. Cover and leave to rise slightly in a warm place for about 10 minutes.

5 Spread the onion and tomato topping over the base. Drain the anchovies, reserving the oil. Split each anchovy in half lengthways and arrange on the pizza in a lattice pattern. Place the olives in between the anchovies and drizzle over a little of the reserved oil. Season to taste.

6 Bake in a preheated oven, at 200°C/ 400°F/Gas Mark 6, for 18–20 minutes, or until the edges are crisp and golden. Cut the pizza into 6 squares and serve immediately.

Cheese & Potato Layer Bake

This really is a great side dish, perfect for serving with main meals cooked in the oven.

NUTRITIONAL INFORMATION

Calories 295	Sugars 5g	
Protein 13g	Fat 17g	
Carbohydrate . . .24g	Saturates 11g	

20 MINS   1½ HOURS

SERVES 4

I N G R E D I E N T S

500 g/1 lb 2 oz potatoes

1 leek, sliced

3 garlic cloves, crushed

50 g/1¾ oz/½ cup grated Cheddar cheese

50 g/1¾ oz/½ cup grated
   mozzarella cheese

25 g/1 oz/⅓ cup grated Parmesan cheese

2 tbsp chopped parsley

150 ml/¼ pint/⅔ cup single (light) cream

150 ml/¼ pint/⅔ cup milk

salt and pepper

chopped flat leaf parsley, to garnish

1 Cook the potatoes in a saucepan of boiling salted water for 10 minutes. Drain well.

2 Cut the potatoes into thin slices. Arrange a layer of potatoes in the base of an ovenproof dish. Layer with a little of the leek, garlic, cheeses and parsley. Season to taste.

3 Repeat the layers until all of the ingredients have been used, finishing with a layer of cheese. Mix the cream and milk together, season with salt and pepper to taste and pour over the potato layers.

4 Cook in a preheated oven, 160°C/325°F/Gas Mark 3, for 1–1¼ hours, or until the cheese is golden brown and bubbling and the potatoes are cooked through and tender.

5 Garnish with chopped fresh flat leaf parsley and serve immediately.

COOK'S TIP

Potatoes make a very good basis for a vegetable accompaniment. They are a good source of complex carbohydrate and contain a number of vitamins. From the point of view of flavour, they combine well with a vast range of other ingredients.

Onion, Ham & Cheese Pizza

This pizza was a favourite of the Romans. It is slightly unusual because the topping is made without a tomato sauce base.

NUTRITIONAL INFORMATION

Calories 333   Sugars 8g
Protein . . . . .12g   Fat 14g
Carbohydrate . . .43g   Saturates 4g

🗄 1 HOUR   ⏱ 40 MINS

SERVES 4

I N G R E D I E N T S

1 portion of Basic Pizza Dough (see
    page 861)

T O P P I N G

2 tbsp olive oil

250 g/9 oz onions, sliced into rings

2 garlic cloves, crushed

1 red (bell) pepper, diced

100 g/3½ oz raw ham (prosciutto), cut into
    strips

100 g/3½ oz Mozzarella cheese, sliced

2 tbsp rosemary, stalks removed and
    roughly chopped

1 Place the yeast and sugar in a measuring jug and mix with 50 ml/2 fl oz/4 tablespoon of water. Put the mixture in a warm place for 15 minutes or until frothy.

2 Mix the flour with the salt and make a well in the centre. Add the oil, the yeast mixture and the remaining water. Using a wooden spoon, mix to form a smooth dough.

3 Turn the dough out on to a floured surface and knead for 4–5 minutes or until smooth. Return the dough to the bowl, cover with an oiled sheet of cling film (plastic wrap) and leave to rise for 30 minutes or until doubled in size.

4 Remove the dough from the bowl. Knead the dough for 2 minutes. Using a rolling pin, roll out the dough to form a square shape, then place it on an oiled baking tray (cookie sheet), pushing out the edges until even. The dough should be no more than 6 mm/¼ inch thick because it will rise during cooking.

5 To make the topping, heat the oil in a pan. Add the onions and garlic and cook for 3 minutes. Add the (bell) pepper and fry for 2 minutes.

6 Cover the pan and cook the vegetables over a low heat for 10 minutes, stirring occasionally, until the onions are slightly caramelized. Leave to cool slightly.

7 Spread the topping evenly over the pizza base. Arrange the ham (prosciutto), Mozzarella and rosemary over the top.

8 Bake in a preheated oven, at 200°C/ 400°F/Gas Mark 6, for 20–25 minutes. Serve hot.

Greek Green Beans

This dish contains many Greek flavours such as lemon, garlic, oregano and olives, for a really flavourful recipe.

NUTRITIONAL INFORMATION

Calories 115   Sugars 4g
Protein . . . . .6g   Fat 4g
Carbohydrate . . .15g   Saturates 0.6g

5 MINS   1 HOUR

SERVES 4

INGREDIENTS

400 g/14 oz can haricot (navy) beans, drained

1 tbsp olive oil

3 garlic cloves, crushed

425 ml/¾ pint/2 cups vegetable stock

1 bay leaf

2 sprigs oregano

1 tbsp tomato purée (paste)

juice of 1 lemon

1 small red onion, chopped

25 g/1 oz pitted black olives, halved

salt and pepper

1 Put the haricot (navy) beans in a flameproof casserole dish.

2 Add the olive oil and crushed garlic and cook over a gentle heat, stirring occasionally, for 4–5 minutes.

3 Add the stock, bay leaf, oregano, tomato purée (paste), lemon juice and red onion, cover and simmer for about 1 hour or until the sauce has thickened.

4 Stir in the olives, season with salt and pepper to taste and serve warm or cold.

VARIATION

You can substitute other canned beans for the haricot (navy) beans – try cannellini or black-eyed beans (peas), or chick-peas (garbanzo beans) instead. Drain and rinse them before use as canned beans often have sugar or salt added.

Stuffed Courgettes (Zucchini)

Hollow out some courgettes (zucchini), fill them with a spicy beef mixture and bake them in the oven for a delicious side dish.

NUTRITIONAL INFORMATION

Calories 208   Sugars 3g
Protein ....12g   Fat 9g
Carbohydrate ...20g   Saturates 4g

 45 MINS   35 MINS

SERVES 4

INGREDIENTS

8 medium courgettes (zucchini)

1 tbsp sesame or vegetable oil

1 garlic clove, crushed

2 shallots, chopped finely

1 small red chilli, deseeded and chopped finely

250 g/9 oz/1 cup lean minced (ground) beef

1 tbsp fish sauce or mushroom ketchup

1 tbsp chopped fresh coriander (cilantro) or basil

2 tsp cornflour (cornstarch), blended with a little cold water

90 g/3 oz/½ cup cooked long-grain rice

salt and pepper

TO GARNISH

sprigs of fresh coriander (cilantro) or basil

carrot slices

1 Slice the courgettes (zucchini) in half horizontally and scoop out a channel down the middle, discarding all the seeds. Sprinkle with salt and set aside for 15 minutes.

2 Heat the oil in a wok or frying pan (skillet) and add the garlic, shallots and chilli. Stir-fry for 2 minutes, until golden. Add the minced (ground) beef and stir-fry briskly for about 5 minutes. Stir in the fish sauce or mushroom ketchup, the chopped coriander (cilantro) or basil and the blended cornflour (cornstarch), and cook for 2 minutes, stirring until thickened. Season with salt and pepper, then remove from the heat.

3 Rinse the courgettes (zucchini) in cold water and arrange them in a greased shallow ovenproof dish, cut side uppermost. Mix the cooked rice into the minced (ground) beef, then use this mixture to stuff the courgettes (zucchini).

4 Cover with foil and bake in a preheated oven at 190°C/375°F/ Gas Mark 5 for 20–25 minutes, removing the foil for the last 5 minutes of cooking time.

5 Serve at once, garnished with sprigs of fresh coriander (cilantro) or basil, and carrot slices.

Cauliflower with Greens

This is a delicious way to cook cauliflower – even without the greens.

NUTRITIONAL INFORMATION

Calories	49	Sugars	........2g
Protein	.........2g	Fat	...........3g
Carbohydrate	....3g	Saturates	.....0.5g

 5 MINS   5 MINS

SERVES 4

INGREDIENTS

175 g/6 oz cauliflower, cut into
   florets

1 garlic clove

½ tsp turmeric

1 tbsp coriander (cilantro) root
   or stem

1 tbsp sunflower oil

2 spring onions (scallions), cut into
   2.5 cm/1 inch pieces

125 g/4½ oz oriental greens, such as
   bok choy or mustard greens,
   tough stalks removed

1 tsp yellow mustard seeds

1 Blanch the cauliflower, rinse in cold running water and drain. Set aside until required.

2 Grind together the garlic, turmeric and coriander (cilantro) root or stem together in a pestle and mortar or spice grinder.

3 Heat the sunflower oil in a wok or large, heavy frying pan (skillet).

4 Add the spring onions (scallions) to the wok or frying pan (skillet) and cook over a high heat for 2 minutes, stirring constantly.

5 Add the oriental greens and stir-fry for 1 minute. Keep warm and set aside until required.

6 Return the wok or frying pan (skillet) to the heat and add the mustard seeds. Stir until they start to pop, then add the turmeric and coriander (cilantro) mixture and the cauliflower, and stir until all the cauliflower is coated.

7 Serve the cauliflower with the greens on a warmed serving plate.

COOK'S TIP

Pestle and mortars are available in wood or stone. The stone mortar gives a finer grind than the wooden mortar. A coffee grinder can also be used, but will need a thorough clean afterwards, as some of the spices used in Chinese cooking can be quite pungent!

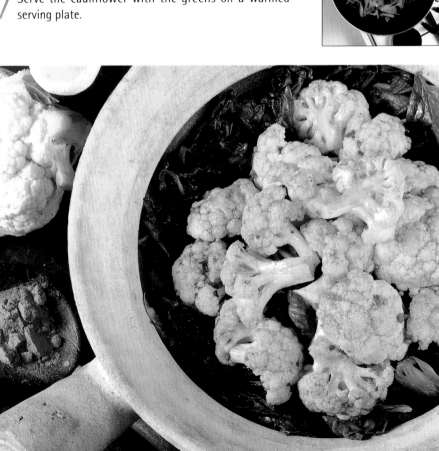

Roast Leeks

Use a good-quality French or Italian olive oil for this deliciously simple yet sophisticated vegetable accompaniment.

NUTRITIONAL INFORMATION

Calories 71   Sugars 2g
Protein . . . . .2g   Fat 6g
Carbohydrate . . . .3g   Saturates 1g

 5 MINS   7 MINS

SERVES 6

INGREDIENTS

4 leeks

3 tbsp olive oil

2 tsp balsamic vinegar

sea salt and pepper

1 Cut the leeks in half lengthways, making sure that you hold the knife straight, so that the leek is held together by the root. Brush each leek liberally with the olive oil.

2 Cook over a hot barbecue (grill) for 6–7 minutes, turning once.

3 Remove the leeks from the barbecue (grill) and brush lightly with the balsamic vinegar.

4 Season to taste with salt and pepper and serve hot or warm.

Lemon Chinese Leaves

These stir-fried Chinese leaves (cabbage) are served with a tangy sauce made of grated lemon rind, lemon juice and ginger.

NUTRITIONAL INFORMATION

Calories	120	Sugars	.........0g
Protein	.........5g	Fat	...........8g
Carbohydrate	....8g	Saturates	.......1g

🍲 5 MINS 🕐 10 MINS

SERVES 4

I N G R E D I E N T S

500 g/1 lb 2 oz Chinese leaves (cabbage)

3 tbsp vegetable oil

1 cm/½ inch piece ginger root, grated

1 tsp salt

1 tsp sugar

125 ml/4 fl oz/½ cup water or vegetable stock

1 tsp grated lemon rind

1 tbsp cornflour (cornstarch)

1 tbsp lemon juice

1 Separate the Chinese leaves (cabbage), wash and drain thoroughly. Pat dry with absorbent kitchen paper (paper towels).

2 Cut the Chinese leaves (cabbage) into 5 cm/2 inch wide slices.

COOK'S TIP

If Chinese leaves (cabbage) are unavailable, substitute slices of savoy cabbage. Cook for 1 extra minute to soften the leaves.

3 Heat the oil in a wok and add the grated ginger root followed by the Chinese leaves (cabbage), stir-fry for 2–3 minutes or until the leaves begin to wilt.

4 Add the salt and sugar, and mix well until the leaves soften. Remove the leaves with a slotted spoon and set aside.

5 Add the water or stock to the wok with the lemon rind. Bring to the boil.

6 Meanwhile, mix the cornflour (cornstarch) to a smooth paste with the lemon juice, then add to the wok. Simmer, stirring constantly, for about 1 minute to make a smooth sauce.

7 Return the cooked Chinese leaves (cabbage) to the pan and mix thoroughly to coat the leaves in the sauce. Arrange on a serving plate and serve immediately.

Spiced Potatoes & Spinach

This is a classic Indian accompaniment for many different curries or plainer main vegetable dishes. It is very quick to cook.

NUTRITIONAL INFORMATION

Calories ....176 Sugars 4g
Protein ....6g Fat 9g
Carbohydrate ...18g Saturates 1g

 10 MINS   20-25 MINS

SERVES 4

INGREDIENTS

3 tbsp vegetable oil

1 red onion, sliced

2 garlic cloves, crushed

½ tsp chilli powder

2 tsp ground coriander

1 tsp ground cumin

150 ml/¼ pint/⅔ cup vegetable stock

300 g/10½ oz potatoes, diced

500 g/1 lb 2 oz baby spinach

1 red chilli, sliced

salt and pepper

1 Heat the oil in a heavy-based frying pan (skillet). Add the onion and garlic and sauté over a medium heat, stirring occasionally, for 2–3 minutes.

2 Stir in the chilli powder, ground coriander and cumin and cook, stirring constantly, for a further 30 seconds.

3 Add the vegetable stock, diced potatoes and spinach and bring to the boil. Reduce the heat, cover the frying pan (skillet) and simmer for about 10 minutes, or until the potatoes are cooked through and tender.

4 Uncover, season to taste with salt and pepper, add the chilli and cook for a further 2–3 minutes. Transfer to a warmed serving dish and serve immediately.

COOK'S TIP

Besides adding extra colour to a dish, red onions have a sweeter, less pungent flavour than other varieties.

Fried Spiced Potatoes

Deliciously good and a super accompaniment to almost any main course dish, although rather high in calories!

NUTRITIONAL INFORMATION

Calories ....430 Sugars 7g
Protein ....4g Fat 35g
Carbohydrate ...26g Saturates 11g

  15 MINS 30 MINS

SERVES 6

INGREDIENTS

2 onions, quartered

5 cm/2 inch piece of root ginger,
   finely chopped

2 garlic cloves

2–3 tbsp mild or medium curry paste

4 tbsp water

750 g/1 lb 10 oz new potatoes

vegetable oil, for deep frying

3 tbsp vegetable ghee or oil

150 ml/¼ pint/⅔ cup strained Greek yogurt

150 ml/¼ pint/⅔ cup double (heavy) cream

3 tbsp chopped mint

salt and pepper

½ bunch spring onions (scallions), chopped,
   to garnish

1 Place the onions, ginger, garlic, curry paste and water in a blender or food processor and process until smooth, scraping down the sides of the machine and processing again, if necessary.

2 Cut the potatoes into quarters – the pieces need to be about 2.5 cm/1 inch in size – and pat dry with absorbent kitchen paper (paper towels). Heat the oil in a deep fryer to 180°C/350°F/Gas 4 or until a cube of bread browns in 30 seconds and fry the potatoes, in batches, for about 5 minutes or until golden brown, turning frequently. Remove from the pan and drain on kitchen paper (paper towels).

3 Heat the ghee or oil in a large frying pan (skillet), add the curry and onion mixture and fry gently, stirring constantly, for 2 minutes. Add the yogurt, cream and 2 tablespoons of mint and mix well.

4 Add the fried potatoes and stir until coated in the sauce. Cook, stirring frequently, for a further 5–7 minutes, or until heated through and sauce has thickened. Season with salt and pepper to taste and sprinkle with the remaining mint and sliced spring onions (scallions). Serve immediately.

COOK'S TIP

When buying new potatoes, look for the freshest you can find. The skin should be beginning to rub off. Cook them as soon after purchase as possible, but if you have to store them, keep them in a cool, dark well-ventilated place.

Gnocchi & Tomato Sauce

Freshly made potato gnocchi are delicious, especially when they are topped with a fragrant tomato sauce.

NUTRITIONAL INFORMATION

Calories 216	Sugars 5g
Protein 5g	Fat 6g
Carbohydrate . . .39g	Saturates 1g

 30 MINS   45 MINS

SERVES 4

I N G R E D I E N T S

350 g/12 oz floury (mealy) potatoes (those
   suitable for baking or mashing), halved

75 g/2¾ oz self-raising flour, plus extra for
   rolling out

2 tsp dried oregano

2 tbsp oil

1 large onion, chopped

2 garlic cloves, chopped

400 g/14 oz can chopped tomatoes

½ vegetable stock cube dissolved in
   100 ml/3½ fl oz/⅓ cup boiling water

2 tbsp basil, shredded, plus whole
leaves to garnish

salt and pepper

Parmesan cheese, grated, to serve

1 Bring a large saucepan of water to the boil. Add the potatoes and cook for 12–15 minutes or until tender. Drain and leave to cool.

2 Peel and then mash the potatoes with the salt and pepper, sifted flour and oregano. Mix together with your hands to form a dough.

3 Heat the oil in a pan. Add the onions and garlic and cook for 3–4 minutes.

Add the tomatoes and stock and cook, uncovered, for 10 minutes. Season with salt and pepper to taste.

4 Roll the potato dough into a sausage about 2.5 cm/1 inch in diameter. Cut the sausage into 2.5 cm/1 inch lengths. Flour your hands, then press a fork into each piece to create a series of ridges on one side and the indent of your index finger on the other.

5 Bring a large saucepan of water to the boil and cook the gnocchi, in batches, for 2–3 minutes. They should rise to the surface when cooked. Drain well and keep warm.

6 Stir the basil into the tomato sauce and pour over the gnocchi. Garnish with basil leaves and season with pepper to taste. Sprinkle with Parmesan and serve at once.

VARIATION

Try serving the gnocchi with pesto for a change.

Dry Moong Dhal

This dhal has a baghaar (seasoned oil dressing) of butter, dried red chillies and white cumin seeds. It is simple to cook and tastes very good.

NUTRITIONAL INFORMATION

Calories 304	Sugars 1g
Protein 9g	Fat 21g
Carbohydrate . . .21g	Saturates 14g

🥘 5 MINS   🕐 30–35 MINS

SERVES 4

INGREDIENTS

150 g/5½ oz/1 cup moong dhal

1 tsp finely chopped root ginger

½ tsp ground cumin

½ tsp ground coriander

1 tsp fresh garlic, crushed

½ tsp chilli powder

600 ml/1 pint/2½ cups water

1 tsp salt

BAGHAAR

100 g/3½ oz/8 tbsp unsalted (sweet) butter

5 dried red chillies

1 tsp white cumin seeds

TO SERVE

chapati

vegetable curry

COOK'S TIP

Moong dhal are tear-drop-shaped yellow split lentils, more popular in northern India than in the south. Dried red chillies are the quickest way to add heat to a dish.

1 Rinse the lentils under cold running water and place them in a large saucepan. Add the ginger, ground cumin, ground coriander, garlic and chilli powder, and stir to mix well.

2 Pour in enough of the water to cover the lentil mixture. Cook over a medium heat, stirring frequently, until the lentils are soft but not mushy.

3 Stir in the salt, transfer to a serving dish and keep warm.

4 Meanwhile, make the baghaar. Melt the butter in a heavy-based saucepan over a fairly low heat. Add the dried red chillies and white cumin seeds and fry, stirring constantly, until they begin to pop.

5 Pour the baghaar over the lentils and serve immediately with chapati and a vegetable curry.

Gingered Potatoes

This is a simple spicy dish which is ideal with a plain main course. The cashew nuts and celery add extra crunch.

NUTRITIONAL INFORMATION

Calories 325	Sugars 1g	
Protein 5g	Fat 21g	
Carbohydrate . . .30g	Saturates 9g	

🥔 20 MINS   🕐 30 MINS

SERVES 4

I N G R E D I E N T S

675 g/1½ lb waxy potatoes, cubed

2 tbsp vegetable oil

5 cm/2 inch piece of root ginger, grated

1 fresh green chilli, chopped

1 celery stick, chopped

25 g/1 oz/¼ cup cashew nuts

few strands of saffron

3 tbsp boiling water

60 g/2 oz/¼ cup butter

celery leaves, to garnish

1 Cook the potatoes in a saucepan of boiling water for 10 minutes, then drain thoroughly.

2 Heat the oil in a heavy-based frying pan (skillet) and add the potatoes. Cook over a medium heat, stirring constantly, for 3-4 minutes.

3 Add the grated ginger, chilli, celery and cashew nuts and cook for 1 minute.

4 Meanwhile, place the saffron strands in a small bowl. Add the boiling water and set aside to soak for 5 minutes.

5 Add the butter to the pan, lower the heat and stir in the saffron mixture. Cook over a low heat for 10 minutes, or until the potatoes are tender.

6 Transfer to a warm serving dish, garnish the gingered potatoes with the celery leaves and serve at once.

COOK'S TIP

Use a non-stick, heavy-based frying pan (skillet) as the potato mixture is fairly dry and may stick to an ordinary pan.

Green Bean Stir-fry

These beans are simply cooked in a spicy, hot sauce for a tasty and very easy recipe.

NUTRITIONAL INFORMATION

Calories 86	Sugars 4g
Protein 2g	Fat 6g
Carbohydrates 6g	Saturates 1g

 5 MINS   5 MINS

SERVES 4

I N G R E D I E N T S

450 g/1 lb thin green beans

2 fresh red chillies

2 tbsp peanut oil

½ tsp ground star anise

1 garlic clove, crushed

2 tbsp light soy sauce

2 tsp clear honey

½ tsp sesame oil

1 Using a sharp knife, cut the green beans in half.

2 Slice the fresh chillies, removing the seeds first if you prefer a milder dish.

3 Heat the oil in a preheated wok or large frying pan (skillet) until the oil is almost smoking.

4 Lower the heat slightly, add the halved green beans to the wok and stir-fry for 1 minute.

5 Add the sliced red chillies, star anise and garlic to the wok and stir-fry for a further 30 seconds.

6 Mix together the soy sauce, honey and sesame oil in a small bowl.

7 Stir the sauce mixture into the wok. Cook for 2 minutes, tossing the beans to ensure that they are thoroughly coated in the sauce.

8 Transfer the mixture in the wok or pan to a warm serving dish and serve immediately.

VARIATION

This recipe is surprisingly delicious made with Brussels sprouts instead of green beans. Trim the sprouts, then shred them finely. Stir-fry the sprouts in hot oil for 2 minutes, then proceed with the recipe from step 4.

Ginger & Orange Broccoli

Thinly sliced broccoli florets are lightly stir-fried and served in a ginger and orange sauce.

NUTRITIONAL INFORMATION

Calories	133	Sugars	.........6g
Protein	.........9g	Fat	...........7g
Carbohydrate	...10g	Saturates	.......1g

5 MINS   10 MINS

SERVES 4

INGREDIENTS

750 g/1 lb 10 oz broccoli

2 thin slices ginger root

2 garlic cloves

1 orange

2 tsp cornflour (cornstarch)

1 tbsp light soy sauce

½ tsp sugar

2 tbsp vegetable oil

1 Divide the broccoli into small florets. Peel the stems, using a vegetable peeler, and then cut the stems into thin slices, using a sharp knife.

2 Cut the ginger root into matchsticks and slice the garlic.

3 Peel 2 long strips of zest from the orange and cut into thin strips. Place the strips in a bowl, cover with cold water and set aside.

4 Squeeze the juice from the orange and mix with the cornflour (cornstarch), light soy sauce, sugar and 4 tablespoons water.

5 Heat the vegetable oil in a wok or large frying pan (skillet). Add the broccoli stem slices and stir-fry for 2 minutes.

6 Add the ginger root slices, garlic and broccoli florets, and stir-fry for a further 3 minutes.

7 Stir the orange sauce mixture into the wok and cook, stirring constantly, until the sauce has thickened and coated the broccoli.

8 Drain the reserved orange rind and stir into the wok before serving.

VARIATION

This dish could be made with cauliflower, if you prefer, or a mixture of cauliflower and broccoli.

Bombay Potatoes

Although virtually unknown in India, this dish is a very popular item on Indian restaurant menus in other parts of the world.

NUTRITIONAL INFORMATION

Calories 307   Sugars 9g
Protein . . . . .9g   Fat 9g
Carbohydrate . . .51g   Saturates 5g

 5 MINS   1 HR 10 MINS

SERVES 4

I N G R E D I E N T S

1 kg/2 lb 4 oz waxy potatoes

2 tbsp vegetable ghee

1 tsp panch poran spice mix

3 tsp ground turmeric

2 tbsp tomato purée (paste)

300 ml/½ pint/1¼ cups natural
    (unsweetened) yogurt

salt

chopped coriander (cilantro), to garnish

1 Put the whole potatoes into a large saucepan of salted cold water, bring to the boil, then simmer until the potatoes are just cooked, but not tender; the time depends on the size of the potato, but an average-sized one should take about 15 minutes.

COOK'S TIP

Panch poran spice mix can be bought from Asian or Indian grocery stores, or make your own from equal quantities of cumin seeds, fennel seeds, mustard seeds, nigella seeds and fenugreek seeds.

2 Heat the ghee in a saucepan over a medium heat and add the panch poran, turmeric, tomato purée (paste), yogurt and salt. Bring to the boil, and simmer, uncovered, for 5 minutes.

3 Drain the potatoes and cut each one into 4 pieces. Add the potatoes to the pan, cover and cook briefly. Transfer to an ovenproof casserole, cover and cook in a preheated oven, 180°C/350°F/Gas Mark 4, for about 40 minutes, or until the potatoes are tender and the sauce has thickened a little.

4 Sprinkle with chopped coriander (cilantro) and serve immediately.

Pizza Margherita

Pizza means 'pie' in Italian. The fresh bread dough is not difficult to make but it does take a little time.

NUTRITIONAL INFORMATION

Calories 456   Sugars 7g
Protein ....16g   Fat 13g
Carbohydrate ...74g   Saturates 5g

 1 HOUR   45 MINS

SERVES 4

I N G R E D I E N T S

BASIC PIZZA DOUGH

7 g/½ oz dried yeast

1 tsp sugar

250 ml/9 fl oz/1 cup hand-hot water

350 g/12 oz strong flour

1 tsp salt

1 tbsp olive oil

TOPPING

400 g/14 oz can tomatoes, chopped

2 garlic cloves, crushed

2 tsp dried basil

1 tbsp olive oil

2 tbsp tomato purée

100 g/3½ oz Mozzarella cheese, chopped

2 tbsp freshly grated Parmesan cheese

salt and pepper

1 Place the yeast and sugar in a measuring jug and mix with 50 ml/2 fl oz/4 tbsp of the water. Leave the yeast mixture in a warm place for 15 minutes or until frothy.

2 Mix the flour with the salt and make a well in the centre. Add the oil, the yeast mixture and the remaining water. Using a wooden spoon, mix to form a smooth dough.

3 Turn the dough out on to a floured surface and knead for 4–5 minutes or until smooth.

4 Return the dough to the bowl, cover with an oiled sheet of cling film (plastic wrap) and leave to rise for 30 minutes or until doubled in size.

5 Knead the dough for 2 minutes. Stretch the dough with your hands, then place it on an oiled baking tray (cookie sheet), pushing out the edges until even. The dough should be no more than 6 mm/¼ inch thick because it will rise during cooking.

6 To make the topping, place the tomatoes, garlic, dried basil, olive oil and salt and pepper to taste in a large frying pan (skillet) and leave to simmer for 20 minutes or until the sauce has thickened. Stir in the tomato purée and leave to cool slightly.

7 Spread the topping evenly over the pizza base. Top with the Mozzarella and Parmesan cheeses and bake in a preheated oven, at 200°C/400°F/Gas Mark 6, for 20–25 minutes. Serve hot.

Spicy Potatoes & Onions

Masala aloo are potatoes cooked in spices and onions. Semi-dry when cooked, they make an excellent accompaniment to almost any curry.

NUTRITIONAL INFORMATION

Calories . . . . .313 Sugars 5g
Protein . . . . .2g Fat 25g
Carbohydrate . . .21g Saturates 3g

 10–15 MINS   10 MINS

SERVES 4

INGREDIENTS

6 tbsp vegetable oil

2 medium-sized onions,
  finely chopped

1 tsp finely chopped
  root ginger

1 tsp crushed garlic

1 tsp chilli powder

1½ tsp ground cumin

1½ tsp ground coriander

1 tsp salt

400 g/14 oz can new potatoes

1 tbsp lemon juice

BAGHAAR

3 tbsp oil

3 dried red chillies

½ tsp onion seeds

½ tsp mustard seeds

½ tsp fenugreek seeds

TO GARNISH

fresh coriander (cilantro) leaves

1 green chilli, finely chopped

1 Heat the oil in a large, heavy-based saucepan. Add the onions and fry, stirring, until golden brown. Reduce the heat, add the ginger, garlic, chilli powder, ground cumin, ground coriander and salt and stir-fry for about 1 minute. Remove the pan from the heat and set aside until required.

2 Drain the water from the potatoes. Add the potatoes to the onion mixture and spice mixture and heat through. Sprinkle over the lemon juice and mix well.

3 To make the baghaar, heat the oil in a separate pan. Add the red chillies, onion seeds, mustard seeds and fenugreek seeds and fry until the seeds turn a shade darker. Remove the pan from the heat and pour the baghaar over the potatoes.

4 Garnish with coriander (cilantro) leaves and chillies, then serve.

Potatoes en Papillotes

New potatoes are perfect for this recipe. The potatoes and vegetables are wrapped in greaseproof (waxed) paper, sealed and steamed in the oven.

NUTRITIONAL INFORMATION

Calories 85	Sugars 4g	
Protein 2g	Fat 0.5g	
Carbohydrate . . .15g	Saturates 0.1g	

 10 MINS 35 MINS

SERVES 4

INGREDIENTS

16 small new potatoes

1 carrot, cut into matchstick strips

1 fennel bulb, sliced

75 g/2¾ oz French (green) beans

1 yellow (bell) pepper, cut into strips

16 tbsp dry white wine

4 rosemary sprigs

salt and pepper

rosemary sprigs, to garnish

1 Cut 4 squares of greaseproof (waxed) paper measuring about 25 cm/10 inches in size.

2 Divide the vegetables equally between the 4 paper squares, placing them in the centre.

3 Bring the edges of the paper together and scrunch them together to encase the vegetables, leaving the top open.

4 Place the parcels in a shallow roasting tin (pan) and spoon 4 tablespoons of white wine into each parcel. Add a rosemary sprig and season.

5 Fold the top of each parcel over to seal it. Cook in a preheated oven, 190°C/375°F/Gas Mark 5, for 30-35 minutes or until the vegetables are tender.

6 Transfer the sealed parcels to 4 individual serving plates and garnish with rosemary sprigs.

7 Open the parcels at the table in order for the full aroma of the vegetables to be appreciated.

COOK'S TIP

If small new potatoes are unavailable, use larger potatoes which have been halved or quartered to ensure that they cook through in the specified cooking time.

Spiced Semolina

A south Indian savoury snack which is very quick and easy to prepare, this should be served warm. It has a really lovely aroma.

NUTRITIONAL INFORMATION

Calories ....556 Sugars 2g
Protein ....9g Fat 41g
Carbohydrate ...40g Saturates 5g

 5 MINS   15 MINS

SERVES 4

INGREDIENTS

150 ml/¼ pint/⅔ cup vegetable oil

1 tsp mixed onion and mustard seeds

4 dried red chillies

4 curry leaves (fresh or dried)

8 tbsp coarse semolina

50 g/1¾ oz/½ cup cashew nuts

1 tsp salt

150 ml/¼ pint/⅔ cup water

1 Heat the vegetable oil in a large, heavy-based frying-pan (skillet) over a fairly low heat.

2 Add the mixed onion and mustard seeds, dried red chillies and curry leaves and fry, stirring constantly, for about 1 minute.

3 Reduce the heat to low and add the coarse semolina and the cashew nuts. Stir-fry for about 5 minutes, moving the mixture around the pan all the time to prevent it from catching and burning on the base.

4 Add the salt to the pan, mixing well, and continue to stir-fry over a low heat, keeping the mixture moving all the time.

5 Add the water and cook, stirring constantly, until the mixture is beginning to thicken.

6 Serve the spiced semolina warm as a delicious snack with Indian tea.

COOK'S TIP

Curry leaves are very similar in appearance to bay leaves but are very different in flavour. They can be bought both fresh and dried. They are mainly used to flavour lentil dishes and vegetable curries.

Garlic Spinach

This has to be one of the simplest recipes, yet it is so tasty. Spinach is fried with garlic and lemon grass and tossed in soy sauce and sugar.

NUTRITIONAL INFORMATION

Calories	118	Sugars	.........6g
Protein	.........7g	Fat	...........7g
Carbohydrate	....7g	Saturates	.......1g

 5 MINS   10 MINS

SERVES 4

I N G R E D I E N T S

2 garlic cloves

1 tsp lemon grass

900 g/2 lb fresh spinach

2 tbsp peanut oil

salt

1 tbsp dark soy sauce

2 tsp brown sugar

1 Peel the garlic cloves and crush them in a pestle and mortar. Set aside until required.

2 Using a sharp knife, finely chop the lemon grass. Set aside until required.

3 Carefully remove the stems from the spinach. Rinse the spinach leaves and drain them thoroughly, patting them dry with absorbent kitchen paper (paper towels).

4 Heat the peanut oil in a preheated wok or large frying pan (skillet) until it is almost smoking.

5 Reduce the heat slightly, add the garlic and lemon grass and stir-fry for 30 seconds.

6 Add the spinach leaves and a pinch of salt to the wok or frying pan (skillet)

and stir-fry for 2–3 minutes, or until the spinach leaves have just wilted.

7 Stir the dark soy sauce and brown sugar into the mixture in the wok or frying pan (skillet) and cook for a further 3–4 minutes.

8 Transfer the garlic spinach to a warm serving dish and serve as an accompaniment to a main dish.

COOK'S TIP

Lemon grass is available fresh, dried and canned or bottled. Dried lemon grass must be soaked for 2 hours before using. The stems are hard and are usually used whole and removed from the dish before serving. The roots can be crushed or finely chopped.

Caramelized New Potatoes

This simple recipe is best served with a plainly cooked main course, as it is fairly sweet and has delicious juices.

NUTRITIONAL INFORMATION

Calories 289	Sugars 18g
Protein 3g	Fat 13g
Carbohydrate . . .43g	Saturates 8g

 5 MINS   ⏱ 20 MINS

SERVES 4

I N G R E D I E N T S

675 g/1½ lb new potatoes, scrubbed

4 tbsp dark brown sugar

60 g/2 oz/¼ cup butter

1 tbsp orange juice

1 tbsp chopped fresh parsley or
  coriander (cilantro)

salt and pepper

orange rind curls, to garnish

1 Cook the new potatoes in a saucepan of boiling water for 10 minutes, or until almost tender. Drain thoroughly.

2 Melt the sugar in a large, heavy-based frying pan (skillet) over a low heat, stirring constantly.

3 Add the butter and orange juice to the pan, stirring the mixture constantly as the butter melts.

4 Add the potatoes to the orange and butter mixture and continue to cook, turning the potatoes frequently until they are completely coated in the caramel.

5 Sprinkle the chopped parsley or coriander (cilantro) over the potatoes and season according to taste with salt and pepper.

6 Transfer the caramelized new potatoes to a serving dish and garnish with the orange rind. Serve immediately.

VARIATION

Lemon or lime juices may be used instead of the orange juice, if preferred. In addition, garnish the finished dish with pared lemon or lime rind, if preferred.

Souffléd Cheesy Potato Fries

These small potato chunks are mixed in a creamy cheese sauce and fried in oil until deliciously golden brown.

NUTRITIONAL INFORMATION

Calories . . . . .614 Sugars 2g
Protein . . . . .12g Fat 46g
Carbohydrate . . .40g Saturates 18g

 20 MINS   25 MINS

SERVES 4

I N G R E D I E N T S

900 g/2 lb potatoes, cut
    into chunks

150 ml/¼ pint/⅔ cup double (heavy) cream

75 g/2¾ oz/¾ cup grated Gruyère
    (Swiss) cheese

pinch of cayenne pepper

2 egg whites

oil, for deep-frying

salt and pepper

chopped flat leaf parsley and grated
    cheese, to garnish

1 Cook the potatoes in a saucepan of boiling lightly salted water for about 10 minutes. Drain thoroughly and pat dry with absorbent kitchen paper (paper towels). Set aside until required.

2 Mix the double (heavy) cream and Gruyère (Swiss) cheese in a large bowl. Stir in the cayenne pepper and season with salt and pepper to taste.

3 Whisk the egg whites until stiff peaks form. Gently fold into the cheese mixture until fully incorporated.

4 Add the cooked potatoes, turning to coat thoroughly in the mixture.

5 Heat the oil for deep-frying to 180°C/350°F or until a cube of bread browns in 30 seconds. Remove the potatoes from the cheese mixture with a slotted spoon and cook in the oil, in batches, if necessary, for 3–4 minutes, or until golden.

6 Transfer the potatoes to a warmed serving dish and garnish with parsley and grated cheese. Serve immediately.

VARIATION

Add other flavourings, such as grated nutmeg or curry powder, to the cream and cheese.

Colcannon

This is an old Irish recipe, usually served with a piece of bacon, but it is equally delicious with a vegetarian main course dish.

NUTRITIONAL INFORMATION

Calories 102   Sugars 4g
Protein . . . . .4g   Fat 4g
Carbohydrate . . .14g   Saturates 2g

🧈 20 MINS   🕐 20 MINS

SERVES 4

INGREDIENTS

225 g/8 oz green cabbage, shredded

5 tbsp milk

225 g/8 oz floury (mealy) potatoes, diced

1 large leek, chopped

pinch of grated nutmeg

15 g/½ oz/1 tbsp butter, melted

salt and pepper

1 Cook the shredded cabbage in a saucepan of boiling salted water for 7–10 minutes. Drain thoroughly and set aside.

2 Meanwhile, in a separate saucepan, bring the milk to the boil and add the potatoes and leek. Reduce the heat and simmer for 15–20 minutes, or until they are cooked through.

3 Stir in the grated nutmeg and thoroughly mash the potatoes and leek together.

4 Add the drained cabbage to the mashed potato and leek mixture and mix well.

5 Spoon the mixture into a warmed serving dish, making a hollow in the centre with the back of a spoon.

6 Pour the melted butter into the hollow and serve the colcannon immediately.

COOK'S TIP

There are many different varieties of cabbage, which produce hearts at varying times of year, so you can be sure of being able to make this delicious cabbage dish all year round.

Corn Cobs & Parsley Butter

There are a number of ways of cooking corn-on-the-cob on the barbecue. Leaving on the husks protects the tender corn niblets.

NUTRITIONAL INFORMATION

Calories 178	Sugars 7g
Protein 2g	Fat 11g
Carbohydrate ...19g	Saturates 7g

 10 MINS   30 MINS

SERVES 4

I N G R E D I E N T S

4 corn cobs, with husks

100 g/3½ oz/½ cup butter

1 tbsp chopped parsley

1 tsp chopped chives

1 tsp chopped thyme

grated rind of 1 lemon

salt and pepper

1 To prepare the corn cobs, peel back the husks and remove the silken hairs.

2 Fold back the husks and secure them in place with string, if necessary.

3 Blanch the corn cobs in a large saucepan of boiling water for about 5 minutes. Remove the cobs with a slotted spoon and drain thoroughly.

4 Barbecue (grill) the cobs over medium hot coals for about 20–30 minutes, turning frequently.

5 Meanwhile, soften the butter and beat in the parsley, chives, thyme, and lemon rind and season with salt and pepper to taste.

6 Transfer the corn cobs to serving plates, remove the string, if used, and

pull back the husks. Serve with a generous portion of herb butter. Eat with two forks or corn cob holders and provide plenty of paper napkins.

COOK'S TIP

If you are unable to get fresh cobs, cook frozen corn cobs on the barbecue (grill). Spread some of the herb butter on to a double thickness of kitchen foil. Wrap the cobs in the foil and barbecue (grill) among the coals for 20–30 minutes.

Pommes Anna

This is a classic potato dish, which may be left to cook unattended while the remainder of the meal is being prepared, so it is ideal with stews.

NUTRITIONAL INFORMATION

Calories	237	Sugars	.........1g
Protein	.........4g	Fat	..........13g
Carbohydrate	...29g	Saturates	.......8g

 15 MINS 2 HOURS

SERVES 4

INGREDIENTS

60 g/2 oz/¼ cup butter, melted

675 g/1½ lb waxy potatoes

4 tbsp chopped mixed herbs

salt and pepper

chopped fresh herbs, to garnish

1 Brush a shallow 1 litre/1¾ pint/4 cup ovenproof dish with a little of the melted butter.

2 Slice the potatoes thinly and pat dry with kitchen paper (paper towels).

3 Arrange a layer of potato slices in the prepared dish until the base is covered. Brush with a little butter and sprinkle with a quarter of the chopped mixed herbs. Season to taste.

4 Continue layering the potato slices, brushing each layer with melted butter and sprinkling with herbs, until they are all used up.

5 Brush the top layer of potato slices with butter, cover the dish and cook in a preheated oven, 190°C/375°F/Gas Mark 5, for 1½ hours.

6 Turn out on to a warm ovenproof platter and return to the oven for a further 25–30 minutes, until golden brown. Serve at once, garnished with fresh herbs.

COOK'S TIP

Make sure that the potatoes are sliced very thinly so that they are almost transparent. This will ensure that they cook thoroughly.

Smoky Bacon & Pepperoni

This more traditional kind of pizza is topped with peperoni, smoked bacon and (bell) peppers covered in a smoked cheese.

NUTRITIONAL INFORMATION

Calories 450	Sugars 6g	
Protein 19g	Fat 24g	
Carbohydrate ...41g	Saturates 6g	

1½ HOURS 20 MINS

SERVES 4

INGREDIENTS

Basic Pizza Dough (see page 861)

1 tbsp olive oil

1 tbsp freshly grated Parmesan

Basic Tomato Sauce (see page 6)

125 g/4½ oz lightly smoked bacon, diced

½ green (bell) pepper, sliced thinly

½ yellow (bell) pepper, sliced thinly

60 g/2 oz pepperoni-style sliced spicy
   sausage

60 g/2 oz smoked Bavarian cheese, grated

½ tsp dried oregano

olive oil, for drizzling

salt and pepper

1 Roll out or press the dough, using a rolling pin or your hands, into a 25 cm/10 inch circle on a lightly floured work surface.

2 Place the dough base on a large greased baking tray (cookie sheet) or pizza pan and push up the edge a little with your fingers, to form a rim.

3 Brush the base with the olive oil and sprinkle with the Parmesan. Cover and leave to rise slightly in a warm place for about 10 minutes.

4 Spread the tomato sauce over the base almost to the edge. Top with the bacon and (bell) peppers. Arrange the pepperoni on top and sprinkle with the smoked cheese.

5 Sprinkle over the oregano and drizzle with a little olive oil. Season well.

6 Bake in a preheated oven, at 200°C/ 400°F/Gas Mark 6, for 18–20 minutes, or until the crust is golden and crisp around the edge. Cut the pizza into wedges and serve immediately.

Aloo Chat

Aloo Chat is one of a variety of Indian foods served at any time of the day. The chickpeas (garbanzo beans) need to be soaked overnight.

NUTRITIONAL INFORMATION

Calories 262	Sugars 6g	
Protein 13g	Fat 4g	
Carbohydrate . . .46g	Saturates 0.5g	

 35 MINS 1 HR 5 MINS

SERVES 4

INGREDIENTS

125 g/4½ oz/generous ½ cup chickpeas
   (garbanzo beans), soaked overnight in
   cold water and drained

1 dried red chilli

500 g/1 lb 2 oz waxy potatoes, boiled in
   their skins and peeled

1 tsp cumin seeds

2 tsp salt

1 tsp black peppercorns

½ tsp dried mint

½ tsp chilli powder

½ tsp ground ginger

2 tsp mango powder

125 ml/4 fl oz/½ cup natural
   (unsweetened) yogurt

oil, for deep frying

4 poppadoms

VARIATION

Instead of chickpeas (garbanzo beans), diced tropical fruits can be stirred into the potatoes and spice mix; add a little lemon juice to balance the sweetness.

1 Boil the chickpeas (garbanzo beans) with the chilli in plenty of water for about 1 hour, until tender. Drain.

2 Cut the potatoes into 2.5 cm/1 inch dice and mix into the chickpeas (garbanzo beans) while they are still warm. Set aside.

3 Grind together the cumin, salt and peppercorns in a spice grinder or with a pestle and mortar. Stir in the mint, chilli powder, ginger and mango powder.

4 Put a small saucepan or frying pan (skillet) over a low heat and add the spice mix. Stir until the spices give off their aroma and then immediately remove the pan from the heat.

5 Stir half of the spice mix into the chickpea (garbanzo bean) and potato mixture and stir the other half into the yogurt.

6 Cook the poppadoms according to the instructions on the packet. Drain on plenty of kitchen paper (paper towels). Break into bite-size pieces and stir into the potatoes and chickpeas (garbanzo beans), spoon over the spiced yogurt and serve immediately.

Pumpkin Parcels with Chilli

This spicy side dish is perfect for a Hallowe'en or Bonfire Night barbecue (grill) party, although it is equally delicious on a summer evening, too.

NUTRITIONAL INFORMATION

Energy 118   Sugar 3g
Protein ....1g   Fat 11g
Carbohydrates ....4g   Saturates 4g

 10 MINS   25-30 MINS

SERVES 4

INGREDIENTS

700 g/1 lb 9 oz pumpkin or squash

2 tbsp sunflower oil

25 g/1 oz/2 tbsp butter

½ tsp chilli sauce

grated rind of 1 lime

2 tsp lime juice

1 Halve the pumpkin or squash and scoop out the seeds. Rinse the seeds and reserve. Cut the pumpkin into thin wedges and peel.

2 Heat the oil and butter together in a large saucepan, stirring constantly, until melted. Stir in the chilli sauce, lime rind and juice.

3 Add the pumpkin or squash and seeds to the pan and toss to coat all over in the flavoured butter.

4 Divide the mixture between 4 double thickness sheets of kitchen foil. Fold over the kitchen foil to enclose the pumpkin or squash mixture completely.

5 Barbecue (grill) the foil parcels over hot coals for 15–25 minutes, or until the pumpkin or squash is tender.

6 Transfer the foil parcels to warm serving plates. Open the parcels at the table and serve at once.

VARIATION

Add 2 teaspoons of curry paste to the oil instead of the lime and chilli. Use butternut squash when pumpkin is not available.

Herby Potatoes & Onion

Fried potatoes are a classic favourite; here they are given extra flavour by frying them in butter with onion, garlic and herbs.

NUTRITIONAL INFORMATION

Calories	413	Sugars	.........4g
Protein	.........5g	Fat	..........26g
Carbohydrate	...42g	Saturates	......17g

 10 MINS   50 MINS

SERVES 4

I N G R E D I E N T S

900 g/2 lb waxy potatoes, cut into cubes

125 g/4½ oz/½ cup butter

1 red onion, cut into 8

2 garlic cloves, crushed

1 tsp lemon juice

2 tbsp chopped thyme

salt and pepper

1 Cook the cubed potatoes in a saucepan of boiling water for 10 minutes. Drain thoroughly.

2 Melt the butter in a large, heavy-based frying pan (skillet) and add the red onion wedges, garlic and lemon juice. Cook, stirring constantly for 2–3 minutes.

3 Add the potatoes to the pan and mix well to coat in the butter mixture.

COOK'S TIP

Keep checking the potatoes and stirring throughout the cooking time to ensure that they do not burn or stick to the base of the frying pan (skillet).

4 Reduce the heat, cover and cook for 25–30 minutes, or until the potatoes are golden brown and tender.

5 Sprinkle the chopped thyme over the top of the potatoes and season.

6 Transfer to a warm serving dish and serve immediately.

Saffron-flavoured Potatoes

Saffron is made from the dried stigma of the crocus and is native to Greece. It is very expensive, but only a very small amount is needed.

NUTRITIONAL INFORMATION

Calories ....197 Sugars 4g
Protein ....4g Fat 6g
Carbohydrate ...30g Saturates 1g

 25 MINS   40 MINS

SERVES 4

INGREDIENTS

1 tsp saffron strands

6 tbsp boiling water

675 g/1½ lb waxy potatoes,
    unpeeled and cut into wedges

1 red onion, cut into 8 wedges

2 garlic cloves, crushed

1 tbsp white wine vinegar

2 tbsp olive oil

1 tbsp wholegrain mustard

5 tbsp vegetable stock

5 tbsp dry white wine

2 tsp chopped rosemary

salt and pepper

1 Place the saffron strands in a small bowl and pour over the boiling water. Set aside to soak for about 10 minutes.

2 Place the potatoes in a roasting tin (pan), together with the red onion wedges and crushed garlic.

3 Add the vinegar, oil, mustard, vegetable stock, white wine, rosemary and saffron water to the potatoes and onion in the tin (pan). Season to taste with salt and pepper.

4 Cover the roasting tin (pan) with kitchen foil and bake in a preheated oven, 200°C/400°F/Gas Mark 6, for 30 minutes.

5 Remove the foil and cook the potatoes for a further 10 minutes until crisp, browned and cooked through. Serve hot.

COOK'S TIP

Turmeric may be used instead of saffron to provide the yellow colour in this recipe. However, it is worth using saffron, if possible, for the lovely nutty flavour it gives a dish.

Easy Cauliflower & Broccoli

Whole baby cauliflowers are used in this recipe. Try to find them if you can, if not use large bunches of florets.

NUTRITIONAL INFORMATION

Calories	433	Sugars	........2g
Protein	.........8g	Fat	..........44g
Carbohydrate	....3g	Saturates	.......9g

10 MINS   20 MINS

SERVES 4

I N G R E D I E N T S

2 baby cauliflowers

225 g/8 oz broccoli

salt and pepper

S A U C E

8 tbsp olive oil

4 tbsp butter or margarine

2 tsp grated root ginger

juice and rind of 2 lemons

5 tbsp chopped coriander (cilantro)

5 tbsp grated Cheddar cheese

1 Using a sharp knife, cut the cauliflowers in half and the broccoli into very large florets.

2 Cook the cauliflower and broccoli in a saucepan of boiling salted water for 10 minutes. Drain well, transfer to a shallow ovenproof dish and keep warm until required.

COOK'S TIP

Lime or orange could be used instead of the lemon for a fruity and refreshing sauce.

3 To make the sauce, put the oil and butter or margarine in a pan and heat gently until the butter melts. Add the grated root ginger, lemon juice, lemon rind and coriander (cilantro) and simmer for 2–3 minutes, stirring occasionally.

4 Season the sauce with salt and pepper to taste, then pour over the vegetables in the dish and sprinkle the cheese on top.

5 Cook under a preheated hot grill (broiler) for 2–3 minutes, or until the cheese is bubbling and golden. Leave to cool for 1–2 minutes and then serve.

Spicy Indian Potatoes

The potato is widely used in Indian cooking and there are many variations of spicy potatoes.

NUTRITIONAL INFORMATION

Calories ....173 Sugars 6g
Protein ....7g Fat 9g
Carbohydrate ...18g Saturates 1g

 15 MINS   40 MINS

SERVES 6

INGREDIENTS

½ tsp coriander seeds

1 tsp cumin seeds

4 tbsp vegetable oil

2 cardamom pods

1 cm/½ inch piece of root ginger, grated

1 red chilli, chopped

1 onion, chopped

2 garlic cloves, crushed

500 g/1 lb 2 oz new potatoes, quartered

150 ml/¼ pint/⅔ cup vegetable stock

675 g/1½ lb spinach, chopped

4 tbsp natural (unsweetened) yogurt

salt

1 Grind the coriander and cumin seeds using a pestle and mortar.

2 Heat the oil in a frying pan (skillet). Add the ground coriander and cumin seeds to the pan, together with the cardamom pods and ginger and cook for about 2 minutes.

3 Add the chopped chilli, onion and garlic to the pan. Cook, stirring frequently, for a further 2 minutes.

4 Add the potatoes to the pan, together with the vegetable stock. Cook gently,

stirring occasionally, for 30 minutes, or until the potatoes are cooked through.

5 Add the spinach to the pan and cook for a further 5 minutes.

6 Remove the pan from the heat and stir in the yogurt. Season with salt and pepper to taste. Transfer the potatoes and spinach to a warmed serving dish and serve immediately.

VARIATION

Use frozen spinach instead of fresh spinach, if you prefer. Thaw the frozen spinach and drain it thoroughly before adding it to the dish, otherwise it will turn soggy.

Potato Crumble

This is a delicious way to liven up mashed potato by topping it with a crumble mixture flavoured with herbs, mustard and onion.

NUTRITIONAL INFORMATION

Calories 451   Sugars 5g
Protein . . . . .13g   Fat 19g
Carbohydrate . . .60g   Saturates 12g

  25 MINS 🕑 30 MINS

SERVES 4

INGREDIENTS

900 g/2 lb floury (mealy) potatoes, diced

25 g/1 oz/2 tbsp butter

2 tbsp milk

50 g/1¾ oz/½ cup grated mature (sharp) cheese or blue cheese

CRUMBLE TOPPING

40 g/1½ oz/3 tbsp butter

1 onion, cut into chunks

1 garlic clove, crushed

1 tbsp wholegrain mustard

175 g/6 oz/3 cups fresh wholemeal (whole wheat) breadcrumbs

2 tbsp chopped parsley

salt and pepper

1 Cook the potatoes in a pan of lightly salted boiling water for 10 minutes, or until cooked through.

2 Meanwhile, make the crumble topping. Melt the butter in a frying pan (skillet). Add the onion, garlic and mustard and fry over a medium heat, stirring constantly, for 5 minutes, until the onion has softened.

3 Put the breadcrumbs in a mixing bowl and stir in the fried onion. Season to taste with salt and pepper.

4 Drain the potatoes thoroughly and place them in another mixing bowl. Add the butter and milk, then mash until smooth. Stir in the grated cheese while the potato is still hot.

5 Spoon the mashed potato into a shallow ovenproof dish and sprinkle with the crumble topping.

6 Cook in a preheated oven, 200°C/400°F/Gas Mark 6, for 10-15 minutes, until the crumble topping is golden brown and crunchy. Serve immediately.

COOK'S TIP

For extra crunch, add freshly cooked vegetables, such as celery and (bell) peppers, to the mashed potato in step 4.

Creamy Green Vegetables

This dish is very quick to make. A dash of cream is added to the sauce, but this may be omitted, if preferred.

NUTRITIONAL INFORMATION

Calories	111	Sugars	...2g
Protein	...5g	Fat	...8g
Carbohydrate	...7g	Saturates	...2g

5 MINS   20 MINS

SERVES 4

I N G R E D I E N T S

450 g/1 lb Chinese leaves (cabbage), shredded

2 tbsp peanut oil

2 leeks, shredded

4 garlic cloves, crushed

300 ml/½ pint/1¼ cups vegetable stock

1 tbsp light soy sauce

2 tsp cornflour (cornstarch)

4 tsp water

2 tbsp single (light) cream or natural (unsweetened) yogurt

1 tbsp chopped coriander (cilantro)

1 Blanch the Chinese leaves (cabbage) in boiling water for 30 seconds. Drain, rinse under cold running water, then drain thoroughly again.

2 Heat the oil in a preheated wok and add the Chinese leaves (cabbage), leeks and garlic. Stir-fry for 2–3 minutes.

3 Add the stock and soy sauce to the wok, reduce the heat to low, cover and simmer for 10 minutes.

4 Remove the vegetables from the wok with a slotted spoon and set aside. Bring the stock to the boil and boil vigorously until reduced by about half.

5 Blend the cornflour (cornstarch) with the water and stir into the wok. Bring to the boil, and cook, stirring constantly, until thickened and clear.

6 Reduce the heat and stir in the vegetables and cream or yogurt. Cook over a low heat for 1 minute.

7 Transfer to a serving dish, sprinkle over the chopped coriander (cilantro) and serve.

COOK'S TIP

Do not boil the sauce once the cream or yogurt has been added, as it will separate.

Crispy Cabbage & Almonds

This dish is better known as crispy seaweed. It does not actually contain seaweed, but consists of spring greens (collard greens) or pak choi.

NUTRITIONAL INFORMATION

Calories 431   Sugars 17g
Protein . . . . .9g   Fat 37g
Carbohydrate . . .17g   Saturates 4g

 10 MINS   10 MINS

SERVES 4

INGREDIENTS

1.25 kg/2 lb 12 oz pak choi or spring
   greens (collard greens)

700 ml/1¼ pints/3 cups vegetable oil

75 g/2¾ oz/¾ cup blanched almonds

1 tsp salt

1 tbsp light brown sugar

pinch of ground cinnamon

1 Separate the leaves from the pak choi or spring greens (collard greens) and rinse them well. Drain thoroughly and pat dry with absorbent kitchen paper (paper towels).

2 Shred the greens (collard greens) into thin strips, using a sharp knife.

3 Heat the vegetable oil in a preheated wok or large, heavy-based frying pan (skillet) until the oil is almost smoking.

4 Reduce the heat and add the pak choi or spring greens (collard greens). Cook for 2–3 minutes, or until the greens begin to float in the oil and are crisp.

5 Remove the greens from the oil with a slotted spoon and leave to drain thoroughly on absorbent kitchen paper (paper towels).

6 Add the blanched almonds to the oil in the wok and cook for 30 seconds. Remove the almonds from the oil with a slotted spoon and drain thoroughly on absorbent kitchen paper (paper towels).

7 Mix together the salt, light brown sugar and ground cinnamon and sprinkle on to the greens.

8 Toss the almonds into the greens.

9 Transfer the greens and almonds to a warm serving dish and serve immediately.

COOK'S TIP

Ensure that the greens are completely dry before adding them to the oil, otherwise it will spit. The greens will not become crisp if they are wet when placed in the oil.

Murkha Dhal

In this dhal recipe, the garlic is intended to burn in the base of the pan, and this flavour permeates the dish.

NUTRITIONAL INFORMATION

Calories 372   Sugars 7g
Protein ....18g   Fat 16g
Carbohydrate ...42g   Saturates 10g

 5 MINS   55 MINS

SERVES 4

I N G R E D I E N T S

60 g/2 oz/¼ cup butter

2 tsp black mustard seeds

1 onion, finely chopped

2 garlic cloves, finely chopped

1 tbsp grated root ginger

1 tsp turmeric

2 green chillies, seeded and
  finely chopped

225 g/8 oz/1 cup red lentils

1 litre/1¾ pints/4 cups water

300 ml/½ pint/1¼ cups coconut milk

1 tsp salt

1 Melt the butter in a large heavy-based saucepan over a moderate heat. Add the mustard seeds and cover the pan. When you can hear the seeds popping, add the onion, garlic and grated ginger. Cook, uncovered, for about 7–8 minutes, until the onion is soft and the garlic is brown.

2 Stir in the turmeric and green chillies and cook for 1–2 minutes, until the chillies soften a little.

3 Add the lentils and cook, stirring frequently, for 2 minutes, until the lentils begin to turn translucent.

4 Stir in the water, coconut milk and salt. Bring to the boil, then reduce the heat and simmer for 40 minutes, or until the desired consistency is reached. However, if you intend to reheat the dhal later rather than eat it straight away, cook it for only 30 minutes to allow for reheating time.

5 Transfer the dhal to a warmed serving dish and serve immediately, while piping hot.

COOK'S TIP

There are many types of lentils used in India, but the two most common are red lentils and green or beige lentils. The red lentils are very useful, as they cook in a relatively short time to form a homogeneous mass. Green and beige lentils stay more separate when cooked.

Steamed Rice in Lotus Leaves

The fragrance of the leaves penetrates the rice, giving it a unique taste. Lotus leaves can be bought from specialist Chinese shops.

NUTRITIONAL INFORMATION

Calories ....163 Sugars 0.1g
Protein ....5g Fat 6g
Carbohydrate ...2.1g Saturates 1g

1 HOUR   40 MINS

SERVES 4

INGREDIENTS

2 lotus leaves

4 Chinese dried mushrooms (if unavailable, use thinly sliced open-cup mushrooms)

175 g/6 oz/generous ¾ cup long-grain rice

1 cinnamon stick

6 cardamom pods

4 cloves

1 tsp salt

2 eggs

1 tbsp vegetable oil

2 spring onions (scallions), chopped

1 tbsp soy sauce

2 tbsp sherry

1 tsp sugar

1 tsp sesame oil

1 Unfold the lotus leaves carefully and cut along the fold to divide each leaf in half. Lay on a large baking sheet and pour over enough hot water to cover. Soak for about 30 minutes until softened.

2 Place the dried mushrooms in a small bowl and cover with warm water. Leave to soak for 20–25 minutes.

3 Cook the rice in a saucepan of boiling water with the cinnamon stick, cardamom pods, cloves and salt for about

10 minutes – the rice should be partially cooked. Drain thoroughly and remove the cinnamon stick. Place the rice in a bowl

4 Beat the eggs lightly. Heat the oil in a wok and cook the eggs quickly, stirring until set. Remove and set aside.

5 Drain the mushrooms, squeezing out the excess water. Remove the tough centres and chop the mushrooms. Stir into

the rice with the cooked egg, spring onions (scallions), soy sauce, sherry, sugar and sesame oil.

6 Drain the lotus leaves and divide the rice into four portions. Place a portion in the centre of each leaf and fold up to form a parcel (packet). Place in a steamer, cover and steam over simmering water for 20 minutes. To serve, cut the tops of the lotus leaves open to expose the rice inside.

Kashmiri Spinach

This is an imaginative way to serve spinach, which adds a little zip to it. It is a very simple dish, which will complement almost any curry.

NUTRITIONAL INFORMATION

Calories 81   Sugars 2g
Protein . . . . .4g   Fat 7g
Carbohydrate . . . .2g   Saturates 1g

 5 MINS   25 MINS

SERVES 4

I N G R E D I E N T S

500 g/1 lb 2 oz spinach or Swiss chard or
   baby leaf spinach

2 tbsp mustard oil

¼ tsp garam masala

1 tsp yellow mustard seeds

2 spring onions (scallions), sliced

1 Remove the tough stalks from the spinach.

2 Heat the mustard oil in a preheated wok or large heavy-based frying pan (skillet) until it smokes. Add the garam masala and mustard seeds. Cover the pan quickly – you will hear the mustard seeds popping inside.

3 When the popping has ceased, remove the cover, add the spring onions (scallions) and spinach. Cook, stirring constantly, until the spinach has wilted.

4 Continue cooking the spinach, uncovered, over a medium heat for 10–15 minutes, until most of the water has evaporated. If using frozen spinach, it will not need to cook for so long – cook it until most of the water has evaporated.

5 Remove the spinach and spring onions (scallions) with a slotted spoon,

draining off any remaining liquid. (This dish is pleasanter to eat when it is served as dry as possible.)

6 Transfer to a warmed serving dish and serve immediately, while it is still piping hot.

COOK'S TIP

Mustard oil is made from mustard seeds and is very fiery when raw. However, when it is heated to this smoking stage, it loses a lot of the fire and takes on a delightful sweet quality.

Chilli Fried Rice

Not so much a side dish as a meal in itself, this delicious fried rice can be served on its own or as an accompaniment to many Chinese dishes.

NUTRITIONAL INFORMATION

Calories 290   Sugars 2g
Protein ....11g   Fat 14g
Carbohydrate ...26g   Saturates 2g

20 MINS   15 MINS

SERVES 4

INGREDIENTS

250 g/9 oz/generous 1 cup long-grain rice

4 tbsp vegetable oil

2 garlic cloves, chopped finely

1 small red chilli, deseeded and chopped finely

8 spring onions (scallions), trimmed and sliced finely

1 tbsp red curry paste or 2 tsp chilli sauce

1 red (bell) pepper, cored, deseeded and chopped

90 g/3 oz/¾ cup dwarf green beans, chopped

250 g/9 oz/1½ cups cooked peeled prawns (shrimp) or chopped cooked chicken

2 tbsp fish sauce

TO GARNISH

cucumber slices

shredded spring onion (scallion)

COOK'S TIP

Cook the rice the day before if you can remember – it will give an even better result. Alternatively, use rice left over from another dish to make this recipe.

1 Cook the rice in plenty of boiling, lightly salted water until tender, about 12 minutes. Drain, rinse with cold water and drain thoroughly.

2 Heat the vegetable oil in a wok or large frying pan (skillet) until the oil is really hot.

3 Add the garlic to the wok and fry gently for 2 minutes until golden.

4 Add the chilli and spring onions (scallions) and cook, stirring, for 3–4 minutes.

5 Add the red curry paste or chilli sauce to the wok or frying pan (skillet) and fry for 1 minute, then add the red (bell) pepper and dwarf green beans. Stir-fry briskly for 2 minutes.

6 Tip the cooked rice into the wok or frying pan (skillet) and add the prawns (shrimp) or chicken and the fish sauce. Stir-fry over a medium-high heat for about 4–5 minutes, until the rice is hot.

7 Transfer the chilli fried rice to warm serving dishes, garnish with cucumber slices and shredded spring onion (scallion) and serve.

Kabli Channa Sag

Pulses such as chickpeas (garbanzo beans) are widely used in India. They need to be soaked overnight so prepare well in advance.

NUTRITIONAL INFORMATION

Calories	217	Sugars	.........5g
Protein	........12g	Fat	...........9g
Carbohydrate	...25g	Saturates	.......1g

10 MINS   1 HOUR

SERVES 6

INGREDIENTS

225 g/8 oz/generous cup chickpeas (garbanzo beans), soaked overnight and drained

5 cloves

2.5 cm/1 inch piece of cinnamon stick

2 garlic cloves

3 tbsp sunflower oil

1 small onion, sliced

3 tbsp lemon juice

1 tsp coriander seeds

2 tomatoes, peeled, seeded and chopped

500 g/1 lb 2 oz spinach, rinsed and any tough stems removed

1 tbsp chopped coriander (cilantro)

TO GARNISH

coriander (cilantro) sprigs

lemon slices

1 Put the chickpeas (garbanzo beans) into a saucepan with enough water to cover. Add the cloves, cinnamon and 1 whole unpeeled garlic clove that has been lightly crushed with the back of a knife to release the juices. Bring to the boil, reduce the heat and simmer for 40–50 minutes, or until the chickpeas (garbanzo beans) are tender when tested with a skewer. Skim off any foam that comes to the surface.

2 Meanwhile, heat 1 tablespoon of the oil in a saucepan. Crush the remaining garlic clove. Put this into the pan with the oil and the onion, and cook over a moderate heat for about 5 minutes.

3 Remove the cloves, cinnamon and garlic from the pan of chickpeas (garbanzo beans). Drain the chickpeas (garbanzo beans). Using a food processor or a fork, blend 90 g/3 oz/½ cup of the chickpeas (garbanzo beans) with the onion and garlic, the lemon juice and 1 tablespoon of the oil until smooth. Stir this purée into the remaining chickpeas (garbanzo beans).

4 Heat the remaining oil in a large frying pan (skillet), add the coriander seeds and stir for 1 minute. Add the tomatoes, stir and add the spinach. Cover and cook for 1 minute over a moderate heat. The spinach should be wilted, but not soggy. Stir in the chopped coriander (cilantro) and remove from the heat.

5 Transfer the chickpeas (garbanzo beans) to a warm serving dish and spoon over the spinach. Garnish with the coriander (cilantro) and slices of lemon and serve immediately.

Deep-fried Courgettes

These courgette (zucchini) fritters are irresistible and could be served as a starter or snack with a chilli dip.

NUTRITIONAL INFORMATION

Calories 117   Sugars 2g
Protein . . . . .3g   Fat 6g
Carbohydrate . . .14g   Saturates 1g

5 MINS   20 MINS

SERVES 4

INGREDIENTS

450 g/1 lb courgettes (zucchini)

1 egg white

50 g/1¾ oz/⅓ cup cornflour (cornstarch)

1 tsp salt

1 tsp Chinese five-spice powder

oil, for deep-frying

chilli dip, to serve

1 Using a sharp knife, slice the courgettes (zucchini) into rings or chunky sticks.

2 Place the egg white in a small mixing bowl. Lightly whip the egg white until foamy, using a fork.

3 Mix the cornflour (cornstarch), salt and Chinese five-spice powder together and sprinkle on to a large plate.

4 Heat the oil for deep-frying in a large preheated wok or heavy-based frying pan (skillet).

5 Dip each piece of courgette (zucchini) into the beaten egg white then coat in the cornflour (cornstarch) and five-spice mixture.

6 Deep-fry the courgettes (zucchini), in batches, for about 5 minutes or until pale golden and crispy. Repeat with the remaining courgettes (zucchini).

7 Remove the courgettes (zucchini) with a slotted spoon and leave to drain on absorbent kitchen paper (paper towels) while deep-frying the remainder.

8 Transfer the courgettes (zucchini) to serving plates and serve immediately with a chilli dip.

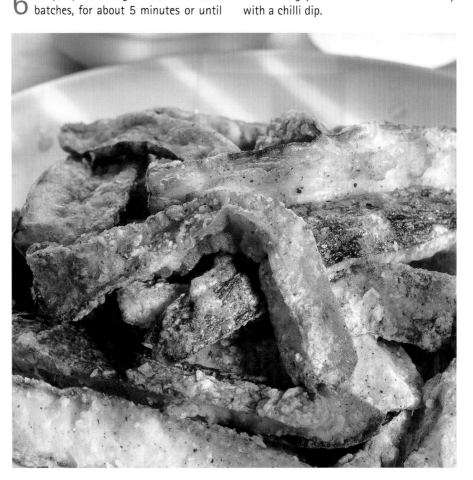

VARIATION

Alter the seasoning by using chilli powder or curry powder instead of the Chinese five-spice powder, if you prefer.

Candied Sweet Potatoes

A taste of the Caribbean is introduced in this recipe, where sweet potatoes are cooked with sugar and lime with a dash of brandy.

NUTRITIONAL INFORMATION

Calories	348	Sugars	........21g
Protein	.........3g	Fat	...........9g
Carbohydrate	...67g	Saturates	.......6g

 15 MINS   25 MINS

SERVES 4

I N G R E D I E N T S

675 g/1½ lb sweet potatoes, sliced

40 g/1½ oz/3 tbsp butter

1 tbsp lime juice

75 g/2¾ oz/½ cup soft dark brown sugar

1 tbsp brandy

grated rind of 1 lime

lime wedges, to garnish

1 Cook the sweet potatoes in a saucepan of boiling water for about 5 minutes. Test the potatoes have softened by pricking with a fork. Remove the sweet potatoes with a perforated spoon and drain thoroughly.

2 Melt the butter in a large frying pan (skillet). Add the lime juice and brown sugar and heat gently, stirring, to dissolve the sugar.

3 Stir the sweet potatoes and the brandy into the sugar and lime juice mixture. Cook over a low heat for about 10 minutes or until the potato slices are cooked through.

4 Sprinkle the lime rind over the top of the sweet potatoes and mix well.

5 Transfer the candied sweet potatoes to a serving plate. Garnish with lime wedges and serve at once.

COOK'S TIP

Sweet potatoes have a pinkish skin and either white, yellow or orange flesh. It doesn't matter which type is used for this dish.

Baked Celery with Cream

This dish is topped with breadcrumbs for a crunchy topping, underneath which is hidden a creamy celery and pecan mixture.

NUTRITIONAL INFORMATION

Calories 237   Sugars 5g
Protein ....7g   Fat 19g
Carbohydrate ....11g   Saturates 7g

 15 MINS   40 MINS

SERVES 4

INGREDIENTS

1 head of celery

½ tsp ground cumin

½ tsp ground coriander

1 garlic clove, crushed

1 red onion, thinly sliced

50 g/1¾ oz/½ cup pecan nut halves

150 ml/¼ pint/⅔ cup vegetable stock

150 ml/¼ pint/⅔ cup single (light) cream

50 g/1¾ oz/1 cup fresh wholemeal
   (whole wheat) breadcrumbs

25 g/1 oz/⅓ cup grated Parmesan cheese

salt and pepper

celery leaves, to garnish

COOK'S TIP

Once grated, Parmesan cheese quickly loses its 'bite' so it is best to grate only the amount you need for the recipe. Wrap the rest tightly in foil and it will keep for several months in the refrigerator.

1 Trim the celery and cut into matchsticks. Place the celery in an ovenproof dish, together with the ground cumin, coriander, garlic, red onion and pecan nuts.

2 Mix the stock and cream together and pour over the vegetables. Season with salt and pepper to taste.

3 Mix the breadcrumbs and cheese together and sprinkle over the top to cover the vegetables.

4 Cook in a preheated oven, 200°C/ 400°F/Gas Mark 6, for 40 minutes, or until the vegetables are tender and the top crispy. Garnish with celery leaves and serve at once.

Thai-Style Stir-Fried Noodles

This dish is considered the Thai national dish, as it is made and eaten everywhere – a one-dish, fast food for eating on the move.

NUTRITIONAL INFORMATION

Calories 407	Sugars 11g
Protein 14g	Fat 16g
Carbohydrate . . .56g	Saturates 3g

15 MINS   5 MINS

SERVES 4

INGREDIENTS

225 g/8 oz dried rice noodles

2 red chillies, seeded and
finely chopped

2 shallots, finely chopped

2 tbsp sugar

2 tbsp tamarind water

1 tbsp lime juice

2 tbsp light soy sauce

1 tbsp sunflower oil

1 tsp sesame oil

175 g/6 oz/¾ cup diced smoked tofu
(bean curd)

pepper

2 tbsp chopped roasted peanuts,
to garnish

1 Cook the rice noodles as directed on the pack, or soak them in boiling water for 5 minutes.

2 Grind together the chillies, shallots, sugar, tamarind water, lime juice, light soy sauce and pepper to taste.

3 Heat both the oils together in a preheated wok or large, heavy frying pan (skillet) over a high heat. Add the tofu (bean curd) and stir for 1 minute.

4 Add the chilli mixture, bring to the boil, and cook, stirring constantly, for about 2 minutes, until thickened.

5 Drain the rice noodles and add them to the chilli mixture. Use 2 spoons to lift and stir them until they are no longer steaming. Serve immediately, garnished with the peanuts.

COOK'S TIP

This is a quick one-dish meal that is very useful if you are catering for a single vegetarian in the family.

Sweet Chilli Pork Fried Rice

This is a variation of egg fried rice which may be served as an accompaniment to a main meal dish.

NUTRITIONAL INFORMATION

Calories 366   Sugars 5g
Protein ....29g   Fat 16g
Carbohydrate ...28g   Saturates 4g

25 MINS   20 MINS

SERVES 4

INGREDIENTS

450 g/1 lb pork tenderloin

2 tbsp sunflower oil

2 tbsp sweet chilli sauce, plus extra
   to serve

1 onion, sliced

175 g/6 oz carrots, cut into thin sticks

175 g/6 oz courgettes (zucchini),
   cut into sticks

100 g/3½ oz/1 cup canned bamboo shoots,
   drained

275 g/9½ oz/4¾ cups cooked long-grain
   rice

1 egg, beaten

1 tbsp chopped fresh parsley

1 Using a sharp knife, cut the pork tenderloin into thin slices.

2 Heat the sunflower oil in a large preheated wok or frying pan (skillet).

3 Add the pork to the wok and stir-fry for 5 minutes.

4 Add the chilli sauce to the wok and allow to bubble, stirring, for 2–3 minutes or until syrupy.

5 Add the onion, carrots, courgettes (zucchini) and bamboo shoots to the wok and stir-fry for a further 3 minutes.

6 Add the cooked rice and stir-fry for 2–3 minutes, or until the rice is heated through.

7 Drizzle the beaten egg over the top of the fried rice and cook, tossing the ingredients in the wok with two spoons, until the egg sets.

8 Scatter with chopped fresh parsley and serve immediately, with extra sweet chilli sauce, if desired.

COOK'S TIP

For a really quick dish, add frozen mixed vegetables to the rice instead of the freshly prepared vegetables.

Sesame Hot Noodles

Plain egg noodles are tossed in a dressing made with sesame oil, soy sauce, peanut butter, coriander (cilantro), lime, chilli and sesame seeds.

NUTRITIONAL INFORMATION

Calories 300	Sugars 1g	
Protein 7g	Fat 21g	
Carbohydrate . . .21g	Saturates 3g	

 5 MINS   10 MINS

SERVES 4

I N G R E D I E N T S

2 x 250 g/9 oz packets medium egg noodles

3 tbsp sunflower oil

2 tbsp sesame oil

1 garlic clove, crushed

1 tbsp smooth peanut butter

1 small green chilli, seeded and very finely chopped

3 tbsp toasted sesame seeds

4 tbsp light soy sauce

½ tbsp lime juice

salt and pepper

4 tbsp chopped fresh coriander (cilantro)

1 Place the noodles in a large pan of boiling water, then immediately remove from the heat. Cover and leave to stand for 6 minutes, stirring once halfway through the time. At the end of 6 minutes the noodles will be perfectly cooked. Alternatively, cook the noodles following the packet instructions.

2 Meanwhile, make the dressing. Mix together the sunflower oil, sesame oil, crushed garlic and peanut butter in a mixing bowl until smooth.

3 Add the chopped green chilli, sesame seeds and light soy sauce to the other dressing ingredients. Add the lime juice, according to taste, and mix well. Season with salt and pepper.

4 Drain the noodles thoroughly then place in a heated serving bowl.

5 Add the dressing and chopped fresh coriander (cilantro) to the noodles and toss well to mix. Serve hot as a main meal accompaniment.

COOK'S TIP

If you are cooking the noodles ahead of time, toss the cooked, drained noodles in 2 teaspoons of sesame oil, then turn into a bowl. Cover and keep warm until required.

Fried Noodles (Chow Mein)

This is a basic recipe for Chow Mein. Additional ingredients such as chicken or pork can be added if liked.

NUTRITIONAL INFORMATION

Calories 716	Sugars 2g	
Protein 4g	Fat 12g	
Carbohydrate . . .14g	Saturates 1g	

 5 MINS   15 MINS

SERVES 4

I N G R E D I E N T S

275 g/9½ oz egg noodles

3-4 tbsp vegetable oil

1 small onion, finely shredded

125 g/4½ oz fresh bean sprouts

1 spring onion (scallion),
   finely shredded

2 tbsp light soy sauce

a few drops of sesame oil

salt

1 Bring a wok or saucepan of salted water to the boil.

2 Add the egg noodles to the saucepan or wok and cook according to the instructions on the packet (usually no more than 4-5 minutes).

COOK'S TIP

Noodles, a symbol of longevity, are made from wheat or rice flour, water and egg. Handmade noodles are made by an elaborate process of kneading, pulling and twisting the dough, and it takes years to learn the art.

3 Drain the noodles well and rinse in cold water; drain thoroughly again, then transfer to a large mixing bowl and toss with a little vegetable oil.

4 Heat the remaining vegetable oil in a preheated wok or large frying pan (skillet) until really hot.

5 Add the shredded onion to the wok and stir-fry for about 30-40 seconds.

6 Add the bean sprouts and drained noodles to the wok, stir and toss for 1 more minute.

7 Add the shredded spring onion (scallion) and light soy sauce and blend well.

8 Transfer the noodles to a warm serving dish, sprinkle with the sesame oil and serve immediately.

Crispy Deep-fried Noodles

This dish requires a certain amount of care and attention to get the crispy noodles properly cooked, but it is well worth the effort.

NUTRITIONAL INFORMATION

Calories 242   Sugars 2g
Protein . . . . .13g   Fat 17g
Carbohydrate . . .10g   Saturates 3g

 35 MINS   25 MINS

SERVES 4

INGREDIENTS

175 g/6 oz thread egg noodles

600 ml/1 pint/2½ cups sunflower oil, for deep-frying

2 tsp grated lemon peel

1 tbsp light soy sauce

1 tbsp rice vinegar

1 tbsp lemon juice

1½ tbsp sugar

250 g/9 oz/1 cup marinated tofu (bean curd), diced

2 garlic cloves, crushed

1 red chilli, sliced finely

1 red (bell) pepper, diced

4 eggs, beaten

red chilli flower, to garnish)

1 Blanch the egg noodles briefly in hot water, to which a little of the oil has been added. Drain the noodles and spread out to dry for at least 30 minutes. Cut into threads about 7 cm/3 inches long.

2 Combine the lemon peel, light soy sauce, rice vinegar, lemon juice and sugar in a small bowl. Set the mixture aside until required.

3 Heat the sunflower oil in a wok or large, heavy frying pan (skillet), and test the temperature with a few strands of noodles. They should swell to many times their size, but if they do not, wait until the oil is hot enough; otherwise they will be tough and stringy, not puffy and light.

4 Cook the noodles in batches. As soon as they turn a pale gold colour, scoop them out and drain on plenty of absorbent kitchen paper (paper towels). Leave to cool.

5 Reserve 2 tablespoons of the oil and drain off the rest. Heat the reserved oil in the wok or pan (skillet).

6 Add the marinated tofu (bean curd) to the wok or frying pan (skillet) and cook quickly over a high heat to seal.

7 Add the crushed garlic cloves, sliced red chilli and diced red (bell) pepper to the wok. Stir-fry for 1–2 minutes.

8 Add the reserved vinegar mixture to the wok, stir to mix well and add the beaten eggs, stirring until they are set.

9 Serve the tofu (bean curd) mixture with the crispy fried noodles, garnished with a red chilli flower.

Chilli Roast Potatoes

Small new potatoes are scrubbed and boiled in their skins, before being coated in a chilli mixture and roasted to perfection in the oven.

NUTRITIONAL INFORMATION

Calories 178	Sugars 2g
Protein 2g	Fat 11g
Carbohydrate ...18g	Saturates 1g

 5–10 MINS   30 MINS

SERVES 4

INGREDIENTS

500 g/1 lb 2 oz small new potatoes, scrubbed

150 ml/¼ pint/⅔ cup vegetable oil

1 tsp chilli powder

½ tsp caraway seeds

1 tsp salt

1 tbsp chopped basil

1 Cook the potatoes in a saucepan of boiling water for 10 minutes, then drain thoroughly.

2 Pour a little of the oil into a shallow roasting tin (pan) to coat the base. Heat the oil in a preheated oven, 200°C/400°F/Gas Mark 6, for 10 minutes. Add the potatoes to the tin (pan) and brush them with the hot oil.

3 In a small bowl, mix together the chilli powder, caraway seeds and salt. Sprinkle the mixture over the potatoes, turning to coat them all over.

4 Add the remaining oil to the tin (pan) and roast in the oven for about 15 minutes, or until the potatoes are cooked through.

5 Using a slotted spoon, remove the potatoes from the the oil, draining them well and transfer them to a warmed serving dish. Sprinkle the chopped basil over the top and serve immediately.

VARIATION

Use any other spice of your choice, such as curry powder or paprika, for a variation in flavour.

Sun-dried Tomato Risotto

A Milanese risotto can be cooked in a variety of ways – but always with saffron. This version with sun-dried tomatoes has a lovely tangy flavour.

NUTRITIONAL INFORMATION

Calories 558   Sugars 2g
Protein ....16g   Fat 19g
Carbohydrate ...80g   Saturates 9g

 10 MINS   30 MINS

SERVES 4

I N G R E D I E N T S

1 tbsp olive oil

25 g/1 oz/2 tbsp butter

1 large onion, finely chopped

350 g/12 oz arborio (risotto) rice, washed

about 15 strands of saffron

150 ml/¼ pint/⅔ cup white wine

850 ml/1½ pints/3¾ cups hot vegetable or
  chicken stock

8 sun-dried tomatoes, cut into strips

100 g/3½ oz frozen peas, defrosted

50 g/1¾ oz Parma ham
  (prosciutto), shredded

75 g/2¾ oz Parmesan cheese, grated

1 Heat the oil and butter in a large frying pan (skillet). Add the onion and cook for 4–5 minutes or until softened.

2 Add the rice and saffron to the frying pan (skillet), stirring well to coat the rice in the oil, and cook for 1 minute.

3 Add the wine and stock slowly to the rice mixture in the pan, a ladleful at a time, stirring and making sure that all the liquid is absorbed before adding the next ladleful of liquid.

4 About half-way through adding the stock, stir in the sun-dried tomatoes.

5 When all of the wine and stock has been absorbed, the rice should be cooked. Test by tasting a grain – if it is still crunchy, add a little more water and continue cooking. It should take 15–20 minutes to cook.

6 Stir in the peas, Parma ham (prosciutto) and cheese. Cook for 2–3 minutes, stirring, until hot. Serve with extra Parmesan.

COOK'S TIP

The finished risotto should have moist but separate grains. This is achieved by adding the hot stock a little at a time, only adding more when the last addition has been absorbed. Don't leave the risotto to cook by itself: it needs constant checking to see when more liquid is required.

Spiced Rice & Lentils

This is a lovely combination of rice and masoor dhal and is simple to cook. You can add a knob of unsalted butter before serving, if liked.

NUTRITIONAL INFORMATION

Calories	394	Sugars 3g
Protein	. . . . .14g	Fat 8g
Carbohydrate	. . .70g	Saturates 1g

  5 MINS   30 MINS

SERVES 4

I N G R E D I E N T S

200 g/7 oz/1 cup basmati rice

175 g/6 oz/³⁄₄ cup masoor dhal

2 tbsp vegetable ghee

1 small onion, sliced

1 tsp finely chopped root ginger

1 tsp crushed garlic

½ tsp turmeric

600 ml/1 pint/2½ cups water

1 tsp salt

1 Combine the rice and dhal and rinse thoroughly in cold running water. Set aside until required.

2 Heat the ghee in a large saucepan. Add the onion and fry, stirring occasionally, for about 2 minutes.

COOK'S TIP

Many Indian recipes specify using ghee as the cooking fat. This is because it is similar to clarified butter in that it can be heated to a very high temperature without burning. Ghee adds a nutty flavour to dishes and a glossy shine to sauces.

3 Reduce the heat, add the ginger, garlic, and turmeric and stir-fry for 1 minute.

4 Add the rice and dhal to the mixture in the pan and blend together, mixing gently, but thoroughly.

5 Add the water to the mixture in the pan and bring to the boil over a

medium heat. Reduce the heat, cover and cook for 20–25 minutes, until the rice is tender and the liquid is absorbed.

6 Just before serving, add the salt and mix to combine.

7 Transfer the spiced rice and lentils to a large warmed serving dish and serve immediately.

Fruity Coconut Rice

A pale yellow rice flavoured with coconut and spices to serve as an accompaniment – or as a main dish with added diced chicken or pork.

NUTRITIONAL INFORMATION

Calories 578	Sugars 17g
Protein 8g	Fat 31g
Carbohydrate 71g	Saturates 15g

5 MINS   35 MINS

SERVES 4

INGREDIENTS

90 g/3 oz creamed coconut

700 ml/1¼ pints/3 cups boiling water

1 tbsp sunflower oil (or olive oil for a stronger flavour)

1 onion, thinly sliced or chopped

250 g/9 oz/generous 1 cup long-grain rice

¼ tsp turmeric

6 whole cloves

1 cinnamon stick

½ tsp salt

60-90 g/2-3 oz/½ cup raisins or sultanas

60 g/2 oz/½ cup walnut or pecan halves, roughly chopped

2 tbsp pumpkin seeds (optional)

1 Blend the creamed coconut with half the boiling water until smooth, then stir in the remainder until well blended.

2 Heat the oil in a preheated wok, add the onion and stir-fry gently for 3-4 minutes until the onion begins to soften.

3 Rinse the rice thoroughly under cold running water, drain well and add to the wok with the turmeric. Cook for 1-2 minutes, stirring all the time.

4 Add the coconut milk, cloves, cinnamon stick and salt and bring to the boil. Cover and simmer very gently for 10 minutes.

5 Add the raisins, nuts and pumpkin seeds, if using, and mix well. Cover the wok again and continue to cook for a further 5-8 minutes or until all the liquid has been absorbed and the rice is tender. Remove from the heat and leave to stand, still tightly covered, for 5 minutes. Remove the cinnamon stick and serve.

COOK'S TIP

250g/9 oz/1 cup cooked chicken or pork cut into dice or thin slivers may be added with the raisins to turn this into a main dish. The addition of coconut milk makes the cooked rice slightly sticky.

Egg Fried Rice

In this classic Chinese dish, boiled rice is fried with peas, spring onions (scallions) and egg and flavoured with soy sauce.

NUTRITIONAL INFORMATION

Calories 203   Sugars 1g
Protein . . . . .9g   Fat 11g
Carbohydrate . . .19g   Saturates 2g

20 MINS   10 MINS

SERVES 4

INGREDIENTS

150 g/5½ oz/⅔ cup long-grain rice

3 eggs, beaten

2 tbsp vegetable oil

2 garlic cloves, crushed

4 spring onions (scallions), chopped

125 g/4½ oz/1 cup cooked peas

1 tbsp light soy sauce

pinch of salt

shredded spring onion (scallion),
   to garnish

1   Cook the rice in a pan of boiling water for 10-12 minutes, until almost cooked, but not soft. Drain well, rinse under cold water and drain again.

2   Place the beaten eggs in a saucepan and cook over a gentle heat, stirring until softly scrambled.

3   Heat the vegetable oil in a preheated wok or large frying pan (skillet), swirling the oil around the base of the wok until it is really hot.

4   Add the crushed garlic, spring onions (scallions) and peas and sauté, stirring occasionally, for 1-2 minutes. Stir the rice into the wok, mixing to combine.

5   Add the eggs, light soy sauce and a pinch of salt to the wok or frying pan (skillet) and stir to mix the egg in thoroughly.

6   Transfer the egg fried rice to serving dishes and serve garnished with the shredded spring onion (scallion).

COOK'S TIP

The rice is rinsed under cold water to wash out the tarch and prevent it from sticking together.

Pesto Rice with Garlic Bread

Try this combination of two types of rice with the richness of pine kernels (nuts), basil, and freshly grated Parmesan.

NUTRITIONAL INFORMATION

Calories 918   Sugars 2g
Protein . . . . .18g   Fat 64g
Carbohydrate . . .73g   Saturates 19g

 20 MINS   🕐 40 MINS

SERVES 4

INGREDIENTS

300 g/10½ oz/1½ cups mixed long-grain
   and wild rice

fresh basil sprigs, to garnish

tomato and orange salad, to serve

PESTO DRESSING

15 g/½ oz fresh basil

125 g/4½ oz/1 cup pine kernels (nuts)

2 garlic cloves, crushed

6 tbsp olive oil

60 g/2 oz/½ cup freshly grated Parmesan

salt and pepper

GARLIC BREAD

2 small granary or whole wheat
   French bread sticks

90 g/3 oz/½ cup butter or
   margarine, softened

2 garlic cloves, crushed

1 tsp dried mixed herbs

1 Place the rice in a saucepan and cover with water. Bring to the boil and cook for 15–20 minutes. Drain well and keep warm.

2 Meanwhile, make the pesto dressing. Remove the basil leaves from the stalks and finely chop the leaves. Reserve 25 g/1 oz/¼ cup of the pine kernels (nuts) and finely chop the remainder. Mix with the chopped basil and dressing ingredients. Alternatively, put all the ingredients in a food processor or blender and blend for a few seconds until smooth. Set aside.

3 To make the garlic bread, slice the bread at 2.5 cm/ 1 inch intervals, taking care not to slice all the way through. Mix the butter or margarine with the garlic, herbs and seasoning. Spread thickly between each slice.

4 Wrap the bread in foil and bake in a preheated oven, 200°C/400°F/Gas Mark 6, for 10–15 minutes.

5 To serve, toast the reserved pine kernels (nuts) under a preheated medium grill (broiler) for 2–3 minutes until golden. Toss the pesto dressing into the hot rice and pile into a warmed serving dish. Sprinkle with toasted pine kernels (nuts) and garnish with basil sprigs. Serve with the garlic bread and a tomato and orange salad.

Coconut Rice with Lentils

Rice and green lentils are cooked with coconut, lemon grass and curry leaves. It will serve 2 people as a main course or 4 as a side dish.

NUTRITIONAL INFORMATION

Calories 511   Sugars 3g
Protein . . . . .12g   Fat 24g
Carbohydrate . . .67g   Saturates 15g

5 MINS   50 MINS

SERVES 4

INGREDIENTS

90 g/3 oz/⅓ cup green lentils

250 g/9 oz/generous 1 cup long-grain rice

2 tbsp vegetable oil

1 onion, sliced

2 garlic cloves, crushed

3 curry leaves

1 stalk lemon grass, chopped (if unavailable, use grated rind of ½ lemon)

1 green chilli, deseeded and chopped

½ tsp cumin seeds

1½ tsp salt

90 g/3 oz/⅓ cup creamed coconut

600 ml/1 pint/2½ cups hot water

2 tbsp chopped fresh coriander (cilantro)

TO GARNISH

shredded radishes

shredded cucumber

1 Wash the lentils and place in a saucepan. Cover with cold water, bring to the boil and boil rapidly for 10 minutes.

2 Wash the rice thoroughly and drain well. Set aside until required.

3 Heat the vegetable oil in a large saucepan which has a tight-fitting lid

and fry the onion for 3–4 minutes. Add the garlic, curry leaves, lemon grass, chilli, cumin seeds and salt, and stir well.

4 Drain the lentils and rinse. Add to the onion and spices with the rice and mix well.

5 Add the creamed coconut to the hot water and stir until dissolved. Stir the coconut liquid into the rice mixture and bring to the boil. Turn down the heat to

low, put the lid on tightly and leave to cook undisturbed for 15 minutes.

6 Without removing the lid, remove the pan from the heat and leave to rest for 10 minutes to allow the rice and lentils to finish cooking in their own steam.

7 Stir in the coriander (cilantro) and remove the curry leaves. Serve garnished with the radishes and cucumber.

Special Fried Rice

This dish is a popular choice in Chinese restaurants. Ham and prawns (shrimp) are mixed with vegetables in a soy-flavoured rice.

NUTRITIONAL INFORMATION

Calories 301   Sugars 1g
Protein . . . . .26g   Fat 13g
Carbohydrate . . .21g   Saturates 3g

5 MINS   30 MINS

SERVES 4

INGREDIENTS

150 g/5½ oz/⅔ cup long-grain rice

2 tbsp vegetable oil

2 eggs, beaten

2 garlic cloves, crushed

1 tsp grated fresh root ginger

3 spring onions (scallions), sliced

75 g/2¾ oz/¾ cup cooked peas

150 g/5½ oz/⅔ cup bean sprouts

225 g/8 oz/1⅓ cups shredded ham

150 g/5½ oz peeled, cooked prawns (shrimp)

2 tbsp light soy sauce

1 Cook the rice in a saucepan of boiling water for about 15 minutes. Drain well, rinse under cold water and drain thoroughly again.

2 Heat 1 tablespoon of the vegetable oil in a preheated wok.

3 Add the beaten eggs and a further 1 teaspoon of oil. Tilt the wok so that the egg covers the base to make a thin pancake.

4 Cook until lightly browned on the underside, then flip the pancake over and cook on the other side for 1 minute. Remove from the wok and leave to cool.

5 Heat the remaining oil in the wok and stir-fry the garlic and ginger for 30 seconds. Add the spring onions (scallions), peas, bean sprouts, ham and prawns (shrimp). Stir-fry for 2 minutes.

6 Stir in the soy sauce and rice and cook for a further 2 minutes. Transfer the rice to serving dishes. Roll up the pancake, slice it very thinly and use to garnish the rice. Serve immediately.

COOK'S TIP

As this recipe contains meat and fish, it is ideal served with simpler vegetable dishes.

Thai Jasmine Rice

Every Thai meal has as its centrepiece a big bowl of steaming, fluffy Thai jasmine rice, to which salt should not be added.

NUTRITIONAL INFORMATION

Calories	239	Sugars	. . . . .0g
Protein	. . . . .5g	Fat	. . . . .2g
Carbohydrate	. . .54g	Saturates	. . . . .0.6g

5 MINS   10–15 MINS

SERVES 4

I N G R E D I E N T S

OPEN PAN METHOD

225 g/8 oz/generous 1 cup
  Thai jasmine rice

1 litre/1¾ pints/4 cups water

ABSORPTION METHOD

225 g/8 oz/generous 1 cup
  Thai jasmine rice

450 ml/16 fl oz/scant 2 cups water

1 For the open pan method, rinse the rice in a strainer under cold running water and leave to drain.

2 Bring the water to the boil. Add the rice, stir once and return to a medium boil. Cook, uncovered, for 8–10 minutes, until tender.

3 Drain thoroughly and fork through lightly before serving.

4 For the absorption method, rinse the rice under cold running water.

5 Put the rice and water into a saucepan and bring to the boil. Stir once and then cover the pan tightly. Lower the heat as much as possible. Cook for 10 minutes. Leave to rest for 5 minutes.

6 Fork through lightly and serve the rice immediately.

COOK'S TIP

Thai jasmine rice can be frozen. Freeze in a plastic sealed container. Frozen rice is ideal for stir-fry dishes, as the process seems to separate the grains.

Fried Rice in Pineapple

This looks very impressive on a party buffet. Mix the remaining pineapple flesh with paw-paw (papaya) and mango for an exotic fruit salad.

NUTRITIONAL INFORMATION

Calories ....197 Sugars 8g
Protein ....5g Fat 8g
Carbohydrate ...29g Saturates 1g

 20 MINS   10 MINS

SERVES 4

INGREDIENTS

1 large pineapple

1 tbsp sunflower oil

1 garlic clove, crushed

1 small onion, diced

½ celery stick, sliced

1 tsp coriander seeds, ground

1 tsp cumin seeds, ground

150 g/5½ oz/1½ cups button
   mushrooms, sliced

250 g/9 oz/1⅓ cups cooked rice

2 tbsp light soy sauce

½ tsp sugar

½ tsp salt

25 g/1 oz/¼ cup cashew nuts

TO GARNISH

1 spring onion (scallion),
   sliced finely

fresh coriander (cilantro) leaves

mint sprig

1 Using a sharp knife, halve the pineapple lengthways and cut out the flesh to make 2 boat-shaped shells.

2 Cut the flesh into cubes and reserve 125 g/4½ oz/1 cup to use in this recipe. (Any remaining pineapple cubes can be served separately.)

3 Heat the sunflower oil in a wok or large, heavy frying pan (skillet).

4 Cook the garlic, onion and celery over a high heat, stirring constantly, for 2 minutes. Stir in the coriander and cumin seeds, and the mushrooms.

5 Add the reserved pineapple cubes and cooked rice to the wok or frying pan (skillet) and stir well.

6 Stir in the soy sauce, sugar, salt and cashew nuts.

7 Using 2 spoons, lift and stir the rice for about 4 minutes until it is thoroughly heated.

8 Spoon the rice mixture into the pineapple boats. Garnish with sliced spring onion (scallion), coriander (cilantro) leaves and a mint sprig.

Pulao Rice

Plain boiled rice is eaten by most people in India every day, but for entertaining, a more interesting rice dish, such as this, is served.

NUTRITIONAL INFORMATION

Calories	265	Sugars 0g
Protein	.........4g	Fat 10g
Carbohydrate	...43g	Saturates 6g

🍲 5 MINS   🕐 25 MINS

SERVES 4

INGREDIENTS

200 g/7 oz/1 cup basmati rice

2 tbsp vegetable ghee

3 green cardamoms

2 cloves

3 peppercorns

½ tsp salt

½ tsp saffron

400 ml/14 fl oz/scant 2 cups water

1 Rinse the rice twice under running water and set aside until required.

2 Heat the ghee in a saucepan. Add the cardamoms, cloves and peppercorns to the pan and fry, stirring constantly, for about 1 minute.

3 Add the rice and stir-fry over a medium heat for a further 2 minutes.

4 Add the salt, saffron and water to the rice mixture and reduce the heat. Cover the pan and simmer over a low heat until the water has been absorbed.

5 Transfer the pulao rice to a serving dish and serve hot.

COOK'S TIP

The most expensive of all spices, saffron strands are the stamens of a type of crocus. They give dishes a rich, golden colour, as well as adding a distinctive, slightly bitter taste. Saffron is sold as a powder or in the more expensive strands.

Oriental-Style Millet Pilau

Millet makes an interesting alternative to rice, which is the more traditional ingredient for a pilau. Serve with a crisp oriental salad.

NUTRITIONAL INFORMATION

Calories ....660 Sugars 28g
Protein ....15g Fat 27g
Carbohydrate ...94g Saturates 5g

20 MINS   30 MINS

SERVES 4

INGREDIENTS

300 g/10½ oz/1½ cups millet grains

1 tbsp vegetable oil

1 bunch spring onions (scallions),
    white and green parts, chopped

1 garlic clove, crushed

1 tsp grated root ginger

1 orange (bell) pepper, seeded and diced

600 ml/1 pint/2½ cups water

1 orange

125 g/4½ oz/¾ cup chopped pitted dates

2 tsp sesame oil

125 g/4½ oz/1 cup roasted cashew nuts

2 tbsp pumpkin seeds

salt and pepper

oriental salad vegetables, to serve

1 Place the millet in a large saucepan and toast over a medium heat, shaking the pan occasionally, for 4–5 minutes, until the grains begin to crack and pop.

2 Heat the oil in another saucepan. Add the spring onions (scallions), garlic, ginger and (bell) pepper and fry, stirring frequently, for 2–3 minutes, until just softened, but not browned. Add the millet and pour in the water.

3 Using a vegetable peeler, pare the rind from the orange and add the rind to the pan. Squeeze the juice from the orange into the pan. Season to taste with salt and pepper.

4 Bring to the boil, reduce the heat, cover and cook gently for 20 minutes, until all the liquid has been absorbed. Remove from the heat, stir in the dates and sesame oil and leave to stand for 10 minutes.

5 Discard the orange rind and stir in the cashew nuts. Pile into a warmed serving dish, sprinkle with pumpkin seeds and serve with oriental salad vegetables.

Spiced Basmati Pilau

The whole spices are not meant to be eaten and may be removed before serving. Omit the broccoli and mushrooms for a plain, spiced pilau.

NUTRITIONAL INFORMATION

Calories 450	Sugars 3g	
Protein 9g	Fat 15g	
Carbohydrate ...76g	Saturates 2g	

20 MINS   25 MINS

SERVES 6

I N G R E D I E N T S

500 g/1 lb 2 oz/2½ cups basmati rice

175 g/6 oz broccoli, trimmed

6 tbsp vegetable oil

2 large onions, chopped

225 g/8 oz/3 cups sliced mushrooms

2 garlic cloves, crushed

6 cardamom pods, split

6 whole cloves

8 black peppercorns

1 cinnamon stick or piece of cassia bark

1 tsp ground turmeric

1.2 litres/2 pints/5 cups boiling vegetable
   stock or water

salt and pepper

60 g/2 oz/⅓ cup seedless raisins

60 g/2 oz/½ cup unsalted pistachios,
   coarsely chopped

VARIATION

For added richness, you could stir a spoonful of vegetable ghee through the rice mixture just before serving. A little diced red (bell) pepper and a few cooked peas forked through at step 4 add a colourful touch.

1 Place the rice in a strainer and wash well under cold running water. Drain. Trim off most of the broccoli stalk and cut into small florets, then quarter the stalk lengthways and cut diagonally into 1 cm/½ inch pieces.

2 Heat the oil in a large saucepan. Add the onions and broccoli stalks and cook over a low heat, stirring frequently, for 3 minutes. Add the mushrooms, rice, garlic and spices and cook for 1 minute, stirring, until the rice is coated in oil.

3 Add the boiling stock and season to taste with salt and pepper. Stir in the broccoli florets and return the mixture to the boil. Cover, reduce the heat and cook over a low heat for 15 minutes without uncovering the pan.

4 Remove from the heat and leave to stand for 5 minutes without uncovering. Add the raisins and pistachios and gently fork through to fluff up the grains. Serve hot.

Curried Rice with Tofu

Cooked rice is combined with marinated tofu (bean curd), vegetables and peanuts to make this deliciously rich curry.

NUTRITIONAL INFORMATION

Calories 598	Sugars 2g	
Protein 16g	Fat 25	
Carbohydrate ...81g	Saturates 4g	

15 MINS   15 MINS

SERVES 4

I N G R E D I E N T S

1 tsp coriander seeds

1 tsp cumin seeds

1 tsp ground cinnamon

1 tsp cloves

1 whole star anise

1 tsp cardamom pods

1 tsp white peppercorns

1 tbsp oil

6 shallots, chopped very roughly

6 garlic cloves, chopped very roughly

5-cm/2-inch piece lemon grass, sliced

4 fresh red chillies, deseeded and chopped

grated rind of 1 lime

1 tsp salt

3 tbsp sunflower oil

250 g/9 oz/1 cup marinated tofu (bean curd), cut into 2.5 cm/1 inch cubes

125 g/4½ oz green beans, cut into 2.5cm/ 1 inch lengths

1 kg/2 lb 4 oz/6 cups cooked rice (300 g/10½ oz/1½ cups raw weight)

3 shallots, diced finely and deep-fried

1 spring onion (scallion), chopped finely

2 tbsp chopped roast peanuts

1 tbsp lime juice

1 To make the curry paste, grind together the seeds and spices in a pestle and mortar or spice grinder.

2 Heat the sunflower oil in a preheated wok until it is really hot. Add the shallots, garlic and lemon grass and cook over a low heat until soft, about 5 minutes. Add the chillies and grind together with the dry spices. Stir in the lime rind and salt.

3 To make the curry, heat the oil in a wok or large, heavy frying pan (skillet). Cook the tofu (bean curd) over a high heat for 2 minutes to seal. Stir in the curry paste and beans. Add the rice and, stir over a high heat for about 3 minutes.

4 Transfer to a warmed serving dish. Sprinkle with the deep-fried shallots, spring onion (scallion) and peanuts. Squeeze over the lime juice.

Savoury (Bell) Pepper Bread

This flavoursome bread contains only the minimum amount of fat.
Serve with a bowl of hot soup for a filling and nutritious light meal.

NUTRITIONAL INFORMATION

Calories 468   Sugars 11g
Protein . . . . .16g   Fat 5g
Carbohydrate . . .97g   Saturates 1g

 2 HOURS 50 MINS

SERVES 4

INGREDIENTS

1 small red (bell) pepper

1 small green (bell) pepper

1 small yellow (bell) pepper

60 g/2 oz dry-pack sun-dried tomatoes

50 ml/2 fl oz/¼ cup boiling water

2 tsp dried yeast

1 tsp caster (superfine) sugar

150 ml/5 fl oz/⅔ cup tepid water

450 g/1 lb/4 cups strong white bread flour

2 tsp dried rosemary

2 tbsp tomato purée (paste)

150 ml/5 fl oz/⅔ cup low-fat natural
     fromage frais (unsweetened yogurt)

1 tbsp coarse salt

1 tbsp olive oil

1 Preheat the oven to 220°C/425°F/Gas Mark 7 and the grill (broiler) to hot. Halve and deseed the (bell) peppers, arrange on the grill (broiler) rack and cook until the skin is charred. Leave to cool for 10 minutes, peel off the skin and chop the flesh. Slice the tomatoes into strips, place in a bowl and pour over the boiling water. Leave to soak.

2 Place the yeast and sugar in a small jug, pour over the tepid water and leave for 10–15 minutes until frothy. Sift the flour into a bowl and add 1 teaspoon of dried rosemary. Make a well in the centre and pour in the yeast mixture.

3 Add the tomato purée (paste), tomatoes and soaking liquid, (bell) peppers, fromage frais (yogurt) and half the salt. Mix to form a soft dough. Turn out on to a lightly floured surface and knead for 3–4 minutes until smooth and elastic. Place in a lightly floured bowl, cover and leave in a warm room for 40 minutes until doubled in size.

4 Knead the dough again and place in a lightly greased 23 cm/9 inch round spring-clip cake tin. Using a wooden spoon, form 'dimples' in the surface. Cover and leave for 30 minutes. Brush with oil and sprinkle with rosemary and salt. Bake for 35–40 minutes, cool for 10 minutes and release from the tin. Leave to cool on a rack and serve.

COOK'S TIP

For a quick, filling snack serve the bread with a bowl of hot soup in winter, or a crisp leaf salad in summer.

Roasted (Bell) Pepper Bread

(Bell) peppers become sweet and mild when they are roasted and make this bread delicious.

NUTRITIONAL INFORMATION

Calories 426	Sugars 4g	
Protein 12g	Fat 4g	
Carbohydrate ...90g	Saturates 1g	

🍞 1¾ HOURS   ⏱ 1 HR 5 MINS

SERVES 4

I N G R E D I E N T S

1 red (bell) pepper, halved and deseeded

1 yellow (bell) pepper, halved and deseeded

2 sprigs of rosemary

1 tbsp olive oil

7 g/¼ oz dried yeast

1 tsp sugar

300 ml/½ pint/1¼ cups hand-hot water

450 g/1 lb strong white flour

1 tsp salt

1 Grease a 23 cm/9 inch deep round cake tin (pan).

2 Place the (bell) peppers and rosemary in a shallow roasting tin (pan). Pour over the oil and roast in a preheated oven, at 200°C/400°F/Gas Mark 6, for 20 minutes or until slightly charred. Remove the skin from the (bell) peppers and cut the flesh into slices.

3 Place the yeast and sugar in a small bowl and mix with 100 ml/3½ fl oz/8 tablespoons of hand-hot water. Leave to ferment in a warm place for 15 minutes.

4 Mix the flour and salt together in a large bowl. Stir in the yeast mixture and the remaining water and mix to form a smooth dough.

5 Knead the dough for about 5 minutes until smooth. Cover with oiled cling film (plastic wrap) and leave to rise for about 30 minutes or until doubled in size.

6 Cut the dough into 3 equal portions. Roll the portions into rounds slightly larger than the cake tin (pan).

7 Place 1 round in the base of the tin (pan) so that it reaches up the sides of the tin (pan) by about 2 cm/¾ inch. Top with half of the (bell) pepper mixture.

8 Place the second round of dough on top, followed by the remaining (bell) pepper mixture. Place the last round of dough on top, pushing the edges of the dough down the sides of the tin (pan).

9 Cover the dough with oiled cling film (plastic wrap) and leave to rise for 30–40 minutes. Return to the oven and bake for 45 minutes until golden or the base sounds hollow when lightly tapped. Serve warm.

Roman Focaccia

Roman focaccia makes a delicious snack on its own or serve it with cured meats and salad for a quick supper.

NUTRITIONAL INFORMATION

Calories 119   Sugars 2g
Protein . . . . .3g   Fat 2g
Carbohydrate . . .24g   Saturates 0.3g

🕐 1 HOUR   🕑 45 MINS

Makes 16 squares

I N G R E D I E N T S

1 tsp sugar

300 ml/½ pint/1¼ cups hand-hot water

450 g/1 lb strong white flour

2 tsp salt

3 tbsp rosemary, chopped

2 tbsp olive oil

450 g/1 lb mixed red and white onions,
    sliced into rings

4 garlic cloves, sliced

1 Place the yeast and the sugar in a small bowl and mix with 100 ml/3½ fl oz/8 tablespoons of the water. Leave to ferment in a warm place for 15 minutes.

2 Mix the flour with the salt in a large bowl. Add the yeast mixture, half of the rosemary and the remaining water and mix to form a smooth dough. Knead the dough for 4 minutes.

3 Cover the dough with oiled cling film (plastic wrap) and leave to rise for 30 minutes or until doubled in size.

4 Meanwhile, heat the oil in a large pan. Add the onions and garlic and fry for 5 minutes or until softened. Cover the pan and continue to cook for 7–8 minutes or until the onions are lightly caramelized.

5 Remove the dough from the bowl and knead it again for 1–2 minutes.

6 Roll the dough out to form a square shape. The dough should be no more than 6 mm/¼ inch thick because it will rise during cooking. Place the dough on to a large baking tray (cookie sheet), pushing out the edges until even.

7 Spread the onions over the dough, and sprinkle with the remaining rosemary.

8 Bake in a preheated oven, at 200°C/400°F/Gas Mark 6, for 25–30 minutes or until a golden brown colour. Cut the focaccia into 16 squares and serve immediately.

Parathas

These triangular shaped breads are so easy to make and are the perfect addition to most Indian meals. Serve hot, spread with a little butter.

NUTRITIONAL INFORMATION

Calories ....127 Sugars 0.5g
Protein ....3g Fat 4g
Carbohydrate ...22g Saturates 0.4g

🍰 50 MINS 🕐 10 MINS

SERVES 6

I N G R E D I E N T S

90 g/3 oz/¾ cup plain (all-purpose)
   wholemeal (whole wheat)flour

90 g/3 oz/¾ cup plain (all-purpose) flour

pinch of salt

1 tbsp vegetable oil, plus extra for greasing

75 ml/3 fl oz/⅓ cup tepid water

1 Place the flours and the salt in a bowl. Drizzle 1 tablespoon of oil over the flour, add the tepid water and mix to form a soft dough, adding a little more water, if necessary. Knead on a lightly floured surface until smooth, then cover and leave for 30 minutes.

2 Knead the dough on a floured surface and divide into 6 equal pieces. Shape each one into a ball. Roll out on a floured surface to a 15 cm/6 inch round and brush very lightly with oil.

3 Fold in half, and then in half again to form a triangle. Roll out to form an 18 cm/7 in triangle (when measured from point to centre top), dusting with extra flour as necessary.

4 Brush a large, heavy-based frying pan (skillet) with a little oil and heat until hot, then add one or two parathas and cook for about 1–1½ minutes. Brush the surfaces very lightly with oil, then turn and cook the other sides for 1½ minutes until completely cooked through.

5 Place the cooked parathas on a plate and cover with foil, or place between the folds of a clean tea towel (dish cloth) to keep warm, while you are cooking the remainder in the same way, greasing the pan between cooking each batch.

VARIATION

If the parathas puff up a lot during cooking, press down lightly with a fish slice. Make parathas in advance if wished: wrap in kitchen foil and reheat in a hot oven for about 15 minutes when required.

Gnocchi Piemontese

Gnocchi, a speciality from northern Italy, are small dumplings that are either poached or baked. Prepare the Espagnole Sauce well in advance.

NUTRITIONAL INFORMATION

Calories 643	Sugars 4g	
Protein 25g	Fat 44g	
Carbohydrate . . .34g	Saturates 21g	

4³/₄ HOURS   15 MINS

SERVES 4

INGREDIENTS

450 g/1 lb warm mashed potato

75 g/2¾ oz/⅝ cup self-raising flour

1 egg

2 egg yolks

1 tbsp olive oil

150 ml/¼ pint/⅝ cup Espagnole Sauce
   (see page 7)

60 g/2 oz/4 tbsp butter

175 g/6 oz/2 cups freshly grated Parmesan
   cheese

salt and pepper

freshly chopped herbs, to garnish

1 In a large bowl, mix together the mashed potato and flour. Add the egg and egg yolks, season with salt and pepper and mix together to form a dough.

VARIATION

Serve with a tomato sauce.
Mix 115 g/4 oz/1 cup chopped sun-dried tomatoes, 1 sliced celery stick, 1 crushed garlic clove and 6 tbsp red wine in a pan. Cook over a low heat for 15–20 minutes. Stir in 8 skinned, chopped plum tomatoes, season and simmer for 10 minutes.

2 Break off pieces of the dough and roll between the palms of your hands to form small balls the size of a walnut. Flatten the balls with a fork into the shape of small cylinders.

3 Bring a large pan of lightly salted water to the boil. Add the gnocchi and olive oil and poach for 10 minutes.

4 Mix together the Espagnole Sauce and the butter in a large saucepan over a gentle heat. Gradually blend in the grated Parmesan cheese.

5 Remove the gnocchi from the pan with a slotted spoon. Toss the gnocchi in the sauce, transfer to 4 serving plates, garnish and serve immediately.

Mixed (Bell) Pepper Pooris

These pooris are easy to make and so good to eat served with a scrumptious topping of spicy mixed (bell) peppers and yogurt.

NUTRITIONAL INFORMATION

Calories 386	Sugars 6g	
Protein 5g	Fat 32g	
Carbohydrate ...21g	Saturates 4g	

 55 MINS 15 MINS

SERVES 6

INGREDIENTS

POORIS

125 g/4½ oz/ 1 cup plain (all-purpose) wholemeal (whole wheat) flour

1 tbsp vegetable ghee or oil

pinch of salt

5 tbsp hot water

vegetable oil, for shallow frying

coriander (cilantro) sprigs, to garnish

natural (unsweetened) yogurt, to serve

TOPPING

4 tbsp vegetable ghee or oil

1 large onion, quartered and thinly sliced

½ red (bell) pepper, seeded and thinly sliced

½ green (bell) pepper, seeded and thinly sliced

¼ aubergine (eggplant), cut lengthways into 6 wedges and thinly sliced

1 garlic clove, crushed

2.5 cm/1 inch piece of root ginger, chopped

½-1 tsp minced chilli

2 tsp mild or medium curry paste

225 g/8 oz can chopped tomatoes

salt

1. To make the pooris, put the flour in a bowl with the ghee or oil and salt. Add hot water and mix to form a fairly soft dough. Knead gently, cover with a damp cloth and leave for 30 minutes.

2. Meanwhile, prepare the topping. Heat the ghee or oil in a large saucepan. Add the onion, (bell) peppers, aubergine (eggplant), garlic, ginger, chilli and curry paste and fry gently for 5 minutes. Stir in the tomatoes and salt to taste and simmer gently, uncovered, for 5 minutes, stirring occasionally until the sauce thickens. Remove from the heat.

3. Knead the dough on a floured surface and divide into 6. Roll each piece to a round about 15 cm/6 inches in diameter. Cover each one as you finish rolling to prevent drying out.

4. Heat about 1 cm/½ inch oil in a large frying pan (skillet). Add the pooris, one at a time, and fry for about 15 seconds on each side, until puffed and golden, turning frequently. Drain on kitchen paper (paper towels) and keep warm while you are cooking the remainder in the same way.

5. Reheat the vegetable mixture. Place a poori on each serving plate and top with the vegetable mixture. Add a spoonful of yogurt to each, garnish with the coriander (cilantro) sprigs and serve.

Italian Bruschetta

It is important to use a good quality olive oil for this recipe. Serve the bruschetta with kebabs (kabobs) or fish for a really summery taste.

NUTRITIONAL INFORMATION

Calories	.415	Sugars	.2g
Protein	.8g	Fat	.24g
Carbohydrate	.45g	Saturates	.4g

10 MINS   10 MINS

Makes 1 loaf

I N G R E D I E N T S

1 ciabatta loaf or small stick of
  French bread

1 plump clove garlic

extra virgin olive oil

fresh Parmesan cheese, grated (optional)

1 Slice the bread in half crossways and again lengthwise to give 4 portions.

2 Do not peel the garlic clove, but cut it in half.

3 Barbecue (grill) the bread over hot coals for 2–3 minutes on both sides or until golden brown.

4 Rub the garlic, cut side down, all over the toasted surface of the bread.

COOK'S TIP

As ready-grated Parmesan quickly loses its pungency and 'bite', it is better to buy small quantities of the cheese in one piece and grate it as needed. Tightly wrapped in cling film (plastic wrap) or foil, it will keep in the refrigerator for several months.

5 Drizzle the olive oil over the bread and serve hot as an accompaniment.

6 If using Parmesan cheese, sprinkle the cheese over the bread.

7 Return the bread to the barbecue (grill), cut side up, for 1–2 minutes or until the cheese just begins to melt. Serve hot.

Naan Bread

There are many ways of making naan bread, but this recipe is very easy to follow. Naan bread should be served immediately after cooking.

NUTRITIONAL INFORMATION

Calories . . . . . . .152 Sugars 1g
Protein . . . . .3g Fat 7g
Carbohydrate . . .20g Saturates 4g

 2¼ HOURS   10 MINS

SERVES 8

I N G R E D I E N T S

1 tsp sugar

1 tsp fresh yeast

150 ml/¼ pint/⅔ cup warm water

200 g/7 oz/1½ cups plain (all-purpose) flour

1 tbsp ghee

1 tsp salt

50 g/1¾ oz/4 tbsp unsalted butter

1 tsp poppy seeds

1 Put the sugar and yeast in a small bowl or jug together with the warm water and mix thoroughly until the yeast has completely dissolved. Set aside for about 10 minutes, or until the mixture is frothy.

2 Place the flour in a large mixing bowl. Make a well in the centre of the flour, add the ghee and salt and pour in the yeast mixture. Mix thoroughly to form a dough, using your hands and adding more water if required.

3 Turn the dough out on to a floured work surface (counter) and knead for about 5 minutes, or until smooth.

4 Return the dough to the bowl, cover and set aside to rise in a warm place for 1½ hours, or until doubled in size.

5 Turn the dough out on to a floured surface and knead for a further 2 minutes. Break off small balls with your hand and pat them into rounds about 12 cm/ 5 inches in diameter and 1 cm/ ½ inch thick.

6 Place the dough rounds on a greased sheet of foil and grill (broil) under a very hot preheated grill (broiler) for 7–10 minutes, turning twice and brushing with the butter and sprinkling with the poppy seeds.

7 Serve warm immediately, or keep wrapped in foil until required.

Lightly Fried Bread

This is perfect with egg dishes and vegetable curries. Allow 2 portions of bread per person. The nutritional information is for each portion.

NUTRITIONAL INFORMATION

Calories 133   Sugars 1g
Protein ....3g   Fat 7g
Carbohydrate ...17g   Saturates 4g

 35 MINS   20-25 MINS

MAKES 10

INGREDIENTS

225 g/8 oz/1½ cups wholemeal (whole wheat) ata or chapati flour

½ tsp salt

1 tbsp ghee

300 ml/½ pint/1¼ cups water

1 Place the flour and the salt in a large mixing bowl and mix to combine.

2 Make a well in the centre of the flour. Add the ghee and rub in well. Gradually pour in the water and work to form a soft dough. Set the dough aside to rise for 10–15 minutes.

3 Carefully knead the dough for about 5-7 minutes. Divide the dough into about 10 equal portions.

4 On a lightly floured surface, roll out each dough portion to form a flat pancake shape.

5 Using a sharp knife, lightly draw lines in a criss-cross pattern on each rolled-out dough portion.

6 Heat a heavy-based frying pan (skillet). Gently place the dough portions, one by one, into the pan.

7 Cook the bread for about 1 minute, then turn over and spread with 1 teaspoon of ghee. Turn the bread over again and fry gently, moving it around the pan with a spatula, until golden. Turn the bread over once again, then remove from the pan and keep warm while you cook the remaining batches.

COOK TIP

In India breads are cooked on a tava, a traditional flat griddle. A large frying pan (skillet) makes an adequate substitute.

Sun-dried Tomato Loaf

This delicious tomato bread is great with cheese or soup or to make an unusual sandwich. This recipe makes one loaf.

NUTRITIONAL INFORMATION

Calories 403	Sugars 5g
Protein 12g	Fat 2g
Carbohydrate ...91g	Saturates 0.3g

1¾ HOURS | 35 MINS

SERVES 4

INGREDIENTS

7 g/¼ oz dried yeast

1 tsp sugar

300 ml/½ pint/1¼ cups hand-hot water

1 tsp salt

2 tsp dried basil

450 g/1 lb strong white flour

2 tbsp sun-dried tomato paste or tomato purée (paste)

12 sun-dried tomatoes, cut into strips

1 Place the yeast and sugar in a bowl and mix with 100 ml/3½ fl oz/ 8 tablespoons of the water. Leave to ferment in a warm place for 15 minutes.

2 Place the flour in a bowl and stir in the salt. Make a well in the dry ingredients and add the basil, the yeast mixture, tomato paste and half of the remaining water. Using a wooden spoon, draw the flour into the liquid and mix to form a dough, adding the rest of the water gradually.

3 Turn out the dough on to a floured surface and knead for 5 minutes or until smooth. Cover with oiled cling film (plastic wrap) and leave in a warm place to rise for about 30 minutes or until doubled in size.

4 Lightly grease a 900 g/2 lb loaf tin (pan).

5 Remove the dough from the bowl and knead in the sun-dried tomatoes. Knead again for 2–3 minutes.

6 Place the dough in the tin (pan) and leave to rise for 30–40 minutes.or until it has doubled in size again,. Bake in a preheated oven, at 190°C/375°F/Gas Mark 5, for 30–35 minutes or until golden and the base sounds hollow when tapped.

COOK'S TIP

You could make mini sun-dried tomato loaves for children. Divide the dough into 8 equal portions, leave to rise and bake in mini-loaf tins (pans) for 20 minutes. Alternatively, make 12 small rounds, leave to rise and bake as rolls for 12–15 minutes.

Olive Oil Bread with Cheese

This flat cheese bread is sometimes called *foccacia*. It is delicious served with *antipasto* or simply on its own. This recipe makes one loaf.

NUTRITIONAL INFORMATION

Calories	586	Sugars 3g
Protein	. . . . .22g	Fat 26g
Carbohydrate	. . .69g	Saturates 12g

 1 HOUR   🕐 30 MINS

SERVES 4

I N G R E D I E N T S

15 g/½ oz dried yeast

1 tsp sugar

250 ml/9 fl oz hand-hot water

350 g/12 oz strong flour

1 tsp salt

3 tbsp olive oil

200 g/7 oz pecorino cheese, cubed

½ tbsp fennel seeds, lightly crushed

1 Mix the yeast with the sugar and 100 ml/3½ fl oz/8 tbsp of the water. Leave to ferment in a warm place for about 15 minutes.

2 Mix the flour with the salt. Add 1 tablespoon of the oil, the yeast mixture and the remaining water to form a smooth dough. Knead the dough for 4 minutes.

COOK'S TIP

Pecorino is a hard, quite salty cheese, which is sold in most large supermarkets and Italian delicatessens. If you cannot obtain pecorino, use strong Cheddar or Parmesan cheese instead.

3 Divide the dough into 2 equal portions. Roll out each portion to a form a round 6 mm/¼ inch thick. Place 1 round on a baking tray (cookie sheet).

4 Scatter the cheese and half of the fennel seeds evenly over the round.

5 Place the second round on top and squeeze the edges together to seal so that the filling does not leak during the cooking time.

6 Using a sharp knife, make a few slashes in the top of the dough and brush with the remaining olive oil.

7 Sprinkle with the remaining fennel seeds and leave the dough to rise for 20–30 minutes.

8 Bake in a preheated oven, at 200°C/400°F/Gas Mark 6, for 30 minutes or until golden brown. Serve immediately.

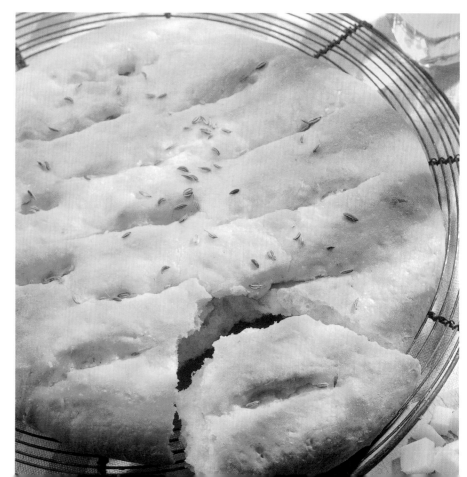

Garlic Bread

A perennial favourite, garlic bread is perfect with a range of barbecue (grill) meals.

NUTRITIONAL INFORMATION

Calories 261   Sugars 1g
Protein ....3g   Fat 22g
Carbohydrate ...15g   Saturates 14g

 10 MINS   15 MINS

SERVES 6

INGREDIENTS

150 g/5½ oz butter, softened

3 cloves garlic, crushed

2 tbsp chopped, fresh parsley

pepper

1 large or 2 small sticks of French bread

1 Mix together the butter, garlic and parsley in a bowl until well combined. Season with pepper to taste and mix well.

2 Cut the French bread into thick slices.

3 Spread the flavoured butter over one side of each slice and reassemble the loaf on a large sheet of thick kitchen foil.

4 Wrap the bread well and barbecue (grill) over hot coals for 10–15 minutes until the butter melts and the bread is piping hot.

5 Serve as an accompaniment to a wide range of dishes.

Desserts

Not everyone has a sweet tooth or is a great pudding fanatic, but most people will have a longing for some type of sweet from time to time, and a dessert is always a good way to round off a meal. Here is a selection of all-time classic desserts from around the world. Bread & Butter Pudding, Syrup Sponge and Summer Pudding are great British favourites while classics from other countries include Tiramisu and Zabaglione from Italy and Cherry Clafoutis from France. There is also a selection of Indian desserts for those who have a very sweet tooth: Sweet Carrot Halva, Semolina Dessert and Indian Vermicelli Pudding are just a few. Fruit is always a good way to end a meal as it is naturally rich in sugar and this chapter contains various fruit and fruit-based desserts including several variations on fruit salad.

Cherry Clafoutis

This is a hot dessert that is simple and quick to put together. Try the batter with other fruits. Apricots and plums are particularly delicious.

NUTRITIONAL INFORMATION

Calories	.261	Sugars	.24g
Protein	.10g	Fat	.6g
Carbohydrate	.40g	Saturates	.3g

10 MINS   40 MINS

SERVES 6

INGREDIENTS

125 g/4½ oz/1 cup plain (all-
    purpose) flour

4 eggs, lightly beaten

2 tbsp caster (superfine) sugar

pinch of salt

600 ml/1 pint/2½ cups milk

butter, for greasing

500 g/1 lb 2 oz black cherries,
    fresh or canned, stoned (pitted)

3 tbsp brandy

1 tbsp sugar, to decorate

1 Sift the flour into a large mixing bowl. Make a well in the centre and add the eggs, sugar and salt. Gradually, draw in the flour from around the edges and whisk.

2 Pour in the milk and whisk the batter thoroughly until very smooth.

3 Thoroughly grease a 1.75 litre/3 pint/7½ cup ovenproof serving dish with butter and pour in about half of the batter.

4 Spoon over the cherries and pour the remaining batter over the top. Sprinkle the brandy over the batter.

5 Bake in a preheated oven, 180°C/ 350°F/Gas Mark 4, for 40 minutes, until risen and golden.

6 Remove from the oven and sprinkle over the sugar just before serving. Serve warm.

Tiramisu Layers

This is a modern version of the well-known and very traditional chocolate dessert from Italy.

NUTRITIONAL INFORMATION

Calories 798	Sugars 60g
Protein 12g	Fat 50g
Carbohydrate ...76g	Saturates 25g

1¼ HOURS   5 MINS

SERVES 6

INGREDIENTS

300 g/10½ oz dark chocolate

400 g/14 oz mascarpone cheese

150 ml/¼ pint/⅔ cup double (heavy) cream, whipped until it just holds its shape

400 ml/14 fl oz black coffee with 50 g/ 1¾ oz caster (superfine) sugar, cooled

6 tbsp dark rum or brandy

36 sponge fingers (lady-fingers), about 400 g/14 oz

cocoa powder, to dust

1 Melt the chocolate in a bowl set over a saucepan of simmering water, stirring occasionally. Leave the chocolate to cool slightly, then stir it into the mascarpone and cream.

2 Mix the coffee and rum together in a bowl. Dip the sponge fingers (lady-fingers) into the mixture briefly so that they absorb the coffee and rum liquid but do not become soggy.

3 Place 3 sponge fingers (lady-fingers) on 3 serving plates.

4 Spoon a layer of the mascarpone and chocolate mixture over the sponge fingers (lady-fingers).

5 Place 3 more sponge fingers (lady-fingers) on top of the mascarpone layer. Spread another layer of mascarpone and chocolate mixture and place 3 more sponge fingers (lady-fingers) on top.

6 Leave the tiramisu to chill in the refrigerator for at least 1 hour. Dust all over with a little cocoa powder just before serving.

VARIATION

Try adding 50 g/1¾ oz toasted, chopped hazelnuts to the chocolate cream mixture in step 1, if you prefer.

Coconut Cream Moulds

Smooth, creamy and refreshing – these tempting little custards are made with an unusual combination of coconut milk, cream and eggs.

🍧 10 MINS 🕐 45 MINS

SERVES 8

INGREDIENTS

CARAMEL

125 g/4½ oz/½ cup granulated sugar

150 ml/¼ pint/⅔ cup water

CUSTARD

300 ml/½ pint/1¼ cups water

90g/3 oz creamed coconut, chopped

2 eggs

2 egg yolks

1½ tbsp caster (superfine) sugar

300 ml/½ pint/1¼ cups single (light) cream

sliced banana or slivers of fresh pineapple

1-2 tbsp freshly grated or desiccated
(shredded) coconut

1 Have ready 8 small ovenproof dishes about 150 ml/¼ pint/⅔ cup capacity. To make the caramel, place the granulated sugar and water in a saucepan and heat gently to dissolve the sugar, then boil rapidly, without stirring, until the mixture turns a rich golden brown.

2 Immediately remove the pan from the heat and dip the base into a bowl of cold water in order to stop it cooking further. Quickly, but carefully, pour the caramel into the ovenproof dishes to coat the bases.

3 To make the custard, place the water in the same saucepan, add the coconut and heat, stirring constantly, until the coconut dissolves. Place the eggs, egg yolks and caster (superfine) sugar in a bowl and beat well with a fork. Add the hot coconut milk and stir well to dissolve the sugar. Stir in the cream and strain the mixture into a jug.

4 Arrange the dishes in a roasting tin (pan) and fill with enough cold water to come halfway up the sides of the dishes. Pour the custard mixture into the caramel-lined dishes, cover with greaseproof paper or foil and cook in a preheated oven, 150°C/300°F/Gas Mark 2, for about 40 minutes, or until set.

5 Remove the dishes, set aside to cool and then chill overnight. To serve, run a knife around the edge of each dish and turn out on to a serving plate. Serve with slices of banana or slivers of fresh pineapple sprinkled with freshly grated or desiccated coconut.

Exotic Fruit Parcels

Delicious pieces of exotic fruit are warmed through in a deliciously scented sauce to make a fabulous barbecue (grill) dessert.

NUTRITIONAL INFORMATION

Calories 43	Sugars 9g
Protein 2g	Fat 0.3g
Carbohydrate 9g	Saturates 0.1g

40 MINS   20 MINS

SERVES 4

I N G R E D I E N T S

1 paw-paw (papaya)

1 mango

1 star fruit

1 tbsp grenadine

3 tbsp orange juice

single (light) cream or natural yogurt, to serve

1 Cut the paw-paw (papaya) in half, scoop out the seeds and discard them. Peel the paw-paw (papaya) and cut the flesh into thick slices.

2 Prepare the mango by cutting it lengthways in half either side of the central stone.

3 Score each mango half in a criss-cross pattern. Push each mango half inside out to separate the cubes and cut them away from the peel.

4 Using a sharp knife, thickly slice the star fruit.

5 Place all of the fruit in a bowl and mix them together.

6 Mix the grenadine and orange juice together and pour over the fruit. Leave to marinate for at least 30 minutes.

7 Divide the fruit among 4 double thickness squares of kitchen foil and gather up the edges to form a parcel that encloses the fruit.

8 Place the foil parcel on a rack set over warm coals and barbecue (grill) the fruit for 15–20 minutes.

9 Serve the fruit in the parcel, with the low-fat natural yogurt.

COOK'S TIP

Grenadine is a sweet syrup made from pomegranates. If you prefer you could use pomegranate juice instead. To extract the juice, cut the pomegranate in half and squeeze gently with a lemon squeezer – do not press too hard or the juice may become bitter.

Aromatic Fruit Salad

The fruits in this salad are arranged attractively on serving plates with a spicy syrup spooned over.

NUTRITIONAL INFORMATION

Calories 125   Sugars 29g
Protein . . . . .3g   Fat 1g
Carbohydrate . . .29g   Saturates 0.2g

25 MINS   5 MINS

SERVES 6

INGREDIENTS

60 g/1½ oz/3 tbsp granulated sugar

150 ml/¼ pint/⅔ cup water

1 cinnamon stick or large piece of cassia bark

4 cardamom pods, crushed

1 clove

juice of 1 orange

juice of 1 lime

½ honeydew melon

a good-sized wedge of watermelon

2 ripe guavas

3 ripe nectarines

about 18 strawberries

a little toasted, shredded coconut, for sprinkling

sprigs of mint or rose petals, to decorate

strained low-fat (unsweetened) yogurt, for serving

1 First prepare the syrup. Put the sugar, water, cinnamon, cardamom pods and cloves into a pan and bring to the boil, stirring to dissolve the sugar. Simmer for 2 minutes, then remove from heat.

2 Add the orange and lime juices to the syrup and leave to cool and infuse while preparing the fruits.

3 Peel and remove the seeds from the melons and cut the flesh into neat slices.

4 Cut the guavas in half, scoop out the seeds, then peel and slice the flesh neatly.

5 Cut the nectarines into slices and hull and slice the strawberries.

6 Arrange the slices of fruit attractively on 6 serving plates.

7 Strain the prepared cooled syrup and spoon over the sliced fruits.

8 Sprinkle the fruit salad with a little toasted coconut. Decorate each serving with sprigs of mint or rose petals and serve with yogurt.

Coconut Bananas

This elaborate dessert is the perfect finale for a Chinese banquet.
Bananas are fried in a citrus-flavoured butter and served with coconut.

NUTRITIONAL INFORMATION

Calories 514   Sugars 70g
Protein . . . . .4g   Fat 21g
Carbohydrate . . .75g   Saturates 14g

10 MINS   10 MINS

SERVES 4

INGREDIENTS

3 tbsp shredded fresh coconut

60 g/2 oz/¼ cup unsalted butter

1 tbsp grated ginger root

grated zest of 1 orange

60 g/2 oz/¼ cup caster (superfine) sugar

4 tbsp fresh lime juice

6 bananas

6 tbsp orange liqueur (Cointreau or Grand Marnier, for example)

3 tsp toasted sesame seeds

lime slices, to decorate

ice-cream, to serve (optional)

1 Heat a small non-stick frying pan (skillet) until hot. Add the coconut and cook, stirring constantly, for 1 minute until lightly coloured. Remove from the pan and allow to cool.

2 Melt the butter in a large frying pan (skillet) and add the ginger, orange zest, sugar and lime juice. Mix well.

3 Peel and slice the bananas length-ways (and halve if they are very large). Place the bananas cut-side down in the butter mixture and cook for 1-2 minutes or until the sauce mixture starts to become sticky. Turn the bananas to coat in the sauce.

4 Remove the bananas and place on heated serving plates. Keep warm.

5 Return the pan to the heat and add the orange liqueur, blending well. Ignite with a taper, allow the flames to die down, then pour over the bananas.

6 Sprinkle with the reserved coconut and sesame seeds and serve at once, decorated with slices of lime.

COOK'S TIP

For a very special treat try serving this with a flavoured ice-cream such as coconut, ginger or praline.

Tropical Fruit Rice Mould

A rice pudding with a twist. Light flakes of rice with a tang of pineapple and lime. You can serve it with any selection of your favourite fruits.

NUTRITIONAL INFORMATION

Calories 145	Sugars 18g
Protein 7g	Fat 1g
Carbohydrate ...30g	Saturates 0.3g

4¼ HOURS   25 MINS

SERVES 8

I N G R E D I E N T S

225 g/8 oz/1 cup + 2 tbsp short-grain or pudding rice, rinsed

850 ml/1½ pints/3¾ cups skimmed milk

1 tbsp caster (superfine) sugar

4 tbsp white rum with coconut or unsweetened pineapple juice

175 ml/6 fl oz/¾ cup low-fat natural yogurt

400 g/14 oz can pineapple pieces in natural juice, drained and chopped

1 tsp grated lime rind

1 tbsp lime juice

1 sachet/1 envelope powdered gelatine dissolved in 3 tbsp boiling water

lime wedges, to decorate

mixed tropical fruits such as passion-fruit, baby pineapple, paw-paw (papaya), mango, carambola (star fruit), to serve

COOK'S TIP

Try serving this dessert with a light sauce made from 300 ml/ ½ pint/1¼ cups tropical fruit or pineapple juice thickened with 2 tsp arrowroot.

1 Place the rice and milk in a saucepan. Bring to the boil, then simmer gently, uncovered, for 20 minutes until the rice is soft and the milk is absorbed.

2 Stir the mixture occasionally and keep the heat low to prevent sticking. Transfer to a mixing bowl and leave to cool.

3 Stir the sugar, white rum with coconut or pineapple juice, yogurt, pineapple pieces, lime rind and juice into the rice. Fold into the gelatine mixture.

4 Rinse a 1.5 litre/2½ pint/1½ quart non-stick ring mould or ring cake tin (pan) with water and spoon in the rice mixture. Press down well and chill for 2 hours until firm.

5 To serve, loosen the rice from the mould with a small palette knife (spatula) and invert on to a serving plate.

6 Decorate with lime wedges and fill the centre with assorted tropical fruits.

Poached Allspice Pears

These pears are moist and delicious after poaching in a sugar and all-spice mixture. They are wonderful served hot or cold.

NUTRITIONAL INFORMATION

Calories 157	Sugars 17g
Protein 5g	Fat 19g
Carbohydrate ...17g	Saturates 12g

5 MINS   15 MINS

SERVES 4

INGREDIENTS

4 large, ripe pears

300 ml/½ pint/1¼ cups orange juice

2 tsp ground allspice

60 g/2 oz/⅓ cup raisins

2 tbsp light brown sugar

grated orange rind, to decorate

1 Using an apple corer, core the pears.

2 Using a sharp knife, peel the pears and cut them in half.

3 Place the pear halves in a large saucepan.

4 Add the orange juice, ground allspice, raisins and light brown sugar to the saucepan and heat gently, stirring, until the sugar has dissolved.

5 Bring the mixture in the saucepan to the boil and continue to boil for 1 minute.

6 Reduce the heat to low and leave to simmer for about 10 minutes, or until the pears are cooked, but still fairly

firm. Test whether the pears are cooked or not by inserting the tip of a sharp knife.

7 Remove the pears from the pan with a slotted spoon and transfer to serving plates.

8 Decorate with grated orange rind and serve hot with the syrup.

COOK'S TIP
The Chinese do not usually have desserts to finish off a meal, except at banquets and special occasions. Sweet dishes are usually served in between main meals as snacks, but fruit is refreshing at the end of a big meal.

Mango Dumplings

Fresh mango and canned lychees fill these small steamed dumplings, making a really colourful and tasty treat.

NUTRITIONAL INFORMATION

Calories	434	Sugars	........16g
Protein	........12g	Fat	...........4g
Carbohydrate	...93g	Saturates	.......1g

 1¾ HOURS 25 MINS

SERVES 4

I N G R E D I E N T S

D O U G H

2 tsp baking powder

1 tbsp caster (superfine) sugar

150 ml/¼ pint/⅔ cup water

150 ml/¼ pint/⅔ cup milk

400 g/14 oz/3½ cups plain
(all-purpose) flour

FILLING AND SAUCE

1 small mango

100 g/3½ oz can lychees, drained

1 tbsp ground almonds

4 tbsp orange juice

ground cinnamon, for dusting

1 To make the dough, place the baking powder and caster (superfine) sugar in a large mixing bowl.

2 Mix the water and milk together and then stir this mixture into the baking powder and sugar mixture until well combined. Gradually stir in the plain (all-purpose) flour to make a soft dough. Set the dough aside in a warm place for about 1 hour.

3 To make the filling, peel the mango and cut the flesh from the stone (pit). Roughly chop the mango flesh; reserve half and set aside for the sauce.

4 Chop the lychees and add to half of the chopped mango, together with the ground almonds. Leave to stand for 20 minutes.

5 Meanwhile, make the sauce. Blend the reserved mango and the orange juice in a food processor until smooth. Using the back of a spoon, press the mixture through a sieve to make a smooth sauce.

6 Divide the dough into 16 equal pieces. Roll each piece out on a lightly floured surface into 7.5-cm/ 3-inch rounds.

7 Spoon a little of the mango and lychee filling on to the centre of each round and fold the dough over the filling to make semi-circles. Pinch the edges together to seal firmly.

8 Place the dumplings on a heatproof plate in a steamer, cover and steam for about 20-25 minutes, or until cooked through.

9 Remove the mango dumplings from the steamer, dust with a little ground cinnamon and serve with the mango sauce.

Rosemary Biscuits (Cookies)

Do not be put off by the idea of herbs being used in these crisp biscuits (cookies) – try them and you will be pleasantly surprised.

NUTRITIONAL INFORMATION

Calories 50	Sugars 2g
Protein 1g	Fat 2g
Carbohydrate 8g	Saturates 1g

45 MINS   15 MINS

MAKES 25

INGREDIENTS

50 g/1¾ oz/10 tsp butter, softened

4 tbsp caster (superfine) sugar

grated rind of 1 lemon

4 tbsp lemon juice

1 egg, separated

2 tsp finely chopped fresh rosemary

200 g/7 oz/1¾ cups plain (all-purpose)
   flour, sieved (strained)

caster (superfine) sugar, for sprinkling
   (optional)

1 Lightly grease 2 baking trays (cookie sheets).

2 In a large mixing bowl, cream together the butter and sugar until pale and fluffy.

3 Add the lemon rind and juice, then the egg yolk and beat until they are thoroughly combined. Stir in the chopped fresh rosemary.

4 Add the sieved (strained) flour, mixing well until a soft dough is formed. Wrap and leave to chill for 30 minutes.

5 On a lightly floured surface, roll out the dough thinly and then stamp out 25 circles with a 6 cm/2½ inch biscuit (cookie) cutter. Arrange the dough circles on the prepared baking trays (cookie sheets).

6 In a bowl, lightly whisk the egg white. Gently brush the egg white over the surface of each biscuit (cookie), then sprinkle with a little caster (superfine) sugar, if liked.

7 Bake in a preheated oven, at 180°C/ 350°F/Gas Mark 4, for about 15 minutes.

8 Transfer the biscuits (cookies) to a wire rack and leave to cool before serving.

COOK'S TIP

Store the biscuits (cookies) in an airtight container for up to 1 week.

Mangoes with Sticky Rice

These delightful rice puddings make a lovely dessert or afternoon snack. You can have fun experimenting with different-shaped rice moulds.

NUTRITIONAL INFORMATION

Calories ....202 Sugars 31g
Protein ....2g Fat 2g
Carbohydrate ...47g Saturates 0.3g

  12³/4 HOURS 50 MINS

SERVES 4

INGREDIENTS

125 g/4½ oz/generous ½ cup glutinous (sticky) rice

250 ml/9 fl oz/1 cup coconut milk

60 g/2 oz/⅓ cup light muscovado sugar

½ tsp salt

1 tsp sesame seeds, toasted

4 ripe mangoes, peeled, halved, stoned (pitted) and sliced

1 Put the glutinous (sticky) rice into a colander and rinse well with plenty of cold water until the water runs clear. Transfer the rice to a large bowl, cover with cold water and leave to soak overnight, or for at least 12 hours. Drain the rice thoroughly.

2 Line a bamboo basket or steamer with muslin (cheesecloth) or finely woven cotton cloth. Add the rice and steam over a pan of gently simmering water until the rice is tender, about 40 minutes.

3 Remove the rice from the heat and transfer to a large mixing bowl.

4 Reserve 4 tablespoons of the coconut milk and put the remainder into a small saucepan with the light muscovado sugar and salt. Heat and simmer gently for about 8 minutes until reduced by about one third.

5 Pour the coconut milk mixture over the rice, fluffing up the rice with a fork so that the mixture is absorbed. Set aside for 10–15 minutes.

6 Pack the rice into individual moulds and then invert them on to serving plates.

7 Pour a little reserved coconut milk over each rice mound and sprinkle with the sesame seeds.

8 Arrange the sliced mango on the plates and serve, decorated with pieces of mango cut into different shapes with tiny cutters.

COOK'S TIP

Glutinous or sticky rice is available from stockists of Thai ingredients, although you can try making this recipe with short-grain pudding rice instead.

Sticky Sesame Bananas

These tasty morsels are a real treat. Pieces of banana are dipped in caramel and then sprinkled with a few sesame seeds.

NUTRITIONAL INFORMATION

Calories 215   Sugars 38g
Protein ....6g   Fat 3g
Carbohydrate ...41g   Saturates 1g

10 MINS   20 MINS

SERVES 4

I N G R E D I E N T S

4 ripe medium bananas

3 tbsp lemon juice

125 g/4¹/₂ oz caster (superfine) sugar

4 tbsp cold water

2 tbsp sesame seeds

150 ml/5 fl oz/⅔ cup low-fat natural fromage frais (unsweetened yogurt)

1 tbsp icing (confectioners') sugar

1 tsp vanilla essence (extract)

lemon and lime rind, shredded, to decorate

1 Peel the bananas and cut into 5 cm/ 2 inch pieces. Place the banana pieces in a bowl, spoon over the lemon juice and stir well to coat – this will help prevent the bananas from discoloring.

2 Place the sugar and water in a small saucepan and heat gently, stirring, until the sugar dissolves. Bring to the boil and cook for 5–6 minutes until the mixture turns golden-brown.

3 Meanwhile, drain the bananas and blot with kitchen paper (paper towels) to dry. Line a baking sheet or board with baking parchment and arrange the bananas, well spaced out, on top.

4 When the caramel is ready, drizzle it over the bananas, working quickly because the caramel sets almost instantly. Sprinkle the sesame seeds over the caramelized bananas and leave to cool for 10 minutes.

5 Mix the fromage frais (unsweetened yogurt) together with the icing (confectioner's) sugar and vanilla essence (extract).

6 Peel the bananas away from the paper and arrange on serving plates.

7 Serve the fromage frais (unsweetened yogurt) as a dip, decorated with the shredded lemon and lime rind.

Chocolate Brownies

You really can have a low-fat chocolate treat. These moist bars contain a dried fruit purée, which enables you to bake without adding any fat.

NUTRITIONAL INFORMATION

Calories . . . . .271 Sugars 45g
Protein . . . . .5g Fat 4g
Carbohydrate . . .57g Saturates 2g

 30 MINS   40 MINS

MAKES 12

INGREDIENTS

60 g/2 oz unsweetened pitted dates, chopped

60 g/2 oz no-need-to-soak dried prunes, chopped

6 tbsp unsweetened apple juice

4 medium eggs, beaten

300 g/10½ oz dark muscovado sugar

1 tsp vanilla essence (extract)

4 tbsp low-fat drinking chocolate powder, plus extra for dusting

2 tbsp cocoa powder

175 g/6 oz plain (all-purpose) flour

60 g/2 oz dark chocolate chips

ICING

125 g/4½ oz icing (confectioners') sugar

1–2 tsp water

1 tsp vanilla essence (extract)

COOK'S TIP

Make double the amount, cut one of the cakes into bars and open freeze, then store in plastic bags. Take out pieces of cake as and when you need them - they'll take no time at all to defrost.

1 Preheat the oven to 180°C/350°F/Gas Mark 4. Grease and line a 18 x 28 cm/7 x 11 inch cake tin with baking parchment. Place the dates and prunes in a small saucepan and add the apple juice. Bring to the boil, cover and simmer for 10 minutes until soft. Beat to form a smooth paste, then set aside to cool.

2 Place the cooled fruit in a mixing bowl and stir in the eggs, sugar and vanilla essence. Sift in 4 tbsp drinking chocolate, the cocoa and the flour, and fold in along with the chocolate chips until well incorporated.

3 Spoon the mixture into the prepared tin and smooth over the top. Bake for 25–30 minutes until firm to the touch or until a skewer inserted into the centre comes out clean. Cut into 12 bars and leave to cool in the tin for 10 minutes. Transfer to a wire rack to cool completely.

4 To make the icing (frosting), sift the sugar into a bowl and mix with sufficient water and the vanilla essence (extract) to form a soft, but not too runny, icing (frosting).

5 Drizzle the icing (frosting) over the chocolate brownies and allow to set. Dust with the extra chocolate powder before serving.

Zabaglione

This well-known dish is really a light but rich egg mousse flavoured with Marsala.

NUTRITIONAL INFORMATION

Calories 158   Sugars 29g
Protein ....1g   Fat 1g
Carbohydrate ...29g   Saturates 0.2g

5 MINS   15 MINS

SERVES 4

INGREDIENTS

5 egg yolks

100 g/3½ oz caster (superfine) sugar

150 ml/¼ pint/⅔ cup Marsala or
    sweet sherry

amaretti biscuits (cookies), to serve
    (optional)

1 Place the egg yolks in a large mixing bowl.

2 Add the caster (superfine) sugar to the egg yolks and whisk until the mixture is thick and very pale and has doubled in volume.

3 Place the bowl containing the egg yolk and sugar mixture over a saucepan of gently simmering water.

4 Add the Marsala or sherry to the egg yolk and sugar mixture and continue whisking until the foam mixture becomes warm. This process may take as long as 10 minutes.

5 Pour the mixture, which should be frothy and light, into 4 wine glasses.

6 Serve the zabaglione warm with fresh fruit or amaretti biscuits (cookies), if you wish.

Orange & Almond Cake

This light and tangy citrus cake from Sicily is better eaten as a dessert than as a cake. It is especially good served after a large meal.

NUTRITIONAL INFORMATION

Calories . . . . . . .399 Sugars 20g
Protein . . . . .8g Fat 31g
Carbohydrate . . .23g Saturates 13g

30 MINS 40 MINS

SERVES 8

INGREDIENTS

4 eggs, separated

125 g/4½ oz caster (superfine) sugar, plus
   2 tsp for the cream

finely grated rind and juice of 2 oranges

finely grated rind and juice of 1 lemon

125 g/4½ oz ground almonds

25 g/1 oz self-raising flour

200 ml/7 fl oz/¾ cup whipping (light) cream

1 tsp cinnamon

25 g/1 oz flaked (slivered) almonds, toasted

icing (confectioners') sugar, to dust

1 Grease and line the base of a 18 cm/ 7 inch round deep cake tin (pan).

2 Blend the egg yolks with the sugar until the mixture is thick and creamy. Whisk half of the orange rind and all of the lemon rind into the egg yolks.

VARIATION

You could serve this cake with a syrup. Boil the juice and finely grated rind of 2 oranges, 75 g/2¾ oz caster (superfine) sugar and 2 tbsp of water for 5–6 minutes until slightly thickened. Stir in 1 tbsp of orange liqueur just before serving.

3 Mix the juice from both oranges and the lemon with the ground almonds and stir into the egg yolks. The mixture will become quite runny at this point. Fold in the flour.

4 Whisk the egg whites until stiff and gently fold into the egg yolk mixture.

5 Pour the mixture into the tin (pan) and bake in a preheated oven, at 180°C/350°F/Gas Mark 4, for 35–40

minutes, or until golden and springy to the touch. Leave to cool in the tin (pan) for 10 minutes and then turn out. It is likely to sink slightly at this stage.

6 Whip the cream to form soft peaks. Stir in the remaining orange rind, cinnamon and sugar.

7 Once the cake is cold, cover with the almonds, dust with icing (confectioners') sugar and serve with the cream.

Summer Puddings

A wonderful mixture of summer fruits encased in slices of white bread which soak up all the deep red, flavoursome juices.

NUTRITIONAL INFORMATION

Calories 250	Sugars 41g
Protein 4g	Fat 4g
Carbohydrate ...53g	Saturates 2g

10 MINS   10 MINS

SERVES 6

INGREDIENTS

vegetable oil or butter, for greasing

6–8 thin slices white bread, crusts removed

175 g/6 oz/¾ cup caster (superfine) sugar

300 ml/½ pint/1¼ cups water

225 g/8 oz/2 cups strawberries

500 g/1 lb 2 oz/2½ cups raspberries

175 g/6 oz/1¼ cups black-
    and/or redcurrants

175 g/6 oz/¾ cup blackberries
    or loganberries

mint sprigs, to decorate

pouring cream, to serve

1 Grease six 150 ml/¼ pint/⅔ cup moulds (molds) with butter or oil.

2 Line the moulds (molds) with the bread, cutting it so it fits snugly.

3 Place the sugar in a saucepan with the water and heat gently, stirring frequently until dissolved, then bring to the boil and boil for 2 minutes.

4 Reserve 6 large strawberries for decoration. Add half the raspberries and the rest of the fruits to the syrup, cutting the strawberries in half if large, and simmer gently for a few minutes, until

beginning to soften but still retaining their shape.

5 Spoon the fruits and some of the liquid into moulds (molds). Cover with more slices of bread. Spoon a little juice around the sides of the moulds (molds) so the bread is well soaked. Cover with a saucer and a heavy weight, leave to cool, then chill thoroughly, preferably overnight.

6 Process the remaining raspberries in a food processor or blender, or press through a non-metallic strainer. Add enough of the liquid from the fruits to give a coating consistency.

7 Turn on to serving plates and spoon the raspberry sauce over. Decorate with the mint sprigs and reserved strawberries and serve with cream.

Mocha Swirl Mousse

A combination of feather-light yet rich chocolate and coffee mousses, whipped and attractively served in serving glasses.

NUTRITIONAL INFORMATION

Calories . . . . . . .130 Sugars 10g
Protein . . . . .5g Fat 8g
Carbohydrate . . . .11g Saturates 5g

1¼ HOURS   0 MINS

SERVES 4

INGREDIENTS

1 tbsp coffee and chicory essence (extract)

2 tsp cocoa powder, plus extra for dusting

1 tsp low-fat drinking chocolate powder

150 ml/5 fl oz/⅔ cup low-fat crème fraîche, plus 4 tsp to serve

2 tsp powdered gelatine

2 tbsp boiling water

2 large egg whites

2 tbsp caster (superfine) sugar

4 chocolate coffee beans, to serve

1 Place the coffee and chicory essence (extract) in one bowl, and 2 teaspoons cocoa powder and the drinking chocolate in another bowl. Divide the crème fraîche between the 2 bowls and mix both well.

2 Dissolve the gelatine in the boiling water and set aside. In a grease-free bowl, whisk the egg whites and sugar until stiff and divide this evenly between the two mixtures.

3 Divide the dissolved gelatine between the 2 mixtures and, using a large metal spoon, gently fold until well mixed.

4 Spoon small amounts of the 2 mousses alternately into 4 serving glasses and swirl together gently. Chill for 1 hour or until set.

5 To serve, top each mousse with a teaspoonful of crème fraîche, a chocolate coffee bean and a light dusting of cocoa powder. Serve immediately.

COOK'S TIP

Vegetarians should not be denied this delicious chocolate dessert. Instead of gelatine use the vegetarian equivalent, gelozone, available from health-food shops. However, be sure to read the instructions on the packet first as it is prepared differently from gelatine.

Baked Coconut Rice Pudding

A wonderful baked rice pudding cooked with flavoursome coconut milk and a little lime rind. Serve hot or chilled with fresh or stewed fruit.

NUTRITIONAL INFORMATION

Calories	211	Sugars	........27g
Protein	.........5g	Fat	..........2g
Carbohydrate	...46g	Saturates	.......1g

 5 MINS   2¹⁄₂ HOURS

SERVES 4–6

INGREDIENTS

90 g/3 oz/scant ⅓ cup short or round-grain pudding rice

600 ml/1 pint/2½ cups coconut milk

300 ml/½ pint/1¼ cups milk

1 large strip lime rind

60 g/2 oz/¼ cup caster (superfine) sugar

knob of butter

pinch of ground star anise (optional)

fresh or stewed fruit, to serve

1 Lightly grease a 1.4 litre/2½ pint shallow ovenproof dish.

2 Mix the pudding rice with the coconut milk, milk, lime rind and caster (superfine) sugar until all the ingredients are well blended.

3 Pour the rice mixture into the greased ovenproof dish and dot the surface with a little butter. Bake in the oven for about 30 minutes.

4 Remove the dish from the oven. Remove and discard the strip of lime from the rice pudding.

5 Stir the pudding well, add the pinch of ground star anise, if using, return to the oven and cook for a further 1-2

hours or until almost all the milk has been absorbed and a golden brown skin has baked on the top of the pudding.

6 Cover the top of the pudding with foil if it starts to brown too much towards the end of the cooking time.

7 Serve the baked coconut rice pudding warm, or chilled if you prefer, with fresh or stewed fruit.

COOK'S TIP

As the mixture cools it thickens. If you plan to serve the rice chilled then fold in about 3 tablespoons cream or extra coconut milk before serving to give a thinner consistency.

Pink Syllabubs

The pretty pink colour of this dessert is achieved by adding blackcurrant liqueur to the wine and cream before whipping.

NUTRITIONAL INFORMATION

Calories 536	Sugars 17g
Protein 2g	Fat 48g
Carbohydrate ...17g	Saturates 30g

45 MINS   0 MINS

SERVES 2

INGREDIENTS

5 tbsp white wine

2–3 tsp blackcurrant liqueur

finely grated rind of ½ lemon or orange

1 tbsp caster (superfine) sugar

200 ml/7 fl oz/scant 1 cup double
(heavy) cream

4 boudoir biscuits (lady-fingers) (optional)

TO DECORATE

fresh fruit, such as strawberries,
raspberries or redcurrants, or pecan
or walnut halves

mint sprigs

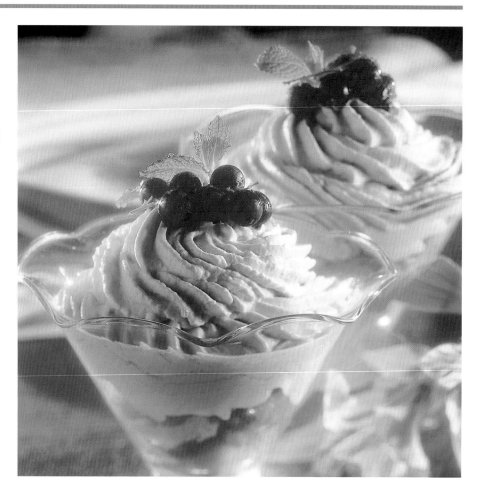

1 Mix together the white wine, blackcurrant liqueur, grated lemon or orange rind and caster (superfine) sugar in a bowl and set aside for at least 30 minutes.

COOK'S TIP

These syllabubs will keep in the refrigerator for 48 hours, so it is worth making more than you need, and keeping the extra for another day.

2 Add the cream to the wine mixture and whip until the mixture has thickened enough to stand in soft peaks.

3 If you are using the boudoir biscuits (lady-fingers), break them up roughly and divide them between 2 glasses.

4 Put the mixture into a piping bag fitted with a large star or plain nozzle (tip) and pipe it over the biscuits (lady-fingers). Alternatively, simply pour the syllabub over the biscuits (lady-fingers). Chill until ready to serve.

5 Before serving, decorate each syllabub with slices or small pieces of fresh soft fruit or nuts, and sprigs of mint.

Pear Tart

Pears are a very popular fruit in Italy. In this recipe from Trentino they are flavoured with almonds, cinnamon, raisins and apricot jam.

NUTRITIONAL INFORMATION

Calories ....629 Sugars 70g
Protein ....7g Fat 21g
Carbohydrate ..109g Saturates 13g

1½ HOURS   50 MINS

SERVES 6

INGREDIENTS

275 g/9½ oz/2¼ cups plain (all-purpose)
    flour

pinch of salt

125 g/4½ oz/½ cup caster (superfine) sugar

125 g/4½ oz/½ cup butter, diced

1 egg

1 egg yolk

few drops of vanilla essence (extract)

2–3 tsp water

sifted icing (confectioners') sugar, for
    sprinkling

FILLING

4 tbsp apricot jam

60 g/2 oz amaretti or ratafia biscuits
    (cookies), crumbled

850–1 kg/1¾–2 lb 4 oz pears, peeled
    and cored

1 tsp ground cinnamon

90 g/3 oz/½ cup raisins

60 g/2 oz/⅓ cup soft brown or demerara
    sugar

1 Sift the flour and salt on to a flat
surface, make a well in the centre and
add the sugar, butter, egg, egg yolk, vanilla
essence (extract) and most of the water.

2 Using your fingers, gradually work the
flour into the other ingredients to give
a smooth dough, adding more water if
necessary. Wrap in cling film (plastic
wrap) and chill for 1 hour or until firm.
Alternatively, put all the ingredients into a
food processor and work until smooth.

3 Roll out three-quarters of the dough
and use to line a shallow 25 cm/
10 inch cake tin (pan) or deep flan tin
(pan). Spread the jam over the base and
sprinkle with the crushed biscuits (cookies).

4 Slice the pears very thinly. Arrange
over the biscuits (cookies) in the
pastry case. Sprinkle with cinnamon then
with raisins, and finally with brown sugar.

5 Roll out a thin sausage shape using
one-third of the remaining dough, and
place around the edge of the pie. Roll the
remainder into thin sausages and arrange
in a lattice over the pie, 4 or 5 strips in
each direction, attaching them to the strip
around the edge.

6 Cook in a preheated oven, at 200°C/
400°F/Gas Mark 6, for 50 minutes
until golden and cooked through. Leave to
cool, then serve warm or chilled, sprinkled
with sifted icing (confectioners') sugar.

New Age Spotted Dick

This is a deliciously moist low-fat pudding. The sauce is in the centre of the pudding, and will spill out when the pudding is cut.

NUTRITIONAL INFORMATION

Calories	529	Sugars	41g
Protein	9g	Fat	31g
Carbohydrate	58g	Saturates	4g

  25 MINS   1¼ HOURS

SERVES 6–8

INGREDIENTS

125 g/4½ oz/¾ cup raisins

125 ml/4 fl oz/generous ½ cup corn oil, plus a little for brushing

125 g/4½ oz/generous ½ cup caster (superfine) sugar

25 g/1 oz/¼ cup ground almonds

2 eggs, lightly beaten

175 g/6 oz/1½ cups self-raising flour

SAUCE

60 g/2 oz/½ cup walnuts, chopped

60 g/2 oz/½ cup ground almonds

300 ml/½ pint/1¼ cups semi-skimmed milk

4 tbsp granulated sugar

1 Put the raisins in a saucepan with 125 ml/4 fl oz/½ cup water. Bring to the boil, then remove from the heat. Leave to steep for 10 minutes, then drain.

2 Whisk together the oil, sugar and ground almonds until thick and syrupy; this will need about 8 minutes of beating (on medium speed if using an electric whisk).

3 Add the eggs, one at a time, beating well after each addition. Combine the flour and raisins. Stir into the mixture. Brush a 1 litre/1¾ pint/4 cup pudding basin with oil, or line with baking parchment.

4 Put all the sauce ingredients into a saucepan. Bring to the boil, stir and simmer for 10 minutes.

5 Transfer the sponge mixture to the greased basin and pour on the hot sauce. Place on a baking tray (cookie sheet).

6 Bake in a preheated oven at 170°C/340°F/Gas Mark 3½ for about 1 hour. Lay a piece of baking parchment across the top if it starts to brown too fast.

7 Leave to cool for 2–3 minutes in the basin before turning out on to a serving plate.

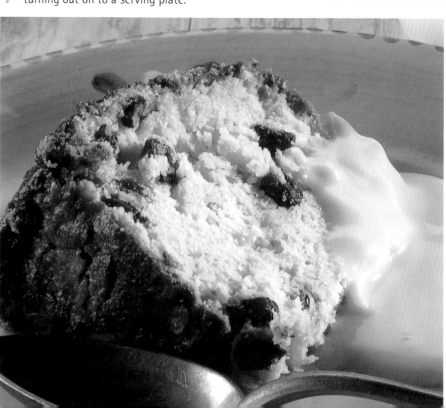

COOK'S TIP

Always soak raisins before baking them, as they retain their moisture nicely and you taste the flavour of them instead of biting on a dried-out raisin.

Exotic Fruit Pancakes

These pancakes are filled with an exotic array of tropical fruits. Decorate lavishly with tropical flowers or mint sprigs.

NUTRITIONAL INFORMATION

Calories 382   Sugars 24g
Protein ....7g   Fat 17g
Carbohydrate ...53g   Saturates 3g

40 MINS   35 MINS

SERVES 4

I N G R E D I E N T S

BATTER

125 g/4½ oz/1 cup plain flour

pinch of salt

1 egg

1 egg yolk

300 ml/½ pint/1¼ cups coconut milk

4 tsp vegetable oil, plus oil for frying

FILLING

1 banana

1 paw-paw (papaya)

juice of 1 lime

2 passion fruit

1 mango, peeled, stoned and sliced

4 lychees, stoned and halved

1-2 tbsp honey

flowers or mint sprigs, to decorate

1 Sift the flour and salt into a bowl. Make a well in the centre and add the egg, egg yolk and a little of the coconut milk. Gradually draw the flour into the egg mixture, beating well and slowly adding the remaining coconut milk to make a smooth batter. Stir in the oil. Cover and chill for 30 minutes.

2 Peel and slice the banana and place in a bowl. Peel and slice the paw-paw (papaya), discarding the seeds. Add to the banana with the lime juice and mix well. Cut the passion-fruit in half and scoop out the flesh and seeds into the fruit bowl. Stir in the mango, lychees and honey.

3 Heat a little oil in a 15 cm/6 inch frying pan (skillet). Pour in just enough of the pancake batter to cover the base of the pan and tilt so that it spreads thinly and evenly. Cook until the pancake is just set and the underside is lightly browned, turn and briefly cook the other side. Remove from the pan and keep warm. Repeat with the remaining batter to make a total of 8 pancakes.

4 To serve, place a little of the prepared fruit filling along the centre of each pancake and then roll it into a cone shape. Lay seam-side down on warmed serving plates, decorate with flowers or mint sprigs and serve.

Mascarpone Cheesecake

The mascarpone gives this baked cheesecake a wonderfully tangy flavour. Ricotta cheese could be used as an alternative.

NUTRITIONAL INFORMATION

Calories	327	Sugars	.......25g
Protein	.........9g	Fat	..........18g
Carbohydrate	...33g	Saturates	......11g

 15 MINS   50 MINS

SERVES 8

INGREDIENTS

50 g/1¾ oz/1½ tbsp unsalted butter

150 g/5½ oz ginger biscuits (cookies), crushed

25 g/1 oz stem ginger (candied), chopped

500 g/1 lb 2 oz mascarpone cheese

finely grated rind and juice of 2 lemons

100 g/3½ oz caster (superfine) sugar

2 large eggs, separated

fruit coulis (see Cook's Tip), to serve

1 Grease and line the base of a 25 cm/10 inch spring-form cake tin (pan) or loose-bottomed tin (pan).

2 Melt the butter in a pan and stir in the crushed biscuits (cookies) and chopped ginger. Use the mixture to line the tin (pan), pressing the mixture about 6 mm/¼ inch up the sides.

COOK'S TIP

Fruit coulis can be made by cooking 400 g/14 oz fruit, such as blueberries, for 5 minutes with 2 tablespoons of water. Sieve the mixture, then stir in 1 tablespoon (or more to taste) of sifted icing (confectioners') sugar. Leave to cool before serving.

3 Beat together the cheese, lemon rind and juice, sugar and egg yolks until quite smooth.

4 Whisk the egg whites until they are stiff and fold into the cheese and lemon mixture.

5 Pour the mixture into the tin (pan) and bake in a preheated oven, at 180°C/350°F/Gas Mark 4, for 35–45

minutes until just set. Don't worry if it cracks or sinks – this is quite normal.

6 Leave the cheesecake in the tin (pan) to cool. Serve with fruit coulis (see Cook's Tip).

Italian Chocolate Truffles

These are flavoured with almonds and chocolate, and are simplicity itself to make. Served with coffee, they are the perfect end to a meal.

NUTRITIONAL INFORMATION

Calories	82	Sugars	........7g
Protein	.........1g	Fat	..........5g
Carbohydrate	....8g	Saturates	.......3g

 5 MINS   5 MINS

MAKES 24

I N G R E D I E N T S

175 g/6 oz dark chocolate

2 tbsp almond-flavoured liqueur (amaretto)
   or orange-flavoured liqueur

40 g/1½ oz/3 tbsp unsalted butter

50 g/1¾ oz icing (confectioners') sugar

50 g/1¾ oz/½ cup ground almonds

50 g/1¾ oz grated milk chocolate

1 Melt the dark chocolate with the liqueur in a bowl set over a saucepan of hot water, stirring until well combined.

2 Add the butter and stir until it has melted. Stir in the icing (confectioners') sugar and the ground almonds.

3 Leave the mixture in a cool place until firm enough to roll into 24 balls.

4 Place the grated chocolate on a plate and roll the truffles in the chocolate to coat them.

5 Place the truffles in paper sweet (candy) cases and chill.

Chinese Custard Tarts

These small tarts are irresistible – a custard is baked in a rich, sweet pastry. The tarts may be served warm or cold.

NUTRITIONAL INFORMATION

Calories 474	Sugars 30g
Protein 9g	Fat 22g
Carbohydrate ...64g	Saturates 12g

20 MINS   30 MINS

SERVES 4

INGREDIENTS

DOUGH

175 g/6 oz/1½ cups plain (all-purpose) flour

3 tbsp caster (superfine) sugar

60 g/2 oz/4 tbsp unsalted butter

25 g/1 oz/2 tbsp lard (shortening)

2 tbsp water

CUSTARD

2 small eggs

60 g/2 oz/¼ cup caster (superfine) sugar

175 ml/6 fl oz/¾ cup pint milk

½ tsp ground nutmeg, plus extra for sprinkling

cream, to serve

1 To make the dough, sift the plain (all-purpose) flour into a bowl. Add the caster (superfine) sugar and rub in the butter and lard (shortening) until the mixture resembles breadcrumbs. Add the water and mix to form a firm dough.

2 Transfer the dough to a lightly floured surface and knead for 5 minutes, until smooth. Cover with cling film (plastic wrap) and leave to chill in the refrigerator while you prepare the filling.

3 To make the custard, beat the eggs and sugar together. Gradually add the milk and ground nutmeg and beat until well combined.

4 Separate the dough into 15 even-sized pieces. Flatten the dough pieces into rounds and press into shallow patty tins (pans).

5 Spoon the custard into the pastry cases (tart shells) and cook in a preheated oven, at 150°C/300°F/Gas 2, for 25-30 minutes.

6 Transfer the Chinese custard tarts to a wire rack, leave to cool slightly, then sprinkle with nutmeg. Serve hot or cold with cream.

COOK'S TIP

For extra convenience, make the dough in advance, cover and leave to chill in the refrigerator until required.

Baked Apples with Berries

This winter dessert is a classic dish. Large, fluffy apples are hollowed out and filled with spices, almonds and blackberries.

NUTRITIONAL INFORMATION

Calories ....228 Sugars 31g
Protein ....1g Fat 2g
Carbohydrate ...31g Saturates 0.2g

10 MINS   45 MINS

SERVES 4

I N G R E D I E N T S

4 medium-sized cooking apples

1 tbsp lemon juice

100 g/3½ oz prepared blackberries, thawed if frozen

15 g/½ oz flaked (slivered) almonds

½ tsp ground allspice

½ tsp finely grated lemon rind

2 tbsp demerara (brown crystal) sugar

300 ml/½ pint/1¼ cups ruby port

1 cinnamon stick, broken

2 tsp cornflour (cornstarch) blended with 2 tbsp cold water

low-fat custard, to serve

1 Preheat the oven to 200°C/400°F/Gas Mark 6. Wash and dry the apples. Using a small sharp knife, make a shallow cut through the skin around the middle of each apple – this will help the apples to cook through.

2 Core the apples, brush the centres with the lemon juice to prevent browning and stand in an ovenproof dish.

3 In a bowl, mix together the blackberries, almonds, allspice, lemon rind and sugar. Using a teaspoon, spoon the mixture into the centre of each apple.

4 Pour the port into the dish, add the cinnamon stick and bake the apples in the oven for 35–40 minutes or until tender and soft. Drain the cooking juices into a pan and keep the apples warm.

5 Discard the cinnamon and add the cornflour (cornstarch) mixture to the cooking juices. Heat, stirring, until thickened.

6 Heat the custard until piping hot. Pour the sauce over the apples and serve with the custard.

Eggless Sponge

This is a healthy variation of the classic Victoria sponge cake (sponge layer cake) and is suitable for vegans.

NUTRITIONAL INFORMATION

Calories	273	Sugars	........27g
Protein	.........3g	Fat	...........9g
Carbohydrate	...49g	Saturates	......1g

🍰 1¼ HOURS   🕐 30 MINS

1 x 8" CAKE

I N G R E D I E N T S

225 g/8 oz/1¾ cups self-raising wholemeal (whole wheat) flour

2 tsp baking powder

175 g/6 oz/¾ cup caster (superfine) sugar

6 tbsp sunflower oil

250 ml/9 fl oz/1 cup water

1 tsp vanilla flavouring (extract)

4 tbsp strawberry or raspberry reduced-sugar spread

caster (superfine) sugar, for dusting

1 Grease two 20 cm/8 inch sandwich cake tins (layer pans) and line them with baking parchment.

2 Sieve (strain) the self-raising flour and baking powder into a large mixing bowl, stirring in any bran remaining in the sieve. Stir in the caster (superfine) sugar.

3 Pour in the sunflower oil, water and vanilla flavouring (extract). Mix well with a wooden spoon for about 1 minute until the mixture is smooth, then divide between the prepared tins (pans).

4 Bake in a preheated oven, 180°C/ 350°F/Gas Mark 4, for about 25-30 minutes until the centre springs back when lightly touched.

5 Leave the sponges to cool in the tins (pans) before turning out and transferring to a wire rack.

6 To serve, remove the baking parchment and place one of the sponges on to a serving plate. Spread with the jam and place the other sponge on top.

7 Dust the eggless sponge cake with a little caster (superfine) sugar before serving.

Caramelized Oranges

The secret of these oranges is to allow them to marinate in the syrup for at least 24 hours, so the flavours amalgamate.

NUTRITIONAL INFORMATION

Calories 235	Sugars 59g	
Protein 2g	Fat 0.2g	
Carbohydrate ...59g	Saturates 0g	

3¹/₄ HOURS   20 MINS

SERVES 6

INGREDIENTS

6 large oranges

225 g/8 oz/1 cup sugar

250 ml/9 fl oz/1 cup water

6 whole cloves (optional)

2–4 tbsp orange-flavoured liqueur
  or brandy

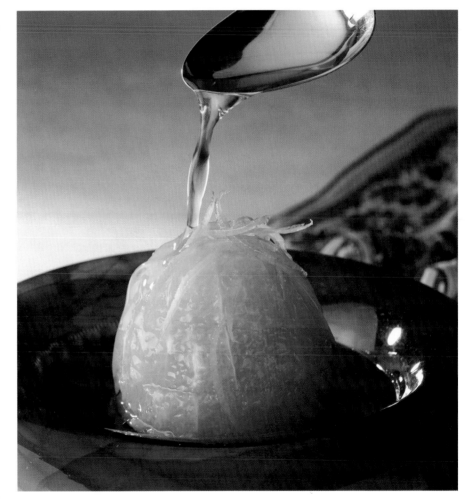

1 Using a citrus zester or potato peeler, pare the rind from 2 of the oranges in narrow strips without any white pith attached. If using a potato peeler, cut the peel into very thin julienne strips.

2 Put the strips into a small saucepan and barely cover with water. Bring to the boil and simmer for 5 minutes. Drain the strips and reserve the water.

3 Cut away all the white pith and peel from the remaining oranges using a very sharp knife. Then cut horizontally into 4 slices. Reassemble the oranges and hold in place with wooden cocktail sticks (toothpick). Stand in a heatproof dish.

4 Put the sugar and water into a heavy-based saucepan with the cloves, if using. Bring to the boil and simmer gently until the sugar has dissolved, then boil hard without stirring until the syrup thickens and begins to colour. Continue to cook until a light golden brown, then quickly remove from the heat and carefully pour in the reserved orange rind liquid.

5 Place over a gentle heat until the caramel has fully dissolved again, then remove from the heat and add the liqueur or brandy. Pour over the oranges.

6 Sprinkle the orange strips over the oranges, cover with cling film (plastic wrap) and leave until cold. Chill for at least 3 hours and preferably for 24–48 hours before serving. If time allows, spoon the syrup over the oranges several times while they are marinating. Discard the cocktail stick (toothpick) before serving.

Vanilla Ice Cream

This home-made version of real vanilla ice cream is absolutely delicious and so easy to make. A tutti-frutti variation is also provided.

NUTRITIONAL INFORMATION

Calories 626   Sugars 33g
Protein . . . . .7g   Fat 53g
Carbohydrate . . .33g   Saturates 31g

   5 MINS   15 MINS

SERVES 6

I N G R E D I E N T S

600 ml/1 pint/2½ cups double
  (heavy) cream

1 vanilla pod

pared rind of 1 lemon

4 eggs, beaten

2 egg, yolks

175 g/6 oz caster (superfine) sugar

1 Place the cream in a heavy-based saucepan and heat gently, whisking.

2 Add the vanilla pod, lemon rind, eggs and egg yolks to the pan and heat until the mixture reaches just below boiling point.

3 Reduce the heat and cook for 8–10 minutes, whisking the mixture continuously, until thickened.

4 Stir the sugar into the cream mixture, set aside and leave to cool.

5 Strain the cream mixture through a sieve.

6 Slit open the vanilla pod, scoop out the tiny black seeds and stir them into the cream.

7 Pour the mixture into a shallow freezing container with a lid and freeze overnight until set. Serve the ice cream when required.

VARIATION

For tutti frutti ice cream, soak 100 g/3½ oz mixed dried fruit in 2 tbsp Marsala or sweet sherry for 20 minutes. Follow the method for vanilla ice cream, omitting the vanilla pod, and stir in the Marsala or sherry-soaked fruit in step 5, just before freezing.

Battered Bananas

These bananas are quite irresistible, therefore it may be wise to make double quantities for weak-willed guests!

NUTRITIONAL INFORMATION

Calories	562	Sugars	.......79g
Protein	.........6g	Fat	..........10g
Carbohydrate	...118g	Saturates	.......1g

10 MINS　　20 MINS

SERVES 4

INGREDIENTS

8 medium bananas

2 tsp lemon juice

75 g/2¾ oz/⅔ cup self-raising flour

75 g/2¾ oz/⅔ cup rice flour

1 tbsp cornflour (cornstarch)

½ tsp ground cinnamon

250 ml/9 fl oz/1 cup water

oil, for deep-frying

4 tbsp light brown sugar

cream or ice cream, to serve

1 Cut the bananas into even-sized chunks and place them in a large mixing bowl.

2 Sprinkle the lemon juice over the bananas to prevent discoloration.

3 Sift the self-raising flour, rice flour, cornflour (cornstarch) and cinnamon into a mixing bowl. Gradually stir in the water to make a thin batter.

4 Heat the oil in a preheated wok until almost smoking, then reduce the heat slightly.

5 Place a piece of banana on the end of a fork and carefully dip it into the

batter, draining off any excess. Repeat with the remaining banana pieces.

6 Sprinkle the light brown sugar on to a large plate.

7 Carefully place the banana pieces in the oil and cook for 2-3 minutes, until golden. Remove the banana pieces from the oil with a slotted spoon and roll them in the sugar.

8 Transfer the bananas to serving bowls and serve with cream or ice cream.

COOK'S TIP

Rice flour can be bought from wholefood shops or from Chinese supermarkets.

Christmas Shortbread

Make this wonderful shortbread and then give it the Christmas touch by cutting it into shapes with seasonal biscuit (cookie) cutters.

NUTRITIONAL INFORMATION

Calories 162	Sugars 10g
Protein 1g	Fat 9g
Carbohydrate . . .21g	Saturates 6g

  45 MINS   15 MINS

MAKES 24

I N G R E D I E N T S

125 g/4½ oz/½ cup caster
   (superfine) sugar

225 g/8 oz/1 cup butter

350 g/12 oz/3 cups plain (all-purpose)
   flour, sifted

pinch of salt

T O   D E C O R A T E

60 g/2 oz/½ cup icing
   (confectioners') sugar

silver balls

glacé (candied) cherries

angelica

1 Beat the sugar and butter together in a large bowl until combined (thorough creaming is not necessary).

2 Sift in the flour and salt and work together to form a stiff dough. Turn out on to a lightly floured surface. Knead lightly for a few moments until smooth, but avoid overhandling. Chill in the refrigerator for 10–15 minutes.

3 Roll out the dough on a lightly floured work surface and cut into shapes with small Christmas cutters, such as bells, stars and angels. Place on greased baking trays (cookie sheets).

4 Bake the biscuits (cookies) in a preheated oven, 180°C/350°F/Gas Mark 4 for 10–15 minutes, until pale golden brown. Leave on the baking trays (cookie sheets) for 10 minutes, then transfer to wire racks to cool completely.

5 Mix the icing (confectioners') sugar with a little water to make a glacé icing (frosting), and use to ice (frost) the biscuits (cookies). Decorate with silver balls, tiny pieces of glacé (candied) cherries and angelica. Store in an airtight container or wrap the biscuits (cookies) individually in cellophane, tie with coloured ribbon or string and then hang them on the Christmas tree as edible decorations.

Semolina Dessert

This dish is eaten with pooris and potato curry for breakfast in northern India, but you can serve it with fresh cream for a delicious dessert.

NUTRITIONAL INFORMATION

Calories 676   Sugars 66g
Protein ....10g   Fat 31g
Carbohydrate ...96g   Saturates 19g

5 MINS   10 MINS

SERVES 4

INGREDIENTS

6 tbsp pure ghee

3 whole cloves

3 whole cardamoms

8 tbsp coarse semolina

½ tsp saffron

50 g/1¾ oz/½ cup sultanas (golden raisins)

10 tbsp sugar

300 ml/½ pint/1¼ cups water

300 ml/½ pint/1¼ cups milk

cream, to serve

TO DECORATE

25 g/1 oz/½ cup desiccated (shredded)
   coconut, toasted

25 g/1 oz/¼ cup chopped almonds

25 g/1 oz/¼ cup pistachio nuts,
   soaked and chopped (optional)

1 Place the ghee in a saucepan and melt over a medium heat.

2 Add the cloves and the whole cardamoms to the melted butter and reduce the heat, stirring to mix.

3 Add the semolina to the mixture in the pan and stir-fry until it turns a little darker.

4 Add the saffron, sultanas (golden raisins) and the sugar to the semolina mixture, stirring to mix well.

5 Pour in the water and milk and stir-fry the mixture continuously until the semolina has softened. Add a little more water if required.

6 Remove the pan from the heat and transfer the semolina to a warmed serving dish.

7 Decorate the semolina dessert with the toasted coconut, flaked almonds and pistachios. Serve with a little cream drizzled over the top.

Banana & Lime Cake

A substantial cake that is ideal served for tea. The mashed bananas help to keep the cake moist, and the lime icing gives it extra zing and zest.

NUTRITIONAL INFORMATION

Calories	235	Sugars	.......31g
Protein	.........5g	Fat	...........1g
Carbohydrate	...55g	Saturates	.....0.3g

 35 MINS   45 MINS

SERVES 10

INGREDIENTS

300 g/10½ oz plain (all-purpose) flour

1 tsp salt

1½ tsp baking powder

175 g/6 oz light muscovado sugar

1 tsp lime rind, grated

1 medium egg, beaten

1 medium banana, mashed with 1 tbsp
    lime juice

150 ml/5 fl oz/⅔ cup low-fat natural
    fromage frais (unsweetened yogurt)

115 g/4 oz sultanas

banana chips, to decorate

lime rind, finely grated, to decorate

TOPPING

115 g/4 oz icing (confectioners') sugar

1–2 tsp lime juice

½ tsp lime rind, finely grated

VARIATION

For a delicious alternative,
replace the lime rind and juice with
orange and the sultanas with
chopped apricots.

1 Preheat the oven to 180°C/350°F/Gas Mark 4. Grease and line a deep 18 cm/7 inch round cake tin with baking parchment.

2 Sift the flour, salt and baking powder into a mixing bowl and stir in the sugar and lime rind.

3 Make a well in the centre of the dry ingredients and add the egg, banana, fromage frais (yogurt) and sultanas. Mix well until thoroughly incorporated.

4 Spoon the mixture into the tin and smooth the surface. Bake for 40–45 minutes until firm to the touch or until a skewer inserted in the centre comes out clean. Leave to cool for 10 minutes, then turn out on to a wire rack.

5 To make the topping, sift the icing (confectioners') sugar into a small bowl and mix with the lime juice to form a soft, but not too runny, icing. Stir in the grated lime rind. Drizzle the icing over the cake, letting it run down the sides.

6 Decorate the cake with banana chips and lime rind. Let the cake stand for 15 minutes so that the icing sets.

Baked Pears with Cinnamon

This simple recipe is easy to prepare and cook but is deliciously warming. For a treat, serve hot on a pool of low-fat custard.

NUTRITIONAL INFORMATION

Calories 207	Sugars 35g
Protein 3g	Fat 6g
Carbohydrate . . .37g	Saturates 2g

 10 MINS   25 MINS

SERVES 4

I N G R E D I E N T S

4 ripe pears

2 tbsp lemon juice

4 tbsp light muscovado sugar

1 tsp ground cinnamon

60 g/2 oz low-fat spread

low-fat custard, to serve

lemon rind, finely grated, to decorate

1 Preheat the oven to 200°C/400°F/Gas Mark 6. Core and peel the pears, then slice them in half lengthwise and brush all over with the lemon juice. Place the pears, cored side down, in a small non-stick roasting tin (pan).

2 Place the sugar, cinnamon and low-fat spread in a small saucepan and heat gently, stirring, until the sugar has melted. Keep the heat low to stop too much water evaporating from the low-fat spread as it gets hot. Spoon the mixture over the pears.

3 Bake for 20–25 minutes or until the pears are tender and golden, occasionally spooning the sugar mixture over the fruit during the cooking time.

4 To serve, heat the custard until it is piping hot and spoon over the bases of 4 warm dessert plates. Arrange 2 pear halves on each plate.

5 Decorate with grated lemon rind and serve.

VARIATION

For alternative flavours, replace the cinnamon with ground ginger and serve the pears sprinkled with chopped stem ginger in syrup. Alternatively, use ground allspice and spoon over some warmed dark rum to serve.

Honeyed Rice Puddings

These small rice puddings are quite sweet, but have a wonderful flavour because of the combination of ginger, honey and cinnamon.

NUTRITIONAL INFORMATION

Calories ....199 Sugars 15g
Protein ....3g Fat 1g
Carbohydrate ...46g Saturates 0g

10 MINS   50 MINS

SERVES 4

INGREDIENTS

300 g/10½ oz/1½ cups pudding rice

2 tbsp clear honey, plus extra
    for drizzling

large pinch of ground cinnamon

15 no-need-to-soak dried apricots,
    chopped

3 pieces stem (preserved) ginger, drained
    and chopped

8 whole no-need-to-soak dried apricots,
    to decorate

1 Put the rice in a saucepan and just cover with cold water. Bring to the boil, reduce the heat, cover and cook for about 15 minutes, or until the water has been absorbed. Stir the honey and cinnamon into the rice.

2 Grease 4 x 150 ml/¼ pint/⅔ cup ramekin dishes.

3 Blend the chopped dried apricots and ginger in a food processor to make a smooth paste.

4 Divide the paste into 4 equal portions and shape each into a flat round to fit into the base of the ramekin dishes.

5 Divide half of the rice between the ramekin dishes and place the apricot paste on top.

6 Cover the apricot paste with the remaining rice. Cover the ramekins with greaseproof (wax) paper and foil and steam for 30 minutes, or until set.

7 Remove the ramekins from the steamer and let stand for 5 minutes.

8 Turn the puddings out on to warm serving plates and drizzle with honey. Decorate with dried apricots and serve.

COOK'S TIP

The puddings may be left to chill in their ramekin dishes in the refrigerator, then turned out and served with ice cream or cream.

Bread & Butter Pudding

Everyone has their own favourite recipe for this dish. This one has added marmalade and grated apples for a really rich and unique taste.

NUTRITIONAL INFORMATION

Calories ....427 Sugars 63g
Protein ....9g Fat 13g
Carbohydrate ...74g Saturates 7g

45 MINS   1 HOUR

SERVES 6

I N G R E D I E N T S

about 60 g/2 oz/¼ cup butter, softened

4–5 slices white or brown bread

4 tbsp chunky orange marmalade

grated rind of 1 lemon

90–125 g/3–4½ oz/½–¾ cup raisins or
    sultanas (golden raisins)

40 g/1½ oz/¼ cup chopped mixed
    (candied) peel

1 tsp ground cinnamon or mixed spice
    (apple spice)

1 cooking apple, peeled,
    cored and coarsely grated

90 g/3 oz/scant ½ cup light brown sugar

3 eggs

500 ml/18 fl oz/2 cups milk

2 tbsp demerara (brown crystal) sugar

1 Use the butter to grease an ovenproof dish and to spread on the slices of bread, then spread the bread with the marmalade.

2 Place a layer of bread in the base of the dish and sprinkle with the lemon rind, half the raisins or sultanas (golden raisins), half the mixed (candied) peel, half the spice, all of the apple and half the light brown sugar.

3 Add another layer of bread, cutting so it fits the dish.

4 Sprinkle over most of the remaining raisins or sultanas (golden raisins) and the remaining peel, spice and light brown sugar, sprinkling it evenly over the bread. Top with a final layer of bread, again cutting to fit the dish.

5 Lightly beat together the eggs and milk and then carefully strain the mixture over the bread in the dish. If time allows, set aside to stand for 20–30 minutes.

6 Sprinkle the top of the pudding with the demerara (brown crystal) sugar and scatter over the remaining raisins or sultanas (golden raisins) and cook in a preheated oven, 200°C/400°F/Gas Mark 6, for 50–60 minutes, until risen and golden brown. Serve immediately or allow to cool and then serve cold.

Strawberry Roulade

Serve this moist, light sponge rolled up with an almond and strawberry fromage frais (yogurt) filling for a delicious tea-time treat.

NUTRITIONAL INFORMATION

Calories . . . . . . .166 Sugars 19g
Protein . . . . .6g Fat 3g
Carbohydrate . . .30g Saturates 1g

 30 MINS 10 MINS

SERVES 8

INGREDIENTS

3 large eggs

125 g/4½ oz caster (superfine) sugar

125 g/4½ oz plain (all-purpose) flour

1 tbsp hot water

FILLING

200 ml/7 fl oz/¾ cup low-fat natural fromage frais (unsweetened yogurt)

1 tsp almond essence (extract)

225 g/8 oz small strawberries

15 g/½ oz toasted almonds, flaked (slivered)

1 tsp icing (confectioners') sugar

1 Preheat the oven to 220°C/425°F/Gas Mark 7. Line a 35 x 25 cm/14 x 10 inch Swiss roll tin with baking parchment. Place the eggs in a mixing bowl with the caster (superfine) sugar. Place the bowl over a pan of hot water and whisk until pale and thick.

2 Remove the bowl from the pan. Sift in the flour and fold into the eggs with the hot water. Pour the mixture into the tin and bake for 8–10 minutes, until golden and set.

3 Transfer the mixture to a sheet of baking parchment. Peel off the lining paper and roll up the sponge tightly along with the baking parchment. Wrap in a tea towel (dish towel) and let cool.

4 Mix together the fromage frais (yogurt) and the almond essence (extract). Reserving a few strawberries for decoration, wash, hull and slice the rest.

Leave the mixture to chill in the refrigerator until required.

5 Unroll the sponge, spread the fromage frais (yogurt) mixture over the sponge and sprinkle with strawberries. Roll the sponge up again and transfer to a serving plate. Sprinkle with almonds and lightly dust with icing (confectioners') sugar. Decorate with the reserved strawberries.

Boston Chocolate Pie

This lighter version of the popular chocolate cream pie is made with yogurt and crème fraîche.

NUTRITIONAL INFORMATION

Calories 795   Sugars 73g
Protein . . . . .13g   Fat 40g
Carbohydrate . . .99g   Saturates 21g

 25 MINS   35 MINS

SERVES 6

INGREDIENTS

225 g/8 oz shortcrust pastry (see page 988)

CHOCOLATE CARAQUE

225 g/8 oz dark chocolate

FILLING

3 eggs

125 g/4½ oz/½ cup caster sugar

60 g/2 oz/½ cup flour, plus extra for dusting

1 tbsp icing (confectioners') sugar

pinch of salt

1 tsp vanilla essence (extract)

400 ml/14 fl oz/1⅔ cups milk

150 ml/¼ pint/⅔ cup natural
  (unsweetened) yogurt

150 g/5½ oz dark chocolate, broken
  into pieces

2 tbsp kirsch

TOPPING

150 ml/¼ pint/⅔ cup crème fraîche

 Roll out the pastry and use to line a 23 cm/9 inch loose-based flan tin (pan). Prick the base with a fork, line with baking parchment and fill with dried beans. Bake blind for 20 minutes. Remove the beans and paper and return to the oven for 5 minutes. Remove from the oven and place on a wire rack to cool.

2 To make the chocolate caraque, put pieces of chocolate on a plate over a pan of simmering water until melted. Spread on a cool surface with a palette knife (spatula). When cool, scrape it into curls with a sharp knife.

3 To make the filling, beat the eggs and sugar until fluffy. Sift in the flour, icing (confectioners') sugar and salt. Stir in the vanilla essence (extract).

4 Bring the milk and yogurt to the boil in a small pan and strain on to the egg mixture. Pour into a double boiler or set over a pan of simmering water. Stir until it coats the back of a spoon.

5 Gently heat the chocolate and kirsch in a small pan until melted. Stir into the custard. Remove from the heat and stand the double boiler or bowl in cold water. Leave it to cool .

6 Pour the chocolate mixture into the pastry case. Spread the crème fraîche over the chocolate, and arrange the caraque rolls on top.

Frozen Citrus Soufflés

These delicious desserts are a refreshing way to end a meal. They can be made in advance and kept in the freezer until required.

NUTRITIONAL INFORMATION

Calories ....364 Sugars 27g
Protein ....11g Fat 24g
Carbohydrate ...27g Saturates 14g

35 MINS   0 MINS

SERVES 4

I N G R E D I E N T S

1 tbsp vegetarian gelatine (gelozone)

6 tbsp very hot water

3 eggs, separated

90 g/3 oz/⅓ cup caster (superfine) sugar

finely grated rind and juice of 1 lemon,
  ½ lime and ½ orange

150 ml/¼ pint/⅔ cup double (heavy) cream

125 g/4½ oz/½ cup plain fromage frais

thin lemon, lime and orange slices
  to decorate

1 Tie greaseproof paper collars around 4 individual soufflé or ramekin dishes or around 1 large (15 cm/6 inch diameter) soufflé dish.

2 Sprinkle the gelatine (gelozone) into the very hot (not boiling) water, stirring well to disperse. Leave to stand for 2–3 minutes, stirring occasionally, to give a completely clear liquid. Leave to cool for 10–15 minutes.

3 Meanwhile, whisk the egg yolks and sugar, using a hand-held electric mixer or wire whisk until very pale and light in texture. Add the rind and juice from the fruits, mixing well. Stir in the cooled gelatine (gelozone) liquid, making sure that it is thoroughly incorporated.

4 Put the cream in a large chilled bowl and whip until it holds its shape. Stir the fromage frais and then add it to the cream, mixing it in gently. Fold the cream mixture into the citrus mixture, using a large metal spoon.

5 Using a clean whisk, beat the egg whites in a clean bowl until stiff and then gently fold them into the citrus mixture, using a metal spoon.

6 Pour the mixture into the prepared dishes, almost to the top of their collars. Allow some room for the mixture to expand on freezing. Transfer the dishes to the freezer and open-freeze for about 2 hours, until frozen.

7 Remove from the freezer 10 minutes before serving. Peel away the paper collars carefully and decorate with the slices of lemon, lime and orange.

Peaches in White Wine

A very simple but incredibly pleasing dessert, which is especially good for a dinner party on a hot summer day.

NUTRITIONAL INFORMATION

Calories . . . . .89 Sugars 14g
Protein . . . . .1g Fat 0g
Carbohydrate . . .14g Saturates 0g

1¼ HOURS   0 MINS

SERVES 4

INGREDIENTS

4 large ripe peaches

2 tbsp icing (confectioners') sugar, sifted

pared rind and juice of 1 orange

200 ml/7 fl oz/¾ cup medium or sweet
  white wine, chilled

1 Using a sharp knife, halve the peaches, remove the stones and discard them. Peel the peaches, if you prefer. Slice the peaches into thin wedges.

2 Place the peach wedges in a serving bowl and sprinkle over the sugar.

3 Using a sharp knife, pare the rind from the orange. Cut the orange rind into matchsticks, place them in a bowl of cold water and set aside.

4 Squeeze the juice from the orange and pour over the peaches together with the wine.

5 Let the peaches marinate and chill in the refrigerator for at least 1 hour.

6 Remove the orange rind from the cold water and pat dry with paper towels.

7 Garnish the peaches with the strips of orange rind and serve immediately.

Pavlova

This fruit meringue dish was created for Anna Pavlova, and it looks very impressive. Use fruits of your choice to make a colourful display.

NUTRITIONAL INFORMATION

Calories	321	Sugars	. . . . .37g
Protein	. . . . .3g	Fat	. . . . .18g
Carbohydrate	. . .37g	Saturates	. . . . .11g

1¹/₂ HOURS   1¹/₂ HOURS

SERVES 8

INGREDIENTS

6 egg whites

½ tsp cream of tartar

225 g/8 oz/1 cup caster (superfine) sugar

1 tsp vanilla flavouring (extract)

300 ml/½ pint/1¼ cups whipping cream

400 g/14 oz/2½ cups strawberries, hulled and halved

3 tbsp orange-flavoured liqueur

fruit of your choice, to decorate

1 Line a baking (cookie) sheet with baking parchment and mark out a circle to fit your serving plate. The recipe makes enough meringue for a 30 cm/12 inch circle.

2 Whisk the egg whites and cream of tartar together until stiff. Gradually beat in the caster (superfine) sugar and vanilla flavouring (extract). Whisk well until glossy and stiff.

3 Either spoon or pipe the meringue mixture into the marked circle, in an even layer, slightly raised at the edges, to form a dip in the centre.

4 Baking the meringue depends on your preference. If you like a soft chewy meringue, bake at 140°C/275°F/ Gas Mark 1 for about 1¹/₂ hours until dry but slightly soft in the centre. If you prefer a drier meringue, bake in the oven at 110°C/225°F/Gas Mark ¹/₄ for 3 hours until dry.

5 Before serving, whip the cream to a piping consistency, and either spoon or pipe on to the meringue base, leaving a border of meringue all around the edge.

6 Stir the strawberries and liqueur together and spoon on to the cream. Decorate with fruit of your choice.

COOK'S TIP

If you like a dry meringue, you can leave it in the oven on the lowest setting overnight. However, do not use this technique with a gas oven – but in an electric oven or solid fuel cooker it would be fine.

Ginger & Apricot Alaskas

No ice cream in this Alaska but a mixture of apples and apricots poached in orange juice enclosed in meringue.

NUTRITIONAL INFORMATION

Calories 442   Sugars 77g
Protein ....7g   Fat 9g
Carbohydrate ...83g   Saturates 3g

 15 MINS   10 MINS

SERVES 2

INGREDIENTS

2 slices rich, dark ginger cake,
   about 2 cm/¾ inch thick

1–2 tbsp ginger wine or rum

1 eating apple

6 ready-to-eat dried apricots, chopped

4 tbsp orange juice or water

15 g/½ oz/1 tbsp flaked (slivered) almonds

2 small egg whites

100 g/3½ oz/⅓ cup caster (superfine) sugar

1 Place each slice of ginger cake on an ovenproof plate and sprinkle with the ginger wine or rum.

2 Quarter, core and slice the apple into a small saucepan. Add the chopped apricots and orange juice or water, and simmer over a low heat for about 5 minutes, or until tender.

3 Stir the almonds into the fruit and spoon the mixture equally over the slices of soaked cake, piling it up in the centre.

4 Whisk the egg whites until very stiff and dry, then whisk in the sugar, a little at a time, making sure the meringue has become stiff again before adding any more sugar.

5 Either pipe or spread the meringue over the fruit and cake, making sure that both are completely covered.

6 Place in a preheated oven, 200°C/ 400°F/Gas Mark 6, for 4–5 minutes, until golden brown. Serve hot.

VARIATION

A slice of vanilla, coffee or chocolate ice cream can be placed on the fruit before adding the meringue, but this must be done at the last minute and the dessert must be eaten immediately after it is removed from the oven.

Exotic Fruit Salad

This is a sophisticated fruit salad that makes use of some of the exotic fruits that can now be seen in the supermarket.

NUTRITIONAL INFORMATION

Calories 149	Sugars 39g	
Protein 1g	Fat 0.1g	
Carbohydrate ...39g	Saturates 0g	

10 MINS   15 MINS

SERVES 6

INGREDIENTS

3 passion-fruit

125 g/4 oz/½ cup caster (superfine) sugar

150 ml/¼ pint/⅔ cup water

1 mango

10 lychees, canned or fresh

1 star-fruit

1 Halve the passion-fruit and press the flesh through a sieve (strainer) into a saucepan.

2 Add the sugar and water to the saucepan and bring to a gentle boil, stirring frequently.

3 Cut a thick slice from either side of the mango, cutting as near to the stone (pit) as possible. Cut away as much flesh as possible in large chunks from the stone (pit) section.

COOK'S TIP

A delicious accompaniment to any exotic fruit dish is cardamom cream. Crush the seeds from 8 cardamom pods, add 300 ml/½ pint/1¼ cups whipping cream and whip until soft peaks form.

4 Take the 2 side slices and make 3 cuts through the flesh but not the skin, and 3 more at right angles to make a lattice pattern.

5 Push inside out so that the cubed flesh is exposed and you can easily cut it off.

6 Peel and stone (pit) the lychees and cut the star-fruit into 12 slices.

7 Add all the mango flesh, the lychees and star-fruit to the passion-fruit syrup and poach gently for 5 minutes. Remove the fruit with a perforated spoon.

8 Bring the syrup to the boil and cook for 5 minutes until it thickens slightly.

9 To serve, transfer all the fruit to individual serving glasses, pour over the sugar syrup and serve warm.

Lime Mousse with Mango

Lime-flavoured cream moulds, served with a fresh mango and lime sauce, make a stunning dessert.

NUTRITIONAL INFORMATION

Calories 254   Sugars 17g
Protein ....5g   Fat 19g
Carbohydrate ...17g   Saturates 12g

10 MINS   0 MINS

SERVES 4

INGREDIENTS

250 g/9 oz/1 cup fromage frais

grated rind of 1 lime

1 tbsp caster (superfine) sugar

125 ml/4 fl oz/½ cup double (heavy) cream

MANGO SAUCE

1 mango

juice of 1 lime

4 tsp caster (superfine) sugar

TO DECORATE

4 Cape gooseberries

strips of lime rind

1 Put the fromage frais, lime rind and sugar in a bowl and mix together.

2 Whisk the double (heavy) cream in a separate bowl and fold into the fromage frais.

3 Line 4 decorative moulds or ramekin dishes with muslin (cheesecloth) or cling film (plastic wrap) and divide the mixture evenly between them. Fold the muslin (cheesecloth) over the top and press down firmly.

4 To make the sauce, slice through the mango on each side of the large flat stone, then cut the flesh from the stone. Remove the skin.

5 Cut off 12 thin slices and set aside. Chop the remaining mango, put into a food processor with the lime juice and sugar. Blend until smooth. Alternatively, push the mango through a sieve (strainer) then mix with the lime juice and sugar.

6 Turn out the moulds on to serving plates. Arrange 3 slices of mango on each plate, pour some sauce around, decorate and serve.

COOK'S TIP

Cape gooseberries have a tart and mildly scented flavour and make an excellent decoration for many desserts. Peel back the papery husks to expose the bright orange fruits.

Brown Bread Ice Cream

Although it sounds unusual, this yogurt-based recipe is delicious. It contains no cream and is ideal for a low-fat diet.

NUTRITIONAL INFORMATION

Calories 264	Sugars 25g
Protein 12g	Fat 6g
Carbohydrate . . .43g	Saturates 1g

2¼ HOURS   5 MINS

SERVES 4

I N G R E D I E N T S

175 g/6 oz fresh wholemeal
    breadcrumbs

25 g/1 oz finely chopped walnuts

60 g/2 oz caster (superfine) sugar

½ tsp ground nutmeg

1 tsp finely grated orange rind

450 ml/16 fl oz/2 cups low-fat natural
    (unsweetened) yogurt

2 large egg whites

TO DECORATE

walnut halves

orange slices

fresh mint

1 Preheat the grill (broiler) to medium. Mix the breadcrumbs, walnuts and sugar and spread over a sheet of foil in the grill (broiler) pan.

2 Grill (broil), stirring frequently, for 5 minutes until crisp and evenly browned. (Take care that the sugar does not burn.) Remove from the heat and leave to cool.

3 When cool, transfer to a mixing bowl and mix in the nutmeg, orange rind and yogurt. In another bowl, whisk the egg whites until stiff. Gently fold into the breadcrumb mixture, using a metal spoon.

4 Spoon the mixture into 4 mini-basins, smooth over the tops and freeze for 1½–2 hours until firm.

5 To serve, hold the bases of the moulds (molds) in hot water for a few seconds, then turn on to serving plates.

6 Serve immediately, decorated with the walnuts, oranges and fresh mint.

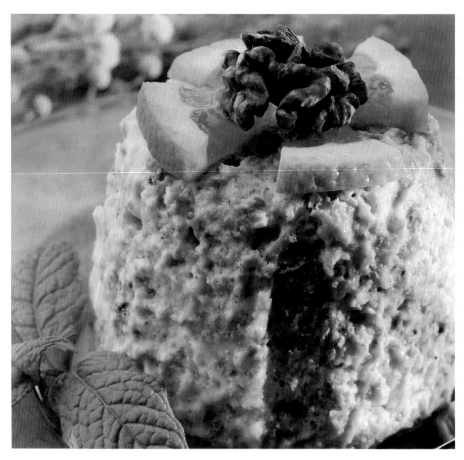

COOK'S TIP

If you don't have mini-basins, use ramekins or teacups or, if you prefer, use one large bowl. Alternatively, spoon the mixture into a large, freezing container to freeze and serve the ice cream in scoops.

Sweet Mascarpone Mousse

A sweet cream cheese dessert that complements the tartness of fresh summer fruits rather well.

NUTRITIONAL INFORMATION

Calories 542	Sugars 31g
Protein 14g	Fat 41g
Carbohydrate ...31g	Saturates 24g

1 ¹/₂ HOURS   ⏱ 0 MINS

SERVES 4

INGREDIENTS

450 g/1 lb mascarpone cheese

100 g/3½ oz caster (superfine) sugar

4 egg yolks

400 g/14 oz frozen summer fruits, such as
   raspberries and redcurrants

redcurrants, to garnish

amaretti biscuits (cookies), to serve

1 Place the mascarpone cheese in a large mixing bowl. Using a wooden spoon, beat the mascarpone cheese until quite smooth.

2 Stir the egg yolks and sugar into the mascarpone cheese, mixing well. Leave the mixture to chill in the refrigerator for about 1 hour.

3 Spoon a layer of the mascarpone mixture into the bottom of 4 individual serving dishes. Spoon a layer of the summer fruits on top. Repeat the layers in the same order, reserving some of the mascarpone mixture for the top.

4 Leave the mousses to chill in the refrigerator for about 20 minutes. The fruits should still be slightly frozen.

5 Serve the mascarpone mousses with amaretti biscuits (cookies).

Coconut Sweet

Quick and easy to make, this sweet is very similar to coconut ice. Pink food colouring may be added towards the end if desired.

NUTRITIONAL INFORMATION

Calories	338	Sugars 5g
Protein	. . . . .4g	Fat 34g
Carbohydrate	. . . .5g	Saturates 26g

1¼ HOURS   15 MINS

SERVES 6

INGREDIENTS

75 g/2¾ oz/6 tbsp butter

200 g/7 oz/3 cups desiccated
  (shredded) coconut

175 ml/6 fl oz/¾ cup condensed milk

a few drops of pink food colouring (optional)

1 Place the butter in a heavy-based saucepan and melt over a low heat, stirring constantly so that the butter doesn't burn on the base of the pan.

2 Add the desiccated (shredded) coconut to the melted butter, stirring to mix.

3 Stir in the condensed milk and the pink food colouring (if using) and mix continuously for 7–10 minutes.

VARIATION

If you prefer, you could divide the coconut mixture in step 2, and add the pink food colouring to only one half of the mixture. This way, you will have an attractive combination of pink and white coconut sweets.

4 Remove the saucepan from the heat, set aside and leave the coconut mixture to cool slightly.

5 Once cool enough to handle, shape the coconut mixture into long blocks and cut into equal-sized rectangles. Leave to set for about 1 hour, then serve.

Ricotta Ice Cream

The ricotta cheese adds a creamy flavour, while the nuts add a crunchy texture. This ice cream needs to be chilled in the freezer overnight.

NUTRITIONAL INFORMATION

Calories 438   Sugars 39g
Protein ....13g   Fat 25g
Carbohydrate ...40g   Saturates 9g

 20 MINS   0 MINS

SERVES 6

INGREDIENTS

25 g/1 oz/¼ cup pistachio nuts

25 g/1 oz/¼ cup walnuts or pecan nuts

25 g/1 oz/¼ cup toasted
   chopped hazelnuts

grated rind of 1 orange

grated rind of 1 lemon

25 g/1 oz/2 tbsp crystallized or stem ginger

25 g/1 oz/2 tbsp glacé cherries

25 g/1 oz/¼ cup dried apricots

25 g/1 oz/3 tbsp raisins

500 g/1 lb 2 oz/1½ cups Ricotta

2 tbsp Maraschino, Amaretto or brandy

1 tsp vanilla essence (extract)

4 egg yolks

125 g/4½ oz/½ cup caster (superfine)
   sugar

TO DECORATE

whipped cream

a few glacé cherries, pistachio nuts or

mint leaves

1 Roughly chop the pistachio nuts and walnuts and mix with the toasted hazelnuts, orange and lemon rind.

2 Finely chop the ginger, cherries, apricots and raisins, and add to the bowl.

3 Stir the Ricotta evenly through the fruit mixture, then beat in the liqueur and vanilla essence (extract).

4 Put the egg yolks and sugar in a bowl and whisk hard until very thick and creamy – they may be whisked over a saucepan of gently simmering water to speed up the process. Leave to cool if necessary.

5 Carefully fold the Ricotta mixture evenly through the beaten eggs and sugar until smooth.

6 Line a 18 x 12 cm/7 x 5 inch loaf tin (pan) with a double layer of cling film (plastic wrap) or baking parchment. Pour in the Ricotta mixture, level the top, cover with more cling film (plastic wrap) or baking parchment and chill in the freezer until firm – at least overnight.

7 To serve, carefully remove the ice-cream from the tin (pan) and peel off the paper. Place on a serving dish and decorate with whipped cream, glacé cherries, pistachio nuts and/or mint leaves. Serve in slices.

Steamed Coffee Sponge

This sponge pudding is very light and is quite delicious served with a sweet chocolate sauce.

NUTRITIONAL INFORMATION

Calories 300   Sugars 21g
Protein ....8g   Fat 13g
Carbohydrate ...40g   Saturates 4g

10 MINS   1¼ HOURS

SERVES 4

INGREDIENTS

25 g/1 oz/2 tbsp margarine

2 tbsp soft brown sugar

2 eggs

50 g/1¾ oz/⅓ cup plain (all-purpose) flour

¾ tsp baking powder

6 tbsp milk

1 tsp coffee flavouring (extract)

SAUCE

300 ml/½ pint/1¼ cups milk

1 tbsp soft brown sugar

1 tsp cocoa powder
   (unsweetened) cocoa

2 tbsp cornflour (cornstarch)

1 Lightly grease a 600 ml/1 pint/2½ cup pudding basin (heatproof bowl). Cream the margarine and sugar until light and fluffy and beat in the eggs.

2 Gradually stir in the flour and baking powder and then the milk and coffee flavouring (extract) to make a smooth batter.

3 Spoon the mixture into the prepared pudding basin (heatproof bowl) and cover with a pleated piece of baking parchment and then a pleated piece of foil, securing around the bowl with string. Place in a steamer or large pan and half fill with boiling water. Cover and steam for 1–1¼ hours, or until cooked through.

4 To make the sauce, put the milk, soft brown sugar and cocoa powder (unsweetened cocoa) in a pan and heat , stirring constantly, until the sugar dissolves. Blend the cornflour (cornstarch) with 4 tablespoons of cold water to make a smooth paste and stir into the pan. Bring to the boil, stirring constantly until thickened. Cook over a gentle heat for 1 minute.

5 Turn the pudding out on to a warmed serving plate and spoon the sauce over the top. Serve immediately.

COOK'S TIP

The pudding is covered with pleated paper and foil to allow it to rise. The foil will react with the steam and must therefore not be placed directly against the pudding.

Sweet Saffron Rice

This is a traditional dessert, which is quick and easy to make and looks very impressive, especially decorated with pistachio nuts and *varq*.

NUTRITIONAL INFORMATION

Calories ....460 Sugars 57g
Protein ....4g Fat 9g
Carbohydrate ...97g Saturates 5g

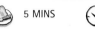

🧈 5 MINS   🕐 35 MINS

SERVES 4

INGREDIENTS

200 g/7 oz/1 cup basmati rice

200 g/7 oz/1 cup sugar

1 pinch saffron strands

300 ml/½ pint/1¼ cups water

2 tbsp vegetable ghee

3 cloves

3 cardamoms

25 g/1 oz/2 tbsp sultanas (golden raisins)

TO DECORATE

a few pistachio nuts (optional)

varq (silver leaf) (optional)

1 Rinse the rice twice and bring to the boil in a saucepan of water, stirring constantly. Remove the pan from the heat when the rice is half-cooked, drain the rice thoroughly and set aside.

2 In a separate saucepan, boil the sugar and saffron in the water, stirring constantly, until the syrup thickens. Set the syrup aside until required.

3 In another saucepan, heat the ghee, cloves and cardamoms, stirring occasionally. Remove the pan from the heat.

4 Return the rice to a low heat and stir in the sultanas (golden raisins).

5 Pour the syrup over the rice mixture and stir to mix.

6 Pour the ghee mixture over the rice and simmer over a low heat for about 10–15 minutes. Check to see whether the rice is cooked. If it is not, add a little boiling water, cover and continue to simmer until tender.

7 Serve warm, decorated with pistachio nuts and varq (silver leaf), if desired.

VARIATION

Basmati rice is the 'prince of rices' and comes from the Himalayan foothills. Its name means fragrant and it has a superb texture and flavour.

Tropical Fruit Fool

Fruit fools are always popular, and this light, tangy version will be no exception. Use your favourite fruits in this recipe if you prefer.

NUTRITIONAL INFORMATION

Calories 149	Sugars 25g
Protein 6g	Fat 0.4g
Carbohydrate . . .32g	Saturates 0.2g

 35 MINS   0 MINS

SERVES 4

INGREDIENTS

1 medium ripe mango

2 kiwi fruit

1 medium banana

2 tbsp lime juice

½ tsp finely grated lime rind, plus extra to
   decorate

2 medium egg whites

425 g/15 oz can low-fat custard

½ tsp vanilla essence (extract)

2 passion fruit

1 To peel the mango, slice either side of the smooth, flat central stone. Roughly chop the flesh and blend the fruit in a food processor or blender until smooth. Alternatively, mash with a fork.

VARIATION

Other tropical fruits to try include paw-paw (papaya) purée, with chopped pineapple and dates or pomegranate seeds to decorate. Or make a summer fruit fool by using strawberry purée, topped with raspberries and blackberries and cherries.

2 Peel the kiwi fruit, chop the flesh into small pieces and place in a bowl. Peel and chop the banana and add to the bowl. Toss all of the fruit in the lime juice and rind and mix well.

3 In a grease-free bowl, whisk the egg whites until stiff and then gently fold in the custard and vanilla essence (extract) until thoroughly mixed.

4 In 4 tall glasses, alternately layer the chopped fruit, mango purée and custard mixture, finishing with the custard on top. Leave to chill in the refrigerator for 20 minutes.

5 Halve the passion fruits, scoop out the seeds and spoon the passion fruit over the fruit fools. Decorate each serving with the extra lime rind and serve.

Florentines

These luxury biscuits (cookies) will be popular at any time of the year, but make a particularly wonderful treat at Christmas.

NUTRITIONAL INFORMATION

Calories 186   Sugars 19g
Protein ....2g   Fat 11g
Carbohydrate ...22g   Saturates 5g

20 MINS   15 MINS

MAKES 10

INGREDIENTS

50 g/1¾ oz/ 10 tsp butter

50 g/1¾ oz/¼ cup caster (superfine) sugar

25 g/1 oz/¼ cup plain (all-purpose) flour, sieved (strained)

50 g/1¾ oz/⅓ cup almonds, chopped

50 g/1¾ oz/⅓ cup chopped mixed peel

25 g/1 oz/¼ cup raisins, chopped

25 g/1 oz/2 tbsp glacé (candied) cherries, chopped

finely grated rind of ½ lemon

125 g/4½ oz dark chocolate, melted

1 Line 2 large baking trays (cookie sheets) with baking parchment.

2 Heat the butter and caster (superfine) sugar in a small saucepan until the butter has just melted and the sugar dissolved. Remove the pan from the heat.

3 Stir in the flour and mix well. Stir in the chopped almonds, mixed peel, raisins, cherries and lemon rind. Place teaspoonfuls of the mixture well apart on the baking trays (cookie sheets).

4 Bake in a preheated oven, at 180°C/350°F/Gas Mark 4, for 10 minutes or until lightly golden.

5 As soon as the florentines are removed from the oven, press the edges into neat shapes while still on the baking trays (cookie sheets), using a biscuit (cookie) cutter. Leave to cool on the baking trays (cookie sheets) until firm, then transfer to a wire rack to cool completely.

6 Spread the melted chocolate over the smooth side of each florentine. As the chocolate begins to set, mark wavy lines in it with a fork. Leave the florentines until set, chocolate side up.

VARIATION

Replace the dark chocolate with white chocolate or, for a dramatic effect, cover half of the florentines in dark chocolate and half in white.

Autumn Fruit Bread Pudding

This is like a summer pudding, but it uses fruits which appear later in the year. This dessert requires chilling overnight so prepare in advance.

NUTRITIONAL INFORMATION

Calories ....177 Sugars 29g
Protein ....3g Fat 1g
Carbohydrate ...42g Saturates 0.1g

10 MINS   15 MINS

SERVES 8

INGREDIENTS

900 g/2 lb/4 cups mixed blackberries,
  chopped apples, chopped pears

150 g/5½ oz/¾ cup soft light brown sugar

1 tsp cinnamon

225 g/8 oz white bread, thinly sliced,
  crusts removed (about 12 slices)

1 Place the fruit in a large saucepan with the soft light brown sugar, cinnamon and 7 tablespoons of water, stir and bring to the boil. Reduce the heat and simmer for 5–10 minutes so that the fruits soften but still hold their shape.

2 Meanwhile, line the base and sides of a 900 ml/1½ pint/3¾ cup pudding basin (bowl) with the bread slices, ensuring that there are no gaps between the pieces of bread.

3 Spoon the fruit into the centre of the bread-lined bowl and cover the fruit with the remaining bread.

4 Place a saucer on top of the bread and weigh it down. Chill the pudding in the refrigerator overnight.

5 Turn the pudding out on to a serving plate and serve immediately.

COOK'S TIP

This pudding would be delicious served with vanilla ice cream to counteract the tartness of the blackberries. Stand the pudding on a plate when chilling to catch any juices that run down the sides of the basin (bowl).

Green Fruit Salad

This delightfully refreshing fruit salad is the perfect finale for a Chinese meal. It has a lovely light syrup made with fresh mint and honey.

NUTRITIONAL INFORMATION

Calories ....157 Sugars 34g
Protein ....1g Fat 0.2g
Carbohydrate ...34g Saturates 0g

30 MINS   15 MINS

SERVES 4

INGREDIENTS

1 small Charentais or honeydew melon

2 green apples

2 kiwi fruit

125 g/4½ oz/1 cup seedless white grapes

fresh mint sprigs, to decorate

SYRUP

1 lemon

150 ml/¼ pint/⅔ cup white wine

150 ml/¼ pint/⅔ cup water

4 tbsp clear honey

few sprigs of fresh mint

1 To make the syrup, pare the rind from the lemon using a potato peeler.

2 Put the lemon rind in a saucepan with the white wine, water and clear honey. Bring to the boil, then simmer gently for 10 minutes.

3 Remove the syrup from the heat. Add the sprigs of mint and leave to cool.

4 To prepare the fruit, first slice the melon in half and scoop out the seeds. Use a melon baller or a teaspoon to make melon balls.

5 Core and chop the apples. Peel and slice the kiwi fruit.

6 Strain the cooled syrup into a serving bowl, removing and reserving the lemon rind and discarding the mint sprigs.

7 Add the apple, grapes, kiwi fruit and melon to the serving bowl. Stir through gently to mix.

8 Serve the fruit salad, decorated with sprigs of fresh mint and some of the reserved lemon rind.

COOK'S TIP

Single-flower honey has a better, more individual flavour than blended honey. Acacia honey is typically Chinese, but you could also try clove, lemon blossom, lime flower or orange blossom.

Passion-Fruit Rice

This creamy rice pudding, adapted for the microwave, is spiced with cardamom, cinnamon and bay leaf and served with passion-fruit.

NUTRITIONAL INFORMATION

Calories	534	Sugars	........42g
Protein	.........9g	Fat	..........22g
Carbohydrate	...80g	Saturates	......13g

1¼ HOURS   30 MINS

SERVES 4

INGREDIENTS

175 g/6 oz/scant 1 cup jasmine fragrant rice

600 ml/1 pint/2½ cups milk

125 g/4½ oz/½ cup caster (superfine) sugar

6 cardamom pods, split open

1 dried bay leaf

1 cinnamon stick

150 ml/¼ pint/⅔ cup double (heavy) cream, whipped

4 passion-fruit

soft berry fruits, to decorate

1 Place the jasmine fragrant rice in a large bowl with the milk, caster (superfine) sugar, cardamom pods, bay leaf and cinnamon stick. Cover and cook on medium power for 25–30 minutes, stirring occasionally. The rice should be just tender

and have absorbed most of the milk. Add a little extra milk, if necessary.

2 Leave the rice to cool, still covered. Remove the bay leaf, cardamom husks and cinnamon stick.

3 Gently fold the cream into the cooled rice mixture.

4 Halve the passion-fruits and scoop out the centres into a bowl.

5 Layer the rice with the passion-fruit in 4 tall glasses, finishing with a layer of passion-fruit. Leave to chill in the refrigerator for 30 minutes.

6 Decorate the passion-fruit rice with soft berry fruits and serve immediately.

COOK'S TIP

If you are unable to obtain passion-fruit, you can use a purée of another fruit of your choice, such as kiwi fruit, raspberry or strawberry.

Apricot & Orange Jellies

These bright fruity little desserts are easy to make and taste so much better than shop-bought jellies. Serve them with low-fat ice cream.

NUTRITIONAL INFORMATION

Calories	206	Sugars	........36g
Protein	.........8g	Fat	...........5g
Carbohydrate	...36g	Saturates	......3g

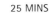

4¼ HOURS   25 MINS

SERVES 4

INGREDIENTS

225 g/8 oz no-need-to-soak dried apricots

300 ml/½ pint/1¼ cups unsweetened orange juice

2 tbsp lemon juice

2–3 tsp clear honey

1 tbsp powdered gelatine

4 tbsp boiling water

TO DECORATE

orange segments

sprigs of mint

CINNAMON 'CREAM'

125 g/4½ oz medium-fat ricotta cheese

125 g/4½ oz low-fat natural fromage frais (unsweetened yogurt)

1 tsp ground cinnamon

1 tbsp clear honey

1 Place the apricots in a saucepan and pour in the orange juice. Bring to the boil, cover and simmer for 15–20 minutes until plump and soft. Cool for 10 minutes.

2 Transfer the mixture to a blender or food processor and blend until smooth. Stir in the lemon juice and add the honey. Pour the mixture into a measuring jug and make up to 600 ml/ 1 pint /2½ cups with cold water.

3 Dissolve the gelatine in the boiling water and stir into the apricot mixture.

4 Pour the mixture into 4 individual moulds (molds), each 150 ml/5 fl oz/²/₃ cup, or 1 large mould, 600 ml/ 1 pint/2½ cups. Leave to chill until set.

5 Meanwhile, make the cinnamon 'cream'. Mix all the ingredients together and place in a small bowl. Cover the mixture and leave to chill until

6 To turn out the jellies, dip the moulds (molds) in hot water for a few seconds and invert on to serving plates.

7 Decorate with the orange segments and sprigs of mint. Serve with the cinnamon 'cream' dusted with extra cinnamon.

Orchard Fruits Bristol

An elegant fruit salad of poached pears and apples, oranges and strawberries in a wine and caramel syrup topped with crumbled caramel.

NUTRITIONAL INFORMATION

Calories	395	Sugars	.......94g
Protein	.........3g	Fat	..........0.5g
Carbohydrate	...94g	Saturates	......0g

30 MINS   20 MINS

SERVES 4

INGREDIENTS

4 oranges

175 g/6 oz/¾ cup granulated sugar

4 tbsp water

150 ml/¼ pint/⅔ cup white wine

4 firm pears

4 dessert (eating) apples

125 g/4½ oz/¾ cup strawberries

 1 Pare the rind thinly from 1 orange and cut into narrow strips. Cook in the minimum of boiling water for 3–4 minutes until tender. Drain and reserve the liquor. Squeeze the juice from this and 1 other orange.

2 Lay a sheet of non-stick baking parchment on a baking sheet or board.

3 Heat the sugar gently in a pan until it melts, then continue without stirring until it turns a pale golden brown. Pour half the caramel quickly on to the parchment and leave to set.

4 Add the water and squeezed orange juice immediately to the caramel left in the pan with 150 ml/¼ pint/ ⅔ cup orange rind liquor. Heat until it melts, then add the wine and remove from the heat.

5 Peel, core and slice the pears and apples thickly (you can leave the apple skins on, if you prefer) and add to the caramel syrup. Bring gently to the boil and simmer for 3–4 minutes until just beginning to soften – they should still be firm in the centre. Transfer the fruits to a bowl.

6 Cut away the peel and pith from the remaining oranges and either ease out the segments or cut into slices, discarding any pips (seeds). Add to the other fruits. Hull the strawberries and halve, quarter or slice thickly depending on the size and add to the other fruits.

7 Add the orange strands to the syrup and bring back to the boil for 1 minute, then pour over the fruits. Leave until cold, then break up the caramel and sprinkle over the fruit. Cover and chill until ready to serve.

COOK'S TIP

The caramel will begin to melt when added to the fruit, so do this as near to serving as possible.

Brown Sugar Pavlovas

This simple combination of fudgey meringue topped with fromage frais (yogurt) and raspberries is the perfect finale to any meal.

NUTRITIONAL INFORMATION

Calories	155	Sugars	........34g
Protein	.........5g	Fat	..........0.2g
Carbohydrate	...35g	Saturates	......0g

   1 HOUR   1 HOUR

SERVES 4

I N G R E D I E N T S

2 large egg whites

1 tsp cornflour (cornstarch)

1 tsp raspberry vinegar

100 g/3½ oz light muscovado sugar, crushed free of lumps

2 tbsp redcurrant jelly

2 tbsp unsweetened orange juice

150 ml/5 fl oz/¾ cup low-fat natural fromage frais (unsweetened yogurt)

175 g/6 oz raspberries, thawed if frozen

rose-scented geranium leaves, to decorate (optional)

1 Preheat the oven to 150°C/300°F/Gas Mark 2. Line a large baking tray (cookie sheet) with baking parchment. Whisk the egg whites until very stiff and dry. Fold in the cornflour (cornstarch) and vinegar.

2 Gradually whisk in the sugar, a spoonful at a time, until the mixture is thick and glossy.

3 Divide the mixture into 4 and spoon on to the baking sheet, spaced well apart. Smooth each into a round, about 10 cm/4 inches across, and bake in the oven for 40–45 minutes until lightly browned and crisp. Leave to cool on the baking tray (cookie sheet).

4 Place the redcurrant jelly and orange juice in a small pan and heat, stirring, until melted. Leave to cool for 10 minutes.

5 Using a palette knife, carefully remove each pavlova from the baking parchment and transfer to a serving plate. Top with the fromage frais (unsweetened yogurt) and the raspberries. Glaze the fruit with the redcurrant jelly, and decorate with the geranium leaves (if using).

COOK'S TIP

Make a large pavlova by forming the meringue into a round, measuring 18 cm/7 inches across, on a lined baking tray (cookie sheet) and bake for 1 hour.

Upside-down Cake

This recipe shows how a classic favourite can be adapted for vegans by using vegetarian margarine and oil instead of butter and eggs.

NUTRITIONAL INFORMATION

Calories	354	Sugars	........31g
Protein	.........3g	Fat	..........15g
Carbohydrate	...56g	Saturates	.......2g

15 MINS   50 MINS

SERVES 6

INGREDIENTS

50 g/1¾ oz/¼ cup vegan margarine,
    cut into small pieces, plus extra
    for greasing

425 g/15 oz can unsweetened pineapple
    pieces, drained and juice reserved

4 tsp cornflour (cornstarch)

50 g/1¾ oz/¼ cup soft brown sugar

125 ml/4 fl oz/½ cup water

rind of 1 lemon

SPONGE

50 ml/2 fl oz/¼ cup sunflower oil

75 g/2¾ oz/⅓ cup soft brown sugar

150 ml/¼ pint/⅔ cup water

150 g/5½ oz/1¼ cups plain
    (all-purpose) flour

2 tsp baking powder

1 tsp ground cinnamon

1 Grease a deep 18 cm/7 inch cake tin (pan). Mix the reserved juice from the pineapple with the cornflour (cornstarch) until it forms a smooth paste. Put the paste in a saucepan with the sugar, margarine and water and stir over a low heat until the sugar has dissolved. Bring to the boil and simmer for 2–3 minutes, until thickened. Set aside to cool slightly.

2 To make the sponge, place the oil, sugar and water in a saucepan. Heat gently until the sugar has dissolved; do not allow it to boil. Remove from the heat and leave to cool. Sift the flour, baking powder and ground cinnamon into a mixing bowl. Pour over the cooled sugar syrup and beat well to form a batter.

3 Place the pineapple pieces and lemon rind on the base of the prepared tin (pan) and pour over 4 tablespoons of the pineapple syrup. Spoon the sponge batter on top.

4 Bake in a preheated oven, 180°C/ 350°F/Gas Mark 4, for 35–40 minutes, until set and a fine metal skewer inserted into the centre comes out clean. Invert on to a plate, leave to stand for 5 minutes, then remove the tin (pan). Serve with the remaining syrup.

Almond Slices

A mouth-watering dessert that is sure to impress your guests, especially if it is served with whipped cream.

NUTRITIONAL INFORMATION

Calories . . . . .416 Sugars 37g
Protein . . . . .11g Fat 26g
Carbohydrate . . .38g Saturates 12g

5 MINS   5 MINS

SERVES 8

INGREDIENTS

3 eggs

75 g/2¾ oz/½ cup ground almonds

200 g/7 oz/1½ cups milk powder

200 g/7 oz/1 cup sugar

½ tsp saffron strands

100 g/3½ oz/½ cup unsalted butter

25 g/1 oz/1 tbsp flaked (slivered) almonds

1 Beat the eggs together in a bowl and set aside.

2 Place the ground almonds, milk powder, sugar and saffron in a large mixing bowl and stir to mix well.

3 Melt the butter in a small saucepan. Pour the melted butter over the dry ingredients and mix well until thoroughly combined.

4 Add the reserved beaten eggs to the mixture and stir to blend well.

5 Spread the mixture in a shallow 15–20 cm/7–9 inch ovenproof dish and bake in a preheated oven, 160°C/325°F/Gas Mark 3, for 45 minutes. Test whether the cake is cooked through by piercing with the tip of a sharp knife or a skewer – it will come out clean if it is cooked thoroughly.

6 Cut the almond cake into slices. Decorate the almond slices with flaked (slivered) almonds and transfer to serving plates. Serve hot or cold.

COOK'S TIP

These almond slices are best eaten hot, but they may also be served cold. They can be made a day or even a week in advance and re-heated. They also freeze beautifully.

Fruit & Nut Loaf

This loaf is like a fruit bread which may be served warm or cold, perhaps spread with a little margarine or butter or topped with jam (jelly).

NUTRITIONAL INFORMATION

Calories 354   Sugars 36g
Protein ....8g   Fat 9g
Carbohydrate ...64g   Saturates 1.2g

35 MINS   40 MINS

SERVES 6

I N G R E D I E N T S

225 g/8 oz/1¾ cups white bread flour,
   plus extra for dusting

½ tsp salt

1 tbsp margarine, plus extra for greasing

2 tbsp light brown sugar

100 g/3½ oz/⅔ cup sultanas (golden raisins)

50 g/1¾ oz/¼ cup ready-to-eat
   dried apricots, chopped

50 g/1¾ oz/½ cup chopped hazelnuts

2 tsp easy-blend dried (active dry) yeast

6 tbsp orange juice

6 tbsp natural (unsweetened) yogurt

2 tbsp strained apricot jam (jelly)

VARIATION

You can vary the nuts according to whatever you have at hand – try chopped walnuts or almonds.

1 Sift the flour and salt into a mixing bowl. Add the margarine and rub in with the fingertips. Stir in the sugar, sultanas (golden raisins), apricots, nuts and yeast.

2 Warm the orange juice in a saucepan, but do not allow to boil.

3 Stir the warm orange juice into the flour mixture, together with the natural (unsweetened) yogurt and bring the mixture together to form a dough.

4 Knead the dough on a lightly floured surface for 5 minutes, until smooth and elastic. Shape into a round and place on a lightly greased baking tray (cookie sheet). Cover with a clean tea towel (dish cloth) and leave to rise in a warm place until doubled in size.

5 Cook the loaf in a preheated oven, 220°C/425°F/Gas Mark 7, for 35–40 minutes, until cooked through. Transfer to a wire rack and brush with the apricot jam. Leave to cool before serving.

Baked Sweet Ravioli

These scrumptious little parcels are the perfect dessert for anyone with a really sweet tooth.

NUTRITIONAL INFORMATION

Calories 765   Sugars 56g
Protein . . . . .16g   Fat 30g
Carbohydrate . . .114g   Saturates 15g

 1½ HOURS   20 MINS

SERVES 4

I N G R E D I E N T S

PASTA

425 g/15 oz/3¾ cups plain
  (all purpose) flour

140 g/5 oz/10 tbsp butter, plus extra
  for greasing

140 g/5 oz/¾ cup caster (superfine) sugar

4 eggs

25 g/1 oz yeast

125 ml/4 fl oz warm milk

FILLING

175 g/6 oz/⅔ cup chestnut purée (paste)

60 g/2 oz/½ cup cocoa powder

60 g/2 oz/¼ cup caster (superfine) sugar

60 g/2 oz/½ cup chopped almonds

60 g/2 oz/1 cup crushed amaretti
  biscuits (cookies)

175 g/6 oz/⅝ cup orange marmalade

1 To make the sweet pasta dough, sift the flour into a mixing bowl, then mix in the butter, sugar and 3 eggs.

2 Mix together the yeast and warm milk in a small bowl and when thoroughly combined, mix into the dough.

3 Knead the dough for 20 minutes, cover with a clean cloth and set aside in a warm place for 1 hour to rise.

4 Mix together the chestnut purée (paste), cocoa powder, sugar, almonds, crushed amaretti biscuits (cookies) and orange marmalade in a separate bowl.

5 Grease a baking tray (cookie sheet) with butter.

6 Lightly flour the work surface (counter). Roll out the pasta dough into a thin sheet and cut into 5 cm/2 inch rounds with a plain pastry cutter.

7 Put a spoonful of filling on to each round and then fold in half, pressing the edges to seal. Arrange on the prepared baking tray (cookie sheet), spacing the ravioli out well.

8 Beat the remaining egg and brush all over the ravioli to glaze. Bake in a preheated oven, at 180°C/350°F/Gas Mark 4, for 20 minutes. Serve hot.

Tropical Salad

Paw-paws (papayas) are ready to eat when they yield to gentle pressure.
Serve in the shells of baby pineapples for a stunning effect.

NUTRITIONAL INFORMATION

Calories 69	Sugars 13g
Protein 1g	Fat 0.3g
Carbohydrate . . .14g	Saturates 0g

10 MINS   0 MINS

SERVES 8

I N G R E D I E N T S

1 paw-paw (papaya)

2 tbsp fresh orange juice

3 tbsp rum

2 bananas

2 guavas

1 small pineapple or 2 baby
   pineapples

2 passion-fruit

pineapple leaves to decorate

1 Cut the paw-paw (papaya) in half and remove the seeds. Peel and slice the flesh into a bowl.

2 Pour over the orange juice together with the rum.

3 Slice the bananas, peel and slice the guavas, and add both to the bowl.

4 Cut the top and base from the pineapple, then cut off the skin.

5 Slice the pineapple flesh, discard the core, cut into pieces and add to the bowl.

6 Halve the passion-fruit, scoop out the flesh with a teaspoon, add to the bowl and stir well to mix.

7 Spoon the salad into glass bowls and decorate with pineapple leaves.

COOK'S TIP

Guavas have a heavenly smell when ripe – their scent will fill a whole room. They should give to gentle pressure when ripe, and their skins should be yellow. The canned varieties are very good and have a pink tinge to the flesh.

Mixed Fruit Brûlées

Traditionally a rich mixture made with cream, this fruit-based version is just as tempting using natural (unsweetened) yogurt as a topping.

NUTRITIONAL INFORMATION

Calories 165	Sugars 21g	
Protein 5g	Fat 7g	
Carbohydrate ...21g	Saturates 5g	

 5 MINS   5 MINS

SERVES 4

I N G R E D I E N T S

450 g/1 lb prepared assorted summer fruits (such as strawberries, raspberries, blackcurrants, redcurrants and cherries), thawed if frozen

150 ml/5 fl oz/¾ cup half-fat double (heavy) cream alternative

150 ml/5 fl oz/¾ cup low-fat natural fromage frais (unsweetened yogurt)

1 tsp vanilla essence (extract)

4 tbsp demerara (brown crystal) sugar

1 Divide the prepared strawberries, raspberries, blackcurrants, redcurrants and cherries evenly among 4 small heatproof ramekin dishes.

2 Mix together the half-fat cream alternative, fromage frais (unsweetened yogurt) and vanilla essence (extract) until well combined.

3 Generously spoon the mixture over the fruit in the ramekin dishes, to cover the fruit completely.

4 Preheat the grill (broiler) to hot.

5 Top each serving with 1 tbsp demerara (brown crystal) sugar and grill (broil) the desserts for 2–3 minutes, until the sugar melts and begins to caramelize. Leave to stand for a couple of minutes before serving.

COOK'S TIP

Look out for half-fat creams, in single and double (light and heavy) varieties. They are good substitutes for occasional use. Alternatively, in this recipe, omit the cream and double the quantity of fromage frais (yogurt) for a lower fat version.

Rich Chocolate Loaf

Another rich chocolate dessert, this loaf is very simple to make and can be served as a tea-time treat as well.

NUTRITIONAL INFORMATION

Calories 180   Sugars 16g
Protein ....3g   Fat 11g
Carbohydrate ...18g   Saturates 5g

1¼ HOURS   5 MINS

MAKES 16 SLICES

INGREDIENTS

150 g/5½ oz dark chocolate

75 g/2¾ oz/6 tbsp butter, unsalted

210 g/7¼ oz tin of condensed milk

2 tsp cinnamon

75 g/2¾ oz almonds

75 g/2¾ oz amaretti biscuits (cookies), broken

50 g/1¾ oz dried no-need-to-soak apricots, roughly chopped

1 Line a 675 g/1½ lb loaf tin (pan) with a sheet of kitchen foil.

2 Using a sharp knife, roughly chop the almonds.

3 Place the chocolate, butter, milk and cinnamon in a heavy-based saucepan.

4 Heat the chocolate mixture over a low heat for 3–4 minutes, stirring with a wooden spoon, or until the chocolate has melted. Beat the mixture well.

5 Stir the almonds, biscuits and apricots into the chocolate mixture, stirring with a wooden spoon, until well mixed.

6 Pour the mixture into the prepared tin (pan) and leave to chill in the refrigerator for about 1 hour or until set.

7 Cut the rich chocolate loaf into slices to serve.

COOK'S TIP

To melt chocolate, first break it into manageable pieces. The smaller the pieces, the quicker it will melt.

Fresh Fruit Compôte

Elderflower cordial is used in the syrup for this refreshing fruit compôte, giving it a delightfully summery flavour.

NUTRITIONAL INFORMATION

Calories 255   Sugars 61g
Protein . . . . .4g   Fat 1g
Carbohydrate . . .61g   Saturates 0.2g

20 MINS   15 MINS

SERVES 4

I N G R E D I E N T S

1 lemon

60 g/2 oz/¼ cup caster (superfine) sugar

4 tbsp elderflower cordial

300 ml/½ pint/1¼ cups water

4 eating apples

225 g/8 oz/1 cup blackberries

2 fresh figs

T O P P I N G

150 g/5½ oz/⅔ cup thick natural (unsweetened) yogurt

2 tbsp clear honey

1 Thinly pare the rind from the lemon using a swivel vegetable peeler. Squeeze the juice. Put the lemon rind and juice into a saucepan, together with the sugar, elderflower cordial and water. Set over a low heat and simmer, uncovered, for 10 minutes.

2 Peel, core and slice the apples. Add the apples to the saucepan. Simmer gently for about 4–5 minutes, until just tender. Remove the pan from the heat and set aside to cool.

3 When cold, transfer the apples and syrup to a serving bowl and add the blackberries. Slice and add the figs. Stir gently to mix. Cover and chill in the refrigerator until ready to serve.

4 Spoon the yogurt into a small serving bowl and drizzle the honey over the top. Cover and chill before serving.

COOK'S TIP

Greek-style yogurt may be made from cow's or ewe's milk. The former is often strained to make it more concentrated and has a high fat content, which perfectly counterbalances the sharpness and acidity of fruit.

Index